KT-227-419

CLINICAL ASSESSMENT AND INTERVENTION FOR AUTISM SPECTRUM DISORDERS

EDITED BY

JOHNNY L. MATSON

AMSTERDAM • BOSTON • HEIDELBERG • LONDON
NEW YORK • OXFORD • PARIS • SAN DIEGO
SAN FRANCISCO • SINGAPORE • SYDNEY • TOKYO

Academic Press is an imprint of Elsevier

ELSEVIER

Academic Press is an imprint of Elsevier
30 Corporate Drive, Suite 400, Burlington, MA 01803, USA
Linacre House, Jordan Hill, Oxford OX2 8DP, UK
84 Theobald's Road, London WC1X 8RR, UK

First edition 2008.

Copyright © 2008, Elsevier Inc., All rights reserved

Published by Elsevier Inc., All rights reserved

No part of this publication may be reproduced, stored in a retrieval system or transmitted
in any form or by any means electronic, mechanical, photocopying, recording
or otherwise without the prior written permission of the publisher

Permissions may be sought directly from Elsevier's Science & Technology Rights
Department in Oxford, UK: phone (+44) (0) 1865 843830; fax (+44) (0) 1865 853333;
email: permissions@elsevier.com. Alternatively you can submit your request online by
visiting the Elsevier web site at http://elsevier.com/locate/permissions, and selecting
Obtaining permission to use Elsevier material

Notice
No responsibility is assumed by the publisher for any injury and/or damage to persons
or property as a matter of products liability, negligence or otherwise, or from any use
or operation of any methods, products, instructions or ideas contained in the material
herein. Because of rapid advances in the medical sciences, in particular, independent
verification of diagnoses and drug dosages should be made

British Library Cataloguing in Publication Data
A catalogue record for this book is available from the British Library

Library of Congress Cataloging-in-Publication Data
A catalog record for this book is available from the Library of Congress

For information on all Academic Press publications
visit our web site at books.elsevier.com

Printed and bound in United States of America
08 09 10   10 9 8 7 6 5 4 3 2 1

ISBN: 978-0-12-373606-2

Cover image reproduced by kind permission of Getty Images

Working together to grow
libraries in developing countries

www.elsevier.com | www.bookaid.org | www.sabre.org

ELSEVIER   BOOK AID International   Sabre Foundation

Clinical Assessment and Intervention for Autism Spectrum Disorders

CONTENTS

PART I

INTRODUCTION

1

ASSESSMENT AND INTERVENTION IN AUTISM: AN HISTORICAL PERSPECTIVE

AMANDA L. RICHDALE AND KIMBERLY A. SCHRECK

2

EVIDENCE-BASED PRACTICE FOR AUTISM SPECTRUM DISORDERS

MARY JANE WEISS, KATE FISKE, AND SUZANNAH FERRAIOLI

3

AUTISM SPECTRUM DISORDERS: A LIFESPAN PERSPECTIVE

LINDA A. LEBLANC, ANDREW R. RILEY AND TINA R. GOLDSMITH

PART II

ASSESSMENT

4

DIFFERENTIAL DIAGNOSIS

MARIE S. NEBEL-SCHWALM AND JOHNNY L. MATSON

5

___

ASSESSMENT OF CHALLENGING BEHAVIORS IN PEOPLE WITH AUTISM SPECTRUM DISORDERS

PETER STURMEY, LAURA SEIVERLING, AND JOHN WARD-HORNER

6

___

COMMUNICATION AND SOCIAL SKILLS ASSESSMENT

JEFF SIGAFOOS, RALF W. SCHLOSSER, VANESSA A. GREEN, MARK O'REILLY, AND GIULIO E. LANCIONI

7

ASSESSMENT OF INDEPENDENT LIVING/ADAPTIVE SKILLS

NAOMI SWIEZY, MELISSA STUART, PATRICIA KORZEKWA, AND STACIE POZDOL

8

PHARMACOLOGY EFFECTS AND SIDE EFFECTS

LUC LECAVALIER AND KENNETH GADOW

PART III

INTERVENTIONS

9

CHALLENGING BEHAVIORS

OLIVER C. MUDFORD, ANGELA M. ARNOLD-SARITEPE,
KATRINA J. PHILLIPS, JANINE MAARI LOCKE, I-CHEN SHARON HO,
AND SARAH ANN TAYLOR

10

COMMUNICATION INTERVENTION FOR CHILDREN WITH AUTISM SPECTRUM DISORDERS

RALF W. SCHLOSSER AND JEFF SIGAFOOS

11

TEACHING ADAPTIVE SKILLS TO PEOPLE WITH AUTISM

KAREN SHERIDAN AND TROY RAFFIELD

12

COMPREHENSIVE TREATMENT PACKAGES FOR ASD: PERCEIVED VS PROVEN EFFECTIVENESS

RAYMOND G. ROMANCZYK, JENNIFER M. GILLIS, SARA WHITE, AND FLORENCE DIGENNARO

13

PHARMACOTHERAPY

LUKE Y. TSAI

PREFACE

The Autism Spectrum Disorders (ASD) as a field has engendered dramatic increases in attention in recent years. As a result, there has been an exponential growth in information, and a dramatic increase in services. Early identification continues to be the primary focus of study and service provision. However, there is also a growing recognition that lifelong service provision needs to be a greater priority. Furthermore, the developmental nature of ASD makes it necessary to develop a range of programs and services which meet the needs of persons with ASD across the life span.

The purpose of the present volume then is to provide the reader with an overview of recent developments in the ASD field. Chapter 1 provides a historical overview to provide context for recent developments. Chapters on methodological issues, the linchpin for evidence-based intervention, and a chapter on the conceptual issues for a life span approach follow. The remainder of the book is broken into two major sections: one on assessment and the other on treatment. Our section on assessment begins with a chapter on methods for differentially diagnosing ASD. This goal is particularly important given the evolving nature of ASD and the various methods used to assess it. The remaining chapters in the book cover key deficit areas in assessment and treatment such as challenging behaviors, communication and social behavior, independent and adaptive living. Given the special status of a few interventions, we have denoted a chapter to comprehensive treatment programs and to pharmacotherapy.

There is a rapid development of intervention methods for persons with ASD. While most efforts are on early intervention, a very worthy goal, a major theme of this book is the need to look at the entire course of the persons life with respect to assessment and treatment. Hopefully this volume will help underscore this critical issue.

Johnny Matson
Baton Rouge, LA
September, 2007

CONTRIBUTORS

Angela M. Arnold-Saritepe Department of Psychology (Tamaki Campus), University of Auckland, Auckland, New Zealand.

Florence Digennaro State University of New york at Binghamton, Binghamton, NY, USA.

Suzannah Ferraioli Rutgers, The State University of New Jersey, NJ, USA.

Kate Fiske Rutgers, The State University of New Jersey, NJ, USA.

Kenneth Gadow State University of New York-Stony Brook, Stony Brook, NY, USA.

Jennifer M. Gillis Auburn University.

Tina R. Goldsmith Department of Psychology, Western Michigan University, MI, USA.

Vanessa A. Green School of Education, University of Tasmania, Hobart, Tasmania 7001, Australia.

I-Chen Sharon Ho Department of Psychology (Tamaki Campus), University of Auckland, Auckland, New Zealand.

Patricia Korzekwa Christian Sarkine Autism, Treatment Center, Riley Hospital for Children, Indiana University School of Medicine, Indianapolis, IN 46202-5000, USA.

Giulio E. Lancioni University of Bari, Bari, Italy.

Linda A. LeBlanc Department of Psychology, Co-Director, WMU Center for Autism, Western Michigan University, Kalamazoo, MI 49008-5439, USA.

Luc Lecavalier Department of Psychology and Nisonger Center, Ohio State University, Columbus, OH 43210, USA.

Janine Maari Locke Department of Psychology (Tamaki Campus), University of Auckland, Auckland, New Zealand.

Johnny L. Matson Department of Psychology, Louisiana State University, Baton Rouge, LA 70803, USA.

Oliver C. Mudford Director of Applied Behavior Analysis Programme, Department of Psychology (Tamaki Campus), University of Auckland, Auckland, New Zealand.

Marie S. Nebel-Schwalm Department of Psychology, Louisiana State University, Baton Rouge, LA 70803, USA.

Mark O'Reilly University of Texas at Austin, Austin, TX, USA.

Katrina J. Phillips Department of Psychology (Tamaki Campus), University of Auckland, Auckland, New Zealand.

Stacie Pozdol Christian Sarkine Autism, Treatment Center, Riley Hospital for Children, Indiana University School of Medicine, Indianapolis, IN 46202-5000, USA.

Troy Raffield Department of Psychology, Pinecrest Developmental Center, Pineville, LA 71361, USA.

Amanda L. Richdale Division of Psychology, School of Health Sciences, RMIT University, Victoria, Australia.

Andrew R. Riley Department of Psychology, Western Michigan University, MI, USA.

Raymond G. Romanczyk Director, Institute for Child Development, and Professor, Department of Psychology, State University of New York at Binghamton, Binghamton, NY 13902-6000, USA.

Ralf W. Schlosser Department of Speech-Language Pathology and Audiology, Northeastern University, Boston, MA 02115, USA.

Kimberly A. Schreck Penn State University, USA.

Laura Seiverling Psychology Department, City University of New York, NY 11367, USA.

Karen Sheridan Department of Psychology, Pinecrest Developmental Center, Pineville, LA 71361, USA.

Jeff Sigafoos Victoria University of Wellington, New Zealand.

Melissa Stuart Christian Sarkine Autism Treatment Center, Riley Hospital for Children, Indiana University School of Medicine, Indianapolis, IN 46202-5000, USA.

Peter Sturmey Psychology Department, City University of New York, NY 11367, USA.

Naomi Swiezy Clinical Psychology in Clinical Psychiatry, Clinical Director, Christian Sarkine Autism Treatment Center, Riley Hospital for Children,

Indiana University School of Medicine, Indianapolis, IN 46202-5000, USA.

Sarah Ann Taylor Department of Psychology (Tamaki Campus), University of Auckland, Auckland, New Zealand.

Luke Y. Tsai Professor of Psychiatry and Pediatrics, Child and Adolescent Psychiatry Hospital, University of Michigan Medical Center, 2385 Placid Way, Ann Arbor, MI 48105, USA.

John Ward-Horner Psychology Department, City University of New York, NY 11367, USA.

Mary Jane Weiss Director of Research and Training, Douglas Developmental Disabilities Center, Rutgers, the State University of New Jersey, New Brunswick/Piscataway, NJ 08901, USA.

Sara White State University of New York at Binghamton, Binghamton, NY, USA.

INTRODUCTION

1

ASSESSMENT AND INTERVENTION IN AUTISM: AN HISTORICAL PERSPECTIVE

AMANDA L. RICHDALE[1] AND KIMBERLY A. SCHRECK[2]

[1]RMIT University, Victoria, Australia
[2]Penn State University, USA

INTRODUCTION

Writing a complete historical account of the assessment, diagnosis, and treatment of autism has been a daunting task. Since the inception of autism as a distinctive diagnosis, debates have dominated the field in almost every area – from diagnosis to assessment methodology to treatments. We have attempted to provide a history of autism while revealing some of the debates and controversies related to this developmental disorder throughout this chapter. We have included the evolution of the concept of "autism", from Kanner's and Asperger's syndromes to the development of the more recent term "autism spectrum disorder" (ASD). We have attempted to elucidate the historical context and debates related to the emergence of autistic disorder and Asperger's disorder as clinical diagnostic categories. We have then discussed the assessment methods used within ASD, attempting to avoid any of the diagnostic debates. As in most venues, the debates concerning etiology and diagnostic categories have influenced treatment choices for people with autism. This chapter concludes with a brief discussion of the historical evolution of interventions for ASD and the debate concerning treatment methodologies.

AUTISM AND ASPERGER'S DISORDER: HISTORICAL ASPECTS

Historical accounts indicate that autism has always formed part of the human condition. For example, "bear", "wolf", and "leopard" children who reportedly had exhibited restricted eating habits, sensory insensitivities and oversensitivities, lack of social skills and speech, and stereotypic behaviors have been cited as far back as the mid-1300s (See Itard, 1962; Malson, 1972). J.K. Wing (1976), Wing (1997), Frith (2003), and Waltz and Shattock (2004) also have provided historical examples, the most famous being Itard's (1962) wild boy of Aveyron, Victor, in 1799. Victor was apparently abandoned in the forest some two years before he was "rescued" at about age 12 and educated for 5 years by Itard. Itard (1962), Malson (1972) and Frith (2003) have provided accounts of Victor's behavior that are consistent with current diagnostic criteria for autistic disorder.

Historical accounts also have provided evidence of people who would today probably receive a diagnosis of Asperger's disorder (Frith, 2003). One example, *John Howard*, a sheriff who lived in the mid to late 18th century and wrote several books on prison reform, was described as meticulous, rigid, rule bound, impaired in social communication, and solitary – possibly fitting the diagnostic category of Asperger's disorder (Lucas, 2001). Most recently Waltz and Shattock (2004) provided clinical accounts of three cases from the historical case notes of Dickinson (1861–1874) at the Great Ormond Street Hospital for Children in London. According to Waltz and Shattock, 24 of Dickinson's cases had exhibited at least some symptoms characteristic of what we now know as ASDs based on current diagnostic criteria.

KANNER'S AUTISM

Until Leo Kanner (1943) first recognized autism as a separate syndrome in his now classic paper *Autistic Disturbances of Affective Contact*, descriptions of such children had not been recognized as different from the general category of childhood psychosis (Wing, 1976) or childhood schizophrenia (Rimland, 1964). Kanner (1943) described a group of apparently physically normal children from highly intelligent, professional families, who had poor social and language skills from infancy, failed to communicate or show interest in people, and who had obsessive dislike for change in their routines. Carefully drawing together the specific features of these cases, he defined the syndrome "autism". In a summary of the primary symptoms that he thought differentiated his children from other psychotic children, Kanner described:

1. An inability to relate to other people from the beginning of life, which he referred to as an *extreme autistic aloneness*.
2. Failure as infants to adapt their posture to being picked up [e.g., "passive as if he were a sack of flour" (p. 243)].

3. Abnormalities of language including no speech, a failure to use speech to convey meaning, delayed echolalia and/or the confusion of personal pronouns.
4. *Excellent rote memories*, which were reflected in the children's ability to remember things such as rhymes, lists, and numbers.
5. Problems with feeding and food, and fear reactions to loud noise, or moving objects.
6. *Anxiously obsessive desire for the maintenance of sameness* (e.g., resisting change in routines or objects being moved, and engaging in rituals).
7. Relating well to objects but not to people (e.g., ignoring the presence or absence of their mothers and lack of eye contact).
8. *Impression of serious-mindedness* (i.e., appearance of intelligence).
9. Physical normality.

Debate 1: Etiology

Kanner's early papers (1943; 1949) contributed to the focus on the contributions of parent characteristics, particularly mothers, to the symptoms of autism. He believed that, while not uncaring, the mothers of children with autism lacked warmth towards their children; and the fathers, while seeming friendly, did not play with their children. Overall, he felt that the parents themselves lacked interest in people (cf. more recent views on the autism behavioral phenotype, e.g., Piven, 1999). Within the psychoanalytic framework of his time, this was viewed as a problem that the infant had in differentiating the self from the mother, and a reaction to the quality of mothering.

These early descriptions of parents with similar characteristics to their children and detached mothers initiated the notion that early infantile autism was caused by an early failure in the mother–child relationship, so-called "refrigerator mothers" (Bettelheim, 1967). Faulty attachment and bonding theories persisted into the 1980s with Tinbergen and Tinbergen's (1983) theory that the cause of autism was the pressures and abnormal socialization patterns encouraged by modern society. Sanua (1983) continued the argument that little support existed for biological theories of autism and that the potential impact of social–cultural factors was neglected.

The impression that mothers were to blame for autism was to be damaging for many years (Mesibov et al., 2005). However, with societal shifts towards science and a renewed interest in the biological basis of autism, based on Kanner's (1943) and Asperger's (1944/1991) original work, researchers began to argue against the prevailing psychogenic theories (Rimland, 1964). Over the years, several theories have postulated neurobiological impacts, including neurological, neurochemical, and genetic influences (see Rapin and Katzman, 1998; Schopler and Mesibov, 1987; Volkmar, et al., 2005 for reviews). Developing from these theories, psychological theories of autism have attempted to link observations of the children's behavior [e.g., difficulty taking others' perspectives (Baron-Cohen,

Leslie, and Frith, 1986)] with possible psychobiological etiologies. For further accounts of psychological theories of autism see Jordan (1999) and Volkmar et al. (2005a).

These biological and psychological theories in conjunction with possible conditioning effects (e.g., impact of an odd and unresponsive child from birth, which may itself negatively affect the mother's responses to that child) provided solid evidence against the psychogenic theories. Consequently, emotional theories of autism related to parent–child bonding or interaction no longer retain credence: autism is now considered a biologically based disorder (Roberts and Prior, 2006).

Debate 2: Is Autism distinct from Schizophrenia?

Kanner's (1943) use of the term "autism" to describe his children created difficulties. The word autism previously had been used by Bleuler to describe the active withdrawal from the real world to an inner, presumably fantasy world seen in schizophrenia (as cited in J.K. Wing, 1976). The confusion between Bleuler's and Kanner's use of the word autism, together with the severe and early onset of the disorder, led to a continued confusion of Kanner's autism with childhood schizophrenia, and more generally an amorphous group of childhood psychoses.

Debate in the ensuing years emerged regarding whether or not early infantile autism was or was not a form of childhood schizophrenia (see Creak et al., 1961; Rimland, 1964). Kanner (1949) speculated that: "Early infantile autism may therefore be looked upon as the earliest possible manifestation of childhood schizophrenia" (p. 419). Thus, at that point he believed that autism was one of the schizophrenias, but lacked any normal period of development because of its onset in the first year of life.

In 1961 Creak and colleagues examined the records of psychotic children who had attended the Great Ormond Hospital in London. They found that the children had received a variety of classifications (e.g., "autistic", "schizophrenic", "atypical", "brain damaged", "epileptic", and "mentally defective"), and treatment locales (e.g., child guidance clinics, hospitals, facilities for people with mental retardation). The committee determined that nine diagnostic points, which essentially mirrored the early points of Kanner (1943, 1949) best described these children, naming the disorder "schizophrenic syndrome in childhood". Creak et al.'s nine points were influential in the literature; for example, the autistic children in Hermelin and O'Conner's work (1970) met Creak's criteria.

Problems with a strict adherence to Kanner's criteria (1943, 1949), or indeed the nine points of Creak et al. (1961) remained and the debate continued. Rutter (1978) reviewed the evidence regarding autism as a diagnostic entity and concluded that there were four main criteria that defined the disorder: (1) onset before 30 months; (2) impaired social development that was inconsistent with general ability; (3) delayed and deviant language inconsistent with general ability; and (4) insistence on sameness.

Wing and Gould's (1979) epidemiological study of children with mental retardation in the London borough of Camberwell examined patterns of social interaction, speech abnormalities, imaginative activities, and routines and interests. Evidence for three groups of children with impaired social interaction (aloof, passive, and odd) was found. A proportion of these socially impaired children were likely to have had a diagnosis of autism but these children fell within all three socially impaired subgroups; social impairment was more common at lower IQ.

Thus, by the late 1970s it seemed clear that there was a distinct pattern of social, language, and behavioral symptoms that, clustered together, were usually associated with mental retardation and were first evident in infancy or early childhood. These children appeared to be reliably distinguished from children with other childhood psychoses and their behavior was consistent with Kanner's (1943) autism. From at least 20 years ago, follow-up reports showed little or no association between autism and schizophrenia in adulthood (e.g., Rumsey, Rapoport, and Sceery, 1985).

ASPERGER'S AUTISTIC PSYCHOPATHY

Shortly after Kanner's (1943) description of children with autism, Hans Asperger published his original paper (1944; trans. in Frith, 1991) describing four boys with autistic psychopathy (meaning personality disorder, Wolff, 2000) who he referred to as "autistic children" (p. 69). Asperger's boys all had good speech and had relatively normal intelligence. Nevertheless his descriptions of the boys' social–communication difficulties and behavior were reminiscent of Kanner's autism. The case histories also indicated the presence of developmental delay and/or social and behavioral difficulties from an early age.

Asperger's work remained relatively unknown (though referred to by Rimland, 1964; Rutter, 1978; Van Krevelen, 1971; and Wing, 1976) in English-speaking countries until Wing (1981) introduced the term Asperger syndrome to describe children with symptoms similar to those seen in autism, but who had good language and cognitive skill. Wing described 34 cases similar to Asperger's boys, including 6 with mild retardation who were discovered in the Camberwell epidemiological study (Wing and Gould, 1979). Wing (1981) noted subtle difficulties of (a) *verbal communication* (e.g., "pedantic" and long talks on favorite topics of interest and difficulties with understanding humor other than that which is obvious (e.g., slap-stick); (b) *nonverbal communication* (e.g., the use and understanding of gestures and facial expression; (c) *repetitive behavior* (e.g., spinning objects, insistence on routines, etc.); (d) *motor movement*; and (e) *learning skills* (e.g. academic difficulties).

Wing (1981) also described impairments for two-way social interaction for people with Asperger syndrome, as they "did not understand the rules governing social behaviour" (p. 116). Like Kanner (1943), she reported excellent rote memory, but for information and facts gathered on diverse topics (e.g., maps). The children could talk endlessly about their current topic of interest. Due to their subtle differences from typically developing children's communication, their severe difficulties with social interactions, and their odd and eccentric behaviors, these children had been highly likely to be bullied at school.

With two similar, yet somewhat distinctly detailed versions of autistic behavior, professionals began hypothesizing about the diagnostic characteristics, etiologies, and underlying symptoms of autism.

Debate 3: Is autism distinct from Asperger's disorder?

Although many overlaps existed in descriptions of children with autism or Asperger's syndrome, debates over etiology and diagnostic differentiation made an early appearance. Van Krevelen (1971) argued that Kanner's autism was a psychotic process while Asperger's autistic psychopathy was a personality trait, concluding that they were nosologically different. Points of difference between Kanner's autism and Asperger's autistic psychopathy as described by Van Krevelen seemed to be more a function of intelligence (i.e., language and IQ) than of a description of different disorders. Additionally, he described Asperger's syndrome as being recognized later in development than Kanner's autism, from a child's third year of life or older. However Asperger (1944/1991) himself stated that "the characteristic features" were found from the second year of life. From his analysis, Van Krevelen concluded that: (1) Kanner's autism may arise due to brain damage in the presence of autistic psychopathy and (2) Asperger's syndrome may be an inherited personality type.

Many questions remained regarding the influence of medical conditions, IQ, and children with lesser degrees of symptoms of autism (Rutter, 1978). Whether or not autism and Asperger syndrome are different disorders has remained a point of contemporary dispute (see Manjiviano and Prior, 1999; Ozonoff et al., 2000; Wolff, 2000). For example, Wing (1981) described a case that met criteria for autism in early life and later fit Asperger syndrome. More recent accounts have described people who fit the criteria for autism earlier in childhood but, by late adolescence or adulthood, resemble Asperger's cases (Howlin, 2003). Although the dispute continues, Asperger's disorder is now included in the Diagnostic and Statistical Manual (DSM) (American Psychiatric Association [APA], 1994) with autistic disorder as a pervasive developmental disorder. Since this debate over the distinction between autism and Asperger's disorder continues, we have chosen to combine the information on early diagnostic signs, assessment, and treatment.

THE HISTORICAL DEVELOPMENT OF STANDARD DIAGNOSTIC CRITERIA

Clinical assessment and diagnosis of an ASD today has involved the criteria in the *Diagnostic and Statistical Manual of Mental Disorders, Fourth Edition, Text Revision* (DSM-IV-TR; APA, 2000) or the *International Classification of Diseases, Tenth Edition* (ICD-10; WHO, 1992). We have concentrated on describing the diagnostic criteria most commonly used in our countries, the DSM. Since the two diagnostic systems are compatible, readers of all nationalities should be able to relate to the diagnostic history provided here (see Volkmar and Klin, 2005 for a discussion of DSM-IV and ICD-10).

INCLUDING AUTISM IN THE DSM

Despite Kanner's (1943) and Asperger's (1944/1991) clear elucidation of an apparently new disorder, autism did not initially appear in the Diagnostic and Statistical Manual of Mental Disorders (DSM). In *DSM-II* (APA, 1968) diagnostic information for childhood schizophrenia referred to a number of symptoms that were reminiscent of the then existing criteria for autism including "autistic, atypical and withdrawn behavior" (p. 35), uneven development, and possible co-occurring mental retardation. Nevertheless, it was not equivalent to the diagnostic features Kanner (1943) described for autism.

Autism first appeared as a Pervasive Developmental Disorder (PDD), Infantile Autism, in DSM-III (APA, 1980). This version of the DSM differentiated autism from schizophrenia. The diagnosis required that the features associated with autism (i.e., social problems, communication difficulties, and bizarre behavior) be present within the first 30 months of life. An atypical form, reflecting the findings of Wing and Gould (1979) and a residual state, where the individual no longer met full criteria, but did at one time, were included in this version. A childhood-onset PDD was also included where symptoms appeared after 30 months but before 12 years, and did not meet all the symptoms for infantile autism. Thus DSM-III covered the major areas of developmental concern first described by Kanner (1943), but allowed for later development and for a residual state.

In 1987 the DSM-III-Revised appeared (APA) and Asperger's work was now known, particularly since Wing's (1981) publication. However, the DSM-III-R (APA) noted that: "no generally recognized subtypes have emerged" (p. 34). Impairments in social interaction, verbal and non-verbal communication, restrictive activities and interests (replacing bizarre behavioral responses) were still the qualifying characteristics of autism. The categories again reflected Kanner's descriptions but had become more clearly defined and refined, providing descriptions of items that were indicative of each major criterion, half of which must be present for diagnosis.

In the DSM-III-R (APA, 1987) atypical autism was replaced by Pervasive Developmental Disorder Not Otherwise Specified (PDDNOS) to account for those individuals who did not meet the full diagnostic criteria for autism. Disintegrative forms were also classified under Autistic Disorder or PDDNOS. However, in this edition of the DSM, the broadening of the age criteria, and the potential for inclusion of disintegrative forms, meant that children who may not previously have received a diagnosis of autism may now do so. The preamble to the diagnostic criteria began to reflect the increased biological and genetic knowledge about autism, including the association with a large number of organic conditions, and the increased risk of the disorder amongst siblings.

ADDING ASPERGER'S DISORDER TO THE DSM

For the first time, the latest revisions of the DSM (DSM-IV: APA, 1994 & DSM-IV-TR: APA, 2000) included Asperger's disorder with autistic disorder and PDDNOS as one of five pervasive developmental disorders. Essentially, the same diagnostic features as those found in DSM-III-R were included in the DSM-IV criteria for Autistic Disorder, except (a) age of onset for at least one of the social–communicative symptoms was now before age 3 years; (b) fewer, more broadly defined items relating to the three major criteria were included; and (c) disintegrative forms were now a separate diagnosis. The DSM-IV was also designed to be compatible with ICD-10 (WHO, 1992).

Thus, a consensus had gradually formed, beginning with DSM-III (APA, 1980) and culminating with DSM-IV (APA, 1994), about what the primary characteristics of autism were – social, communication and behavior deficits that affected all areas of development. Although a consensus was reached for Debates 1 and 2, diagnosis continues to be clouded by Debate 3 – the separateness or otherwise of autism and Asperger's disorder (e.g., Miller and Ozonoff, 1997), and whether or not autism forms a spectrum or a group of clearly distinguishable but overlapping disorders (e.g., Prior et al., 1998). For a more complete discussion of the current debates and issues and development of the DSM criteria for autism and Asperger's disorder see APA (1980, 1987, 1994) and Volkmar and Klin (2005).

HISTORICAL ASPECTS OF ASSESSING ASDs

As we have represented, prevailing social and theoretical views historically have guided people's thoughts and ideas about autism. They have also guided assessment. Early theoretical perspectives regarding causal mechanisms in autism differed markedly with no consensus regarding whether autism was a biological or a psychogenic disorder; and thus, no consensus about assessment tools (Parks, 1988). The tendency of differing perspectives to focus on particular features of autism to the exclusion of others meant that comprehensive assessment related to all areas of the children's functioning was not often achieved. These factors then influenced assessment processes – whether it was essentially qualitative or quantitative and whether or not it was derived primarily from naturalistic observation, interview, observation within a clinical setting, using standardized measures, or some combination of these.

These seemingly historical issues and debates still guide assessments today. However, professionals have agreed that assessment has served two related purposes: (1) to arrive at a diagnosis and/or (2) for intervention and educational planning and evaluation. These different purposes have dictated the focus of the assessment process and the tools used.

DIAGNOSTIC ASSESSMENT AND PLANNING

The development of diagnostic assessment has been addressed for at least 30 years (e.g., Rutter, 1978; Schopler and Mesibov, 1988; Volkmar et al., 1999). Since a comprehensive evaluation of historical and current assessment methods for autism is not possible in this chapter, readers are encouraged to read Volkmar et al. (2005b) for a thorough review of autism assessment.

Although historically, many believed that children with autism were untestable (Parks, 1988; Rutter, 1978), with proper choice of assessment materials (DeMeyer, 1976) and choice of reinforcers for performance (Freeman and Ritvo, 1976), professionals could conduct very thorough diagnostic assessments for autism (DeMeyer, 1976; Freeman and Ritvo, 1976; Rutter, 1978). Despite the debates concerning etiology and diagnosis, recommendations for a thorough assessment for children suspected of an ASD involved a multidisciplinary assessment that may include:

a. Comprehensive medical examination

Where indicated genetic and other medical tests may be ordered due to the co-occurrence of autism at a greater than expected rate with epilepsy and rare disorders such as tuberous sclerosis and chromosomal disorders such as fragile X and other organic conditions (Gillberg and Coleman, 2000; Rimland, 1964). Audiology is often indicated to rule out any hearing loss, and occupational or physical therapy assessment to address the commonly occurring gross and/or fine motor difficulties.

b. Developmental history

Early historical accounts believed to fit criteria for autism refer to professionals and parents of children noticing problems from infancy (Coonrod and Stone, 2005; Kanner, 1943) or early childhood (Asperger, 1944/1991; Short and Schopler, 1988; Waltz and Shattock, 2004). Wing (1976) argued that some children experienced a period of apparently normal development with the first concerns not raised until the child was in its second or third year. Behaviors noted to develop as early as infancy for children later diagnosed as autistic included apathy, or conversely continual crying, and failure to (a) anticipate being picked up, (b) mold to the parent's body when being carried, (c) take interest in other people, (d) respond to their name, (e) use the toilet, and (f) eat like other children. These children also engaged in repetitive behaviors and preoccupations, had a need for preserving sameness, and cried for reasons that were not obvious (Rimland, 1964). Careful questioning of these developmental patterns and behaviors may assist in diagnostic and educational planning.

c. Psychological examination

As the diagnosis of autism evolved, cognitive, behavioral, and language assessments using standardized tools were recommended to assist with diagnosis and future planning. The psychological assessment was of primary importance, as cognitive and adaptive skills underpin so much of what the child will need and can currently do (Klin et al., 2005). Researchers showed that contrary to earlier beliefs, educational opportunities together with verbal and cognitive skills positively influenced later adaptive skills and academics (e.g., Venter et al., 1992). Knowing a child's level of functioning enabled appropriate goals and expectations to be incorporated into future intervention or educational planning.

To enable appropriate future planning, assessments that address all areas of the child's functioning are needed. Children with autism showed uneven test performance and an overall score did not reflect strengths and weakness, which were important to know for educational planning (Flaharty, 1976). Professionals need to consider the difficulties of children with autism taking standardized testing, such as fine motor control issues, lack of verbal behavior, and attention problems. In school-age children of normal IQ, academic assessments have also been indicated to rule out specific learning difficulties (Reitzel and Szatmari, 2003).

ASSESSING OR MEASURING THE SYMPTOMS OF AUTISM

Over the years, psychological tests useful to diagnose autism and to assist with treatment planning have included autism symptom questionnaires, semistructured autism interviews and observations, IQ tests, language tests, and adaptive behavior questionnaires and structured interviews (see Baker, 1983; Klin et al., 2005; Parks, 1988 for reviews).

Although these diagnostic measures were available, it was and continues to be difficult to find direct information on assessment for the purposes of ongoing education and treatment (Luiselli et al., 2001). Generally such assessment tool information was embedded within texts without being explicitly addressed, for example, descriptions of the TEACCH program (Mesibov et al., 2005) and of behavioral programs (e.g., Maurice et al., 1996).

Checklists, Questionnaires and Observations

Over the past 40 or more years, a large number of questionnaires or checklists were developed that address symptoms and behaviors in autism consistent with the social, communication and behavioral diagnostic criteria (for a review see Lord and Corsello, 2005). They served a variety of purposes, including diagnostic screening, describing the child's behaviors and their severity, and allowing professionals to gauge behavior change in response to programming. A description of the wide variety of such instruments available was beyond the scope of this chapter; consequently, familiarity and history guided our brief offering.

One of the earliest autism diagnostic questionnaires was Rimland's E-2 Checklist (Prior and Bence, 1975; Rimland, 1964).

The Childhood Autism Rating Scale (CARS; Schopler et al., 1980) developed into a popular observational and interview instrument to assess the severity of behaviors associated with autism and is still widely used. The Autism Real Life Rating Scale (Freeman et al., 1986) was developed as an observational checklist where professionals recorded frequencies of behaviors over a 30-minute period to assess behavior change. A more recent addition to the autism symptom measures was the Social Communication Questionnaire (SCQ; Rutter et al., 2003) which was developed from the Autism Diagnostic Interview (ADI-R) (Lord et al., 1994). The SCQ has grown into a useful screening and behavioral change instrument, particularly in the social–communication domains. There were also a number of questionnaires over the past decade or more specifically addressing Asperger's disorder, for example, the Australian Scale for Asperger's Syndrome (Attwood, 1997); Campbell (2005) has provided a comparison of several scales.

In contemporary history, the ADI-R (Le Couter et al., 1989; Lord et al., 1994) and the Autism Diagnostic Observation Schedule (ADOS) (Lord et al., 2000) prevailed in the assessment of autism symptoms. The ADI-R, a structured parent interview, was developed to probe the child's developmental history and current behavior centering on autism diagnostic criteria. The ADOS was developed as a structured observational system using situations such as a pretend birthday party, story telling, and miming, and covering from early childhood through to adolescence across a range of ability. Algorithms based on DSM-IV criteria produce cutoff scores for ASD and autism for both instruments but cannot distinguish between autism and Asperger's disorder. Training is required for administration of both the ADI-R and the ADOS.

Cognitive, Developmental and Educational Evaluations

Within typical assessment protocols, traditional cognitive tests have relied heavily on verbal skills and instructions, but children with autism have long been observed to perform better on performance items than verbal items on IQ tests (e.g., Freeman and Ritvo, 1976). The Weschler scales (Weschler Preschool and Primary Scale of Intelligence [WPPSI] and the Weschler Intelligence Scale for Children [WISC]) were most useful scales for estimating cognitive skills and observing behavior in school-age children with an ASD who were not severely to profoundly retarded. The WISC (Weschler, 2003) is currently in its 4th edition. Profiles for children with autism or Asperger's disorder showed the expected verbal advantage in Asperger's disorder and performance advantage in autism, with both groups doing relatively poorly on the processing speed index. The Stanford-Binet also was useful to assess IQ but had a focus on verbal skills (Freeman and Ritvo, 1976); Mayes and Calhoun (2003) provide a comparison of the 4th edition with the WISC-III.

Other tests that were favored for the intellectual assessment of children with autism were the Merrill-Palmer Scale of Mental Tests (Stutsman, 1931 as cited in Sattler, 1982) and the Leiter International Performance Scale (Leiter, 1948 as cited in Sattler, 1982). The Merrill-Palmer was used for children aged 18 months to 6 years and contained items on which many young and lower functioning children with autism showed interest and performed well (e.g., puzzles and form boards). The Leiter covered the age range 2 years to 18 years, giving a non-verbal IQ. It correlated well with the WISC and WISC-Revised performance IQ (Sattler, 1982; Shah and Holmes, 1985). The Leiter was particularly useful for children with autism who were considered "untestable" (Shah and Holmes). There were no spoken instructions and items involved activities including matching, counting, shapes and sequencing. A more recent version of the Leiter (Roid and Miller, 1997) is now available which has some advantages over the original Leiter, but the 1948 version can still be useful with very low-functioning children (Tsatsanis et al., 2003).

Testing young and very developmentally delayed children with autism has always been challenging. The Bayley-III (Bayley, 2005) and its earlier editions and the Psychoeducational Profile-Revised (PEP-R; Schopler et al., 1990) were useful for assessing the development in very young and very delayed children under 6 years (the 3rd edition has just been released). The PEP-R had a flexible administrative procedure and assessed the child's performance across imitation, perception, cognitive language and fine and gross motor domains as well as behavior. Current and emerging skills were scored, making it useful for educational planning and for assessing progress as well as estimating current level of functioning.

In addition to cognitive assessments, a range of educational assessments exists that have been used to assess both learning difficulties and academic progress, including criterion-referenced developmental scales for pre-school children, observations, and records of progress. Standardized achievement tests (see Mayes and Calhoun, 2003) or tests of performance in reading, writing, spelling and mathematics also have been used. A review of these types of assessments was outside the scope of this chapter; however Mayes and Calhoun have provided some guidance on the use of IQ and academic achievement tests for planning educational intervention.

Language Evaluation

Because of the inherent language problems for children with ASD, clinicians required both informal (history, observation, and interaction) and formal (standardized) tests of language when assessing these children with an ASD. While the former have generally been sufficient to arrive at a diagnosis, the latter has been essential for planning intervention.

Language assessment had long been used to assess progress in response to intervention (Davis, 1967). Standardized language assessments such as the Clinical Evaluation of Language Fundamentals (Sennel et al., 2003), the Pre-School Language Scale (Zimmerman et al., 2003), and the Reynell Developmental Language Scale (Edwards et al., 1999) in their various editions had been used to assess the level of receptive and expressive language development in children with an ASD. Other assessments, which proved useful were parent questionnaires such as the MacArthur Communication Development Inventories (Fenson et al., 1993) which provided information about both verbal and nonverbal communication for quite young children with autism, and the Children's Communication Checklist (Bishop, 1998) which also provided information about pragmatic communication. Tests of vocabulary such as the Peabody Picture Vocabulary Test (Dunn and Dunn, 1997) also became helpful and were used in their several editions for many years. A more formal assessment of pragmatic language remains an important area (e.g., Bishop and Norbury, 2002), which was often ignored in earlier times. For a more thorough discussion of the approaches to language assessment, readers are encouraged to read Paul (2005).

Adaptive Behavior

Adaptive behavior has remained an important measure of level of functioning in social, communicative and self-care domains (Volkmar et al., 1999), and for some young and/or very low-functioning children with autism it may have been the best means of assessing their current level of functioning and assessing their intervention progress (e.g., Davis, 1967). Historically, adaptive behavior has been assessed using the Vineland Adaptive Behavior Scales (VABS; Sparrow et al., 1984a,b), and the majority of published research pertains to these scales.

Children with autism typically have performed poorly on measures of adaptive behavior relative to IQ (Tsatsanis et al., 2003), with even very high-functioning children performing more poorly in all domains than would be predicted by their IQ (Klin et al., 2000). Thus, adaptive behavior has been useful for illustrating the deficits in ASDs relative to intellectual functioning, particularly for high-functioning children. Adaptive behavior measures also have assisted educators to understand the extent of a child's problems. However, while useful, the comprehensiveness and equivalence of the various measure of adaptive behavior need to be considered (Sattler, 2002); thus care needs to be taken in the interpretation of results from different scales or informants.

AUTISM TREATMENT

Like the early history of diagnostic issues in autism, prevailing societal views and theories (e.g., psychodynamics, physiological, etc.) have greatly influenced treatments for people with autism symptoms (see Jacobson, 2005; Scheerenberger, 1983). For example, during periods of history when demonic possessions were the current rage, people with intellectual disabilities were exposed to exorcisms and prayer treatments (Scheerenberger, 1983). When psychodynamic theories reigned, treatment unsuccessfully involved attachment and "rebonding" of the mother and child (Bettelheim, 1967; Lovaas, 1987; Schreibman and Ingersoll, 2005). Changes in the underlying theories of autism etiology from refrigerator mothers to neurological/organic etiology also influenced the use of interventions (see Jacobson, 2005 for a review). For example, Bettelheim advocated removal of the child from the family and his/her placement in a residential institution; Delacato (1974) treated the sensory–behavioral symptoms of autism; physiological theorists (e.g., neurotransmitter and neurohormonal theorists) proposed pharmacologic interventions (see Campbell et al., 1987) and dietary manipulations (e.g., Barthélémy et al., 1988). Other values and theories of humanity led practitioners to psychological and educational interventions. For example, Itard and Seguin concentrated on teaching practical skills to people with intellectual disabilities (Scheerenberger, 1983).

Within these reports of general treatments for people with intellectual disabilities, anecdotal accounts of treatments for people with autism symptoms were intermixed. Discussions of the treatment progress with "isolated" children with autism, like Itard's Victor, were recorded without a definitive autism diagnosis. Although detailed documents remained of the results of some of the treatments for these children with autism-like behaviors, less than detailed reports existed for the *exact* treatments that were implemented (Itard, 1962; Jacobson, 2005; Malson, 1972).

The records that existed for early historical treatments for people with autism symptoms seem to have indicated that therapists concentrated on treatments that attempted to increase or decrease individual behaviors and skills and to teach comprehensive sets of skills, such as adaptive behavior skills, communication (e.g., sign language and speech), and social skills (Itard, 1962, Jacobson, 2005). With the evolution of skills teaching, behaviorally based treatments returned to teaching the skills taught by Itard (1962) and his generation – concentrating on teaching individual categories of skills (e.g., social skills), decreasing inappropriate behaviors and/or on teaching comprehensive skill repertoires (Olley, 2005).

Although these distinct categories of treatments returned within the Applied Behavior Analysis (ABA) literature, a newer societal swing toward complementary and alternative medicine (CAM) resulted in a buffet of unsupported or fad treatments for people with ASDs. This buffet approach of combinations of treatments for children with autism sparked yet another bitter scientific and social debate concerning autism.

DEBATE 4: SCIENTIFIC TREATMENTS VERSUS THE BUFFET APPROACH

Side 1: The Scientific Side of the Debate

On one side of the issue, scientific practitioners contended that treatments during critical periods for learning should involve only treatments with scientific support. If too much time was spent attempting to implement a variety of treatments that had no evidence of effectiveness, critical intervention time was lost. The American Psychological Association (APsA) succinctly acknowledged this

purpose of scientifically supporting autism treatments by stating "If psychological research does not always give us hoped-for answers, it does help us *sift potent
reality from wishful thinking* [emphasis added], and focus our energy on real
solutions" (APsA, 2007). As Favell (2005) and the APsA (2007) elaborated, the
scientific method allowed practitioners and caregivers to sort "the wheat from
the chaff" or the ". . . potent reality from wishful thinking".

Use of the scientific method to evaluate autism treatments was always an
exercise in objectivity. With the CAM movement many people moved away from
science and objectivity because of what was perceived as unnecessary and incom-
prehensible jargon. However, scientifically supporting that a treatment caused
changes and improvements for people with autism really only required an understanding of a few basics: (a) providing clear, precise definitions of the behaviors
to be changed; (b) using testable methods of making the change; (c) eliminating
other possible reasons for a change in behavior (e.g., changing sleep time and diet
at the same time); and (d) replicating results (Green, 1996; Kay and Vyse, 2005;
Newsom and Hovanitz, 2005b). These basic principles allowed modern practitioners and caregivers to objectively develop and refine methods for teaching
individual skills, decreasing excessive behavior, and instructing comprehensive
skill repertoires for people with autism.

In accordance with using the scientific method for developing and refining
specific interventions, specific criteria were developed for determining specific
treatments to be scientifically supported. Although many different versions of
criteria existed, the basic criteria continued to require that a treatment (a) be
supported through multiple published, scientifically controlled reports, (b) contain clearly defined treatment techniques and protocols, and (c) be cost-effective
(see Chambless and Hollon, 1998; Green, 1996; Lonigan et al., 1998; Newsom,
and Hovanitz, 2005b for a description of the scientific method and treatment
efficacy criteria). The only treatment to meet these criteria and be endorsed by
the Surgeon General of the United States for teaching individual skills, comprehensive learning skill repertoires and for decreasing behavioral excesses (e.g.,
self-injurious behavior, stereotypy, etc.) for people with autism was Applied
Behavior Analysis (ABA) (New York State Department of Health, Early Intervention Program, 1999; Shook, 2005; U.S. Department of Health and Human
Services, 1999).

Decades of scientifically supported articles reporting ABA-based treatments
for decreasing behavior excesses, increasing individual skill categories, and for
educating comprehensive learning skill repertoires were published illustrating
the effects of behavioral techniques for treating people with autism (Matson
et al., 1996). Unfortunately, with the pseudoscientific societal movements and
the widespread dissemination and application of components of ABA by people
with a wide variety of training, misunderstandings about ABA developed (Metz
et al., 2005). Although some detractors misunderstood ABA treatment for people
with autism to only involve Discrete Trial Instruction (DTI) as described in
Lovaas's 1987 study (see Steege et al., 2007), a wide variety of behavioral

methods and treatments that incorporate components of ABA methods were used to teach individual skills, to reduce behavior excesses, and to teach the comprehensive learning skill repertoires for people with autism.

Scientific Support for Using ABA to Teach Specific Skill Categories

The Committee on Educational Interventions for Children with Autism (National Research Council, 2001) dictated that appropriate education/treatment for children with autism must involve teaching and generalizing functional skills, such as: (a) communication, (b) cognitive skills, (c) adaptive behavior, (d) social and play skills, and (e) reduction of behavioral excesses. Interventions using components of ABA instruction within each of the skill areas (i.e., communication, adaptive behavior, academic/cognitive skills, and social/play skills) were numerous. Some of the approaches to teaching these skills included (a) using incidental teaching for elaborating skills in a natural environment (Fenske et al., 2001; Hart and Risley, 1982); (b) using ABA to teach augmentative communication methods, such as picture exchange and sign language (Frost and Bondy, 2000; Schreibman and Ingersoll, 2005); (c) implementing Skinner's theories on verbal behavior to teach language (Newsom and Hovanitz, 2006a; Sundberg and Partington, 1998); (d) applying adult and peer mediation for play skills (Taylor, 2001; Taylor and Jasper, 2001); and (e) incorporating video modeling to teach social, communication, and daily living skills (Charlop and Milstein, 1989; Taylor, 2001).

As mentioned previously, Metz et al. (2005) and Steege et al. (2007) cautioned readers in interpreting ABA as being one of these specific technique (e.g., verbal behavior, DTI, etc.). Teaching skills and reducing inappropriate behavior for people with autism involved a variety of behavioral techniques based upon operant and respondent learning (see Cooper et al., 2006 for an explanation of general behavioral principles). Some of these behavioral interventions for teaching people with autism included: (a) making environmental changes, such as providing structure and reducing distraction in teaching situations; (b) using specific prompts and prompting strategies (e.g., modeling, gestural, mechanical, etc.); (c) requiring repeated practice of behaviors (e.g., DTI); (d) employing reinforcement for correct responses; (e) decreasing behavior through reinforcement manipulation and punishment procedures; (f) implementing naturalistic teaching (e.g., incidental learning, delayed cue prompting, etc.); (g) using task analyses, chaining, and shaping to teach new skills; (h) planning for generalization and maintenance; and (i) exposing children to typical learning environments based on skills (see Cooper et al., 2006; Foxx, 1982a,b, for information concerning behavioral interventions).

Scientific evidence for using ABA to reduce behavioral excesses

Frequently for people with autism the large array of behavioral excesses and related behavior problems, such as self-injurious behavior, stereotypic behavior, extreme tantrums, aggression, sleep disorders, and feeding problems (APA,

1994), must be reduced for skill building to occur. Countless articles were published within the ABA literature describing behavioral interventions for reducing these behavioral excesses. Depending on the severity of the behavioral excess and the type of behavior problem, a variety of behavioral strategies were scientifically supported (see Cooper et al., 2006; Foxx, 1982a; Konarksi et al., 1997).

Scientific evidence for using ABA to teach comprehensive skills

Eventually ABA's concentration on teaching specific skills and reducing behavioral excesses evolved into comprehensive behavioral treatments for teaching young children with autism the prerequisite skills for learning in general (Olley, 2005). Lovaas (1987) provided the seminal article on implementing these comprehensive behavioral interventions to teach young children with autism (see Lovaas, 1983, 2003; Maurice et al., 1996; Maurice, Green, and Foxx, 2001 for curricular and methodology examples of comprehensive behavioral interventions). Although controversial to some, Lovaas (1987) reported that 47 percent of the children treated with a comprehensive behavioral approach for teaching fundamental learning skills no longer exhibited autism symptoms and were able to be educated in typical classroom settings.

Lovaas's (1987) results were not *fully* replicated in the scientific literature. However, prior and subsequent studies examining comprehensive behavioral treatments for people with autism reported significant gains for these people in intellectual skills, communication, and adaptive behavior (Birnbauer and Leach, 1993; Butter et al., 2006; Cohen et al., 2006; Eikeseth et al., 2002; Howard, Sparkman et al., 2005; Schreck, 2000; Sheinkopf and Siegel, 1998; Smith et al., 1997; Smith et al., 2000; Weiss, 1999). The substantial gains or prevention of deterioration in functioning for children in comprehensive ABA programs were significant compared to children who received other types of treatments, such as eclectic treatment, public school special education, or no treatment at all (Cohen et al., 2006; Eikeseth et al., 2002; Eldevik et al., 2006; Howard et al., 2005; Lovaas, 1987; Sheinkopf and Siegel, 1998). As these noteworthy results evolved, so have recommendations on the critical components related to the effectiveness of comprehensive behavioral treatments. Table 1.1 summarizes the current research indicating the necessary components of a comprehensive behavioral program (see Green, 1996).

Although the behaviorally based treatments for specific skill categories, reductions in inappropriate behaviors, and comprehensive instruction of learning repertoires had research support, these treatments were widely debated and not universally applied. Possible reasoning for this may be that: (a) the research on these treatments has been incomplete (e.g., predictions on treatment outcome cannot be reliably made based on symptomatology); (b) the treatments have been time-consuming; (c) the interventions have required extensive training and experience to implement; and (d) the treatments have not tended to be related to a specific theory of the origin of autism (thus, contradicting people's a priori

TABLE 1.1   Variables related to effectiveness of comprehensive behavioral treatment

Variable	Description	Research
Age at onset of treatment	Research indicates that starting treatment before age 5 years relates to better outcomes. Best outcomes seem to be related to children who start by age 2 or 3 years. However, older children have shown significant benefits.	Eikeseth et al. (2002) Fenske et al. (1985) Harris and Handleman (2000) Lovaas (1987)
Types of treatment	Comparisons of ABA to other eclectic and special education structured teaching approaches indicate that ABA alone is more effective.	Cohen et al. (2006) Eikeseth et al. (2002) Eldevik et al. (2006) Howard et al. (2005) Sheinkopf and Siegel (1998) Smith et al. (2000)
Intensity of ABA treatment	Best outcomes have been reported for children who receive at least 40 hours per week of behavioral treatment. However, Lovaas (1987) utilized parent training "so that treatment could take place for almost all of the subjects' waking hours, 365 days a year" (p. 5). Significant outcomes also have been reported for children who receive between 20 and 30 hours per week.	Anderson et al. (1987) Birnbrauer and Leach (1993) Eldevik et al. (2006) Howard et al. (2005) Sheinkopf and Siegel (1998) Smith et al. (1997) Smith et al. (2000) Weiss (1999)
Duration of intervention	Current consensus recommends at least 2 years of intensive behavioral intervention (for at least 40 hours per week).	Lovaas (1987) Smith et al. (1997)
Quality of ABA services	Since Lovaas's (1987) article, debate has occurred concerning who is qualified to supervise comprehensive ABA programs. Consultants minimally should have a master's or doctoral degree in ABA or related field and supervised experience in ABA autism consultation. The Behavior Analyst Certification Board also certifies some (but not all) behavior analysts.	Shook and Favell (1996) Behavior Analyst Certification Board http://www.bacb.com

beliefs about autism). These characteristics (Vyse, 2005) of behavioral interventions could possibly lead to the rapid development and assimilation of fad therapies for the treatment of autism and the buffet approach to autism treatment.

Side 2: The Buffet Approach to Autism Treatment

The other side of the debate contended that a little bit of everything in treatment ensures that you miss nothing. This philosophy resulted in the prolific dissemination of fad therapies for people with autism. Caregivers were bombarded by professionals, role models, internet sites, and TV documentaries with

TABLE 1.2 Current fashionable autism treatments[a]

Treatment	Treatment description[a]	Research/recommendations	Example references related to topic[b]
Physiological			
Sensory integration	Supposes autism behavior due to sensory organization, hyper/hyposensitivity problems. Treatment involves exposure to sensory stimuli and reducing sensory distractions. Typically used by occupational therapists.	No scientific research support. Anecdotal reports.	Kay and Vyse (2005) Metz et al. (2005) Smith et al. (2005) New York State Department of Health, Early Intervention Program (1999)
Auditory integration	Assumes people with autism are oversensitive to sounds. Treatment involves listening to filtered sounds and music to reduce hypersensitivity.	No scientific research support. **May cause harm.**	Mudford and Cullen (2005) New York State Department of Health, Early Intervention Program (1999)
Chelation therapy	Assumes autism due to excessive heavy metals (e.g. mercury) in blood. Frequently related to the autism/vaccine debate. Treatment involves injection of medication to bind to metals and assist the body with purging the metals.	No scientific research support. Anecdotal reports. **May cause harm due to side effects.**	Metz et al. (2005) Roberts and Prior (2006)
Gluten-free and/or - Casein-free diet	Gluten-free diets exclude proteins found in wheats. Casein-free diets exclude milk products. Supporters report improvements in behavior.	No scientific research support. Anecdotal reports. **May cause harm due to malnutrition.**	Metz et al. (2005) Irvin (2006)

(Continues)

TABLE 1.2 (*Continued*)

Treatment	Treatment description[a]	Research/recommendations	Example references related to topic[b]
Vitamin therapy	Assumes that deficiencies in vitamins (typically B_6 and magnesium) increase autism symptoms.	Little to no research support. Excessive amounts of vitamins may have long-term physiological effects.	Metz et al. (2005) Neisworth and Wolfe (2005) New York State Department of Health, Early Intervention Program (1999)
Chiropractic	Adjustments of the spine and joints are used to realign the body; thus relieving autism symptoms.	No scientific research.	
Hyperbaric oxygen	Treatment involves spending time in a pressurized chamber while breathing pure oxygen.	No scientific research.	
Secretin	Treatment involves injecting a hormone that assists with digestion.	Scientific research refuted relationships.	Roberts and Prior (2006)
Educational/Teaching Methods			
Positive behavioral support	A reaction to the anti-aversive movement, this treatment approach concentrates on environmental changes and "supports".	No research beyond basic ABA science.	Mulick and Butter (2005)
TEACCH/ Structured teaching	Believes that autism is a permanent disability that requires highly structured, unchanging routines. Treatment typically involves structured classrooms with visual schedules and workstations.	Some research support as more effective than standard special education.	Metz et al. (2005)
Social stories	Stories about common social situations that include descriptions of the situation and how the person with autism is to respond.	Little to no scientific research. Anecdotal accounts.	Olley (2005)

Treatment	Description	Scientific status	References
Developmental, individual-difference, relationship-based (DIR) model/floor time	Theory based on developmental theory and social relationships. Treatment commonly involves floortime where parents and child progress through development of social and emotional development.	Little to no scientific research. Anecdotal accounts.	Metz et al. (2005)
Son-rise program	Parents teach their child by imitating the child's stereotypic behavior to build a "non-judgmental" relationship that assists with learning.	No scientific research. Anecdotal accounts.	Paul and Sutherland (2005)
Music therapy	Assumes that musical treatment will help develop communication, social, emotional, and intellectual development.	No scientific research.	New York State Department of Health, Early Intervention Program (1999)
Facilitated communication	Assumes motor problems hinder people with autism from communicating. Treatment involves an adult holding the hand of the person with autism to keyboard messages.	**No Support.** Scientifically refuted.	Jacobson et al. (2005)[b] New York State Department of Health, Early Intervention Program (1999
Psychodynamic methods			
Holding therapy	Assumes a lack of mother-child bond. Treatment involves comforting children, physically restraining a resistant child, or "rebirthing".	No scientific research. **Could be dangerous.**	Metz et al. (2005)

[a] See Neisworth and Wolfe (2005); New York State Department of Health, Early Intervention Program (1999); Paul and Sutherland (2005); Remedyfind (2007); Roberts and Prior (2006).

[b] Since a comprehensive review of every unsupported treatment was beyond the scope of this chapter, representative references (e.g., literature reviews) were provided for further study. Additionally, some treatments had no references to report.

a buffet treatment approach to caring for their children. They were advised to "Pick a little of this and/or a little of that" to help treat the underlying *causes or etiologies* of autism, such as audiological or sensory problems, dietary incompatibilities, metal poisonings, etc. Unfortunately, people in authority (or likeable role models) pushed these buffet approaches; providing caregivers with hundreds of treatments (Dawson, 2001; Remedyfind, 2007) with little or no research support of their relationship to autism or to improvement in skill acquisition or behavior reduction.

As previously discussed, research did not support the use of these eclectic, buffet approaches to autism treatment (Cohen et al., 2006; Eikeseth et al., 2002; Eldevik et al., 2006; Howard et al., 2005; Sheinkopf and Siegel, 1998). However, within our practice these buffet approaches have been commonly observed. Although it was impossible to include all of the hundreds of unsupported treatments proclaimed to treat people with autism, we listed some of the most in vogue treatments that are currently used for people with autism (see Table 1.2), many of which have been influential for up to two decades or more (e.g., vitamin therapy).

CONCLUSION

As the diagnosis of an ASD becomes more and more prevalent in our societies, the debates over the appropriate autism diagnosis, assessment, and treatment will undoubtedly continue. As we have illustrated, many of the issues that arose from when Kanner (1943) and Asperger (1944/1991) first published descriptions of their cases still exist today, while others such as psychogenic theories of autism have been abandoned. Although the contemporary behavioral diagnostic criteria of autism continue to resemble Kanner's and Asperger's descriptions of their children, researchers and clinicians still debate whether or not the ASDs form a spectrum or a group of related disorders. Some of these diagnostic and assessment issues continue to fuel contentious treatment debates. Most now agree that early intensive educational and behavioral intervention provides the best evidence for good outcomes; however, scientifically unsupported and potentially dangerous approaches to intervention are still peddled and many potentially promising interventions require further research before being safe for children with autism.

REFERENCES

American Psychiatric Association (1968). *Diagnostic and Statistical Manual of Mental Disorders (2nd ed.)*. Washington DC: Author.

American Psychiatric Association (1980). *Diagnostic and Statistical Manual of Mental Disorders (3rd ed.)*. Washington DC: Author.

American Psychiatric Association (1987). *Diagnostic and Statistical Manual of Mental Disorders (3rd ed.) – Revised.* Washington DC: Author.

American Psychiatric Association (1994). *Diagnostic and Statistical Manual of Mental Disorders (4th ed.).* Washington DC: Author.

American Psychiatric Association (2000). *Diagnostic and Statistical Manual of Mental Disorders (4*th ed.*) – Text revision.* Washington DC: Author.

American Psychological Association (2007). *Psychology Matters: Facilitated Communication: Sifting the Psychological Wheat from the Chaff.* Retrieved February 22 from http://www.psychologymatters.org/facilitated.html

Anderson, S.R., Avery, D.L., DiPietro, E.K., Edwards, G.L. and Christian, W.P. (1987). Intensive home-based early intervention with autistic children. *Education and Treatment of Children,* **10,** 352–366.

Asperger, H. (1944/1991). Autistic psychopathy in childhood (Translated by U. Frith). In *Autism and Asperger Syndrome* (U. Frith, ed.) pp. 37–92. Cambridge, UK: Cambridge University Press.

Attwood, T. (1997). *Asperger's Syndrome: A Guide for Parents and Professionals.* London, UK: Jessica Kingsley.

Baker, A.F. (1983). Psychological assessment of autistic children. *Clinical Psychology Review,* **3,** 41–59.

Baron-Cohen, S., Leslie, A., and Frith, U. (1986). Mechanical, behavioural and intentional understanding of pictures stories in autistic children. *British Journal of Developmental Psychology,* **4,** 113–125.

Barthélémy, C., Garreau, B., Bruneau, N., Martineau, J., Jouve, J., Roux, S., et al. (1988). Biological and behavioural effects of magnesium + vitamin B6, folates and fenfluramine in autistic children. In *Aspects of autism: Biological research* (L. Wing, ed.) London, UK: The Royal College of Psychiatrists.

Bayley, N. (2005). *The Bayley Scales of Infant and Toddler Development* 3rd ed. Marrickville, Australia: Harcourt Assessment.

Bettelheim, B. (1967). *The Empty Fortress.* New York, NY: The Free Press.

Birnbauer, J.S. and Leach, D.J. (1993). The Murdoch early intervention program after 2 years. *Behaviour Change,* **10,** 63–74.

Bishop, D.V.M (1998). Development of the children's communication checklist (CCC): A method for assessing qualitative aspects of communicative impairment in children. *Journal of Child Psychology and Psychiatry,* **39,** 879–891.

Bishop, D.V.M and Norbury, C.F. (2002). Exploring the borderlands of autistic disorder and specific language impairment: a study using standardized diagnostic instruments. *Journal of Child Psychology and Psychiatry,* **43,** 917–929.

Butter, E.M., Mulick, J.A., and Metz, B. (2006). Eight case reports of learning recovery in children with pervasive developmental disorders after early intervention. *Behavioral Interventions,* **21,** 227–243.

Campbell, J.M. (2005). Diagnostic assessment of Asperger's disorder: A review of five third-party rating scales. *Journal of Autism and Developmental Disorders,* **35,** 25–35.

Campbell, M. Perry, R., Small, A.M., and Green, W.H. (1987). Overview of drug treatment in autism. In *Neurobiological issues in autism* (E. Schopler and G.B. Mesibov, eds.) pp. 341–356. New York, NY: Plenum Press.

Chambless, D.L. and Hollon, S.D. (1998). Defining empirically supported therapies. *Journal of Consulting and Clinical Psychology,* **66,** 7–18.

Charlop, M.H., and Milstein, J.P. (1989). Teaching autistic children conversation speech using video modeling. *Journal of Applied Behavior Analysis,* **23,** 275–285.

Cohen, H., Amerine-Dickens, M., and Smith, T. (2006). Early intensive behavioral treatment: Replication of the UCLA model in a community setting. *Journal of Developmental and Behavioral Pediatrics,* **27,** S145–S155.

Coonrod, E.E. and Stone, W.L. (2005). Screening for autism in young children. In *Handbook of Autism and Pervasive Developmental Disorders: Volume Two. Assessment, Interventions, and*

Policy (F.R. Volkmar, R. Paul, A. Klin, and D. Cohen, eds.) pp. 707–729. Hoboken, NJ: John Wiley and Sons.

Cooper, J.O., Heron, T.E., and Heward, W.L. (2006). *Applied Behavior Analysis.* 2nd ed. Columbus, OH: Prentice Hall.

Creak, M., Cameron, K., Cowie, V., Ini, S., MacKeith, R., Mitchell, G., et al. (1961). Schizophrenic syndrome in childhood. Progress report of a working party (April, 1961). *Cerebral Palsy Bulletin,* **3,** 501–504.

Davis, B.J. (1967). A clinical method of appraisal of the language and learning behavior of young autistic children. *Journal of Communication Disorders,* **1,** 277–296.

Dawson, P. (2001). The search for effective autism treatment: Options or insanity. In *Making a difference: Behavioral intervention for autism* (C. Maurice, G. Green, and R. M. Foxx, eds.) pp. 11–22. Austin, TX: Pro-Ed.

Delacato, C.H. (1974). *The Ultimate Stranger. The Autistic Child.* New York, NY: Doubleday and Company Inc.

DeMeyer, M.K. (1976). Motor, perceptual-motor and intellectual disabilities of autistic children. In *Early childhood autism, 2nd ed.* (L. Wing, ed.) pp. 169–193. Oxford, UK: Pergamon Press.

Dunn, L. and Dunn, L. (1997). *Peabody Picture Vocabulary Test – III.* Circle Pines, MN: American Guidance Service.

Edwards, S., Fletcher, P., Garman, M., Highes, A., Letts, C., and Sinka, I. (1999). *Reynell Developmental Language Scale-III.* Windsor, UK: NFER-Nelson.

Eikeseth, S., Smith, T., Jahr, E., and Eldevik, S. (2002). Intensive behavioral treatment at school for 4- to 7-year-old children with autism: A 1-year comparison controlled study. *Behavior Modification,* **26,** 49–68.

Eldevik, S., Eikeseth, S., Jahr, E., and Smith, T. (2006). Effects of low-intensity behavioral treatment for children with autism and mental retardation. *Journal of Autism and Developmental Disorders,* **36,** 211–224.

Favell, J.E. (2005). Sifting sound practice from snake oil. In *Controversial Therapies for Developmental Disabilities: Fad, Fashion, and Science in Professional Practice* (J.W. Jacobson, R.M. Foxx and J.A. Mulick, eds.) pp. 19–30. Mahwah, NJ: Lawrence Erlbaum Associates.

Fenske, E. C., Zalenski, S., Krantz, P.J., and McClannahan, L. E. (1985). Age at intervention and treatment outcome for autistic children in a comprehensive intervention program. *Analysis and Intervention in Developmental Disabilities,* **5,** 49–58.

Fenske, E.C., Krantz, P.J., and McClannahan, L.E. (2001). Incidental teaching: A not-discrete-trial teaching procedure. In *Making a Difference: Behavioral Intervention for Autism* (C. Maurice, G. Green, and R.M. Foxx, eds.) pp. 11–22. Austin, TX: Pro-Ed.

Fenson, L., Dale, P.S., Reznick, J.S., Thal, D., Bates, E., Hartung, J.P., et al. (1993). *MacArthur Communication Development Inventories: Users' Guide and Technical Manual.* CA: Singular Publishing Company.

Flaharty, R. (1976). EPEC: Evaluation and prescription for exceptional children. In *Autism. Diagnosis, Current Research and Management* (E.R. Ritvo, B.J. Freeman, E.M. Ornitz, and P.E. Tanguay, eds.) pp. 35–56. New York, NY: Spectrum Publications, Inc.

Foxx, R. (1982a). *Decreasing Behaviors of Severely Retarded and Autistic Persons.* Champaign, IL: Research Press.

Foxx, R. (1982b). *Increasing Behaviors of Severely Retarded and Autistic Persons.* Champaign, IL: Research Press.

Freeman, B.J., Ritvo, E.R., Yokota, A., and Ritvo, A. (1986). A scale for rating symptoms of patients with the syndrome of autism in real life settings. *Journal of the American Academy of Child Psychiatry,* **25,** 130–136.

Freeman, B.J. and Ritvo, E.R. (1976). Cognitive assessment. In *Autism. Diagnosis, Current Research and Management* (E.R. Ritvo, B.J. Freeman, E.M. Ornitz, and P.E. Tanguay, eds.) pp. 27–33. New York, NY: Spectrum Publications, Inc.

Frith, U. (2003). *Autism. Explaining the Enigma* (2nd ed.). Melbourne, Australia: Blackwell Publishing.

Frost, L. and Bondy, A. (2000). *The Picture Exchange Communication System* (PECS) *Training Manual* (2nd ed.). Newark, DE: Pyramid Products.

Gillberg, C. and Coleman, M. (2000). *The Biology of the Autistic Syndromes* (3rd ed.). London, UK: MacKeith Press.

Green, G. (1996). Evaluating claims about treatments for autism. In *Behavioral Intervention for Young Children with Autism: A Manual for Parents and Professionals* (C. Maurice, G. Green, and S.C. Luce, eds.) pp. 15–28. Austin, TX: Pro-Ed.

Harris, S.L. and Handleman, J.S. (2000). Age and IQ at intake as predictors of placement for young children with autism: A four-to six-year follow-up. *Journal of Autism and Developmental Disorders*, **30**, 137–142.

Hart, B.M. and Risley, T.R. (1982). *How to Use Incidental Teaching for Elaborating Language.* Austin, TX: Pro-Ed.

Hermelin, B.A. and O'Connor, N. (1970). *Psychological Experiments with Autistic Children.* Oxford, UK: Pergamon Press.

Howard, J.S., Sparkman, C.R., Cohen, H.G., Green, G., and Stanislaw, H. (2005). A comparison of behavior analytic and eclectic treatments for young children with autism. *Research in Developmental Disabilities*, **26**, 359–383.

Howlin, P. (2003). Outcome in high-functioning adults with autism with and without early language delays: Implications for the differentiation between autism and Asperger syndrome. *Journal of Autism and Developmental Disorders*, **33**, 3–13.

Irvin, D.S. (2006). Using analog assessment procedures for determining the effects of gluten-free and casein-free diet on rate of problem behaviors for an adolescent with autism. *Behavioral Interventions*, **21**, 281–286.

Itard, J.M.G (1962). *The Wild Boy of Aveyron.* New York, NY: Appleton Century Crofts.

Jacobson, J. (2005). Historical Approaches to Developmental Disabilities. In *Controversial Therapies for Developmental Disabilities: Fad, Fashion, and Science in Professional Practice* (J.W. Jacobson, R.M. Foxx, and J.A. Mulick, eds.) pp. 61–84. Mahwah, NJ: Lawrence Erlbaum Associates.

Jacobson, J.W., Foxx, R.M., and Mulick, J.A. (2005). Facilitated communication: The ultimate fad treatment. In *Controversial Therapies for Developmental Disabilities: Fad, Fashion, and Science in Professional Practice* (J.W. Jacobson, R.M. Foxx, and J.A. Mulick, eds.) pp. 363–384. Malwah, NJ: Lawrence Erlbaum Associates.

Jordon, R. (1999). *Autistic Spectrum Disorders. An Introductory Handbook for Practitioners.* London, UK: David Fulton Publishing.

Kanner, L. (1943). Autistic disturbances of affective contact. *Nervous Child*, **2**, 217–250.

Kanner, L. (1949). Problems of nosology and psychodynamics of early infantile autism. *American Journal of Orthopsychiatry*, **19**, 416–426.

Kay, S. and Vyse, S. (2005). Helping parents separate the wheat from the chaff: Putting autism treatments to the test. In *Controversial Therapies for Developmental Disabilities: Fad, Fashion, and Science in Professional Practice* (J.W. Jacobson, R.M. Foxx and J.A. Mulick, eds.) pp. 265–277. Mahwah, NJ: Lawrence Erlbaum Associates.

Klin, A., Saulnier, C., Tsatsanis, K., and Volkmar, F.R. (2005). Clinical evaluation in autism spectrum disorders: Assessment within a transdisciplinary framework. In *Handbook of Autism and Pervasive Developmental Disorders: Volume Two Assessment, Interventions, and Policy (3rd ed.)* (F.R. Volkmar, R., Paul, A., Klin, and D. Cohen, eds.) pp. 772–798. Hoboken, NJ: John Wiley and Sons, Inc.

Klin, A., Sparrow, S.S., Marans, W.D., Carter, A., and Volkmar, F.R. (2000). Assessment issues in children and adolescents with Asperger syndrome. In *Asperger syndrome* (A. Kiln, F.R. Volkmar, and S.S. Sparrow, eds.) pp. 309–339. New York, NY: The Guilford Press.

Konarksi, E.A., Favell, J.E.,and Favell, J.E. (1997). *Manual for the Assessment and Treatment of the Behavior Disorders of People with Mental Retardation.* Morganton, NC: West Carolina Center Foundation.

Le Couter, A., Rutter, M., Lord, C., Rios, P., Roberston, S., Holdgarfer, M. et al. (1989). Autism diagnostic interview: A standardized investigator-based instrument. *Journal of Autism and Developmental Disorders*, **19**, 363–387.

Lonigan, C.J., Elbert, J.C., and Johnson, S.B. (1998). Empirically supported psychosocial interventions for children: An overview. *Journal of Clinical Child Psychology*, **27**, 138–14.

Lord, C. and Corsello, C. (2005). Diagnostic instruments in autistic spectrum disorders. In *Handbook of Autism and Pervasive Developmental Disorders: Volume 2 Assessment, Interventions, and Policy (3rd ed.)* (F.R. Volkmar. R. Paul, A. Klin, and D. Cohen, eds.) pp. 730–771. Hoboken, NJ: John Wiley and Sons Inc.

Lord, C., Risi, S., Lambrecht, L., Cook, E.H., Leventhal, B.L., DiLavore, P.C., et al. (2000). The autism diagnostic observation schedule – generic: A standard measure of social and communication deficits associated with the spectrum of autism. *Journal of Autism and Developmental Disorders*, **30**, 205–233.

Lord, C., Rutter, M., and Le Couter, A. (1994). Autism diagnostic interview-revised: A revised version of a diagnostic interview for caregivers of individuals with possible pervasive developmental disorders. *Journal of Autism and Developmental Disorders*, **24**, 659–685.

Lovaas, O.I. (1983). *Teaching Developmentally Disabled Children: The ME Book*. Austin, TX: Pro-Ed.

Lovaas, O.I. (1987). Behavioral treatment and normal educational and intellectual functioning in young autistic children. *Journal of Consulting and Clinical Psychology*, **55**, 3–9.

Lovaas. O., I. (2003). *Teaching Individuals with Developmental Delays: Basic Intervention Techniques*. Austin, TX: Pro-Ed.

Lucas, P. (2001). John Howard and Asperger's syndrome: Psychopathology or philanthropy. *History of Psychiatry*, **12**, 73–101.

Luiselli, J.K., Cambell, S., Cannon, B., DiPietro, E., Ellis, J.T., Taras, M. et al. (2001). Assessment instruments used in the education and treatment of persons with autism: brief report of a survey of national service centers. *Research in Developmental Disabilities*, **22**, 389–398.

Malson, L. (1972). *Wolf Children and the Problem of Human Nature*. New York, NY: Monthly Review Press.

Manjiviano, J. and Prior, M. (1999). Neuropsychological profiles of children with Asperger syndrome and autism. *Autism*, **3**, 327–356.

Matson, J.L., Benavidez, D.A., Compton, L.S., Pacloawsky, T., and Baglio, C. (1996). Behavioral treatment of autistic persons: A review of research from 1980 to the present. *Research in Developmental Disabilities*, **17**, 433–465.

Maurice, C., Green, G., and Foxx, R.M. (eds.) (2001). *Making a Difference: Behavioral Interventions for Autism*. Austin, TX: Pro-Ed.

Maurice, C., Green, G., and Luce, S.C. (eds.). (1996). *Behavioral Intervention for Young Children with Autism: A Manual for Parents and Professionals*. Austin, TX: Pro-Ed.

Mayes, S.D. and Calhoun, S.L. (2003). Analysis of WISC-III, Stanford-Binet:IV, and academic achievement test scores in children with autism. *Journal of Autism and Developmental Disorders*, **33**, 329–341.

Mesibov, G.B., Shea, V., and Schopler, E. (2005). *The TEACCH Approach to Autism Spectrum Disorders*. New York, NY: Kluwer Academic/Plenum Press.

Metz, B., Mulick, J.A., and Butter, E.M. (2005). Autism: A late-20th-century fad magnet. In *Controversial Therapies for Developmental Disabilities: Fad, Fashion, and Science in Professional Practice* (J.W. Jacobson, R.M. Foxx and J.A. Mulick, eds.) pp. 237–263. Mahwah, NJ: Lawrence Erlbaum Associates.

Miller, J.N. and Ozonoff, S. (1997). Did Asperger's cases have Asperger disorder? A research note. *Journal of Child Psychology and Psychiatry*, **38**, 247–251.

Mudford, O.C. and Cullen, C. (2005). Auditory Integration Training: A Critical Review. In *Controversial Therapies for Developmental Disabilities: Fad, Fashion, and Science in Professional Practice* (J.W. Jacobson, R.M. Foxx and J.A. Mulick, eds.) pp. 351–362. Mahwah, NJ: Lawrence Erlbaum Associates.

Mulick, J.A. and Butter, E.M. (2005). Positive behavior support: A paternalistic utopian delusion. In *Controversial Therapies for Developmental Disabilities: Fad, Fashion, and Science in Professional Practice* (J.W. Jacobson, R.M. Foxx and J.A. Mulick, eds.) pp. 385–404. Mahwah, NJ: Lawrence Erlbaum Associates.

National Research Council (2001). *Educating Children with Autism* (Committee on educational interventions for children with autism, division of behavioral and social sciences and education). Washington DC: National Academy Press.

Neisworth, J.T. and Wolfe, P.S. (eds.) (2005). *The Autism Encyclopedia*. Baltimore: Brookes.

Newsom, C. and Hovanitz, C.A. (2005a). Autism spectrum disorders. In *Treatment of Childhood Disorders (3rd ed.)* (E.J. Mash and R.A. Barkley, eds.) pp. 455–511. New York, NY: Guilford Press.

Newsom, C. and Hovanitz, C.A. (2005b). The nature and value of empirically validated interventions. In *Controversial Therapies for Developmental Disabilities: Fad, Fashion, and Science in Professional Practice* (J.W. Jacobson, R.M. Foxx and J.A. Mulick, eds.) pp. 31–57. Mahwah, NJ: Lawrence Erlbaum Associates.

New York State Department of Health, Early Intervention Program (1999). *Clinical Practice Guideline: The Guideline Technical Report. Autism/pervasive Developmental Disorders: Assessment and Intervention for Young Children (age 0–3 years).* Publication No. 4217. Albany. Author.

Olley, J.G. (2005). Curriculum and classroom structure. In *Handbook of Autism and Pervasive Developmental Disorders: Volume Two Assessment, Interventions, and Policy* (F.R. Volkmar, R. Paul, A. Klin, and D. Cohen, eds.) pp. 882–896. Hoboken, NJ: John Wiley and Sons.

Ozonoff, S., South, M, and Miller, J.N. (2000). DSM-IV-defined Asperger syndrome: Cognitive, behavioral and early history differentiation from high-functioning autism. *Autism*, **4**, 29–46.

Parks, S.L. (1988). Psychometric instruments available for the assessment of autistic children. In *Diagnosis and Assessment in Autism* (E. Schopler and G. B. Mesibov, eds.) pp. 123–138. New York, NY: Plenum Press.

Paul, R. (2005). Assessing communication in autism spectrum disorders. In *Handbook of Autism and Pervasive Developmental Disorders: Volume Two Assessment, Interventions, and Policy (3rd ed.)* (F.R. Volkmar, R. Paul, A. Klin, and D. Cohen, eds.) pp. 799–816. Hoboken, NJ: John Wiley and Sons, Inc.

Paul, R. and Sutherland, D. (2005). Enhancing early language in children with autism spectrum disorders. In *Handbook of Autism and Pervasive Developmental Disorders: Volume Two Assessment, Interventions, and Policy* (F.R. Volkmar, R. Paul, A. Klin, and D. Cohen, eds.) pp. 946–976. Hoboken, NJ: John Wiley and Sons.

Piven, J. (1999). Genetic liability for autism: The behavioural expression in relatives. *International Review of Psychiatry*, **11**, 299–308.

Prior, M. and Bence, R. (1975). A note on the validity of the Rimland diagnostic checklist. *Journal of Clinical Psychology*, **31**, 510–513.

Prior, M., Eisenmajer, R., Leekam, S., Wing, L., Gould, J. Ong, B., et al. (1998). Are there subgroups within the autistic spectrum? A cluster analysis of a group of children with autistic spectrum disorders. *Journal of Child Psychology and Psychiatry*, **39**, 893–902.

Rapin, I., and Katzman, R. (1998). Neurobiology of autism. *Annals of Neurology*, **43**, 7–14.

Remedyfind: *Autism (Autistic Disorder) Complete List of Treatments* (2007). Retrieved February 22, 2007, from http://www.remedyfind.com/HealthConditions/45/hc_display.aspx?&lHCID=45& All=1&

Reitzel, J-A. and Szatmari, P. (2003). Cognitive and academic problems. In *Learning and Behavior Problems in Asperger Syndrome* (M. Prior, ed.) pp. 35–54. New York, NY: The Guilford Press.

Rimland, B. (1964). *Infantile Autism. The Syndrome and its Implications for a Neural Theory of Behavior.* Englewood Cliffs, NJ: Prentice-Hall Inc.

Roberts, J.M.A and Prior, M.R. (2006). *A Review of the Research to Identify the Most Effective Models of Practice in Early Intervention of Children with Autism Spectrum Disorders.* Australian Government Department of Health and Ageing, Canberra: Australia.

Roid, G.M. and Miller, L.J. (1997). *Leiter International Performance Scale-revised*. Wood Dale, IL: Stoetling.

Rumsey, J.M, Rapoport, J.L., and Sceery, W.R. (1985). Autistic children as adults: Psychiatric, social and behavioral outcomes. *Journal of the American Academy of Child Psychiatry*, **24**, 465–473.

Rutter, M. (1978). Diagnosis and definition of childhood autism. *Journal of Autism and Childhood Schizophrenia*, **8**, 139–161.

Rutter, M., Bailey, A., Berument, S.K., Lord, C., and Pickles, A. (2003). *The Social Communication Questionnaire*. Los Angeles, CA: Western Psychological Services.

Sanua, V.D. (1983). Infantile autism and childhood schizophrenia: Review of the issues from the sociocultural point of view. *Social Science and Medicine*, **17**, 1633–1651.

Sattler, J.M. (1982). *Assessment of Children's Intelligence and Special Abilities 2nd ed.*. Boston, MS: Allyn & Bacon.

Sattler, J.M. (2002). *Assessment of Children: Behavioral and Clinical Applications 4th ed.*. La Mesa, CA: Author.

Scheerenberger, R.C. (1983). *A History of Mental Retardation*. Baltimore, MD: Brookes.

Schopler, E. and Mesibov, G.B., (eds.) (1987). *Neurobiological Issues in Autism*. New York, NY: Plenum Press.

Schopler, E. and Mesibov, G.B. (eds.) (1988). *Diagnosis and Assessment in Autism*. New York, NY: Plenum Press.

Schopler, E., Reichler, R.J., DeVellis, R., and Daly, K. (1980). Toward objective classification of childhood autism: Childhood autism rating scale. *Journal of Autism and Developmental Disorders*, **10**, 91–103.

Schopler, E., Reichler, R.J., Bashford, Lansing, A., and Marcus, L.M. (1990). *Psychoeducational Profile – Revised*. Austin, TX: ProEd.

Schreck, K.A. (2000). It can be done: An example of a Behavioral Individualized Education Program (IEP) for a child with autism. *Behavioral Interventions*, **15**, 279–300.

Schreibman, L. and Ingersoll, B. (2005). Behavioral interventions to promote learning in individuals with autism. In *Handbook of Autism and Pervasive Developmental Disorders: Volume Two Assessment, Interventions, and Policy* (F.R. Volkmar, R. Paul, A. Klin, and D. Cohen, eds.) pp. 882–896. Hoboken, NJ: John Wiley and Sons, Inc.

Sennel, E., Wiig, E.H., and Secord, W.A. (2003). *Clinical Evaluation of Language Fundamentals 4th ed*. San Antonia, TX: The Psychological Corporation.

Sheinkopf, S.J. and Siegel, B. (1998). Home-based behavioral treatment of young children with autism. *Journal of Autism and Developmental Disorders*, **28**, 15–23.

Shah, A. and Holmes, N. (1985). Brief report: The use of the Leiter international performance scale with autistic children. *Journal of Autism and Developmental Disorders*, **15**, 195–203.

Shook, G. (2005). Applied Behavior Analysis. In *The Autism Encyclopedia*. (J.T. Neisworth and P.S. Wolfe, eds.) Baltimore, MD: Brookes.

Shook. G.L. and Favell, J.E. (1996). Identifying qualified professionals in behavior analysis. In *Behavioral Interventions for Young Children with Autism: A Manual for Parents and Professionals* (C. Maurice, G. Green, and S.C. Luce, eds.) pp. 221–230. Austin, TX: Pro-Ed.

Short, A.B. and Schopler, E. (1988). Factors relating to age of onset in autism. *Journal of Autism and Developmental Disorders*, **18**, 207–216.

Smith, T., Eikeseth, S., Klevstrand, M., and Lovaas, O.I. (1997). Intensive behavioral treatment for preschoolers with severe mental retardation and pervasive developmental disorder. *American Journal on Mental Retardation*, **102**, 238–249.

Smith, T., Groen, A.D., and Wynn, J.W. (2000). Randomized trial of intensive behavioral treatment for preschoolers with severe mental retardation and pervasive developmental disorder. *American Journal on Mental Retardation*, **102**, 238–249.

Smith, T., Mruzek, D.W., and Mozingo, D. (2005). Sensory integrative therapy. In *Controversial therapies for developmental disabilities: Fad, fashion, and science in professional practice* (J.W. Jacobson, R.M. Foxx and J.A. Mulick, eds.) pp. 341–350. Mahwah, NJ: Lawrence Erlbaum Associates.

Sparrow, S.S., Balla, D., and Cicchetti, D. (1984a). *Vineland Adaptive Behavior Scales, Survey Edition.* Circle Pines, MN: American Guidance Service.

Sparrow, S.S., Balla, D., and Cicchetti, D. (1984b). *Vineland Adaptive Behavior Scales, Expanded Edition.* Circle Pines, MN: American Guidance Service.

Steege, M.W., Mace, F.C., Perry, L., and Longenecker, H. (2007). Applied behavior analysis: beyond discrete trial teaching. *Psychology in the Schools. Special Issue: The Practitioner's Edition on Promoting Behavioral Competence*, **44**, 91–99.

Sundberg, M.L. and Partington, J.W. (1998). *Teaching Language to Children with Autism or Other Developmental Disabilities.* Danville, CA: Behavior Analysts, Inc.

Taylor, B. (2001). Teaching peer social skills to children with autism. In *Making a difference: Behavioral Intervention for Autism* (C. Maurice, G. Green, and R.M. Foxx, eds.) (pp. 83–96). Austin, TX: Pro-Ed.

Taylor, B. and Jasper, S. (2001). Teaching programs to increase peer interaction. In *Making a difference: Behavioral intervention for autism* (C. Maurice, G. Green, and R.M. Foxx, eds.) pp. 97–162. Austin, TX: Pro-Ed.

Tinbergen, N. and Tinbergen, E.A. (1983). *Autistic Children New Hope for a Cure.* London, UK: George Allen & Unwin.

Tsatsanis, K.D., Dartnall, N., Cicchetti, D., Sparrow, S.S., Kin, A., and Volkmar, F.R. (2003). Concurrent validity and classification accuracy of the Leiter and the Leiter-R in low-functioning children with autism. *Journal of Autism and Developmental Disorders*, **33**, 23–30.

U.S. Department of Health and Human Services (1999). *Mental Health: A Report of the Surgeon General.* Retrieved February 22, 2007 from http://www.surgeongeneral.gov/library/mentalhealth/chapter3/sec6.html

Van Krevelen, D.A. (1971). Early infantile autism and autistic psychopathy. *Journal of Autism and Childhood Schizophrenia*, **1**, 82–86.

Venter, A., Lord, C., and Schopler, E. (1992). A follow-up study of high-functioning autistic children. *Journal of Child Psychology and Psychiatry*, **33**, 489–507.

Volkmar, F., Cook, E.H., Pomeroy, J., Realmuto, G., Tanguay, P., Bernet, W. et al. (1999). Practice parameters for the assessment and treatment of children, adolescents and adults with autism and other pervasive developmental disorders. *Journal of the American Academy of Child and Adolescent Psychiatry*, **38** (Supp.), 32S–45S.

Volkmar, F.R. and Klin, A. (2005). Issues in the classification of autism and related conditions. In *Handbook of Autism and Pervasive Developmental Disorders: Volume One. Diagnosis, Development, Neurobiology, and Behavior 3rd ed.* pp. 5–41. Hoboken, NJ: John Wiley and Sons, Inc.

Volkmar, F.R. Paul, R., Klin, A., and Cohen, D. (eds.) (2005a). *Handbook of Autism and Pervasive Developmental Disorders: Volume One. Diagnosis, Development, Neurobiology, and Behavior (3rd ed.)* Hoboken, NJ: John Wiley and Sons, Inc.

Volkmar, F.R. Paul, R., Klin, A., and Cohen, D. (eds.) (2005b). *Handbook of Autism and Pervasive Developmental Disorders: Volume Two Assessment, Interventions, and Policy 3rd ed.)* Hoboken, NJ: John Wiley and Sons, Inc.

Vyse, S. (2005). Where do fads come from? In *Controversial Therapies for Developmental Disabilities: Fad, Fashion, and Science in Professional Practice* (J.W. Jacobson, R.M. Foxx, and J.A. Mulick, eds.) pp. 3–18. Mahwah, NJ: Lawrence Erlbaum Associates.

Waltz, M. and Shattock, P. (2004). Autistic disorder in nineteenth-century London. *Autism*, **8**, 7–20.

Weiss, M.J. (1999). Differential rates of skill acquisition and outcomes of early intensive behavioral intervention for autism. *Behavioral Interventions*, **14**, 3–22.

Weschler, D. (2003). *Weschler Intelligence Scale for Children-fourth edition: Administration and Scoring Manual.* San Antonio, TX: The Psychological Corporation.

Wing, J.K. (1976). Kanner's syndrome: A historical introduction. In *Early childhood autism 2nd ed.* (L. Wing, ed.) pp. 3–14. Oxford, UK: Pergamon Press.

Wing, L. (1976). Diagnosis, clinical description and prognosis. In *Early childhood autism 2nd ed.* (L. Wing (ed.)) pp. 15–48. Oxford, UK: Pergamon Press.

Wing, L. (1981). Asperger syndrome: a clinical account. *Psychological Medicine*, **11**, 115–129.

Wing, L. (1997). The history of ideas on autism: legends, myths and reality. *Autism*, **1**, 13–21.

Wing, L. and Gould, J. (1979). Severe impairments of social interaction and associated abnormalities in children: epidemiology and classification. *Journal of Autism and Developmental Disorders*, **9**, 11–29.

Wolff. S. (2000). Schizoid personality in childhood and Asperger syndrome. In *Asperger syndrome* (A. Klin, F.R. Volkmar, and S.S. Sparrow, eds.) pp. 278–305. New York, NY: The Guilford Press.

World Health Organization. (1992). *International Classification of Diseases: Diagnostic criteria for research 10th ed*. Geneva, Switzerland: Author.

Zimmerman, I., Steiner, V., and Pond, R. (2003). *Pre-school language scale-IV*. San Antonio, TX: Psychological Corporation.

2

EVIDENCE-BASED PRACTICE FOR AUTISM SPECTRUM DISORDERS

MARY JANE WEISS, KATE FISKE, AND
SUZANNAH FERRAIOLI

Rutgers, The State University of New Jersey, NJ, USA

INTRODUCTION

The identification of effective programs and methods for children with autism is a daunting task for many parents and professionals. The severe impact that the disorder has on so many affected individuals and their families, as well as the dearth of information regarding the etiology of the disorder, is fertile ground for the continual development of hypotheses regarding the origin of the disorder and promising treatments. Those who live with children and adults with autism understand the severe impact of the disorder on both the individual and the family, and many wish for a breakthrough that will cure the individual with autism. This understandable desire for a "cure" leaves many vulnerable and susceptible to the appeal of treatments that are based solely on hearsay, anecdotal evidence, and biased report.

In the field of clinical psychology, increased emphasis has been placed on the use of empirically supported treatment for psychological disorders. This call for evidence-based treatment extends to the field of autism and, as a result, researchers and professionals have taken steps to identify the comprehensive programs and focal methods that are most effective in treating autism and its accompanying symptoms. This chapter will review the current state of information regarding evidence-based treatment for autism. Various definitions of evidence-based treatment, along with the criteria used to evaluate different treatments will be reviewed. Several strategies in applied behavior analysis (ABA) will be highlighted, as they clearly have the largest preponderance of evidence supporting their effectiveness. In addition, a variety of strategies that are not empirically validated, but which are in common use will be reviewed. Finally, recommendations for both professionals advising consumers and for consumers navigating treatment decisions will be delineated.

AUTISM SPECTRUM DISORDERS: AN OVERVIEW

The most widely accepted criteria for autism are contained in the *Diagnostic and Statistical Manual of Mental Disorders – Fourth Edition Text Revision* (DSM-IV-TR; American Psychiatric Association, 2000). According to this resource, autism has three central defining characteristics, namely:

1. Qualitative impairment in reciprocal social interaction
2. Qualitative impairment in verbal and nonverbal communication and in imaginative ability
3. Markedly restricted and repetitive repertoire of behavior, activities, and interests.

The ways in which these characteristics are manifested, however, are highly variable. While some individuals with autism are not interested in social interaction, others are affectionate and attached to others. While some individuals with autism lack vocal language ability, others use vocal speech communicatively. When speech is used communicatively, however, there are often unusual qualities of the speech, or their vocal speech ability may lag behind their communication potential. For example, a child may only request for wanted items and not be able to hold conversations, or may converse only about topics of special interest. Restricted behaviors and interests may manifest themselves as classically autistic rocking or flapping. However, it may also present as adhering to rituals or routines, or becoming fixated on a single object or topic.

It is estimated that about 75 percent of children with autism have developmental delays (APA, 2000). There is also a tendency for their development to be uneven or scattered, with clear strengths and weaknesses evident. Behavioral difficulties are common, occurring in about 90 percent of individuals with autism. At least 10 to 20 percent of individuals with autism exhibit severe behaviors such as aggression and self-injury (Lovaas, 1987; Smith et al., 2007).

DSM-IV-TR (APA, 2000) also classifies other Pervasive Developmental Disorders (PDDs) along with autism: Rett's Disorder, Childhood Disintegrative Disorder, Asperger's Disorder, and Pervasive Developmental Disorder – Not Otherwise Specified (PDD-NOS). Rett's Disorder is a degenerative disorder that occurs in girls, and is distinct from autism in course and prognosis (Kerr and Ravine, 2003). Childhood Disintegrative Disorder is poorly understood and is rare (Mouridsen, 2003).

The current diagnostic criteria for Asperger's Disorder highlight impairments in nonverbal communication and in social interaction with an absence of delays in cognitive or language skills (APA, 2000). However, individuals with Asperger's

Disorder do experience a variety of problems in communication and interaction, such as poor reciprocal conversational abilities, difficulties in comprehending abstract language, and perseveration on topics of special interest that interfere with true reciprocity. Individuals classified as PDD-NOS generally exhibit features of autism, but fail to meet the full diagnostic criteria for Autistic Disorder.

In recent years, many clinicians and researchers have discussed autism, PDD-NOS and Asperger's Disorder as a spectrum. While there are not yet reliable criteria for distinguishing between these groups, and it may be that the same disorder essentially varies in presentation and severity along the continuum (Wing, 1988), the concept of a continuum seems to have utility.

GUIDELINES FOR CONSUMERS OF TREATMENTS FOR INDIVIDUALS WITH AUTISM

Guidelines have been developed to help consumers caring for individuals with autism to identify those research studies that offer the strongest support for a given treatment (Lonigan et al., 1998; New York State Department of Health, Early Intervention Program, 1999; National Research Council, 2001). Such guidelines, however, do not provide a clear methodology for identifying therapies as either evidence-based or non-evidence based. Rather, the multiple guidelines currently used in the field give rise to varying levels of scientific strength and support on which treatments may be based. This continuum, from the broad identification of science to the more specific identification of empirically supported treatment, will be described here.

SCIENCE, PSEUDOSCIENCE, AND ANTISCIENCE

When examining the evidence for the effectiveness of an intervention for individuals with autism, a distinction can first be made between what is clearly science, and what is not. To identify therapies that are evidence based, it is helpful to ensure that the elements of science and the scientific method have been used to demonstrate support for the effectiveness of a given intervention. Science is based in part on (1) the direct and objective observation of measurable events, (2) a systematic manipulation of conditions, (3) procedures that rule out alternative explanations for results, and (4) replication of the results (Green, 1996). In contrast, pseudoscience promotes specific phenomena without the use of the scientific method and without providing evidence of efficacy or effectiveness (Green, 1996). While scientific findings rest on the solid base of the scientific method, pseudoscience relies heavily on the use of persuasive marketing that appeals to consumers. A treatment that is not supported either by the scientific method or by direct evidence of its effectiveness may still be adopted by a consumer either because the treatment was promoted using scientific terminology or because it was supported by an authority in the field, such as a doctor or a scientist.

An even more extreme phenomenon, antiscience, constitutes the body of treatments that reject the use of scientific methods altogether (Green, 1996). In contrast to pseudoscience, antiscience demonstrates a complete disregard for any type of data and suggests that empirical testing of the treatment is a violation of the treatment. Interventions supported by antiscience are based on belief alone.

While these basic definitions are helpful to begin an evaluation of the evidence for an intervention, a more in-depth review of the components of science will further delineate the differences between science, pseudoscience, and antiscience. The first distinction lies in data collection procedures. Science relies on the objective observation and measurement of observable events. Such measurement is accomplished using operational definitions, by which phenomena and treatments are defined in observable terms such that the use of the treatment and the measurement of the phenomena are unbiased and nonsubjective (Cooper et al., 1987, 2007; Green, 1996). To further strengthen the impartial measurement of phenomena, scientific investigations are conducted by professionals who are well-trained in the implementation of the treatment and the data collection method, and who are often unaware of the hypotheses guiding the research (Green, 1996). Such steps protect against the possibility of bias influencing the results of the research. This provides a stark contrast to pseudoscience and antiscience, in which treatment effects are speculative and subjective. In these approaches, treatments are supported by testimony, anecdotal reports, and subjective reports rather than on observed and measured phenomena.

Another distinction between science and pseudoscience or antiscience is the former's commitment to ensuring that confounding variables are not responsible for the perceived effectiveness of the intervention. To maintain this internal validity, science makes use of comparative research, in which the treatment in question is compared to other treatments or to lack of treatment to ensure that other variables – such as the passage of time or significant events in the environment – are not responsible for the observed effect on the targeted phenomena. Scientific research is well controlled to ensure that the treatment variables are responsible for change, rather than external variables that – if not held constant – may impact the treatment effects (Cooper et al., 2007; Green, 1996). Additionally, external validity is maintained by assessing the generalization of treatment effects across settings different from the treatment setting. In contrast, pseudoscience approaches are often noncomparative, relying only on indirect reports or pre-post measures in which the same child is evaluated before and after treatment. In these instances, extraneous variables may be responsible for changes in behavior, though they are infrequently cited as possible agents of change (Green, 1996).

While one may be able to easily differentiate between science and pseudoscience – or easier yet, science and antiscience – further discrimination is required to define that which has been termed "evidence-based treatment" within the more global area of science. Researchers and professionals have been grappling with the degree of support required for a treatment to be considered evidence-based, and have – perhaps inadvertently – created a continuum of degrees of evidence by which treatments can be assessed. The spectrum of support for various treatments extends from those that are based on only one well-conducted research study to those that rest on a large body of convincing evidence. Those that are based on the most convincing evidence earn the distinction of "empirically supported treatments," though a variety of somewhat less convincingly supported treatments rest on a significant enough body of evidence to still be considered evidence-based.

EMPIRICALLY SUPPORTED TREATMENTS

With the increased focus on and need for evidence-based treatments among the population of children with psychological disorders, Division 12 of the American Psychological Association assembled the Task Force on Promotion and Dissemination of Psychological Procedures to develop guidelines by which a treatment could be identified as an "empirically supported treatment." Lonigan et al. (1998) report on these guidelines, citing criteria for both "well-established interventions" (p. 141) and "probably efficacious treatments" (p. 141). Well-established interventions for childhood disorders are supported by a body of evidence comprised of at least two well-conducted group design studies implemented by at least two different investigators that indicate that the treatment is either more effective than pill placebo or an alternative treatment, or is equivalent to previously established treatments evaluated in studies with adequate statistical power.

Another acceptable form of empirical support comes from single-subject research designs, used by many researchers within the field of behavior analysis to measure the effects of treatment on individuals. In these designs, researchers use graphed representations of the measurement of behavior to compare an individual's level of behavior prior to and following treatment to determine the efficacy of the intervention (Green, 1996). Each single-subject design is constructed to ensure that the results of the treatment are not due to external, or confounding, variables. Unlike group designs, single-subject design studies are often comprised of a small number of participants, allowing researchers to examine the effects of treatment on each individual (Cooper et al., 2007). Within applied behavior analysis – and especially in the field of autism – researchers utilize single-subject design to examine the effects of treatment at an individual level. Lonigan et al. (1998) account for the fact that many treatments for children are supported by single-subject design research. To include these designs in the identification of well-established treatments, the authors stipulate that a body of evidence that includes more than nine single-case design studies that use good experimental design, utilize treatment manuals, and clearly specify sample characteristics may constitute well-established evidence. To qualify, these single-case design studies must compare the intervention in question to an alternative treatment.

Probably efficacious treatments are supported by bodies of evidence in which either (1) two studies indicate that the studied treatment is more effective than a no-treatment control group, (2) two group-design studies that meet the criteria mentioned above for well-established interventions but are conducted by the same investigator offer support for the treatment, or (3) a series of three or more single-subject design studies that fit the criteria described above support the effectiveness of the treatment (Lonigan et al., 1998).

The criteria for well-established treatments and probably efficacious treatments, as described by Lonigan et al. (1998), are lofty. While many focal treatments that target specific skill deficits within the autistic population (e.g., motor deficits, communication deficits, social deficits) meet the above criteria, no comprehensive treatment program – a program that seeks to improve the overall functioning of individuals with autism – currently meets criteria for an empirically supported treatment as per Lonigan et al.'s definition (Rogers, 1998). Rogers identifies several difficulties in meeting these criteria, including the challenge of designing a research study or series of research studies to examine the efficacy of a comprehensive treatment for autism. As Rogers points out, treatment for many childhood disorders can be disseminated over a short period of time, but comprehensive treatments for children with autism are much more time- and labor-intensive. The author notes that the study of a comprehensive treatment for autism requires the implementation of a treatment delivered for 20 to 30 hours per week for at least 24 months to a minimum of 25 children. The pre- and post-treatment assessments and delivery of treatment would require countless hours and personnel, and the use of control groups and random assignment creates both ethical and practical difficulties (Rogers, 1998).

Fortunately, several organizations have recognized the challenges in assessing comprehensive programs for children with autism and have developed guidelines that, while not as strict as those developed by Lonigan et al. (1998), identify comprehensive evidence-based effective treatments specifically for these individuals. Such guidelines for evidence-based therapy are necessary in this field to hedge the use of potentially ineffective therapies based on pseudoscience and antiscience.

EVIDENCE-BASED PRACTICE FOR THE TREATMENT OF AUTISM

The National Research Council (2001) organized a committee to identify both comprehensive and focal interventions for individuals with autism supported by scientific evidence. In the committee's report, research in support of various treatments for individuals with autism was evaluated based on the strength in each of three areas: internal validity, external validity, and generalization. For instance, a study was ranked highly if it was a prospective study comparing the proposed treatment to an alternative treatment or placebo, in which evaluators were blind to the hypotheses of the study. In addition, the participants in the study would have been assigned to conditions randomly, samples would have been well defined, and the sample size would have been large enough to allow for comparison. The effects of the study, to achieve the highest rating in generalization, would have been documented in at least one natural setting outside of the treatment setting, and a measure of social validity must have been included.

In contrast, a weaker study might have used a pre-post, historical, or single-subject design in which evaluators were not blind to the hypotheses of the study nor the treatment conditions, three or more subjects in a single-subject design or an adequate size for group design were included, and generalization was not addressed.

In addition to national guidelines, individual state governments have also taken it upon themselves to publish procedures for identifying best practice for working with individuals with autism. For example, the California Department of Education (1997) published a list of treatments available for children with autism, though without identifying those that had empirical support. The New York Early Intervention Program, however, has published a comprehensive resource of evidence-based practice recommendations for working with children with autism and developmental disorders between the ages of 0 and 3 years (New York State Department of Health, Early Intervention Program, 1999). The selection of studies included in the review of treatments was based on a set of guidelines used to identify well-conducted scientific research. The following criteria were used: All studies were published in English in a peer-reviewed scientific or academic publication and evaluated the effectiveness of a well-described intervention currently available for the treatment of children with autism. Additionally, all intervention studies were required to evaluate functional outcomes related to the health and development of the child and/or the outcomes important to the family or society. Studies using group designs must have been based on controlled trials comparing the intervention to an alternative treatment or no treatment, in which participants were assigned to conditions in a way that did not bias the results of the study. The baseline for all children included in the group design study must have been equivalent. For studies using a single-subject design, the use of an appropriate research design – multiple baseline, alternating treatment, ABAB, or a combination of these – was required, and the authors must have reported on at least three participants.

Guidelines such as those published by the New York State Department of Health and the National Research Committee offer wonderful resources to parents and professionals seeking informed criteria for evidence-based practice. As previously noted, the procedures for distinguishing empirically supported treatments for childhood disorders (Lonigan et al., 1998) limits the identification of such evidenced-based practice for autism treatment. Therefore, guidelines developed specifically for individuals with autism are necessary both to increase the utilization of effective treatment and to limit the dissemination of ineffective or unsupported treatments. What follows is a review of evidence-based treatments, as well as a number of treatments that have not been empirically validated but are currently in use. Those treatments described as evidence-based have been supported by bodies of well-conducted scientific research, while those that are described as non-evidence based have received little or no support in scientific research. One should note that interventions that do not have empirical evidence may not be ineffective; rather, it may be that these interventions have not been evaluated using the scientific method and should be used with extreme caution. At best, these treatments may be effective, but at worst, these treatments may be seriously detrimental to the health or well-being of the individual with autism. Even benign ineffective treatments may be detrimental if the treatment replaces, reduces the intensity of, or delays access to an evidenced-based treatment that could potentially benefit the child (Green, 1996).

TREATMENT OF AUTISM SPECTRUM DISORDERS

The next sections of this chapter will provide an overview of the wide variety of treatments available for individuals with autism spectrum disorders. In particular, we will focus on the supporting evidence for available treatments. While treatments for autism abound, there is great variability in the strength of evidence, ranging from an absence of evidence to anecdotal evidence to empirical validation of varying extents. It is really not surprising that so many treatments for autism have received attention in recent years; as prevalence estimates of autism are suggesting increased incidence, new treatments emerge on a continual basis, and claims for effective treatment flourish. Consumers are faced with seemingly countless choices for treatment. Furthermore, consumers often have difficulty understanding the opinions of professionals from multiple perspectives and disciplines, and may struggle with evaluating the claims made by professionals regarding the successes of various interventions. In the next sections of this chapter, we will review the varying levels of evidence for the effectiveness of behavior analytic and nonbehavior analytic interventions for autism. It is important to note that this chapter is not an exhaustive review of extant literature in each of the areas noted. A thorough and comprehensive literature review of each and every treatment is beyond the scope of this chapter. Such literature reviews would be helpful additions to the present literature, and it is our hope that such comprehensive reviews will be done. What we have endeavored to do is to describe common treatments, and suggest which evidence-based category a treatment may fall into, based on available knowledge at this point in time. It may be that our categorizations are imperfect, but they represent an attempt to describe the current state of knowledge on a variety of treatments.

BEHAVIORAL TREATMENT OF AUTISM SPECTRUM DISORDERS

Behavior analytic treatment of children with autism began in the 1960s, and is currently the treatment with the greatest evidential support regarding its effectiveness for learners with autism spectrum disorders. Decades of research have underscored how ABA intervention can teach skills and reduce the degree to which challenging behaviors interfere with learning. Ferster and DeMyer (1962) published the first demonstration of the use of behavioral principles to increase appropriate behavior in children with autism. In the years that followed, behavioral intervention was demonstrated to be effective in increasing skills (e.g., Wolf et al., 1964) and in reducing challenging behaviors (e.g., Lovaas et al., 1965).

Over time, it became clear that children with autism were capable of learning and of altering their behavior, and that certain procedures worked better in helping children with autism learn than did others (e.g., Lovaas et al., 1971). In particular, researchers indicated that individuals with autism learned well in a form of teaching in which there were clear instructions, repetition and practice, and immediate reinforcement for correct responses. This form of teaching – well-established through numerous historical descriptions and single-case design studies (e.g., Lovaas, 1977, 1981; Wolf et al., 1964), described in a variety of treatment manuals (e.g., Anderson et al., 1996; Leaf and McEachin, 1999), and investigated in recent research (e.g., Crockett et al., 2007; Delprato, 2001; Grindle and Remington, 2002; Miranda-Linne and Melin, 1992; Sarakoff and Sturmey, 2004; Sigafoos et al., 2006; Taubman et al., 2001) – is termed "discrete trial training."

Discrete trial training. Discrete trial training (DTT) uses repetition and sequenced instruction to build a variety of skills in students with autism (Lovaas, 1981; Lovaas et al., 1973; Smith, 1993). It has been effective in teaching a wide variety of core skills in a structured, formalized context, and is a well-established intervention for learners with ASDs. Early applications of DTT often utilized blocks of identical target trials and procedures that allowed for repeated errors. Research has identified effective elements of use, which include errorless learning procedures (e.g., Etzel and LeBlanc, 1979; Lancioni and Smeets, 1986; Terrace, 1963; Touchette and Howard, 1984) and task variation and interspersal (e.g., Dunlap, 1984; Mace et al., 1988; Winterling et al., 1987; Zarcone et al., 1993). Current state-of-the-art clinical application of DTT procedures generally involves mixing of new and mastered material, as well as the prevention and interruption of errors.

In general, clinicians view DTT as well matched to teaching skills requiring repetition, to teaching skills that are not intrinsically motivating, and to building solid repertoires of tacting, imitation, and receptive skills (e.g., Sundberg and Partington, 1998, 1999). In addition, discrete trial teaching has been shown to be much more effective when combined with strategies for effective generalization to the natural environment (Smith et al., 2007; Stokes and Baer, 1977). Skill acquisition is better when instruction is conducted across environments, when significant others are involved in training, and when discrete trial teaching is used along with other, more naturalistic approaches.

DTT is clearly a well-established intervention, with dozens of single-case design studies which utilize good experimental design and clearly describe participants supporting its efficacy. Many of these studies do compare DTT to alternate treatments or to the absence of treatment. Furthermore, the specific characteristics of instruction (such as errorless learning) associated with improved outcomes have been well-documented.

Naturalistic teaching methods. Over the past 25 years within ABA, there has been a strong focus on the development and use of naturalistic teaching methodologies to teach skills to learners with autism. The best researched and oldest of these approaches is incidental teaching. Incidental teaching emphasizes requiring an elaborated response from the individual, after they have initiated interest in an item or a topic (Hart and Risley, 1982). Incidental teaching has been shown to be a successful method for increasing initiation skills and for teaching a wide variety of language and conversation skills (e.g., Farmer-Dougan, 1994; McGee et al., 1985, 1986). Incidental teaching procedures have substantial generalization benefits, compared to discrete trial teaching (McGee et al., 1985). This is a significant advantage, as the strength of DTT is in building responsivity, and DTT is relatively weak in building initiations. Furthermore, it is well known that DTT results in little generalization without additional training.

In incidental teaching, the teacher arranges the environment to create or contrive learner interest. The learner initiates a request or a conversation about a particular item or topic, and the teacher then prompts an elaboration of that initiation. The learner's more elaborate communication results in immediate access to the desired item (Fenske et al., 2001). One of the advantages to an incidental approach over a DTT approach is that the learner is leading the exchange. It is the learner's interest that creates the opportunity for the instruction (Fenske et al., 2001). Incidental teaching is an excellent means of increasing initiation and spontaneity, and is by far the most successful and well-documented naturalistic teaching strategy within ABA. It can be described as a well-established treatment, with many published single-case studies outlining its effectiveness across multiple targets of instruction and participants (e.g., Charlop et al., 1985; Farmer-Dougan, 1994; Krantz and McClannahan, 1993; MacDuff et al., 1988; McGee et al., 1992; McGee et al., 1983; McGee et al., 1985, 1986).

Other naturalistic methodologies within ABA have also emphasized learner interests. Pivotal Response Training (PRT) and Natural Language Paradigm (NLP) have emphasized using very motivating materials, teaching in natural contexts, and following the child's lead to target deficits in language (Koegel and Koegel, 2005; Koegel et al., 1987, 1992; Laski et al., 1988). These strategies likely fall into the classification of well-established or probably efficacious treatments, based upon available definitions. There are a variety of studies documenting the effectiveness of PRT, in particular.

Natural Environment Training (NET; Sundberg and Partington, 1998), like NLP and PRT, emphasizes the use of intrinsically motivating materials and following the child's lead in language instruction. It also, however, uses Skinner's Verbal Behavior language classification system to guide language instruction (Skinner, 1957). The use of this classification system ensures comprehensive attention to the functions of language. Sundberg and Partington's emphasis on building manding (requesting) skills targets this very important response class of initiations. Other behavior analytic approaches to building communication skills have also used Skinner's classification system, with good results. One example of this is the Picture Exchange Communication System (Frost and Bondy, 2002), which teaches individuals with autism to interact with a listener in order to communicate through the exchange of pictorial representations. This system has been shown to increase functional communication and reduce behavior problems (Bondy et al., 2004; Charlop-Christy et al., 2002). Based on the current body of research, PECS could be called a probably efficacious treatment, and evidence on its effectiveness continues to increase. As the number of single case studies documenting the effectiveness grows, PECS will move into the category of a well-established intervention.

As of yet, however, a strong body of research on the use of Natural Environment Training does not exist. Though NET uses elements of instruction that are efficacious and well established, there is not as yet a large body of evidence that attests to its utility as an instructional package.

Outcome data. The loftiest category of strength of evidence is an empirically supported treatment. To date, most of the currently available comprehensive ABA treatments have not been tested at this level. The only ABA treatment that approaches this degree of support and accountability is the Lovaas/UCLA model. Lovaas' (1987) study is clearly the most ambitious and most extensive in the existing literature, and the gains documented are by far the most impressive (Lovaas, 1987; McEachin et al., 1993). Lovaas (1987) compared a group of children under age 4 who received 40 hours of intervention per week for 2 or more years with groups of children who received either fewer hours of such intervention or no intervention. Following intensive intervention, nearly half of the children in the intensive intervention group were able to be placed in regular education classes without assistance and had IQs in the average range.

Other researchers have similarly documented that early intensive behavioral intervention results in significant gains for some children (e.g., Green et al., 2002; Smith, 1999). However, precise replications of Lovaas' initial studies have not been done. This would lead some to say that Lovaas' study itself does not meet the standards of an empirically supported treatment, although others would describe it in this way (e.g., Green, 1996; Rogers, 1998). Overall, when ABA is implemented by qualified practitioners, there is a clear consensus that it leads to important improvements. In fact, there are dramatic improvements for about 50 percent of children who receive such intervention (Sallows and Graupner, 2005). More research is still needed to identify essential elements and intensity levels of intervention, and how such variables impact outcome. Outcome remains quite variable, and researchers seek more reliable predictors of how children respond to intensive intervention.

Other directions. In recent years, some behavior analysts have begun to incorporate elements of rate-building to achieve fluency. Fluency has been defined as responding correctly, quickly, and without hesitation (Binder, 1996; Dougherty and Johnston, 1996). While fluency has been a goal of Precision Teaching, a field within the discipline of ABA instruction that has served many populations for many years (e.g. Lindsley, 1992), it has only recently been discussed as relevant for learners with autism (Fabrizio and Moors, 2003). Rate-building procedures are used to build fluency in the demonstration and availability of skills.

Rate-building addresses the motor dysfluencies and long response latencies characteristic of many earners with autism spectrum disorders. Many learners on the autism spectrum exhibit motor dysfluencies. While they may be able to achieve mastery when accuracy is used to assess skill acquisition, they may still perform the task laboriously, inefficiently, or with inadequate speed. Many individuals with ASD demonstrate a long latency to respond to instructions or to social initiations and bids. These slowed response times can lead to missed opportunities, especially in social contexts with peers and in group learning situations (Weiss, 2001, 2005).

Rate-building procedures focus on rate of response as the performance variable of interest. Coaching is often used to speed performance. Practice sessions typically begin as very short sprints (e.g., 10 seconds), and lengthen as performance improves. A performance aim is used to guide daily progress (Fabrizio and Moors, 2003), and may be determined by a celeration line on a Standard Celeration Chart (or may be more individually determined by a learner's own rate.) Progress is tracked and evaluated on a daily basis, and the learner is actively engaged in tracking his or her own progress.

The attainment of fluency has been associated with a number of outcomes of learning, which are said to represent true mastery (Binder, 1996; Fabrizio and Morrs, 2003; Haughton, 1980; Johnson and Layng, 1996). Johnson and Layng (1996) emphasized the outcomes of stability (capacity to engage in behavior in face of distraction); endurance (capacity to engage in behavior for extended periods); application (broadly, ability to generalize and combine skills); and retention (ability to maintain skills).

Most instructional models for children with autism attend only to accuracy (and not to rate) to evaluate mastery (Fabrizio and Moors, 2003). Fabrizio and Moors (2003) have suggested the use of frequency aims in teaching students with autism, and have provided suggested aim ranges for core skills in this population of learners. Potential advantages to rate-building, and to achieving fluency, include the outcomes of fluency instruction (stability, endurance, application, retention), the addition of rate data, and the capacity to track and target errors separately from correct responses.

There is some controversy within the field about whether fluency is achieved as a consequence of rate building or whether it is a result of some other element of instruction (Doughty et al., 2004). Several alternate, potential explanatory variables may be responsible for the effects, including practice itself and the rate of reinforcement. Practice has been shown to facilitate learning (Samuels, 2002), and the kind and amount of practice opportunities given do affect mastery (Ericsson et al., 1993). Learners given specific, immediate feedback and multiple trials improve both their accuracy and speed. In addition, the high rates of reinforcement used in rate-building could also lead to the positive outcomes. Finally, it may be that some of the benefits of rate-building are attributable to training staff in procedures that build fluency and facilitate speed of response (Binder, 1996).

As of this point in time, rate-building to achieve fluency with learners with autism (specifically) is likely best described as a probably efficacious treatment. There are single-subject studies documenting its effectiveness with this population, but they are infrequent. More research is needed to increase our understanding of its application to this group of learners.

Another related instructional approach that has been recently discussed as relevant for learners on the autism spectrum is Direct Instruction. Direct Instruction's use of specific behavioral targets, scripted teaching formats, and data-based decision is similar in scope and focus to other ABA approaches used to teach skills to this population of learners.

Direct Instruction has been applied to a variety of curricular areas, including language, reading, mathematics, and writing with a wide variety of learners. While the intervention and research done in these areas exists outside the realm of Austism Spectrum Disorders (ASDs), there may be utility for these procedures with learners on the autism spectrum. However, the data regarding its application to this population specifically are sparse at this time. Direct Instruction approaches may meet the needs of learners with ASDs in effective ways, but scripted available curricula may need to be modified for learners with autism spectrum disorders. This is an area for future research. The utility of this approach may be great, but there is not as yet a substantial body of evidence regarding its effectiveness with this population.

SUMMARY OF ABA TREATMENTS

The treatment of autism spectrum disorders continues to receive a great deal of attention in professional circles, in the media, and in the culture at large. Applied Behavior Analysis has been extensively documented as effective in addressing the deficits associated with autism. Though the amount of research on ABA as a comprehensive treatment does not provide enough support to categorize ABA as a well-established treatment, no other treatment approach comes close to ABA in empirical validation or strength of scientific evidence.

Lovaas' study alone is not evidence for an empirically supported treatment – replications are needed by independent research groups. However, it is by far the closest approach within ABA autism treatment to an empirically supported treatment. It clearly exceeds the requirements for a treatment study by the guidelines of well-established and probably efficacious treatments, but must be joined by additional studies that are equally well-controlled and provide support for ABA as a comprehensive treatment package before ABA can be conclusively categorized as an empirically supported treatment.

Within ABA, there are a variety of well-established treatments that are in wide use. Discrete Trial Training (DTT) is a well-established treatment that has been used to build core skills. In recent years, there have been increased emphases on using task interspersal procedures, errorless learning procedures, embedded generalization strategies, and high rates of instruction (Weiss, 2001, 2005). Discrete Trial Training continues to be effective in building responsivity to instruction and in establishing a wide variety of core skills, and is best used in combination with other ABA procedures that target different deficits.

Naturalistic ABA teaching procedures such as Incidental Teaching improve generalization and build initiation. Incidental teaching is a well-established treatment that has been shown to have great utility for this population. Other naturalistic strategies, such as Pivotal Response Training, are probably best described as probably efficacious, as there are several well-designed single-case studies published on its effectiveness. Pivotal behaviors are viewed as potentially very important, as they are behaviors that may produce changes in other, untrained behaviors (Cooper et al., 2007). Pivotal behaviors include behaviors such as self-initiation, motivation, and responsivity to multiple cues. Pivotal behavior has been described as an "interesting and promising concept in behavioral research" (Cooper et al., 2007, p. 59), and may result in widespread positive changes in individuals with autism (Koegel et al., 2003). They may increase the efficiency of instruction and the generalization of training, and have relevance for self-monitoring and self-initiation. Some newer naturalistic strategies, such as Natural Environment Training, use well-established elements of instruction but have yet to be empirically verified as a package intervention, and cannot yet be considered to have been documented as a well-established treatment.

Rate-building procedures may help to address problems in speed and/or in latency to respond, which are critically important to ensure the functional availability of responses in the natural environment. This is likely best described as a probably efficacious treatment, and the data are encouraging and increasing. Furthermore, Direct Instruction's use of effective instructional design, individual assessment of progress, and scripted curricula may also benefit this population, although data on the application to learners with ASDs are lacking.

The use of all of these procedures provides a comprehensive approach to addressing the diverse profiles and characteristics encountered among learners with ASDs. ABA in general, and specifically in regard to the focal treatments discussed above, has an impressive body of evidence documenting its effectiveness.

Derby Hospitals NHS Foundation
Trust
Library and Knowledge Service

While there are some applications and extensions of ABA treatment that have not been fully explicated for this population, it is a highly effective and efficient treatment for autism spectrum disorders. It stands in stark contrast to all other treatments for autism, both in terms of the evidence that exists and in terms of its commitment to accruing more evidence to inform clinical practice.

NONBEHAVIORAL INTERVENTIONS

Despite the wealth of research identifying evidence-based treatments for children with autism, a variety of interventions are currently in use that do not fit the definition. Anecdotal evidence and methodologically flawed studies may be partly responsible for the continued implementation of these treatments. Even though non-evidence based practice has declined in the past years, as many as 74 percent of parents may be administering supplemental treatments that do not have empirical evidence for their use (Hanson et al., 2006).

Biomedical Interventions

The Gluten-Free Casein-Free (GFCF) Diet

Children with autism historically experience gastrointestinal difficulties. Increased levels of peptides resulting from an incomplete breakdown of gluten, a cereal protein, and casein, a milk protein, in urine samples from children with autism suggest that these compounds pose a specific problem in their digestion (Knivsberg et al., 2003; Reichelt et al., 1981; Shattock et al., 1990). It has been theorized that incompletely digested gluten and casein may have opioid-like properties in the body. Prolonged exposure to these peptides is proposed to have adverse effects on the brain that may be responsible for some of the core features of autism including social relatedness deficits and stereotypic behaviors.

The GFCF diet is intended as a supplemental treatment to other social and educational interventions. It involves the removal from the diet of all gluten products including wheat, rye, oats, and barley, and casein including all dairy-related products. Casein typically takes up to 3 weeks to eliminate from the body, but it may take up to 3 months for all traces of gluten to leave the body (Shattock and Whiteley, 2000); thus the diet should be systematically introduced and considered long-term. Other practical considerations include keeping all gluten and casein products out of reach from individuals on the diet. Because the diet removes an addictive substance from the system, children may still intensely crave wheat and dairy products. Individuals on the diet should also avoid touching products containing gluten and casein, such as Play-Doh®, because these products need not be ingested to have an effect.

There are many resources available for parents who put their children on the diet; recently a variety of GFCF food has been made accessible. Nutritionists should work in conjunction with parents to assure that children on the diet are getting adequate nourishment. In addition to behavioral changes, other aspects of their lives should also be monitored (e.g., stool type, sleep patterns, concurrent allergies).

Evidence regarding the efficacy of the GFCF diet is mixed. Many positive accounts of dietary benefits are based on parent and teacher report (Cade et al., 2000; Whiteley et al., 1999). Empirical analyses have found some optimistic results (Kinvsberg et al., 1990; Lucarelli et al., 1995), mixed evidence (Whiteley et al., 1999), and a lack of improvement related to the diet. This lack of consensus and, in some cases, reliance on biased report indicates that more randomized controlled trials are needed before the GFCF diet should be considered an empirically based intervention.

Medical Interventions

The use of medication has been proposed to target aggressions, compulsions, ritualistic behavior, and attention deficits. Many children with autism currently take a variety of selective serotonin reuptake inhibitors (SSRIs), atypical antipsychotics, and psychotropics. SSRIs such as fluoxetine (Prozac®) and paroxetine (Paxil®) are generally administered to address compulsive and ritualistic behaviors. Their use is predicated upon the success of these medications with individuals with obsessive–compulsive disorder. Empirical analyses are promising; the use of SSRIs has been linked to decreases in stereotypy (McDougle et al., 1996) and aggressive and self-injurious behavior (Posey et al., 1999; Steingard et al., 1997), although these benefits may not be elicited in all individuals. Although researchers have found few side effects in response to SSRIs, further empirical analysis is needed to replicate these results.

Atypical antipsychotics are also administered as a popular supplemental intervention. The most common, risperidone (Risperdal®), is a dopamine blocker that has effected a variety of positive changes in aggression, self-injurious behavior, communication and socialization skills, and overall autism severity in the literature (Barnard et al., 2002; Luby et al., 2006; Williams et al., 2006). Side effects such as weight gain and hypersalivation are more reliably present, and as with any anti-psychotic, there is a potential risk of developing tardive dyskenesia.

There are several concerns regarding indiscriminate administration of medications to children with autism. Firstly, more randomized controlled trials (RCTs) – or extensively controlled single-subject case designs – are necessary before these can be considered evidence-based treatments. Secondly, additional research on side effects in children is warranted. Lastly, drugs can be effective for only as long as a person continues to take them; long-term maintenance of positive behavior change is eliminated as soon as medication is discontinued. Accordingly, medication regimes should be utilized as a supplemental intervention to an evidence-based treatment. Furthermore, because these drugs are administered to children, enduring side effects become of utmost importance. Hopefully, future research will further explicate the guidelines to which we will adhere in promoting this medical intervention.

An alternative approach to a medical or dietary intervention is the administration of specific vitamins to children with autism. Proponents of vitamin therapy assert that nutritional deficiencies may be partly responsible for processing difficulties and aberrant behaviors. The most commonly dispensed vitamins include a B-6 (pyridoxine) and magnesium compound marketed as Super Nu Thera, vitamin B-12, and Omega-3 fatty acids. The method of administration varies. For example, Omega-3 and pyridoxine–magnesium are noninvasive; they are ingested in pill or liquid form. In contrast, B-12 is typically injected directly into the blood stream at a high rate at onset of treatment, and is eventually faded to a monthly shot. Salutary effects can take up to several months to fully emerge, and there are many reports of concomitant increases in irritability in children.

The literature offers some evidence of decreases in symptomatic behavior (Barthelemy et al., 1981; Lelord et al., 1981) and aberrant sensory-motor behavior (Dolske et al., 1993). However, all currently published randomized controlled trials have found no explicit benefits to vitamin therapy (Findling et al., 1997; Tolbert et al., 1993). Because the procedure can be invasive, time-consuming, and expensive, vitamin therapy is not a recommended intervention for children with autism.

Secretin Therapy

This peptide hormone was first introduced to alleviate gastrointestinal (GI) difficulties in children. Secretin is produced in the duodenum to regulate increased acidity in the stomach. Because children with autism commonly experience GI problems, many were treated with secretin after its approval by the Food and Drug Administration in 1981. Subsequent reports of recovery from autistic symptoms generated hype for this new "cure," but the evidence suggests that secretin therapy is ineffective (Carey et al., 2002; Dunn-Geier et al., 2000; Sandler et al., 1999). Indeed, when combined with other medications, secretin may even be linked to increases in autism severity (Ratcliff-Schaub et al., 2005). The invasive nature of secretin injections and side effects – such as diarrhea, vomiting, constipation, and irritability – should also be considered.

Chelation

Chelation is a detoxification process to remove heavy metals from the bloodstreams of individuals who have suffered metal poisoning. It was first introduced to populations with autism in response to the theory that autism is caused by elevated levels of mercury and other heavy metals in the body. Chelation can occur through ingestion of pills, through creams, or intravenously. Although parent reports of chelation-related improvements have fueled the continuing use of this procedure, it is not an evidence-based treatment (Shannon et al., 2001; Sinha et al., 2006). There is also a potential for severe side effects, such as kidney and liver damage and allergic reaction. The alarming death of a 5-year-old boy during a chelation session (DeNoon, 2005) also cautions against the use of this treatment until more controlled trials have demonstrated its efficacy and safety.

Sensory-Motor Interventions

It is widely thought that children with autism experience difficulties in processing visual, auditory, and sensory stimuli, and that these atypical processes may be responsible for social and attentional deficits and maladaptive behaviors. Consequently, a variety of treatment options aimed specifically at these sensory processes have been made available.

Auditory Integration Training (AIT)

Individuals with autism may experience heightened sensitivity to frequencies tolerated by most people; auditory integration training aims to correct abnormal reactions to common auditory stimuli. Berard, following anecdotal evidence suggesting that 48 children with whom he attempted this treatment experienced complete recovery from their symptoms, developed AIT in 1993.

The treatment contains two mechanisms by which it purportedly alleviates adverse reactions to sensory signals. During modulation, the child listens to a recording that is filtered through an electronic device. The device randomly presents alternating high and low frequencies to "exercise" the inner ear and the brain. In the second phase, filtering, frequencies are identified that fall on either side of the individual's comfort level. These frequency borders are attenuated around those sounds to which the individual is sensitive, the result of which "can be likened to that of a poorly tuned transistor radio" (Link, 1997, p. 106). AIT typically requires twenty 20-minute sessions (ideally twice daily over 10 days), with an intermediate assessment of the individual's progress. Although treatment is considered complete after the twentieth session, Berard and colleagues advise that positive changes in behavior may not be fully realized for up to one year.

Although some empirical analyses have presented encouraging results for AIT (Rimland and Edelson, 1994; Zollweg et al., 1997), the majority of the data suggest a lack of treatment benefits (Gillberg et al., 1997; Link, 1997; Mudford et al., 2000). In addition, there are no randomized controlled trials evidencing the efficacy of this intervention in the extant literature.

Sensory Integration

Sensory integration offers the similar possibility of normalizing an individual's response to tactile stimuli through manipulation of the proprioceptive, tactile, and vestibular systems. Manipulation of these structures is theorized to increase attention and extinguish the regulatory function of self-stimulatory behavior. Proprioceptive interventions include methods such as deep pressure massage and joint compression; their purpose is to hone the child's awareness of how his body interacts in the space around him. Tactile interventions target more superficial sensations through light touch and brushing. Vestibular interventions include swinging, rolling, and jumping to regulate the child's sense of balance and how his body interrelates with gravity.

As with AIT, the literature presents only equivocal evidence at best for the efficacy of sensory integration. Although some analysts found behavioral gains as a result of sensory integration (Field et al., 1997), the majority reported either no change (Gillberg et al., 1997) or adverse effects (i.e., increased stereotypy) in response to treatment (Kane et al., 2004).

Facilitated Communication (FC)

Facilitated communication has been an empirically validated intervention for individuals with physical disabilities; in 1993 the methodology was adapted for children with autism. The theory underlying FC posits that individuals have the motivation and desire to communicate, but they are physically unable to do so. It is also suggested that using FC will reveal previously unexpressed levels of academic and emotional intelligence in the population.

During FC the child types on a keyboard or similar communication device with the physical assistance of a person positioned behind him. These facilitators purportedly offer only physical assistance and emotional encouragement; however the evidence suggests that they may significantly influence the individual's responses (Kezuka, 1998; Oswald, 1994; Perry et al., 1998; Shane and Kearns, 1994). There is little experimental support for collateral gains with FC, and other methods of encouraging communication have been empirically established (e.g., Picture Exchange Communication System). Thus, the utilization of this intervention is not recommended.

Social-Educational Interventions/Psycho-social interventions

Treatment and Education of Autistic and related Communication Handicapped Children (TEACCH)

This North Carolina-based intervention offers lifelong treatment and support to individuals on the autism spectrum. As a global model, TEACCH targets gains that can be built upon an individual's existing skill repertoire, rather than following a predetermined set of instructional goals. As an individualized treatment, TEACCH capitalizes on a child's interests and strengths through continuing assessment and through teacher and parent participation. TEACCH thus provides a flexible, individual-based environment to promote independence across the life span. The literature cautions, however, that established gains may not easily generalize to other settings.

Rather than an academic intervention targeting specific skills, TEACCH is more a program to create an environment to manage behavior and foster real-world success. For example, structured activity schedules and visual instructional agendas are implemented to increase a child's understanding of his or her environment and consequently decrease inappropriate behaviors. To increase academic and social behaviors, general antecedent management and reinforcement systems are preferred over reactivity to behavior-specific feedback to promote an enriched environment. Ideally, manipulations of the environment will encourage child motivation to learn and create a system in which he or she understands what is expected of him or her. TEACCH also includes a successful supported employment program that matches adults with community job opportunities.

The few empirical analyses of TEACCH in publication present mixed results (Francke and Geist, 2003; Schopler and Hennike, 1990; Van Bourgondien et al., 2003), but parent satisfaction with the model has been well documented (Van Bourgondien et al., 2003). Despite this support, until its efficacy is better demonstrated in the literature it is unlikely that TEACCH will be become a consistently applied early intervention model.

Learning Experiences . . . an Alternative Program (LEAP)

Contrary to most early intervention programs, LEAP is based upon a single core deficit in autism. Predicated upon social learning theory, this model proposes that remediation of social deficits will lead to ancillary gains in other aspects of a child's development. Children in the LEAP program attend integrated classrooms for opportunities to benefit from peer modeling and a systematic instructional environment. Concurrently, parents participate in behavioral skill training, so that their children may encounter similar learning environments across a variety of settings. A typical classroom contains six children with autism and ten of their typical peers (Erba, 2000). Target children are taught sets of individualized instructional goals through ABA techniques (e.g., contingent reinforcement), but in a socially enriched environment. Frequent group activities, for example, present many opportunities for peer imitations, interactions, and play.

Currently, there are no controlled studies evaluating the efficacy of LEAP; nor has it been determined if LEAP is a more effective intervention than similar programs, such as TEACCH. Because key components are predicated upon well-established principles (e.g., social learning theory, naturalistic teaching strategies, etc.) we would expect positive outcomes. Future research should address the mechanisms of LEAP to evaluate whether it offers a unique model or whether it performs similarly to more well-established interventions.

Developmental Individual Difference Relationship-Based Model (DIR)

Also referred to as "floortime" or the "Greenspan approach," DIR is a child-directed, play-based intervention that capitalizes upon social interactions to facilitate skill acquisition. Its founders propose a developmental approach; DIR attempts to recreate the developmental process with the acquisition of newly established milestone skills. Parents, speech pathologists, occupational therapists, and classroom teachers are all included in the floortime process. In a one-on-one setting, a teacher sits on the floor with the target child and is directed to follow the child's lead in play while providing an emotionally supportive environment. The teacher is encouraged to mimic the child's choice of activity; if he wants to engage in stereotypic play with the wheels of a car, the teacher should also spin the wheels. Theoretically, by entering into a child's preferred activity the teacher creates an affective interaction, and the child will be more likely to emotionally engage in the future. The only published literature on DIR is limited by nonexperimental design and a lack of information on concurrent treatments

(Greenspan and Wieder, 1997; Wieder and Greenspan, 2005), so randomized controlled trials are warranted for future research.

Relationship Development Intervention (RDI)

Steven Gutstein created this intervention based on the theory that inflexible thinking and theory of mind deficits are the most salient core deficits in autism. His approach targets perspective-taking and the processing of nonverbal cues through naturalistic strategies. Children in RDI engage in "games" in which the target response can only be reached through the interpretation of a companion's gestures and facial expressions. For example, a child may have to follow his teacher's point to decipher where she wants him to sit. These objectives can also be attained through an understanding of facial expressions; a child walking toward a small precipice must interpret the look of shock on his teacher's face to realize that he should stop. The hierarchy of gestural and emotional referencing is systematically introduced to teach the motivation for "experience sharing."

In a nonrandomized trial of 17 children with autism, Gutstein (2005) reported positive outcomes on the ADOS following an RDI intervention. Future outcome research should employ a more controlled methodology and larger sample sizes.

CONCLUSION: NON-BEHAVIORAL TREATMENTS

The overwhelming lack of empirical evidence to support these alternative treatments is alarming. Ideally, parents, educators, and practitioners should look to the extant literature to guide positive practice. Until knowledge about the shortcomings and contraindicated nature of many treatments is more established in the public eye, further rigorous analyses of these interventions are recommended.

SUMMARY AND FUTURE DIRECTIONS

Autism continues to attract tremendous attention from the media. Increasing incidence estimates further fuel interest in the disorder and increase claims of cures. Parents and educators are confronted with a plethora of treatments, many supported only by anecdotal reports of progress. Consumers have difficulty effectively navigating treatment options in this environment, especially in the light of discussions of urgency in early intervention and continual reports of "cures." Parents fear that failure to try various treatments will result in lesser outcomes.

Furthermore, some interventions, in contrasting themselves with evidence-based treatments (namely ABA), lead parents to believe that they must supplement the evidence based practices with ancillary treatments. Thus, many children

with autism receive a combination of empirically validated treatment and experimental treatment. Providers may or may not be aware of which treatments are
being used, and may be asked to assist consumers in navigating decisions about
treatments. We will suggest a few necessary steps in both research and practice
to aid parents and professionals in the identification and use of evidence-based
treatments for individuals with autism.

NEXT STEPS: RESEARCH

It is imperative that more information on the efficacy of all behavioral and
nonbehavioral treatments be made available to consumers. One major deficit in
the existing literature is a comprehensive literature review of all of the studies
on focal treatments within ABA. While we tried to classify each focal treatment
according to the available categories, this was not an exhaustive review of all
studies published on every treatment. Such an extensive review would be a great
service to the field.

In addition, continued research on the different interventions within ABA
will help elucidate which interventions are most effective in remediating specific
deficits associated with the disorder. Research should also target interventions
that have not yet been widely applied to this population in a research context,
such as Direct Instruction. ABA strategies currently best categorized as probably efficacious may likely be best described as well-established with additional
studies in the next few years. Finally, while we require additional data on focal
treatments, increased emphasis should be placed on researching the effectiveness
of comprehensive treatment programs. More analysis of these types of packaged
interventions would provide additional information on treatments shown to be
effective at the highest level of research evidence–empirically supported treatments for autism. This is an area that has not received much research attention
outside of the Lovaas/UCLA model. Ultimately, empirically supported treatments provide the greatest benefit, and instill the highest levels of confidence
among both professionals and consumers. It is hoped that more comprehensive,
targeted studies will yield more data at this level of evidence.

NEXT STEPS: EDUCATIONAL IMPLICATIONS FOR
PROFESSIONALS AND CONSUMERS

Perhaps the greatest challenge that exists for clinicians addressing this disorder
is the extent of misinformation to which consumers are exposed (Holburn, 2007).
It may be the most important responsibility of professionals to be accurate and
honest with consumers about the evidence that exists for various treatments
(Holburn, 2007). Toward that end, we have developed a list of guidelines to
help clinicians responsibly communicate with consumers and to help consumers
navigate difficult treatment decisions.

1. Ensure that clinicians are well-versed in evidence-based practices. Professionals need to promote and implement effective interventions (Holburn, 2007). Specifically, effectiveness needs to be a professional standard. In fact, ABA has long held effectiveness to be a dimension of the discipline of ABA (Baer et al., 1968). Furthermore, effectiveness is a requirement for professional integrity. In their training, behavior analysts are taught to monitor effectiveness on a daily basis, to alter their approach when progress is not substantial, and to discontinue ineffective treatments. Thus, the only interventions that behavior analysts should be implementing are effective interventions. The same ethical guidelines would also extend to the promotion of interventions. Behavior analysts should not encourage consumers to pursue treatments that lack empirical evidence or which have been shown to be ineffective.

These goals can be partially addressed through training of professionals. A scientist–practitioner approach is essential for developmental disabilities (Jacobsen et al., 2006). More attention could be paid in training to help behavior analysts understand the varying degrees of evidence for treatments within ABA and for those outside the discipline of ABA. Most behavior analysts know little about the continuum of evidence for non-behavior analytic interventions, yet they are often in a position to advise consumers or to comment on alternative treatments. Behavior analysts need to be well-versed in the nonbehavior analytic treatments of autism. This need may be especially important for the autism field, in comparison to other disabilities, as people with autism continue to be subjected to myriad ineffective therapies (Holburn, 2007).

2. Teach consumers about degrees of evidence.   In the same way that professionals need to be well-versed in understanding degrees of evidence, consumers need to be educated about levels of scientific evidence. Consumers may be especially helped by information regarding distinguishing science, pseudoscience, and antiscience. Understanding these distinctions can empower consumers to detect fraudulent or overstated claims, and can help them to seek more objective evidence of success. In addition, consumers are helped in making treatment decisions by being maximally informed about the state of information regarding all treatments.

It may be especially important to highlight for consumers the differences between anecdotal evidence and scientific evidence. Unfortunately, anecdotal evidence of success is abundant and is readily available. Efforts can be made to educate consumers on where to seek the best and most objective information about treatment. While the Internet has been wonderful in increasing the amount of information available, it has also substantially increased the amount of and ease of access to misinformation. Similarly, stories in television programs and magazines are often compelling, but they remain simply one person's story. In most cases, there is no discussion of the scientific merit of the approach described.

Even within the professional realm, there is variability in quality and in the scientific basis for claims made. Many consumers may think that if a professional is lecturing on a topic or presenting at a professional conference, they must have scientific evidence of the effectiveness of the approach they are describing. This is not necessarily the case. Consumers need to understand the difference between information presented at a lecture and information presented in a peer-reviewed journal. Informing them about such differences assists them in wading through the plethora of mixed quality information widely available in both the lay and professional arenas.

3. Encourage consumers to share information and to evaluate the effectiveness of specific treatments.   A discouraging aspect to some parent–professional collaboration is the frequent failure of parents to disclose their child's participation in alternative or ancillary treatments. Parents often cite a fear that their use of such treatments will not be supported or will be met with criticism. At times, parents opt to quietly pursue such treatments, rather than risk the awkwardness of disclosure.

There are, sometimes, negative consequences to this course of action. It may be that failure to disclose information on the ancillary treatments makes it difficult for educators to evaluate what is happening with skill acquisition and/or behavioral challenges. It is always in the best interests of the learner for the staff to have complete information regarding variables that may affect performance or behavior. Perhaps most importantly, in the absence of disclosure, an opportunity may be lost to objectively evaluate the impact of an alternative treatment. When such information is shared, it is often possible to design a means of evaluating the objective impact of the treatment for the learner. In this way, data can be used to guide decisions about continuing, altering, or stopping the treatment, depending on the impact it has on the learner.

Professionals can work collaboratively with parents to identify what symptoms are supposed to be affected by the treatment, and design a method for objectively evaluating the impact of the treatment. In addition, parents can be trained to be more impartial and independent consumers of services. Kaye and Vyse (2006) have outlined how to teach parents to identify target behaviors, collect data, and judicially evaluate the results of treatment. The goal of such an approach would be to provide a framework for making decisions based on information that is objective (Holburn, 2007).

4. Use data to assess effectiveness.   Parents and professionals can be encouraged to evaluate treatments claims by using data to assess the efficacy of any and all interventions. Data-based decision-making is one of the greatest contributions of ABA, and it can be extended to treatments within and outside of the discipline. ABA's foci on objective target behaviors, precise descriptions of treatments, objective evaluation of progress, and evaluating change at an individual level match perfectly with the goal of evaluating the relevance of treatments for specific individuals. In addition, ABA is in a unique position to also evaluate potential unwanted side effects of such treatments, using the same strategies used to assess for a positive effect.

5. Publish reports of success and failure of all treatments.   As a field, we can also do much to advance the understanding of all treatments by sharing results in public forums. In particular, it is important to publish studies documenting both the effectiveness and ineffectiveness of procedures. Contrary to current practice, the documentation of the failure of treatments is as important as the documentation of the success of treatments in affecting change.

CLOSING THOUGHTS

The treatment of autism spectrum disorders remains a very confusing topic for consumers. Claims of effective treatments abound, and few consumers understand how to accurately interpret the available information. ABA remains the only intervention with substantial documentation of effectiveness. A variety of focal ABA treatments have been shown to be highly effective, and evidence exists for the Lovaas/UCLA comprehensive treatment package though more research is needed to provide additional empirical support for this model. ABA is committed to continually increasing knowledge regarding effective intervention. Unfortunately, many ineffective treatments for autism are currently available, and consumers often invest time and energy in these treatments. Professionals need to become more aware of the evidence for and against behavioral and non-behavioral treatments. Consumers, too, must be educated about how to evaluate treatment claims and how to assess whether an intervention is effective for a particular learner.

REFERENCES

American Psychiatric Association (2000). *Diagnostic and Statistical Manual of Mental Disorders* (4th edition text revision). Washington DC: Author.

Anderson, S.R., Taras, M., and O'Malley Cannon, B. (1996). Teaching new skills to children with autism. In *Behavioral Interventions for Young Children with Autism: A Manual for Parents and Professionals* (C. Maurice, G. Green, and S.C. Luce, eds.) Austin, TX: Pro-Ed.

Baer, D.M., Wolf, M.M., and Risley, T. (1968). Some current dimensions of applied behavior analysis. *Journal of Applied Behavior Analysis*, 1, 91–97.

Barnard, L., Young, A.H., Pearson, J., Geddes, J., and O'Brien, G. (2002). A systematic review of the use of atypical antipsychotics in autism. *Journal of Psychopharmacology*, 16(1), 93–101.

Barthélémy, C., Garreau, B., Leddet, I., Ernouf, D., Muh, J.P., and LeLord, G. (1981). Behavioral and biological effects of oral magnesium, vitamin B6, and combined magnesium-B6 administration in autistic children. *Magnesium Bulletin*, 3, 150–153.

Berard, G. (1993). *Hearing Equals Behavior*. New Canaan, CT: Keats.

Binder, C. (1996). Behavioral fluency: Evolution of a new paradigm. *The Behavior Analyst*, 19, 163–197.

Bondy, A., Tincani, M., and Frost, L. (2004). Multiply controlled verbal operants: An analysis and extension to the Picture Exchange Communication System. *The Behavior Analyst*, **27**, 247–261.

Cade, R., Privette, M., Fregley, M., Rowland, N., Sun, Z., Zele, V., et al. (2000). Autism and schizophrenia: Intestinal disorders. *Nutritional Neuroscience*, **3**, 57–72.

California Department of Education. (1997). *Best Practices for Designing and Delivering Effective Programs for Individuals with Autism Spectrum Disorders: Recommendations of the Collaborative Workshop on Autism Spectrum Disorders*. Sacramento, CA: Author.

Carey, T., Ratliff-Schaub, K., Funk, J., Weinle, C., Myers, M., and Jenks, J. (2002). Double-blind placebo-controlled trial of secretin: Effects on aberrant behavior in children with autism. *Journal of Autism and Developmental Disorders*, **32**(3), 161–167.

Charlop, M.H., Schreibman, L., and Thibodeau, M.G. (1985). Increasing spontaneous verbal responding in autistic children using a time delay procedure. *Journal of Applied Behavior Analysis*, **18**, 155–166.

Charlop-Christy, M.H., Carpenter, M., Le, L., LeBlanc, L.A., and Kellet, K. (2002). Using the Picture Exchange Communication System (PECS) with children with autism: Assessment of PECS acquisition, speech, social-communicative behavior and problem behavior. *Journal of Applied Behavior Analysis*, **35**, 213–231.

Cooper, J.O., Heron, T.E., and Heward, W.L. (2007). *Applied Behavior Analysis* (2nd edition). Upper Saddle River, NJ: Merrill Prentice Hall.

Cooper, J.O., Heron, T.E., and Heward, W.L. (1987). *Applied Behavior analysis*. Upper Saddle River, NJ: Merrill Prentice Hall.

Crockett, J.L., Fleming, R.K., Doepke, K.J., and Steven, J.S. (2007). Parent training: Acquisition and generalization of discrete trial teaching skills with parents of children with autism. *Research in Developmental Disabilities*, **28**, 23–26.

Delprato, D.J. (2001). Comparisons of discrete trial and normalized behavioral language intervention for young children with autism. *Journal of Autism and Developmental Disorders*, **31**, 315–325.

DeNoon, D. Boy dies after controversial treatment for autism. Online document at: http://www.webmd.com/content/Article/110/109785.html. Accessed February 11, 2007.

Dolske, M.C., Spollen, J., McKay, S., Lancashire, E., and Tolbert, L. (1993). A preliminary trial of ascorbic acid as supplemental therapy for autism. *Progress in Neuro-Psychopharmacology & Biological Psychiatry*, **17**(5), 765–774.

Dougherty, K.M. and Johnston, J.M. (1996). Overlearning, fluency, and automaticity. *The Behavior Analyst*, **19**, 289–292.

Doughty, S.S., Chase, P.N., and O'Shields, E.M. (2004). Effects of rate building on fluent performance: A review and commentary. *The Behavior Analyst*, **27**, 7–23.

Dunlap, G. (1984). The influence of task variation and maintenance tasks on the learning of autistic children. *Journal of Experimental Child Psychology*, **37**, 41–64.

Dunn-Geier, J., Ho, H.H., Auersperg, E., Doyle, D., Eaves, L., Matsuba, C. et al. (2000). Effect of secretin on children with autism: A randomized controlled trial. *Developmental Medicine and Child Neurology*, **42**, 796–802.

Elder, J.H., Shankar, M., Shuster, J., Theriaque, D., Burns, S., and Sherrill, L. (2006). The gluten-free, casein-free diet in autism: Results of a preliminary double blind clinical trial. *Journal of Autism and Developmental Disorders*, **36**(3), 413–420.

Erba, H.W. (2000). Early intervention programs for children with autism: Conceptual frameworks for implementation. *American Journal of Orthopsychiatry*, **70**(1), 82–94.

Ericsson, K.A., Krampe, R.T., and Tesch-Romer, C. (1993). The role of deliberate practice in the acquisition of expert performance. *Psychological Review*, **100**, 363–406.

Etzel, B.C. and LeBlanc, J.M. (1979). The simplest treatment alternative: The law of parsimony applied to choosing appropriate instructional control and errorless learning procedures for the difficult-to-teach child. *Journal of Autism and Developmental Disorders*, **9**, 361–382.

Fabrizio, M.A. and Moors, A.L. (2003). Evaluating mastery: Measuring instructional outcomes for children with autism. *European Journal of Behavior Analysis*, **4**, 23–36.

Farmer-Dougan, V. (1994). Increasing requests by adults with developmental disabilities using incidental teaching by peers. *Journal of Applied Behavior Analysis*, **27**, 533–544.

Fenske, E.C., Krantz, P.J., and McClannahan, L.E. (2001). Incidental teaching: A not-so-discrete-trial teaching procedure. In *Making a Difference: Behavioral Intervention for Autism* (C. Maurice, G. Green, and R.M. Foxx, eds.) Austin, Texas: Pro-Ed.

Ferster, C.B. and DeMeyer, M.K. (1962). The development of performances in autistic children in an automatically controlled environment. *Journal of Chronic Diseases*, **13**, 312–345.

Field, T., Lasko, D., Mundy, P., Henteleff, T., Kabat, S., Talpins, S., et al. (1997). Brief report: Autistic children's attentiveness and responsivity improve after touch therapy. *Journal of Autism and Developmental Disorders*, **27**(3), 333–338.

Findling, R.L., Maxwell, K., Scotese-Wojtila, L., Huang, J., Yamashita, T., and Wiznitzer, M. (1997). High-dose pyridoxine and magnesium administration in children with autistic disorder: An absence of salutary effects in a double-blind, placebo-controlled study. *Journal of Autism and Developmental Disorders*, **27**(4), 467–478.

Francke, J. and Geist, E.A. (2003). The effects of teaching play strategies on social interaction for a child with autism: A case study. *Journal of Research in Childhood Education*, **18**(2), 125–140.

Frost, L. and Bondy, A. (2002). *The Picture Exchange Communication System Training Manual*. Newark, DE: Pyramid Educational Products.

Gillberg, C., Johansson, M., Steffenburg, S., and Berlin, O. (1997). Auditory integration training in children with autism. *Autism*, **1**(1), 97–100.

Green, G. (1996). Evaluating claims about treatments for autism. In *Behavioral Intervention for Young Children with Autism: A Manual for Parents and Professionals* (C. Maurice, G. Green, and S.C. Luce, eds.) Austin, TX: Pro-Ed.

Green, G., Brennan, L.C., and Fein, D. (2002). Intensive behavioral treatment for a toddler at high risk for autism. *Behavior Modification*, **26**, 69–192.

Greenspan, S.I. and Wieder, S. (1997). Developmental patterns and outcomes in infants and children with disorders in relating and communicating: A chart review of 200 cases of children with autistic spectrum diagnoses. *Journal of Developmental and Learning Disorders*, **1**(1), 87–141.

Grindle, C.F., and Remington, B. (2002). Discrete trial teaching for autistic children when reward is delayed: A comparison of conditioned cue value and response marking. *Journal of Applied Behavior Analysis*, **35**, 187–190.

Gutstein, S.E. (2005). Preliminary evaluation of the relationship developmental intervention program. *Journal of Autism and Developmental Disorders*. Available online from http://www.rdiconnect.com/download

Hanson, E., Kalish, L.A., Bunce, E., Curtis, C., McDaniel, S., Ware, J., et al. (2006). Use of complementary and alternative medicine among children diagnosed with autism spectrum disorder. *Journal of Autism and Developmental Disorders*. Available from http://www.springerlink.com/content/25w074k876041432/

Hart, B.M., and Risley, T.R. (1982). *How to Use Incidental Teaching for Elaborating Language*. Austin, TX: Pro-Ed.

Haughton, E.C. (1980). Practicing practices: Learning by activity. *Journal of Precision Teaching*, **1**, 3–20.

Holburn, C.S. (2007). Counter the mistreatments for autism with professional integrity. *Intellectual and Developmental Disabilities*, **45**, 136–137.

Jacobson, J.W., Foxx, R.M., and Mulick, J.A. (2006). Fad, dubious, controversial, pseudoscientific and politically correct treatments in developmental disability services. In *Controversial Therapies for Developmental Disabilities: Fad, Fashion, and Science in Professional Practice* (J. Jacobson, R. Foxx, and J. Mulick, eds.) (pp. xi–xviii). Mahwah, NJ: Erlbaum.

Johnson, K. and Layng, T.V.J. (1996). On terms and procedures: Fluency. *The Behavior Analyst*, **19**, 281–288.

Kane, A., Luiselli, J.K., Dearborn, S., and Young, N. (2004) Wearing a weighted vest as intervention for children with autism/pervasive developmental disorder. *The Scientific Review of Mental Health Practice*, **3**(2), 19–24.

Kaye, S., and Vyse, S. (2006). Helping parents separate the wheat from the chaff: putting autism treatments to the test. In *Controversial Therapies for Developmental disabilities: Fad, Fashion, and Science in Professional Practice* (J. Jacobson, R. Foxx, and J. Mulick, eds.) pp. 265–277. Mahwah, NJ: Erlbaum.

Kerr, A.M. and Ravine, D. (2003). Review article: Breaking new ground with Rett syndrome. *Journal of Intellectual Disability Research*, **47**, 580–587.

Kezuka, E. (1998). The role of touch in facilitated communication. *Journal of Autism and Developmental Disorders*, **27**, 571–593.

Knivsberg, A., Reichelt, K-L., Hoien, T., and Nodland, M. (2003). Effect of a dietary intervention on autistic behavior. *Focus on Autism and Other Developmental Disabilities*, **18**(4), 247–256.

Knivsberg, A., Wiig, K., Lind, G., Nodland, M., and Reichelt, K.L. (1990). Dietary intervention in autistic syndromes. *Brain Dysfunction*, **3**, 315–327.

Koegel, L.K., Carter, C.M., and Koegel, R.L. (2003). Teaching children with autism self-initiations as a pivotal response. *Topics in Language Disorders*, **23**, 134–145.

Koegel, R.L. and Koegel, K.L. (2005). *Pivotal Response Treatments for Autism: Communication, Social, and Academic Development*. Baltimore, MD: Brookes.

Koegel, R.L., Koegel, L.K., and Surrat, A. (1992). Language intervention and disruptive behavior in preschool children with autism. *Journal of Autism and Developmental Disorders*, **22**, 141–153.

Koegel, R.L., O'Dell, M.C., and Koegel, L.K. (1987). A natural language teaching paradigm for nonverbal autistic children. *Journal of Autism and Developmental Disorders*, **17**, 187–200.

Krantz, P.J. and McClannahan, L.E. (1993). Teaching children with autism to initiate to peers: Effects of a script-fading procedure. *Journal of Applied Behavior Analysis*, **26**, 121–132.

Laski, K.E., Charlop, M.H., and Schreibman, L. (1988). Training parents to use the natural language paradigm to increase their children's speech. *Journal of Applied Behavior Analysis*, **21**, 391–400.

Lancioni, G.E. and Smeets, P.M. (1986). Procedures and parameters of errorless discrimination training with developmentally impaired individuals. In *International review of research in mental retardation*, **14**, (N.R. Ellis and N.W. Bray, eds.) pp. 135–164. Orlando, FL: Academic Press.

Leaf, R. and McEachin, J. (1999). *A Work in Progress: Behavior Management Strategies and a Curriculum for Intensive Behavioral Treatment of Autism*. New York: DRL Books.

Lelord, G., Muh, J.P., Barthelemy, C., Martineau, J., Garreau, B., and Callaway, E. (1981). Effects of pyridoxine and magnesium on autistic symptoms – initial observations. *Journal of Autism and Developmental Disorders*, **11**(2), 219–230.

Lindsley, O.R. (1992). Precision teaching: Discoveries and effects. *Journal of Applied Behavior Analysis*, **25**, 51–57.

Link, H.M. (1997). Auditory integration training (AIT): Sound therapy? Case studies of three boys with autism who recereived AIT. *British Journal of Learning Disabilities*, **25**, 106–110.

Lonigan, C.J., Elbert, J.C., Johnson, S.B. (1998). Empirically supported psychosocial interventions for children: An overview. *Journal of Clinical Child Psychology*, **27**(2), 138–145.

Lovaas, O.I. (1987). Behavioral treatment and normal intellectual functioning in young autistic children. *Journal of Consulting and Clinical Psychology*, **55**, 3–9.

Lovaas, O.I. (1981). *Teaching Developmentally Disabled Children: The ME Book*. Baltimore: University Park Press.

Lovaas, O.I. (1977). *The Autistic Child: Language Development Through Behavior Modification*. New York: Irvington.

Lovaas, O.I., Freitag, G., Gold, V.J., and Kassorla, I.C. (1965). Recording apparatus and procedure for observation of behaviors of children in free play settings. *Journal of Experimental Child Psychology*, **2**, 108–120.

Lovaas, O.I., Koegel, R.L., Simmons, J.Q., and Long, J. (1973). Some generalization and follow up measures on autistic children in behavior therapy. *Journal of Applied Behavior Analysis*, **6**, 131–166.

Lovaas, O.I., Schreibman, L., Koegel, R.L., and Rehm, R. (1971). Selective responding by autistic children to multiple sensory input. *Journal of Abnormal Psychology*, **77**, 211–222.

Luby, J., Mrakotsky, C., Stalets, M.M., Belden, A., Heffelfinger, A., Williams, M., and et al. (2006). Risperidone in preschool children with autistic spectrum disorders: An investigation of safety and efficacy. *Journal of Child and Adolescent Psychopharmacology*, **16**(5), 575–587.

Lucarelli, S., Frediani, T., and Zingoni, A.M. (1995). Food allergy and infantile autism. *Panminerva Medica*, **3**, 137–141.

MacDuff, G.S., Krantz, P.J., MacDuff, M.A., and McClannahan, L.E. (1988). Providing incidental teaching for autistic children: A rapid training procedure for therapists. *Education and Treatment of Children*, **11**, 207–211.

Mace, F.C., Hock, M.L., Lalli, J.S., West, B.J., Belfiore, P., Pinter, E., and Brown, D.F. (1988). Behavioral momentum in the treatment of noncompliance. *Journal of Applied Behavior Analysis*, **21**, 123–141.

McDougle, C.J., Naylor, S.T., Cohen, D.J., Volkmar, F.R., Heninger, G.R., and Price, L.H. (1996). A double-blind, placebo-controlled study of fluvoxamine in adults with autistic disorder. *Archives of General Psychiatry*, **53**, 1001–1008.

McEachin, J., Smith, T., and Lovaas, I. (1993). Long-term outcome for children with autism who received early intensive behavioral treatment. *American Journal of Mental Retardation*, **97**, 359–372.

McGee, G.G., Almeida, M.C., Sulzer-Azaroff, B., and Feldman, R.S. (1992). Promoting reciprocal interaction via peer incidental teaching. *Journal of Applied Behavior Analysis*, **25**, 117–126.

McGee, G.G., Krantz, P.J., Mason, D., and McClannahan, L.E. (1983). A modified incidental teaching procedure for autistic youth: Acquisition and generalization of receptive object labels. *Journal of Applied Behavior Analysis*, **16**, 329–338.

McGee, G.G., Krantz, P.J., and McClannahan, L.E. (1985). The facilitative effects of incidental teaching on preposition use by autistic children. *Journal of Applied Behavior Analysis*, **18**, 17–31.

McGee, G.G., Krantz, P.J., and McClannahan, L.E. (1986). An extension of incidental teaching procedures to reading instruction for autistic children. *Journal of Applied Behavior Analysis*, **19**, 147–157.

Miranda-Linne, F., and Melin, L. (1992). Acquisition, generalization, and spontaneous use of color adjectives: A comparison of incidental teaching and traditional discrete trial procedures for children with autism. *Research in Developmental Disabilities*, **13**, 191–210.

Mouridsen, S.E. (2003). Review article: Childhood disintegrative disorder. *Brain and Development*, **25**, 225–228.

Mudford, O.C., Cross, B.A., Breen, S., Cullen, C., Reeves, D., Gould, J., et al. (2000). Auditory integration training for children with autism: No behavioral benefits detected. *American Journal on Mental Retardation*, **105**(2), 118–129.

National Research Council (2001). *Educating Children with Autism*. Washington D.C.: National Academy Press.

Clinical Practice Guideline: The Guideline Technical Report for Autism/Pervasive Developmental Disorders, Assessment and Intervention for Young Children (Age 0–3 Years) (New York State Department of Health Early Intervention Program, 1999). Albany, NY: Author

Oswald, D.P. (1994). Facilitator influence in facilitated communication. *Journal of Behavioral Education*, **4**, 191–199.

Perry, A., Bryson, S., and Bebko, J. (1998). Brief report: Degree of facilitator influence in facilitated communication as a function of facilitator characteristics, attitudes, and beliefs. *Journal of Autism and Developmental Disorders*, **28**, 87–90.

Posey, D.J., Litwiller, M., Koburn, A., and McDougle, C.J. (1999). Paroxetine in autism. *Journal of the American Academy of Child Adolescent Psychiatry*, **38**(2), 111–112.

Ratcliff-Schaub, K., Carey, T., Reeves, G.D., and Rogers, M.A. (2005). Randomized controlled trial of transdermal secretin on behavior of children with autism. *Autism*, **9**(3), 256–265.

Reichelt, K.L., Hole, K., Hamberger, A., Saelid, G., Edminsson, P.D., Braestrup, C.B., et al. (1981). Biologically active peptide containing fractions in schizophrenia and childhood autism. *Advances in Biochemical Psychopharmacology*, **28**, 627–643.

Rimland, B. and Edelson, S.M. (1994). The effects of auditory integration training on autism. *American Journal of Speech-Language Pathology*, **5**, 16–24.

Rogers, S.J. (1998). Empirically supported comprehensive treatments for young children with autism. *Journal of Clinical Child Psychology*, **27**(2), 168–179.

Sallows, G.O. and Graupner, T.D. (2005). Intensive behavioral treatment for children with autism: Four-year outcome and predictors. *American Journal on Mental Retardation*, **100**, 417–438.

Samuels, S.J. (2002). Reading fluency: Its development and assessment. In *What Research has to say About Reading Instruction* (A.E. Farstrup and S.J. Samuels, eds.) pp. 166–183. Newark, DE: International Reading Association.

Sandler, A.D., Kelly, A.S., DeWeese, J., Girardi, M., Sheppard, V., and Bodfish, J.W. (1999). Lack of benefit of a single dose of synthetic human secretin in the treatment of autism and pervasive developmental disorder. *New England Journal of Medicine*, **341**(24), 1801–1806.

Sarakoff, R.A. and Sturmey, P. (2004). The effects of behavioral skills training on staff implementation of discrete trial teaching. *Journal of Applied Behavior Analysis*, **37**, 535–538.

Schopler, E. and Hennike, J.M. (1990). Past and present trends in residential treatment. *Journal of Autism and Developmental Disorders*, **20**, 291–298.

Shane, H.C. and Kearns, K. (1994). An examination of the role of the facilitator in "Facilitated Communication". *American Journal of Speech-Language Pathology*, **3**, 48–54.

Shannon, M., Levy, S.E., and Sandler, A. (2001). Chelation therapy neither safe nor effective as autism treatment. *American Academy of Pediatric News*, **19**, 63.

Shattock, P., Kennedy, A., Rowell, F., and Berney, T. (1990). The role of neuropeptides in autism and their relationships with classical neurotransmitters. *Brain Dysfunction*, **3**, 328–345.

Shattock, P. and Whiteley, P. (2000). The Sunderland protocol: A logical sequencing of biomedical interventions for the treatment of autism and related disorders. *From Proceedings of Conference held at the University of Durham*, April 10, 2000.

Sigafoos, J., O'Reilley, M.O., Ma, C.H., Edrinsha, C., Cannella, H., and Lancioni, G.E. (2006). Effects of embedded instruction versus discrete trial training on self-injury, correct responding, and mood in a child with autism. *Journal of Intellectual and Developmental Disabilities*, **31**, 196–203.

Sinha, Y., Silove, N., and Williams, K. (2006). Letter to the editor: Chelation therapy and autism. *British Medical Journal*, **333**(7571), 756.

Skinner, B.F. (1957). *Verbal Behavior.* New York: Appleton-Century-Crofts.

Smith, T. (1993). Autism. In *Effective Psychotherapies* (T.R. Giles, ed.) pp. 107–113. New York: Plenum.

Smith, T. (1999). Outcome of early intervention for children with autism. *Clinical Psychology: Science and Practice*, **6**, 33–49.

Smith, T., McAdam, D., and Napolitano, D. (2007). Autism and applied behavior analysis. In *Autism Spectrum Disorders: Applied Behavior Analysis, Evidence, and Practice* (P. Sturmey and A. Fitzer, eds.) pp. 1–29. Austin, TX: Pro-Ed.

Steingard, R.J., Zimnitzky, B., DeMaso, D.R., Bauman, M.L., and Bucci, J.P. (1997). Sertraline treatment of transition-associated anxiety and agitation in children with autistic disorder. *Journal of Child and Adolescent Psychopharmacology*, **7**(1), 9–15.

Stokes, T. and Baer, D.M. (1977). An implicit technology of generalization. *Journal of Applied Behavior Analysis*, **10**, 349–367.

Sundberg, M.L. and Partington, J.W. (1998). *Teaching Language to Children with Autism or Other Developmental Disabilities*. Pleasant Hill, CA: Behavior Analysts, Inc.

Sundberg, M.L. and Partington, J.W. (1999). The need for both DT and NE training for children with autism. In *Autism: Behavior Analytic Approaches* (P.M. Ghezzi, W.L. Williams, and J.E. Carr, eds.) Reno, NV: Context Press.

Terrace, H. (1963). Discrimination learning with and without errors. *Journal of the Experimental Analysis of Behavior*, **6**, 1–27.

Taubman, M., Brierly, S., Wishner, J., Baker, D., McEachin, J., and Leaf, R.B. (2001). The effectiveness of a group discrete trial instructional approach for preschoolers with developmental disabilities. *Research in Developmental Disabilities*, **22**, 205–219.

Tolbert, L.C., Haigler, T., Waits, M.M., and Dennis, D. (1993). Brief report: Lack of response in an autistic population to a low dose clinical trial of pyridoxine plus magnesium. *Journal of Autism and Developmental Disorders*, **23**(1), 193–199.

Touchette, P.E. and Howard, J. (1984). Errorless learning: Reinforcement contingencies and stimulus control transfer in delayed prompting. *Journal of Applied Behavior Analysis*, **17**, 175–181.

Van Bourgondien, Reichler, R.J., and Schopler, E. (2003). Effects of a model treatment approach on adults with autism. *Journal of Autism and Developmental Disorders*, **33**(2), 131–140.

Weider, S. and Greenspan, S.I. (2005). Can children with autism master the core deficits and become empathetic, creative, and reflective? A ten to fifteen year follow-up of a subgroup of children with autism spectrum disorders (ASD) who received comprehensive developmental, individual-difference, relationship-based (DIR) approach. *Journal of Developmental and Learning Disorders*, **9**, 39–51.

Weiss, M.J. (2001). Expanding ABA intervention in intensive programs for children with autism: The inclusion of natural environment training and fluency based instruction. *The Behavior Analyst Today*, **2**, 182–187.

Weiss, M.J. (2005). Comprehensive ABA Programs: Integrating and evaluating the implementation of varied instructional approaches. *Behavior Analyst Today*, **6**, 249–256.

Whiteley, P., Rodgers, J., Savery, D., and Shattock, P. (1999). A gluten-free diet as an intervention for autism and associated spectrum disorders: Preliminary findings. *Autism*, **3**(1), 45–65.

Williams, S.K., Scahill, L., Vitiello, B., Aman, M.G., Arnold, E., McDougle, C.J., et al. (2006). Risperidone and adaptive behavior in children with autism. *Journal of the American Academy of Child and Adolescent Psychiatry*, **45**(4), 431–564.

Wing, L. (1988). The continuum of autistic characteristics. In *Diagnosis and Assessment in Autism* (E. Schopler and G. Mesibov, eds.) pp. 91–110. New York: Plenum.

Winterling, V., Dunlap, G., and O'Neill, R.E. (1987). The influence of task variation on the aberrant behaviors of autistic students. *Education and Treatment of Children*, **10**, 105–119.

Wolf, M.M., Risley, T.R., and Mees, H. (1964). Application of operant conditioning procedures to the behaviour problems of an autistic child. *Behavior Research and Therapy*, **1**, 305–312.

Zarcone, J.R., Iwata, B.A., Hughes, C.E., and Vollmer, T.R. (1993). Momentum versus extinction effects in the treatment of self-injurious escape behavior. *Journal of Applied Behavior Analysis*, **26**, 135–136.

Zollweg, W., Palm, D., and Vance, V. (1997). The efficacy of auditory integration training: A double blind study. *American Journal of Audiology*, **6**, 39–47.

3

Autism Spectrum Disorders: A Lifespan Perspective

Linda A. LeBlanc, Andrew R. Riley
and Tina R. Goldsmith

Western Michigan University, MI, USA

INTRODUCTION

There is a growing importance about lifespan issues for individuals with autism spectrum disorders (ASDs). Practices such as transition planning during secondary education, supports for independent community living and employment, and higher education supports have become common. The 2007 proposed Commission on Accreditation of Rehabilitation Facilities (CARF) Autism standards also reflect the importance of lifespan issues by focusing approximately half of the standards on the degree to which relevant transition and long-term life planning is conducted for individual consumers.

Several factors have contributed to the increasing importance of lifespan developmental issues for individuals with ASDs. First, the deinstitutionalization movement created greater access to community-based services and living arrangements for individuals with developmental disabilities with concurrent increases in life expectancy (Meyers and Balcher, 1987; Seltzer and Krauss, 1987). As a result, late life issues associated with aging with a developmental disability have received unprecedented attention with respect to research, policy issues, and program development (Bigby, 2003; McCallion and McCarron, 2004). Second, educational advocacy and legislation such as the Individuals with Disabilities Education Act (IDEA) and the 1997 Amendments have facilitated access to effective educational services (Annino, 1999). Today's student with an ASD is more likely to experience effective instruction and meaningful integration into general education environments than ever before (Zager, 2005). Third, effective early intensive behavioral intervention programs have frequently produced dramatic increases in language, social skills, and scholastic aptitude for children with ASDs with a subset of individuals achieving functioning in the average range (Harris, 1986; Lovaas, 1987; McEachin et al., 1993).

The purpose of this chapter is to highlight the importance of the lifespan approach to ASDs and to provide a review of problems and supports provided at critical times in the lifespan. An introduction to lifespan developmental theories is followed by a review of outcomes evidence and exploration of commonly encountered concerns and successes in key developmental periods. Since early childhood has been the subject of so many comprehensive reviews and texts (Volkmar et al., 2005; Zager, 2005), this chapter will focus on critical developmental periods that have been examined less frequently: adolescence, young adulthood, and adulthood.

LIFESPAN THEORIES

Many psychological theories, referred to as lifespan theories, acknowledge that people continue to grow and change throughout their lives as they are faced with new tasks, challenges, and opportunities (Smith and Baltes, 1999). An influential lifespan theorist, Paul Baltes, defines the lifespan developmental approach as a family of theoretical perspectives that attempt to describe and understand the patterns of growth and change across an entire lifetime (Baltes, 1987; Baltes and Smith, 2004). Lifespan theories often seek to understand general developmental trajectories as well as aspects of the environmental context that might be altered at different points during the life course to impact developmental trajectory and improve developmental outcomes.

Erik Erickson is often termed the first lifespan theorist based on his psychosocial stages, which spanned infancy to old age (Erikson, 1950, 1959). His theory of development emphasized the importance of stage-specific social tasks that facilitate interpersonal development and the importance of periods of transition between the stages. Each transition point is marked by a change in values, goals, and primary social activities (Papalia et al., 2007). For example, adolescence is marked by various physical changes associated with puberty and by the establishment of relationships and social values that are independent of (but impacted by) the values of the parent. Young adulthood (age 20–40 years) is marked by a shift in values and activities towards establishment of the next generation of nuclear family and mastery of spousal and parenting roles. Finally, late life (65 years and older) is marked by revaluing of the uses of one's time, and search for meaningfulness in life based on reflection upon one's prior contributions to the lives of others and to society as a whole.

Charlotte Buhler (1933, 1968), a contextualist, introduced the concept that individuals set personal goals based on their own particular context and are constantly setting new goals based on their changing contexts and their own abilities. Her theory highlights the importance of individual differences in planning, aspirations, and achievements rather than a uniform lifepath for all. Finally, Sansone and Berg (1993) present the "activated lifespace" model, an extension of the contextualist approach that suggests that people use only the personal resources and contextual features within his or her lifespace at the relevant moment. This theory illustrates the importance of creating life contexts that facilitate ongoing learning and effective problem-solving.

In summary, lifespan theories offer several tenets that can guide assessment and intervention planning activities for individuals with ASDs. First, certain transitional periods are critical times for planning and promoting acquisition of skills critical to the next social milestones in life. Second, individual goal setting and incorporation of individual aspirations and interests should guide planning for the future with the goal of creating meaningful quality of life outcomes throughout adulthood. Finally, individuals must exist in contexts that present challenges and simultaneously provide resources for meeting those challenges in order to continue to develop across the lifespan.

OUTCOMES ACROSS THE LIFESPAN

A developmental lifespan approach is predicated on the notion that individual development follows a trajectory over the course of the lifespan and that various factors (e.g., early intervention, resilience factors) can impact that trajectory and the subsequent life outcomes experienced by the individual (Seltzer et al., 2004; Smith and Baltes, 1999). Thus, outcome studies typically involve identification of participants with certain characteristics or experiences and tracking of those individuals over a specific interval (Tsatsanis, 2003). Subsequently, analysts attempt to identify variables that predict positive outcomes. The majority of outcome studies differentiate between individuals on the autism spectrum based on their intellectual abilities. The data for those individuals with autism who are "higher functioning" (Ventner et al., 1992) are often collapsed with individuals with Asperger's Disorder based on the absence of intellectual disability. This group is often contrasted with individuals with autism with IQ scores below 60–70 (i.e., intellectual disability), limited to nonexistent speech, and increased frequency of problem behaviors including aggression, self-injury, tantrums, and stereotypies (Burack and Volkmar, 1992; Johnson et al., 1995; Kraijer, 2000). The terms "autism" and "Asperger's Disorder" will be used from this point forward when specific studies examine only one of the groups and the general term ASDs will be used when a specific diagnostic subcategory is not specified.

Several studies have examined outcomes of children with ASD in attempts to identify the effects of intervention, predictor variables associated with better or poorer outcome, and average levels of functioning achieved at different ages (Tsatsanis, 2003). Unfortunately, many of the studies have used relatively short follow-up intervals of 2–7 years after a specific event such as diagnosis or delivery of a given intervention (Jonsdottir et al., 2007; Sallows and

Graupner, 2005) such that the participants are still children. For example, Turner et al. (2006) examined developmental outcomes 7 years after initial diagnosis at age 2. At follow-up (age 9), the vast majority of children still met the criteria for an ASD and over 50 percent had cognitive scores above 70 compared to only 16 percent at age 2. Children with higher outcomes on intellectual achievement, and language testing were generally diagnosed at younger ages, had higher cognitive and language skills at age 2, and received more speech and language therapy than children with poorer outcomes. A higher proportion of individuals achieved typical intellectual functioning than in previous studies (Stone and Ousley, 1999) suggesting that overall outcomes for children may be improving related to intellectual and academic outcomes. However, this follow-up interval does not span even the first critical developmental transition period (i.e., adolescence) and does not sample other critical indicators of meaningful outcomes (e.g., social functioning).

Some outcome studies have examined individuals with ASDs in adulthood with the preponderance of these studies focusing on higher functioning individuals. Early studies of adults with Asperger's and high-functioning autism indicated that approximately 8–22 percent of individuals were employed, few pursued or completed higher education, and the vast majority remained living at home with family or in institutional settings (Kanner, 1971; Tantam, 1991). Ventner et al. (1992) conducted an 8-year follow-up of 58 higher functioning (IQ Mean = 80) autistic children during their adolescence and adulthood. Of the 22 adult participants at follow-up, 6 were competitively employed, 13 were in sheltered or supervised employment or school programs, and 3 were unemployed and not in school. None were married and only 2 lived on their own. Employed individuals were in low-level jobs in service industries generally obtained with assistance, and language measures discriminated the competitively employed group from others suggesting that literacy and comprehension skills are critical targets during school years. Other follow-up studies that tracked higher functioning individuals with ASD into adulthood reveal similar to slightly better outcomes with 7–50 percent pursuing higher education, 16–50 percent living semi-independently and 5–44 percent gainfully employed (Howlin et al., 2004; Larsen and Mouridsen, 1997; Mahwood and Howlin, 1999; Rumsey et al., 1985; Szatmari et al., 1989).

ADOLESCENCE

Adolescence is defined as the period from onset to completion of physiological maturation (i.e., puberty) and is characterized by increased hormonal variability, spurts of rapid growth, and development of sexual physical features (DeRose and Brooks-Gunn, 2006). Puberty is associated with behavioral deterioration in approximately one-tenth to one-third of adolescents with ASDs, with females and individuals with intellectual disabilities primarily affected (Gillberg, 1984;

Knickmeyer et al., 2006). At least two unusual patterns of pubertal development have been noted in females with ASD. Knickmeyer et al. recently surveyed a cross-sectional sample of women with ASDs and discovered that their average age for onset of menarche was significantly higher than non-ASD women, which they hypothesized is related to the influence of prenatal androgen in extreme cases (i.e., onset above age 17). Lee (2004) described two teenagers with autism diagnosed with Premenstrual Dysphoric Disorder (PMDD) resulting in onset or a dramatic increase in agitation and problem behavior at menarche, with cyclical amplification of autistic symptoms (e.g., stereotypies, sensitivity to change and noise) for the older teen. A cyclical pattern was evident with increased agitation, self-injurious behavior, and mood symptoms beginning 4 to 5 days before menstruation and abating within 4 days.

In addition to physiological changes, adolescence is marked by various other changes in psychosocial development, access to community activities and the related safety issues that can accompany those activities, and changing educational structure associated with the transition to middle and high school. During adolescence, students shift from the relative stasis of elementary education to middle and high school, which are marked by increased academic demands and structural differences such as frequent changes in classes and teachers. Often, interest in the opposite sex increases without commensurate knowledge about safety and relationship issues. The impact of these changes on the core features of ASDs, comorbid problems, and peer relationships can be quite notable and are reviewed below. Though they are included in the section on adolescence because of the increased probability of onset during this period, each issue persists into adulthood.

CORE ASD SYMPTOMS EXHIBITED BY ADOLESCENTS

The life course of individuals with ASDs is heterogeneous with some individuals losing skills over time, others reaching a plateau in adolescence, and still others manifesting a pattern of continued development into adulthood. Seltzer et al. (2004) found that the core symptoms of autism often abate to some degree during adolescence and young adulthood, particularly for individuals without intellectual disabilities (Piven et al., 1996). Some individuals experience improvements that are limited to certain core features of ASD with variable timing of improvements across behaviors (e.g., Seltzer et al., 2003). Shattuck et al. (2007) found that adult participants had fewer maladaptive behaviors (i.e., self-injury, noncompliance, aggression) and experienced more improvement in these behaviors over time than adolescents. Seltzer et al. (2003) examined ASD symptoms across a wide age span (ages 10–53 years) and found that only 55 percent met the criteria for autism in adolescence (compared with virtually 100 percent in early childhood) with the greatest improvements in basic language and the least symptom improvement in friendship development.

For those individuals who do not experience symptom improvement, several patterns are common. Gillberg and Steffenberg (1987) found that 35 percent of a sample of 23 people (16–23 years) with ASD experienced 1–2 year periods of aggravation of behavioral symptoms (e.g., aggression, hyperactivity, insistence on sameness) and 22 percent exhibited continuing deterioration throughout puberty. Shattuck et al. (2007) found that approximately 50 percent of their sample showed stable nonverbal communication impairments, impairments in social reciprocity, and maladaptive behaviors over time with worsening of symptoms for only a small minority of their sample.

Differences in patterns of improvement across age groups may be reflective of several cohort factors that have not been controlled in previous studies, so findings must be interpreted with caution. For example, diagnostic practices and DSM editions have differed over the decades (Volkmar et al., 1992), and the availability of effective treatment services has increased (Lord and McGee, 2001). However, developmental changes occurring during adolescence and adulthood may well account for changes in core ASD symptoms above and beyond these cohort effects (Howlin et al., 2000; Mahwood et al., 2000). There is a need for continued prospective research on the symptoms of ASDs in adolescence and adulthood to enhance basic understanding of the life course trajectory of this disorder, to facilitate service development, and to support families in their long-range planning efforts.

COMORBID MENTAL HEALTH ISSUES

As children progress towards adolescence, parents and clinicians should be alert to the possible onset of various mental health problems that co-occur with ASDs. Individuals with ASDs exhibit many behavioral difficulties including hyperactivity, attentional problems, obsessive–compulsive phenomena, self-injury and stereotypies, tics, and affective symptoms (Ghaziuddin et al., 1992, 1995; Jaselskis et al., 1992; McDougle et al., 1995; Realmuto and Main, 1982; Stone and Ousley, 1999). The possible comorbidity of Depression, Anxiety, and Attention Deficit/Hyperactivity Disorder with ASDs has been examined in several recent studies with particular focus on the increase in these comorbid disorders as children move into adolescence.

To date, one empirical review (Stewart et al., 2006) and two studies have examined the prevalence and characteristics of anxiety and mood problems among children diagnosed with ASDs compared with a community sample (Kim et al., 2000; Szatmari et al., 1989). Depression and generalized anxiety are more common in high-functioning ASD groups than same age adolescents in the general community (Kim et al.) suggesting that screening for these problems should be common practice as untreated anxiety and depression will typically persist or worsen throughout adolescence and into adulthood (Stewart et al.). Mood problems occurred most frequently with 17 percent of participants scoring at clinically relevant levels of depression (Kim et al.) and similar levels of internalizing problems for those with ASD diagnoses. Participants with mood problems were also more aggressive, limited their parents' social activities, and had poorer relationships with others than nonanxious/nondepressed teens with ASDs.

Three studies have examined the prevalence and types of anxiety exhibited by high-functioning adolescents with ASDs and factors related to anxiety. Adolescents with ASDs exhibit anxiety levels that are significantly higher than those of the general population with a low negative correlation between assertive social skills and social anxiety and a moderate curvilinear relationship between empathetic skills and social anxiety (Bellini, 2004). Bellini (2006) examined 41 high-functioning adolescents with ASDs and found that elevated physiological arousal combined with social skills deficits contributes significantly to the variance in social anxiety. Biederman et al. (1995) proposed that children who are less able to regulate their own physiological arousal are more vulnerable to stressful social encounters and are more likely to experience adverse conditioning by negative social encounters. Finally, Farrugia and Hudson (2006) compared anxiety symptoms in adolescents (age 12–16) with Asperger's Disorder, nonclinical adolescents, and adolescents with anxiety disorders. Adolescents with Asperger's Disorder have levels of anxiety equivalent to adolescents with anxiety disorders and significantly higher than those in the general population; and the correlated negative automatic thoughts, behavioral problems, and life interference were significantly higher for adolescents with Asperger's than for the comparison groups.

As children diagnosed with ASDs move towards adolescence, parents and clinicians may see the development of symptoms associated with attention-deficit and disruptive behavior disorders. Problems with impulse control, attentional deficits, hyperactivity, disorganized behavior, aggression and disruption should be addressed so that developmental progression through adolescence is not impeded and parents are not unduly stressed. Disruptive behavior left untreated during later childhood and early adolescence increases parental stress and the likelihood of placement into residential care programs (Howlin, 1997) and prohibition of students from participating in a fully integrated school day (Einfeld and Tonge, 1996; King et al., 1995).

Future research on comorbid problems during adolescence and adulthood should emphasize development of reliable and valid diagnostic instruments for identifying comorbid psychiatric disorders in this population (Tsai, 1996) and subsequently developing effective prevention and treatment strategies. Additionally, future research should investigate how comorbid conditions change as the child progresses through adolescence and adulthood. Given that negative consequences of untreated early symptoms of comorbid conditions are probable, clinicians and caregivers should be vigilant about treating symptoms as they emerge rather than waiting for symptom presentation at a level of significance that would warrant an additional diagnosis.

PEER INTERACTIONS AND VICTIMIZATION

Longitudinal research indicates that many individuals with ASDs show increased social skill development and interest in social relationships during adolescence (Mesibov, 1983; Mesibov and Handlan, 1997; Rutter, 1970; Volkmar and Klin, 1995) with improved relations with teachers and parents (Travis and Sigman, 1998; Volkmar, 1987), but most continue to have great social difficulty into adolescence and adulthood (Church et al., 2000; DeMyer et al., 1981; Seltzer et al., 2003). Individuals with ASD initiate fewer interactions than their typically developing peers and their peers with other disabilities (Attwood et al., 1988; Hauck et al., 1995; Lord, 1990; Lord and Magill-Evans, 1995; Sigman and Ruskin, 1999). Even when individuals with ASDs develop friendships, there is often more reported loneliness compared to typically developing children (Bauminger and Kasari, 2000). Higher functioning individuals with ASDs are more likely to report having friendships than children with less developed skills, but their friendships often focus on common circumscribed interests rather than social interactions (Bauminger and Kasari, 2000; Church et al., 2000). Orsmond et al. (2004) studied families of over 200 adolescents and adults with ASDs and found low prevalence of friendships and participation in social and recreational activities. Having peer relationships was predicted by younger age and better social skills while greater functional independence, better social skills, greater maternal participation in social and recreational activities, and inclusion in integrated settings while in school predicted greater participation in activities.

Bauminger et al. (2003) compared 18 high-functioning preadolescents and adolescents with same aged typically developing individuals. They found that high-functioning children with autism initiated and responded to peers at about half the rate of typical controls, and that level of functioning was positively correlated with peer-based social involvement. Bauminger et al. also evaluated the construct of loneliness and found that children with autism self-reported greater levels of emotional and social loneliness, and, quite notably, their increased participation in social interaction did not result in decreased levels of loneliness. The authors speculate that this may be because individuals on the spectrum may not make positive attributions to the interactions that they have, they may simply want more interactions than they are currently experiencing, and/or individuals on the autism spectrum may not understand or experience social behavior and loneliness in the same way as typically developing children.

Individuals diagnosed with an ASD are at risk for victimization throughout their lifespan. While there is no conclusive data that supports a correlation between increased rates of victimization and developmental period, there are data to confirm that the form or type of victimization changes across the lifespan. For example, filicide (i.e., murder by parent) occurs rarely but almost exclusively in early childhood (Palermo, 2003), bullying or peer victimization is most common in adolescence, and robbery is associated with adulthood (Wilson and Brewer, 1992). The developmental period of particular concern for parents of individuals with ASDs is typically adolescence because the victimization often occurs at school away from parental protection. Self-report data for all high school students (not ASD specific) indicate that approximately 9 percent of children reported being victimized frequently, and 13 percent report bullying others frequently (Klomek et al., 2007). Frequent exposure to victimization or bullying others is related to high risks of depression, ideation, and suicide attempts compared with adolescents not involved in bullying behavior, while involvement in bullying behavior is related to increased risk of depression and suicidality, particularly among girls.

Little (2001) examined the prevalence of peer shunning and victimization of children and adolescents with Asperger's Disorder and found a yearly prevalence rate of peer victimization at 94 percent. Peers or siblings had hit 73 percent and 10 percent reported being attacked by a gang. Peer shunning was also common, with 33 percent of the children being excluded from birthday parties, 11 percent eating alone at lunch every day, and 31 percent always or almost always picked last for games and teams. While assault by siblings and peers decreased slowly with age, bullying remained high regardless of age, and gang attacks were the most frequent in middle school and high school. Younger children were more likely to be assaulted by peers or siblings with boys at greater risk for assault than girls. Older children were at greater risk for emotional bullying by peers or siblings and shunning by peers.

ROMANCE AND SEXUALITY

The sexuality of individuals with ASDs has been largely unexamined, perhaps because some consider those with ASDs to be sexually immature or incapable of intimacy (Konstantareas and Lunsky, 1997). However, many individuals with ASDs, particularly males, show interest in developing intimate sexual relationships and marriage (Ousley and Mesibov, 1991). A recent highly publicized novel and movie (Newport et al., 2007) describes the marriage of two adults with Asperger's Disorder and may spark an interest in research in this area. In spite of this well-publicized example of the marriage of two very competent adults with Asperger's Disorder, only a small proportion of individuals with an ASD develop intimate relationships in adolescence or adulthood (Ousley and Mesibov, 1991). For instance, in a 30-year follow up of subjects hospitalized as children, Larsen and Mouridsen (1997) found that just two of nine individuals with Asperger's Disorder were married, and none of the nine individuals with autism were married. The centrality of social impairments in ASDs may cause difficulties in initiating and maintaining intimate relationships, making them challenging or unappealing for potential partners.

Individuals with ASDs have less sexual knowledge and experience than their typically developing peers (Ousley and Mesibov, 1991) and the discrepancy can prove problematic. Sexual knowledge is positively correlated with cognitive functioning (Konstantareas and Lunsky, 1997) such that those with greater cognitive impairments exhibit more inappropriate sexual behavior (Haracopos and Pederson, 1992), engage in fewer privacy-seeking behaviors, and have less sexual education (Stokes and Kaur, 2005) than typically developing peers.

The available data suggest the sexual knowledge of individuals with ASDs is not adequate for their level of interest. While the sexual knowledge of typical peers tends to improve with age, this is not the case for adolescents with ASDs (Stokes and Kaur, 2005). Of particular concern is the likelihood that interest on the part of higher functioning individuals with ASDs will be interpreted, accurately or inaccurately, as threatening or predatory behavior (Stokes et al., 2007). Some authors (e.g., Stokes and Kaur, 2005) have suggested that specialized sexual education combined with social skills training for adolescents with ASDs may be beneficial. Such education would focus on making sexual mores concrete and salient so that inappropriate activity may be avoided, and quality of life might be enhanced (Konstantareas and Lunsky, 1997).

ADULTHOOD: TRANSITION PLANNING

In recent years, interest in adult outcomes for individuals with ASDs has increased dramatically (Howlin, 2000, 2004, 2005; Howlin and Goode, 1998). Research in this area typically focuses on descriptive outcome domains that contribute to quality of life (e.g., health, employment, education, residential). Awareness of the need for facilitating the transition from adolescence to adulthood and subsequent individualized programming has greatly increased (Schall et al., 2006). There are key elements of successful programs that target employment, education, and independent living and these elements are somewhat different for pre-transition planning than for ongoing support during and after transitions.

Effective planning that focuses on exploring interests and abilities and teaching appropriate skills to high school students prior to post-high school settings can facilitate transition to adult life (Wehman and Thoma, 2006). When designing an individual education program (IEP), curricula should be designed to maximize the potential of each individual student and engender independence whenever possible. Schall et al. (2006) cite three key attributes of successful curricula: (1) person-centered, (2) functional, and (3) flexible.

Person-centered curricula focus on creating personalized activities and goals for each student. Those goals should be established in a collaborative approach that incorporates input from the individual, parents, and involved professionals. Given the heterogeneity in abilities and personalities of individuals with ASD, a uniform intervention or curriculum is unlikely to be effective for all individuals. For instance, an individual with Asperger's Disorder may aspire to attend a major university, whereas someone with more severe cognitive deficits may have a goal of obtaining any vocation that facilitates social contact and provides income. Tailoring curricula to the goals and interests of individuals helps to utilize school resources in the manner most relevant to those individuals.

A curriculum is functional to the degree that it improves an individual's ability to live and work independently and meets his or her goals. In other words, the later practical utility of the skills learned during transition planning are the critical factors for determining functionality. Thus, one must examine the environments in which the person would like to operate and address behavioral deficits or excesses that may limit the individual's ability to succeed in those environments. Targeted skills will vary with individual characteristics and environments and may include social skills, problem-solving skills, and specific job training.

It is also important that a student's IEP remain flexible and sensitive to change. As students develop new skills and encounter novel environments, goals may change and new challenges will arise. Constant reevaluation of goals and teaching strategies is essential to maximize the impact of schooling on subsequent employment, education, and functional independent living. For instance, a young man with Asperger's Disorder with a keen interest in fish may have the original goal of working at an aquarium or pet store. As his knowledge and skills increase, he may develop a new goal to attend a university to study wildlife and fisheries or ichthyology. New possibilities for interest and employment may exist, but new planning must occur in preparation for the stressors and challenges associated with the social and organizational demands of higher education.

As awareness of ASDs continues to grow, so will the need to effectively transition adolescents into a more independent adult life. While recent research (e.g., Iovannone et al., 2003; Rogan et al., 2000) has begun to examine this process, it is still a relatively unexplored area. A further understanding of the educational and transitional services required for successful adaptation to new environments is needed. Ostensibly, this knowledge base will continue to expand, and, as it does, more opportunities for engagement in society should become available for adults with ASDs.

ADULTHOOD: ONGOING FUNCTIONAL SUPPORTS

Several researchers (e.g., Howlin et al., 2005; Keel et al., 1997; Mahwood and Howlin, 1999; Muller et al., 2003) have demonstrated the effectiveness of supportive programs for adults with ASDs in their work, living, and higher education endeavors. The majority of programs focus on supported employment; however, their basic principles should apply in multiple arenas. Supports may vary in structure and mode of implementation, but three elements are central to all successful programming: tailoring the level of proximal support, providing environmental supplements, and incorporation of personal goals and interests.

The level of proximal support provided to an individual should correspond to both the magnitude and specific areas of skill strengths and deficits (Schall et al., 2006). For instance, an individual with an ASD may require very little support in basic living skills (e.g., food preparation, personal hygiene, cleaning), but may need some intervention in order to complete more administrative tasks (e.g., paying bills, making doctor's appointments, acquiring auto insurance). Providing excessive proximal supports when they are not needed can lead to dependence, while an inadequate number of supports can lead to failure. Many programs provide a "liaison" or "job coach" in the target environment to keep the individual on task, explain unclear expectations, monitor progress, and provide helpful mentoring on issues such as social effectiveness (Smith, 1999).

Because individuals with ASDs are less apt to pick up on "unwritten" rules, they may benefit from supplemental information in their environment. One form of supplementation includes schedules, task sheets, or various other aids. Textual or pictorial aids may be used to address problem behaviors and to provide subtle reminders about rules of the environment and task requirements (Schall et al., 2006). Supplementing the environment may also include educating coworkers or neighbors about different behaviors they might observe from a person with an ASD. Such preparations purportedly increase knowledge and readiness of coworkers for the atypical behavior of the person with an ASD (Rogan et al., 2000).

Finally, effective support structures evaluate the interests and personal goals of the individual and attempt to match them with corresponding work, educational, and living environments. The more tailored a particular environment is to the profile of the consumer with an ASD, the more one can expect success (Hawkins, 2004). Consider the example of a young man who excels in organizational tasks, has strong arithmetic skills, relatively poor social interaction skills, and has an interest in computers. An office job that requires him to do some filing and computer-based data-entry would correspond to his attributes nicely.

These types of supports are exemplary and should not be considered exhaustive. Ultimately, the characteristics of the individual and the demands of the environment will determine the intensity and nature of any intervention. Furthermore, supports should be implemented with the terminal goal of increased autonomy, allowing the individual to function more effectively with less invasive assistance.

EMPLOYMENT AND HIGHER EDUCATION

When transitioning from adolescence into adulthood, it is typical to pursue entrance into the workforce or post-secondary education (Carter and McGoldrick, 1980; Gerhardt and Holmes, 2005), a process that can be particularly challenging for individuals with ASDs. Even those with high intellectual ability and impressive education are often unsuccessful (Mahwood and Howlin, 1999; Muller et al., 2003). Those who do find employment, on average, do not earn as much as their typically developing peers (Jennes-Coussens et al., 2006) as a result of skill deficits of the person with ASD or reluctance and lack of preparation of employers to hire disabled individuals (Nesbitt, 2000). Similarly, the unstructured university environment presents many challenges (e.g., low levels of supervision, high social demands, increased independence, academics pressures) that may overwhelm those with an ASD (Glennon, 2001). However, with proper support, high-functioning individuals with ASDs can succeed in the workplace and other post-high school environments (Keel et al., 1997; Mahwood and Howlin; Nesbitt, 2000; Smith and Philippen, 2005).

Employment of individuals with ASDs may provide numerous benefits for the employee and the hiring organization. For the individual, being successful in a skill-level appropriate environment increases autonomy and provides access to otherwise unavailable reinforcers (e.g., money, interpersonal relationships, etc). In our society, one's job can be a defining feature and provide an important way to earn respect from others (Berkell and Gaylord-Ross, 1989). Furthermore, Garcia-Villamisar and Hughes (2007) found that supported employment is associated with improved cognitive functioning in adults with autism. Employers may take advantage of particular strengths that people with ASDs possess in order to increase productivity (Hawkins, 2004; Mahwood and Howlin, 1999). Many higher functioning individuals with ASDs excel in mathematics and computing, recall facts readily or perform visuo-motor skills admirably while possessing desirable traits such as perseverance, precision, truthfulness, and punctuality. All of these skills and behavioral tendencies can facilitate success as long as the work or educational environment can support the concurrent deficits or rigidity.

Society at large may also benefit from the employment and further education of disabled persons. The cost of educating a person with an ASD is much higher than that of the general population (Howlin et al., 2005). To best capitalize on this investment, people with ASDs should be given the opportunity to contribute to their community by applying relevant skills learned in school to contribute to the economy, enrich the social environment, and offer new ideas in academics and industry. In addition, people with disabilities who participate fully in the workforce have the opportunity to enhance society's perception of individuals with disabilities and their societal value.

Social skills deficits often contribute to trouble in employment situations, and matriculation and academic success in university and college environments (Glennon, 2001; Muller et al., 2003; Schall et al., 2006). The inability to make conversation, detect and respond to social cues, use problem-solving strategies effectively, as well as general disinterest in socialization may all be detrimental to success in work and school environments. Additionally, communication difficulties such as a limited verbal repertoire, abnormal speech rhythm, flat affect, and difficulty understanding abstract concepts can further exacerbate social problems by alienating coworkers and fellow students.

Individual employers' attitudes about hiring individuals with disabilities are generally favorable (Nesbitt, 2000); however, organizations are often unprepared to provide the needed supports (Parent and Everson, 1986). In resolution of this dilemma, third-party adult vocational service providers have emerged as facilitators of the transition from school to work (Howlin et al., 2005; Keel et al., 1997; Mahwood and Howlin, 1999; Muller et al., 2003). For a listing of such services and other resources, see Table 3.1. These providers use the elements described above (i.e., tailored level of proximal support, environmental supplements, and incorporation of personal goals and interest) to facilitate positive outcomes.

Tailoring the level of support for an individual in the workplace might involve providing oral instructions to someone with poor reading skills or a picture-based

TABLE 3.1   Resources for successful transition planning for individuals with ASDs

Title	Citation	Description
Career training and personal planning for students with autism spectrum disorders: A practical resource for schools	Lundine and Smith (2006)	This book outlines a program to assess ASD students' strengths and abilities and help them acquire the skills necessary for a smooth transition from school to employment.
How to find work for people with Asperger syndrome	Hawkins (2004)	This book describes programming to assist persons with Asperger's Syndrome in finding and maintaining appropriate work.
Planning to learn: creating and using a personal planner with young people on the autism spectrum	Harper-Hill and Lord (2007)	This book provides guidance for teaching people with ASDs to plan and contains materials such as schedules and planners.
The autism spectrum and further education	Breakey (2006)	This book provides guidelines and practical advice on guiding young adults with ASDs, emphasizing the development of resources and practical skills for use specifically in university settings.
Effective educational practices for students with autism spectrum disorders	Iovannone et al. (2003)	This article provides a description of 6 core elements that have empirical support and should be included in instructional programs students with ASD
A guide to successful employment for individuals with autism	Smith et al. (1995)	This handbook describes how to effectively find and keep work for individuals with ASDs
TEACCH-supported employment program	Keel et al. (1997)	This article described the structure of and outcome data for the TEACCH model of supported employment

job-aid to someone with no reading skills and poor verbal comprehension. Alternatively, task-related skills may be adequate, but a prompting or redirection intervention may be required to ensure that the person is able to stay on task throughout the day. Environmental supplementation to increase productivity might involve eliminating distractions common in a typical office environment (e.g., machine noises, conversations, foot traffic) by switching to a cubicle-style desk removed from main corridors or developing explicit schedules of tasks and responsibilities to remove some of the ambiguity from the environment.

Efforts to incorporate individual goals and interests are typically implemented prior to job placement by selecting prospective jobs that are well suited. For an individual with an interest in horticulture, for instance, arranging employment in landscaping work or at a tree nursery might increase motivation to retain the job to a level that will ensure persistence in trying to master difficult social or organizational aspects of the job.

Supportive strategies can similarly be applied to the higher education setting. Often the university office of support services for students with special needs can coordinate many of the environmental supplements or proximal supports. It is likely, however that the individual with an ASD will need facilitation in contacting and sustaining a relationship with such an organization and may have to educate the staff of the university office about ASDs to ensure effective support. Some individuals may succeed in solitary residence in an apartment or house off-campus while attending school, while others may benefit from a dormitory environment because of the amenities it provides (e.g., cafeterias, minimal cleaning, proximity to campus) and the opportunity for structured social activities. The classroom environment may be supplemented to facilitate learning for the individual with an ASD by eliminating the need for real-time note taking if handouts and audio-taping of lectures facilitate accuracy and completeness of understanding. Some students may benefit from tests that are without time-limits, specially formatted, or administered on a computer in an isolated setting. In addition, special pains should be taken to incorporate goals and interests by ensuring that the prospective university offers a course of study that will be interesting and useful in the student's future endeavors.

INDEPENDENT LIVING

Achieving the highest level of independence in living is an important goal for adults with ASDs (Ruef and Turnbull, 2002), as well as their parents and support staff (Krauss et al., 2005; Petry et al., 2005). Mothers of individuals with ASDs cite calmer family life, better married life, more free time, and less stress as several benefits of having their adult offspring live outside the home (Krauss, et al.). Perceived benefits for the individual with an ASD include the acquisition of new skills, better access to appropriate services, a better social life, and a more age-appropriate lifestyle (Krauss et al.). While complete autonomy is not a feasible goal for many individuals, increased self-reliance and self-determination are universally desirable.

Perhaps due to increased access to services and greater understanding of needs and abilities, individuals with ASD are increasingly living more independent lives though many still require support. In a review of the available outcome data, Howlin (1997) found that less than 10 percent of individuals with ASDs after 1980 were hospitalized, as opposed to over 50 percent prior to 1980. However, residing outside of a hospital setting does not ensure that one will live indepen-dently and less than 15 percent of individuals with ASD live independently in their own home. In most studies, less than 10 percent of adults with an ASD are found to perform "well" on measures of independence (Moxon and Gates, 2001).

Many studies have reported residential characteristics as a demographic variable (Bennett et al., 2005; Engstrom et al., 2003; Jennes-Coussens et al., 2006; Krauss et al., 2005; Renty and Roeyers, 2005), but these findings often include only high-functioning individuals with an ASD who may be most likely to gain independence. Based on data from state agencies in New York and Massachusetts, Seltzer et al. (2000) estimated that only one-third to one-fourth of adults in their 30s with autism continue to live with their parents. Most reports, however, are less optimistic, generally suggesting that 60 percent of children with autism will remain dependent on others into adulthood (Moxon and Gates, 2001). To our knowledge, the largest outcome study to date reporting residential status was conducted in Sweden by Billstedt et al. (2005). Of 108 individuals at all levels of functioning originally diagnosed with autism or autism-like features in childhood, only 4 were found to be living independently as adults.

Several barriers to independent residence exist for individuals with ASDs. First, low employment rates may create difficulties affording independent residence for the highest functioning individuals. Even those with adequate finances may have deficits in basic living skills that make tasks such as preparing food or cleaning difficult. Further, obtaining a house or apartment and sustaining neighborly relations requires a reasonable amount of social interaction that many individuals with ASDs may find challenging. While these and other obstacles are formidable, there is evidence to suggest that with proper support they are surmountable as well (Luce and Dyer, 1995; Smith, 1985).

Supporting the transition to a new residence will vary greatly according to the characteristics of the individual but will generally incorporate the above-mentioned strategies of providing proximal supports, supplementing the environment, and incorporating interests and goals. A generally effective working person who has a goal to live in an urban environment may do so in spite of lacking many basic self-help skills such as food preparation and laundry skills. An appropriate level of proximal supports for this individual might involve weekly or twice weekly visits from parents or support staff to assess living conditions and provide feedback, assist with shopping for easy self-prepared foods, and assist with laundry. Supplementing the environment for this individual might mean finding a place of residence where a cafeteria or restaurants and a dry cleaner are nearby.

CONCLUSIONS AND AREAS FOR FUTURE RESEARCH

In summary, a reasonable body of evidence has begun to document the positive outcomes that can be associated with effective programming across the lifespan of individuals with ASD. There are changes evident in the core characteristics of ASDs and comorbid conditions suffered by individuals with

ASD, particularly during adolescence. There are also conceptual models for providing effective planning and supports through the transition to adulthood and throughout young adulthood. However, several research areas need to continue to be developed to ensure an adequate understanding of ASDs across the entire lifespan.

First, additional follow-up studies need to be conducted. Prospective longitudinal studies provide the best opportunity for comprehensive evaluation of multiple aspects of functioning across major developmental transition periods. Those follow-up studies also need to focus on meaningful indicators of functional outcome in addition to standardized measures of intelligence and adaptive functioning. Second, studies need to examine later adulthood to determine if individuals with ASDs experience aging with any unique challenges. At this point, no studies have examined individuals with ASD over the age of 60 years leaving us with no information about residential characteristics, retirement pursuits, or age-related and/or condition-related declines in functioning. Third, most supported employment programs are based on conceptual models and are created based on a philosophy of service delivery and support. Few studies have experimentally evaluated the effects of supported employment programs to determine if the features that are considered critical to success are actually associated with improved outcomes. In addition, studies that examine cost–benefit ratios for supported employment programs should be conducted. Finally, the literature and service providers would benefit from the development and experimental evaluation of programs for treating comorbid mental health problems in adults with ASDs and of programs for specialized sexual education and relationship preparation as a part of transition to adulthood services.

REFERENCES

Annino, P.G. (1999). The new IDEA regulations: The next step in improving the quality of special education. *Mental & Physical Disability Law Reporter*, **23**, 439–442.

Attwood, A., Frith, U., and Hermelin, B (1988). The understanding and use of interpersonal gestures by autistic and Down's syndrome children. *Journal of Autism and Developmental Disorders*, **18**, 241–257.

Baltes, P.B. (1987). Theoretical propositions of life-span development psychology: On the dynamics between growth and decline. *Developmental Psychology*, **23**, 611–626.

Baltes, P.B. and Smith, J. (2004). Lifespan psychology: From developmental contextualism to developmental biocultural co-constructionism. *Research in Human Development*, **1**, 123–144.

Bauminger, N. and Kasari, C. (2000). Loneliness and friendship in high-functioning children with autism. *Child Development*, **71**, 447–456.

Bauminger, N., Shulman, C., and Agam, G. (2003). Peer interaction and loneliness in high-functioning children with autism. *Journal of Autism and Developmental Disorders*, **33**, 489–507.

Bellini, S. (2004). Social skill deficits and anxiety in high-functioning adolescents with autism spectrum disorders. *Focus on Autism and Other Developmental Disabilities*, **19**, 78–86.

Bellini, S. (2006). The development of social anxiety in adolescents with autism spectrum disorders. *Focus on Autism and Other Developmental Disabilities*, **21**, 138–145.

Bennett, H.E., Wood, C.L., and Hare, D.J. (2005). Providing care for adults with autistic spectrum disorders in learning disability services: Needs-based or diagnosis-driven? *Journal of Applied Research in Intellectual Disabilities*, **18**, 57–64.

Berkell, D. and Gaylord-Ross, R. (1989). The concept of transition: Historical and current developments. In *Transition From School to Work for Persons with Disabilities* (D.E. Berkell and J.M. Brown, eds.) pp. 1–17. White Plains, NY: Longman.

Biederman, J., Rosenbaum, J.F., Chaloff, J., and Kagan, J. (1995). Behavioral inhibition as a risk factor for anxiety disorders. In *Anxiety in Children and Adolescents* (J.S. March, ed.) (pp. 61–81). New York: Guilford Press.

Bigby, C. (2003). *Ageing with a Lifelong Disability: A Guide for Practice, Program and Policy Issues for Human Services Professionals*. London: Jessica Kingsley.

Billstedt, E., Gillberg, C., and Gillberg, C. (2005). Autism after adolescence: Population-based 13- to 22-year follow-up study of 120 individuals with autism diagnosed in childhood. *Journal of Autism and Developmental Disabilities*, **35**, 351–360.

Breakey, C. (2006). *The autism spectrum and further education: A guide to good practice*. London: Jessica Kingsley.

Buhler, C. (1933). *Der menschliche lebenslauf als psychologisches problem*. Leipzig: Verlag von S. Hirzel.

Buhler, C. (1968). The general structure of the human life cycle. In *The Course of Human Life* (C. Buhler and F. Massarik, eds.) (pp. 12–26). New York: Springer.

Burack, J.A. and Volkmar, F.R. (1992). Development of low- and high-functioning autistic children. *Journal of Child Psychology and Psychiatry*, **33**, 607–616.

Carter, E.A., and McGoldrick, M. (1980). *The Family Cycle: A Framework for Family Therapy*. New York: Gardner Press.

Church, C., Alinsanski, S., and Amanullah, S. (2000). The social, behavioral, and academic experiences of children with Asperger syndrome. *Focus on Autism and Other Developmental Disabilities*, **15**, 12–20.

DeMyer, M.K., Hingtgen, H., and Jackson, K. (1981). Infantile autism reviewed: A decade of research. *Schizophrenia Bulletin*, **7**, 388–451.

DeRose, L.M. and Brooks-Gunn, J. (2006). Transition into adolescence: The role of pubertal processes. In *Child Psychology: A Handbook of Contemporary Issues (2nd ed.)* (L. Balter and C.S. Tamis-LeMonda, eds.) (pp. 385–414). New York, NY: Psychology Press.

Einfeld, S.L. and Tonge, J. (1996). Population prevalence of psychopathology in children and adolescents with intellectual disabilities. *Journal of Intellectual Disability Research*, **40**, 99–109.

Engstrom, I., Ekstrom, L., and Emilsson, B. (2003). Psychosocial functioning in a group of Swedish adults with Asperger syndrome or high-functioning autism. *Autism*, **7**, 99–110.

Erikson, E.H. (1950). *Childhood and Society*. New York: Norton.

Erikson, E.H. (1959). Identity and the life cycle. *Psychological Issues, I* (whole volume).

Farrugia, S. and Hudson, J. (2006). Anxiety in adolescents with Asperger syndrome: Negative thoughts, behavioral problems, and life interference. *Focus on Autism and other Developmental Disabilities*, **21**, 25–35.

Garcia-Villamisar, D. and Hughes, C. (2007). Supported employment improves cognitive performance in adults with Autism. *Journal of Intellectual Disability Research*, **51**, 142–150.

Gerhardt, P.F. and Holmes, D.L. (2005). Employment: Options and issues for adolescents and adults with autism spectrum disorders. In *Handbook of Autism and Pervasive Developmental Disorders (Third Edition) Volume Two: Assessment, Interventions, and Policy* (F.R. Volkmar, R. Paul, A. Klin, and D. Cohen, eds.) pp. 1087–1101. Hoboken, NJ: John Wiley & Sons.

Ghaziuddin, M. Alessi, N., and Greden, J.F. (1995). Life events and depression in children with pervasive developmental disorders. *Journal of Autism and Developmental Disorders*, **25**, 495–502.

Ghaziuddin, M., Tsai, L., and Ghaziuddin, N. (1992). Comorbidity of autistic disorder in children and adolescents. *European Journal of Child and Adolescent Psychiatry*, **1**, 209–213.

Gillberg, C. (1984). Autistic children growing up: Problems during puberty and adolescence. *Developmental Medicine & Child Neurology*, **26**, 125–129.

Gillberg, C. and Steffenberg, S. (1987). Outcome and prognostic factors in infantile autism and similar conditions: A population-based study of 46 cases followed through puberty. *Journal of Autism and Developmental Disorders*, **17**, 273–287.

Glennon, T.J. (2001). The stress of the university experience for students with Asperger syndrome. *Work: Journal of Prevention, Assessment & Rehabilitation*, **17**, 183–190.

Haracopos, D. and Pedersen, L. (1992). *Sexuality and Autism: A Nationwide Survey in Denmark. Preliminary Report*. Copenhagen. Unpublished manuscript (in press).

Harper-Hill, K. and Lord, S. (2007). *Planning to learn: creating and using a personal planner with young people on the autism spectrum*. London: Jessica Kingsley.

Harris, S.L. (1986). Brief report: A 4- to 7-year questionnaire follow-up of participants in a training program for parents of autistic children. *Journal of Autism and Developmental Disorders*, **16**, 377–383.

Hauck, M., Fein, D., Waterhouse, L., and Feinstein, C. (1995). Social initiations by autistic children to adults and other children. *Journal of Autism and Developmental Disorders*, **25**, 579–595.

Hawkins, G. (2004). *How to Find Work for People with Asperger Syndrome*. New York: Jessica Kingsley.

Howlin, P. (1997). Prognosis in autism: do specialist treatments affect long-term outcome? *European Child & Adolescent Psychiatry*, **6**, 55–72.

Howlin, P. (2000). Outcome in adult life for more able individuals with autism or Asperger syndrome. *Autism*, **4**, 63–83.

Howlin, P. (2004). *Autism and Asperger syndrome: Preparing for adulthood (Second Edition)*. London: Routledge.

Howlin, P. (2005). Outcomes in autism spectrum disorders. In *Handbook of Autism and Pervasive Developmental Disorders, Volume One: Diagnosis, Development, Neurobiology, and Behavior (Third Edition)* (F.R. Volkmar, R. Paul, A. Klin, and D. Cohen, eds.) pp. 201–220. Hoboken, NJ: John Wiley & Sons.

Howlin, P. and Goode, S. (1998). Outcome in adult life for people with autism and Asperger's syndrome. In *Autism and Pervasive Developmental Disorders* (F.R. Volkmar, ed.). New York: Cambridge University Press.

Howlin, P., Alcock, J, and Burkin, C. (2005). An 8-year follow-up of a specialist supported employment service for high-ability adults with autism or Asperger's syndrome. *Autism*, **9**, 533–549.

Howlin, P., Goode, S., Hutton, J. and Rutter, M. (2004). Adult outcome for children with autism. *Journal of Child Psychology and Psychiatry*, **45**, 212–229.

Howlin, P., Mawhood, L., and Rutter, M. (2000). Autism and developmental receptive language disorder – a follow-up comparison in early adult life II: Social, behavioural, and psychiatric outcomes. *Journal of Child Psychology and Psychiatry, and Allied Disciplines*, **41**, 561–578.

Iovannone, R., Dunlap, G., Huber, H., and Kincaid, D. (2003). Effective educational practices for students with autism spectrum disorders. *Focus on Autism and Other Developmental Disabilities*, **18**, 150–165.

Jaselskis, C.A., Cook, E.H., and Fletcher, K.E. (1992). Clonidine treatment of hyperactive and impulsive children with autistic disorder. *Journal of Clinical Psychopharmacology*, **12**, 322–327.

Jennes-Coussens, M., Magill-Evans, J. and Koning, C. (2006). The quality of life of young men with Asperger syndrome. *Autism*, **10**, 403–414.

Johnson, C.R., Lubetsky, M.J., and Sacco, K.A. (1995). Psychiatric and behavioral disorders in hospitalized preschoolers with developmental disabilities. *Journal of Autism and Developmental Disorders*, **25**, 169–182.

Jonsdottir, S.L., Saemundsen, E., Asmundsdottir, G., Hjartardottir, S., Asgeirdottir, B.B., Smaradottir, H.H., Sigurdardottir, S., and Smari, J. (2007). Follow-up of children diagnosed with pervasive developmental disorders: Stability and change during the preschool years. *Journal of Autism and Developmental Disorders*, **37**, 1361–1374.

Kanner, L. (1971). Follow-up study of eleven autistic children originally reported in 1943. *Journal of Autism and Childhood Schizophrenia*, **1**, 119–145.

Keel, J.H., Mesibov, G.B., and Woods, A.V. (1997). TEACCH-supported employment program. *Journal of Autism and Developmental Disabilities*, **27**, 3–9.

Kim, J.A., Szatmari, P., Bryson, S.E., Streiner, D.L., and Wilson, F.J. (2000). The prevalence of anxiety and mood problems among children with autism and Asperger syndrome. *Autism*, **4**, 117–132.

King, N.J., Ollendick, T.H., and Tonge, B.J. (1995). *School Refusal: Assessment and Treatment.* Needham, MA: Allyn & Bacon.

Klomek, A.B., Marrocco, F., Kleinman, M., Schonfeld, I.S., and Gould, M.S. (2007). Bullying, depression, and suicidality in adolescents. *Journal of American Academy of Child and Adolescent Psychiatry*, **46**, 40–49.

Knickmeyer, R.C., Wheelwright, S., Hoekstra, R., and Baron-Cohen, S. (2006). Age of menarche in females with autism spectrum conditions. *Developmental Medicine & Child Neurology*, **28**, 1007–1008.

Konstantareas, M.M. and Lunsky, Y.J. (1997). Sociosexual knowledge, experience, attitudes, and interests of individuals with autistic disorder and developmental delay. *Journal of Autism and Developmental Disorders*, **27**, 397–413.

Kraijer, D. (2000). Review of adaptive behavior studies in mentally retarded persons with autism/pervasive developmental disorder. *Journal of Autism and Developmental Disorders*, **30**, 39–47.

Krauss, M.W., Seltzer, M.M., and Jacobson, H.T. (2005). Adults with autism living at home or in non-family settings: positive and negative aspects of residential status. *Journal of Intellectual Disability Research*, **49**, 111–124.

Larsen, F.W. and Mouridsen, S.E. (1997). The outcome in children with childhood autism and Asperger syndrome originally diagnosed as psychotic: A 30- year follow-up study of subjects hospitalized as children. *European Child and Adolescent Psychiatry*, **6**, 181–190.

Lee, D.O. (2004). Menstrually related self-injurious behavior in adolescents with autism. *Journal of the American Academy of Child and Adolescent Psychiatry*, **43**, 1193.

Little, L. (2001). Peer victimization of children with Asperger spectrum disorders. *Journal of the American Academy of Child and Adolescent Psychiatry*, **40**, 995–996.

Lord, C. (1990). A cognitive behavioral model for the treatment of social-communicative deficits in adolescents with autism. In *Behavior Disorders of Adolescence: Research, Intervention, and Policy in Clinical and School Settings* (R.J. McMahon and R. DeV. Peters, eds.) pp. 155–174. New York: Plenum Press.

Lord, C. and Magill-Evans, J. (1995). Peer interactions of autistic children and adolescents. *Development and Psychopathology*, **7**, 611–626.

Lord, C. and McGee, W. (2001). *Educating Children with Autism.* Committee on Educational Interventions for Children with Autism. Division of Behavioral and Social Sciences and Education. Washington DC: National Academy Press.

Lovaas, I.O. (1987). Behavioral treatment and normal educational and intellectual functioning in young autistic children. *Journal of Consulting and Clinical Psychology*, **55**, 3–9.

Luce, S.C. and Dyer, K. (1995). Providing effective transitional programming to individuals with autism. *Behavioral Disorders*, **21**, 36–52.

Lundine, V. and Smith, C. (2006). *Career training and personal planning for students with autism spectrum disorders: A practical resource for schools.* London: Jessica Kingsley.

Mahwood, L. and Howlin, P. (1999). The outcome of a supported employment scheme for high-functioning adults with autism or Asperger's syndrome. *Autism*, **3**, 229–254.

Mahwood, L., Howlin, P., and Rutter, M. (2000). Autism and developmental receptive language disorder – comparative follow-up study in early adult life: Cognitive and language outcomes. *Journal of Child Psychology and Psychiatry, and Allied Disciplines*, **41**, 547–559.

McCallion, P. and McCarron, M. (2004). Ageing and intellectual disabilities: A review of recent literature. *Current Opinion in Psychiatry*, **17**, 349–352.

McDougle, C.J., Kresch, L.E., Goodman, W.K., Naylor, S.T., Volkmar, F.R., Cohen, D.J., and Price, L.H. (1995). A case-controlled study of repetitive thoughts and behavior in adults with autistic disorder and obsessive-compulsive disorder. *American Journal of Psychiatry*, **152**, 772–777.

McEachin, J.J., Smith, T. and Lovaas, O.I. (1993). Long-term outcome for children with autism who received early intensive behavioral treatment. *American Journal on Mental Retardation*, **97**, 359–372.

Mesibov, G.B. (1983). Current perspectives and issues in autism and adolescence. In *Autism in Adolescents and Adults* (E. Schopler and G.B. Mesibov, eds.) pp. 37–53. New York: Plenum Press.

Mesibov, G.B. and Handlan, S. (1997). Current perspectives and issues in autism and adolescence. In *Handbook of Autism and Pervasive Developmental Disorders*. 2nd ed. (D.J. Cohen and F.R. Volkmar, eds.) pp. 309–322. New York: John Wiley & Sons.

Meyers, C.E. and Balcher, J. (1987). Historical determinants of residential care. In *Living Environments and Mental Retardation* (S. Landesman, P.M. Vietze, and M.J. Begab, eds.) pp. 3–16. Washington DC: American Association on Mental Retardation.

Moxon, L. and Gates, D. (2001). Children with autism: Supporting the transition to adulthood. *Educational and Child Psychology*, **18**, 28–40.

Muller, E., Schuler, A., Burton, B.A., and Yates, G.B. (2003). Meeting the vocational support needs of individuals with Asperger Syndrome and other autism spectrum disabilities. *Journal of Vocational Rehabilitation*, **18**, 163–185.

Nesbitt, S. (2000). Why and why not? Factors influencing employment for individuals with Asperger syndrome. *Autism*, **4**, 357–369.

Newport, J., Newport, M., and Dodd, J. (2007). *Mozart and the Whale: An Asperger's Love Story*. New York: Touchstone.

Orsmond, G., Krauss, M.W., and Seltzer, M.M. (2004). Peer relationships and social and recreational activities among adolescents and adults with autism. *Journal of Autism and Developmental Disorders*, **34**, 245–256.

Ousley, O. and Mesibov, G. (1991). Sexual attitudes and knowledge of high-functioning adolescents and adults with autism. *Journal of Autism and Developmental Disabilities*, **21**, 471–481.

Palermo, M.T. (2003). Preventing filicide in families with autistic children. *International Journal of Offender Therapy and Comparative Criminology*, **47**, 47–57.

Papalia, D.E., Sterns, H.L., Feldman, R.D., and Camp, C.J. (2007). *Adult Development and Aging (Third Edition)*. Boston: McGraw Hill.

Parent, W.S. and Everson, J.M. (1986). Competencies of disabled workers in industry: A review of business literature. *Journal of Rehabilitation*, **52**, 16–23.

Petry, K., Maes, B., and Vlaskamp, C. (2005). Domains of life of people with profound multiple disabilities: the perspective of parents and direct support staff. *Journal of Applied Research in Intellectual Disabilities*, **18**, 35–46.

Piven, J., Harper, J., Palmer, P., and Arndt, S. (1996). Course of behavioral change in Autism: A retrospective study of High-IQ adolescents and adults. *Journal of the American Academy of Child and Adolescent Psychiatry*, **35**, 523–529.

Realmuto, G.M. and Main, B. (1982). Coincidence of Tourette's disorder and infantile autism. *Journal of Autism and Developmental Disorders*, **12**, 367–372.

Renty, J. and Roeyers, H. (2005). Students with autism spectrum disorders in Special and General Education schools in Flanders. *British Journal of Developmental Disabilities*, **51**, 27–39.

Rogan, P., Banks, B., and Howard, M. (2000). Workplace supports in practice: As little as possible, as much as necessary. *Focus on Autism and Other Developmental Disabilities*, **15**, 2–11.

Ruef, M.B. and Turnbull, A.P. (2002). The perspectives of individuals with cognitive disabilities and/or autism on their lives and their problem behavior. *Research and Practice for Persons with Severe Disabilities*, **27**, 125–140.

Rumsey, J.M., Rapoport, J.L., and Sceery, W.R. (1985). Autistic children as adults: Psychiatric social and behavioural outcomes. *Journal of the American Academy of Child Psychiatry*, **24**, 465–473.

Rutter, M. (1970). Autistic children: Infancy to adulthood. *Seminars in Psychiatry*, **2**, 435–450.

Sallows, G.O. and Graupner, T.D. (2005). Intensive behavioral treatment for children with autism: Four-year outcome and predictors. *American Journal on Mental Retardation*, **110**, 417–438.

Sansone, C. and Berg, C.A. (1993). Adapting to the environment across the life span: Different process or different inputs? *International Journal of Behavioral Development*, **16**, 215–241.

Schall, C., Cortijo-Doval, E., Targett, P.S., and Wehman, P. (2006). Applications for youth with autism spectrum disorders. In *Life Beyond the Classroom: Transition Strategies for Young People with Disabilities* (P. Wehman, ed.) pp. 535–575. Baltimore: Paul H Brooks.

Seltzer, M.M. and Krauss, M.W. (1987). *Aging and Mental Retardation: Extending the Continuum*. Washington DC: American Association on Mental Retardation.

Seltzer, M.M., Krauss, M.W., Orsmond, G.I., and Vestal, C. (2000). Families of adolescents and adults with autism: Uncharted territory. *International Review of Research on Mental Retardation*, **23**, 267–294.

Seltzer, M.M., Krauss, M.W., Shattuck, P.T., Orsmond, G., Swe, A., and Lord, C. (2003). The symptoms of autism spectrum disorders in adolescence and adulthood. *Journal of Autism and Developmental Disorders*, **33**, 565–581.

Seltzer, M.M., Shattuck, P., Abbeduto, L., and Greenberg, J.S. (2004). Trajectory of development in adolescents and adults with autism. *Mental Retardation and Developental Disabilities Research Reviews*, **10**, 234–247.

Shattuck, P.T., Seltzer, M.M., Greenberg, J.S., Orsmond, G.I., Bolt, D., Kring, S., et al. (2007). Change in autism symptoms and maladaptive behaviors in adolescents and adults with an autism spectrum disorder. *Journal of Autism and Developmental Disorders*, **37**, 1735–1747.

Sigman, M. and Ruskin, E. (1999). Continuity and change in the social competence of children with autism, Down syndrome, and developmental delays, *Monographs of the Society for Research in Child Development*, **64**, (1, Serial No. 256) 114.

Smith, M.D. (1985). Teaching life skills to adults disabled by autism. *Journal of Autism and Developmental Disorders*, **15**, 163–175.

Smith, D.M., Belcher, R.G., and Juhrs, P.D. (1995). *A guide to successful employment for individuals with autism*. Baltimore, MD: Brookes.

Smith, M.D. (1999). Community integration and supported employment. In *Autism: Identification, Education, and Treatment*. 2nd ed. (D.B. Zager, ed.) pp. 301–321. Mahwah, NJ: Lawrence Earlbaum.

Smith, J. and Baltes, P.B. (1999). Life span perspectives on development. In *Developmental Psychology: An Advanced Textbook (Fourth Edition)* (M.H. Bornstein and M.E. Lamb, eds.) pp. 47–72. Mahwah, NJ: Lawrence Erlbaum.

Smith, M.D. and Philippen, L.R. (2005). Community integration and supported employment. In *Autism Spectrum Disorders: Identification, Education, and Treatment*. (D. Zager, ed.) pp. 493–514. Mahwah, NJ: Lawrence Earlbaum.

Stewart, M.E., Barnard, L., Pearson, J., Hasan, R., and O'Brien, G. (2006). Presentation of depression in autism and asperger syndrome. *Autism*, **10**, 103–116.

Stokes, M. and Kaur, A. (2005). High-functioning autism and sexuality: A parental perspective. *Autism*, **9**, 266–289.

Stokes, M., Newton, N., and Kaur, A. (2007). Stalking, and Social and Romantic Functioning Among Adolescents and Adults with Autism Spectrum Disorder. *Journal of Autism and Developmental Disorders*, **37**, 1969–1986.

Stone, W.L. and Ousley, O.Y. (1999). Pervasive Developmental Disorders: Autism. In *Disorders of Development and Learning (Second Edition)* (M. Wohraich, ed.) pp. 379–405. St. Louis, MO: Mosby.

Szatmari, P., Bartolucci, G., Bremmer, R.S., Bond, S., and Rich, S. (1989). A follow-up study of high functioning autistic children. *Journal of Autism and Developmental Disorders*, **19**, 213–226.

Tantam, D. (1991). Asperger's syndrome in adulthood. In *Autism and Asperger Syndrome* (U. Frith, ed.) pp. 147–183. Cambridge, England: Cambridge University Press.

Travis, L.L. and Sigman, M. (1998). Social deficits and interpersonal relationships in autism. *Mental Retardation and Developmental Disabilities Research Review*, **4**, 65–72.

Tsai, L.Y. (1996). Brief report: Comorbid psychiatric disorders of autistic disorder. *Journal of Autism and Developmental Disorders*, **26**, 159–163.

Tsatsanis, K.D. (2003). Outcome research in Asperger syndrome and autism. *Child and Adolescent Psychiatric Clinics*, **12**, 47–63.

Turner, L.M., Stone, W.L., Pozdol, S.L., and Coonrod, E.E. (2006). Follow-up of children with autism spectrum disorders from age 2 to age 9. *Autism*, **10**, 243–265.

Ventner, A., Lord, C., and Schopler, E. (1992). A follow-up study of high-functioning autistic children. *Journal of Child Psychology and Psychiatry*, **3**, 489–507.

Volkmar, F.R. (1987). Diagnostic issues in the pervasive developmental disorders. *Journal of Child Psychology and Psychiatry and Allied Disciplines*, **28**, 365–369.

Volkmar, F.R., Cicchetti, D.V., Bregman, J., Cohen, D.J. (1992) Three diagnostic systems for autism: DSM-III, DSM-III-R, and ICD-10. *Journal of Autism and Developmental Disorders*, **22**, 483–492.

Volkmar, F.R. and Klin, A. (1995). Social development in autism: Historical and clinical perspectives. In *Understanding Other Minds: Perspectives From Autism* (S. Baron-Cohen, H. Tager-Flusberg, and D.J. Cohen, eds.) pp. 40–55. New York: Oxford University Press.

Volkmar, F.R., Paul, R., Klin, A., and Cohen, D. (2005), *Handbook of Autism and Pervasive Developmental Disorders (Third Edition)*. Hoboken, NJ: John Wiley & Sons.

Wehman, P. and Thoma, C.A. (2006). Teaching for transition. In *Life Beyond the Classroom: Transition Strategies for Young People with Disabilities* (P. Wehman, ed.) pp. 201–236. Baltimore: Paul H. Brooks.

Wilson, C. and Brewer, N. (1992). The incidence of criminal victimization of individuals with an intellectual disability. *Australian Psychologist*, **27**, 114–117.

Zager, D. (2005). *Autism Spectrum Disorders: Identification, Education, and Treatment (Third Edition)*. Mahwah NJ: Lawrence Erlbaum.

PART

II

ASSESSMENT

4

DIFFERENTIAL DIAGNOSIS

MARIE S. NEBEL-SCHWALM AND
JOHNNY L. MATSON

Louisiana State University, LA, USA

INTRODUCTION

Autism spectrum disorders are a class of five disorders that share features such as impaired social functioning, repetitive or restricted interests and stereotyped behaviors, and language impairment. The *Diagnostic and Statistical Manual of Mental Disorders, 4th edition*, Text Revision (DSM-IV:TR; APA, 2000) categorizes these disorders as pervasive developmental disorders. These include autistic disorder (also referred to as autism), Asperger's disorder (or Asperger's syndrome), pervasive developmental disorder-not otherwise specified (PDD-NOS), Rett's disorder (or Rett's syndrome), and childhood disintegrative disorder. The majority of the literature focuses on the first three to the near exclusion of the latter two. This is likely due to the recency in which Rett's disorder and childhood disintegrative disorder have been added to the DSM (Volkmar and Klin, 2004). Reflecting current changes in the nomenclature, this chapter will refer to these disorders as autism spectrum disorders (ASD) (Akshoomoff, 2006). The shift from PDD to ASD emphasizes the growing consensus in the field that these disorders are aligned along a spectrum and that they are distinguished primarily by the severity and number of symptoms, rather than representing clearly discrete disorders (Meyer and Minshew, 2002).

Families who receive the news that their child has been diagnosed with a disorder on this spectrum are faced with the daunting task of how to maximize the child's quality of life. However, researchers and clinicians do not always agree on the methods with which these diagnoses are based, nor, in some cases, the categorical distinctions between disorders on the spectrum. Clearly then, to best serve these families and to be able to offer the most useful treatments for the children and adults who have been diagnosed with an autism spectrum disorder, more work is needed to build consensus in the field about what these disorders are, how to assess and diagnose them, and, most importantly, how to effectively treat them. This chapter will focus on etiological issues, prevalence estimates, lifespan development, differentially diagnosing within the spectrum, comorbid psychopathology and differential diagnoses, and current assessment methods available to assist in the diagnosis of ASD.

ETIOLOGY

Approximately 80 percent of individuals with ASD do not have a known causality (Steffenburg, 1991). For the small percentage where causality is known, multiple theories exist. Some of the more commonly proposed theories are presented here. A clinician's knowledge of the state of the art in etiological research has assessment and treatment implications. For example, Rett's syndrome is linked to mutations of one gene, thus genetic testing may be warranted in cases where this is a potential diagnosis (Amir et al., 1999). Without that knowledge, clinicians are at an increased risk of misdiagnosing clients who may have this disorder. For individuals who have not been accurately diagnosed, this could lead to less-than-optimal treatments, or even inappropriate treatments. This section highlights etiological theories of ASD including genetic, neurobiological, immunological, and perinatal factors. Also included is the proposed link between MMR vaccinations and autism (Wakefield, 1999).

GENETIC

Several genes and chromosomes have been identified as playing a role in the development of ASD. Some of the most common chromosomal anomalies are Down syndrome and fragile X syndrome (Rasmussen et al., 2001; Steffenburg, 1991). Single-gene diseases, such as tuberous sclerosis and untreated PKU have also been identified in the development of ASD (Baker et al., 1998; Miladi et al., 1992; Smalley, 1998). Rett's syndrome has been linked to a single gene (MECP2; Amir et al., 1999), however, mutations of the same gene have also been associated with other disorders such as autism (Beyer et al., 2002) and encephalopathy (Hoffbuhr et al., 2001). Researchers have concluded that rather than a solitary gene, many genes are involved in the expression of ASD (Pickles et al., 1995).

Rates of ASD among relatives of probands are higher than in the general population and monozygotic twins have a higher rate of concordance (50 percent for diagnostic concordance and 92 percent for concordant features of ASD) (Bailey et al., 1995). These findings suggest that a combination of genetic and environmental factors is involved. Consequently, the idea that genetic factors play a causal role in the development of ASD has been generally accepted (Volkmar et al., 2004). This general consensus is reflected in the shift in hypothesis-testing from whether genetic factors play a role, to which genetic factors are involved (Rutter, 2005; Volkmar et al., 2004).

NEUROBIOLOGICAL

Neurobiological differences, including irregularities in head circumference, brain volume, corpus callosum, hippocampus, amygdala, cerebellum, and the parietal lobes, have been noted in individuals with ASD (Courchesne et al., 2001; Fidler et al., 2000; Haas et al., 1996; Harden et al., 2000; Kemper and Bauman, 1998). Although several studies have found differences in head circumference among those with ASD (e.g., Dawson et al., 2007), others have not (Hultman et al., 2002). Further, although brain volume differences were noted for young children, this was not the case for adolescents or adults (Aylward et al., 2002).

Evidence for irregularities of the hippocampus and amygdala is similarly equivocal (Bailey et al., 1998). Despite these contradictions, there has been more consistent support to show that there are developmentally linked increases in brain volume and reduced sizes of the corpus callosum, indicating that these structural abnormalities may in fact be linked to the development of ASD (Nicolson and Szatmari, 2003). While there is some support that ASD are neurobiological disorders, the equivocal data indicate that more information is needed (Tsai, 2005).

IMMUNOLOGICAL

Neurotransmitters play a vital role in the communication between the immune system and the brain. Among immunologically based theories of etiology, ASD have been associated with abnormal responses to certain antigens, unusual numbers of T-cells (abnormally high or abnormally low), and low activity levels of natural killer cells (Burger and Warren, 1998). Further, abnormal cell-death regulation has also been observed (Engstrom et al., 2003), as well as increased serotonin levels (Coutinho et al., 2004; Leboyer et al., 1999) and the presence of serotonin antibodies (Singh et al., 1997). Leboyer and colleagues (1999) reported that 25–50 percent of individuals with autism have abnormally high levels of serotonin; however, these results are not unique to individuals with ASD (Gupta, 2004).

It has been proposed that increased levels of dopamine are associated with higher rates of restricted, repetitive and stereotyped behaviors (Klinger et al., 2003). Studies have reported lower levels of a dopamine metabolite (homovanillic acid; HVA) among autistic individuals (Tani et al., 1994), and, conversely, some have shown no differences (Minderaa et al., 1989). Levels of HVA have not been shown to correlate with autistic behaviors or individuals with autism, thus, clear support for the etiological role of dopamine in ASD is lacking (Tsai, 2005).

Norepinephrine (NE) plays a critical role in how one responds to stress, anxiety, and arousal. The link of NE to ASD is based on reports that some individuals with ASD are hyperresponsive to stress and anxiety (Anderson and

Hoshino, 2005). However, support for this has been weak and comes primarily from reports of the effectiveness of clonidine (a drug that lessens the effect of NE) in individuals with autism (Frankhauser et al., 1992).

Endogenous opioids and the gastrointestinal (GI) tract have been identified as playing a role in the etiology of ASD (Gupta, 2004). Theories regarding gastrointestinal abnormalities originated when high frequencies of GI problems were reported among individuals with ASD, such as esophageal reflux and colitis (D'Eufemia et al., 1996). However, these claims are not consistently supported. Black et al. (2002) found no evidence of increased levels of GI disturbances among individuals with ASD.

Other research on GI factors has found metabolic problems of dietary opioids in the GI tract among those with ASD (Furlano et al., 2001). The proposed mechanism is that nonmetabolized opioid peptides can cross the blood-brain barrier and bind to opioid receptors which results in behavioral problems such as short attention span, learning problems, and social problems (Reichelt et al., 1991; Sandman, 1991). However, some have found higher rates of endorphins (Tordjman et al., 1997) while others have found lower rates (Sandman et al., 1990). The conflicting literature highlights the need for additional research to clarify the relationship between endorphins and the etiology of ASD.

Overall, the evidence for immunologically based etiologies of ASD is limited due to the fact that few replicated differences exist (Anderson and Hoshino, 2005). Also, some of the abnormalities noted are found among individuals without ASD and it cannot be certain whether these differences are a causal factor or the result of having ASD (Gupta, 2004). Unfortunately, the presence of methodological problems, such as small sample sizes and the lack of consistent definitions of ASD further hamper conclusions that may be drawn (Tsai, 2005).

PERINATAL

Several studies have looked into whether various perinatal factors are associated with the development of ASD. These factors include induced labor, prolonged labor, obstetrical complications, prematurity, oxygen at birth, and jaundice (Bolton et al., 1997; Cryan et al., 1996). None of these factors, however, have received strong or consistent support (Gupta, 2004). While individuals with low-functioning autism were found to have more complications than those with high-functioning autism, these individuals did not have more obstetrical complications than their non-autistic siblings (Deb et al., 1997). Although there is some evidence for the correlation between perinatal variables and functioning level of individuals with autism, there is no evidence that perinatal variables cause autism to develop (Cryan et al., 1996; Piven et al., 1993). Other hypotheses suggest that, rather than being a casual factor of autism, obstetrical complications result from the presence of an abnormally developing fetus (Gupta, 2004), or that they may be due to a third unknown factor (Bolton et al., 1997).

MMR VACCINATIONS

A very controversial and well-known theory proposed by Wakefield (1999) suggested that the MMR vaccination was causally linked to the development of ASD. Subsequently, several researchers have not found support for this hypothesis (DeStefano and Chen, 2001; Herbert et al., 2002; Goin-Kochel and Myers, 2005). Further, rates of autism and related disorders have increased over the past several decades, while rates of MMR vaccination use have remained constant (Dales et al., 2001). In Japan, the MMR vaccination has been discontinued, however, rates of autism are increasing (Honda et al., 2005). Unfortunately, despite the mounting evidence, this theory has continued to be perpetuated (Herbert et al., 2002; Rutter, 2005).

SUMMARY

Although there appears to be consensus that genetic factors play a role in the etiology of ASD, the specific etiological pathways are not well understood. Some evidence exists for neurobiological differences (i.e., brain volume and the corpus callosum) and, although differences have been found with respect to perinatal factors, there is no evidence that these factors are causal. One of the more consistent findings is that MMR vaccinations do not play a causal role in the development of ASD. Unfortunately, despite the evidence, belief that MMR vaccinations cause autism remains.

Among the immunological theories of etiology (i.e., theories involving dopamine, norepinephrine, serotonin, and endorphins), consistent empirical results are lacking. In many cases this is due to methodological factors such as small sample sizes, inconsistent inclusion and/or exclusion criteria, inaccuracies in assessment, and variations in how factors were measured. Taken together, these studies highlight the degree to which little is known about the causality of ASD.

PREVALENCE AND INCIDENCE

There has been an increase in the reported prevalence and incidence of ASD. In the past, estimates were approximately 4 to 5 in 10 000 (CDC, 2007a). A recent study carried out by the Center for Disease Control and Prevention reported a much higher prevalence estimate of autism and related spectrum disorders than previously thought. Two multistate studies found that approximately 6.6 in 1000 children had a diagnosis of autism, Asperger's or PDD-NOS (CDC, 2007a; CDC, 2007b). These studies employed clinicians who were defined as having "an advanced degree and/or certification in the assessment and diagnosis of children with developmental disabilities, especially ASDs" (p. 4). Clinicians reviewed charts to determine if a particular child met DSM-IV-TR criteria for an ASD. Despite limitations to this methodology, the rates found by this study were similar to the rates from other studies that did not rely on chart review, but utilized clinical interviews with a subsample. For example, Baird and colleagues (2006) reported the prevalence of autistic disorder to be 38.9 per 10 000, other ASD to be 77.2 per 10 000. These findings were based on a population of almost 57 000, of which, 1770 had received a diagnosis of ASD in their communities. Of the 1770 individuals, 255 were selected and administered a clinical interview resulting in 81 individuals diagnosed with autism, 77 with another ASD, and 97 with a non-ASD diagnosis. Some possible explanations for the change in prevalence include the fact that diagnostic criteria have changed over time, awareness of these disorders has increased, and that more sensitive measures of ASD exist.

LIFESPAN DEVELOPMENT

EARLY IDENTIFICATION

There are two key factors that have inspired and influenced efforts to reliably diagnose ASD in very young children. The first is the belief that the earlier one can identify a child with developmental difficulties, the earlier one can provide treatment. While it may seem intuitive that beginning treatment when children are very young will yield the most robust results, it is possible that too much early intervention may have adverse effects. For example, a child may experience burnout as the result of too many intensive interventions, which could impede progress. A second factor is that many parents of children with autism report that they noticed changes in their child's behavior between 1 and 2 years of age (Calhoun and Mayes, 1999; Rogers, 2004). Changes that have been reported include a lack of progress, and, in some cases, a loss of skill that had been present (e.g., language). Although this stagnation and/or decline in functioning is not reported by all parents of children with ASD, its presence is noteworthy and has contributed to the belief that these disorders are due to events occurring during toddlerhood.

Therefore, in an effort to provide families with accurate early diagnoses so that they may access appropriate services, researchers have developed measures used to assess the functioning of very young children, ranging in age from 18 months to 3 years. Examples of these include the Checklist for Autism in Toddlers (CHAT; Baron-Cohen et al., 1992) and the Screening Tool for Autism in Two-Year-Olds (STAT; Stone et al., 2000) (see the review of assessment measures section for details of these measures). However, researchers suggest that clinicians are not able to reliably diagnose ASD until children are closer to 3 years of age and that autism is more reliably diagnosed at younger ages than Asperger's disorder or PDD-NOS (Matson et al., 2006). This is most likely due to the more severe symptomatology of autism versus Asperger's or PDD-NOS than years of age With increasing age, more social interactions, and the increased complexity of skills that are required, individuals with Asperger's and PDD-NOS begin to manifest more difficulties and become more readily identifiable compared to their regularly developing peers.

ADOLESCENCE AND ADULTHOOD

The majority of literature on ASD, including diagnostic and treatment concerns, focuses on children, even though the pervasiveness of these disorders indicates that almost all of these individuals will require treatment as adolescents and adults (Shea and Mesibov, 2005). While some individuals with ASD experience significant improvements in their social, communication, and/or repetitive and restricted behaviors, these improvements do not indicate a decreased need for services, but rather, the need for services that are appropriate to their particular developmental level (Seltzer et al., 2003).

Other researchers have also noted improvements in ASD core symptomatology (e.g., Schopler et al., 1980), language use (Ballaban-Gil et al., 1996), and restricted and repetitive behaviors (Seltzer et al., 2003). Indeed, some researchers have suggested that adult assessment may be warranted for individuals who do not currently meet criteria for ASD, but did when they were children (Piven et al., 1996). Unfortunately, improvement is not always the observed outcome. Deterioration has also been documented in cognitive and behavioral symptoms (Venter et al., 1992), including reports of individuals who met ASD criteria as adults, but lacked such symptoms as children (Seltzer et al., 2003). Thus, the ability to conduct adult assessments of ASD is helpful for individuals where changes in symptomatology have occurred across the lifespan. Although most measures only assess children and adolescents, one measure that assesses ASD in adults is the ASD-Diagnostic Adult version (ASD-DA) (Matson et al., 2007). The ASD-DA is an interview that is done with an informant (such as a relative or caregiver). More details of this measure can be found in the ASD assessment measures section.

DIFFERENTIAL DIAGNOSES WITHIN THE SPECTRUM

Determining whether an individual meets criteria for an ASD can be challenging. Broadly speaking, a diagnosis of autism reflects more severe impairment, followed by Asperger's disorder and then PDD-NOS. Having said this, differentiating between these disorders, particularly autism and Asperger's syndrome, can be difficult. The DSM specifies that clinicians must not diagnose Asperger's if the individual meets criteria for autism, and yet the criteria are very similar for these two disorders. The differences are that there must not be evidence of delays in language, cognitive abilities, or adaptive behavior (except social interactions) in those with Asperger's disorder; however, individuals meeting criteria for autism may or may not have cognitive delays (APA, 2000). Therefore, having a high IQ does not preclude the diagnosis of autism. Yet, in reality, the presence of a high IQ increases the chance that a clinician will diagnose an individual with Asperger's disorder (Sciutto and Cantwell, 2005).

It is no surprise, then, that debate exists as to whether autism and Asperger's are discrete categories. Some researchers have gone so far as to conclude that Asperger's should be removed from the DSM (Mayes and Calhoun, 2004). Others have proposed that a developmental approach to diagnosing within the spectrum be adopted (Gillham et al., 2000). Specifically, Gillham and colleagues suggest that measuring socialization skills within a developmental context can more readily distinguish individuals with autism from controls than traditional methods of assessment that rely on symptom counts without reference to developmental norms.

Ironically, some researchers have proposed that all of the individuals originally described by Hans Asperger actually meet criteria for autistic disorder rather than Asperger's disorder (Miller and Ozonoff, 1997). This finding was underscored by Tryon et al. (2006). They asked parents of 26 individuals with an Asperger's diagnosis to complete a checklist containing DSM-IV-TR criteria for autism and Asperger's. The vast majority of these individuals ($n = 20$) actually met criteria for autism. These results highlight two problem areas: the confusing diagnostic overlap and whether clinicians are adhering to the hierarchical rule of not diagnosing Asperger's if the individual meets criteria for autism. Tryon and colleagues (2006) suggest that these two disorders are dimensionally related rather than discrete entities. These authors propose renaming Asperger's syndrome high-functioning autistic disorder to clarify the relationship between autism and the current Asperger's diagnostic group.

In an attempt to find empirical evidence of differences between individuals meeting criteria for autism, Asperger's syndrome, and PDD-NOS, 159 individuals were given measures of executive functioning (Verte et al., 2006). Individuals with high-functioning autism (defined as having autistic disorder and an IQ of 80 or higher), Asperger's disorder, and PDD-NOS differed significantly from the control group on several measures of executive functioning, including verbal fluency, cognitive flexibility, and inhibition of a response. However, there was much less variation within the spectrum. Individuals in the high-functioning autistic group did not differ from the Asperger group, whereas the PDD-NOS group obtained scores that fell between the autistic/Asperger groups and participants in the control group.

Another contributor to the confusion of these categories is the term high-functioning autistic disorder. This term is defined variably, and is sometimes used interchangeably with Asperger's disorder. Attwood (2006) provides an explanation about the relationships between Asperger's disorder, classical autistic disorder, and high-functioning autistic disorder. Attwood purports that high-functioning and classical autistic disorder are manifested in similar ways during the individual's first months and years. However, individuals with

high-functioning autistic disorder improve, partially as a result of early intervention, to the point where their skill levels are in line with those who never
displayed language delays in the early years (i.e., their functioning is congruent
with those who have Asperger's disorder). In a study that compared individuals with high-functioning autistic disorder (defined as having an IQ of 70 or
higher) and Asperger's disorder, meaningful differences were not found (Howlin,
2003).

Additional research has compared high-functioning autism and Asperger's.
For example, Sciutto and Cantwell (2005) used fictional descriptions and presented them to clinicians for their diagnostic impressions. They found that clinicians primarily rely on the DSM-IV criteria regarding these two disorders, but
that they also tend to take into account additional information that is not related
to the core symptoms necessary for a diagnosis.

Taken together, these data highlight the difficulties inherent in differentially
diagnosing between the similar constructs of autism and Asperger's syndrome.
Although diagnostic differences between these two disorders exist in the current
DSM nosology, along with a hierarchical standard, not all clinicians abide by
these rules. This further blurs the distinction between the disorders. It remains
to be seen whether future editions of the DSM will alter the way in which
these disorders are conceptualized and whether any future changes will assist
with the diagnostic process. At present, care must be taken to ascertain early
language and adaptive developmental history in order to best assist with making
an accurate distinction.

COMORBID PSYCHOPATHOLOGY AND DIFFERENTIAL DIAGNOSES

More attention is being paid to the possibility that comorbid diagnoses exist
among individuals with ASD (Gillberg and Billstedt, 2000). Giving such diagnoses can be difficult due to the lack of knowledge of prevalence estimates among
this sample. In the DSM-IV-TR, for example, it is stated that one cannot give a
comorbid diagnosis of ADHD to an individual with ASD (APA, 2000), and yet
rates of inattention and hyperactivity are reportedly higher among these children
as compared to same-aged peers with a diagnosis of ADHD (Gadow et al., 2004).
Can children with ASD have comorbid ADHD, or are these behaviors features
of ASD? Although controversy exists over these questions, a consensus appears
to be emerging that comorbid disorders can occur, as it does for other Axis I
disorders. In support of this, Gadow and colleagues (2004) found that almost
half of the children with ASD met criteria for ADHD and that children with
ASD were more likely to display symptoms of tics than their non-ASD peers.
The following sections briefly summarize some common comorbid diagnoses
and differential diagnostic concerns for individuals with ASD.

INTELLECTUAL DISABILITIES

Approximately 75 percent of individuals with ASD also have an intellectual disability (ID) (Fombonne, 1999). The notion that the majority of individuals with ASD have an ID has been widely cited; however, this estimate has been recently challenged by Edelson (2006) who reviewed literature from the past 60 years. She concluded that many of the high estimates of comorbidity among children with ASD were either not empirically based, were based on studies that used inappropriate measures of intelligence for individuals with ASD, and/or were based on research more than 25 years old. Edelson's review of the data challenges some of the assumed features of individuals with ASD (Ritvo and Ritvo, 2006). In line with these findings, more recent studies have found lower rates of ID (i.e., approximately 40–50 percent) (Chakrabarti and Fombonne, 2001). One reason given for the lower rates of ID is that these decreases reflect a change in inclusion criteria for ASD (that is, children with PDD-NOS and Asperger's, in general, are more likely to have higher cognitive functioning, but were excluded from earlier estimates) (Bryson and Smith, 1998). Also, it is possible that early diagnosis and interventions may have resulted in some gains and/or lack of deterioration in cognitive development (Shea and Mesibov, 2005). Although recent studies have estimated approximately 50 percent have comorbid ID, this is still a significant portion of the ASD population.

ASSESSING INTELLECTUAL DISABILITIES

Making a diagnosis of ID (or, as it is listed in the DSM-IV-TR, mental retardation; APA, 2000) requires the use of a cognitive/intelligence test as well as an assessment of adaptive skills. Several of the most well-established cognitive tests include the Wechsler Primary Preschool Scale of Intelligence-III (WPPSI-III; Wechsler, 2002), Wechsler Intelligence Scale for Children-IV (WISC-IV; Wechsler, 2003), Wechsler Adult Intelligence Scale-III (WAIS-III; Wechsler, 1997), and Stanford-Binet, 5th Edition (SB5; Roid, 2003). Of these, the SB5 is more often used when diagnosing ID due to its broader potential range of scores. For nonverbal individuals, alternative tests such as the Peabody Picture Vocabulary Test, 4th Edition (PPVT-IV; Dunn and Dunn, 2007) and the Test of Non-Verbal Intelligence, 3rd Edition (TONI-3; Brown et al., 1997) are options. A commonly used measure of adaptive skills is the Vineland Adaptive Behaviors Scales, 2nd Edition (VABS-II; Sparrow et al., 2005). This assessment yields scores in communication, social interactions, daily living skills, maladaptive behaviors, and a total score. In order to meet criteria for an ID, the individual must score more than 2 standard deviations (SD) below the mean on a test of intelligence, display significant difficulties with adaptive living skills, and have an onset prior to age 18 years.

LANGUAGE DISORDERS

Expressive language disorder and mixed expressive–receptive language disorder have features that are similar to ASD, including communication impairments and social impairments (Mildenberger et al., 2001). Both categories also share a distinction of being quite heterogeneous; however, children with language impairments are less impaired overall than their same-aged peers with ASD (Bishop and Norbury, 2002; Mildenberger et al., 2001).

Using questionnaire and observational data, researchers attempted to discern whether children who were clinically diagnosed with a language disorder but displayed autistic features could be distinguished from children with autism (Barrett et al., 2004). With a sample of 37 children (22 of whom met criteria for autism and the remaining 15 were diagnosed with a language disorder), cluster analyses revealed that these two groups were similar in language impairment and social deficits; however, children with autism engaged in more frequent repetitive and stereotyped patterns of behavior. Thus, features of repetitive and stereotypic behaviors were more distinguishing between these two groups than social deficits.

ASSESSING LANGUAGE DISORDERS

There are numerous measures available to assess language ability. These measures cover aspects of language including expressive language, receptive language, and phonological skills. For infants and young children, two measures include the Receptive–Expressive Emergent Language Scale, 3rd edition (REEL-3; Bzoch et al., 2003) and the Preschool Language Scale, 4th edition (PLS-4; Zimmerman et al., 2002). The REEL-3 assesses developing language and the PLS-4 measures receptive and expressive language among children ages "birth" through 6.11 years.

For older individuals, the Clinical Evaluation of Language Fundamentals, 4th edition (CELF-4; Semel et al., 2003) and the Test of Adolescent and Adult Language, 4th edition (TOAL-4; Hammill et al., 2006) assess receptive and expressive language. The CELF is appropriate for people 6–21 years of age, and the TOAL is designed for individuals 12–24 years of age.

SLEEP PROBLEMS

Sleep disturbances, including parasomnias and dyssomnias, among children with ASD have been widely noted (e.g., Polimeni et al., 2005; Williams et al., 2004; Durand, 2002). It is estimated that 44–83 percent of children with autism have comorbid sleep disorders (Williams et al., 2004). In a study that compared rates of sleep disturbance among children with ASD and typically developing peers, 50 percent of typically developing peers experienced problems with sleep compared to 73 percent of children with ASD (Polimeni et al., 2005). Explanations for the high co-occurrence of sleep problems in individuals with ASD have implicated serotonin and melatonin dysregulation; however, the actual mechanisms are not well understood (Malow, 2004).

Assessing Sleep Problems

In addition to a clinical interview, a parent report on sleep problems that distinguishes between those with sleep disorders and normal controls is the Children's Sleep Habits Questionnaire (Owens et al., 2000); however, this scale was not specifically designed to be used with individuals with ASD. Additional assessments include a sleep study (or polysomnography) and the multiple sleep latency test (Carskadon et al., 1986). More simplistically, but also effective, is a "sleep log" that can be filled out by the individual or that person's caregiver regarding their sleep patterns over a week or more.

FEEDING PROBLEMS

Feeding difficulties, including food refusal, texture restrictions, and nonmedically based behaviors such as choking and expulsion have been noted among children with ASD. In fact, Leo Kanner's seminal work in 1943 listed feeding difficulties as a key trait (Ledford and Gast, 2006). Rates of feeding problems in children with ASD have ranged from 33–74 percent, as compared to 25 percent in typically developing children (Burklow et al., 1998; Patel and Piazza, 2001). Coercive parenting practices for children with food refusal may reinforce the negative feeding behaviors (Sanders et al., 1993). In these families, children are more likely to be oppositional and complain more frequently. This, coupled with high levels of negative comments issued by parents, as well as frequent parent commands, is further reinforced by intermittent compliance by the child (Sanders et al., 1993). Therefore, when assessing for feeding problems, it is important to ask detailed questions about parental responses to the child's behaviors.

Assessing Feeding Problems

A food diary is a simple and informative method for assessing problems with feeding. Children's Eating Behavior Inventory (CEBI; Archer et al., 1991) is a 40-item parent report of eating and mealtime behaviors for children ages 2 to 12 years. Items are rated on a 5-point scale (i.e., never, seldom, sometimes, often, always). It also measures whether a particular behavior is a problem (yes or no). The Screening Tool of Feeding Problems (STEP; Matson and Kuhn, 2001) was developed specifically for individuals with intellectual disabilities. The STEP has 23 items that span 5 domains: aspiration risks, selectivities, feeding skills, food refusal, and nutrition-related feeding problems. Items are completed by caregivers who rate frequencies and severities for each question on a 3-point scale. Results of the STEP may indicate whether an individual should be further assessed for such problems as pica and rumination.

ELIMINATION DISORDERS

Although there is much research on sleep disturbances and feeding problems among individuals with ASD, similar evidence about elimination disorders (i.e., enuresis and encopresis) does not exist. Lainhart (1999) noted that individuals with ASD have more delays in being toilet trained, however, the reference cited in support of this was from 1967 (i.e., Rutter et al., 1967, as cited in Lainhart, 1999). For individuals with ASD who also have severe intellectual disabilities, there are more recent documented reports of enuresis (Saloviita, 2002). However, the literature does not address elimination problems among those with ASD who do not have an intellectual disability.

Assessing Elimination Disorders

Unlike the other disorders mentioned, there appears to be a lack of normative standardized measures for assessing enuresis and encopresis. The clinician, therefore, must rely on parent report via a clinical interview and probe for frequency of incidence of wetting or soiling. It is also important to probe for potential precursors and medical conditions that may be affiliated with such behavior. The DSM-IV states that enuresis is the presence of repeated wetting (daytime and/or nighttime) at least twice a week for 3 months, or at a level that is distressing or impairing to the child, and the child is at least 5 years old or the equivalent developmental level (APA, 2000). General medication conditions that are rule-outs include diabetes, spina bifida, seizure disorders and the use of diuretics. Encopresis is defined as repeated voiding (either involuntary or intentional) that occurs at least once a month for three months in a child at least 4 years of age (or developmental equivalent) and is not due exclusively to substance use or medical conditions, with the exception of constipation (APA, 2000).

TICS AND TOURETTE'S SYNDROME

It has been well documented that children with ASD are at an increased risk for developing tics (Barnhill and Horrigan, 2002; Bolton et al., 1998; Canitano and Vivanti, 2007; Gadow and DeVincent, 2005; Ringman and Jankovic, 2000). Estimates of individuals with comorbid ASD and tic disorders range from 25 percent to 60 percent (Gadow and DeVincent, 2005). Features of ASD and tics (including Tourette's syndrome) overlap in the areas of ritualistic behaviors and echolalia, thus differential diagnoses can be difficult (Baron-Cohen et al., 1999). Some research has been published that indicates tics may be primarily genetically transmitted and that they frequently co-occur with obsessive and compulsive behaviors (Frankel, 1986; Eapen et al., 1993), however, other explanations include that tics are independent from the etiologies of ASD, and that they may result from the use of medications (Lainhart, 1999). Therefore, it is important to get a detailed history of medication use (e.g., a time line of medications, dosage information, and side effects) when assessing for tic disorders.

Assessing Tic Disorders

Because of the similarities between stereotypies and tics, it can be difficult to differentiate between them. Generally, some differences that have been noted include the rate and presentation of the movements. Specifically, tics are more likely to be brief, sudden, rapid, and are distressful to the individual, whereas stereotypies are often more fluid, continuous, and do not appear to distress the individual (Lainhart, 1999). Although tic disorders are primarily assessed via interview and observation, an assessment measure that has been shown to have acceptable psychometric properties is the Yale Global Tic Severity Scale (YGTSS; Leckman et al., 1989; Storch et al., 2005). Storch and colleagues (2005) reported the YGTSS to have good internal consistency, test–retest reliability, and convergent and discriminant validity. The YGTSS is a clinician-rated checklist of several possible motor and phonic tics that takes approximately 15–20 minutes to complete. Tics are rated for their number, frequency, intensity, complexity, interference and impairment.

ANXIETY DISORDERS

There are several studies that have evaluated the relationship between anxiety disorders and ASD. Anxiety disorders, such as phobias and obsessive-compulsive disorder, have been studied in this population. Questions addressed include comorbidity issues and concerns about differential diagnoses (e.g., does an individual's repetitive behavior appear more consistent with symptoms of ASD or obsessive-compulsive disorder).

Among individuals with ASD, comorbidity rates of phobias range from 17 percent to 23 percent (Ando and Yoshimura, 1979; Chung et al., 1990 respectively). Rates of obsessive-compulsive disorder appear to be bimodal with some studies finding low rates (2.3 percent, Tantam, 1991; and 2.8 percent, Ghaziuddin et al., 1998) and others finding rates that are much higher (i.e., approximately 20 percent; Bejerot et al., 2001). Higher rates of comorbid anxiety have been reported for people with Asperger's versus those with autism (Klin et al., 2005). This difference may be because individuals with Asperger's are typically more willing to attempt social interactions; however, because they lack social skills, this increased willingness results in more frequent negative interactions (Klin et al., 2005). Below is a more detailed review of phobias and obsessive-compulsive disorder.

FEARS AND PHOBIAS

Several studies have reported increased levels of fears and phobias among children with ASD as compared to typically developing peers (Leyfer et al., 2006; Matson and Love, 1990). Matson and Love (1990) found qualitative differences in that children with ASD were more fearful of thunderstorms, big crowds, the dark, enclosed places, and of being punished, whereas non-ASD peers were more fearful of criticism, injuries, and small animals.

Some researchers have proposed that individuals with ASD display differences in social behaviors, including fears and phobias, due to abnormal functioning of the amygdala (Schultz and Robins, 2005). These data, however, are mixed. Some studies show support for the amygdala dysfunction hypothesis (Ashwin et al., 2007), and others have documented no such relationship (Bernier et al., 2005).

Evans et al. (2005) found that children with ASD were significantly more likely to have medical, situational, and animal fears as compared to same-aged peers, children with Down syndrome, and peers matched by mental age, and they were less likely to have fears that involved harm and injury. Further, these children had externalizing behaviors that were associated with the phobias, such as impulsivity, hyperactivity, and conduct problems, whereas children in the other groups did not have the same associations. Although certain fears and phobias may be more "normative" among individuals with ASD, children and adults with ASD display more symptoms compared to their peers, which implies that these individuals are more likely to need treatment (Evans et al., 2005).

Assessing Fears and Phobias

Similar to the assessment of other disorders, a multimethod, multiinformant approach enhances the validity of diagnostic decisions. For children, the Anxiety Disorder Interview Schedule for DSM-IV, Child and Parent Interview Versions (ADIS-IV-C/P; Silverman and Albano, 1996) is a semistructured interview that assesses phobias as well as other anxiety disorders, depression, and externalizing disorders. Broadband rating scales to be completed by parents and/or teachers include the Behavior Assessment System for Children-Second Edition (BASC-2; Reynolds and Kamphaus, 2004), the Child Behavior Checklist (CBCL; Achenbach, 1991a) and Teacher Report Form (TRF; Achenbach, 1991b). The BASC has internal consistency and test–retest reliabilities that range from 0.70s to 0.90s for the various subscales whereas the CBCL and TRF have lower reported internal consistency (ranging from 0.54 to 0.96) and a less variable test–retest reliability (ranging from 0.86 to 0.89; Silverman and Ollendick, 2005).

A child-completed rating scale that is specific to phobias is the Fear Survey Schedule for Children (FSS-C; Ollendick, 1983) which has 80 items about various stimuli. It has test–retest reliability of 0.82 for the total scale and internal consistency that ranges from 0.92 to 0.95 (Ollendick, 1983). Some fears and phobias may closely resemble other anxiety disorders and require a careful clinical interview in order to make an accurate diagnosis. For example, fear of the dark may behaviorally mimic separation anxiety. In this situation, some helpful questions to ask when trying to discern whether a child has separation anxiety and/or fear of the dark are the following: can the child be in the dark with a parent and can they be alone in the room with the lights on? Other measures that address fears and phobias include the Pediatric Anxiety Rating Scale (PARS; RUPP Study Group, 2002). This is a clinician-based measure with 50 items that cover specific phobias as well as generalized anxiety, social situations, separation, and physical symptoms. It has a total scale internal consistency of 0.64 and interrater reliability for the total scale of 0.97.

For adults, the semistructured Anxiety Disorder Interview Schedule for DSM-IV: Lifetime Version (ADIS-IV-L; Di Nardo et al., 1994) assesses the presence of phobias as well as other anxiety disorders. The adult-rated Fear Survey Schedule–II (Geer, 1965) is a rating scale specifically designed to assess phobias.

OBSESSIVE-COMPULSIVE DISORDER

There is mounting evidence to suggest that ASD and obsessive-compulsive disorder (OCD) are associated (Bejerot et al., 2001; Bolton et al., 1998; Cook et al., 1994; Green et al., 2000; Hollander et al., 2003). Specifically, the restrictive, repetitive, and stereotyped patterns of interest and behaviors component of ASD shares some resemblance with compulsions in individuals with OCD. For example, children with ASD may line up toys and become very distraught when the order is not preserved. Similarly, some of them wish to rely on a strict schedule for their daily routine. Although rates of OCD diagnoses among individuals with ASD were reportedly bimodal (2–3 percent, Tantam, 1991, and Ghaziuddin et al., 1998; close to 20 percent, Bejerot et al., 2001), symptoms of OCD (e.g., compulsive actions, reported obsessions) ranged from 16 percent to 81 percent (Lainhart, 1999). With such a wide range, it is difficult to know if symptom rates are closer to 16 percent, 81 percent, or somewhere in between.

In further consideration of the potential link between ASD and OCD, one study found differences in parental behaviors when measuring restrictive and repetitive behaviors among children with ASD (Hollander et al., 2003). Parents of children with high rates of restrictive and repetitive behaviors were more likely to have symptoms and/or a diagnosis of OCD as compared to parents of children with low rates of these behaviors (Hollander et al., 2003). Further, some studies have found that first-degree relatives of children with ASD were more likely to have OCD as compared to first-degree relatives of children with Down syndrome (Bolton et al., 1998; Cook et al., 1994). This association is compelling and further investigation will hopefully clarify the potential link between ASD and OCD.

ASSESSING OBSESSIVE-COMPULSIVE DISORDER

Symptoms that appear to overlap between ASD and OCD (i.e., repetitive behaviors) may have differing functions. The examiner must determine whether the repetitive acts or compulsions cause distress and are undesirable or if the behaviors lack this quality. Behaviors that cause distress are more indicative of a compulsion rather than restricted and repetitive behaviors typically seen in individuals with ASD (Thomsen, 1998).

Similar to the assessment of other disorders, a multimethod, multiinformant approach enhances the validity of diagnostic decisions. The ADIS-IV-C/P, as previously mentioned, is a semistructured clinical interview that assesses internalizing and externalizing disorders in children (Silverman and Albano, 1996). Alternatively, the Schedule for Affective Disorders and Schizophrenia for School-Age Children (K-SADS; Ambrosini, 2000), a semistructured interview, provides diagnostic information about internalizing disorders, mood disorders, and externalizing disorders.

For adults, the ADIS-IV-L (Di Nardo et al., 1994) assesses current and lifetime disorders, particularly anxiety disorders, mood disorders, and substance use disorders. An alternative is the Structured Clinical Interview for DSM-IV Axis I Disorders: Clinician Version (SCID-CV; First, Spitzer et al., 1997) which also assesses these disorders, but is less extensive regarding anxiety disorders.

Broadband rating scales designed to assess internalizing and externalizing symptoms in children and adolescents include the BASC-2 (Reynolds and Kamphaus, 2004), CBCL (Achenbach, 1991a) and TRF (Achenbach, 1991b). Clinician-completed assessments specific to OCD in adults and children are the Yale-Brown Obsessive Compulsive Scale (Y-BOCS; Goodman et al., 1989a,b) and the Children's Yale-Brown Obsessive Compulsive Scale (CY-BOCS; Scahill et al., 1997).

The Y-BOCS is a semistructured interview that assesses the severity of obsessions and compulsions rather than emphasizing the actual content of the thoughts or actions. It has reportedly excellent interrater reliability and internal consistency (Goodman et al., 1989a). Like the Y-BOCS, the CY-BOCS assesses the severity of obsessions and compulsions based on parent and/or child input. The CY-BOCS has high internal consistency (0.87 for the total scale) and variable interrater reliability (0.66 to 0.91) (Scahill et al., 1997). More recently, the Children's Yale-Brown Obsessive Compulsive Scale Modified for Pervasive Developmental Disorders (CY-BOCS-PDD; Scahill et al., 2006) was developed. This scale consists of five severity items relating to compulsions. Preliminary reports indicate that it has excellent interrater reliability and internal consistency (Scahill et al., 2006).

Self-report scales include the Spence Children's Anxiety Scale (Spence, 1998), a 44-item scale that assesses the frequency of symptoms associated with OCD, separation anxiety, social phobia, generalized anxiety, panic disorder, and fears of injury. Unfortunately, it has low test–retest reliability (0.45 to 0.60) and variable internal consistency among the subscales (0.60 to 0.92) (Spence, 1998). The Revised Child Anxiety and Depression Scales (Chorpita et al., 2000) assesses OCD, separation anxiety, social phobia, generalized anxiety, panic disorder and major depressive disorder. However, of the subscales, OCD had the lowest reported internal consistency at 0.65 (Chorpita et al., 2000).

Children between the ages of 3 years and puberty who experience a dramatic onset of tics and/or OCD symptoms should be assessed for the presence of pediatric autoimmune neuropsychiatric disorders associated with streptococcal infection (or PANDAS; Swedo et al., 1997). A detailed developmental history (including whether the child's symptoms were preceded by a streptococcal infection) is helpful in discerning whether the tics and/or OCD symptoms are better explained as being an autoimmune disorder or a psychiatric disorder.

ATTENTION-DEFICIT/HYPERACTIVITY DISORDER (ADHD)

Despite the declaration in the DSM-IV-TR that ADHD cannot be diagnosed in individuals with ASD, research suggests otherwise (Goldstein and Schwebach, 2004; Yoshida and Uchiyama, 2004). Hastings et al. (2005) looked at individuals with intellectual disabilities, including those with and without ASD. They found that having an ASD increased the likelihood that the child had symptoms of ADHD. They also discuss the fact that there are no known studies that demonstrate base-rates of symptoms of ADHD among children with ASD (Hastings et al., 2005). Without these data, it is difficult for clinicians to reliably determine if an individual's inattentive and/or hyperactive symptoms are appropriate considering an ASD diagnosis or severe enough to warrant a comorbid diagnosis of ADHD.

Assessing Attention-Deficit/Hyperactivity Disorder

A comprehensive protocol for assessing ADHD must include measures that evaluate alternative hypotheses for why a child may display symptoms of inattention and/or hyperactivity. For this reason, it is important to use broad-based measures as well as more specific measures of ADHD. The diagnosis of ADHD, regardless of the subtype, requires the presence of disturbances in more than one setting (e.g., at work, home, school, and/or with peers); thus, input from several sources (i.e., parents, teachers, and the individual) across multiple methods (interviews, rating scales, and observations) is key. Diagnostic interviews include the Diagnostic Interview Schedule for Children, 4th Edition (DISC-IV; Shaffer et al., 2000) and the ADIS-IV-C/P (Silverman and Albano, 1996). Both the DISC-IV and the ADIS-IV-C/P assess for the presence of internalizing and externalizing disorders; however, because the DISC-IV is a structured interview, it can be completed by paraprofessionals, whereas the ADIS-IV-C/P must be completed by a trained clinician due to its semistructured nature. Broadband rating scales such as the BASC-2 (Reynolds and Kamphaus, 2004) and Achenbach protocols (i.e., CBCL; Achenbach 1991a, and the TRF; Achenbach, 1991b) include parent, teacher, and adolescent rating scales. Rating scales specific to ADHD include the Conners scales for parents, teachers, and adolescent (Conners, 1997) as well as the Brown Attention Deficit Disorder Scales (Brown, 1996).

Although less commonly done, observations of children in academic settings can be very helpful in obtaining a glimpse of their behaviors when they are among peers. Observational systems include the broad-based Direct Observation Form (DOF; Achenbach, 1986) which corresponds with the Child Behavior Checklist's internalizing, externalizing, and total problems scales and ADHD

Derby Hospitals NHS Foundation
Trust
Library and Knowledge Service

specific protocols such as the State University of New York at Stony Brook observation system (Abikoff et al., 1980).

McGough and Barkely (2004) noted that the DSM-IV does not have a developmentally appropriate criteria set for assessing ADHD in adults. Although the Wender Utah Rating Scale (Ward et al., 1993) is designed to be completed by adults to report retrospectively on their behaviors as children, it was not found to highly correlate with the current conceptualization of ADHD, per the DSM-IV.

SUMMARY

Clearly differential diagnosis between ASD and other disorders presents many challenges to the clinician. It can be very difficult to determine whether an individual has an autism spectrum disorder and/or another disorder. Careful clinical interviewing, including a detailed developmental history and the use of empirically based measures are critical. Some disorders mimic symptoms and/or features of ASD such as intellectual deficits, language problems, tics, feeding problems, sleeping problems, repetitive behaviors, and hyperactivity, and further complexity is added when comorbidity is considered. The field is not in agreement as to the possibility of comorbidity (e.g., the DSM does not allow an autism spectrum disorder and ADHD to be simultaneously diagnosed). Prevalence estimates and base rate information regarding comorbidity among individuals with ASD are sorely lacking. Although these data are not readily available, clinicians will enhance their ability to determine an accurate diagnosis and comorbid diagnoses when relying on empirically based measures, multiple informants (i.e., the individual, parents, teachers, caregivers) and multiple methods (i.e., interviews, rating scales, observations).

AUTISM SPECTRUM DISORDERS ASSESSMENT MEASURES

The following section is an overview of measures (i.e., interviews, observation systems, clinician-rated scales, and informant-rated scales) used to assess and diagnose ASD. It includes measures that are more commonly used as well as some newly developed measures. Although most are developed for the assessment of children, some are designed for assessing adults (e.g., ASD-DA, Matson et al., 2007).

INTERVIEWS

Autism Diagnostic Interview-Revised (ADI-R) (Lord et al., 1994)

The ADI-R is a revision of the original ADI which was published in 1989 (Le Couteur et al., 1989). The ADI-R is a semistructured interview that assesses the triad of core domains in the ASD (i.e., deficits in social interactions, communication, and repetitive, limited, and/or stereotyped behaviors or interests) as well as other features, including whether skills (linguistic abilities, for example) ever regressed. The ADI-R requires extensive training for the clinician and the actual administration lasts 2 to 3 hours. It is appropriate for use regarding individuals ages 1½ years to adulthood.

The authors of the ADI-R report good interrater reliability, adequate test–retest reliability, and good validity compared to diagnoses made using the ICD-10 and DSM-IV criteria. However, the test–retest reliability was computed using only six families (Lord et al., 1994). Tadevosyan-Leyfer and colleagues (2003) conducted a principal components analysis with 292 families. Their results suggest that the ADI-R has good internal consistency, face validity, discriminant validity, and construct validity.

Autism Spectrum Disorders-Diagnostic Adult (ASD-DA; Matson et al., 2007)

The ASD-DA was designed to aid in the diagnosis of autistic disorder and PDD-NOS. It is a brief measure that was developed to be used for adults with intellectual disabilities. Examiners complete the ratings via interviews with the individuals' caregiver. This measure has 31 items that are scored either 0 or 1 (0 = no impairment and 1 = some impairment is present). Items include questions about body posture, motor coordination, and restricted interests.

The authors of this measure collected reliability and validity data on 192 adults with intellectual disabilities who are living in residential centers. The average interrater reliability kappa coefficient was 0.295 (ranging from 0.20 to 0.49) and the average test–retest kappa coefficient was 0.386 (ranging from 0.311 to 0.606). A factor analysis yielded three factors which had excellent internal consistency (Matson et al., 2007).

The ASD-DA has also been demonstrated to have robust convergent and divergent validity (Matson, Wilkins, Boisjoli, and Smith, in press). Additional reports of psychometric properties include those of excellent internal consistency and good interrater and test–retest reliability (Matson et al., in press).

Diagnostic Interview for Social and Communication Disorders (DISCO; Wing et al., 2002)

The DISCO is a semistructured interview designed to aid the clinician in diagnosing an ASD, atypical ASDs, non-ASD developmental disorders, and/or the presence of a psychiatric disorder and takes approximately two to four hours to administer. The DISCO offers several algorithms to assist with diagnosing a disorder based on DSM-III-R, DSM-IV, and ICD-10 criteria. Additional algorithms include Kanner's early infant autism criteria, Wing and Gould's autism spectrum disorder criteria, and Gillberg's Asperger syndrome criteria (Wing et al., 2002).

An interrater reliability study for the coding of DISCO items completed by the authors of this measure revealed high agreement (kappa coefficient or intraclass correlation greater or equal to 0.75). This study included data from parents of 82 children 3 to 11 years of age (Wing et al., 2002). Convergent validity was evaluated by comparing 67 clinically-diagnosed children who met criteria for autism (high- or low-functioning), language disorder, or intellectual/learning disability (Leekam et al., 2002). Results indicated that the DISCO ICD-10 algorithm failed to accurately discriminate between some children with ASD and some without ASD (kappa $= 0.57$). The authors propose a revision of their ICD-10 algorithm and recommend the use of the autism spectrum disorder algorithm (Leekam et al., 2002).

OBSERVATION SYSTEMS

Autism Diagnostic Observation Schedule-Generic (ADOS-G; Lord et al., 2000)

The ADOS-G is a revised measure that combines the previously published observation systems known as the Autism Diagnostic Observation Schedule (ADOS; Lord et al., 1989) and the Pre-Linguistic Autism Diagnostic Observation Schedule (PL-ADOS; DiLavore et al., 1995). The ADOS-G consists of four modules based on developmental and language abilities: (1) preverbal/ single words/simple phrase (no consistent spontaneous speech), (2) flexible phrase speech (prefluent speech with some phrases), (3) fluent speech, child and adolescent, and (4) fluent speech, adolescent and adult. The examiner chooses one module to administer to an individual; however, if it is determined that an advanced module would be more appropriate, the examiner may then administer that additional module. Modules take approximately 30 minutes to complete. The first two modules entail the use of toys and other interactive methods, whereas the third and fourth modules are more interview-based. Similar to the ADI-R, the ADOS-G requires extensive training, including attendance at a training workshop, demonstrated interrater reliability, and convergence with training materials prior to being used for research purposes. It contains algorithms for autistic disorder and PDD-NOS.

The following psychometric data were reported by the authors of the ADOS-G (Lord et al., 2000). Across the domains of social, stereotyped behaviors and restricted interests, communication, and nonspecific abnormal behaviors, the interrater item reliability for exact agreement ranged from adequate to substantial. For the four modules, the mean weighted kappas were 0.78, 0.70, 0.65, and 0.66 respectively. Diagnostic classification agreement among raters, when considering individuals with autistic disorder, PDD-NOS, and non-ASDs, ranged from 81 percent to 93 percent across the four modules. Test–retest reliability yielded adequate to excellent stability for the domains. Validity tests revealed that the ADOS-G correctly classified 95 percent of individuals with autistic disorder and 92 percent of those not having an ASD. However, only 33 percent of the PDD-NOS sample received a correct diagnosis (53 percent of this sample received a classification of autistic disorder). The authors acknowledge the limitations of attributing a diagnosis based solely on an observational method (Lord et al., 2000).

Behavior Observation Scale (BOS; Freeman et al., 1981)

This observation system measures 67 behaviors associated with autistic disorder such as grinding teeth, looking at hands, head banging, covering ears, ignoring object, clinging, eye contact, echolalia, and ignoring examiner. The examiner records whether the behavior occurred regularly (3), two times (2), one time (1) or not at all (0). The BOS is conducted across nine 3-minute long sessions, including two baseline periods and one period where the examiner actively tries to engage the child in play. In the remaining 3-minute sessions, the examiner presents stimuli without interacting with the child (Freeman et al., 1981).

Freeman and colleagues (1981) reported good interrater agreement on 60 of the 67 behaviors ($r > 0.80$). Using a sample of 140 children, the authors matched participants based on their cognitive functioning level (i.e., control participants were matched with individuals with autistic disorder who had IQs above 70 and individuals with mental retardation were matched with individuals with autistic disorder who had IQs below 70). Results yielded significant differences in frequencies of 21 behaviors and the percentages of 19 behaviors among high-IQ matched participants as well as significant differences in frequencies of 9 behaviors and the percentages of 6 behaviors among the low-IQ matched participants. Thus, low-IQ individuals were much more similar than high-IQ individuals (Freeman et al., 1981).

RATING SCALES: CLINICIAN COMPLETED

Autism Spectrum Disorders-Diagnostic Child (ASD-DC; Matson et al., 2007)

This newly developed measure is a parent report that is designed to assess symptoms of autistic disorder, Asperger's disorder, and PDD-NOS. It has 71 items that assess social impairments, communication problems, and restricted, repetitive, or stereotyped behaviors, as well as exceptional skills. The latter topic includes questions about whether the child possesses abilities that are beyond expectations based on the child's age, including reading ability, exceptional memory, and artistic ability.

The scale has proven to have robust reliability (Matson, Gonzales and Wilkins, 2007).

Childhood Autism Rating Scale (CARS) (Schopler et al., 1980)

This measure consists of 15 domains that the clinician rates based on interviews, parent report, teacher report, clinic observations, and chart reviews. It was designed by individuals affiliated with the statewide program for individuals with autism in North Carolina. Each item can be rated on a 7-point scale that range across the following levels: normal functioning, mildly abnormal and/or inappropriate, moderately abnormal and/or inappropriate, and severely abnormal and/or inappropriate. Total scores are used to determine whether a child is autistic or not. Scores over 30 indicate the presence of autistic symptoms; however, depending on the score, an individual may have a classification of mild, moderately autistic, or severely autistic. Mesibov et al. (1989) documented differences in total scores over time. They compared CARS scores collected when individuals were 10 years of age or younger with those taken when these individuals were 13 years of age or older and found that these individuals improved by nearly 3 points. Thus, they recommend the use of a cutoff score of 27 compared to the original cutoff of 30 when rating individuals 13 years of age or older.

Much research has been done evaluating this clinician-rated scale. Garfin et al. (1988) found the CARS to have adequate internal consistency and adequate convergent validity, however, they found age-related differences in scores of some items which indicate that these items may be age-limited when considering responses about children and adolescents. They recommend its use as a screening instrument. Van Bourgondien et al. (1992) compared CARS ratings, DSM-III-R criteria, and independent clinical ratings to assess convergent validity. There was total agreement across all 3 methods 78 percent of the time (107 of the 138 individuals). The remaining 22 percent of the cases ($n = 31$) had varying results: 12 were categorized as autistic by the CARS and clinical ratings, 11 by clinical ratings alone, 4 by clinical ratings and DSM-III-R, 2 by CARS and DSM-III-R, 1 by CARS alone, and 1 by DSM-III-R alone. Thus, the CARS had higher convergence with clinical assessment than the DSM-III-R, which appeared to underdiagnose autistic disorder.

DiLalla and Rogers (1994) conducted a principal components analysis based on data collected on 69 children. Assessment was done at baseline and at a 6-month follow-up. Their results yielded three factors: social impairment, negative emotionality, and distorted sensory response. Social impairment was most accurate at discriminating among individuals with autism, PDD-NOS, and regularly developing peers. Test–retest analysis revealed that social impairment and distorted sensory response were more stable over time, whereas negative emotionality showed greater variability, suggesting that it may be more sensitive to developmental changes and treatment intervention.

A more recent study found that the CARS displayed 100 percent sensitivity of children with autistic disorder within a sample of 65 children with and without ASDs, however, it did not correctly identify individuals with Asperger's disorder or PDD-NOS (Rellini et al., 2004).

Screening Tool for Autism in Two-Year-Olds (STAT; Stone et al., 2000)

The STAT was developed to be able to identify children ages 24 to 35 months with autistic disorder from those who have other developmental disorders.

The authors caution that the items on the STAT are developmentally sensitive (i.e., they were written specifically for young children) and thus may not be appropriate for use with older children. It is a play-like interactive assessment consisting of 12 items. The administrator uses tools such as toys, candy, balloon, puppets, and noise makers. Ratings are based on whether the child engages in behaviors such as turn-taking, functional play, making requests, directing attention, and imitation (Stone et al., 2004).

Authors of this measure, Stone and colleagues (2000), evaluated convergent validity with a sample of 33 children who had either an ASD or a non-ASD developmental disorder (e.g., language impairment). In their sample, the STAT had specificity rate of 0.86 and a sensitivity rate of 0.83 in correctly classifying children compared to a clinical diagnosis.

RATING SCALES: INFORMANT-COMPLETED

Asperger Syndrome Diagnostic Scale (ASDS; Myles et al., 2001)

This 50-item informant-completed scale yields an Asperger Syndrome Quotient (ASQ) with a mean of 100 and a standard deviation of 15. It also yields scores in five domains: language, social, maladaptive, cognitive, and sensorimotor and takes approximately 10 minutes to complete.

The manual presents the following reliability evidence: coefficient alpha $= 0.83$ for the ASQ and interrater reliability (based on 14 individuals) of $r = 0.93$ and low correlation with a measure of autism (i.e., the GARS) of $r = 0.46$, indicating discriminant validity (Mirenda, n.d.); however, researchers have expressed serious concerns with this test due to the lack of an independent diagnosis in the standardization sample, as well as psychometric properties that do not meet standards (i.e., the ASQ failed to meet the standard internal consistency of 0.90 or higher) (Campbell, 2005; Goldstein, 2002).

AUTISM BEHAVIOR CHECKLIST (ABC; KRUG ET AL., 1980)

The ABC is a 57-item checklist designed to assess the level of autistic behaviors among individuals with autistic disorder as well as those with mental retardation, emotional disturbance, and the deaf/blind. It was intended to be used by school personnel; however, it is frequently used by parents (Szatmari et al., 1994). It is unique in its use of weighted scores, which were determined based on an analysis of the items (Krug et al., 1980). Items range in weighted scores from 1 to 4. Teachers or parents are to circle the items that describe the child. Each item belongs to one of five scales: sensory, relating, body and object use, language, and social/self help. Scores are totaled for each of the five scales and the checklist also yields a total score.

Several data exist regarding the psychometric properties of this rating scale. The authors of the ABC reported high interrater reliability (i.e., $r = 0.87$) and interrater agreement (95 percent). They also cited evidence of discriminant validity based on the findings that normal control participants scored significantly lower on all scales, individuals with autistic disorder score significantly higher, and the remaining groups (severely emotionally disturbed, deaf blind, and severely mentally retarded) scored in the middle of the range between these two groups, but not significantly different from one another (Krug et al., 1980).

However, when comparing the ABC with clinically diagnosed autistic individuals, it was found to have a 20 percent false negative rate (Volkmar et al., 1988). Further, Volkmar and colleagues found poor interrater reliability and that parents tended to have higher ratings than teachers. Given the high false negative rate of this measure, they recommend using parent report over teacher report.

Sevin et al. (1991) evaluated the ABC and determined that half of their sample of individuals with autism were not accurately diagnosed according to the proposed cutoff scores on the ABC. As a result, they proposed that the cutoff scores were too high, a sentiment echoed by Wadden et al. (1991).

Miranda-Linne and Melin (2002) conducted a factor analysis which yielded a different 5-factor structure of the ABC from the original 5-factor structure adopted by the ABC originators. They noted the difficulties inherent when researchers determine factor structures based on face validity rather than empirical support.

A recent analysis evaluated the ABC with children who were diagnosed according to DSM-IV criteria by a clinician. In this study, the ABC had a 54 percent sensitivity rate, indicating poor ability to accurately identify individuals with ASDs (Rellini et al., 2004).

Autism Spectrum Screening Questionnaire (ASSQ; Ehlers et al., 1999)

This 27-item scale assesses behaviors in the following domains: social interactions, communication problems, restricted and repetitive behavior, motor clumsiness, and associate symptoms (such as tics). It takes approximately 10 minutes to complete and is intended to be used as a screener rather than a diagnostic instrument.

The authors report excellent test–retest and interrater reliability (Campbell, 2005). Mean scores comparing samples of individuals without ASD and those with ASD were 0.7 (SD 2.6) and 26.2 (SD 10.3) respectively. Validity studies showed adequate discriminant and good convergent validity with sensitivity ratings of 62 percent based on parent report cutoff score of 19 and 70 percent based on teacher report cutoff rating of 22 (Ehlers et al., 1999). As a screener, it provides adequate specificity, but has poor sensitivity (Campbell, 2005).

CHECKLIST FOR AUTISM IN TODDLERS (CHAT; BARON-COHEN ET AL., 1992)

The CHAT was designed to be used by a healthcare provider as a very brief (i.e., 5–10 minute) screening measure during a toddler's 18-month well-visit. It consists of two sections: (a) 9 questions to ask the parent and (b) 5 areas to assess via observation by the healthcare provider.

The authors measured predictive validity and test–retest reliability using a longitudinal design (Baron-Cohen et al., 2000). Results indicate excellent reliability among the high- and low-risk groups and good reliability among the medium-risk individuals. Although sensitivity was low, the CHAT had high levels of specificity and good predictive validity.

Childhood Asperger Syndrome Test (CAST; Scott et al., 2002)

The CAST is a 37-item parent or teacher report designed to be used as a screener for the presence of Asperger's disorder. Items are scored either present or absent and a total score is determined. Individuals who obtain score equal to or greater than 15 warrant further evaluation.

Test–retest reliability was reportedly good (correlation 0.83) (Williams et al., 2006). Validity data demonstrated sensitivity of 0.88 and specificity of 0.98 (Campbell, 2005). Results from an epidemiological study indicate that the CAST has demonstrated utility in this setting, but that more data are needed to evaluate its use in clinical settings (Williams et al., 2006).

Gilliam Asperger's Disorder Scale (GADS; Gilliam, 2003)

This 32-item parent or teacher report assesses social interactions, restricted patterns, cognitive patterns, and pragmatic skills of individuals ages 3 to 22. It takes approximately 5 to 10 minutes to complete, and it yields an Asperger's Diagnostic Quotient (ADQ) with a mean of 100 and a standard deviation of 15.

Unlike the following measure by the same author (the Gilliam Autism Rating Scale), there is much less research on the GADS. Small samples were used to assess reliability (i.e., 10 individuals for test–retest, and 16 individuals for interrater) and validity findings were not robust (England, n.d.). Unfortunately, the ADQ of the GADS does not meet the standard of internal consistency reliability of 0.90 or higher (Campbell, 2005).

Gilliam Autism Rating Scale (GARS; Gilliam, 1995)

This parent-report measure consists of 56 items from four domains: social interaction, communication, stereotyped behaviors, and developmental disturbances. It was normed and is intended for individuals ages 3 to 22. Each item is rated on a 4-point scale. A total score, or autism quotient (AQ) with a mean of 100 and a standard deviation of 15, is determined. AQs above 90 indicate probable autistic disorder.

Parents of 119 participants with clinical diagnoses of autistic disorder were given the GARS along with other measures (e.g., ADI-R, and ADOS-G) (South et al., 2002). The results indicated that the GARS underdiagnosed autistic disorder, displaying a sensitivity rate of only 0.48; specificity could not be determined based on the fact that only individuals with an autistic disorder diagnosis were included. These authors proposed a lowering of the threshold from 90 to 80 which would increase the sensitivity to 0.80 (South et al., 2002).

A factor analysis of the GARS revealed that only a low percentage of the variance was explained (i.e., 38 percent) (Lecavalier, 2005). Further, in line with studies mentioned previously, sensitivity was low. Alpha coefficients on three of the four scales were good, but on the final scale (developmental disturbance) it was unacceptable. Finally, Lecavalier (2005) noted that the number of items on the GARS that relate to restrictive and repetitive behaviors are overemphasized as compared to the other domains. Because the DSM-IV requires two social impairment symptoms and only one symptom from the other domains, this emphasis appears to be not in line with the current diagnostic standards.

Krug Asperger's Disorder Index (KADI; Krug and Arick, 2003)

This 32-item informant-based scale is organized in two sections: section one (consisting of 11 items) was developed to differentiate between individuals without impairment and those with Asperger's disorder. If scores on this section are sufficiently high, the rater then completes the second section (consisting of 21 items) which is designed to differentiate between Asperger's and high-functioning autistic disorder.

Although test–retest and interrater agreement were reportedly high ($r = 0.89$ and $r = 0.98$ respectively), the manner in which interrater agreement was measured allowed ratings of "low likelihood" and "high likelihood" (Krug and Arick, 2003). This percentage-based agreement (versus correlation-based agreement) may inflate interrater reliability (Campbell, 2005). The authors did not have independent confirmation of the subjects' diagnoses in the sample, a problem that has been noted in other measures as well (Campbell, 2005). Although the authors refer to the scale as a screening instrument, the presentation of this measure as an aid for differentially diagnosing Asperger's from autistic disorder implies that it can be used to diagnose these disorders (Nellis n.d.).

Modified Checklist for Autism in Toddlers (M-CHAT; Robins et al., 2001)

As its name implies, the M-CHAT is a modification of the CHAT (see above) by Baron-Cohen and colleagues (1992). It is a 23-item parent report that is designed for 24-month-olds and it was developed initially by retaining the 9 parent-report items of the CHAT and substituting additional parent-report items for the health-provider observation items (or, section "b" of the original CHAT).

Internal reliability was reportedly adequate (specifically, Cronbach's alpha = 0.85 for the entire checklist and 0.83 for the critical items). The authors reported that the M-CHAT had slightly better predictive validity than the CHAT based on their study of 1293 children that included follow-up data on 58 who qualified for a more extensive evaluation (Robins et al., 2001).

Pervasive Developmental Disorder Behavior Inventory (PDDBI; Cohen et al., 2003)

The PDDBI is a parent and teacher report developed to assess children 1 to 17 years of age for the presence of ASDs, namely autistic disorder, Asperger's disorder, PDD-NOS, and childhood disintegrative disorder. A unique feature of this scale is that it was designed to assess adaptive as well as maladaptive behaviors, which allows it to be used for progress monitoring in treatment. Separate versions exist for parents and teachers. This scale also provides age-based standard scores that reflect developmental changes. Cumulatively, between the parent and teacher versions there are six maladaptive subscales: aggressiveness/behavior problems, arousal problems, semantic/pragmatic problems, sensory/perceptual approach behaviors, social pragmatic problems, and specific fears. The adaptive subscales include the following: learning, memory, and receptive language, phonological skills, semantic/pragmatic ability, and social approach behaviors.

The authors of this inventory (Cohen et al., 2003) found only weak evidence that the PDDBI accurately discriminates between individuals with autistic disorder and those with PDD-NOS; however, it was able to discriminate between individuals with autistic disorder and those with language impairment. The PDDBI has good internal consistency in both parent and teacher versions and good interrater reliability; however, agreement tended to be lower when comparing teacher–parent agreement versus teacher–teacher agreement. Also, the PDDBI significantly correlated the ADI-R and the CARS, indicating evidence of criterion-related validity (Cohen et al., 2003).

Rett Syndrome Behavior Questionnaire (RSBQ; Mount et al., 2002)

This informant-based measure consists of 100 items that cover symptoms and features associated with Rett syndrome. Each item is rated on a 3-point scale (not true, somewhat true, or very true). Topics include self-injury, hand movements, hand skills, repetitive movements, breathing difficulties, and sleeping problems.

The authors provide the following psychometric properties (Mount et al., 2002). The questionnaire was able to differentiate between a group of individuals with Rett's ($n = 143$) from a comparison group of individuals with severe intellectual disabilities ($n = 85$). Internal consistency for the total score was 0.90, and for the subscales ranged from moderate to high ($0.60 - >0.90$) except for the walking/standing factor which was 0.45, which is comprised of two items. Using a cutoff score of 30, the scale had a sensitivity level of 86.3 percent and a specificity level of 86.8 percent. Test–retest reliability ranged from moderate to high ($0.60 - >0.80$). However, independent testing is needed to further evaluate the convergent and discriminant validity of this measure.

CONCLUSIONS

Shifts in terminology, increases in the prevalence estimates of ASD, early identification, and interest in the assessment of adults with ASD have been key characteristics in recent decades of research. The current debate regarding diagnostic distinctions within the spectrum, particularly between autism and Asperger's disorder, has drawn several suggestions, including that Asperger's be renamed high-functioning autistic disorder, that it be more developmentally based, and that it be dropped altogether from the DSM. The categorical distinction between autism and Asperger's remains problematic. Comorbidity is receiving more attention despite DSM claims that ASD can not be comorbid with certain disorders (e.g., ADHD).

More research has focused on identifying comorbid disorders for individuals with ASD, yet clearly still more is needed. Diagnosing comorbid disorders or deciding between differential diagnoses presents significant challenges to clinicians when discrepancies exist.

Numerous assessment measures exist for ASD, including interviews, observation systems, and rating scales (both clinician- and informant-based). Good assessment techniques start with broad-based measures and use multiple informants and multiple methods whenever possible.

The practical matters of length of administration time (ranging from 5 minutes to 4 hours) and whether extensive training is required will have an impact on which measures clinicians will adopt. Ideally, one would be able to use measures that are thorough, brief, and psychometrically sound to aid in the diagnosis of ASDs. Several rating scales show promise, but currently lack a foundation of psychometric data. The clinician, therefore, must weigh the pros and cons of what is currently known about a particular measure, the presenting problem they are attempting to address, and what is practical.

REFERENCES

Abikoff, H., Gittelman, R., and Klein, D.F. (1980). Classroom observation code for hyperactive children: A replication of validity. *Journal of Consulting and Clinical Psychology*, **48**, 555–565.

Achenbach, T.M. (1986). *Child Behavior Checklist-Direct Observation Form*. Burlington, BT: University of Vermont.

Achenbach, T.M. (1991a). *Manual for the Child Behavior Checklist and 1991 Profile*. Burlington: University of Vermont, Department of Psychiatry.

Achenbach, T.M. (1991b). *Manual for the Teachers Report Form and 1991 Profile*. Burlington: University of Vermont, Department of Psychiatry.

Akshoomoff, N. (2006). Autism Spectrum Disorders: Introduction. *Child Neuropsychology*, **12**, 245–246.

Ambrosini, P.J. (2000). Historical development and present status of the Schedule for Affective Disorders and Schizophrenia for School-Age Children (K-SADS). *Journal of the American Academy of Child and Adolescent Psychiatry*, **39**, 49–58.

American Psychiatric Association. (2000). *Diagnostic and Statistical Manual of Mental Disorders (4th ed. – Text revision)*. Washington DC: Author.

Amir, R.E., Van den Veyver, I.B., Wan, M. et al. (1999). Rett syndrome is caused by mutations in X-linked MECP2, encoding methyl-CpG-binding protein 2. *Nature Genetics*, **23**, 185–188.

Anderson, G.M. and Hoshino, Y. (2005). Neurochemical studies of autism. In *Handbook of Autism and Pervasive Developmental Disorders, Vol. 1: Diagnosis, Development, Neurobiology, and Behavior* (F.R. Volkmar, R. Paul, A. Klin, and D. Cohen, eds.) 3rd ed. pp. 453–472. Hoboken, NJ: John Wiley & Sons, Inc.

Ando, H. and Yoshimura, I. (1979). Comprehension skill levels and prevalence of maladaptive behaviors in autistic and mentally retarded children. *Child Psychiatry and Human Development*, **9**, 131–136.

Archer, L.A., Rosenbaum, P.L., and Streiner, D.L. (1991). The Children's Eating Behavior Inventory: Reliability and validity. *Journal of Pediatric Psychology*, **16**, 629–642.

Ashwin, C., Baron-Cohen, S., Wheelwright, S., O'Riordan, M., and Bullmore, E.T. (2007). Differential activation of the amygdala and the 'social brain' during fearful face-processing in Asperger Syndrome. *Neuropsychologia*, **45**, 2–14.

Attwood, T. (2006, October). Encouraging social understanding and emotion management. In *Autism and Asperger's Syndrome*. Presentation conducted at the meeting of Future Horizons, Port Allen, Louisiana.

Aylward, E.H., Minshew, N.J., Field, K. et al. (2002). Effects of age on brain volume and head circumference in autism. *Neurology*, **59**, 175–183.

Bailey, A., Palferman, S., Heavey, L., and Le Couteur, A. (1998). Autism: The phenotype in relatives. *Journal of Autism and Developmental Disorders*, **28**, 369–392.

Bailey, A., Le Couteur, A., Gottesman, I., and Bolton, P. (1995). Autism as a strongly genetic disorder: Evidence from a British twin study. *Psychological Medicine*, **25**, 63–77.

Baird, G., Simonoff, E., Pickles, A., Chandler, S., Loucas, T., Meldrum, D., et al. (2006). Prevalence of disorders of the autism spectrum in a population cohort of children in South Thames: The Special Needs and Autism Project (SNAP). *Lancet*, **368**, 210–215.

Baker, P., Piven, J., and Sato, Y. (1998). Autism and tuberous sclerosis complex: Prevalence and clinical features. *Journal of Autism and Developmental Disorders*, **28**, 279–285.

Ballaban-Gil, K., Rapin, I., Tuchman, R., and Shinnar, S. (1996). Longitudinal examination of the behavioral, language, and social changes in a population of adolescents and young adults with autistic disorder. *Pediatric Neurology*, **15**, 217–223.

Barnhill, J., and Horrigan, J.P. (2002). Tourette's syndrome and autism: A search for common ground. *Mental Health Aspects of Developmental Disabilities*, **5**, 7–15.

Baron-Cohen, S., Mortimore, C., Moriarty, J., et al. (1999). The prevalence of Gilles de la Tourette's syndrome in children and adolescents with autism. *Journal of Child Psychology and Psychiatry*, **40**, 213–218.

Baron-Cohen, S., Allen, J., and Gillberg, C. (1992). Can autism be detected at 18 months? The needle, the haystack, and the CHAT. *British Journal of Psychiatry*, **161**, 839–843.

Baron-Cohen, S., Wheelwright, S., Cox, A., et al. (2000). The early identification of autism: The Checklist for Autism in Toddlers (CHAT). *Journal of the Royal Society of Medicine*, **93**, 521–525.

Barrett, S., Prior, M., and Manjiviona, J. (2004). Children on the borderlands of autism. *Autism*, **8**, 61–87.

Bejerot, S., Nylander, L., and Lindstrom, E. (2001). Autistic traits in obsessive-compulsive disorder. *Nordic Journal of Psychiatry*, **55**, 169–176.

Bernier, R., Dawson, G., Panagiotides, H., and Webb, S. (2005). Individuals with autism spectrum disorder show normal responses to a fear potential startle paradigm. *Journal of Autism and Developmental Disorders*, **35**, 575–583.

Beyer, K.S., Blasi, F., Bacchelli, E., Klauck, S.M., Maestrini, E., and Poustka, A. (2002). Mutation analysis of the coding sequence of the MECP2 gene in infantile autism. *Human Genetics*, **111**, 305–9.

Bishop, D.V.M. and Norbury, C.F. (2002). Exploring the borderlands of autistic disorder and specific language impairment: A study using standardized diagnostic instruments. *Journal of Child Psychology and Psychiatry*, **43**, 917–929.

Black, C., Kaye, J.A., and Jick, H. (2002). Relation of childhood gastrointestinal disorders to autism: Nested case control study using data from the UK general practice research database. *British Medical Journal*, **325**, 419–421.

Bolton, P.F., Pickles, A., Murphy, M., and Rutter, M. (1998). Autism, affective and other psychiatric disorders: Patterns of familial aggregation. *Psychological Medicine*, **28**, 385–395.

Bolton, P.F., Murphy, M., and MacDonald, H. (1997). Obstetric complications in autism: Consequences or causes of the condition. *Journal of the American Academy of Child & Adolescent Psychiatry*, **36**, 272–281.

Brown, T.E. (1996). *Brown Attention-Deficit Disorder Scales*. San Antonio, TX: Psychological Corporation Harcourt Brace Jovanovich.

Brown, L., Sherbenou, R.J., and Johnson, S.K. (1997). *Test of Non-Verbal Intelligence-3rd Edition*. Austin, TX: Pro-Ed.

Bryson, S.E. and Smith, I.M. (1998). Epidemiology of autism: Prevalence, associated characteristics, and implications for research and service delivery. *Mental Retardation and Developmental Disabilities Research Reviews*, **4**, 97–103.

Burger, R.A. and Warren, R.P. (1998). Possible immunogenetic basis for autism. *Mental Retardation and Developmental Disabilities Research Reviews*, **4**, 137–141.

Burklow, K.A., Phelps, A.N., Schultz, J.R., McConnell, K., and Rudolph, C. (1998). Classifying complex pediatric feeding disorders. *Journal of Pediatric Gastroenterology and Nutrition*, **27**, 143–147.

Bzoch, K.R., League, R., and Brown, V.L. (2003). *Receptive-Expressive Emergent Language Test, 3rd Edition (REEL-3)*. Austin, TX: Pro-Ed.

Calhoun, S.L. and Mayes, S.D., (1999). Symptoms of autism in young children and correspondence with the DSM. *Infants and Young Children*, **12**, 90–97.

Campbell, J.M. (2005). Diagnostic assessment of Asperger's disorder: A review of five third-party rating scales. *Journal of Autism and Developmental Disorders*, **35**, 25–35.

Canitano, R. and Vivanti, G. (2007). Tics and Tourette syndrome in autism spectrum disorders. *Autism*, **11**, 19–28.

Carskadon, M.A., Dement, W.C., Mitler, M.M., Roth, T., Westbrook, P., and Keenan, S. (1986). Guidelines for the multiple sleep latency test (MSLT): A standard measure of sleepiness. *Sleep*, **9**, 519–524.

Centers for Disease Control and Prevention. (2007a). Prevalence of autism spectrum disorders and developmental disabilities monitoring 14 sites, United States, 2002. *Morbidity and Mortality Weekly Report*, **56**, 12–28.

Centers for Disease Control and Prevention. (2007b). Prevalence of autism spectrum disorders: autism and developmental disabilities monitoring network, six sites, United States, 2000. *Morbidity and Mortality Weekly Report*, **56**, 1–11.

Chakrabarti, S. and Fombonne, E. (2001). Pervasive developmental disorders in preschool children. *Journal of the American Medical Association*, **285**, 3093–3099.

Chorpita, B.F., Yim, L., Moffitt, C., Umemoto, L.A., and Francis, S.E. (2000). Assessment of symptoms of DSM-IV anxiety and depression in children: A revised child anxiety and depression scale. *Behaviour Research and Therapy*, **38**, 835–855.

Chung, S.Y., Luk, S.L., and Lee, P.W. (1990). A follow-up study of infantile autism in Hong Kong. *Journal of Autism and Developmental Disorders*, **20**, 221–232.

Cohen, I.L., Schmidt-Lackner, S., Romanczyk, R. and Sudhalter, V. (2003). The PDD Behavior Inventory: A rating scale for assessing response to intervention in children with pervasive developmental disorder. *Journal of Autism and Developmental Disorders*, **33**, 31–45.

Conners, C.K. (1997). *Conners Rating Scales-Revised*. North Tonawanda, NY: Multi-Health Systems.

Cook, E.H., Charak, D.A., Arida, J., and Spohn, J.A. (1994). Depressive and obsessive-compulsive symptoms in hyperserotonemic parents of children with autistic disorder. *Psychiatry Research*, **52**, 25–33.

Courchesne, E., Karns, C.M., and Davis, H.R. (2001). Unusual brain growth patterns in early life in patients with autistic disorder: An MRI study. *Neurology*, **57**, 245–254.

Coutinho, A.M., Oliveira, G., Morgadinho, T., et al. (2004). Variants of the serotonin transporter gene (SLC6A4) significantly contribute to hyperserotonemia in autism. *Molecular Psychiatry*, **9**, 264–271.

Cryan, E., Byrne, M., O'Donovan, A., and O'Callaghan, E. (1996). Brief report: A case-control study of obstetric complications and later autistic disorder. *Journal of Autism and Developmental Disorders*, **26**, 453–460.

Dales, L., Hammer, S.J., and Smith, N.J. (2001). Time trends in autism and in MMR immunization coverage in California. *Journal of the American Medical Association*, **285**, 1183–1185.

Dawson, G., Munson, J., Webb, S.J., et al. (2007). Rate of head growth decelerates and symptoms worsen in the second year of life in autism. *Biological Psychiatry*, **61**, 458–464.

Deb, S., Prasad, K.B.G., Seth, H., and Eagles, J.M. (1997). A comparison of obstetric and neonatal complications between children with autistic disorder and their siblings. *Journal of Intellectual Disability Research*, **41**, 81–86.

DeStefano, F. and Chen, R.T. (2001). Autism and measles-mumps-rubella vaccination: Controversy laid to rest? *CNS Drugs*, **15**, 831–837.

D'Eufemia, P., Celli, M., Finocchiaro, R. et al. (1996). Abnormal intestinal permeability in children with autism. *Acta Paediatrica*, **85**, 1076–1079.

DiLalla, D.L. and Rogers, S.J. (1994). Domains of the childhood autism rating scale: relevance for diagnosis and treatment. *Journal of Autism and Developmental Disorders*, **24**, 115–128.

DiLavore, P.C., Lord, C., and Rutter, M. (1995). Pre-linguistic autism diagnostic observation schedule. *Journal of Autism and Developmental Disorders*, **25**, 355–379.

Di Nardo, P.A., Brown, T.A., and Barlow, D.H. (1994). *Anxiety Disorders Interview Schedule for DSM-IV: Lifetime Version (ADIS-IV-L)*. San Antonio, TX: Psychological Corporation.

Dunn, L. and Dunn, L. (2007). *Peabody Picture Vocabulary Test-IV (PPVT-IV)*. Circle Pines, MN: American Guidance Service, Inc.

Durand, V.M. (2002). Treating sleep terrors in children with autism. *Journal of Positive Behavior Interventions*, **4**, 66–72.

Eapen, V., Pauls, D.L., and Robertson, M.M. (1993). Evidence for autosomal dominant transmission in Tourette's syndrome: United Kingdom cohort study. *British Journal of Psychiatry*, **162**, 593–596.

Edelson, M.G. (2006). Are the majority of children with autism mentally retarded? A systematic evaluation of the data. *Focus on Autism and Other Developmental Disabilities*, **21**, 66–83.

Ehlers, S., Gillberg, C., and Wing, L. (1999). A screening questionnaire for Asperger syndrome and other high-functioning autism spectrum disorders in school age children. *Journal of Autism and Developmental Disorders*, **29**, 129–141.

England, C.T. (n.d.) [Review of the Gilliam Asperger's Disorder Scale]. In *The Sixteenth Mental Measurements Yearbook*. Retrieved February 15, 2007, from EBSCOHost Mental Measurements Yearbook database.

Engstrom, H.A., Ohlson, S., Stubbs, E.G. et al. (2003). Decreased expression of CD95 (Fas/APO-1) on CD4 + T-lymphocytes from participants with autism. *Journal of Developmental and Physical Disabilities*, **15**, 155–163.

Evans, D.W., Canavera, K., Kleinpeter, F.L., Maccubbin, E., and Taga, K. (2005). The fears, phobias and anxieties of children with autism spectrum disorders and Down syndrome: Comparisons with developmentally and chronologically age matched children. *Child Psychiatry and Human Development*, **36**, 3–26.

Fidler, D.J., Bailey, J.N., and Smalley, S.L. (2000). Macrocephaly in autism and other pervasive developmental disorders. *Developmental Medicine and Child Neurology*, **42**, 737–740.

First, M.B., Spitzer, R.L., Gibbon, M., and Williams, J.B.W. (1997). *Structured Clinical Interview for DSM-IV Axis I Disorders – Clinician Version (SCID-CV)*. Washington DC: American Psychiatric Press.

Fombonne, E. (1999). The epidemiology of autism: A review. *Psychological Medicine*, **29**, 769–786.

Frankel, M. (1986). Obsessions and compulsions in Gilles de la Tourette's syndrome. *Neurology*, **36**, 378–382.

Frankhauser, M.P., Karumanchi, V.C., German, M.L., Yates, A., and Karumanchi, S.D. (1992). A double-blind, placebo-controlled study of the efficacy of transdermal clonidine in autism. *Journal of Clinical Psychiatry*, **53**, 77–82.

Freeman, B.J., Ritvo, E.R., Schroth, P.C., Tonick, I., Guthrie, D., and Wake, L. (1981). Behavioral characteristics of high- and low-IQ autistic children. *American Journal of Psychiatry*, **138**, 25–29.

Furlano, R.I., Anthony, A., Day, R., et al. (2001). Colonic CD8 and gamma delta T-cell infiltration with epithelial damage in children with autism. *Journal of Pediatrics*, **138**, 366–372.

Gadow, K.D. and DeVincent, C.J. (2005). Clinical significance of tics and attention-deficit hyperactivity disorder (ADHD) in children with pervasive developmental disorder. *Journal of Child Neurology*, **20**, 481–488.

Gadow, K.D., DeVincent, C.J., Pomeroy, J., and Azizian, A. (2004). Psychiatric symptoms in preschool children with PDD and clinic and comparison samples. *Journal of Autism and Developmental Disorders*, **34**, 379–393.

Garfin, D.G., McCallon, D., and Cox, R. (1988). Validity and reliability of the childhood autism rating scale with autistic adolescents. *Journal of Autism and Developmental Disorders*, **18**, 367–378.

Geer, J.H. (1965). The development of a scale to measure fear. *Behavior Research and Therapy*, **3**, 45–53.

Ghaziuddin, M., Weidmer-Mikhail, E., and Ghaziuddin, N., (1998). Comorbidity of Asperger syndrome: A preliminary report. *Journal of Intellectual Disability Research*, **42**, 279–283.

Gillberg, C. and Billstedt, E. (2000). Autism and Asperger syndrome: Coexistence with other clinical disorders. *Acta Psychiatrica Scandinavica*, **102**, 321–330.

Gilliam, J.E. (1995). *Gilliam Autism Rating Scale*. Austin, TX: Pro-Ed.

Gilliam, J.E. (2003). *Gilliam Asperger's Disorder Scale*. Austin, TX: Pro-Ed.

Gillham, J.E., Carter, A.S., Volkmar, F.R., and Sparrow, S.S. (2000). Toward a developmental operational definition of autism. *Journal of Autism and Developmental Disorders*, **30**, 269–278.

Goin-Kochel, R.P., and Myers, B.J. (2005). Congenital versus regressive onset of autism spectrum disorders: parents' beliefs about causes. *Focus on Autism and Other Developmental Disabilities*, **20**, 169–179.

Goldstein, S. (2002). Review of the Asperger Syndrome diagnostic scale. *Journal of Autism and Developmental Disorders*, **32**, 611–614.

Goldstein, S. and Schwebach, A.J. (2004). The comorbidity of pervasive developmental disorder and attention deficit hyperactivity disorder: Results of a retrospective chart review. *Journal of Autism and Developmental Disorders*, **34**, 329–339.

Goodman, W.K., Price, L.H., Rasmussen, S.A., et al., (1989a). The Yale-Brown obsessive compulsive scale: I. Development, use, and reliability. *Archives of General Psychiatry*, **46**, 1006–1011.

Goodman, W.K., Price, L.H., Rasmussen, S.A., et al., (1989b). The Yale-Brown obsessive compulsive scale (Y-BOCS): II. Validity. *Archives of General Psychiatry*, **46**, 1012–1016.

Green, J., Gilchrist, A., Burton, D., and Cox, A. (2000). Social and psychiatric functioning in adolescents with Asperger syndrome compared with conduct disorder. *Journal of Autism and Developmental Disorders*, **30**, 279–293.

Gupta, V.B. (2004). *Autistic Spectrum Disorders in Children: Pediatric Habilitation*. V. 12. New York: Marcel Dekker, Inc.

Haas, R.H., Townsend, J. Courchesne, E., and Lincoln, A.J. (1996). Neurologic abnormalities in infantile autism. *Journal of Child Neurology*, **11**, 84–92.

Hammill, D.D., Brown, V.A., Larsen, S.C., and Wiederholt, J.L. (2006). *Test of Adolescent and Adult Language-Intermediate, 4th ed.* Austin: PRO-ED.

Harden, A.Y., Minshew, N.J., and Keshavan, M.S. (2000). Corpus callosum size in autism. *Neurology*, **55**, 1033–1036.

Hastings, R.P., Beck, A., Daley, D. and Hill, C. (2005). Symptoms of ADHD and their correlates in children with intellectual disabilities. *Research in Developmental Disabilities*, **26**, 456–468.

Herbert, J.D., Sharp, I.R., and Gaudiano, B.A. (2002). Separating fact from fiction in the etiology and treatment of autism: A scientific review of the evidence. *The Scientific Review of Mental Health Practice*, **1**, 23–43.

Hoffbuhr, K., Devaney, J.M., LeFleur, B., et al. (2001). MeCP2 mutations in children with and without the phenotype of Rett syndrome. *Neurology*, **56**, 1486–1495.

Hollander, E., King, A., Delaney, K., et al. (2003). Obsessive-compulsive behaviors in parents of multiplex autism families. *Psychiatry Research*, **117**, 11–16.

Honda, H., Shimizu, Y., Rutter, M. (2005). No effect of MMR withdrawal on the incidence of autism: a total population study. *Journal of Child Psychology and Psychiatry*, **46**, 572–579.

Howlin, P. (2003). Outcome in high-functioning adults with autism with and without early language delays: Implications for the differentiation between autism and Asperger syndrome. *Journal of Autism and Developmental Disorders*, **33**, 3–13.

Hultman, C.M., Sparén, P., and Cnattingius, S. (2002). Perinatal risk factors for infantile autism. *Epidemiology*, **13**, 417–23.

Kemper, T.L. and Bauman, M. (1998). Neuropathology of infantile autism. *Journal of Neuropathology and Experimental Neurology*, **57**, 645–52.

Klin, A., McPartland, J., and Volkmar, F.R. (2005). Asperger Syndrome. In *Handbook of Autism and Pervasive Developmental Disorders, Vol. 1: Diagnosis, Development, Neurobiology, and Behavior*. 3rd ed. (F.R. Volkmar, R. Paul, A. Klin, and D. Cohen, eds.) pp. 88–125. Hoboken, NJ: John Wiley & Sons, Inc.

Klinger, L.G., Dawson, G., and Renner, P. (2003). Autistic disorder. In *Child psychopathology*. 2nd ed. (E.J. Mash and R.A. Barkley, eds.) pp. 409–454. New York: Guilford Press.

Krug, D.A., Arick, J., and Almond, P. (1980). Behavior checklist for identifying severely handicapped individuals with high levels of autistic behavior. *Journal of Child Psychology and Psychiatry*, **21**, 221–229.

Krug, D. and Arick, J. (2003). *Krug Asperger Disorder Index*. Austin, Texas: Pro-Ed.

Lainhart, J.E. (1999). Psychiatric problems in individuals with autism, their parents and siblings. *International Review of Psychiatry*, **11**, 278–298.

Leboyer, M., Philippe, A., Bouvard, M., et al. (1999). Whole blood serotonin and plasma beta-endorphin in autistic probands and their first-degree relatives. *Biological Psychiatry*, **45**, 158–163.

Lecavalier, L. (2005). An evaluation of the Gilliam autism rating scale. *Journal of Autism and Developmental Disorders*, **35**, 795–805.

Leckman, J.F., Riddle, M.A., Hardin, M.T., et al. (1989). The Yale global tic severity scale: Initial testing of a clinician-rated scale of tic severity. *Journal of the American Academy of Child and Adolescent Psychiatry*, **28**, 566–573.

Le Couteur, A., Rutter, M., Lord, C., and Rios, P. (1989). Autism diagnostic interview: A standardized investigator-based instrument. *Journal of Autism and Developmental Disorders*, **19**, 363–387.

Ledford, J.R. and Gast, D.L. (2006). Feeding problems in children with autism spectrum disorders: A review. *Focus on Autism and Other Developmental Disabilities*, **21**, 153–166.

Leekam, S.R., Libby, S.J., Wing, L., et al. (2002). The diagnostic interview for social and communication disorders: Algorithms for icd-10 childhood autism and Wing and Gould autistic spectrum disorder. *Journal of Child Psychology and Psychiatry*, **43**, 327–342.

Leyfer, O.T., Folstein, S.E., Bacalman, S., et al. (2006). Comorbid psychiatric disorders in children with autism: Interview development and rates of disorders. *Journal of Autism and Developmental Disorders*, **36**, 849–861.

Lord, C., Risi, S., Lambrecht, L., et al. (2000). The autism diagnostic observation schedule – Generic: A standard measure of social and communication deficits associated with the spectrum of autism. *Journal of Autism and Developmental Disorders*, **30**, 205–223.

Lord, C., Rutter, M., Goode, S., et al. (1989). Autism diagnostic observation schedule: A standardized observation of communicative and social behavior. *Journal of Autism and Developmental Disorders*, **19**, 185–212.

Lord, C., Rutter, M., and Le Couteur, A., (1994). Autism diagnostic interview – Revised: A revised version of a diagnostic interview for caregivers of individuals with possible pervasive developmental disorders. *Journal of Autism and Developmental Disorders*, **24**, 659–685.

Malow, B.A. (2004). Sleep disorders, epilepsy, and autism. *Mental Retardation and Developmental Disabilities Research Reviews*, **10**, 122–125.

Matson, J.L., Boisjoli, J.A., Gonzalez, M.L., et al. (2007). Norms and cut off scores for the autism spectrum disorders diagnosis for adults (ASD-DA) with intellectual disability, *Research in Autism Spectrum Disorders*, doi:10.1016/j.rasd.2007.01.001.

Matson, J.L. and Kuhn, D.E. (2001). Identifying feeding problems in mentally retarded persons: Development and reliability of the screening tool of feeding problems (STEP). *Research in Developmental Disabilities*, **22**, 165–172.

Matson. J.L. and Love, S.R. (1990). A comparison of parent-reported fear for autistic and nonhandicapped age-matched children and youth. *Australia and New Zealand Journal of Developmental Disabilities*, **16**, 349–357.

Matson, J.L., Nebel-Schwalm, M.S., and Matson, J.L. (2006). A review of methodological issues in the differential diagnosis of autism spectrum disorders in children: Diagnostic systems and scaling methods. *Research in Autism Spectrum Disorders*, doi:10.1016/j.rasd.2006.07.004.

Matson, J.L., Terlonge, C., and Gonzalez, M.L. (2007). *Autism spectrum disorders-diagnostic child*. Baton Rouge, LA: Disability Consultants, LLC.

Matson, J.L., Wilkins, J., Boisjoli, J.A., and Smith, K.R. (in press). The convergent and divergent validity of the autism spectrum disorders-diagnosis scale for intellectually disabled adults (ASD-DA). *Research in Autism Spectrum Disorders*.

Matson, J.L., Wilkins, J., and Gonzalez, M.L. (2007). Reliability and factor structure of the autism spectrum disorders-diagnosis scale for intellectually disabled adults (ASD-DA). *Research in Autism Spectrum Disorders. Journal of Developmental and Physical Disabilities*, **19**, 565–577.

Mayes, S.D., and Calhoun, S.L. (2004). Influence of IQ and age in childhood autism: Lack of support for DSM-IV Asperger's disorder. *Journal of Autism and Physical Disabilities*, **16**, 257–272.

McGough, J.J. and Barkley, R.A. (2004). Diagnostic controversies in adult attention deficit hyperactivity disorder. *American Journal of Psychiatry*, **161**, 1948–1956.

Mesibov, G.B., Schopler, E., Schaffer, B., and Michal, N. (1989). Use of the childhood autism rating Scale with autistic adolescents and adults. *Journal of the American Academy of Child and Adolescent Psychiatry*, **28**, 538–541.

Meyer, J.A., and Minshew, N.J. (2002). An update on neurocognitive profiles in Asperger syndrome and high-functioning autism. *Focus on Autism and Other Developmental Disabilities*, **17**, 152–160.

Miladi, N., Larnaout, A., Kaabachi, N., Helayem, M., and Ben Hamida, M. (1992). Phenylketonuria: An underlying etiology of autistic syndrome: A case report. *Journal of Child Neurology*, **7**, 22–23.

Mildenberger, K., Sitter, S., Norterdaeme, M., and Amorosa, H. (2001). The use of the ADI-R as a diagnostic tool in the differential diagnosis of children with infantile autism and children with a receptive language disorder. *European Child and Adolescent Psychiatry*, **10**, 248–255.

Miller, J.N. and Ozonoff, S. (1997). Did Asperger's cases have Asperger disorder? A research note. *Journal of Child Psychology and Psychiatry, and Allied Disciplines*, **38**, 247–251.

Minderaa, R.B., Anderson, G.M., Volkmar, F.R., and Akkerhuis, G.W. (1989). Neurochemical study of dopamine functioning in autistic and normal subjects. *Journal of the American Academy of Child and Adolescent Psychiatry*, **28**, 190–194.

Miranda-Linne, F.M., and Melin, L. (2002). A factor analytic study of the autism behavior checklist. *Journal of Autism and Developmental Disorders*, **32**, 181–188.

Mirenda, P. (n.d.). [Review of the Asperger Syndrome Diagnostic Scale]. In *The Fifteenth Mental Measurements Yearbook*. Retrieved February 15, 2007, from EBSCOHost Mental Measurements Yearbook database.

Mount, R.H., Charman, T., Hastings, R.P., et al. (2002). The Rett Syndrome Behaviour Questionnaire (RSBQ): refining the behavioural phenotype of Rett syndrome. *Journal of Child Psychology and Psychiatry*, **43**, 1099–1110.

Myles, B., Bock, S., and Simpson, R. (2001). *Asperger Syndrome Diagnostic Scale*. Austin, Texas: Pro-Ed.

Nellis, L.M. (n.d.) [Review of the Krug Asperger's Disorder Index]. In *The Sixteenth Mental Measurements Yearbook*. Retrieved February 15, 2007, from EBSCOHost Mental Measurements Yearbook database.

Nicolson, R. and Szatmari, P. (2003). Genetic and neurodevelopmental influences in autistic disorder. *Canadian Journal of Psychiatry*, **48**, 526–537.

Ollendick, T.H. (1983). Reliability and validity of the Revised Fear Survey Schedule for Children (FSSC-R). *Behaviour Research and Therapy*, **21**, 685–692.

Owens, J.A., Spirito, A., and McGuinn, M. (2000). Sleep habits and sleep disturbance in elementary school-aged children. *Journal of Developmental and Behavioral Pediatrics*, **21**, 27–36.

Patel, M.R., Piazza, C.C., and Kelly, M.L. (2001). Using a fading procedure to increase fluid consumption in a child with feeding problems. *Journal of Applied Behavior Analysis*, **34**, 357–360.

Piven, J., Harper, J., Palmer, P., and Arndt, S. (1996). Course of behavioral change in autism: A retrospective study of high-IQ adolescents and adults. *Journal of the American Academy of Child and Adolescent Psychiatry*, **35**, 523–529.

Piven, J., Simon, J., Chase, G.A., et al. (1993). The etiology of autism: pre-, peri-, and neonatal factors. *Journal of the American Academy of Child and Adolescent Psychiatry*, **32**, 1256–1263.

Pickles, A., Bolton, P., MacDonald, H., et al. (1995). Latent class analysis of recurrence risk for complex phenotypes with selection and measurement error: A twin and family history study of autism. *American Journal of Human Genetics*, **57**, 717–726.

Polimeni, M.A., Richdale, A.L., and Francis, A.J.P. (2005). A survey of sleep problems in autism, Asperger's disorder and typically developing children. *Journal of Intellectual Disability Research*, **49**, 260–268.

Rasmussen, P., Borjesson, O., Wentz, E., and Gillberg, C. (2001). Autistic disorders in Down syndrome: Background factors and clinical correlates. *Developmental Medicine and Child Neurology*, **43**, 750–754.

Reichelt, K.L., Knivsberg, A., Lind, G., and Nodland, M. (1991). Probable etiology and possible treatment of childhood autism. *Brain Dysfunction*, **4**, 308–319.

Rellini, E., Tortolani, D., Trillo, S., Carbone, S. et al. (2004). Childhood autism rating scale (CARS) and autism behavior checklist (ABC) correspondence and conflicts with DSM-IV criteria in diagnosis of autism. *Journal of Autism and Developmental Disorders*, **34**, 703–708.

Research Units on Pediatric Psychopharmacology Anxiety Study Group. (2002). The Pediatric Anxiety Rating Scale (PARS): Development and psychometric properties. *Journal of the American Academy of Child and Adolescent Psychiatry*, **41**, 1061–1069.

Reynolds, C.R. and Kamphaus, R.W. (2004). *Behavior Assessment System for Children: Second Edition*. Circle Pines, MN: AGS Publishing.

Ringman, J.M. Jankovic, J. (2000). Occurrence of tics in Asperger's syndrome and autistic disorder. *Journal of Child Neurology*, **15**, 394–400.

Ritvo, E.R. and Ritvo, R.A. (2006). Are the majority of children with autism mentally retarded? *Focus on Autism and Other Developmental Disabilities*, **21**, 84–85.

Robins, D.L., Fein, D., Barton, M., and Green, J.A. (2001). The modified checklist for autism in toddlers: An initial study investigating the early detection of autism and pervasive developmental disorders. *Journal of Autism and Developmental Disorders*, **31**, 131–151.

Rogers, S.J. (2004). Developmental regression in autism spectrum disorders. *Mental Retardation and Developmental Disabilities Research Reviews*, **10**, 139–143.

Roid, G.H. (2003). *Stanford-Binet Intelligence Scales, Fifth Edition*. Itasca, IL: Riverside Publishing.

Rutter, M. (2005). Aetiology of autism: Findings and questions. *Journal of Intellectual Disability Research*, **49**, 231–238.

Saloviita, T. (2002). Dry bed training method in the elimination of bed-wetting in two adults with autism and severe mental retardation. *Cognitive Behaviour Therapy*, **31**, 135–140.

Sanders, M., Patel, R., K., LeGrice, B., and Shepherd, R.W. (1993). Children with persistent feeding difficulties: An observational analysis of the feeding interactions of problem and non-problem eaters. *Health Psychology*, **12**, 64–73.

Sandman, C.A. (1991). The opiate hypothesis in autism and self-injury. *Journal of Child and Adolescent Psychopharmacology*, **1**, 237–248.

Sandman, C.A., Barron, J.L., Chicz-Demet, A., and Demet, E.M. (1990). Plasma b-endorphin levels in patients with self-injurious behavior and stereotypy. *American Journal on Mental Retardation*, **95**, 84–92.

Scahill, L., McDougle, C.J., Williams, S.K., Dimitropoulos, A., et al. (2006). Children's Yale-Brown obsessive compulsive scale modified for pervasive developmental disorders. *Journal of the American Academy of Child and Adolescent Psychiatry*, **45**, 1114–1123.

Scahill, L., Riddle, M.A., McSwiggin-Hardin, M., et al., (1997). Children's Yale-Brown obsessive compulsive scale: Reliability and validity. *Journal of the American Academy of Child and Adolescent Psychiatry*, **36**, 844–852.

Schopler, E., Reichler, R.J., DeVellis, R.F., and Daly, K. (1980). Toward objective classification of childhood autism: Childhood autism rating scale (CARS). *Journal of Autism and Developmental Disorders*, **10**, 91–103.

Schultz, R.T. and Robins, D.L. (2005). Functional neuroimaging studies of autism spectrum disorders. In *Handbook of Autism and Pervasive Developmental Disorders, Vol. 1: Diagnosis, Development, Neurobiology, and Behavior* 3rd ed. (F.R. Volkmar, R. Paul, A. Klin, and D. Cohen, eds.) pp. 515–533. Hoboken, NJ: John Wiley & Sons, Inc.

Sciutto, M.J. and Cantwell, C. (2005). Factors influencing the differential diagnosis of Asperger's disorder and high-functioning autism. *Journal of Developmental and Physical Disabilities*, **17**, 345–359.

Scott, F.J., Baron-Cohen, S., Bolton, P., and Brayne, C. (2002). The CAST (Childhood Asperger Syndrome Test): Preliminary development of a UK screen for mainstream primary-school-age children. *Autism*, **6**, 9–31.

Seltzer, M., Mailick, K., Marty, W., et al. (2003). The symptoms of autism spectrum disorders in adolescence and adulthood. *Journal of Autism and Developmental Disorders*, **33**, 565–581.

Semel, E.M., Wiig, E.H., and Secord, W.A. (2003). *Clinical Evaluation of Language Fundamentals – 4*. San Antonio, TX: Psych Corp/Harcourt.

Sevin, J.A., Matson, J.L., Coe, D.A., Fee, V.E., and Sevin. B.M. (1991). A comparison and evaluation of three commonly used autism scales. *Journal of Autism and Developmental Disorders*, **21**, 417–432.

Shaffer, D., Fisher, P., Lucas, C., Dulcan, M., et al. (2000). NIMH Diagnostic Interview Schedule for Children, Version IV (NIMH DISC-IV): Description, differences from previous versions, and reliability of some common diagnoses. *Journal of the American Academy of Child and Adolescent Psychiatry*, **39**, 28–38.

Shea, V. and Mesibov, G.B. (2005). Adolescents and adults with autism. In *Handbook of Autism and Pervasive Developmental Disorders, Vol. 1: Diagnosis, Development, Neurobiology, and Behavior*. 3rd ed. (F.R. Volkmar, R. Paul, A. Klin, and D. Cohen, eds.) pp. 288–311. Hoboken, NJ: John Wiley & Sons, Inc.

Silverman, W.K., and Albano, A.M. (1996). *The Anxiety Disorders Interview Schedule for Children for DSM-IV: Child and Parent Versions*. San Antonio, TX: Psychological Corporation.

Silverman, W.K. and Ollendick, T.H. (2005). Evidenced-based assessment of anxiety and its disorders in children and adolescents. *Journal of Clinical Child and Adolescent Psychology*, **34**, 380–411.

Singh, V.K., Singh, E.A., and Warren, R.P. (1997). Hyperserotoninemia and serotonin receptor antibodies in children with autism but not mental retardation. *Biological Psychiatry*, **41**, 753–755.

Smalley, S.L. (1998). Autism and tuberous sclerosis. *Journal of Autism and Developmental Disorders*, **28**, 407–414.

South, M., Williams, B.J., McMahon, W.M., et al., (2002). Utility of the Gilliam autism rating scale in research and clinical populations. *Journal of Autism and Developmental Disorders*, **32**, 593–599.

Sparrow, S.S., Cicchetti, D.V., and Balla, D.A. (2005). *Vineland Adaptive Behavior Scale, Second Edition*. Circle Pines, MN: American Guidance Service.

Spence, S.H. (1998). A measure of anxiety symptoms among children. *Behaviour Research and Therapy*, **36**, 545–566.

Steffenburg, S. (1991). Neuropsychiatric assessment of children with autism: A population-based study. *Developmental Medicine and Child Neurology*, **33**, 495–511.

Stone, W.L., Coonrod, E.E., and Ousley, O.Y. (2000). Screening Tool for Autism Two-Year-Olds (STAT): Development and preliminary data. *Journal of Autism and Developmental Disorders*, **30**, 607–612.

Stone, W.L., Coonrod, E.E., Turner, L.M., and Pozdol, S.L. (2004). Psychometric Properties of the STAT for Early Autism Screening. *Journal of Autism and Developmental Disorders*, **34**, 691–701.

Storch, E.A., Murphy, T.K., Geffken, G.R., et al. (2005). Reliability and validity of the Yale Global Tic Severity Scale. *Psychological Assessment*, **17**, 486–491.

Swedo, S.E., Leonard, H.L., Mittleman, B.B., et al. (1997). Identification of children with pediactric autoimmunie neuropsychiatric disorders associated with streptococcal infections by a marker associated with rheumatic fever. *American Journal of Psychiatry*, **154**, 110–112.

Szatmari, P., Archer, L., Fisman, S., and Streiner, D.L. (1994). Parent and teacher agreement in the assessment of pervasive developmental disorders. *Journal of Autism and Developmental Disorders*, **24**, 703–717.

Tadevosyan-Leyfer, O., Dowd, M., Mankoski, R., et al., (2003). A principal of components analysis of the Autism Diagnostic Interview-Revised. *Journal of the American Academy of Child and Adolescent Psychiatry*, **42**, 864–872.

Tani, Y., Fernell, E., Watanabe, Y., et al. (1994). Decrease in 6R-5,6,7,8-tetrahydrobiopterin content in cerebrospinal fluid of autistic patients. *Neuroscience Letters*, **181**, 169–172.

Tantam, D. (1991). Asperger syndrome in adulthood. In *Autism and Asperger Syndrome* (U. Frith, ed.) pp. 147–183. London: Cambridge University Press.

Thomsen, P.H. (1998). Obsessive-compulsive disorder in children and adolescents: Clinical guidelines. *European Child & Adolescent Psychiatry*, **7**, 1–11.

Tordjman, S., Anderson, G.M., McBride, P.A., et al. (1997). Plasma β-endorphin, adrenocorticotropin hormone, and cortisol in autism. *Journal of Child Psychology and Psychiatry*, **38**, 705–715.

Tryon, P.A., Mayes, S.D., Rhodes R.L., and Waldo, M. (2006). Can Asperger's disorder be differentiated from autism using DSM-IV criteria? *Focus on Autism and Other Developmental Disabilities*, **21**, 2–6.

Tsai, L.Y. (2005). Recent neurobiological research in autism. In *Autism Spectrum Disorders: Identification, Education, and Treatment*. 3rd ed. (D. Zager, ed.) pp. 47–87. Mahwah, NJ: Lawrence Erlbaum Associates Publishers.

Van Bourgondien, M.E., Marcus, L.M., and Schopler, E. (1992). Comparison of DSM-III–R and Childhood Autism Rating Scale diagnoses of autism. *Journal of Autism and Developmental Disorders*, **22**, 493–506.

Venter, A., Lord, C., and Schopler, E. (1992). A follow-up study of high-functioning autistic children. *Journal of Child Psychology and Psychiatry*, **33**, 489–507.

Verte, S., Geurts, H.M., Roeyers, H., et al. (2006). Executive functioning in children with an autism spectrum disorder: Can we differentiate within the spectrum? *Journal of Autism and Developmental Disorders*, **36**, 351–372.

Volkmar, F.R., Cicchetti, D.V., Dykens, E., et al. (1988). An evaluation of the autism behavior checklist. *Journal of Autism and Developmental Disorders*, **18**, 81–97.

Volkmar, F.R. and Klin, A. (2004). Issues in the classification of autism and related conditions. In *Handbook of Autism and Pervasive Developmental Disorders* (F.R. Volkmar, R. Paul, A. Klin, and D. Cohen, eds.) pp. 5–41. Hoboken, NJ: John Wiley & Sons, Inc.

Volkmar, F.R., Lord, C., Bailey, A., et al. (2004). Autism and pervasive developmental disorders. *Journal of Child Psychology and Psychiatry*, **45**, 135–170.

Wadden, N.P., Bryson, S.E., and Rodger, R.S. (1991). A closer look at the Autism Behavior Checklist: Discriminant validity and factor structure. *Journal of Autism and Developmental Disorders*, **21**, 529–541.

Wakefield, A.J. (1999). MMR vaccination and autism. *Lancet*, **354**, 949–950.

Ward, M.F., Wender, P.H., and Reimherr, F.W. (1993). The Wender Utah Rating Scale: An aid in the retrospective diagnosis of childhood attention deficit hyperactivity disorder. *American Journal of Psychiatry*, **150**, 885–890.

Wechsler, D. (1997). *Wechsler Adult Intelligence Scale – 3rd Edition (WAIS-III)*. San Antonio, TX: Harcourt Assessment.

Wechsler, D. (2002). *Wechsler Primary and Preschool Scale of Intelligence – Third edition (WPPSI-III)*. San Antonio, TX: Harcourt Assessment.

Wechsler, D. (2003). *Wechsler Intelligence Scale for Children – 4th Edition (WISC-IV)*. San Antonio, TX: Harcourt Assessment.

Williams, J., Allison, C., Scott, F., et al. (2006). The childhood Asperger syndrome test (CAST): Test-retest reliability. *Autism*, **10**, 415–427.

Williams, P.G., Sears, L.L., and Allard, A. (2004). Sleep problems in children with autism. *Journal of Sleep Research*, **13**, 265–268.

Wing, L., Leekam, S.R., Libby, S.J., et al. (2002). The diagnostic interview for social and communication disorders: Background, inter-rater reliability and clinical use. *Journal of Child Psychology and Psychiatry*, **43**, 307–325.

Yoshida, Y. and Uchiyama, T. (2004). The clinical necessity for assessing attention-deficit/hyperactivity disorder (ADHD) symptoms in children with high-functioning pervasive developmental disorder (PDD). *European Child and Adolescent Psychiatry*, **13**, 307–314.

Zimmerman, I.L., Steiner, V.G., and Pond, R.E. (2002). *Preschool language scale – Fourth edition*. San Antonio, TX: The Psychological Corporation.

5

ASSESSMENT OF CHALLENGING BEHAVIORS IN PEOPLE WITH AUTISM SPECTRUM DISORDERS

PETER STURMEY, LAURA SEIVERLING, AND JOHN WARD-HORNER

Queens College and The Graduate Center, City University of New York, NY, USA

INTRODUCTION

Emerson (2005) defined challenging behavior (CB) as "... culturally abnormal behaviour(s) of such intensity, frequency or duration that the physical safety of the person or others is placed in serious jeopardy, or behaviour which is likely to seriously limit or deny access to the use of ordinary community facilities ... ". Hence, Emerson defined CB without reference to its topography, but rather in terms of its context and its effects on the person's life. For example, lacerating one's body may be either a culturally appropriate behavior, as when some religious people atone for their own or others' sins, or in other cultures in may be considered pathological, as when adolescents lacerate themselves in response to a trip being cancelled.

A number of psychiatric disorders may be related to CB. The American Psychiatric Association (APA, 1994) defined psychiatric disorders as

> a clinically significant behavioral or psychological syndrome or pattern that occurs in an individual and that is associated with present distress (e.g., a painful symptom) or disability (i.e. impairment in one or more important areas of functioning) or with a significant increased risk of suffering death, pain, disability, or an important loss of freedom. In addition, this syndrome or pattern must not be merely an expectable and culturally sanctioned response to a particular event for example, loss of a loved one ... (p. xxi).

The APA defined several psychiatric disorders related to CB. These include Conduct Disorder, Oppositional Defiant Disorder, Disruptive Behavior Disorder, Not Otherwise Specified (NOS), Pica, Rumination Disorder, Stereotypical Movement Disorder, Stereotypic Movement Disorder with Self-Injurious Behavior (SIB), Trichotillomania and Impulse Control Disorder NOS. These disorders are often directly related to CB as many of these diagnostic criteria use topographical definitions of symptoms.

Others have inferred the presence of psychiatric disorders from presenting CB. For example, Tsiouris et al. (2003) diagnosed and treated SIB in 26 people with ID, only 7 of whom had a psychiatric diagnosis before this study. They diagnosed depressive disorders, impulse control disorders and anxiety disorders and then modified their psychotropic medication accordingly, for example, tapering antipsychotics and replacing them with SSRIs. They reported that they eliminated SIB in 12 participants and the overall reduction was statistically significant. The notion that CB may be a "behavioral equivalent" of a psychiatric disorder is commonly espoused. (See Charlot [2005] for a review.) However, empirical data are often contradictory (Tsiouris et al., 2003).

Rather than viewing CB as a symptom of an underlying mental illness, applied behavior analysis (ABA) views all behavior, including unusual and pathological behavior, as the outcomes of biological evolution, social evolution and evolution of the operant within the lifespan of the organism (Skinner, 1953). Independent variables in the current environment that can be manipulated, have large effects on the behavior of interest and are causal (Haynes and O'Brien, 1990). This model has now been applied successfully to the full range of psychopathology (Sturmey, 2007a) including autism (Fitzer and Sturmey in press; Sturmey and Fitzer, 2007).

Basic behavioral research supports this view. For example, self-injury can be shaped and brought under stimulus control rapidly in rhesus monkeys (Schaefer, 1970). Similarly, head banging in pigeons can be shaped and experimentally analyzed to identify its controlling variables (Layng et al., 1999) Further, the hundreds of ABA experimental studies have shown that intervention based on ABA is effective (Didden et al., 1997), including in people with mild ID (Didden et al., 2006) and people with ASD (Campbell, 2003). Further, ABA interventions have also been effective for treatment of psychiatric disorders in people with developmental disabilities, including depression (Sturmey, 2005a,b), anxiety disorders (Matson, 1981) and psychoses (Travis and Sturmey, in review). These observations allow us to conclude that (a) learning is an important process in the development and maintenance of CB and (b) behavioral treatments are highly effective for a wide range of CB and psychiatric disorders in people with a variety of developmental disabilities, including autism.

Researchers often distinguish extra-personal and intra-personal maladaptive behavior. Extra-personal maladaptive behaviors include behavior such as aggression, verbal threats, tantrums and property destruction. In contract, intra-personal maladaptive behaviors include fearful, anxious and withdrawn behavior. The precise nature of this distinction is unclear. However, one feature that may be shared by extra-personal maladaptive behavior is that they interfere with caretaker goal-directed behavior. For instance, when a client engages in CB, caretakers often stop their ongoing activity to attend to the problem behavior of the client. Hence, client extra-personal maladaptive behavior may result in the negative side effects of extinction in caretaker behavior. By contrast, intra-personal maladaptive behaviors do not interfere with other people's ongoing activities. This, distinction may have some important implications. For example, the termination of extra-personal maladaptive behavior may be highly reinforcing to caretakers as their ongoing, presumably reinforcing, activities will no longer be terminated and they can return to their preferred ongoing activities. Thus, termination of client extra-personal maladaptive behavior may be implicated in its development and maintenance and may result in shaping of inappropriate management practices in some circumstances. In contrast, it may be difficult to motivate family members and staff to intervene with intra-personal maladaptive behavior as *treatment* results in effort and interruption of ongoing caretaker reinforced behavior.

Challenging behavior is common in children and adults with ASD (Dunlap et al., 1994; Gadow et al., 2004; Lecavalier, 2006) and people with ASD are at special risk for CB. For example, McClintock, Hall, and Oliver (2003) investigated risk factors for CB in people with developmental disabilities. They reported a meta-analysis of 22 studies conducted over 30 years and found that children and adults with ASD were more likely than other people with ID to display self-injury, disruption, and aggression. Thus, CB is common in people with ASD and they are at greater risk for CB than other people with ID.

Challenging behavior has many negative impacts on people with autism, their family members, staff and society. For example, CB is stigmatizing to the person and may result in rejection by peers, siblings, other family members and staff. It may also interfere with learning and expression of adaptive behavior. It is associated with exclusion from typical settings, such as family homes, mainstream educational and typical work settings. Consequently, CB may result in placement in restricted settings, such as specialized education, segregated residential settings and institutionalization. Challenging behavior may result in treatment practices that are both restrictive and potentially harmful, such as psychotropic medications, polypharmacy, emergency psychotropic medications (Aman et al., 2005) and restrictive and risky behavioral interventions, such as loss of personal property, physical and personal restraint, seclusion and time-out. It carries significant health risks, such as sutures, lacerations, fractures, recurrent infections and death. Also, CB may have negative impacts on family members, such as parental distress, depression and anxiety, the effects of chronic sleep deprivation, and may be associated with divorce. Additionally, siblings may be embarrassed or required to participate in behavior management. Finally, CB result in extensive costs to society. These include the additional costs of specialized and expensive services, such as early intervention, special education and adult residential and other services. The costs associated with higher staffing and one- or two-to-one staffing and additional staffing at night are particularly significant. Thus, CB has many negative impacts on the person, their family and significant others and society in general. Therefore, services should design and implement effective and efficient interventions to reduce CB.

Many current treatments for people with ASD are unevaluated, have been shown to be ineffective but continue to be used, and/or have harmful side effects (Jacobson et al., 2005; Mudford et al., in press; Smith, 1996; Smith et al., 2007). Sturmey (2005c, 2006a,b,c) has argued that ABA treatments should be preferred and should be based on functional assessments and functional analyses because they are the most likely to be effective for a wide range of problems and least likely to have harmful side effects, such as those associated with psychotropic medication.

This chapter reviews various aspects of assessment of CB. These include the reasons for assessment, assessment of topographies, assessment of function and its implications for treatment. Subsequent sections go on to review common problems including aggression, stereotypy, and eating problems in people with ASD.

FUNCTIONS OF ASSESSMENT

It is not uncommon to observe services engage in standardized assessment procedures which may be extensive. However, the reasons why these assessment procedures are used may be unclear leading to the appearance that sometimes assessment is an end in itself. This confusion may arise out of the lack of clarity of the reasons for assessment and the multiple functions that assessments may serve.

Sturmey (2007b) identified at least 12 reasons for assessing CB and mental health disorders. These are listed and described in Table 5.1. Certain questions can be contrasted with each other as these different questions require different kinds of information. For example, service eligibility may sometimes be answered quickly if the person does or does not meet certain highly reliable criteria, such as age, residence or diagnosis. Other questions concerning service eligibility, such as having CB of sufficient severity to require additional funding, additional staffing or access to specialized services, may be less reliable and more complex. Such questions cannot be answered by some simple demographic variables. Thus, when assessing CB the assessors should be explicit as to the reason why they are conducting the assessment: the reason for the assessment will direct the assessment procedure. For example, when assessing a client's aggressive behavior for residential placement, one might be interested in the current and potentially available supports in the current setting and the availability and nature of any future placements. In contrast, if one were assessing the same client for behavioral support, then the assessment would be directed at identifying

TABLE 5.1   Some Common Problems in Making Psychiatric Diagnoses in People with Intellectual Disabilities (Reproduced from N. Bouras and G. Holt (eds.) *Psychiatric and Behavioral Disorders in Intellectual and Developmental Disabilities* (p. 5) Cambridge University Press. ©

Phenomenon	Definition	Example
Intellectual Distortion (Sovner, 1986)	Concrete thinking and impaired communication result in poor communication about their own experience.	Client describes self as "scared" instead of "mad" because of poor verbal skills.
Psychosocial Masking (Sovner, 1986)	Impoverished social skills and life experiences result in unsophisticated presentation of a disorder or misdiagnosis of unusual behavior as a psychiatric disorder.	Giggling and silliness is misdiagnosed as psychosis.
Cognitive Disintegration (Sovner, 1986)	Bizarre behavior is presented in response to minor stressors that could be misdiagnosed as a psychiatric disorder.	A client is highly disruptive and complains a lot after a preferred staff member leaves, but is diagnosed with schizophrenia.
Baseline Exaggeration (Sovner, 1986)	Prior to the onset of a disorder there are high levels of unusual behaviors making it difficult to recognize the onset of a new disorder.	A person who already had poor social skills and was withdrawn becomes more so and begins to experience other signs and symptoms of depression. This is missed because staff reports are inaccurate and staff turnover means that no one is aware of the overall change in the person's functioning.
Misdiagnosis of developmentally appropriate phenomenon (Hurley, 1996)	Developmentally appropriate behaviors that are unusual for the client's chronological age are misdiagnosed as a psychiatric disorder.	Solitary play, talking to oneself and imaginary friends are taken as evidence of psychosis.
Passing (Edgerton, 1996)	People with ID learn to cover up disability and pass for normal.	Unusual persons' experiences are not reported or are ascribed to physical problems.
Diagnostic overshadowing	Unusual behavior is erroneously ascribed to ID, rather than a true mental disorder.	Poor social skills and withdrawal are ascribed to ID rather than a psychosis.

the functions of the behavior, previous treatment plans and their outcomes, the resources available to intervene and the skills of staff and family members.

ASSESSMENT OF TOPOGRAPHY

One apparently elementary type of assessment is to determine the presenting CB topographies. Interviews, psychometric measures and informal direct observations can all be useful for this purpose. Assessment of the topographies of CB is however complicated by two other issues relating to multiple topographies. First, when a client presents with more than one topography, the assessor(s) have to decide which, if any, of the problems should be treated. This may involve decisions concerning treatment priorities and the significance of a problem. For example, it can be useful to distinguish which problems are dangerous to self or other people and hence should probably be treatment priorities, and which are offensive and irritating and hence can be given a lower priority. Second, when a person presents with multiple topographies the possible relationship between the topographies should be considered. For example, some topographically distinct CBs may be functionally equivalent, that is they may all be controlled by the same independent variables. For example, attention may maintain crying, property destruction and aggression, even though all three topographies are quite distinct. Related to this is the possibility that topographically distinct forms of CB may form a response chain. Thus, a maladaptive response may be lawfully preceded by other CB, and the reinforcer maintaining the terminal maladaptive response may be responsible for maintaining the entire sequence of CB. For example, Fisher et al. (1998) demonstrated that property destruction was reinforced by access to stereotypy, involving manipulation of broken items. Harding et al. (2001) demonstrated that both earlier, less intense forms of CB and later, more intense forms of CB were all maintained by the same reinforcer. Others have reported similar findings (Lalli et al., 1995; Richman et al., 1999).

Many assessments include some form of interviews, which may be formal, such as an appointment with a family member or case conferences, or informal, such as a casual conversation with a staff person. The kinds of questions used during interviews greatly affect the kinds of information that informants provide. Open questions, such as "Tell me what problems you are having with Vicky" are likely to be followed by voluminous and perhaps unstructured responses. Closed questions, such as "Does she self-injure?", are likely to be followed by short answers, such as "yes" or "no". A useful interviewing strategy can be to systematically use open-ended questions to elicit a lot of information and to use closed questions to clarify specific points. Minimal interviewer verbal responses, such as "uh huh" can be used to encourage more information. Reflections and checks for accuracy can be helpful. For example, after using a series of open questions, an interviewer might reflect "So she yells, pinches other clients, and body rocks" and then check for completeness by asking "Is that everything?".

Sometimes such reflecting and checking for completeness can reveal additional significant problems that are not initially apparent. Miltenberger and Fuqua (1985) and Miltenberger and Veltum (1988) provided a useful task analysis of these interviewing strategies and also demonstrated how to train clinicians to use these interviewing skills competently using behavioral skills training.

There are many questionnaires to assess the presenting topographies of CB. Most are relatively quick and convenient to administer. They often consist of 10–100 items. Sometimes they are part of a larger instrument that assesses both adaptive and maladaptive behaviors. The informant then rates these items on scales that may estimate the frequency, severity or intensity of each item. Some may be administered by non-professional staff. Respondents may be family members and staff who are familiar with the client. Often the scores from individual items are combined into scales or totals. Sometimes norms are available that may assist in judging the significance of the presenting problem.

There are a very large number of such instruments. Aman (1991) and Sturmey et al. (1991) reviewed these instruments, but such reviews are now incomplete and outdated. Currently, no comprehensive review of these instruments is available. Therefore, this section will select one illustrative measure – the *Behavior Problem Inventory* (BPI: Rojahn et al., 2001).

The BPI is an empirically constructed instrument that assesses three domains of CB: self-injurious behavior (SIB), stereotyped behavior and aggressive/destructive behaviors. The current version has 49 items of which 14 are related to SIB, 24 to stereotyped behavior and 11 to aggression/destruction. Each item is rated on Likert scales for frequency and severity, if the behavior has occurred over the last 2 months. The BPI can be administered to residential staff who know the client well and to family members. There has been extensive research into the reliability and validity of the BPI (Aman et al., 2002; Bodfish et al., 1999; Rojahn et al., 2001, 2003; Sturmey et al., 1993, 1995).

SUMMARY

There are now many psychometric measures to assess CB topographies. They can be quick and efficient in the early stages of assessing CB, in screening larger populations, and in periodic screening of individuals, such as during admission to services and annual evaluations. However, although they may be quick and relatively cheap to administer, they may not always identify all the relevant topographies. Further, they do not tell us much about the person's strengths or the functions of the target behaviors. Hence, they are a place to begin assessment of CB in people with autism, but by themselves they are insufficient.

INFORMAL OBSERVATION

Information obtained from third parties through interview and observation may be relatively coarse. Direct observation in the natural environment, including informal observation, can yield new information or clarify ambiguities that result from third party assessments. For example, informal observation may identify (a) topographies that third parties fail to mention, (b) hypotheses concerning the organization of different topographies, and (c) hypotheses concerning the functions of the CBs. In order to obtain the maximally useful information it is good practice to observe in several settings, across several different activities, and on more than one occasion.

ASSESSMENT OF FUNCTION

In *Science and Human Behavior*, Skinner (1953) wrote, "The external variables of which behavior is a function provide for what may be called a causal or functional analysis" (p. 35). Later, Baer et al. (1968) extended this notion to its use in ABA. They stressed that ABA should be analytic, meaning that the researcher should be able to exercise control over a particular behavior and turn it on and off through manipulation of independent variables. In an experimental assessment of behavior, this is exactly what occurs. According to Miltenberger (2003), experimental or functional analysis involves the manipulation of antecedents and consequences to evaluate the functions of behavior. Miltenberger further discussed how behavioral problems can be maintained through social positive reinforcement, social negative reinforcement, automatic positive reinforcement, and automatic negative reinforcement. A behavior is maintained by social positive reinforcement if another person delivers a positively reinforcing consequence following the target behavior. When a behavior is maintained by social negative reinforcement, a person terminates an aversive stimulus, such as an interaction, activity, or task, contingent on the problem behavior. A behavior can also be maintained through automatic positive or negative reinforcement. Automatic positive reinforcement occurs if a behavior produces a reinforcing consequence automatically. For example, eye poking in someone who is blind may produce visual consequences by stimulating the optic nerve. Automatic negative reinforcement occurs if the occurrence of a behavior automatically terminates or reduces an aversive stimulus following a behavior. For example, persons may intentionally fall out of wheel chairs to terminate physical discomfort associated with sitting in the wheel chair.

EXPERIMENTAL ASSESSMENT METHODS

A functional analysis can be conducted in a variety of ways. Generally, a series of conditions are presented in either a multielemental design, in which conditions are randomly or sequentially alternated in rapid succession, or in a reversal design, in which test and control conditions are alternated until behavior levels are stable. A sequential test control, in which test conditions are individually presented while control conditions are interspersed, may also be used to conduct a functional analysis (Smith, 2007). Following Carr's earlier work (Carr, 1977; Carr et al., 1980), Iwata et al. (1982/1994) developed methods and experimental designs to determine the function of self-injury. Researchers have extended and modified these methods to determine the functions of many forms of CB and psychopathology (Sturmey, 2007a).

In this analysis, Iwata et al. (1982/1994) compared the effects of four conditions on self-injury. In the social disapproval condition, to determine self-injurious behavior was maintained by positive social reinforcement, the experimenter directed the child to play with toys and the experimenter then engaged in other work. Only when the child engaged in self-injurious behavior did the experimenter provide attention to the child, for example, by saying "Don't do that!". If high rates of the problem behavior occured during attention, the experimenter concluded that the behavior was maintained by social positive reinforcement. To determine if the behavior was maintained through social negative reinforcement, Iwata et al. implemented an academic demand or escape condition in which the experimenter and participant were seated at a table and the experimenter verbally instructed the participant to initiate an appropriate educational activity. If the participant did not respond, the experimenter repeated the instructions, modeled the response, and then used physical guidance if necessary to assist the participant in completing the task. Contingent on any self-injurious behavior, the experimenter terminated the task and turned away for 30 seconds. If high rates of self-injurious behavior occurred during the demand conditions, the experimenter surmised that the behavior was maintained through social negative reinforcement. Next, Iwata et al. implemented an unstructured play condition to serve as an enriched environment control condition that they used to compare to all other conditions. In this play condition, the experimenter remained within 1 meter of the participant. The experimenter did not present educational tasks; rather various toys were available to the participant. The experimenter ignored self-injurious behavior and provided social praise and physical contact contingent on the absence of the problem behavior. To assess whether the behavior was maintained by automatic reinforcement, Iwata et al. conducted an alone condition in which the participant was placed alone in the treatment room without any objects. The alone condition attempts to simulate a deprived environment. If the participant exhibited high levels of problem behavior during an alone condition, it was concluded that the behavior was not maintained by social reinforcement. Experimenters may also make further inferences about whether a behavior is maintained through automatic positive reinforcement or automatic negative reinforcement. Behavior maintained by automatic positive reinforcement generally will occur at high rates exclusively during the alone condition. In contrast, behavior maintained by automatic negative reinforcement will most likely occur across all conditions, since the internal aversive event is presented throughout all conditions.

Iwata et al.'s (1982/1994) methodology has been used most commonly in research. However, several other researchers have developed different methods and procedural variations. For example, Carr and Durand (1985) developed a way to assess educational situations in which problems occurred. They used a reversal design in which a baseline condition was immediately followed by either an easy or a difficult condition. In the baseline condition, the student was presented an easy academic task and given adult attention during 100 percent of time intervals. In the easy condition, the student was given an easy academic task to complete and was provided with adult attention during 33 percent of the time intervals. In the difficult condition, the student was asked to complete a difficult academic task and received attention during 100 percent of the session intervals. This design was used to determine if problem behavior was maintained by level of adult attention and or level of task difficulty. Smith et al. (2007) provide a useful review of these methods.

Due to time or setting constraints, researchers and practitioners may not conduct a lengthy functional analysis. Rather, brief variations of this approach are implemented. For example, Iwata (1987) initially implemented a multielement design across alone, escape, attention, demand, and tangible conditions. However, during replication of phases, they only examined the conditions in which the most and least aberrant behaviors occurred. Similarly, Derby et al. (1992) evaluated brief functional analyses in 79 outpatients. They found that while most brief functional assessments identified a maintaining condition for aberrant behavior, aberrant behavior only occurred in 63 percent of the cases. Thus, brief functional assessments may be limited to those who exhibit high-frequency behavior in the clinic setting and that brief assessments are most valid when they closely approximate more extended assessment procedures.

Some people exhibit problem behaviors so severe that conducting a functional analysis in which environmental contingencies are directly manipulated to increase the likelihood of problem behaviors during particular conditions may be dangerous both to those conducting the analysis as well as to the participant. For example, Smith and Churchill (2002) conducted a functional analysis to identify contingencies for precursor behaviors that were reliably preceded by problem behaviors. They first conducted an experimental assessment similar to Iwata et al.'s (1982/1994). They then applied the contingencies maintaining the target behaviors to precursor behaviors such as screaming, foot-stomping, and grabbing. The experimental analyses of both problem and precursor behaviors produced the same conclusions. Therefore, conducting experimental analyses of precursor behaviors may be a safe alternative to experimental analyses of severe problem behaviors.

AGGRESSION, TANTRUMS, AND RELATED BEHAVIOR

Aggressive behavior includes responses such as kicking, screaming, pinching, hitting, and property destruction. A variety of environmental variables may control aggressive behavior including consequences, such as escape, attention, and automatic reinforcement (Sigafoos and Tucker, 2000; Thompson et al., 1998) and antecedent stimuli, such as presentation of requests, removal of reinforcers, and deprivation and satiation of the consequence maintaining aggression. The multitude of functions that may control aggressive behavior and the different treatments that these functions indicate and contraindicate imply the use of functional assessment and functional analysis procedures to determine the best treatment. Meta-analyses of outcome studies have repeatedly found that interventions based on functional assessments and analyses result in larger treatment effects (Didden et al., 1997, 2006). Treating aggressive behavior without conducting the appropriate assessments to identify variables associated with the behavior may result in ineffective or harmful treatments, consumer and staff injury, and the unnecessary use of restrictive procedures.

Descriptive assessments identify environmental variables causing the target behaviors, but do not manipulate those variables. They include interviews, questionnaires, and observation in the natural environment. A variety of descriptive assessments have been used to determine what variables are associated with the occurrence of aggressive behavior. For example, Touchette et al. (1985) used a scatter-plot assessment to identify variables associated with a 14 year-old girl's aggression. The aggression consisted of kicking, hitting, and head butting staff and peers. They collected data throughout the day and identified that aggression occurred during specific times. Based on these data, Touchette et al. identified the activities in which the aggressive behavior was most likely to occur and rearranged the girl's schedule to remove the activities associated with which aggression. This resulted in a rapid decrease in aggression. They then gradually faded the activities associated with aggression back into the girl's schedule without any increase in aggression.

Sasso et al. (1992) used the Motivation Assessment Scale (MAS) and ABC observations (Bijou et al., 1968) to identify the functions of CBs including hitting, pinching, and slapping others in three children with intellectual disabilities (ID) and autism. The MAS is a 16-item questionnaire that asks raters to rate the likely function of the target behavior on Likert scales. The MAS results for two of the children suggested that escape maintained aggression and for the third child the results indicated that CB was likely maintained by *both* escape and attention. The authors then conducted an experimental functional analysis consisting of baseline, attention, and demand conditions that supported the results of the MAS. Treatment based on these descriptive and experimental analyses were effective in reducing all three participants' CB. These results illustrate that in this study descriptive and experimental analyses converged on the same conclusion and that these results lead to valid and effective treatments.

Matson and Vollmer (1995) developed *The Questions About Behavioral Function* (QABF) to assess five behavioral functions: attention, escape, non-social, tangible, and physical. The QABF has been extensively evaluated by its developers in terms of its reliability, internal consistency, (Dawson et al., 1998; Matson and Boisjoli, 2007) and ability to predict effective treatment (Matson et al., 1999). Further, several independent researchers have found similar results (e.g., Freeman et al., 2007; Nicholson et al., 2006; Shogren and Rojahn, 2003). Thus, the QABF should also be considered as a measure to use in functional assessment of aggression in people with autism.

Although descriptive assessment can be helpful in identifying the variables associated with aggressive behavior, these assessment procedures may not always identify the consequence maintaining the aggression. In fact, the utility of descriptive assessments has been questioned on the grounds that the assessments do not reliably correspond to the results of functional analyses (Arndorfer and Miltenberger, 1994; Lerman and Iwata, 1993). For example, Arndorfer and Miltenberger (1994) compared the results of the MAS, Functional Analysis Interview (FAI), and ABC observations with the results of a brief experimental functional analysis. The results of the FAI and ABC observations both corresponded with the functions identified in the experimental functional analysis. However, the functions identified by the MAS did not correspond to those of the functional analysis. By contrast, Lerman and Iwata (1993) found that ABC observations did not correspond well with the results of the functional analyses. Paclawskyj et al. (2001), observing that the results of the QABF and MAS correlated more closely with each other than with the results of analog baselines, expressed a contrary opinion, namely, that experimental methods may be insensitive to the functions of low frequency/high intensity behaviors if they do not appear in the functional analyses.

Despite some limitations and inconsistencies with descriptive assessments, they have proven to be useful tools (Sasso et al., 1992; Thompson et al., 1998) and many practitioners use them rather than experimental methods (Desrochers et al., 1997). As noted above, aggressive behavior may have multiple functions, which may result in undifferentiated findings of functional analyses. That is, aggressive behavior may remain high in two or more of the conditions of a functional analysis, leading to inconclusive results. In such cases, descriptive assessments may be helpful in identifying events that could be included or removed from a functional analysis to enhance sensitivity to changes across conditions. For example, Thompson et al. (1998) conducted a functional analysis of the aggressive behavior of a boy with Pervasive Developmental Disabilities (PDD) and ID. Aggressive behavior consisted of hitting, scratching, kicking, pinching, and chin grinding (pushing chin into caregivers). The functional analysis used play, attention, tangible, and demand conditions. The rate of aggressive behavior was low and about equal for the demand and tangible conditions, and aggressive behavior occurred at a higher, but similar rate for the attention and play conditions. Because the results of the functional analysis were inconclusive, Thompson et al. then collected additional data using ABC data and informal observation. Based on the results of the descriptive assessments, it was hypothesized that chin grinding, although topographically similar to aggressive behavior, might be maintained by automatic reinforcement, whereas the other aggressive behavior was maintained by social-positive reinforcement. Given the results of the descriptive assessment, a second functional assessment was conducted and confirmed Thompson et al's hypothesis. Based on the results of these combined experimental and descriptive analyses, they successfully treated aggression using functional communication training (FCT) and extinction of aggression. Importantly, this treatment was ineffective for chin grinding. Since chin grinding appeared to be maintained by automatic reinforcement, they used response blocking and access to a device that the participant could use for chin grinding. This combined treatment was effective in reducing chin grinding against people. Again, the results of the descriptive assessments and experimental analyses led to effective treatments based on the functions of individual topographies.

Thompson et al.'s (1998) results suggest that, when conducting descriptive assessments and functional analyses, it is important to record different CB topographies since different topographies may be maintained by different consequences. In other situations, however, it has been demonstrated that classes of aggressive behavior can be maintained by more than one consequence (Hagopian et al., 2001) and that one CB topography may have several functions (Labelle and Charlop-Christy, 2002). For example, hitting behavior might be maintained by escape and attention functions. A second concern for many practitioners is the length of time it may take to complete functional analyses. In many situations it may be neither practical nor desirable to conduct extensive analyses, as they may delay treatment implementation. A third issue is that functional analyses require that the problem behavior is reinforced, which can lead to increases in aggression that can increase the probability of injury to the client and staff members, at least during assessment which may be unacceptable in some situations.

For these reasons, a number of studies have examined the utility of brief functional analyses (Arndorfer and Miltenberger, 1994; Sigafoos and Tucker, 2000). Brief functional analyses are an abridged version of a traditional functional analysis, which may include either all or a subset of the same conditions as a traditional functional analysis. When all of the original conditions are included in a brief analysis, the client is exposed to each of the conditions for shorter periods of time and the order of conditions may initially be sequential followed by a brief reversal between conditions that may influence the target behavior. When brief functional analyses include only a subset of the original conditions, descriptive assessments and/or interviews are generally conducted prior to the functional analysis to determine the conditions that will be included in the functional analysis.

Arndorfer and Miltenberger (1994) conducted a brief functional analysis of the aggressive behavior of a child with autism. (Other children also participated, but did not have autism). The child's aggressive behavior consisted of hitting, grabbing, screaming, and crying. They used ABC, scatter-plot, MAS, and FAI data to determine the conditions used in the functional analysis. Based on the information from the assessments, Arndorfer and Miltenberger hypothesized that escape maintained CB. Therefore, they used only high- and low-demand conditions. The results confirmed Arndorfer and Miltenberger's hypothesis in that challenging behavior was maintained by escape. Sigafoos and Tucker (2000) also used a brief functional analysis to identify the function of challenging behavior for a 19-year-old with autism. The participant's challenging behavior consisted of spitting, self-injury, hitting, and property destruction. The brief functional analysis included five conditions: a task, ignore, access to tangibles, wait for tangibles, and alone conditions. During the first phase of the analysis, they presented the task and ignore conditions twice for 3 minutes in an ABAB reversal design, and during the second experiment, they presented the wait for tangibles and access to tangibles conditions twice for 3 minutes in an ABAB reversal design. During the final phase, they implemented the alone condition in which the participant was simply observed for 12 minutes. CB served multiple functions as it occurred at high rates during the task, ignore, wait for tangibles, and alone conditions. These two studies demonstrate that brief functional analyses can be efficiently applied to determine the functions of CB in people with ASD.

An interesting application of functional analysis methodology for assessing environmental events associated with aggressive behavior of an individual with autism is an analysis of establishing operations (EO). Michael (1993) defined an EO as ". . . an environmental event, operation, or stimulus condition that affects an organism by momentarily altering (a) the reinforcing effectiveness of other events and (b) the frequency of occurrence of that part of the organism's repertoire relevant to those events as consequences" (p. 192). EOs are different from discriminative stimuli, since discriminative stimuli indicate the presence or absence of a reinforcement contingency, whereas EOs are stimuli that are not differentially associated with consequent events, but are stimuli that make the consequences effective as reinforcers.

Hoch et al. (2000) used an EO analysis to identify environmental events that made destructive behavior reinforcing. Three boys with autism who displayed destructive behavior participated. Their destructive behavior consisted of shirt biting, chin pressing (against oneself or staff member's body part), hitting, pinching, and noncompliance with tasks. The procedure consisted of a traditional functional analysis, which was followed by a descriptive assessment to generate hypotheses about EOs associated with the destructive behavior. Finally, they conducted an EOs analysis in which they manipulated environmental events without changing the consequence that followed the destructive behavior. For example, the functional analysis for one child's destructive behavior indicated that escape from task demands maintained the destructive behavior. The child's descriptive assessment indicated that destructive behavior occurred most frequently when the child was required to repeat tasks that were previously performed incorrectly. The EO assessment therefore consisted of manipulating whether the child was required to repeat tasks, while maintaining the escape contingencies in both conditions. A large decrement in destructive behavior occurred when they did not require the child to repeat tasks, even though the occurrence of destructive behavior could result in escape from demands.

Researchers have shown that both descriptive and experimental analyses of aggression may result in successful identification of the independent variables of which aggression is a function. Further, the results of these analyses may result in effective interventions that results in the reduction of aggression and replacement with functionally equivalent and socially valid alternate behavior.

RESTRICTIVE INTERVENTION PROCEDURES AND ASSESSMENT

Aggression and related extra-personal CB is often associated with restrictive management practices. Restrictive procedures refer to a range of behavior management practices that restrict clients' freedom, or are painful or demeaning. Restrictions of clients' freedom may include loss or restriction of access to personal property, movement and programming. Personal restraints may include basket holds, wraps, hugs, and physical takedowns. Physical restraints may include ties, papoose boards, mittens, splints, individually built devices such as casts or braces to restrict movement and modified seating devices, furniture, and clothing. Chemical restraints can also include emergency ("prn") medication, such as needed sedating antipsychotics or antihistamines, which may be used for behavioral emergencies, dental, and medical procedures.

Unfortunately, these procedures are widely used in educational, community and institutional adults services and during medical and dental procedures. Feldman et al. (2004) surveyed caretakers of 6235 person with ID of whom 92 percent lived in various community settings and 8 percent in institutional settings in Ontario, Canada. They found that 56 percent of the sample experienced intrusive interventions of some kind. For example, 12 percent have experienced restraint, 11 percent time-out, 6 percent mechanical restraint, 5 percent seclusion. Emerson (2002) reported a series of studies in special education settings in Britain that also showed high rates of restrictive behavior management practices. Recent scandals over inadequate care for adults with ID in community settings often involve inappropriate use of restraint and other restrictive behavior management practices, such as community services in Cornwall, United Kingdom (Healthcare Commission, 2006), Sutton and Merton Primary Healthcare Trust, United Kingdom (Learning Disabilities Care Slammed, 2007) and Washington DC, USA (Boo, 1999). The use of restraint does not seem strongly related to client characteristics, such as behavior severity (Sturmey, 1999; Sturmey et al., 2005), suggesting that other factors, such policies, staff training, and supervision practices may be more important than client factors. Despite this recent history of exposés of inappropriate use of restrictive procedures, there has not yet been any extensive documentation of procedures to reduce these practices in contemporary educational or community settings.

There is a small amount of literature on restrictive procedures for children and adults with autism. Sourander et al. (2002) found that children with autism who exhibit aggressive behavior towards themselves and others are potentially placing themselves and those around them at risk, especially in an environment such as an in-patient child or adolescent unit. Therefore, if alternative strategies have been implemented and have been found to be ineffective, an argument to use holding restraints to protect the individual and others in certain environments may find support. For example, Ramm (1990) discussed the use of duvet (quilt) to restrain people with autism who were aggressive. Nevertheless, relatively little is know about restrictive procedures in services for people with autism.

The use of these procedures is undesirable for many reasons. First, their extended use suggests that the CB is both serious and that current interventions continue to be ineffective. Second, often these procedures are used when other less restrictive procures have not been implemented competently or at all, such as when service providers have not conducted adequate functional assessments, stimulus preferences assessments, and staff or family training. Third, many staff members and other people (McDonnell and Sturmey, 2000; McDonnell et al., 1993), including clients (Cunningham et al., 2003) view these procedures negatively. Professional standards, such as those espoused by the American Association on Intellectual Disabilities (American Association on Mental Retardation, 2005) have called for the reduction and elimination of such procedures while simultaneously promoting effective behavior management practices. These contemporary calls echo similar sentiments that have been expressed for hundreds of years (Deutsch, 1946, Chapter 11). These procedures also pose significant risk of client injury and even death (General Accounting Office, 1999), injury to staff and family members and legal action, including class action law suits in the USA. Thus, service providers should strive to identify and effectively reduce the use of these procedures.

Despite the frequent calls for elimination of these procedures, the precise technology by which such procedures can be effectively eliminated is unclear. Indeed, safety concerns may inhibit practitioners from attempting to eliminate restrictive procedures. When directly asked about the use of restrictive procedures, service providers and managers may deny any such use, but they may use euphemisms to describe restrictive procedures. For example, service providers might say that a child is placed in the "the quiet chair", which really means that restraints are used to keep the child seated. In other situations, staff may explain that the procedures are not restrictive; rather, they are a part of socially acceptable programs. For instance, service providers or managers may claim that the restrictive procedures are part of medical or behavioral programs, such as physical or occupational therapy.

There is a growing body of empirical studies, some of which are well controlled, to develop and evaluate effective behavioral technologies to eliminate these restrictive procedures safely. These include both studies of individual clients and interventions for groups of clients and entire services. For example, Wong et al. (1991) reported treatment of aggressive and self-injurious behavior in a man with autism which had failed to respond to psychotropic medication and repeated restraint. They found that DRO resulted in reductions of restraint from more than once per day to less than once per month, and that this reduction was maintained at one year follow-up. Reduction of restraint and related restrictive procedures is also possible on a large scale. For example, in Connelly (1856, cited in Deutsch, 1946) reported complete elimination of mechanical restraints within 4 months in a mental health facility. More recently, Sturmey and McGlynn (2002) reported two examples of large-scale restraint reduction. They used policy change, identifying at-risk clients, staff training in treatment implementation, and feedback to staff and supervisors. These procedures were associated with large reductions in restraint that were maintained over a 3-year period in one case. So far, there have been no reports of large-scale restraint reduction in educational or community services for people with autism.

Restrictive procedures continue to be used inappropriately in a wide variety of contemporary services for people with developmental disabilities. Competent behavioral services, effective staff training and feedback, and effective service policy, oversight and vigilance can result in effective and safe elimination of these restrictive procedures.

STEREOTYPY

Stereotypies are highly repetitive rhythmic motor activities that are topographically invariant and appear to have no adaptive function (Repp and Karsh, 1992). Stereotypy occurs in both motor and vocal forms. Examples of the most common stereotypies among persons with developmental disabilities are body rocking, object mouthing, complex hand and finger movements, limb or body posturing, thumb or limb sucking, and object manipulation (LaGrow and Repp, 1984). Some forms of self-injurious behavior are also considered a type of stereotypy (APA, 1994). Stereotypy can interfere with learning new skills or academic tasks as well as inhibit one's ability to socially interact with peers (Repp and Karsh, 1992). When conducting prevalence studies with those who have autism, both Campbell et al. (1990) and Bodfish et al. (2002) found that 100 percent of those studied with autism engage in at least one stereotypic behavior.

MOTOR STEREOTYPY

Direct observation methods have been used to assess the functions of stereotypy. For example, Jung-Chang et al. (2002) conducted a direct observation prior to conducting a functional analysis to assess stereotypical ear covering in a 5-year-old boy with autism. They videotaped 43, 30-min. sessions across 4 days and then used a 30-s. partial-interval paper-and-pencil system to record occurrences of stereotypy. Observers also recorded any change in adult behavior following the occurrence of the child's ear covering. Jung-Chang et al. found that ear covering occurred at similar levels throughout the day and during greater than 60 percent of the observed intervals. In addition, no antecedents or social consequences, except for a classmate's scream, were associated with the behavior. The functional analysis conducted following the descriptive analysis confirmed that the ear covering occurred only when the classmate screamed. The researchers concluded that the ear covering was maintained by negative sensory reinforcement – noise attenuation – and that the descriptive assessment was helpful in exposing this idiosyncratic event that was involved in behavioral maintenance.

Kennedy et al. (2000) also conducted functional analyses with 5 students with autism, ranging from 9 to 17 years old, who exhibited various forms of stereotypy, such as hand waving, nose touching, rocking, head movements, object manipulation, and tapping objects. Using a multielement design, they compared the effects of attention, demand, no attention, and a recreation control condition. Stereotypy occurred most frequently in demand, attention, and recreation conditions for two students, across all conditions for two other students, and occurred most frequently during the demand and recreation condition for one student. They then implemented FCT procedures for one of the students whose behavior served multiple functions. In the attention, demand, and no attention condition, this student learned to sign "break" and "more" respectively. Stereotypy reduced only when the student learned the communication response in each condition and the effects did not generalize to other conditions. Thus, FCT was effective, but only for specific response–reinforcer relations.

Rehfeldt and Chambers (2003) conducted a functional analysis and treatment for a 23-year-old man who engaged in verbal perseveration on specific topics such as sirens, alarms, dentist and doctor appointments, or coughing. In the functional analysis, experimenters randomly alternated the attention: demand, alone, and tangible conditions. Rates of perseverative speech were highest in the attention condition. Thus, Rehfeldt and Chambers (2003) concluded that the participant's speech was positively reinforced by social attention. As a result, they introduced a differential reinforcement of alternative (DRA) verbal responses and attention–extinction procedure for perseverative speech that was successful in increasing appropriate speech and reducing perseverative speech. However, results did not generalize to the participant's daily work environment. A number of other studies have also shown that functional assessments and analyses can identify the functions of stereotypy and be useful for developing effective interventions (Hanley et al., 2000; Jung-Chang et al., 2002; Sidener et al., 2005).

The studies reviewed demonstrate the importance of both descriptive and experimental methods for assessing stereotypy in those with autism. Treatment can be more effective when the function of the behavior is demonstrated through assessment prior to intervention.

ECHOLALIA

Echolalia is a type of vocal stereotypy (Charlop, 1992). There are both immediate and delayed forms. In immediate echolalia, a person repeats part or all of what another person said. For example, if another person asks "How are you today?", the person with autism immediately echoes "How are you today?". In delayed echolalia, a person will repeat something that he or she heard in the past. For example, a person might repeat something from a commercial such as, "This sale won't last!" Schreibman and Charlop (1987) found that approximately half of all people with autism demonstrate echolalia. Those with echolalia may have difficulty following directions and learning (Mancina et al., 2000). In addition, they may have problems socially interacting with others in an appropriate manner. Echolalia is not entirely problematic. It indicates that the person has already acquired some imitations skills, and has acquired some control of the respiratory and other muscle systems while talking. Further, if the person emits echolalia with appropriate prosody, then they may also have some good discrimination skills relevant to learning language. Thus, echolalia can be incorporated into treatment strategies to teach appropriate language (Poulson, in press; Brown and Poulson, in press).

Like other problem behaviors, echolalia is typically assessed through direct observation and other descriptive assessments. These assessment have demonstrated that various features of adult speech may be related to echolalia. For example, Rydell and Mirenda (1994) assessed the functions of echolalia by conducting 1-hour observation periods during preexperimental play sessions of 7 boys with autism ranging from 5 to 6 years old. These authors examined the relationship between adult's high and low constraint utterances during a free play environment on echolalia in the male students with autism. High constraint utterances were mostly directive and included wh-questions and verbal prompts. Low utterances were considered facilitative and were used to follow the child's lead. Positive responses and reflective statements were considered low utterances. The participants' immediate echolalia mostly occurred following high constraint utterances of adults while delayed echolalia mostly occurred following low constraint utterances. Violette and Swisher (1992) examined lexical familiarity on levels of echolalia in children with autism and found that immediate echolalia was more likelty when lexical stimuli were unknown and given in a directive manner. Charlop (1986) evaluated setting effects on echolalia and found that echolalia was most likely to occur in children with autism when an unfamiliar person presented an unfamiliar task. Echolalia levels were also high when a familiar person presented an unfamiliar task stimuli.

As with motor and vocal stereotypy, assessment of echolalia also provides helpful information regarding the function of behavior. The studies discussed did not examine treatment following assessments. Nevertheless, the assessments indicated the times at which high levels of echolalia occurred, thus providing helpful information for possible future interventions.

EATING PROBLEMS

Feeding problems are relatively common in people with developmental disabilities. Up to one-third of persons with mental retardation may display some form of feeding problems (Palmer et al., 1975). Hove (2007) surveyed

311 adults with mental retardation living in community settings and found that approximately two-thirds had some form of eating problems. The most frequent problems were eating too fast, bolting food (eating food quickly with little chewing), food refusal, excessive eating, and noncompliance during meals.

Matson and Kuhn (2001) developed the Screening Tool of Feeding Problems (STEP) to identify risk of aspiration, food selectivity, feeding skills, food refusal, and associated CB and nutrition related CB. The STEP can be a useful starting point to identify important topographies of feeding problems.

Several studies have used the QABF to identify the functions of various feeding problems (Applegate et al., 1999). For example, Matson et al. (2005) administered the QABF to 125 individuals with various feeding problems and severe and profound mental retardation and found interesting interactions between topography and function. For example, they found that CB and food refusal were most likely to be maintained by attention, whereas food stealing and pica were least likely to be maintained by attention. Similarly, pica and rumination were more likely to have a nonsocial function than CB, food stealing, and food refusal. This study suggests that certain functions may be correlated with the topography of feeding problems and that the QABF might be a useful starting point for a descriptive analysis of these problems.

FOOD OVER-SELECTIVITY AND REFUSAL

A common feeding problem amongst both children and adults with autism is food selectivity, in which a person eats a very limited variety of food or eats few types of food, such as only food with low texture. Food selectivity is often linked to food refusal in which a person refuses to eat a particular type of food or foods. Ahearn et al. (2001) conducted an assessment of food acceptance in children with ASD and found that approximately half of the participants demonstrated food selectivity by food category or texture. Child food selectivity can often lead to disruptions during family mealtimes and health risks such as weight loss or gain and malnutrition.

Schreck and Williams (2005) used descriptive assessment techniques to examine food selectivity in children with ASD. They used the *Children's Eating Behavior Inventory* (Archer et al., 1991), which is given to caregivers to report their child's mealtime behaviors, eating behaviors, and the disruption of feeding problems on family dynamics. They also used the *Food Preference Inventory*, which is a checklist filled out by caregivers to report the typically accepted food items from each of the five food groups as well as the family food preferences. Food selectivity was defined as a child who ate less than half of the listed food items in each food group. Seventy-two percent of the children engaged in restricted food acceptance (selectivity) and 57 percent engaged in food refusal. In addition, family eating preferences also influenced child selectivity: Families that ate fewer foods tended to have children who were more selective eaters, suggesting that opportunity to eat varied food and modeling might be relevant factors. Schreck et al. (2004) used similar descriptive assessment methods to compare eating behaviors of children with and without autism. Children with autism had significantly more feeding problems and eat a narrower range of food compared to children without autism.

Najdowski et al. (2003) evaluated the functions of food selectivity using an experimental functional analysis and treatment of food selectivity in a 5-year-old child with autism in which they taught the child's parent to deliver antecedents and consequences during several conditions. The experiment included no-interaction, attention, play, and escape conditions modified for food selectivity. In the no-interaction condition, the parent provided a plate with one bite of five nonpreferred foods, determined by a preference assessment, and did not provide any demands to take a bite or consequences for food refusal. In the attention condition, the parent provided a plate of food with five nonpreferred items and gave attention if food refusal occurred. For example, if the child engaged in food refusal behavior, the parent might say "I know the food is gross.". In the play condition, the parent provided both a plate of nonpreferred foods and a plate of preferred foods and the parent gave noncontingent positive attention every 30 seconds. During the escape condition, the parent provided a plate of nonpreferred foods and made requests to self-feed, modeled how to take a bite, and physically prompted the child to take a bite by putting the food in the child's mouth. Najdowski et al. (2003) found that the child engaged in food refusal most often in the escape condition and concluded that the behavior was most likely maintained by negative reinforcement. As a result, they implemented a package consisting of differential reinforcement of an alternative behavior, escape extinction, and demand fading. After the intervention, the child increased food acceptance in the home and in a restaurant. His food acceptance continued during follow-up visits. Thus, treatment was considered effective.

Assessments of food selectivity have been especially helpful in determining prevalence of food selectivity in those with autism and other developmental disabilities. In addition, treatments have been successfully implemented following functional analysis of food selectivity (Najdowski et al., 2003; Piazza and Addison, 2007).

RUMINATION AND REGURGITATION

Rumination Disorder is the repeated regurgitation and rechewing of food (American Psychiatric Association [DSM-IV-TR], 2000). Prevalence estimates among people with developmental disabilities range from 6 to 10 percent (Heering et al., 2003). Rumination can lead to many health problems, such as malnutrition, weight loss, dehydration, gastric disorders, aspiration, pneumonia, and even death (Dudley et al., 2002). In addition, severe rumination may interfere with one's educational program and social skills, such as integration into the community (Johnston and Greene, 1992).

Several studies have been conducted with parametric analyses of independent variables that control rumination. Rast et al. (1981) compared the effects of large portions of food and satiation on rumination. During the large portion condition, the participant consumed approximately twice a typical meal. During satiation, the participant had free access to as much potatoes, grits, cream of wheat and bread as the person wished to consume, and in this condition the participant consumed approximately 3 to 8 times a typical meal. This procedure was compared to both typical mealtime procedures and a control procedure – spaced baseline regular diet–during which the usual amount of food was served, but was spaced out over time to control for the duration of the meal. Rast et al. (1981) observed that large quantities of food and satiation, but not longer mealtimes, had large and significant reductions in rumination in all the participants. Subsequently, Rast et al. (1984) examined the effects of increasing the weight of meals, by adding 5 to 50 ounces of starch to the meals, on the rumination behavior of three adults with intellectual disabilities. To demonstrate experimental control, starch was added in 10 oz increments and in others they began with 50 oz of starch added to the meal and then decreased the quantity of starch in 10 oz steps. They found a reliable relationship between quantity of starch and rate of rumination during meals in all three participants. The results from the six participants in these two experiments demonstrate that rumination is a function of quantity of food consumed during meals.

Several studies have demonstrated similar effects, often incorporating idiosyncratic variables. Heering et al. (2003) conducted a functional analysis to assess rumination in a 19-year-old man with autism and profound ID. In the preintervention assessment, the experimenters manipulated the amount of liquid and consistency of food intake of the participant throughout five conditions in a multielemental design. In the baseline condition, the participant was served one half-pint of chocolate milk and one sausage. Next, in the free liquid condition, the experimenters increased the amount of liquid given to the participant by serving an additional half-pint of chocolate milk and three 6 oz apple juices. In the third condition, no liquid was served to the participant. In the fourth condition, the participant was served two 4 oz yogurts and one half-pint of chocolate milk. Lastly, in the peanut butter condition, the participant was given a piece of wheat toast with peanut butter on it and a half-pint of chocolate milk. Assessment took place over a 2-week period and each condition was conducted twice. The participant ruminated most, 18.5 times per hour, following the free liquid condition. Thus, the researchers treated the rumination by implementing rescheduling procedure in which liquids were not presented during mealtimes. Following intervention, the client did not ruminate for 90 minutes following meals or when presented with liquids 90 minutes after the completion of a meal. Thus, the researchers considered the treatment a success.

PICA

Pica is another eating problem which is commonly found in those with autism as well as other developmental disabilities. The APA (1994) defined pica as eating a nonnutritive substance for at least one month, that is inappropriate to the person's developmental level, not part of a culturally sanctioned practice, and not due to any other mental disorder. Prevalence studies estimate between 9.2 and 25 percent of those with developmental disabilities display pica and that the prevalence rates may be higher if less severe pica is considered (Ali, 2001). People with developmental disabilities may ingest both organic items, such as leaves, twigs, coffee grounds or cigarette butts, and inorganic items, such as matches or paint chips. Some people who display pica eat items indiscriminately while others have very strong preferences for specific items. The health risks associated with pica include toxicity in which a person can suffer from lead poisoning, nicotine or caffeine toxicity; parasitic infections; malnutrition; oral and dental problems; gut obstructions and perforations; and choking and asphyxiation (Stiegler, 2005). Those with pica can also exhibit aggression and engage in dangerous behavior in attempts to seek out items to ingest or be at risk for injuries when others attempt to redirect them away from their preferred item. Due to the severe health risks to some people, they may also experience very restrictive and stigmatizing preventative strategies, such as helmets and fencing masks to prevent pica. Such management strategies may prevent the problem from occurring in the short term, but do not constitute treatment. Indeed, such preventative strategies may function as establishing operations in which the person is deprived of highly preferred items related to pica. This may lead to intense seeking of those items and increasing the reinforcing value of the pica items still further (Michael, 1993).

Researchers have reported several functional assessments and analyses of pica in children and adults with ASD. For example, Rapp et al. (2001) conducted a functional analysis and treatment of pica in a 6-year-old girl with autism. They used no-interaction, attention, demand, and control (play) conditions. The participant engaged in pica most often in the no-interaction and control (play) condition. Thus, Rapp et al. concluded that the behavior was maintained through automatic reinforcement. The second phase of the experiment was a preference assessment to determine which foods might compete with the reinforcement paired with pica and thus make treatment more effective. However, the function-based interventions, including non-contingent reinforcement, and less restrictive punishment procedures, including response blocking and verbal reprimands were all ineffective. Therefore, the authors implemented an intervention involving contingent, varied auditory stimulation in both the child's natural and clinical setting, which led to a suppression in pica. This study attests to the extreme difficulty and the limits to functional analytic technology in treating pica in some people.

Piazza et al. (1998) also conducted functional analysis of pica in three subjects, one of which was a 17-year-old girl with autism, ID, and Cornelia De Lange Syndrome and another of which was a 5-year-old boy diagnosed with autism, attention-deficit hyperactive disorder, moderate ID, and severe esophagitis. They found that pica was maintained through automatic reinforcement for one participants and social and automatic reinforcement for the second participants.

Next, the authors conducted preference and treatment analyses to determine stimuli that would compete with pica. They then implemented treatments addressing the socially motivated components of two of the participants' pica which led to a significant reduction in pica of both participants. The researchers considered treatment effective and emphasized the importance of functional analysis and the advantages of indirect analyses to determine sources of reinforcement for automatically reinforced behavior.

Piazza et al. (1996) conducted two functional analyses and treatment of cigarette pica in a 17-year-old man with severe mental retardation and autism. They observed that (a) pica was most frequent during the alone condition and (b) when the cigarettes contained nicotine rather than herbs. A choice assessment found that tobacco was more preferred than other parts of the cigarette. A second functional analysis that included alone, social attention, and toy play conditions indicated that cigarette pica was maintained independent of social consequences. Researchers then implemented a treatment that interrupted the supposed response–reinforcer relationship, which led to a reduction of consumed cigarettes to zero. Non-contingent access to preferred foods, without response blocking was ineffective at preventing pica, only the combined treatment of noncontingent food and response blocking was effective. However, because this procedure would be very difficult to implement in practice, the researchers developed a stimulus control procedure in which the effective treatment was repeatedly implemented in the presence of a purple card but not a yellow card for 180 10-minute training sessions conducted over 18 days. Subsequently, the presentation of the purple card alone reliably suppressed pica in a variety of community settings indicating that the purple card exerted stimulus control over pica. Treatment gains were maintained across community and home settings and blood levels of nicotine were consistent with no consumption of tobacco. The researchers suggested that such procedures may be effective in reducing other typically covert aberrant behaviors.

Several studies reviewed here have indicated that pica is a difficult problem to treat and hence have sometimes used punishment procedures. Kern et al. (2006) developed an interesting alternate approach. They were unable to identify the function of pica in two boys with developmental disabilities. Rather than use punishment, they taught the boys to hand over inedible items in exchange for preferred food items. This intervention was effective for one boy, while the second boy required further training.

PSYCHIATRIC DISORDERS AND CHALLENGING BEHAVIORS

Children and adults with ASD and CB are often diagnosed with additional psychiatric disorders, although Tsakanikos et al. (2006) did not find higher rates of psychiatric disorders in adults with autism compared to adults with ID.

However, Tsakanikos et al. (2006) did find higher rates of CB and higher rates of antipsychotic medication in adults with ASD than in a control sample of people with ID only. Externalizing CB predicted restricted practices such as prescription of antipsychotics and further involvement in psychiatric services. Reflecting these psychiatric diagnoses, the use of psychotropic medication is very prevalent (Tsakanikos et al., 2006), including in children and adolescents. Polypharmacy is also commonly reported in people with ASD (Aman et al., 2005).

Many challenging behaviors, such as SIB and aggression, are treated primarily with psychotropic medication. Sometimes this is done on the basis that the observed CB may be a symptom of an underlying psychiatric disorder that cannot be diagnosed in a person with ASD, for example, if they are nonverbal (Tsiouris et al., 2003). Audits of practice reveal worrying results. For example, Marshall (2004) surveyed the charts of 102 people with ID and found that practitioners failed to follow local practice consensus guidelines in *all* cases of people taking psychotropic medications. Further, in 96 percent of people who took psychotropic or antipsychotics medication, practitioners rarely defined the CB for which the medication was prescribed and rarely provided adequate monitoring of, and warnings about, the side effects associated with the medication.

There are now a growing number of randomized controlled trials (RCTs) of several psychotropic medications for CB, such as risperidone for aggression and irritability. Jesner et al. (2007) reported a Cochrane database review and only identified three adequate RCT's of risperidone with at least one standardized dependent variable. Although, they concluded that there was some evidence of effect on irritability, repetition, and social withdrawal. However, they were unclear if these benefits were worth the risks associated with weight gain and also noted the absence of long-term studies. Kolevzon et al. (2006) also conducted a systematic literature review on the sue of Serotonin Selective Reuptake Inhibitors (SSRIs), which are sometimes used to treat compulsive behaviors and stereotypies. They found only three RCTs which reported significant effects on ratings of global functioning. However, SSRIs also have negative side effects, such as increased activation and agitation in some participants. Thus, although very commonly used, the status of psychotropic medications for CB in people for ASD is unclear. For example, although these RCTs have demonstrated that the medication was superior to placebos, they did not necessarily demonstrate the clinical or educational significance of the change. Further, the emphasis on statistically significant change in group means hides important individual differences in response to medication, including perhaps negative responses. Further, the choice of medication over alternative treatments should reflect careful consideration of the overall costs and benefits of this approach, not merely the change in behavior. For example, when selecting risperidone or FCT and extinction for aggression, practitioners must weigh the short-and long-term benefits of each approach. Thus, Lerman et al. (1999) reported data on extinction bursts and aggression in 41 participants with self-injury. They found these negative side effects in 62 percent of applications of extinction alone, but in only

15 percent of extinction combined with differential reinforcement, noncontingent reinforcement or antecedent manipulations. However, risperidone carries the known short-term risk of sedation with the long-term risks of weight gain such as possible diabetes, and potentially life-threatening hyperglycemia and other as yet unknown risks when it is used on a long-term basis in developing children. Drug companies have often suppressed or minimized information in order to make larger profits, pay physicians directly and indirectly for the prescription of new psychotropic medications, and greatly influence the content of medical education, professional continuing education and state prescription guidelines. Hence, the knowledge we have of negative side effects of psychotropic medications may be incomplete.

CONCLUSIONS AND PRACTITIONER RECOMMENDATIONS

Children and adults with ASD are at much greater risk of showing a wide range of CB than typically developing people. Of most immediate concern are extra-personal maladaptive behaviors, such as aggression and tantrums, because of their negative and sometimes severe consequences for the person and those around them. Intra-personal maladaptive behaviors may also be significant as they may be stigmatizing and may interfere with learning and the expression of adaptive behavior.

The CB topographies can be readily assessed with screening questionnaires, but these questionnaires are limited in that they do not provide all the information necessary to design an effective intervention plan. Information regarding the EOs, discriminative stimuli, functionally equivalent adaptive and maladaptive behaviors, and contingencies maintaining the CB greatly improve the design of an effective treatment plan (Didden et al., 1997, 2006). Despite the efficacy of this approach to treatment of CB in people with ASD, certain problems, such as pica, remain more difficult to treat. Additionally, more research involving the dissemination of this technology to routine care providers and practitioners is needed (National Research Council, 2001).

REFERENCES

Ahearn, W.H., Castine, T., Nault, K., and Green, G. (2001). An assessment of food acceptance in children with autism or pervasive developmental disorder-not otherwise specified. *Journal of Autism and Developmental Disabilities*, **31**, 505–511.

Ali, Z. (2001). Pica in people with intellectual disability: A literature review of aetiology, epidemiology and complications. *Journal of Intellectual and Developmental Disability*, **26**, 205–215.

Aman, M.G. (1991). Review and evaluation of instruments for assessing emotional and behavioural disorders. *Journal of Intellectual and Developmental Disabilities*, **17**, 127–145.

Aman, M.G., De Smedt, G., Derivan, B., Lyons, B., and Findling, R.L. (2002). Double-blind, placebo controlled study of risperidone for treatment of disruptive behavior in children with subaverage intelligence. *American Journal of Psychiatry*, **159**, 1337–1346.

Aman, M.G., Lam, K.S., and van Bourgondien, M.E. (2005). Medication patterns in patients with autism: temporal regional and demographic influences. *Journal of Child and Adolescent Psychopharmacology*, **15**, 116–126.

American Association on Mental Retardation (2005). *Aversive procedures*. Downloaded on Sunday, May 13, 2007 from www.aamr.org/Policies/aversive.shtml

American Psychiatric Association. (1994). *Diagnostic and Statistical Manual of Mental Disorders*. 4th ed. Washington, DC: Author.

Applegate, H., Matson, J.L., and Cherry, K.E. (1999). An evaluation of functional variables affecting severe problem behavior in adults with mental retardation by using the Questions About Behavioral Function Scale (QABF). *Research in Developmental Disabilities*, **20**, 229–237.

Archer, L.A., Rosenbaum, P.L., and Streiner, D.L. (1991). The children's eating behavior inventory. *Journal of Pediatric Psychology*, **16**, 629–642.

Arndorfer, R.E. and Miltenberger, R.G. (1994). Home-based descriptive and experimental analysis of problem behaviors in children. *Topics in Early Childhood Special Education*, **14**, 64–87.

Baer, D.M., Wolf, M.M., and Risley, T.R. (1968). Some current dimensions of applied behavior analysis. *Journal of Applied Behavior Analysis*, **1**, 91–97.

Bijou, S.W., Peterson, R.F., and Ault, M.H. (1968). A method to integrate descriptive and experimental field studies at the level of data and empirical concepts. *Journal of Applied Behavior Analysis*, **1**, 175–191.

Bodfish, J.W., Symons, F.W., Parker, D.E., and Lewis, M.H. (2000). Varieties of repetitive behaviors in autism: Comparisons to mental retardation. *Journal of Autism and Developmental Disorders*, **30**, 237–243.

Boo, K. (1999). *Forest Haven is Gone, but the Agony Remains*. Washington Post, Sunday March 14, 1999. Downloaded Sunday, May 13, 2007 from www.washingtonpost.com/wp-srv/local./daily/march99/grouphome14.htm.

Brown, J.L. and Poulson, C.L. (in press). Speech prosody intervention in Autism. In *Applied Behavior Analysis and Language Acquisition in People with Autism Spectrum Disorders*. (A. Fitzer and P. Sturmey, eds. In press) Austin: PROED Inc.

Campbell, J.M. (2003). Efficacy of behavioral interventions for reducing problem behavior in persons with autism. A quantitative synthesis of single-subject research. *Research in Developmental Disabilities*, **24**, 120–138.

Campbell, M., Locascio, J., Choroco, M.C., Spencer, E.K., Malone, R.P., and Kafantaris, V. (1990). Stereotypies and tardive dyskinesia: Abnormal movements in autistic children. *Psychopharmacology Bulletin*, **26**, 260–266.

Carr, E.G. (1977). The motivation of self-injurious behavior. A review of some hypotheses. *Psychological Bulletin*, **84**, 800–816.

Carr, E.G. and Durand, V.M. (1985). Reducing problem behavior through functional communication training. *Journal of Applied Behavior Analysis*, **18**, 111–126.

Carr, E.G., Newsom, C.D., and Binkoff, J.A. (1980). Escape as a factor in the aggressive behavior of two retarded children. *Journal of Applied Behavior Analysis*, **13**, 101–117.

Charlop, M.H. (1992). Echolalia. In *Manual for the Assessment and Treatment of the Behavior Disorders of People with Mental Retardation* (E.A. Konarski, J.E., Favell, and J.E. Favell, eds.) (Tab BD10, pp. 1–13). Morganton, NC: Western Carolina Center Foundation.

Charlop, M.H. (1986). Setting effects on the occurrence of autistic children's immediate echolalia. *Journal of Autism and Developmental Disorders*, **16**, 473–483.

Charlot, L. (2005). Use of behavioral equivalents for symptoms of mood disorders. In *Mood Disorders in People with Mental Retardation* (P. Sturmey, ed.) pp. 17–46. Kingston, NY: NADD Press.

Cunningham, J., McDonald, A., Easton, S., and Sturmey, P. (2003). Social validation data on three methods of physical restraint: Views of consumers, staff and students. *Research in Developmental Disabilities*, **24**, 307–316.

Dawson, J.E., Matson, J.L., and Cherry, K.E. (1998). An analysis of maladaptive behaviors in persons with autism, PDD-NOS, and mental retardation. *Research in Developmental Disabilities*, **19**, 439–448.

Derby, K.M., Wacker, D.P., Sasso, G., et al. (1992). Brief functional assessments techniques to evaluate aberrant behavior in an outpatient setting: A summary of 79 cases. *Journal of Applied Behavior Analysis*, **25**, 713–721.

Desrochers, M.N., Hile, M.G., and Williams-Moseley, T.L. (1997). Survey of functional assessment procedures used with individuals who display mental retardation and severe problem behaviors. *American Journal on Mental Retardation*, **101**, 535–566.

Deutsch, A. (1946). *The Mentally Ill in America*. New York: Columbia University Press.

Didden, R., Duker, P., and Korzilius, H. (1997). Meta-analytic study on treatment effectiveness for problem behaviors for individuals who have mental retardation. *American Journal on Mental Retardation*, **101**, 387–399.

Didden, R., Korzilius, H., van Oorsouw, W., and Sturmey, P. (2006). Behavioural treatment of challenging behaviors in individuals with mild mental retardation: Meta-analysis of single subject research. *American Journal on Mental Retardation*, **111**, 290–298.

Dudley, L.L., Johnson, C., and Barnes, R.S. (2002). Decreasing rumination using a starchy food satiation procedure. *Behavioral Interventions*, **17**, 21–29.

Dunlap, G., Robbins, F.R., and Darrow, M.A. (1994). Parents' reports of their children's challenging behaviors: Results of a statewide survey. *Mental Retardation*, **32**, 206–212.

Edgerton, R.D. (1967). The cloak of competence. Los Angeles, CA: University of California Press.

Emerson, E. (2002). The prevalence of reactive management strategies in community-based services in the UK. In. *Ethical Approaches to Physical Interventions. Responding to Challenging Behaviour in People with Intellectual Disabilities* (D. Allen, ed.) pp. 15–30. Plymouth, UK: BILD Publications.

Emerson, E. (2005). *Challenging Behaviour: Analysis and Intervention with People with Learning Difficulties*. Cambridge: Cambridge University Press.

Feldman, M.A., Atkinson, L., Foti-Gervais, L., and Condillac, R. (2004). Formal versus informal interventions for challenging behaviours in persons with intellectual disabilities. *Journal of Intellectual Disabilities Research*, **48**, 60–68.

Fisher, W.W., Lindauer, S.E., Alterson, C.J., and Thompson, R.H. (1998). Assessment and treatment of destructive behavior maintained by stereotypic object manipulation. *Journal of Applied Behavior Analysis*, **31**, 513–527.

Fitzer, A. and Sturmey, P. (in press). *Applied Behavior Analysis and Language Acquisition in People with Autism Spectrum Disorders*. Austin, TX: PROED Inc.

Freeman, K.A., Walker, M., and Kaufman, J. (2007). Psychometric properties of the questions about behavioral function scale in a child sample. *American Journal on Mental Retardation*, **112**, 122–129.

Gadow, K.D., DeVincent, C.J., Pomeroy, J., and Azizian, A. (2004). Psychiatric symptoms in preschool children with PDD and clinic and other comparisons. *Journal of Autism and Developmental Disabilities*, **34**, 379–393.

General Accounting Office (1999). *Improper Restraint or Seclusion use Places People at risk*. Washington DC: General Accounting Office.

Hagopian, L.P., Wilson, D.M., and Wilder, D.A. (2001). Assessment and treatment of problem behavior maintained by escape from attention and access to tangible items. *Journal of Applied Behavior Analysis*, **34**, 229–232.

Hanley, G.P., Iwata, B.A., Thompson, R.H., and Lindberg, J.S. (2000). A component analysis of "stereotypy as reinforcement" for alternative behavior. *Journal of Applied Behavior Analysis*, **33**, 285–297.

Harding, J.W., Wacker, D.P. Berg, W.K., et al. (2001). Analysis of response class hierarchies with attention-maintained problem behaviors. *Journal of Applied Behavior Analysis*, **34**, 61–64.

Haynes, S.N. and O'Brien, W. (1990). The functional analysis in behavior therapy. *Psychological Assessment*, **7**, 238–247.

Healthcare Commission (2006). *Joint Investigation into the Provision of Services for People with Learning Disabilities in Cornwall Partnership NHS Trust*. London, UK: Commission for Healthcare Audit and Inspection.

Heering, P.W., Wilder, D.A., and Ladd, C. (2003). Liquid rescheduling for the treatment of rumination. *Behavioral Interventions*, **18**, 199–207.

Hoch, H., Paone, D., and El-Roy, D. (2000). Escape behavior during academic task: A preliminary analysis of idiosyncratic establishing operations. *Journal of Applied Behavior Analysis*, **33**, 479–493.

Hove, O. (2007). Survey on dysfunctional eating behavior in adult person with intellectual disabilities. *Research in Developmental Disabilities*, **28**, 1–8.

Hurley, A.D. (1996). The misdiagnosis of hallucinations and delusion in adults with mental retardation: A neurodevelopmental perspective. Seminars in Neuropsychology, **1**, 122–133.

Iwata, B. (1987). Negative reinforcement in applied behavior analysis: An emerging technology. *Journal of Applied Behavior Analysis*, **20**, 361–378.

Iwata, B.A., Dorsey, M.F., Slifer, K.J., et al. (1994). Toward a functional analysis of self-injury. *Journal of Applied Behavior Analysis*, **27**, 197–209. (Reprinted from *Analysis and Intervention in Developmental Disabilities*, **2**, 3–20, 1982).

Jacobson, J.W., Foxx, R.M., and Mulick, J.A. (2005). *Controversial Therapies for Developmental Disabilities. Fad, Fashion, and Science in Professional Practice*. Mawah, NJ: Lawrence Erlbaum.

Jesner, O.S., Aref-Adib, M., and Coren, E. (2007). Risperidone for autism spectrum disorder. *Cochrane Database Systematic Review*, **24**, CD005040.

Johnston, J.M. and Greene, K.S. (1992). Relation between ruminating and quantity of food consumed. *Mental Retardation*, **30**, 7–11.

Jung-Chang, T., Kennedy, C.H., Koppekin, A., and Caruso, M. (2002). Functional analysis of stereotypical ear covering in a child with autism. *Journal of Applied Behavior Analysis*, **25**, 95–98.

Kennedy, C.H., Meyer, K.A., Knowles, T., and Shukla, S. (2000). Analyzing the multiple functions of stereotypical behavior of students with autism: Implications for assessment and treatment. *Journal of Applied Behavior Analysis*, **33**, 339–571.

Kern, L., Starosta, K., and Adelman, B.E. (2006). Reducing pica by teaching children to exchange inedible items for edibles. *Behavior Modification*, **30**, 135–158.

Kolevzon, A., Matherson, K.A., and Hollander, E. (2006). Selective serotonin reuptake inhibitors in autism: A review of efficacy and tolerability. *Journal of Clinical Psychiatry*, **67**, 407–414.

Labelle, C.A. and Charlop-Christy, M.H. (2002). Individualizing functional analysis to assess multiple and changing functions of severe behavior problems in children with autism. *Journal of Positive Behavioral Support*, **4**, 231–241.

LaGrow, S.J. and Repp, A.C. (1984). Stereotypic responding: A review of intervention research. *American Journal of Mental Deficiency*, **88**, 595–609.

Lalli, J.S., Mace, F.C., Wohn, T., and Livezy, K. (1995). Identification and modification of a response-class hierarchy. *Journal of Applied Behavior Analysis*, **28**, 551–559.

Layng, T.V., Andronis, P.T., and Goldiamond, I. (1999). Animal models of psychopathology: The establishment, maintenance, attenuation, and persistence of head-banging in pigeons. *Journal of the Experimental Analysis of Behavior*, **30**, 45–61.

Learning Disabilities Care Slammed (2007). Downloaded Sunday, May 13, 2007 http://news.bbc,co, uk/2/hi/health/6266923.stm.

Lecavalier, L. (2006). Behavioral and emotional problems in young people with pervasive developmental disorders: Relative prevalence, effects of subject characteristics, and empirical classification. *Journal of Autism and Developmental Disabilities*, **36**, 1101–1114.

Lerman, D.C. and Iwata, B.A. (1993). Descriptive and experimental analysis of variables maintaining self-injurious behavior. *Journal of Applied Behavior Analysis*, **26**, 293–319.

Lerman, D.C., Iwata, B.A., and Wallace, M.D. (1999). Side effects of extinction: Prevalence of bursting and aggression during the treatment of self-injurious behavior. *Journal of Applied Behavior Analysis*, **32**, 1–8.

Mancina, C., Tankersley, M., Kamps, D., et al. (2000). Brief report: Reduction of inappropriate vocalizations for a child with autism using a self-management treatment program. *Journal of Autism and Developmental Disorders*, **30**, 599–606.

Marshall, T. (2004). Audit of the use of psychotropic medication for challenging behaviour in a community learning disability service. *British Journal of Psychiatry*, **28**, 447–450.

Matson, J.L. (1981). A controlled outcome study of phobias in mentally retarded adults. *Behaviour, Research and Therapy*, **19**, 101–107.

Matson, J.L., Bamburg, J.W., Cherry, K.E., and Paclawskyj, T.R. (1999). A validity study on the Questions About Behavioral Function (QABF) Scale: Predicting treatment success for self-injury aggression and stereotypies. *Research in Developmental Disabilities*, **20**, 163–175.

Matson, J.L. and Boisjoli, J.A. (2007). Multiple versus single maintaining factors of challenging behaviors as assessed by the QABF for adults with intellectual disabilities. *Journal of Intellectual and Disabilities*, **32**, 39–44.

Matson, J.L. and Kuhn, D.E. (2001). Identifying feeding problems in mentally retarded persons: developing and reliability of the Screening Tool of Feeding Problems (STEP). *Research in Developmental Disabilities*, **22**, 165–172.

Matson, J.L., Mayville, S.B., Kuhn, D.E., et al. (2005). The behavioral function of feeding problems as assessed by the Questions About Behavior Functions (QABF). *Research in Developmental Disabilities*, **26**, 399–408.

Matson, J.L. and Vollmer, T.R. (1995). *User's Guide. Questions About Behavioral Function* (QABF). Baton Rouge: Scientific Publishers.

McClintock, K., Hall, S., and Oliver, C. (2003). Risk markers associated with challenging behaviours in people with intellectual disabilities: A meta-analysis study. *Journal of Intellectual Disabilities Research*, **47**, 405–416.

McDonnell, A.J., Dearden, R., and Sturmey, P. (1993). The acceptability of physical restraint procedures for people with learning disabilities. *Behavioural and Cognitive Psychotherapy*, **21**, 255–264.

McDonnell, A. and Sturmey, P. (2000). The social validation of physical restraint procedures with people with developmental disabilities: A comparison of young people and professional groups. *Research in Developmental Disabilities*, **21**, 85–92.

Michael, J. (1993). Establishing operations. *The Behavior Analyst*, **16**, 191–206.

Miltenberger, R.G. (2003). *Behavior Modification. Principles and Procedures.* Third edition. Belmont, CA: Wadsworth.

Miltenberger, R.G. and Fuqua, R.W. (1985). Evaluation of a training manual for the acquisition of behavioral assessment interviewing skills. *Journal of Applied Behavior Analysis*, **18**, 323–328.

Miltenberger R.G. and Veltum, L.G. (1988). Evaluation of an instructions and modeling procedure for training behavioral assessment interviewing. *Journal of Behavior Therapy and Experimental Psychiatry*, **19**, 31–41.

Mudford, O.C., Ford, E., and Arnold-Saritepe A.M. (in press). Efficacy of interventions to promote language. In *Applied Behavior Analysis and Language Acquisition in People with Autism Spectrum Disorders*. (A. Fitzer and P. Sturmey, eds.) Austin, TX: PROED Inc.

Najdowski, A.C., Wallace, M.D., Doney, J.K., and Ghezzi, P.M. (2003). Parental assessment and treatment of food selectivity in natural settings. *Journal of Applied Behavior Analysis*, **36**, 383–386.

National Research Council (2001). *Educating Children with Autism*. Washington DC: National Academies Press.

Nicholson, J., Konstantinidi, E., and Furniss, F. (2006). On some psychometric properties of the Questions About behavior Function (QABF) scale. *Research in Developmental Disabilities*, **27**, 337–352.

Paclawskyj, T.R., Matson, J.L., Rush, K.S., et al. (2001). Assessment of the convergent validity of the Questions About Behavioral Function scale with analog functional analysis and the Motivational Assessment Scale. *Journal of Intellectual Disabilities Research*, **45**, 484–494.

Palmer, S., Thompson, R.J., and Linscheid, T.R. (1975). Applied behavior analysis in the treatment of childhood feeding problems. *Developmental Medicine and Child Neurology*, **17**, 333–339.

Piazza, C.C. and Addison, L.R. (2007). Function-based assessment and treatment of pediatric feeding disorders. In *Functional Analysis in Clinical Treatment* (P. Sturmey, ed.) pp. 129–150. New York: Academic Press.

Piazza, C.C., Fisher, W.W., Hanley, G.P., et al. (1998). Treatment of pica through multiple analyses of its reinforcing functions. *Journal of Applied Behavior Analysis*, **31**, 165–189.

Piazza, C.C., Hanley, H.P., and Fisher, W.W. (1996). Functional analysis and treatment of cigarette pica. *Journal of Applied Behavior Analysis*, **29**, 437–450.

Poulson C.L. (in press). Behavioral theory and language acquisition. In *Applied Behavior Analysis and Language Acquisition in People with Autism Spectrum Disorders* (A. Fitzer and P. Sturmey, eds.) Austin: PROED Inc.

Ramm, S. (1990). The use of the duvet (quilt) for the treatment of autistic, violent behaviors (an experiential account). *Journal of Autism and Developmental Disorders*, **20**, 279–280.

Rapp, J.T., Dozier, C.L., and Carr, J.E. (2001). Functional assessment and treatment of pica: A single-case experiment. *Behavioral Interventions*, **16**, 111–125.

Rast, J., Johnston J.M., and Drum, C. (1984). A parametric analysis of the relationship between food quantity and rumination. *Journal of the Experimental Analysis of Behavior*, **41**, 125–134.

Rast, J., Johnston J.M. Drum, C., and Conrin, J. (1981). The relation of food quantity to rumination behavior. *Journal of Applied Behavior Analysis*, **14**, 121–130.

Rehfeldt, R.A. and Chambers, M.R. (2003). Functional analysis and treatment of verbal perseverations displayed by an adult with autism. *Journal of Applied Behavior Analysis*, **36**, 259–261.

Repp, A.C. and Karsh, K.G. (1992). Stereotypy. In *Manual for the assessment and treatment of the behavior disorders of people with mental retardation* (E.A. Konarski, J.E. Favell and J.E. Favell, eds.) Tab BD2, pp. 1–14. Morganton, NC: Western Carolina Center Foundation.

Richman, D.M., Wacker, D.P., Asmus, J.M., et al. (1999). Further analysis of problem behavior in response class hierarchies. *Journal of Applied Behavior Analysis*, **32**, 269–283.

Rojahn, J., Aman, M.G., Matson, J.L., and Mayville, E. (2003). The Aberrant behavior checklist and the behavior problems inventory: Convergent and divergent validity. *Research in Developmental Disabilities*, **24**, 391–404.

Rojahn, J., Matson, J.L., Lott, D., et al. (2001). The Behavior Problem Inventory: An instrument for the assessment of self-injury, stereotyped behavior, and aggression/destructive in individuals with developmental disabilities. *Journal of Autism and Developmental Disabilities*, **31**, 577–588.

Rydell, P.J. and Mirenda, P. (1994). Effects of high and low constraint utterances on the production of immediate and delayed echolalia in young children with autism. *Journal of Autism and Developmental Disorders*, **24**, 719–735.

Sasso, G.M., Reimers, T.M., Cooper, L.J., et al. (1992). Use of descriptive and experimental analysis to identify the functional properties of abberant behavior in school settings. *Journal of Applied Behavior Analysis*, **25**, 809–821.

Schaefer, H.H. (1970). Self-injurious behavior: Shaping head-banging in monkeys. *Journal of Applied Behavior Analysis*, **3**, 111–116.

Schreck, K.A. and Williams, K. (2005). Food preferences and factors influencing food selectivity for children with autism spectrum disorders. *Research in Developmental Disabilities*, **27**, 353–363.

Schreck, K.A., Williams, K., and Smith, A.F. (2004). A comparison of eating behaviors between children with and without autism. *Journal of Autism and Developmental Disorders*, **34**, 433–438.

Schreibman, L. and Charlop, M.H. (1987). Autism. In *Psychological Evaluation of the Developmentally and Physically Disabled* (V.B. Van Hasselt and M. Hersen, eds.) pp. 155–177. New York: Plenum Press.

Shogren, K.A. and Rojahn, J. (2003). Convergent reliability and validity of the Questions About Behavioral Function and Motivation Assessment Scale: A replication study. *Journal of Developmental and Physical Disabilities*, **15**, 367–375.

Sidener, T.M., Carr, J.E., and Firth, A.M. (2005). Superimposition and withholding of edible consequences as treatment for automatically reinforced stereotypy. *Journal of Applied Behavior Analysis*, **38**, 121–124.

Sigafoos, J. and Tucker, M. (2000). Brief assessment and treatment of multiple challenging behaviors. *Behavioral Intervention*, **15**, 53–70.

Skinner, B.F. (1953). *Science and Human Behavior*. New York: Macmillan.

Smith, T. (1996). Are other treatments effective? In *Behavioral Intervention of Children with Autism. A Manual for Parents and Professionals* (C. Maurice, C.G., Green, and S.C. Luce, eds.) pp. 45–62. Austin, TX: PROED Inc.

Smith, R.G. and Churchill, R.M. (2002). Identification of environmental determinants of behavior disorders through functional analysis of precursor behaviors. *Journal of Applied Behavior Analysis*, **35**, 125–136.

Smith, T., McAdam, D., and Napolitano, D. (2007). Autism and applied behavior analysis. In *Autism Spectrum Disorders. Applied behavior analysis, evidence and practice* (P. Sturmey and A. Fitzer, eds.) pp. 1–30. Austin, TX: PROED Inc.

Smith, R.G., Vollmer, T.R., and St. Peter Pipkin. C. (2007). Functional approaches to assessment and treatment of problem behavior in persons with autism and related disabilities. In *Autism Spectrum Disorders* (P. Sturmey and A. Fitzer, eds.) pp. 187–234. Austin, Texas: Pro-ed.

Sourander, A., Ellilam, H., Valimaki, M.,and Piha, J. (2002). Use of holding, restraints, seclusion and time-out in child and adolescent psychiatric in-patient treatment. *European Child and Adolescent Psychiatry*, **11**, 162–167.

Sovner, R. (1986). Limiting factors in the use of DSM-II with mentally ill/mentally retarded persons. *Psychopharmacology Bulletin*, **22**, 1055–1059.

Stiegler, L.N. (2005). Understanding pica behavior: A review for clinical and education professionals. *Focus on Autism and Other Developmental Disabilities*, **20**, 27–38.

Sturmey, P. (1999). Correlates of restraint use in an institutional population. *Research in Developmental Disabilities*, **20**, 339–346.

Sturmey, P. (2005a). Treatment of mood disorders in people with mental retardation: A selective review. *NADD Bulletin*, **8**, 33–38.

Sturmey, P. (2005b). Behavioral conceptualization and treatment of depression in people with mental retardation. In *Mood Disorders in People with Mental Retardation* (P. Sturmey, ed.) pp. 293–315. Kingston: NADD Press.

Sturmey, P. (2005c). Against psychotherapy with people with mental retardation. *Mental Retardation*, **43**, 55–57.

Sturmey, P. (2006a). Against psychotherapy with people who have mental retardation: In response to the responses. *Mental Retardation*, **44**, 71–74.

Sturmey, P. (2006b). On some recent claims for the efficacy of cognitive therapy for people with intellectual disabilities. *Journal of Applied Research in Intellectual Disabilities*, **19**, 109–118.

Sturmey, P. (2006c). In response to Lindsay and Emerson. *Journal of Applied Research in Intellectual Disabilities*, **19**, 125–129.

Sturmey, P. (2007a). *Functional analysis in clinical treatment*. New York: Academic Press.

Sturmey, P. (2007b). Diagnosis of mental disorders in people with intellectual disabilities. In *Psychiatric and Behavioral Disorders in Intellectual and Developmental Disabilities*. 2nd ed. (N. Bouras and G. Holt, eds.) pp. 3–24. Cambridge: Cambridge University Press.

Sturmey, P., Fink, C., and Sevin, J.A. (1993). The behavior problem inventory: A replication and extension of its psychometric properties. *Journal of Developmental and Physical Disabilities*, **5**, 327–336.

Sturmey, P. and Fitzer, A. (eds.) (2007). *Autism Spectrum Disorders. Applied Behavior Analysis, Evidence and Practice*. Austin TX: PROED Inc.

Sturmey, P., Lott, J.D., Laud, R., and Matson, J.L. (2005). Correlates of restraint use in an institutional population: A replication. *Journal of Intellectual Disabilities Research*, **49**, 501–506.

Sturmey, P. and McGlynn, A.P. (2002). Restraint reduction. In *Responding to Challenging Behaviour in Persons with Intellectual Disabilities: Ethical Approaches to Physical Intervention*. (D. Allen, ed.) pp. 203–218. Kidderminster: BILD.

Sturmey, P., Reed, J., and Corbett, J. (1991). Assessment of psychiatric disorders in people with learning difficulties: A psychometric review of available measures. *Psychological Medicine*, **21**, 143–155.

Sturmey, P., Sevin, J., and Williams, D.E. (1995). The Behavior Problem Inventory: A further replication of its factor structure. *Journal of Intellectual Disabilities Research*, **39**, 353–356.

Thompson, R.H., Fisher, W.W., Piazza, C.C., and Kuhn, D.E. (1998). The evaluation and treatment of aggression maintained by attention and automatic reinforcement. *Journal of Applied Behavior Analysis*, **31**, 103–116.

Touchette, P.E., MacDonald, R.F., and Langer, S.N. (1985). A scatter plot for identifying stimulus control of problem behavior. *Journal of Applied Behavior Analysis*, **18**, 343–351.

Travis, R. and Sturmey, P. (in review). *A Review of Behavioral Interventions for Psychotic Verbal Behavior in People with Intellectual Disabilities.*

Tsakanikos, E., Costello, H., Holt, G., et al. (2006.) Psychopathology in adults with autism and intellectual disabilities. *Journal of Autism and Developmental Disorders*, **36**, 1123–1129.

Tsakanikos, E., Costello, H., Holt, G., et al. (2007). Behaviour management problems as predictors of psychotropic medication and use of psychiatric services in adults with autism. *Journal of Autism and Developmental Disorders*, **35**, 1080–1085.

Tsiouris, J.A., Cohen, I.L., Patti, P.J., and Korosh, W.M. (2003). Treatment of previously undiagnosed psychiatric disorders in persons with developmental disabilities decreased or eliminated self-injurious behavior. *Journal of Clinical Psychiatry*, **4**, 1081–1090.

Tsiouris, J.A., Mann, R., Patti, P.J., and Sturmey, P. (2003). Challenging behaviours should not be considered a depressive equivalents in individuals with intellectual disability. *Journal of Intellectual Disability Research*, **47**, 14–21.

Violette, J. and Swisher, L. (1992). Echolalic responses by a child with autism to four experimental conditions of sociolinguistic input. *Journal of Speech and Hearing Research*, **35**, 139–147.

Wong, S.E., Floyd, J., Innocent, A.J., and Woolsey, J.E. (1991). Applying a DRO schedule and compliance training to reduce aggressive and self-injurious behavior in an autistic man: A case report. *Journal of Behavior Therapy and Experimental Psychiatry*, **22**, 299–304.

6

COMMUNICATION AND SOCIAL SKILLS ASSESSMENT

JEFF SIGAFOOS[1], RALF W. SCHLOSSER[2],
VANESSA A. GREEN[3], MARK O'REILLY[4],
AND GIULIO E. LANCIONI[5]

[1]*Victoria University of Wellington, New Zealand*
[2]*Northeastern University, Boston, MA, USA*
[3]*University of Tasmania, Hobart, Tasmania, Australia*
[4]*University of Texas at Austin, Austin, TX, USA*
[5]*University of Bari, Bari, Italy*

INTRODUCTION

In 1943, Kanner described 11 children with developmental and behavioral characteristics so aberrant and novel that they appeared to represent the first known cases of a new [autistic] syndrome. Kanner's assessment of these children involved clinical observation and compilation of detailed case histories. Systematic assessment protocols were not available to Kanner, but his case study approach was sufficient to reveal a cluster of unique developmental and behavioral characteristics. Among the more extreme of these characteristics were: (a) the presence of stereotyped behaviors, (b) frequent and prolonged tantrums, (c) an obsessive insistence on the maintenance of sameness, and (d) significant communication and social skills deficits.

Subsequent reports of infants, children, adolescents, and adults diagnosed with autism confirmed the presence of significant communication and social skills deficits. From the emerging evidence, Rutter (1970, 1978) identified a triad of symptoms that appeared unique to autism: (a) qualitative impairment in the ability to relate socially to others, (b) significant deficits in speech, language, and communication development, and (c) aberrant and ritualistic behaviors, such as extreme tantrums, repetitive/stereotyped movements, and an obsessive insistence on sameness. Ritvo and Freeman (1978) identified a fourth characteristic – unusual responses to sensory stimuli – that is also commonly seen in individuals diagnosed with autism. For example, some individuals may seem deaf and fail to attend to auditory stimuli at one time, but exhibit an extreme reaction to low-level noise at other times.

Today the syndrome first described by Kanner (1943) falls within a wider spectrum of pervasive developmental disorders characterized by qualitative impairment in the ability to relate socially to others and significant speech, language, and communication deficits (American Psychiatric Association, 2000). Within this larger class of pervasive developmental disorders is the classic form of autism described by Kanner, as well as Rett's disorder, Childhood Degenerative Disorder, and a seemingly less severe variant known as Asperger's syndrome (American Psychiatric Association, 2000). There is also increasing recognition of a group of children who present with significant problems of social interaction and communication impairment, yet fail to meet all of the diagnostic criteria for one of the pervasive developmental disorders (Hartman et al., 2006). These children often receive a diagnosis of pervasive developmental disorder not otherwise specified. For the purpose of this chapter, all of these types of developmental disabilities can be viewed as falling within the broader category of autism spectrum disorders (ASD).

The characteristic impairments in communication and social skills, so well described by Kanner (1943), retain prominence in contemporary descriptions and definitions of ASD (Akshoomoff, 2006; Osterling et al., 2001). Indeed, the triad of social, communication, and ritualistic behavior, represent core features of ASD (Sturmey and Sevin, 1994). Comprehensive assessment of communication and social skills should therefore be a core component in services for individuals with ASD.

In addition to representing core features of these conditions, deficits in communication and social skills may hold special significance for understanding the nature of ASD and developing more effective treatments. Matson and Wilkins (2007) reviewed literature on the importance of social skill deficits in ASD and noted that social behaviors may represent core deficits or "behavioral cusps" that could significantly impact other areas of adaptive behavior functioning. In a similar argument, Koegel and Koegel (2006) conceptualized communication and social skills as pivotal responses or key behaviors that, once improved, might positively impact adaptive behavior functioning more widely. Assessment of communication and social skills would therefore seem critical if clinicians are to accurately identify the core deficits, key behaviors, or pivotal responses for treatment (Matson and Wilkins, 2007).

Given the prominence of communication and social skills deficits in the description and diagnosis of ASD, comprehensive assessment of communication and social skills is important to ensure accurate diagnoses in young children who first present with symptoms of ASD. Initial screening and follow-up diagnostic assessments will often need to be supplemented in the preschool years to differentiate and classify the severity of the child's condition (e.g., autism versus Asperger's syndrome). This is necessary because ASD is not a homogeneous condition. There is a range in both the severity and qualitative nature of the impairments found within the autism spectrum (Osterling et al., 2001). In terms of variability of communication development, for example, some individuals with ASD may fail to develop any appreciable amount of speech, whereas others may develop quite complex, yet rather odd, speech patterns. Some individuals might, for instance, embark on lengthy monologues on highly specialized topics, such as telling anyone who will listen the intricate details about vacuum cleaners. In terms of variability of social skills, some individuals may fail to attend to the presence of others or act as if they are deaf or blind. Others may eagerly seek out interactions, but then engage in socially unacceptable responses, such as attempting to remove the person's belt or touch the person's shoes. This variability highlights the need for comprehensive assessment of the individual's communication and social skills.

In addition to diagnosis and classification, assessment of communication development and social functioning is also important in facilitating research into both the causes and treatment of ASD. And, as mentioned before, assessing these two domains is necessary for developing effective systems of support for individuals with ASD and their families. Because symptoms and service needs can change over time, it is crucial that assessment occurs at regular intervals throughout the lifespan.

In this chapter, we review the major issues and contemporary approaches to the assessment of communication and social skills for individuals with ASD within a lifespan/developmental perspective. Assessment issues are often similar across the lifespan, but some assessment purposes (e.g., screening, diagnosis) are likely to be more of a priority in infancy and preschool than in adolescence or adulthood. Consideration is given to purposes of assessment and the most relevant communication and social skills to assess at each major life stage. To this end, we include a review of contemporary practices for assessing communication and social skills in individuals with ASD.

This chapter covers basic concepts and procedures that underlie effective assessment of communication and social skills. Specifically, it is important to consider issues related to the definition, conceptualization, and classification of communication and social skills. It is also important to consider the various purposes of communication and social skills assessment and the range of procedures that can be used in an attempt to achieve each specific purpose. Reliability and validity must also be considered in determining which of several procedures, tactics, or assessment tools should be used at each life stage and for the varying assessment purposes.

Exploration of definitional, conceptual, and classification issues is intended to clarify the nature of the communication and social skills deficits and excesses associated with ASD and delineate the range of communication and social skills that are important to assess in individuals with these disorders. This, in turn, should enable professionals to target their assessment activities to relevant skills for each developmental stage. Consideration of various assessment procedures and issues of reliability and validity should facilitate the selection of appropriate assessment tactics and appropriate use of assessment data for its various intended purposes (e.g., screening, diagnosis, treatment evaluation).

DEFINING COMMUNICATION AND SOCIAL SKILLS

There is no single definition of communication or social skills that would be suitable for all purposes. Indeed numerous definitions of these skills have been proposed and refined in response to advances in the assessment of communication impairments and social skill deficits in individuals with ASD (Landa, 2005). Current definitions of communication and social skills range from fairly broad statements of what constitutes communication or social competence to more fine-grained molecular definitions that delineate specific communication and social skills.

MOLAR DEFINITIONS OF COMMUNICATION AND SOCIAL COMPETENCE

At the broad molar level, communication is often defined as the sharing of information using speech, gestures, or other recognizable signs or symbols (Losee, 1999). Consistent with this broad definition, The National Joint Committee for the Communication Needs of Persons with Severe Disabilities defined communication as:

> Any act by which one person gives to or receives from another person information about that person's needs, desires, perceptions, knowledge or affective states. Communication may be intentional or unintentional, may involve conventional or unconventional signals, may take linguistic or nonlinguistic forms, and may occur through spoken or other modes (1992, p. 2).

As illustrated by this definition, communicative competence is dependent to some extent on establishing shared meanings or understandings between speaker and listener. Communication can occur in the absence of speech, which is an important point to emphasize given that approximately 25–33 percent of individuals diagnosed with ASD fail to develop any appreciable amount of speech (Cohen and Volkmar, 1997; Osterling et al., 2001). Communication assessments must therefore include strategies to document nonspeech modes of communication, such as the use of gestures or picture-based communication systems. Assessment of speech and nonspeech modes of communication would in both cases aim to determine deficits in the ability to share information about needs, desires, perceptions, knowledge, and affective states. The extent to which an individual can share this type of information with others in age-appropriate ways represents an important type of assessment data.

It is also important to recognize that what is considered communicatively appropriate and effective is likely to change across the lifespan, hence the need for conducting assessments at regular intervals throughout the lifespan. Leading a person's hand to an object – to indicate a desire for that object – might be tolerated in an infant or preschooler, but not in an adolescent or adult. The same analysis applies to social skills in that the acceptability and effectiveness of specific social responses is also likely to vary across the lifespan.

Molar approaches to defining social skills often focus on the ability to engage successfully in appropriate social interactions that lead to important social outcomes. Social skills, broadly defined, refer in part to a person's ability to get along with others and engage in prosocial behavior (Matson and Ollendick, 1988). Gresham (1986, 2001) defined social skills as behaviors that occur within a given situation and which predict important social outcomes for the individual. Definitions of this type imply that the individual's social competence is assessed by the extent to which they are successful in using appropriate behaviors to engage socially with others across a range of contexts and social partners.

A person is perceived to be socially competent if he or she is able to interact socially with others in ways that are not only effective, but are also likely to be adaptable to multiple social situations (Kennedy, 2004). The socially competent individual should find it relatively easy to vary his or her style of interaction in relation to changing environmental contexts and in response to the feedback received from his/her social partners. Being flexible and adapting to contexts and the responses of social partners is likely to facilitate successful social engagement.

As mentioned before, and as is the case with communication skills, the types of social skills that are perceived as appropriate during one life stage (e.g., infancy or preschool) may become socially unacceptable at later stages (e.g., adolescence or adulthood). An infant may show social recognition of a familiar adult by bouncing up and down and flapping its arms and hands in an excited manner. An adult, in contrast, might be expected to approach, say hello, and shake hands.

Assessment of communication and social competencies based on molar definitions may yield useful information about the general nature of functioning in these two domains, but is perhaps less likely to identify specific skills for treatment (Matson and Wilkins, 2007). In line with a more molar definition of communication, for example, assessment might focus on how well the person can share information or the extent to which the individual is judged to be socially competent. Such information can be useful for gaining a better understanding of overall communication and social functioning. For intervention purposes, however, the assessment process must at some point identify specific skills that are either present or absent from the person's repertoire, appropriate or inappropriate, and effective or ineffective. To this end, molar definitions will probably need to be supplemented with more fine-grained or molecular definitions of communication and social skills.

MOLECULAR DEFINITIONS OF COMMUNICATION AND SOCIAL SKILLS

Molecular definitions of communication and social skills focus on specific responses that exemplify communicative and social competence. This approach essentially involves definition by example. The examples, in this context, are specific, concrete behaviors that can be observed and measured. Saying hello when a familiar person is encountered at work, looking at the person who is talking to you, requesting help from the teacher when presented with a difficult academic task, or introducing yourself when meeting a new person are all examples of observable and measurable communication and social skills. Numerous examples of communication and social skills have been itemized and included on various rating scales, checklists, and assessment protocols (see section **Assessment Procedures**). Matson and Wilkins (2007) defended this approach of defining social skills by example by suggesting that it is perhaps the best method of determining what constitutes social skills in children with ASD. This argument would seem equally valid when applied to the communication domain and individuals other than children (i.e., adolescents and adults).

In addition to existing inventories of communication and social skills found in various rating scales, checklists, and assessment protocols, the content or specific examples that form the basis for defining communication and social skills could be derived using norm-referenced comparisons or a more environment-based assessment (Brown et al., 2006). In a norm-referenced approach, the aim is to identify specific skills used by peers, who are judged to be communicatively and socially competent. The individual with ASD is then assessed to determine which, if any, of the skills exhibited by socially competent peers are present in his/her repertoire. This approach can highlight discrepancies between the skills exhibited by the individual with ASD as compared to his/her socially competent peers. Treatment can then focus on reducing these discrepancies by developing skills in the person with ASD to the level seen in his/her socially competent peers.

Environment-based assessments, combined with an individual norm-referenced assessment, can also help identify performance discrepancies. The goal here is to identify discrepancies between what is required in a given environment or social situation and what the individual with ASD actually does in those environments or situations (Brown et al., 2006). With this approach, the skills needed to function effectively across a range of home, school, vocational, and community settings are inventoried. Maintaining employment in a shoe store, for example, requires the ability to greet customers appropriately and respond to corrective feedback from the boss. Once the required skills have been inventoried, the extent to which the individual with ASD exhibits the necessary skills at the right time and under appropriate conditions can be assessed.

THE RELATION BETWEEN COMMUNICATION AND SOCIAL SKILLS

There is considerable overlap across the communication and social skills domains in the sense that many social skills also require a fair degree of communication and successful communication often requires a fair degree of social interaction. Figure 6.1 illustrates the overlap between social and communication skills. Given this overlap, it would seem useful to coordinate and combine the assessment of communication and social skills rather than view these as distinct activities and separate domains of adaptive behavior. Historically, however, the assessment of communication and social skills has often been conceptualized as distinct activities and conducted independently of one another. Part of this may stem from the fact that there are few assessment tools or procedures that include comprehensive assessment of both communication and social skills.

On the other hand, there appear to be some social skills that do not involve much direct or obvious communication. Opening a door for someone else, for example, does not necessarily require an obligatory communication response. Similarly, some communication interactions involve rather minimal social interaction. To gain access to the playground, for example, a child with ASD might simply walk over and stand near the door. Such acts are often interpreted as a communicative request to go outside and play. While such acts might be interpreted as communicative, they often require little or no social interaction on the part of the child.

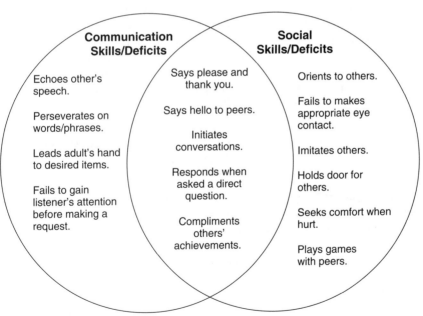

FIGURE 6.1   Venn diagram illustrating the overlap of communication and social skills.

Bruner (1975) referred to this type of seemingly asocial communication in terms of a behavior regulation function. That is, as behaviors that have in the past enabled the individual to fulfill wants and needs through the actions of another person. Requesting access to preferred or needed objects is an example of a communicative act that has a behavior regulation function. In contrast, many important communication and social skills have been ascribed with a more social interaction or declarative function. The function or purpose of social declarative acts is seen as primarily related to initiating and maintaining social interactions, rather than for some more instrumental function such as seeking information. Data indicate that individuals with ASD tend to have more deficits with respect to social interactive and declarative communication, as compared to behavior regulation functions (Cress and Marvin, 2003; Wetherby and Prizant, 1992). Assessment should therefore not only aim to document specific communication and social skills deficits, but also the presence or absence of specific communicative and social functions, such as the behavior regulation versus the social declarative function.

THEORETICAL CONCEPTUALIZATIONS OF COMMUNICATION AND SOCIAL SKILLS

Attempts to conceptualize communication and social skills, and the nature of communication and social skills deficits in ASD, has inspired a considerable amount of research and generated heated debate (Panyan, 1998; Winner, 2002). One tradition conceptualizes communication and social skills as primarily learned or operant behaviors. Another prominent view emphasizes the role of cognitive processes, which are thought to underlie the behavioral manifestations of ASD. While these two conceptualizations are not necessarily mutually exclusive, each nonetheless implies a very different emphasis in relation to the approach taken to assess communication and social functioning.

OPERANT CONCEPTUALIZATIONS OF COMMUNICATION AND SOCIAL SKILLS

Skinner (1957) interpreted communication as a special type of operant behavior that is effective only through the mediation of others. What makes communication special is the fact that such behavior produces reinforcing consequences only indirectly by first affecting the behavior of a partner or listener, who then provides (or mediates access to) reinforcement. Matson and Wilkins (2007) noted how social skills have also been conceptualized as learned or operant behavior. Social skills thus conceptualized are presumably maintained by the reinforcing consequences that derive from successful and positive interaction with others.

Operant explanations for the communication and social skills deficits of individuals with ASD usually refer to either (a) failure to learn appropriate behavior, or (b) lack of motivation to engage in social-communicative interactions (Matson and Wilkins, 2007). That is, skill deficits are considered to stem from a lack of competence (can't do) or a lack of motivation (won't do). With respect to competence, the individual with ASD may have simply failed to learn specific communication and social skills that typically developing children acquire rather incidentally, without much need for deliberate or systematic instruction. The implication is that assessments must therefore identify the skills that are needed, but have not yet been learned, so these can then be directly taught to the individual.

Failure to learn communication and social skills may be related in part to learning difficulties arising from mental retardation, which is also diagnosed in some individuals with ASD (Edelson, 2006). That is, it might simply be more difficult for some individuals with ASD to learn communication and social skills incidentally because they may also have impaired intellectual functioning. Consequently, these individuals might require systematic and deliberate instruction to acquire effective communication and social skills. In addition, their learning difficulties might also stem in part from the failure to provide an appropriate learning environment that matches the unique characteristics or learning styles of individuals with ASD (Lovaas, 2003). The associated intellectual impairments, when present, would no doubt make it more difficult for these individuals to learn the communication and social skills that typically developing children acquire incidentally. And the unique characteristics of ASD no doubt make it more difficult to provide an appropriate and effective learning environment.

In addition to the competence issue, it is possible that the purely social consequences that maintain many communicative and social interactions are simply of no interest to individuals with ASD. This may account for the fact that individuals with ASD often develop effective communication skills for achieving behavior regulation functions, while at the same time having few, if any, effective skills for initiating and maintaining social interactions (Wetherby and Prizant, 1992). Put another way, individuals with ASD may not be strongly motivated to interact with others. In fact, there is evidence to suggest that some individuals with ASD may find social interaction aversive and anxiety provoking (Osterling et al., 2001).

These two explanations (competence versus motivation) are not mutually exclusive, but most likely interact in complex ways. It is possible, for example, that skill acquisition is impaired because social interaction has not acquired conditioned reinforcing properties. Even so, the value of social interaction might emerge as the individual learns various communication and social skills. That is, by deliberately teaching communication and social skills, especially skills that lead to important outcomes for the individual with ASD, that individual may come to value social interaction for its own sake. The implication for assessment is the need to identify skills that produce important social outcomes (Bosch and Fuqua, 2001).

An operant conceptualization of communication and social skills deficits is consistent with data showing that the development of social and communication skills vary as a function of environmental contingencies. Echolalia, for example, has been shown to vary as a function of the communicative partners' level of familiarity (Charlop, 1986), interaction style (Rydell and Mirenda, 1991), and the content of the conversation (Paccia and Curcio, 1982). The success of operant techniques for teaching social and communication skills also supports the conceptualization of these skills as falling within the class of operant behavior (Lovaas, 2003; Matson and Ollendick, 1988).

In relation to assessment, operant conceptualizations imply the need for behavioral measures to identify skill deficits and motivational factors that might account for observed breakdowns in communication and social functioning. That said, it might be difficult to distinguish competence from motivational problems. Assessment must therefore consider both competence and motivation as possible contributors to the communication and social skill deficits of individuals with ASD.

COGNITIVE CONCEPTUALIZATIONS OF COMMUNICATION AND SOCIAL SKILLS

Another prominent theoretical conceptualization, with implications for assessment, is that communication and social skills represent behavioral manifestations of underlying impairments in certain cognitive processing mechanisims (Rogers and Pennington, 1991). The temporal lobe, for example, has been pinpointed as a region that appears specialized for processing social information and therefore presumed to be rather critical for the development of social cognition (Allman and Brothers, 1994). Temporal lobe problems would thus be expected to manifest as social skills deficits, such as failure to orient to social stimuli and establish joint attention (Osterling and Dawson, 1994). Joint attention refers in part to the coordinated exchange that must occur between a speaker and a listener for the dyad to communicate effectively (Cress, 2002). Joint attention is evident when the speaker and listener are jointly focused on, or attending to, the same aspect(s) of the environment during a communicative exchange (Cress, 2002). Children with ASD typically show major impairment in establishing joint attention and responding to the joint attention bids of others (Jones and Carr, 2004). Similarly, problems with executive functioning in the frontal lobe have been linked to key features of ASD, including deficits with initiating communication and attending to relevant social stimuli (Rogers and Pennington, 1991).

In relation to assessment, cognitive conceptualizations imply the need for neurological measures to identify processing impairments that might account for the observed behavioral deficits in communication and social functioning. Assessment might therefore involve procedures to identify neurological anomalies in brain functioning using technology such as Magnetic Resonance Imaging (MRI) and Positron Emission Tomography (PET). While neurologically based assessment may have some future potential, these techniques currently seem difficult to recommend for screening, diagnosis, classification, placement, or treatment planning and evaluation, due to their cost and impracticality for applied settings. It is also the case that these assessment techniques are unlikely to yield data on specific communication or social skills deficits or excesses that could not be obtained more readily by observation, rating scales, or checklists.

On the other hand, the emphasis on the behavioral manifestations of the presumed underlying processes point to important assessment targets that could be overlooked if clinicians focused only on identifying deficits in specific quantifiable responses. Consideration of cognitive processing issues highlight the value of assessing what might be seen as underlying or more qualitative aspects of communication and social functioning. These more qualitative aspects of functioning include the ability to establish joint attention, orient and attend to social stimuli, and understand that others might have thoughts, feelings, beliefs, and intentions that are different from one's own; the so-called theory of mind ability (Osterling et al., 2001).

CLASSIFYING COMMUNICATION AND SOCIAL SKILLS

Lovaas (2003) classified the symptoms of ASD in terms of behavioral deficits and excesses. Individuals with ASD have deficits in their play, communication, social, self-care, academic, and daily living skills. Their excess behaviors include tantrums, stereotyped movements, aggression, and self-injury. Deficits refer to gaps in the person's behavioral repertoire in comparison to typically developing peers and in relation to the demands of everyday social situations that occur in typical home, school, work, and community environments. A behavior that would be expected to occur under certain conditions would be considered deficit if it occurred too infrequently or not at all. Behavioral deficits also include poorly executed responses, such as a child who speaks in a very low volume or stands too far away to participate in group play. Individuals with ASD may present with major communication deficits as evidenced by a complete lack of speech, rarely initiating communication, or consistently failing to respond when asked direct questions. A child with autism may show deficits in social skills by failing to make eye contact, making only fleeting eye contact, ignoring the comings and goings of others, or attending to irrelevant stimuli in a social interaction (e.g., looking at the person's shoes rather than their face). Behavior is excessive if it occurs too frequently (e.g., repeating the answer to a question over and over) or takes a form that is socially unacceptable (e.g., attempting to sniff the hair of a stranger).

Individuals with ASD typically present with a range of communication deficits and excesses (Schopler and Mesibov, 1985). The specific deficits and excesses will vary across individuals because ASD is not a homogeneous condition as mentioned before. The heterogeneity of symptoms within the autism spectrum and the wide variability in symptom expression requires an individualized approach to communication and social skills assessment.

While the communication and social skills problems of individuals with ASD have been classified in terms of deficits and excesses, it is important to note that deficits and excesses are often interrelated and can interact in complex ways to influence overall behavioral development. For example, deficits in communication and social skills have been linked to increased problem behavior in individuals with ASD and related developmental disabilities (Matson et al., 1998; Sigafoos, 2000). This link suggests that some forms of problem behavior may in fact stem from communication and social skills deficits. A child who fails to acquire effective communication skills to gain access to preferred objects, for example, may develop problem behaviors, such as tantrums and self-injury, to fill the communicative void. Assessment of excess behaviors is therefore important for developing effective treatments and should include procedures to identify skill deficits that may be contributing to the expression of problem behavior (O'Neill et al., 1997).

In addition to the possibility of interaction between behavioral deficits and excesses, problems in one specific skill area are likely to negatively affect functioning more generally. Speech and language delay, for example, is typically associated with problems in more than one aspect of communication functioning, including problems with articulation of speech, acquisition of vocabulary, and disorders of syntax, semantics, and pragmatics (Schopler and Mesibov, 1985). Assessment must therefore consider the more general effects of specific communication and social skill deficits on other areas of adaptive behavior functioning.

Identifying behavioral deficits and excesses and their interaction is a major aim of communication and social skills assessment. It is important to identify both skills deficits and their relation to excessive or aberrant forms of communication and social skills, so as to document the individual's existing strengths and gaps in the behavioral repertoire. This information is of direct use in making diagnoses, classifying the severity of the disorder, and selecting treatment priorities. Because educational and behavioral treatment of ASD focuses on building skills and reducing excess behaviors, an individual's specific deficits and excess behaviors must be accurately identified and this can only be done by undertaking comprehensive assessments of communication and social skills. Assessment of an individual's deficits and excesses with respect to communication and social skills assists clinicians in prioritizing treatment targets (Matson and Wilkins, 2007; Sigafoos et al., 2006).

PURPOSES OF ASSESSMENT

Assessment of communication and social skills is undertaken to accomplish several purposes. In clinical contexts, the main purposes of assessment include: (a) screening and diagnosis, (b) classification and placement, (c) selection of treatment targets, and (d) treatment evaluation. For educational contexts, Brown et al. (2006) described the role of assessment data in making educational placement decisions, designing curriculum, planning educational programs, and evaluating student progress. Accomplishing some of these purposes (e.g., screening or diagnosis), might require only a single assessment, but for other purposes (e.g., curriculum development or program evaluation), assessment should be thought of as an ongoing process that will need to occur at regular intervals throughout the lifespan. In most cases, the assessment will involve a combination of approaches and procedures, including interview, behavioral observation, and administration of standardized rating scales or checklists.

SCREENING

Screening can be seen as involving a general assessment of key behaviors that may signal a clinical condition. Screening tests are often used to determine if a person's behavioral development is of sufficient concern to warrant referral for more detailed diagnostic assessment. In screening individuals for developmental delays that may indicate ASD, there is typically a focus on comparing the individual's communication and social skill development to that expected of typically developing peers. Screening and diagnostic assessments are usually implemented during infancy and the preschool years, when the child is suspected of having ASD.

A variety of instruments have been developed that can be used to screen for ASD in young children (see Mawle and Griffiths, 2006 for a review). Two examples, representing commonly used screening instruments, include The Checklist for Autism in Toddlers (CHAT: Baron-Cohen et al., 1992) and the Social Communication Questionnaire (SCQ: Eaves et al., 2006). The original CHAT consisted of nine items, whereas the modified version (M-CHAT) consists of 23 items. Each item takes the form of a question to which informants (usually the parent) answer either yes or no. Many CHAT and M-CHAT questions reference communication and social skills (e.g., Does the child ever use his/her index finger to point, to ask for something?, Does the child look you in the eye for more than a second or two?, Does the child smile in response to your face or your smile?). Results from several studies suggest that the CHAT, and M-CHAT are promising for screening 12–24-month-old children suspected of having autism (Baron-Cohen et al., 1992; Robins et al., 2001; Watson et al., 2007).

The SCQ is based on an earlier instrument called the Autism Screening Questionnaire (Berument, Rutter, Lord, Pickles, and Bailey, 1999). It is also a parent-based screening tool intended to identify children in need of follow-up assessment. The 40-item questionnaire is based on DSM-IV (American Psychiatric Association, 2000) criteria for the diagnosis of autism, including several items to assess the types of communication and social skills problems associated with ASD. While its potential for screening young children for ASD has not yet been fully researched, Eaves et al. (2006) concluded that it could be useful for this purpose.

DIAGNOSIS

When screening results indicate a potential problem, children suspected of having ASD require follow-up assessment, which will usually involve clinical observations and administration of one or more diagnostic protocols. The aim of this follow-up is to make a reliable and valid diagnosis and generally the sooner this is done the better. Parents and professionals require this information to help them understand the child's developmental and behavioral problems, the likely prognosis, and to begin planning interventions and related services.

A variety of instruments have been developed that can be used as part of the diagnostic workup (see Lord and Corsello, 2005 for a review). Two widely used rating scales for diagnosing ASD are The Childhood Autism Rating Scale (CARS: Schopler et al., 1988) and the Gilliam Autism Rating Scale (GARS: Gilliam, 1995). While neither instrument is intended to provide a comprehensive assessment of communication or social functioning, both contain a number of items related to communication and social skills. The CARS, for example, assesses 14 areas of functioning and ends with asking for an overall impression concerning the child's autistic symptoms (i.e., mild, moderate, or severe). Among the 14 areas assessed are several that relate to overall communication (listening responses, verbal and nonverbal communication) and social functioning (e.g., relating to people, emotional response). Instead of obtaining ratings for fairly broad areas of functioning, the GARS consists of 56 items referencing specific behavioral tendencies, including tendencies that could be viewed as examples of communication (uses speech to communicate within the first 36 months, follows simple commands) and social skills (avoids eye contact, resists physical contact, smiles at parents). The CARS and GARS have the advantage of being relatively quick and easy to complete and both appear to provide useful data that can assist clinicians in diagnosing ASD.

Another set of related diagnostic procedures make use of The Autism Diagnostic Interview-Revised (ADI-R: Lord, Rutter and Le Couteur, 1994) and the Autism Diagnostic Observation Schedule (ADOS: Lord et al., 1999), The ADI-R requires informant interviews, whereas the ADOS includes direct observation of behavior. The procedures are intended to assess a range of functioning deficits that define the autism spectrum disorders, including social interaction, communication, and stereotyped behavior. The ADOS in particular has become extremely popular as part of the diagnostic process for young children suspected of having ASD.

Differential Diagnosis

As noted in the Introduction, the term ASD covers a number of more specific developmental disability conditions. While the term can be useful in most applied settings, for diagnostic, classification, and research purposes, it is often important to make distinctions between autism and Asperger's syndrome, for example. Making such distinctions is referred to as differential diagnosis and can be complicated. Differential diagnosis is further complicated by the possibility of distinct subtypes within the autism spectrum. Begliner and Smith (2001) noted the possibility of distinct subtypes within the autism spectrum. If subtypes do in fact exist, then these might be identified through systematic assessment of communication and social skills and subsequent identification of distinct communication and/or social skills, phenotypes or profiles. Identification of distinct subtypes within the autism spectrum could have significant implications for tracking the causes of these conditions and for enhancing treatment efforts.

CLASSIFICATION AND PLACEMENT

Once a diagnosis is made, it can be necessary to conduct additional assessments to provide additional data for making classification and placement decisions. These additional assessments are likely to occur shortly after the diagnostic process has been initiated. Assessments may also need to be repeated at each major transition point in the individual's life, such as the transition from preschool to elementary school or the transition from high school to adult services.

Classification includes documenting the severity of the presenting problems. Scheuermann and Webber (2002) noted that the extent of the individual's presenting language problems is often used to classify the severity of autism and to distinguish autism from other conditions, such as Asperger's syndrome. For example, when the individual is mute, their autism is considered more severe than if speech is present. Scheuermann and Webber also noted, however, that even when a high level of speech and language has developed, the person may still have rather severe communication and social skills problems. It can still be the case that individuals with ASD who have some speech and considerable interest in social interaction may nonetheless present formidable challenges in terms of designing useful assessments and developing effective treatments. For example, the so called "higher-functioning" individuals within the autism spectrum can present with odd and unusual speech characteristics, such as (a) unusual voice tone and inflection, (b) pronoun reversals, (c) lack of variety in sentence structure, and (d) immature grammar (e.g., simple noun–verb formats). These aspects of communication are difficult to assess, although instruments such as the CARS and GARS do include opportunities for informants to rate these types of problems.

It is important to attempt to classify the nature and extent of an individual's communication and social skills deficits at major transition points because severity of symptoms is a primary basis for determining whether or not an individual is eligible for certain types of services, such as special education and supported employment. The level of support that the individual is likely to require is also often based on assessment results, including assessment of communication and social skills (Luckasson et al., 2002). The level of required support, in turn, may influence educational, vocational, and residential placement decisions.

SELECTING TREATMENT TARGETS

As mentioned previously in this chapter, individuals with ASD often present with a wide range of communication and social skills deficits (Lovaas, 2003; Schopler and Mesibov, 1985). They are also likely to present with numerous excess behaviors that are related to their communication and social skills deficits. Treatment priorities therefore need to be identified from among the larger pool of potential targets because it is often impractical to target every presenting deficit. When a number of deficits or excesses have been identified in an assessment, priority should be given to skills that are most likely to influence functioning more widely. Priority should be given to the key skills, behavioral cusps, or pivotal responses that, once acquired, are likely to remain functional for the individual across settings and over time (Bosch and Fuqua, 2001). Functional, in this context, refers to behaviors that are considered appropriate by society at large, important to significant others, and effective in gaining reinforcement for the individual.

Assessments that identify specific communication and social skills deficits and/or excesses are likely to be the most relevant for selecting treatment targets. Because treatment of ASD is likely to be ongoing, these types of assessments will need to be repeated throughout the lifespan to update the treatment plan. To this end, some of the more commonly used screening and diagnostic tools (e.g., M-CHAT, CARS, GARS, ADOS) provide data on some aspects of communication and social functioning, but often contain too few items specific to communication and social skills. This may make it difficult to rely on diagnostic measures alone to assist in identifying and prioritizing treatment targets. Data from diagnostic measures might be supplemented with direct observations and data from rating scales that are specifically focused on communication and social skills (see section **Assessment Procedures**).

TREATMENT EVALUATION

Ongoing assessment can assist in evaluating treatments designed to teach communication and social skills to individuals with ASD. In fact, ongoing assessment is a necessity, but not always sufficient for the evaluation of treatment effects. Data from regularly conducted assessments are used to evaluate whether the individual is making sufficient progress in acquiring the targeted skills. If not, steps can be taken to improve the treatment. For this purpose, assessments will need to be completed and repeated on a regular basis (e.g., every week to 10 days). Intervention studies that focus on teaching adaptive skills to individuals with ASD often rely on very frequent (often daily observations) of a small number of objectively defined target behaviors (Kennedy, 2005). The purpose of these frequent and repeated direct observations is to establish a baseline with respect to performance of target behaviors against which the effects of treatment can be compared. Outside of formal intervention studies, it may be more practical to reduce the frequency of assessment and rely on indirect measures, such as rating scales and checklists. Assessments using rating scales and checklists are generally less time and resource intensive than direct observations. A number of rating scales and checklists that can be used in treatment evaluation are reviewed in the next section of this chapter.

ASSESSMENT PROCEDURES

There are several approaches that can provide useful assessment data on the communication and social skills deficits and excesses of individuals with ASD. These approaches include (a) behavioral observations, (b) role-play tests, (c) and standardized rating scales and behavior checklists. It is important to note that these various assessment procedures or instruments are not mutually incompatible. Each of these procedures has advantages and disadvantages. Consequently, as Frame and Matson (1987) argued, it is often helpful to develop comprehensive assessment protocols that incorporate several procedures, approaches, and instruments.

BEHAVIORAL OBSERVATION

This approach involves direct observations of the individual's behavior. The approach requires trained observers, objectively defined target behaviors, and collection of interobserver agreement data to ensure observations are reliable. Observations must be systematic, repeated at regular intervals, and of sufficient duration to ensure the assessment yields an adequate and representative (i.e., valid) sample of behavior. Assessments that are distributed across the entire day (e.g., from waking in the morning to going to sleep at night), and which occur across several days, are more likely to yield representative samples of behavior. It is also useful to conduct observations in the person's home, school, vocational, and community environments. Doing so can help increase the ecological validity of the data. As indicated by these requirements, behavioral observations can be time and resource intensive. In addition, due to constraints of relying on human observers, it is often the case that only a very few specific behaviors can be assessed. Consequently, it may be difficult to obtain a comprehensive inventory of communication and social skills deficits and excesses using behavioral observations alone. Still, behavioral observations can often provide important details about environmental variables that might be influencing the expression of communication and social skills. These details are often helpful in understanding the function or purpose of behavior and for designing the environment to ensure that it includes effective stimuli to set the occasion for appropriate communication and social skills. With behavioral assessment, the presence or absence of specific communication and social skills, or lack thereof, can be recorded in relation to opportunities for communication (Ogletree et al., 2002). This can occur under naturalistic or more structured, analog conditions.

In a naturalistic observation, an observer may simply record the number and types of communicative behaviors or social acts that occur in a given period of time, with no attempt made to directly evoke communicative or social behavior by creating opportunities to request, reject, comment, greet others, etc. To illustrate, Sigafoos et al. (1994) assessed communication responses in relation to opportunities in 37 children with various types of developmental disabilities. Observers entered the children's classrooms and watched the teacher and children across a number of days. Each daily session of 15 min. was divided into 10-sec. intervals. For each interval, the observer recorded whether or not the teacher provided an opportunity for communication and if so, what type of opportunity was provided, Opportunities were classified into one of four types based on Skinner's (1957) analysis of verbal behavior: (a) tact, (b) mand, (c) intraverbal, and (d) echoic. If an opportunity was provided, the child was then observed for the next 10 seconds to determine his or her response. Child responses were coded as (a) appropriate, (b) inappropriate, or (c) no response. The data from this study enabled the researchers to assess communicative skills in relation to naturally arising opportunities. However, these data are limited because it is not clear if the times selected for the observations provided a representative sample of the children's communicative skills. This is because so much depended on the number and types of opportunities provided by teachers, and these opportunities were not necessarily provided systematically nor consistently across sessions.

With respect to social skills, Anderson et al. (2004) described a naturalistic play-based approach for assessing social skills. The study involved 10 children with autism attending mainstream kindergarten and elementary school class-rooms. The children's social behaviors were observed in free play contexts and compared to the behavior of typically developing peers. As would be predicted, the children with autism differed significantly in terms of their social skills when compared to peers. Differences were noted in both the frequency and quality of play skills and social interaction during play routines. Compared to their typi-cally developing peers, the children with autism exhibited a lower frequency of appropriate play and grossly aberrant social interaction patterns. This naturalistic assessment of social functioning in mainstream classrooms and in the context of unstructured free play enabled the researchers to assess the children's functioning in direct comparison to the behavior of typically developing peers. Comparing the two groups revealed a number of skill discrepancies in the repertoires of the chil-dren with autism. These discrepancies would represent logical treatment targets.

The validity of naturalistic assessments may depend on the number and type of opportunities that arise during the observations. If the environment contains few such opportunities, then the resulting data may underestimate communication and social functioning. One solution is to introduce more structure to the environment by, for example, presenting a predetermined number of opportunities, with each opportunity following a standardized protocol.

Keen et al. (2001) described a more structured procedure for assessing com-munication behaviors in young children with ASD. Observations occurred in preschool settings and consisted of recording the children's responses to three types of opportunities which were designed to assess skills related to making a request, making choices, and responding to social overtures from peers. The assessments involved (a) offering a preferred item, (b) offering a choice of two items, or (c) having a peer approach the child and say hello. These conditions were designed to create the opportunity for requesting, choice making, and greeting, respectively. After creating the opportunity, the child was observed for the next 10 seconds. During this 10-sec. interval, the researchers recorded what, if anything, the child did, such as reaching for the item, leading the adult's hand to the item, or vocalizing as the peer approached. Similar structured opportunities could be created to assess the presence or absence of specific types of social skills, such as greeting others, responding to corrective feedback, or participating in small group activities at school.

In relation to assessing one of the core communication deficits in ASD, MacDonald et al. (2006) described an observational procedure for assessing joint attention deficits in children. To assess the child's ability to respond to joint attention bids from others, for example, an adult pointed to pictures and waited 5 seconds to determine whether the child would follow the adult's pointing gesture to find the picture. To assess the child's ability to initiate joint attention, two tasks were employed: toy activation and picture book. For the toy-activation scenario, a mechanical toy was activated for 5 seconds. In the picture-book scenario, the adults presented a page containing several pictures and asked "What do you see?" After this, the child was observed to determine the frequency of gaze shifts (i.e., alternating gaze between the toy/picture and the adult). A prior assessment of joint attention, such as described by MacDonald et al. may enable the therapist to identify specific joint attention skills for inclusion in the child's speech training curriculum.

ROLE-PLAY TESTS

Role-play tests have long been used to assess social skills (Bellack et al., 1979; Matson and Ollendick, 1988). A role-play test can be viewed as a type of structured behavioral observation, in which various social situations are simulated to allow direct observation of the individual's responses. For example, the scenarios might be structured to simulate meeting new people or approaching co-workers to ask for assistance. Behaviors observed in the simulated situation are assumed to represent valid indications of how the person would respond under similar situations in the home, school, community or workplace (Becker and Heimberg, 1988). However, this aspect of validity has been questioned (Bellack et al., 1979).

Several formal role-play tests have been developed and empirically validated (Van Hasselt et al., 1981). Many of these role-play tests include standardized scenarios to assess a range of conversational and social skills. These tests can provide useful data on social skills for a range of individuals, including children with disabilities (Van Hasselt et al., 1985). However the utility of such tests for children with ASD remains to be determined.

Gresham and Elliott (1984) described four advantages of role-play tests. First, this approach enables clinicians to assess critical social skills that occur at low frequencies in the natural environment. Second, there can be greater control over the situations than might otherwise be possible in unstructured, naturalistic observations. This allows for a more systematic assessment. Third, the resulting data consist of direct observations of behavior, rather than the perceptions or ratings of third-party informants. Fourth, role-play tests can be more efficient and cost effective than naturalistic behavioral observations.

Recent variations, which seem similar in some respects to traditional role-play tests, have been used to assess a range of skills, including communication and social skills in children suspected of having ASD. An example is the diagnostic process involving the Autism Diagnostic Observation Schedule (ADOS: Lord et al., 1999). As part of the process, the assessor seeks to engage the individual in various play routines or simulated social interactions (e.g., a pretend birthday party, bubble play). Observations focus on the individual's reaction to the scenario, such as use of gestures, speech, attending skills, and eye contact. For example, in one part of this assessment protocol, the assessor attempts to engage the child in a pretend birthday party (e.g., putting candles on a cake, pretending to light the candles, blowing out the candles, etc). Assessors look for a variety of behaviors from the child, including any relevant communication and social skills (e.g., expressing empathy as the assessor pretends to burn his/her fingers while lighting the candles). Assessors also rate the extent to which the individual is observed to engage in repetitive behaviors, such as fixation on a specific object of interest. As mentioned before, the ADOS is primarily used in the diagnosis of ASD, but the associated observations, which involve simulated social situations, might also yield useful data on communication and social skills deficits. In addition to its intended diagnostic purpose, the results of these observations during simulated social situations might also prove useful for selecting treatment targets.

Despite the potential advantages of role-play tests, studies have found that the results of role-play tests do not always correlate very highly with other measures of social skills, such as self-report, and teacher ratings (Bellack et al., 1979). In addition, Matson and Wilkins (2007) noted that traditional role-play tests might not always be very well suited to the task of assessing social skills in individuals with ASD. Indeed, successful use of traditional role-play tests, involving simulated social situations, would seem to require a fairly high degree of language comprehension, which may be limited in some individuals with ASD.

RATING SCALES AND BEHAVIOR CHECKLISTS

Rating scales and behavior checklists are frequently used to assess the communication and social skills of individuals with ASD. Rating scales may include measures on the frequency and/or severity of skill deficits and behavioral excesses. Behavior checklists, on the other hand, typically involve recording whether skills are present or absent from the repertoire (Matson and Wilkins, 2007).

Derby Hospitals NHS Foundation Trust
Library and Knowledge Service

Generally, both rating scales and checklists ask informants to make judgments based on their familiarity with the person's behavior over some time frame (e.g., the past 3 or 6 months). Because informants consider average performance over a period of time, the results from rating scales and checklists may be less influenced by transient environmental variables. The results may therefore provide a more representative assessment of communication and social skills than direct observation. However, the resulting data may be potentially biased by the informant's idiosyncratic interpretation of the meaning of items and ratings.

Several rating scales for assessing communication or social skills have been published (see Landa, 2005 and Matson and Wilkins, 2007 for reviews). In terms of communication, one of the more commonly used scales is Bzoch and League's (1991) Receptive-Expressive Emergent Language Scale (REEL-2). Although not specifically designed for children with ASD, the REEL-2 can be useful for assessing early communication development of children suspected of having ASD or for documenting the communication deficits of children with more severe disabilities. The REEL-2 consists of 66 expressive items and 66 receptive items covering language development of typically developing children from birth to 36 months of age. Items are rated as typical of the child (+); emerging or partly exhibited (±); or never observed (−). Ratings are converted into age equivalent scores including a Combined Language Age (CLA), a Receptive Language Age (RLA), and an Expressive Language Age (ELA). These age equivalent scores provide a basis for comparing communication development to typically developing children, which is important for identifying discrepancies and gaps in the communicative repertoires of individuals with ASD. Data show that this device provides a reliable estimate of receptive and expressive language ability in young children with developmental disabilities and severe communication impairment (Sigafoos and Pennell, 1995).

A more recent rating scale that has been validated for assessing communication in children with a variety of developmental disorders, is the *Verbal Behavior Assessment Scale* (VerBAS: Duker et al., 2002). The VerBAS consists of 15 items, each rated for frequency on a 0 to 4 scale. Items were derived from Skinner's (1957) analysis of verbal behavior. The scale therefore ties assessment to an operant conceptualization of communication. The VerBAS includes ratings for a range of communicative functions including requesting (i.e., mands), commenting (i.e., tacts), and imitative responses (i.e., echoics). To assess rejecting, for example, one item asks "If s/he does not want the offered food, drink, or toy(s) any longer, does s/he say this, make the appropriate sign, or pushes it away?" A strength of the scale is that it considers a variety of communication modes including vocal, gesture, and graphic mode.

Partington and Sundberg (1998) also developed a now widely used assessment tool for assessing communication based on Skinner's (1957) analysis of verbal behavior. Their Assessment of Basic Language and Learning Skills (ABLLS) is used to assess communication skills in children with ASD and related developmental disorders. This instrument includes task analyses of a range of expressive and receptive communication skills. The ABLLS can be used for several purposes, including identifying communication deficits in the repertoires of individuals with ASD and treatment evaluation.

For identifying deficits in social skills, some of the more widely used instruments include the Children's Social Behavior Questionnaire (CSBQ: Hartman et al., 2006), the Social Skills Rating System (SSRS: Gresham and Elliott, 1990), and the Matson Evaluation of Social Skills in Youngsters (MESSY: Matson et al., 1986). Each of these scales includes social skill items that have been shown to be deficient or aberrant in individuals with ASD.

The CSBQ, for example, includes items that are often described as problematic for individuals with more mild impairment of communication and social skills functioning. Hence, it may be particularly useful for individuals with high-functioning autism, Asperger's syndrome, or pervasive developmental disorders not otherwise specified.

The SSRS is primarily intended for preschool children. This scale rates how often a child exhibits social skills or problem behaviors, such as (a) follows instructions, (b) answers the phone appropriately, (c) speaks in an appropriate tone of voice at home, and (d) is aggressive toward people or objects. Each of the 49 items in the scale is rated on a 0 (never) to 2 (very often) scale.

Of the available rating scales, the MESSY and the MESSIER, which is a variation of the MESSY for children with more severe impairments (Matson et al., 1999) are among the most well developed and researched scales for assessing social skills. The MESSIER or Matson Evaluation of Social Skills for Individuals with Severe Retardation, for example, consists of 85 social skills, ranging from early infantile responses (e.g., turns head in direction of caregiver, looks at face of caregiver when spoken to) to more advanced social skills that would be expected of older individuals (e.g., thanks or compliments others). Items in the MESSY and MESSIER reference many of the behavioral deficits and excesses that are characteristic of individuals with ASD (e.g., prefers to be alone, avoids eye contact, resists being touched). Each item is rated on a 0 (never) to 3 (often) scale. Research with the MESSY involving children with ASD (Matson et al., 1991) has demonstrated the efficacy of the scale for identifying targets for social skills training. Indeed, it is one of the few rating scales with well-developed reliability and validity that has empirical support for identifying social skills deficits in children with ASD.

RELIABILITY AND VALIDITY

A number of psychometric characteristics should be considered in evaluating the technical adequacy of any given assessment approach, procedure, or instrument. These characteristics fall into the two broad categories of reliability and validity. Assessment of communication and social skills must yield data that is reliable and valid for its intended purpose.

RELIABILITY

Reliability refers to the accuracy of assessment data. In assessing communication and social skills, it is important to obtain data that provide an accurate estimate or inventory of the individual's communication and social skills. To ensure accuracy, the assessment must not only yield a representative sample of behavior, but also a sample that reflects the true extent of the individual's deficits and excesses.

The reliability of assessment data is typically demonstrated through various measures, such as interrater (or interobserver) agreement and test–retest reliability. An assessment result or an assessment procedure is considered reliable if two raters or observers, each of whom completes the assessment independently, obtains comparable results (i.e., 80 percent or better agreement). When interrater agreement is adequate, clinicians can have more confidence that the results represent an accurate sample of behavior, rather than the influence of rater or observer biases or other extraneous variables. Similarly, a test is considered to have good test–retest reliability if it yields similar results across two separate administrations. These separate administrations are usually separated by a 2 to 4-week-interval so as to eliminate any possible improvement in test results due to maturation. Test–retest reliability is important when assessment procedures are to be repeated on a regular basis, as might be done to select new treatment targets or evaluate treatments. When a test has good test–retest reliability, clinicians can be more confident that any changes in results across subsequent administrations (e.g., at 3 or 6-month-intervals) represent true changes in the individual's behavior, rather than measurement error.

VALIDITY

As with reliability, there are a number of aspects to validity that are critical to communication and social skills assessment. Validity, in this context, refers to the extent to which assessment procedures bring about the intended results. A particular assessment procedure or instrument might be intended to identify deficits in social skills in preschoolers. The procedure is valid to the extent that it does in fact provide data on deficits in important social skills that predict successful social integration in the preschool environment. A valid assessment of communication skills is one that measures communication skills and a valid assessment of social skills is one that measures social skills. Face and content validity is determined by judging the extent to which assessment items represent communication or social skills. Diagnostic validity, on the other hand, refers to the extent to which the assessment protocol correctly identifies or classifies clinical cases (Sturmey and Sevin, 1994). Validity is also determined by evaluating the extent to which test results predict actual performance. A child who scores low on an assessment of social skills would be predicted to experience considerable problems in social situations. If the prediction holds, the assessment is said to have good predictive validity. It is important to note that an assessment procedure or instrument cannot be valid unless it is first reliable for its intended purpose. Even if reliable, a given assessment tactic may not be sufficiently valid for its intended purpose or for assessment across the lifespan.

SUMMARY AND CONCLUSION

Given the ubiquity of deficits in communication development among individuals with developmental disabilities, it is not surprising that a considerable amount of research has focused on assessing the communication and language skills of such individuals. However, assessment has often lagged behind treatment efforts, as noted by Matson and Wilkins (2007). Because assessment data on communication and social skills is useful to many aspects of clinical management (e.g., screening, diagnosis, classification and placement, selecting treatment targets, evaluating treatment programs), additional research to develop new assessment procedures, and enhance existing assessment practices, is clearly warranted.

At the present time, there is general consensus that comprehensive assessment of communication and social skills is a vital component in the overall provision of support to individuals with ASD and their families. As indicated in this chapter, a range of useful procedures and assessment tools are available, ranging from rapid screening instruments to fully comprehensive diagnostic work-ups involving standardized measures and direct observations. In this mix, there is likely to be considerable value in using naturalistic and structured observations, role-play scenarios, rating scales, and checklists to identify specific communication and social skills deficits and excesses. Each approach contributes useful information. Familiarity with the basic concepts and procedures that underlie effective assessment of communication and social skills may enable parents and professionals to obtain more useful information to enhance the quality of life for individuals with ASD.

REFERENCES

Akshoomoff, N. (2006). Autism spectrum disorders: Introduction. *Child Neuropsychology*, **12**, 245–246.

Allman, J. and Brothers, L. (1994). Faces, fear, and the amygdala. *Nature*, **372**, 613.

American Psychiatric Association (2000). *Diagnostic and statistical manual of mental disorders* (4th ed., text revision). Washington DC: Author.

Anderson, A., Moore, D.W., Godfrey, R., and Fletcher-Finn, C.M. (2004). Social skills assessment of children with autism in free-play situations. *Autism*, **8**, 369–385.

Baron-Cohen, S., Allen, J., and Gillberg, C. (1992). Can autism be detected at 18 months? The needle, the haystack, and the CHAT. *British Journal of Psychiatry*, **161**, 839–843.

Becker, R.E. and Heimberg, R.G. (1988). Assessment of social skills. In *Behavioral assessment: A practical guidebook*. (3rd ed.) (A.S. Bellack and M. Hersen, eds.) pp. 365–395. New York: Pergamon Press.

Begliner, L.J. and Smith, T.H. (2001). A review of subtyping in autism and proposed dimensional classification model. *Journal of Autism and Developmental Disorders*, **31**, 411–422.

Bellack, A.S., Hersen, M., and Lamparski, D. (1979). Role-play tests for assessing social skills: Are they valid? Are they useful? *Journal of Consulting and Clinical Psychology*, **47**, 335–342.

Berument, S.K., Rutter, M., Lord, C., et al. (1999). Autism screening questionnaire: Diagnostic validity. *British Journal of Psychiatry*, **175**, 444–451.

Bosch, S. and Fuqua, R.W. (2001). Behavioral cusps: A model for selecting target behaviors. *Journal of Applied Behavior Analysis*, **34**, 123–125.

Brown, F., Snell, M.E., and Lehr, D. (2006). Meaningful assessment. In *Instruction for Students with Severe Disabilities* (6th ed.) (M.E. Snell and F. Brown, eds.) pp. 67–110. Upper Saddle River, NJ: Pearson.

Bruner, J.S. (1975). The ontogenesis of speech acts. *Journal of Child Language*, **2**, 1–19.

Bzoch, K.R. and League, R. (1991). *Receptive-expressive Emergent Language Scale* (2nd ed.) Austin, TX: Pro-ed.

Charlop, M.H. (1986). Setting effects on the occurrence of autistic children's immediate echolalia. *Journal of Autism and Developmental Disorders*, **16**, 473–483.

Cohen, D.J. and Volkmar, F.R. (1997). *Handbook of Autism and Pervasive Developmental Disorders*. New York: John Wiley & Sons.

Cress, C.J. (2002). Expanding children's early augmented behaviors to support symbolic development. In *Exemplary Practices for Beginning Communicators* (J. Reichle, D.R. Beukelman, and J.C. Light, eds.) pp. 219–273. Baltimore: Paul H Brookes Publishing Co.

Cress, C.J. and Marvin, C.A. (2003). Common questions about AAC services in early intervention. *Augmentative and Alternative Communication*, **19**, 4, 254–272.

Duker, P.C., van Driel, S., and van de Bercken, J. (2002). Communication profiles of individuals with Down's syndrome, Angelman syndrome and pervasive developmental disorder. *Journal of Intellectual Disability Research*, **46**, 35–40.

Eaves, L.C., Wingert, H.D., Ho, H.H., and Mickelson, E.C. (2006). Screening for autism spectrum disorders with the Social Communication Questionnaire. *Journal of Developmental and Behavioral Pediatrics*, **27**(Suppl. 2), S95–S103.

Edelson, M.G. (2006). Are the majority of children with autism mentally retarded? A systematic evaluation of the data. *Focus on Autism and Other Developmental Disorders*, **21**, 66–83.

Frame, C.L. and Matson, J.L. (1987). *Handbook of Assessment in Childhood Psychopathology: Applied Issues in Differential Diagnosis and Treatment Evaluation*. New York: Plenum.

Gilliam. J.E. (1995). *Gilliam Autism Rating Scale*. Austin, TX: Pro-ed.

Gresham, F.M. (1986). Conceptual and definitional issues in the assessment of children's social skills: Implications for classification and training. *Journal of Clinical Child Psychology*, **15**, 3–15.

Gresham, F.M. (2001). Assessment of social skills in children and adolescents. In *Handbook of Psychoeducational Assessment: Ability, Achievement, and Behavior in Children* (J.W. Andrews, D.H. Saklofske, and H.L. Janzen, eds.) pp. 325–355. San Diego, CA: Academic Press.

Gresham, F.M. and Elliott, S.N. (1984). Assessment and classification of children's social skills: A review of methods and issues. *School Psychology Review*, **13**, 292–301.

Gresham, F.M. and Elliott, S.N. (1990). *Social Skills Rating System*. Circle Pines, MN: American Guidance Service.

Hartman, C.A., Luteijn, E., Serra, M., and Minderaa, R. (2006). Refinement of the children's social behavior questionnaire (CSBQ): An instrument that describes the diverse problems seen in milder forms of PDD. *Journal of Autism and Developmental Disorders*, **36**, 325–342.

Hayden, M.F. and Abery, B.H. (eds.) (1994). *Challenges for a Service System in Transition: Ensuring Quality Community Experiences for Persons with Developmental Disabilities*. Baltimore: Paul H. Brookes Publishing Co.

Jones, E.A. and Carr, E.G. (2004). Joint attention in children with autism: Theory and intervention. *Focus on Autism and Other Developmental Disabilities*, **19**, 13–26.

Kanner, L. (1943). Autistic disturbances of affective contact. *Nervous Child*, **2**, 217–250.

Keen, D., Sigafoos, J., and Woodyatt, G. (2001). Replacing prelinguistic behaviors with functional communication. *Journal of Autism and Developmental Disorders*, **31**, 385–398.

Kennedy, C.H. (2004). Social relationships. In *Including Students with Severe Disabilities* (C.H. Kennedy and E.M. Horn, eds.) pp. 100–119. Boston: Pearson Education.

Kennedy, C.H. (2005). *Single-case Designs for Educational Research*. Boston: Allyn & Bacon.

Koegel, R.L. and Koegel, L.K. (2006). *Pivotal Response Treatments for Autism: Communication, Social, and Academic Development*. Baltimore: Paul H. Brookes Publishing Co.

Landa, R.J. (2005). Assessment of social communication skills in preschoolers. *Mental Retardation and Developmental Disabilities Research Reviews*, **11**, 247–252.

Lord, C. and Corsello, C. (2005). Diagnostic instruments in autism spectrum disorders. In *Handbook of Autism and Pervasive Developmental Disorders, Vol. 2: Assessment, Interventions, and Policy* (3rd ed.) (F.R. Volkmar, R. Paul, A. Klin, and D. Cohen, eds.) pp. 730–771. New York: John Wiley & Sons.

Lord, C., Rutter, M., DiLavore, P.C., and Risi, S. (1999). *Autism Diagnostic Observation Schedule*. Los Angeles: Western Psychological Services.

Lord, C., Rutter, M., and Le Couteur, A. (1994). Autism diagnostic interview-Revised: A revised version of a diagnostic interview for caregivers of individuals with possible pervasive developmental disorders. *Journal of Autism and Developmental Disorders*, **24**, 659–685.

Losee, R. (1999). Communication defined as complementary informative processes. *Journal of Information, Communication, & Library Science*, **5**, 1–15.

Lovaas, O.I. (2003). *Teaching Individuals with Developmental Delays: Basic Intervention Techniques*. Austin, TX: Pro-Ed.

Luckasson, R.A., Schalock, R.L., Spitalnik, D.M., et al. (2002). *Mental Retardation: Definition, Classification, and Systems of Support*. Washington DC: American Association on Mental Retardation.

MacDonald, R., Anerson, J., Dube, W.V., et al. (2006). Behavioral assessment of joint attention: A methodological report. *Research in Developmental Disabilities*, **27**, 138–150.

Matson, J.L., Heinze, A., Helsel, W.J., et al. (1986). Assessing social behaviors in the visually handicapped: The Matson evaluation of social skills with youngsters (MESSY). *Journal of Clinical Child Psychology*, **15**, 78–87.

Matson, J.L., LeBlanc, L.A., Weinheimer, B., and Cherry, K.E. (1999). Reliability of the Matson evaluation of social skills for individuals with severe retardation (MESSIER). *Behavior Modification*, **23**, 647–661.

Matson, J.L. and Ollendick, T.H. (1988). *Enhancing Children's Social Skills: Assessment and Training*. New York: Pergamon Press.

Matson, J.L., Stabinsky-Compton, L., and Sevin, J.A. (1991). Comparison and item analysis of the MESSY for autistic and normal children. *Research in Developmental Disabilities*, **12**, 361–369.

Matson, J.L. and Wilkins, J. (2007). A critical review of assessment targets and methods for social skills excesses and deficits for children with autism spectrum disorders. *Research in Autism Spectrum Disorders*, **1**, 28–37.

Matson, J.L., Smiroldo, B.B., and Bamburg, J.W. (1998). The relationship of social skills to psychopathology for individuals with severe or profound mental retardation. *Journal of Intellectual and Developmental Disability*, **23**, 137–145.

Mawle, E. and Griffiths, P. (2006). Screening for autism in pre-school children in primary care: Systematic review of English Language tools. *International Journal of Nursing Studies*, **43**, 623–636.

National Joint Committee for the Communicative Needs of Persons With Severe Disabilities. (1992). *Guidelines for Meeting the Communication Needs of Persons with Severe Disabilities*, ASHA, **34** (March), 1–8.

Ogletree, B.T., Pierce, K., Harn, W.E., and Fisher, M.A. (2002). Assessment of communication and language in classical autism: Issues and practices. *Assessment for Effective Intervention*, **27**, 61–71.

O'Neill, R.E., Horner, R.H., Albin, R.W., et al. (1997). *Functional Assessment and Program Development for Problem Behavior: A Practical Handbook.* (2nd ed.). Pacific Grove: Brooks/Cole Publishing.

Osterling, J. and Dawson, G. (1994). Early recognition of children with autism: A study of first birthday home videotapes. *Journal of Autism and Developmental Disorders, 24,* 247–257.

Osterling, J., Dawson, G., and McPartland, J. (2001). Autism. In *Handbook of Clinical Child Psychology* (3rd. ed.) (C.E. Walker and M.C. Roberts, eds.) pp. 432–452. New York: John Wiley & Sons.

Paccia, J.M. and Curcio, F. (1982). Language processing and forms of immediate echolalia in autistic children. *Journal of Speech & Hearing Research, 25,* 42–47.

Panyan, M.V. (1998). *How to Teach Social Skills.* Austin, TX: Pro-ed.

Partington, J.W. and Sundberg, M.L. (1998). T*he Assessment of Basic Language and Learning Skills (ABLLS): An Assessment, Curriculum Guide, and Skills Tracking System for Children with Autism and Other Developmental Disabilities: The ABLLS Protocol.* Pleasant Hill, CA: Behavior Analysts, Inc.

Ritvo, E.R. and Freeman, B.J. (1978). National Society for Autistic Children definition of the syndrome of autism. *Journal of Autism and Developmental Disorders, 8,* 162–170.

Robins, D.L., Fein, D., Barton, M.L., and Green, J.A. (2001). The modified checklist for autism in toddlers: An initial study investigating the early detection of autism and pervasive developmental disorders. *Journal of Autism and Developmental Disorders, 31,* 131–144.

Rogers, S. and Pennington, B. (1991). A theoretical approach to the deficits in infantile autism. *Development and Psychopathology, 3,* 137–162.

Rutter, M. (1970). Autistic children: Infancy to adulthood. *Seminars in Psychiatry, 2,* 435–450.

Rutter, M. (1978). Diagnosis and definition of childhood autism. *Journal of Autism and Developmental Disorders, 8,* 139–161.

Rydell, P.J. and Mirenda, P. (1991). The effects of two levels of linguistic constraint on echolalia and generative language production in children with autism. *Journal of Autism and Developmental Disorders, 21,* 131–157.

Scheuermann, B. and Webber, J. (2002). *Autism: Teaching does Make a Difference.* Belmont, CA: Wadsworth/Thomson Learning.

Schopler, E. and Mesibov, G.B. (eds.) (1985). *Communication Problems in Autism.* New York: Plenum Press.

Schopler, E., Reichler, R.J., and Renner, B.R. (1988). *The Childhood Autism Rating Scale.* Los Angeles: Western Psychological Services.

Sigafoos, J. (2000). Communication development and aberrant behavior in children with developmental disabilities. *Education and Training in Mental Retardation and Developmental Disabilities, 35,* 168–176.

Sigafoos, J., Arthur-Kelly, M., and Butterfield, N. (2006). *Enhancing Everyday Communication for Children with Disabilities.* Baltimore: Paul H. Brookes Publishing Co.

Sigafoos, J. and Pennell, D. (1995). Parent and teacher assessment of receptive and expressive language in preschool children with developmental disabilities. *Education and Training in Mental Retardation and Developmental Disabilities, 30,* 329–335.

Sigafoos, J., Roberts, D., Kerr, M., et al. (1994). Opportunities for communication in classrooms serving children with developmental disabilities. *Journal of Autism and Developmental Disorders, 24,* 259–280.

Skinner, B.F. (1957). *Verbal Behavior.* Englewood Cliffs, NJ: Prentice-Hall.

Sturmey, P. and Sevin, J.A. (1994). Defining and diagnosing autism. In *Autism in Children and Adults: Etiology, Assessment, and Intervention* (J.L. Matson, ed.) pp. 13–36. Pacific Grove, CA: Brooks/Cole.

Van Hasselt, V.B., Hersen, M., and Bellack, A.S. (1981). The validity of role play tests for assessing social skills in children. *Behavior Therapy, 12,* 202–216.

Van Hasselt, V.B., Hersen, M., and Kazdin, A.E. (1985). Assessment of social skills in visually-handicapped adolescents. *Behaviour Research & Therapy, 23,* 53–63.

Watson, L.R., Baranek, G.T., Crais, E.R., et al. (2007). The first inventory: Retrospective parent responses to a questionnaire designed to identify one-year-olds at risk for autism. *Journal of Autism and Developmental Disorders*, **37**, 49–61.

Wetherby, A.M. and Prizant, B. (1992). Profiling young children's communicative competence. In *Causes and Effects in Communication and Language Intervention* (S. Warren and J. Reichle, eds.) pp. 217–253. Baltimore: Paul H. Brookes Publishing Co.

Winner, M.G. (2002). Assessment of social skills for students with Asperger syndrome and high-functioning autism. *Assessment for Effective Intervention*, **27**, 73–80.

7

ASSESSMENT OF INDEPENDENT LIVING/ADAPTIVE SKILLS

NAOMI SWIEZY[1], MELISSA STUART[2],
PATRICIA KORZEKWA[3], AND STACIE POZDOL[4]

[1]*Associate Professor of Clinical Psychology in Clinical Psychiatry*
[2]*Behavioral Research Specialist*
[3]*Special Education Liaison*
[4]*Lead Behavioral Specialist, The Christian Sarkine Autism Treatment Center at Riley Hospital for Children and the Indiana University School of Medicine, Indianapolis, IN, USA*

INTRODUCTION

Autism is a developmental disorder distinguished by impairments in three core areas: communication, socialization, and repetitive behavior. These core impairments are often associated with deficits in adaptive functioning (American Psychiatric Association, 1994; Volkmar et al., 1987). Sparrow et al. (1984) define adaptive functioning as the development and application of abilities required for gaining personal independence and social sufficiency. Interest in the assessment of adaptive behavior exploded recently due to convergence in three areas (Winters et al., 2005). First, the Diagnostic and Statistical Manual of Mental Disorders (American Psychiatric Association, 1994) began addressing issues of functional impairment in the diagnosis of several disorders. Additionally, health care providers, caregivers, educators and consumers began advocating for outcomes focused on functionality over symptom relief. Finally, research demonstrating that improvements in adaptive behavior do not necessarily correlate with symptom reduction and that the two can each be assessed and intervened upon independently of the other fueled an increase in interest (Winters et al., 2005).

There are two compelling reasons to assess adaptive behavior in individuals with autism. First is that adaptive behavior is a good indicator of an individual's level of functioning and independence. An individual's level of adaptive skill development, more so than cognitive skill, is often the main factor in determining his or her ability to function independently. Level of adaptive behavior is also easier to determine than level of intellectual functioning, particularly when assessing individuals with severe or profound comorbid mental retardation (Kraijer, 2000). Evidence indicates that for individuals with an autism spectrum disorder (ASD), measures of intelligence are highly variable and likely do not present an accurate picture of actual cognitive potential, especially in younger children (Magiati and Howlin, 2001). These intelligence measures also vary in strength of correlation with measures of adaptive behavior (Roberts et al., 1993). For example, a study of preschool children with autism reported that the scores on two separate measures of intelligence varied significantly, with the Bayley Scales of Infant Development producing the lowest IQ scores and the Merrill-Palmer Intelligence Test producing the highest (Magiati and Howlin, 2001). Further evidence demonstrates that the Leiter-R, a test often used to measure intelligence in individuals with autism, does not consistently correlate with scores on the Vineland Adaptive Behavior Scale (VABS), ranging from $r = 0.49$ to $r = 0.80$ (Szatmari et al., 2002; Tsatsanis et al., 2003). This variability in correlation has also been demonstrated in other measures of intellectual functioning compared to adaptive functioning, including the Kaufman Assessment Battery for Children ($r = 0.39$) and the Woodcock-Johnson ($r = 0.78$, $r = 0.91$) (Roberts et al., 1993). Measures of adaptive functioning provide information about an individual's actual or typical behavior, whereas intelligence is more relevant to potential behavior or ability. Finally, adaptive behavior is easier to modify or change than cognitive functioning, allowing it to function as both a treatment moderator and outcome (Kraijer, 2000).

The second reason to assess adaptive behavior in individuals with autism is that it allows a provider to ascertain directly how well an individual functions in various environments. Adaptive skills are required for successful integration into the community. Through assessment of adaptive skills, clinicians, teachers, and other care providers can develop goals for independence and successful community integration. Data collected from assessment can be used to inform educational and clinical goals in three ways: determining which skills have been mastered, which are emerging, and which are lacking within an individual's repertoire. Additionally, assessment data can aid in prioritizing goals for intervention and instruction. Finally, periodic assessment of adaptive behavior can provide information on skill growth and acquisition. Thus, it is of utmost importance that care providers be able to adequately assess an individual with autism's adaptive functioning in order to supplement diagnosis, and inform treatment planning (Winters et al., 2005).

Several considerations should be made when deciding to test adaptive behavior. First, assessment of adaptive skills for an individual with autism should be one component of a core, comprehensive assessment and should include all relevant areas of adaptive functioning. Such a core battery might include diagnostic measurement, cognitive assessment, language assessment, and adaptive behavior assessment (Ozonoff et al., 2005). Additionally, several important considerations should inform the process. First, one must maintain a developmental perspective. Research has shown that individuals with an ASD display a pattern of adaptive behavior characterized by significant deficits in socialization, moderate deficits in communication, and areas of relative strength in daily living skills (Fenton et al., 2003). However, an individual's developmental stage, areas of strength and weakness, current level of functioning, and changes in form and quality of symptomatology must also be addressed since an ASD is a lifelong disorder characterized by periods of uneven development. Great gains may be made in some areas, while others may be slower to progress. Furthermore, the pattern detected may change over time as adaptive behavior varies with age. Fenton and colleagues (2003), suggest that deficits in adaptive functioning become more evident with age and increasing cognitive ability. More so, in the ASD population, individuals consistently demonstrate adaptive behavior levels lower than their chronological age and intelligence, especially those with a normal IQ (Bolte and Poustka, 2002). Both adaptive behavior and cognitive functioning relate to an individual's ability to cope with and adapt to the environments; hence, they are expected to be related, but not necessarily strongly correlated (Roberts et al., 1993). This finding suggests that assessment of both adaptive behavior and cognitive functioning need to be evaluated to obtain a comprehensive picture of the individual's true abilities. Given the extreme variability both within and across individuals on the spectrum in the presentation of symptomatology, strengths, and weaknesses, it is important to maintain an appropriate perspective when conducting an assessment.

A second consideration is determining which areas of adaptive behavior to measure. An initial assessment should include at least a broad measure of each core domain to inform areas of strength and weakness and to develop individualized goals based on areas of need. These core areas include communication, socialization, and activities of daily living. Each broad domain contains multiple specific sets of skills. Additional broad domains may include physical and motor development, and functional academic skills (Roberts et al., 1993). Communication generally includes both verbal and nonverbal forms of communication, functional, expressive, receptive, written and social communication. Socialization generally includes leisure and play activities, relationships with others, and community functioning such as following rules and social norms. Daily living activities are primarily composed of self-help skills that directly relate to an individual's level of independence, such as feeding and dressing oneself, understanding concepts of money and time, and having good hygiene practices. Once the broad categories listed above have been assessed, more targeted skill-specific measures can be used to further evaluate a specific adaptive behavior.

Another consideration when assessing an individual on the autism spectrum is the inclusion of multiple contexts and sources in the evaluation. Adaptive behaviors are often defined by the expectations or standards of those who interact with the individual. Depending on the environment, symptom expression, strengths, and weaknesses within an individual may vary. Both the structure and demands of the environment as well as the interaction with people present can influence the demonstration of adaptive skills. For individuals with an ASD, the most salient environments are the home, school or work, and community. Additional environments of interest include the therapeutic environment, and other social environments. To obtain a comprehensive picture of the level of functioning, the individual should be assessed in several environments. Additionally, the use of multiple informants, inclusive of family, medical, educational, clinical and other care providers, should be used whenever possible to obtain the most comprehensive view of the individual's level of adaptive functioning. The focus of this chapter will be on the three most salient environments and core informants within those environments: parents, educators, clinicians, and self-report.

A final consideration in assessing adaptive behavior is the manner in which the data are obtained from the source or setting. This chapter will cover four basic methods of obtaining information related to adaptive functioning, each with its own unique advantages and disadvantages. A complete assessment of adaptive behavior can include all four types of assessments both within and across settings. The first method is through surveys and questionnaires. A second way of obtaining information from different sources and settings is through interview. Interviews can be conducted with any caregiver and provide the best way for determining an individual's current skills (Kraijer, 2000). Interviews can be structured or unstructured and may provide protocols for scoring and interpreting responses. Another method of obtaining information from multiple sources and settings is direct observation of the individual while in that setting. This approach provides the best source for observing the context of the adaptive behavior. Observations concern spontaneous behavior in day-to-day situations that can cover extended periods (Kraijer, 2000). A final and arguably less-used way of obtaining information about the individual's adaptive functioning is through self-report.

This chapter will describe measures ascribing to the four methods of obtaining data as relevant to the particular context and informants involved. The first section will discuss assessments conducted in the home or informed by the individual's parent or guardian. The second will focus on the school setting and assessments informed by the individual's teacher. The third will describe assessments conducted by the clinician in clinic or community-based settings. The final section will address self-report measures. The choice of which type of assessment to use in a particular setting or for a particular informant will ultimately be made based on the form, frequency, and quality of the data needed, as well as practical issues such as time, training, and financial resources required.

Scale selection for this chapter reflects a broad perspective in a rapidly evolving field. Multiple sources were reviewed, including peer-reviewed literature, book chapters, and test and measurement databases. Selection of measures was also informed by clinical practice. The selection of scales was intended to give the reader a broad representation of the variety of settings and sources of measurement currently available, without serving as a comprehensive, systematic review. Additionally, efforts were made to include measures appropriate for all ages. While several measures discussed below are applicable across the lifespan, those specifically for adults with autism are lacking in number and quality and thus are not specifically addressed in this review. Table 7.1 presents a brief snapshot of all studies reviewed for this chapter.

HOME-BASED OR PARENT/CAREGIVER-REPORT ASSESSMENTS

A range of adaptive skills has been studied utilizing parent-report measures. One potential advantage is the in-depth knowledge parents have about their children. Parents spend hours per day across developmentally critical years with their children. They have a personal investment in noticing each newly acquired skill and in tracking those skills that appear to be delayed or absent. For these reasons, many measures of adaptive skills have focused on parents or primary caregivers as respondents. All measures that rely on these individuals as respondents will herein be termed parent-report measures.

Some of the adaptive skills addressed by parent-report measures include communication abilities (Aman et al., 1996; Bishop, 1998; Rimland and Edelson, 1999; Salvia et al., 1995), social interaction skills (Harrison and Oakland, 2005; Matson et al., 1983), and self-care skills (MacDonald and Barton, 1986; Salvia et al., 1995). Several measurement tools assess a range of adaptive skills (Salvia et al., 1995), while others focus exclusively on one aspect, such as pragmatic language (Bishop, 1998). A handful of the adaptive measures in existence have been used exclusively in individuals with ASD (Stone and Hogan, 1993), while others have been used in a variety of populations (Matson et al., 1983). The presentation format often used is that of a questionnaire or interview. This section of the chapter will focus on various parent-report measures of adaptive skills frequently used in individuals with ASD.

SURVEYS AND QUESTIONNAIRES

AAMD-Adaptive Behavior Scale (AAMD-ABS)

The AAMD-ABS is a commonly used measure that has been studied extensively in individuals with mental retardation (MR) as well as a wide range of other

TABLE 7.1 Summary of Adaptive Measures.

Measure	Use (population, ages[†])	Respondents/ Alternate Forms	Domains of Adaptive Behavior
AAMD-Adaptive Behavior Scale, Second Edition (ABS-2, ABS-S:2); Lambert et al., 1993)	ASD, Broad, MR, 3–16 years	Parent Teacher Self	Adaptive, AAMR Domains, Maladaptive
Adaptive Behavior Evaluation (ABES; McCarney, 1995)	MR, 5–18 years	Parent Teacher Clinician	Adaptive, AAMR Domains, Diagnostic Screening
Assessment of Adaptive Areas (AAA; Bryant et al., 1996)	Broad, 3–60 years	Parent Teacher Clinician	Adaptive, AAMR Domains
Behavior Assessment System for Children, Second Edition (BASC-2; Reynolds and Kamphaus, 2004)	Broad, 2–21 years	Parent Teacher Self	Adaptive, Externalizing, Internalizing
Behavior Observation Scale-Revised (BOS-R; Freeman et al., 1984)	ASD, MR, Children, Adolescents	Clinician Observation	Adaptive, Leisure
Behavior Rating Instrument for Autistic and Atypical Children (BRIAAC; Ruttenberg et al., 1966)	Broad, Children	Clinician Observation	Communication, Development, Motor, Social Skills
Checklist of Adaptive Living Skills (CALS; Morreau and Bruininks, 1991)	Broad, Lifespan	Observation: Parent Teacher Employer	Community, Daily Living, Independence, Leisure, Residential, Work
Experimental-analogue Functional Assessment (EFA; Iwata et al., 1984)	Broad, Lifespan	Clinician Observation	Maladaptive

Instrument	Population	Respondent/Format	Domains
Scales of Independent Behavior – Revised (SIB-R; Bruininks, Woodcock et al., 1996)	Broad, 3–90 years	Interview: Parent Short-Form	Communication, Community, Motor, Personal, Social Skills
School Function Assessment (SFA; Coster et al., 1998)	Broad, Children, Adolescents	Parent Teacher Observation	Adaptive, Cognitive, Participation, Socialization
Topeka Association for Retarded Citizens Assessment System (TARC; Sailor and Mix, 1975)	MR, 3–16 years	Teacher Parent	Communication, Daily Living, Motor, Social Skills
Vineland Adaptive Behavior Scales, Second Edition (VABS-II; Sparrow et al., 2005)	Broad, birth – 18 years 11 months 30 days; ASD, 2–59 years	Interview: Parent Survey: Parent, Teacher	Communication, Daily Living, Maladaptive, Motor, Socialization

[†] specific ages are provided when readily available, otherwise a more general category of Children, Adolescents, Adults, or Lifespan is used; ASD = Autism Spectrum Disorder; Broad = Broad populations with disabilities; MR = Mental Retardation; AAMR Domains = Communication, Self-care, Home living, Community, Social, Self-direction, Health and safety, Functional academics, Leisure and work.

populations (Nihira et al., 1975). The ABS is most appropriate for school-age children 3–16 years old. A review of this measure indicates average inter-rater reliability estimates of 0.86, internal consistency of 0.91, and test–retest reliability of 0.91 for the adaptive skills portion (Spreat, 1982). These psychometric properties are similar when utilized with a sample of individuals with autism (Perry and Factor, 1989). Though the AAMD-ABS is a highly researched and reliable measure of adaptive skills, research is limited regarding the utility of this measure with the ASD population.

Behavior Assessment System for Children (BASC)

The BASC, recently revised to create the BASC-2, is an in-depth assessment of internalizing and externalizing behavior difficulties as well as adaptive skills in children, adolescents, and adults (Reynolds and Kamphaus, 1992). It includes a parent-report scale, a teacher-report scale, and a self-report scale. The adaptive subscale of the parent form consists of five components: activities of daily living, adaptability, functional communication, leadership, and social skills. Studies of the BASC have revealed alphas for the domains of 0.83–0.95, with test–retest reliability ranging from 0.90 to 0.94 over two months (Reynolds and Kamphaus, 1992). Given its use in a variety of ASD research and the well-established norms (Lopata et al., 2006; Meyer et al., 2006), the BASC shows promise as an adaptive measure for the ASD population. Information regarding the more recently released BASC-2 and its utility in individuals with ASD has yet to be fully documented.

INTERVIEW-BASED ASSESSMENT TOOLS

Vineland Adaptive Behavior Scales (VABS)

The most widely used adaptive measure with individuals with ASD is the Vineland Adaptive Behavior Scales, which consists of three core domains and two optional domains (Sparrow et al., 1984). The core domains are Communication, Daily Living Skills, and Socialization. An optional domain for children under 6 years old is Motor Skills. A Maladaptive Behavior domain for children over 5 years old is also included. The VABS is administered to the parent or caregiver by trained personnel and takes approximately 45 minutes to complete. The examiner begins with a general prompt, and via responses from the caregiver, guides the interview through the various domains. Items are scored by the administrator on a 3-point Likert scale. Scores from each domain are converted to standardized composite scores (mean = 100, standard deviation = 15), and summed to create an adaptive behavior composite. Higher scores indicate better adaptive functioning for all domains, excepting the Maladaptive Behavior domain, where higher scores indicate greater endorsement of problem behaviors. Standardized scores are available for birth to 18 years 11 months. Age equivalents and adaptive levels are also available for each domain, again excepting Maladaptive Behavior. Supplementary norms are also available for individuals with ASD, ages 2 to 59 years making this an appropriate assessment across the lifespan (Carter et al., 1998). The VABS have adequate test–retest reliability and internal consistency estimates (average between 0.80 and 0.90) for both the Adaptive Behavior Composite and domain scores (Sparrow et al., 1984). Inter-rater reliability estimates are also good (Winters et al., 2005). In addition, the validity of the VABS has been well established. Furthermore, the literature demonstrates that it coincides with other measures of adaptive functioning (Roberts et al., 1993; Sparrow et al., 1984). The psychometric properties and thorough use in research (Burack and Volkmar, 1992; Kraijer, 2000; Paul et al., 2004; Volkmar et al., 1987) make VABS the de facto gold standard for both clinical and research use.

Advantages of the VABS are plenty. Given its wide use in research, there are many opportunities for comparison with different populations. The VABS has a good normative base and the availability of supplemental norms is unique. Additionally, the VABS measures the general areas of adaptive behavior needed in a comprehensive assessment, and can track an individual's progress over the lifespan. It requires only moderate training to administer and score.

Disadvantages of the VABS include application of the results in that the pattern of adaptive behavior found is most homogenous within individuals with autism and is less relevant and distinguishing between those on the autism spectrum and those with other disorders (Fenton et al., 2003). Additionally, because of the somewhat lengthy time needed to administer and score, the Vineland does not lend itself well to frequent use but does appear to act as a good indicator of change before and after intervention. Concerns regarding the face validity of some items and use of an outdated normative sample have been addressed in the latest revision (Sparrow and Ciccetti, 2005).

Scales of Independent Behavior-Revised (SIB-R)

The SIB-R is another commonly used interview consisting of 14 subscales in four areas: motor skills, social and communication skills, personal living skills, and community living skills (Bruininks et al., 1996). Each subscale contains between 16 and 20 items, with items presented in ascending level of difficulty. Items are scored on a 4-point scale; and subscales can be averaged to find a Broad Independence Scale score. The SIB-R has been normed on individuals from 3 months to 90 years, making it appropriate for use across the lifespan (Bruininks et al., 1996). A recent study of the SIB-R in 293 children and adolescents (ages 3–18) found internal consistencies ranging from 0.87 to 0.96, with an average estimate of 0.92 (Lecavalier et al., 2006). The SIB-R has been used in various samples with autism, primarily as a measure of change in response to treatment (Keen et al., 2007; Lecavalier et al., 2006). The SIB-R has also been used to verify the social and communication deficits in samples of individuals with ASD (Edgin and Pennington, 2005). One advantage to the SIB-R is that administration does not require extensive training. An interesting component to this measure is the assessment of independence. In lieu of the interview, a short checklist form is also available which may allow for more frequent data collection. A distinct disadvantage is that, despite its solid psychometric standing, it has yet to be adopted as a standard measurement equal to the VABS, and, as such, it is lacking empirical data. Additionally, the scoring system for determining the Broad Independence score is complex and can be time-consuming. Overall, the SIB-R shows promise as an in-depth adaptive skills interview for individuals with ASD.

In summary, there are a variety of parent-report measures of adaptive skills and several others exist (CCC, Bishop, 1998; DAS, Holmes et al., 1982; RISA, Salvia et al., 1995; Tasse et al., 1996). Most typically, survey and questionnaire data are collected from these informants. Some measures have been used far more often in individuals with ASD than have others. Few have been studied extensively in individuals with autism and further research is necessary to ensure that the measures are reliable in individuals with autism and at a variety of age levels.

SCHOOL-BASED OR TEACHER-REPORT ASSESSMENTS

Many of the larger, more commonly used adaptive measures have a teacher report as a component for gathering additional information during the assessment process. These teacher reports typically come in the form of a survey or questionnaire based on informal observations in the school setting. Assessing the adaptive skills of students diagnosed with autism spectrum disorders can be a critical component in the process of determining goals and objectives for general and educational programming and services. Determining areas of strength and weakness within the established domains of adaptive skills is not only part of the initial evaluation process for determining educational programming needs and placement, but it is also a critical component of the ongoing assessment process established to determine student growth and program direction.

Practitioners in the educational setting use a variety of assessment formats for gathering information from parents, teachers and other specialists in the educational setting as a part of the overall assessment process. The areas that are broadly assessed by standardized assessment measures in the educational setting include social skills, communication, living skills, classroom routines, functional academics and motor skills. The following is a sample of measures being utilized in the educational setting to assess adaptive functioning levels, which include a teacher-report component or are designed for use by school personnel.

a. Surveys and Questionnaires
   i. Vineland Adaptive Behavior Scales – Classroom Edition (VABS-CE)
      The Vineland Adaptive Behavior Scales-Classroom Edition, and its most recent revision in 2006, is the most widely utilized measure for assessing adaptive behavior skills within the school setting (Sparrow et al., 1984). The individual's teacher completes the questionnaire based on informal observation in the classroom. This questionnaire can

be utilized with students aged 3–12 years who participate in a variety of school settings including full or partial inclusion, self-contained, preschool placements and structured daycare programs. Four domains matching the structure of the original VABS are assessed, including communication, daily living, socialization, and motor skills. The VABS-CE is structured to include areas that the teacher would most likely observe in a classroom setting. An adaptive behavior composite score is provided when all four domains are administered, which is comparable to the interpretation of the VABS composite.

Studies have been conducted comparing the classroom and parent survey editions of the VABS in samples of students with autism (Szatmari et al., 1994) and those with multiple disabilities (Voelker et al., 1997). Results of those studies were similar indicating parent and teacher ratings were highly correlated including a close agreement on relative ranking of the children in adaptive behavior ability. One notable exception found suggests teachers systematically rated the children as having more skills than did parents (Achenbach et al., 1987). Cicchetti and Sparrow (1989), described several possible reasons for these differences in rating including the differing formats of VABS versions, the amount of time a teacher has worked with the student, teacher dedication to working with students with disabilities, and differences in environments and levels of structure. Teachers who have completed the survey indicate difficulty with the item order, length and need to "guesstimate" on certain items not observable in the school setting (Reynolds, 1987).

ii. AAMR Adaptive Behavior Scale-II School Edition (ABS-S:2)

The AAMR Adaptive Behavior Scale-II-School Edition is the second revision of the original AAMD Adaptive Behavior Scale-Public School Version developed in Lambert et al. (1993). This scale is designed to be utilized in the educational setting to assess levels of independence, social skills and the need for specialized programming. The ABS-S:2 is most widely used to assess the functioning level of children and adolescents with mental retardation and autism spectrum disorders. The test consists of two parts. Part one assesses nine domains including independent functioning, physical development, economic activity, language development, prevocational/vocational activity, numbers and time, self-direction, responsibility and socialization. Part two assesses seven maladaptive behavioral domains, which include social behavior, conformity, trustworthiness, stereotyped and hyperactive behavior, self-abusive behavior, social engagement and disturbing interpersonal behavior. The ABS-S:2 is completed independently by the teacher. The ABS-S:2 can be used in the development of individualized educational plans (IEP), curriculum development, evaluation of training programs and to compare specific behaviors in a variety of settings.

The following measures show promise but have not been traditionally used with the ASD population. The field would benefit from further research related to these measures.

iii. The School Function Assessment (SFA)

The School Functional Assessment (SFA) is a criterion-referenced instrument designed to measure a student's performance of functional tasks as well as his/her participation in the academic and social aspects of elementary school programs (Coster, 1998). This measure is designed to be administered with students in grades K–6 and should be completed by someone who has knowledge of the individual being evaluated including teachers, parents or other school professionals who work closely with the student. This measure relies mostly on observation, but at times may require some value judgments by the rater. The SFA was originally developed as a behavior assessment, but recent reviews have reported that the measure should be classified more as an adaptive behavior rating scale (Piersel, 2001). The SFA is divided into three parts including participation, task supports, and activity performance. Internal consistency reliability coefficients range form 0.92 to 0.98 for each of the 27 scales. Test–retest reliability coefficients range form 0.80 to 0.99 on a sample of 29 participants. Despite promising psychometrics, limitations include lack of data on the scale of structure, lack of an inter-rater agreement coefficient and lack of use with the ASD population specifically (Piersel, 2001).

iv. Checklist of Adaptive Living Skills (CALS)

The CALS is a criterion-referenced measure that can be used as a tool for program planning across the lifespan (Morreau and Bruininks, 1991). It is organized into four broad domains consisting of 800 specific behaviors related to personal independence, self-care, leisure, community skills, work skills and residential environments. The CALS can be used to develop program goals, training objectives and progress made within the specific domains. Skills can be assessed within a variety of settings including classrooms, residential placements and job training sites. The CALS is a checklist observational system that can be administered by a variety of practitioners in the educational and vocational setting including teachers, case managers, social workers and direct care providers. The examiner should have the opportunity to observe the individual in a natural environment for at least three months. Internal consistency was reported for persons with and without disabilities on a sample of 627 subjects from eight different states. The majority of coefficients for persons with disabilities ranged from 0.80 to 0.90. Inter-rater reliability was not assessed (Bachelor, 1995). Respectable psychometric properties suggest the import of further evaluation and consideration of utilization with the ASD population.

v. Assessment of Adaptive Areas (AAA)

The AAA is categorized as a behavior assessment designed to identify deficits in 10 adaptive skills areas defined by the American Association on Mental Retardation (Bryant et al., 2001). These domains include communication, self-care, home living, community use, social, self-direction, health and safety, functional academics, leisure and work. The authors define four purposes for the AAA including identifying individuals with mental retardation, determining adaptive strengths and weaknesses, documenting progress in adaptive domains, and conducting research. The primary purpose is to identify individuals with deficits in adaptive behavior functioning. The AAA is normed for individuals ages 3–60 years and over and is typically administered by someone who is working directly with the individual, including teachers, parents and direct care providers. The AAA does not have a standardization sample separate from the AAMR Adaptive Behavior Scales. The median internal consistency coefficients range from 0.89 to 0.98. The test–retest coefficients range from 0.78 to 0.94 with a median of 0.83 (Cummings, 2001). Promising results for psychometrics suggest the need to research the AAA further, particularly with the ASD population.

vi. Adaptive Behavior Evaluation Scale (ABES)

The ABES is designed to assist in the diagnosis and placement process for individuals with mental retardation, emotional disturbance and behavior disorders (McCarney, 1995). The ABES is also designed to assist in programming decisions for the individual. The ABES is a norm-referenced rating scale intended for use by school personnel and designed for children and adolescents ages 5–18 years. The ABES measures the adaptive behaviors skills within the 10 domains identified by the American Association of Mental Retardation. The goals of the ABES identified by the authors include screening for adaptive problems, providing an adaptive measure for any referred student, providing information for diagnosis of mental retardation, aid in developing goals and objectives in the problem areas, aid in identifying instructional activities in problem areas, and identifying entry and exit points for program documentation. Administration of the ABES should be completed by parents, classroom teachers, or other school personnel familiar with the individual, including counselors and aids. There is a home and school version of the ABES available, both consisting of 104 items.

Scoring consists of a 5-point rating scale that is completed based on observations of the identified skill or by information gathered from other school personnel. Test–retest reliability was evaluated for 109 students on the school version and 83 for the home version over a 30-day interval and resulted in coefficients averaging 0.75 (Kranzler, 2001). Inter-rater reliability for the school version was rated by 57 teachers and coefficients range from 0.77 to 0.84. Limitations of this measure include small samples across age levels for test–retest and inter-rater reliability, no analyses of possible test bias with racial/ethnic groups, and no reported evidence to support use of the ABES with individuals with ASD (Kranzler, 2001).

vii. The Topeka Association for Retarded Citizens Assessment System (TARC)

The TARC is a third-party rating scale which is most frequently completed by the teacher of record (Sailor and Mix, 1975). The TARC consists of four areas including Self-help, Motor, Communication, and social domains. This assessment is most reliable and valid for young children with severe disabilities. It is most discriminative at the lowest levels of functioning and is sensitive to small changes in adaptive functioning. The TARC was developed with a standardization sample of 283 institutionalized children and adolescents who ranged in age from 3 to 16 years. The TARC was utilized in a study that looked at the assessment of play and adaptive behaviors in students with developmental disabilities (Sigafoos et al., 1999). Of the 13 children who participated in the study, four of the children were diagnosed with autistic disorder. The TARC was chosen to assess the adaptive behaviors of the children, because of its validity with individuals with severe disabilities and its reported easy use for teachers and parents as compared to other adaptive behavior scales. This measure would also appear promising for use in the field of ASD.

viii. Behavior Assessment System for Children, Second Edition (BASC-2)

The BASC-2 is a measure focusing on the behaviors and emotions of children and adolescents (Reynolds and Kamphaus, 1998). The teacher-rating scale is used to measure adaptive and problem behaviors in the school setting. By gathering information from a variety of sources, the BASC-2 is helpful in developing behavior intervention plans and IEPs. As previously mentioned, the psychometrics on this measure are not yet sufficiently reported.

In summary, teacher reports and other structured observational measures completed by school professionals are critical components in the assessment process for determining the adaptive behavior skills of students in this setting and overall. Determining a student's strengths and areas of need are a part of the ongoing assessment process aimed at programming effectively. Future research in the area of teacher reports on adaptive behavior skills should include studies focusing on its reliability when utilized with individuals on the autism spectrum.

Further research should also be conducted on how the information gathered from the measure impacts treatment and educational programming.

CLINIC-BASED OR CLINICIAN-REPORT ASSESSMENTS

Measurement of adaptive behavior by clinicians in both community and clinic-based centers has been studied widely due to the potentially far-reaching diagnostic and treatment implications for the individual. As the relationship of the person to the social environment, adaptive behavior can pertain to one's success in such varied domains as school or work, personal relationships, self-care, and leisure skills. As individuals with ASD become further integrated into community settings and the emphasis on functional curriculum and integration increases, the role of adaptive functioning is quickly becoming a key aspect in need of assessment in a variety of modalities inclusive of clinician-administered assessments (Winters et al., 2005).

Direct observation of operationally defined target behaviors provides an opportunity for an alternative means of assessment, to derive information from more than history and reporting. The methodology has been utilized a great deal in single-case research over time, but has lagged behind the use of standardized checklists, ratings, and other informant measures that have been utilized for years (Matson et al., 2006) likely due to the very large time and staff cost associated with the method.

A wide range of adaptive behavior skills have been measured through these means, including but not limited to: play behavior including cooperative play, pretend play, and symbolic play (for more details, see Anderson et al., 2004; Black et al., 1975; Charman et al., 1997; Wulff, 1985); social interaction skills including humor, joint attention, (Anderson et al., 2004; Charman et al., 1997; Van Bourgondien and Mesibov, 1987); functional communication skills, such as phrase speech, appropriate gestures, and eye contact (Charman et al., 2005; Lord et al., 2000); self-help and community skills (Belfiore and Mace, 1994); and other adaptive skills including empathy, imitation, and stereotypies (Charman et al., 1997; Gardenier et al., 2004). Some measurement tools and strategies utilized by clinicians in the clinic and community settings have focused on a broad range of adaptive skills, while others have focused more precisely on specific areas of interest. This section of the chapter will focus on a variety of measures of adaptive skills administered by clinicians for use with the ASD population, specifically highlighting those utilized with the highest rates of prevalence and success.

OBSERVATION-BASED MEASUREMENT

Direct observation of individuals with ASD in both natural and contrived settings has been utilized widely for the assessment of adaptive behavior functioning. Using such methods has distinct advantages in the study of adaptive skills in general and for individuals with an ASD in particular. According to Carter and colleagues (1996), the utilization of the more standardized forms of assessment can assist in: (1) the identification of strengths and weaknesses, (2) planning of educational, clinical intervention, and vocational goals, (3) monitoring progress over time; and (4) documentation of intervention outcomes. Additionally, the utilization of observational modes of assessment can also serve to clearly document the qualitative aspects (key in the area of autism), identify individualized examples, and generally demonstrate more understanding of daily functioning, providing further vital information regarding the implementation of interventions.

Observation-based measurements have often taken the form of standardized protocols and systems developed for distinct functions such as diagnostic assessment. With these measurement tools, the observation is structured according to protocol and standard environmental stimuli are presented, standard behaviors are observed, and standard scoring rubrics are utilized. The defining characteristics of autism (typically including impairments in empathy, pretend play, joint attention, and imitation) are often linked to later problems in social understanding and reciprocal social communication. These adaptive skills are crucial to normalized development in the areas of communication and socialization (Rogers and Pennington, 1991). As such, it is important to look at measures often used for diagnosing ASD that may also provide some measure of these areas of adaptive functioning as well as highlight areas in need of intervention.

Behavior Observation Scale – Revised (BOS-R)

The revised BOS is a revised version from the original developed by Freeman et al. in 1978 (Freeman et al., 1984). The original BOS was developed as a means for the diagnosis and assessment of symptoms over time. The measure involves rating of 67 behaviors that are objectively defined on a scale of 0 to 3 after observing the individual in a standardized play situation. The measure is easily learned, reliable, and accounts for behavioral change as individuals mature and develop. In stepwise discriminant analyses, the measure was seen to discriminate normal individuals from those with autism or mental retardation. However, the discriminative ability was poor in discriminating the disability groups (Freeman et al., 1978).

As such, Freeman et al. (1984), developed the revised BOS inclusive of 24 objectively defined behaviors divided into 4 domains: solitary, relation to objects, relation to people, and language. Inter-observer reliability was noted as greater than 0.70 for all but eight of the items and stepwise discriminative analysis resulted in a mean correct classification of 75 percent between low autism and mental retardation and 87.7 percent between high autism and normalized individuals.

While useful as a diagnostic screening assessment for autism, it could still potentially serve as a useful tool to objectively describe adaptive behavior in individuals with autism (Freeman et al., 1984; Kanner, 1943).

Behavior Rating Instrument for Autistic and Atypical Children (BRIAAC)

The BRIAAC was developed from the observation of children with autism in a psychoanalytically based day care setting (Ruttenberg et al., 1966). The scales of the tool measure communication, social, developmental, and motor repetition related areas. Despite the unique development of the scale with the utilization of actual clinical notes to construct the content and the use of behaviorally defined items, the measure has not been utilized widely. Psychometric properties have not yet been fully established. Inter-rater reliability is noted as 0.85 to 0.88 and internal consistency ranges from 0.54 to 0.86, noting some common attributes of scales but enough differentiation to warrant the use of each scale. Concurrent validity was measured by comparing ratings with those at another child study center. Significant correlation was noted for the total scale but only three of eight subscales. Discriminative validity has been established to distinguish between normal, mental retardation, and autism comparison groups.

Experimental-analogue Functional Assessment (EFA)

The popular use of EFAs also reflects an observational mode of assessment that, though it does not involve direct assessment of adaptive behavior, is certainly relevant and essential to a comprehensive assessment in this area (Iwata et al., 1982). As reflected in Campbell (2003), the core difficulties in social functioning (and other adaptive behaviors) can result in increased anxiety and frustration, thus leading to maladaptive behaviors which can interfere with the further development of adaptive functioning. The importance and relationship of maladaptive behavior problems to adaptive functioning and assessment is reflected in part by the presence of subscales and measurement of maladaptive behavior within the context of some of the most popular adaptive behavior scales.

Undoubtedly, research has shown that individuals with an ASD can learn adaptive social skills (Kohler et al., 2001) and adaptive play behavior as well as learn through modeling, imitation and observation (Lovaas and Buch, 1997). To accomplish this level of learning, however, and allow the individual to reach potential requires the necessity of limiting maladaptive behaviors that might interfere with that progress. In other words, although adaptive behaviors are often found to be more predictive of success in daily life than the level of intelligence or cognition, the presence of maladaptive behaviors can affect competence, success, and general life skills. As such, the measurement of cognition and maladaptive behavior is part of a comprehensive assessment of autism and is essential to the appropriate interpretation of adaptive skills (Carter et al., 1996; Matson et al., 1997).

EFA involves the experimental manipulation of antecedents and/or consequences thought to be maintaining behavior (Matson et al., 1999). It has been utilized with a diversity of behaviors in single-case format (Chapman et al., 1993; Grace et al., 1994; Vollmer et al., 1994). Though the analogue method of EFA has not been researched thoroughly and the test–retest convergent validity has been found to be weak to poor, it has been utilized often (Martin et al., 1999). Further, it is time consuming and not cost-effective (Matson et al., 1999). However, the research and utilization of the method continue and there is a need for more efficient and reliable methods (Horner, 1994).

Other direct observation methods

Accurate assessment of maladaptive and adaptive behaviors is important in establishing the potential impact of problem behaviors on the development of functional and adaptive skills. In addition, direct observation can provide information not otherwise accessed through standardized, informant, or other assessments. Direct observation can be useful for assessment and planning to train such skills as community skills, vocational skills, self-help (e.g., eating, hygiene, dressing, leisure) skills. Such assessment lends information regarding prognosis and effective intervention strategies. Direct observation is a method that can be useful and most precise in such assessment (Belfiore and Mace, 1994).

Direct observation can be systematic or structured (Black et al., 1975; Charman et al., 1997; Kazdin et al., 1984; Stanley and Konstantareas, in press) in the measurement of behaviors and skills as diverse as play, socialization, joint attention, empathy, eye contact, facial expressions, verbalizations and imitation. Such structured observation opportunities typically involve contrived situations or analogues designed to simulate real life events in a controlled setting to elicit potential occurrence of behavior (Kazdin et al., 1984) Providing such structure can elicit behaviors otherwise not elicited by the natural environment and can increase comparability due to norms and standardization availed with this method (Black et al., 1975).

Direct observation can also be conducted as a naturalistic observation in an effort to measure such diverse behaviors and skills as humor, social interaction, play, maladaptive behavior (Anderson et al., 2004; Charman et al., 2005; El-Ghouroury and Romanzyk, 1999; Gardenier et al., 2004; Kazdin et al., 1984; Oke and Schreibman, 1990; Van Bourgondien and Mesibov, 1987). In naturalistic observation, adaptive and other behaviors are assessed through observations of spontaneous behaviors within their natural environments. Kraijer (2000) notes that naturalistic observation can provide information about actual behavior as opposed to potential behavior that might be assessed in more standardized, contrived, or artificial conditions. In addition, naturalistic observation often allows for the assessment of very specific and individualized targets of concern and/or interest that standardized instruments and controlled structured observations cannot capture (Van Bourgondien and Mesibov, 1987). Naturalistic observation provides a means for accessing "representative and reliable data useful in treatment planning by: (1) collecting data external to the traditional assessment situation, (2) observing in multiple settings, (3) conducting multiple observations, and (4) observing during functional activities such that the assessment activities are natural and engaging, setting up for success through individualization of functional activities, motivating activities, and familiar surroundings and events

(Ogletree and Oren, 1998; Ogletree et al., 2001–2002; Stanley and Konstantareas, in press). There is no better way to learn individual strengths and needs to be successful in an environment than to observe the individual interacting in that actual environment, with actual tools, cues, activities and people (Belfiore and Mace, 1994).

Naturalistic observation will likely provide the most insight to an individual's potential as well as other key components of adaptive behavior meaningful for integration such as interfering behaviors, time it takes to complete a skill, and typical errors an individual is likely to make. Adaptive skills build much more quickly, maintain, and generalize easier when natural cues are used. Furthermore, if the individual is taught adaptive skills out of context, this can lead to a reliance on instructional cues that are later more difficult to fade (Belfiore and Mace, 1994).

SELF-REPORT ASSESSMENTS

Although most measures of adaptive skills focus on parent, teacher, or clinician ratings, a few measures also include self-report components. Self-report measures are rare for individuals with ASD possibly because a significant portion of the population may have difficulty providing accurate self-report data. However, in the age of developing more functional curriculum and programming, it can be a meaningful way to assess strengths, weaknesses, and motivating factors. A few self-report measures do exist and have been shown to be effective ways to assess adaptive skills in those individuals able to complete them.

AAMR ADAPTIVE BEHAVIOR SCALE, SECOND EDITION (ABS-2)

The AAMR Adaptive Behavior Scale (ABS, ABS-2), in both its original form and revision allow for self-report of adaptive behaviors in adolescents and adults whose abilities allow them to do so (Lambert et al., 1993). This scale is designed to assess levels of independence, and other functional measures based on the AAMR criteria. Specific psychometric properties of the ABS and ABS-2 are featured in other areas of this review.

BEHAVIOR ASSESSMENT SYSTEM FOR CHILDREN (BASC)

The BASC is described in more detail in the parent and teacher-report sections of this chapter. The newest edition of the BASC, the BASC-2 contains self-report scales for children starting at age 6 (Reynolds and Kamphaus, 2002). The self-report scales tap both adaptive skills and clinical difficulties. The adaptive scales include interpersonal relations, relations with parents, self-esteem, and self-reliance. The self-report scales of the BASC-2 are designed to be conducted as an interview for children under 7 years old and as a survey form for older children and adolescents.

SUMMARY AND CONCLUSIONS

In summary, assessment is critical in the education and treatment of those with ASD as well as in determining an individual's level of independence for community integration. As more individuals with ASD are integrated into the community, programs focusing on functional curriculums and functional integration are essential (Belfiore and Mace, 1994). Effective assessment of adaptive skills is particularly important in diagnosis, outcomes research, and for the provision of functional integration into the community. However, this assessment can also be quite challenging in that various informants see individuals in multiple different settings. Each of these various settings is paired with different people and expectations, and with potentially different behavior. Additionally, typical variability inherent in ASD over the course of development and maturation are likely to influence behaviors seen (Winters et al., 2005). The ability to assess individuals at different stages in development is critical. Using lifespan appropriate measures such as the VABS and SIB-R are useful in being able to track an individual's progress in adaptive skill acquisition over time. As such, to accomplish the assessment successfully, it is important to query from a variety of informants in multiple environments and during different critical developmental periods. An additional area of concern is in the lack of specific measures of adaptive ability for adults with ASD. Most program planning addressing adaptive behaviors is focused on school-age-children where learning these skills is vital. However, issues for addressing adaptive behaviors in adults with autism are scarce despite its importance in determining one's ability to function independently. As mentioned previously, several measures are appropriate for use across the lifespan, but none address areas of concern specific to adults. Future efforts should be made to expand normative samples on currently validated measures or to develop measures focusing more on adaptive behaviors relevant to independent living, and work skills.

As mentioned previously, individuals with autism often demonstrate deficits in adaptive behavior associated with the core diagnostic criteria of autism (American Psychiatric Association, 1994; Volkmar et al., 1987). Because of this demonstrated association, many diagnostic instruments currently available lend themselves to observing and describing adaptive behavior in individuals with autism (Schopler et al., 1988). While these instruments are described elsewhere in the book, it is important to note as they may serve a useful dual purpose as not only a diagnostic tool but also as an outcome measure for future studies (Charman et al., 2005).

Relevant to adaptive behavior assessment and dating to some of the earliest programming, IQ and adaptive skill measures have been common measures of treatment outcome (Lovaas and Buch, 1997). However, in some cases, adaptive behavior has been seen as more predictive of independence than IQ, especially in later development (Lord and Schopler, 1989). In general, there has been a movement away from traditional cognitive assessment practice toward addressing a life skills curriculum which will allow for not only the physical inclusion of the individual into society, but also on functional and adaptive participation in society as a contributing member (Belfiore and Mace, 1994).

Despite the noted importance of adaptive assessment, it has not always been readily clear which standardized assessments are most utilized or considered to be the gold standards for the field (Luiselli et al., 2001). As such, a comprehensive review was conducted of various adaptive assessment measures utilized in the area of autism practice and research. Given the broad base of the literature, this was not an exhaustive review; rather, a sample of representative studies and viewpoints serve as the basis for this chapter. As in any primary area of assessment, the need for multimodal assessment in the area of adaptive functioning has been clear. Gathering information from a variety of informants, with methods appropriate to the information relevant to those individuals and in those settings in which they function is paramount. The formats in which information is provided by informants have their strengths and weaknesses, as do the particular measures utilized to glean information from those informants.

In general, parent-, teacher-, and self-report information have been primarily assessed through the utilization of surveys, questionnaires and interviews. By far the most of utilized measure has been the VABS and newly developed VABS-II for parent and teacher reports, though the measure is lengthy and requires some practice in application. With further research, it is possible that some of the other more recent measures or those that have not yet been utilized with individuals with ASD would show promise in this field of assessment. Self-report measures have been utilized to a far lesser degree in the assessment of adaptive behavior. Certainly, the individual's level of functioning can influence his or her ability to correctly report on behaviors. However, this information is essential in establishing particularly areas of motivation and specific strengths and weaknesses relevant to this area.

The use of surveys and questionnaires, overall, has several advantages. The first advantage is that surveys can be completed by several care providers. Some surveys are provider-specific and some can be completed by anyone familiar with the individual. Depending on the length of the survey or questionnaire, they may be used to track increases in adaptive behavior over time. Many surveys have the benefit of providing a standard or composite score that can be used to compare the individual's level of skill to a greater normative sample. A disadvantage of surveys and questionnaires is that oftentimes only general adaptive behaviors are reported on which may not help in addressing individualized target skills. Additionally, there may be differences in reporting on adaptive behavior based on the raters' definition of the skill, and ability to notice salient features of its presentation. The amount of time needed to complete a survey or questionnaire is also a consideration.

Interview-based assessments are also particularly good as an overall pre- and post intervention measure. A limitation of this strategy is the length of time required of both the respondent and administrator. Oftentimes interview methods are lengthy and thus do not lend themselves to frequent use during intervention. Additional consideration should be paid to the level of training needed to administer, score, and interpret the interview protocol.

Typically, it is recognized that some measure of observation is critical for a comprehensive view of the individual. Some version of direct instruction is oftentimes most useful in tandem with other modes of assessment particularly self-report methods. Such assessment of functional skills is paramount as functional integration and life skills curriculum development take prominence. In that assessment informs direct instruction, it is important to evaluate functional routines and skills within those routines to target a functional curriculum that leads to motivation and learning. Assessing in the natural environment provides the best access to actual skills performed most naturally in the actual setting and with the actual activities and/or curriculum (Belfiore and Mace, 1994).

Direct observation can be done frequently throughout the intervention. Some direct observation measures require specific interactions between the administrator and the individual or require the individual to perform a specific task. For standardized observation assessments, a score or composite can be obtained for use in tracking progress over time and comparing the individual to a larger group. Though not a direct measure of adaptive behavior, challenging behaviors do often occur in ASD and can influence the course and development of adaptive behavior. As such, challenging behaviors are important aspects to assess, particularly through structured and controlled observational measures (Matson et al., 2006). Many structured observations that directly assess the adaptive areas specific to individuals with ASD have been traditionally used as diagnostic screening measures. However, they each have also had their uses in identifying particular skill areas in need of targeted intervention and in providing specific information relevant to specific behavior-targeted programming. Their psychometric properties are well established. Limiting concerns with observation have been the training and resources needed to properly define target behaviors, develop knowledge to correct accurate data, and acquire the time and labor to complete the assessments.

Overall, it is clear that much more research is necessary in the area of adaptive assessment given the area's relevance in a time where functional integration into the community is paramount. To date, it has not been clear as to the progress in this area in the field in that much of the literature has not been systematically and comprehensively reviewed. From this review, it is evident that far more research is necessary to analyze fully the psychometric properties of several promising measures as well as to utilize these measures specifically in the area of ASD. Given the import of assessing adaptive functioning across informants and settings and the fact that various measures are deemed appropriate for the variety of settings, it will be important to establish the various components or criteria of a gold standard multimodal assessment to ensure that this important construct is being optimally assessed.

ACKNOWLEDGMENTS

We would like to acknowledge our Center librarian Heather Coates, Behavioral Program Specialist, for her assistance in the preparation of this chapter.

REFERENCES

Achenbach, T.M., McConaughy, S.H., and Howell, C.T. (1987). Child/adolescent behavioral and emotional problems: Implications of cross-informant correlations for situational specificity. *Psychological Bulletin*, **101**(2), 213–232.

Aman, M.G., Tasse, M.J., Rojahn, J., and Hammer, D. (1996). The Nisonger CBRF: A child behavior rating form for children with developmental disabilities. *Research in Developmental Disabilities*, **17**(1), 41–57.

American Psychiatric Association. (1994). *Diagnostic and Statistical Manual of Mental Disorders-IV* (4th ed.). Washington DC: American Psychological Association.

Anderson, A., Moore, D.W., Godfrey, R., and Fletcher-Flinn, C.M. (2004). Social skills assessment of children with autism in free-play situations. *Autism*, **8**(4), 369–385.

Bachelor, P.A. (1995). Mental Measurements Yearbook, *Review of the Checklist of Adaptive Living Skills* (Vol. 12). Lincoln, NE: University of Nebraska Press.

Belfiore, P.J. and Mace, F.C. (1994). Self-help and community skills. In *Autism in Children and Adults: Etiology, Assessment, and Intervention* (J.L. Matson, ed.) pp. 193–211. Pacific Grove, CA: Brooks/Cole.

Bishop, D.V. (1998). Development of the Children's Communication Checklist (CCC): A method for assessing qualitative aspects of communicative impairment in children. *Journal of Child Psychology & Psychiatry*, **39**(6), 879–891.

Black, M., Freeman, B.J., and Montgomery, J. (1975). Systematic observation of play behavior in autistic children. *Journal of Autism & Childhood Schizophrenia*, **5**(4), 363–371.

Bolte, S. and Poustka, F. (2002). The relation between cognitive level and adaptive behavior domains in individuals with autism with and without co-morbid mental retardation. *Child Psychiatry & Human Development*, **33**, 165–172.

Bruininks, R.H., Woodcock, R.W., Weatherman, R.F., and Hill, B.K. (1996). *Scales of Independent Behavior-Revised*. Itasca, IL: Riverside Publishing Company.

Bryant, B.R., Taylor, R.L., and Rivera, D.P. (2001). *Assessment of adaptive areas* (Vol. 14). Lincoln, NE: University of Nebraska Press.

Burack, J. and Volkmar, F. (1992). Development of low and high functioning autistic children. *Journal of Child Psychology and Psychiatry*, **33**, 607–616.

Campbell, J.M. (2003). Efficacy of behavioral interventions for reducing problem behavior in persons with autism: A quantitative synthesis of single-subject research. *Research in Developmental Disabilities*, **24**, 120–138.

Carter, A.S., Gillham, J.E., Sparrow, S.S., and Volkmar, F.R. (1996). Adaptive behavior in autism. *Child & Adolescent Psychiatric Clinics of North America*, **5**(4), 945–961.

Carter, A.S., Volkmar, F.R., Sparrow, S.S., et al. (1998). The Vineland Adaptive Behavior Scales: Supplementary norms for individuals with autism. *Journal of Autism & Developmental Disorders*, **28**(4), 287–302.

Chapman, S., Fisher, W., Piazza, C.C., and Kurtz, P.F. (1993). Functional assessment and treatment of life-threatening drug ingestion in a dually diagnosed youth. *Journal of Applied Behavior Analysis*, **26**(2), 255–256.

Charman, T., Swettenham, J., Baron-Cohen, S., Cox, A., Baird, G., and Drew, A. (1997). Infants with autism: An investigation of empathy, pretend play, joint attention, and imitation. *Developmental Psychology*, **33**(5), 781–789.

Charman, T., Taylor, E., Drew, A., Cockerill, H., Brown, J., and Baird, G. (2005). Outcome at 7 years of children diagnosed with autism at age 2: Predictive validity of assessments conducted at 2 and 3 years of age and pattern of symptom change over time. *Journal of Child Psychology & Psychiatry*, **46**(5), 500–513.

Cicchetti, D.V. and Sparrow, S.S. (1989). Adaptive functioning at home and in the classroom. *Journal of the American Academy of Child & Adolescent Psychiatry*, **28**(4), 620–623.

Coster, W. (1998). Occupation-centered assessment of children. *American Journal of Occupational Therapy*, **52**(5), 337–344.

Cummings, J.A. (2001). Mental Measurements Yearbook, *Review of the Assesment of Adaptive Areas* (Vol. 14). Lincoln, NE: University of Nebraska Press.

Edgin, J.O. and Pennington, B.F. (2005). Spatial Cognition in Autism Spectrum Disorders: Superior, Impaired, or Just Intact? *Journal of Autism & Developmental Disorders*, **35**(6), 729–745.

El-Ghoroury, N.H. and Romanzyk, R.G. (1999). Play interactions of family members towards children with autism. *Journal of Autism & Developmental Disorders*, **29**(3), 249–258.

Fenton, G., D'Ardia, C., Valente, D., et al. (2003). Vineland adaptive behavior profiles in children with autism and moderate to severe developmental delay. *Autism*, **7**(3), 269–287.

Freeman, B.J., Ritvo, E.R., Guthrie, D., et al. (1978). The Behavior Observation Scale for Autism. *American Academy of Child Psychiatry*, **17**(4), 578–588.

Freeman, B.J., Ritvo, E.R., and Schroth, P.C. (1984). Behavioral observation system. *Journal of the American Academy of Child Psychiatry*, **23**(5), 588–594.

Gardenier, N.C., MacDonald, R., and Green, G. (2004). Comparison of direct observational methods for measuring stereotypic behavior in children with autism spectrum disorders. *Research in Developmental Disabilities*, **25**, 99–118.

Grace, N.C., Kahng, S.W., and Fisher, W.W. (1994). Balancing social acceptability with treatment effectiveness of an intrusive procedure: A case report. *Journal of Applied Behavior Analysis*, **27**(1), 171–172.

Harrison, P.L. and Oakland, T. (2005). *Adaptive Behavior Assessment System – Second Edition* (Vol. 16). Lincoln, NE: University of Nebraska Press.

Holmes, N., Shah, A., and Wing, L. (1982). The Disability Assessment Schedule: A brief screening device for use with the mentally retarded. *Psychological Medicine*, **12**(4), 879–890.

Horner, R.H. (1994). Functional assessment: Contributions and future directions. *Journal of Applied Behavior Analysis*, **27**, 401–404.

Iwata, B., Dorsey, M., Slifer, K., Bauman, K., and Richman, G. (1982). Toward a functional analysis of self-injury: Analysis and intervention in developmental disorders. *Analysis & Intervention in Developmental Disorders* **2**, 3–22.

Kanner, L. (1943). Autistic disturbances of affective contact. *Nervous Child*, **2**, 217–250.

Kazdin, A.E., Matson, J.L., and Esveldt-Dawson, K. (1984). The relationship of role-play assessment of children's social skills to multiple measures of social competence. *Behavior Research & Therapy*, **22**(2), 129–139.

Keen, D., Rodger, S., Doussin, K., and Braithewaite, M. (2007). A pilot study of the effects of a social-pragmatic intervention on the communication and symbolic play of children with autism. *Autism*, **11**(1), 63–71.

Kohler, F.W., Anthony, L.J., Steighner, S.A., and Hoyson, M. (2001). Teaching social interaction skills in the integrated preschool: An examination of naturalistic tactics. *Topics in Early Childhood Special Education*, **21**(2), 93–104.

Kraijer, D. (2000). Review of adaptive behavior studies in mentally retarded persons with autism/pervasive developmental disorder. *Journal of Autism & Developmental Disorders*, **30**(1), 39–47.

Kranzler, J.H. (2001). Mental measurements yearbook *Review of the Adaptive Behavior Evaluation Scale, Revised*. Lincoln, NE: University of Nebraska Press.

Lambert, N., Nihira, K., and Leland, H. (1993). *Adaptive Behavior Scale*: School. Austin, TX: Pro-Ed.

Lecavalier, L., Leone, S., and Wiltz, J. (2006). The impact of behaviour problems on caregiver stress in young people with autism spectrum disorders. *Journal of Intellectual Disability Research*, **50**(3), 172–183.

Lopata, C., Thomeer, M.L., Volker, M.A., and Nida, R.E. (2006). Effectiveness of a cognitive-behavioral treatment on the social behaviors of children with asperger disorder. *Focus on Autism & Other Developmental Disabilities*, **21**(4), 237–244.

Lord, C., Risi, S., Lambrecht, L., et al. (2000). The Autism Diagnostic Observation Schedule-Generic: A standard measure of social and communication deficits associated with the spectrum of autism. *Journal of Autism & Developmental Disorders*, **30**(3), 205–223.

Lord, C. and Schopler, E. (1989). Stability of assessment results of autistic and non-autistic language-impaired children from preschool years to early school age. *Journal of Child Psychology & Psychiatry*, **30**(4), 575–590.

Lovaas, O.I. and Buch, G. (1997). *Intensive Behavioral Intervention with Young Children with Autism*. Pacific Grove, CA: Brooks/Cole Publishing Co.

Luiselli, J.K., Campbell, S., Cannon, B., et al. (2001). Assessment instruments used in the education and treatment of persons with autism: Brief report of a survey of national service centers. *Research in Developmental Disabilities*, **22**, 389–398.

MacDonald, L. and Barton, L.E. (1986). Measuring severity of behavior: A revision of part II of the Adaptive Behavior Scale. *American Journal of Mental Deficiency*, **90**(4), 418–424.

Magiati, I. and Howlin, P. (2001). Monitoring the progress of preschool children with autism in early intervention programmes. *Autism*, **5**(4), 399–406.

Martin, N.T., Gaffan, E.A., and Williams, T. (1999). Experimental functional analysis for challenging behavior: A study of validity and reliability. *Research in Developmental Disabilities*, **20**(2), 125–146.

Matson, J.L., Bamburg, J.W., Cherry, K.E., and Paclawskyj, T.R. (1999). A validity study on the Questions About Behavioral Function (QABF) Scale: Predicting treament success for self-injury, aggression, and stereotypies. *Research in Developmental Disabilities*, **20**, 163–176.

Matson, J.L., Kiely, S.L., and Bamburg, J.W. (1997). The effect of stereotypies on adaptive skills as assessed with the DASH-II and Vineland Adaptive Behavior Scales. *Research in Developmental Disabilities*, **18**(6), 471–476.

Matson, J.L., Minshawi, N.F., Gonzalez, M.L., and Mayville, S.B. (2006). The relationship of comorbid problem behaviors to social skills in persons with profound mental retardation. *Behavior Modification*, **30**(4), 496–506.

Matson, J.L., Rotatori, A.F., and Helsel, W.J. (1983). Development of a rating scale to measure social skills in children: The Matson Evaluation of Social Skills with Youngsters (MESSY). *Behaviour Research & Therapy*, **21**(4), 335–340.

McCarney, S.B. (1995). *Adaptive Behavior Evaluation Scale: School Version Technical Manual, Revised*. Columbia, MO: Hawthorne Educational Services, Inc.

Meyer, J.A., Mundy, P.C., Van Hecke, A.V., and Durocher, J.S. (2006). Social attribution processes and comorbid psychiatric symptoms in children with Asperger syndrome. *Autism*, **10**(4), 383–402.

Morreau, L.E. and Bruininks, R.H. (1991). *Checklist of adaptive living skills* (Vol. 12). Lincoln, NE: University of Nebraska Press.

Nihira, K., Foster, R., Shellhaas, M., and Leland, H. (1975). *AAMD Adaptive Behavior Scale-Revised*. WashingtonDC: American Association on Mental Deficiency.

Ogletree, B.T. and Oren, T. (1998). Structured yet functional: An alternative conceptualization of treatment for communication impairment in autism. *Focus on Autism & Other Developmental Disabilities*, **13**(4), 228–233.

Ogletree, B.T., Pierce, K., Harn, W.E., and Fischer, M.A. (2001–2002). Assessment of communication and language in classical autism: Issues and practices. *Assessment for Effective Intervention*, **27**(1&2), 61–71.

Oke, N.J. and Schreibman, L. (1990). Training social initiations to a high-functioning autistic child: Assessment of collateral behavior change and generalization in a case study. *Journal of Autism & Developmental Disorders*, **20**(4), 479–497.

Ozonoff, S., Goodlin-Jones, B.L., and Solomon, M. (2005). Evidence-based assessment of autism spectrum disorders in children and adolescents. *Journal of Clinical Child and Adolescent Psychology*, **34**(3), 523–540.

Paul, R., Miles, S., Cicchetti, D., et al. (2004). Adaptive behavior in autism and pervasive developmental disorder-not otherwise specified: Microanalysis of scores on the Vineland Adaptive Behavior Scales. *Journal of Autism & Developmental Disorders*, **34**(2), 223–228.

Perry, A. and Factor, D.C. (1989). Psychometric validity and clinical usefulness of the Vineland Adaptive Behavior Scales and the AAMD Adaptive Behavior Scale for an autistic sample. *Journal of Autism & Developmental Disorders*, **19**(1), 41–55.

Piersel, W.C. (2001). Mental measurements yearbook. *Review of the School Function Assessment* (Vol. 14). Lincoln, NE: University of Nebraska Press.

Reynolds, C.R. (1987). Critiques of school psychological materials. *Journal of School Psychology*, **25**(1), 97–100.

Reynolds, C.R. and Kamphaus, R.W. (1992). *Behavior Assessment System for Children*. Circle Pines, MN: American Guidance Service.

Reynolds, C.R. and Kamphaus, R.W. (1998). *Behavior Assessment System for Children (BASC)*. Circle Pines, MN: American Guidance Service.

Reynolds, C.R. and Kamphaus, R.W. (2002). *The Clinician's Guide to the Behavior Assessment for Children (BASC)*. London: The Guilford Press.

Rimland, B. and Edelson, S.M. (1999). *Autism Treatment Evaluation Checklist (ATEC)*. San Diego, CA: Autism Research Institute.

Roberts, C., McCoy, M., Reidy, D., and Cruciti, F. (1993). A comparison of methods of assessing adaptive behaviour in pre-school children with developmental disabilities. *Australia and New Zealand Journal of Developmental Disabilities*, **18**(4), 261–272.

Rogers, S.J. and Pennington, B.F. (1991). A theoretical approach to the deficits in infantile autism. *Development & Psychopathology*, **3**(2), 137–162.

Ruttenberg, B.A., Dratman, M.L., Fraknoi, J., and Wenar, C. (1966). An instrument for evaluating autistic children. *Journal of the American Academy of Child & Adolescent Psychiatry*, **5**(3), 453–478.

Sailor, W. and Mix, B. (1975). *The Topeka Association for Retarded Citizens Assessment System*. Austin, TX: Pro-Ed.

Salvia, J., Neisworth, J.T., and Schmidt, M.W. (1995). *Responsibility and Independence Scale for Adolescents* (Vol. 12). Lincoln, NE: University of Nebraska Press.

Schopler, E., Reichler, R.J., and Renner, B.R. (1988). *The Childhood Autism Rating Scale (CARS)*. Los Angeles: Western Psychological Services.

Sigafoos, J., Roberts-Pennell, D., and Graves, D. (1999). Longitudinal assessment of play and adaptive behavior in young children with developmental disabilities. *Research in Developmental Disabilities*, **20**(2), 147–162.

Sparrow, S.S., Balla, D.A., and Cicchetti, D.V. (1984). *Vineland Adaptive Behavior Scales-II (2nd ed.)*. Circle Pines, MN: American Guidance Service.

Sparrow, S.S., Balla, D. and Ciccetti, D. (2005). *Vineland Adaptive Behavior Scales (Vineland-II)*. New York: Pearson Assessments.

Spreat, S. (1982). An empirical analysis of item weighting on the Adaptive Behavior Scale. *American Journal on Mental Deficiency*, **87**(2), 159–163.

Stanley, G.C. and Konstantareas, M.M. (in press). Symbolic play in children with autism spectrum disorder. *Journal of Autism & Developmental Disorders*.

Stone, W.L. and Hogan, K.L. (1993). A structured parent interview for identifying young children with autism. *Journal of Autism & Developmental Disorders*, **23**(4), 639–652.

Szatmari, P., Archer, L., Fisman, S., and Streiner, D.L. (1994). Parent and teacher agreement in the assessment of pervasive developmental disorders. *Journal of Autism & Developmental Disorders*, **24**(6), 703–717.

Szatmari, P., Merette, C., Bryson, S.E., et al. (2002). Quantifying dimensions in autism: A factor-analytic study. *Journal of the American Academy of Child & Adolescent Psychiatry*, **41**(4), 467–474.

Tasse, M.J., Aman, M.G., Hammer, D., and Rojahn, J. (1996). The Nisonger child behavior rating form: Age and gender effects and norms. *Research in Developmental Disabilities*, **17**(1), 59–75.

Tsatsanis, K.D., Dartnall, N., Cicchetti, D., et al. (2003). Concurrent validity and classification accuracy of the Leiter and Leiter-R in low-functioning children with autism. *Journal of Autism & Developmental Disorders*, **33**(1), 23–30.

Van Bourgondien, M.E. and Mesibov, G.B. (1987). Humor in high-functioning autistic adults. *Journal of Autism & Developmental Disorders*, **17**(3), 417–424.

Voelker, S.L., Shore, D.L., Hakim-Larson, J., and Bruner, D. (1997). Discrepancies in parent and teacher ratings of adaptive behavior of children with multiple disabilities. *Mental Retardation*, **35**, 10–17.

Volkmar, F.R., Sparrow, S.S., Goudreau, D., et al. (1987). Social deficits in autism: An operational approach using the Vineland Adaptive Behavior Scales. *Journal of the American Academy of Child & Adolescent Psychiatry*, **26**(2), 156–161.

Vollmer, T.R., Marcus, B.A., and LeBlanc, L. (1994). Treatment of self-injury and hand mouthing following inconclusive functional analyses. *Journal of Applied Behavior Analysis*, **27**(2), 331–344.

Winters, N., Collett, B.R., and Myers, K.M. (2005). Ten-year review of rating scales VII: Scales assessing functional impairment. *Journal of the American Academy of Child & Adolescent Psychiatry*, **44**(4), 309–338.

Wulff, S.B. (1985). The symbolic and object play of children with autism: A review. *Journal of Autism & Developmental Disorders*, **15**(2), 139–148.

8

PHARMACOLOGY EFFECTS AND SIDE EFFECTS

LUC LECAVALIER[1] AND KENNETH GADOW[2]

[1]*Ohio State University, Columbus, OH, USA*
[2]*State University of New York-Stony Brook, Stony Brook, NY, USA*

INTRODUCTION

Although it can be argued that currently there are no well-established, biologic therapies to effect clinically significant improvement in the core features (language and social impairments) of autism spectrum disorders (ASD), clinicians who specialize in the medical management of these individuals are often called upon to treat impairing behaviors associated with the disorder, which in many instances are highly similar to the symptoms of conventional child psychiatric syndromes. In the United States, for example, psychotropic drugs are often prescribed for people with ASD to ameliorate behavioral disturbances (Langworthy-Lam et al., 2002; Witwer and Lecavalier, 2005), and there is evidence that pharmacotherapy is on the increase (Aman et al., 2005). For these and other reasons, the primary focus of this chapter is on instruments for assessing response to psychotropic medication for impairing behaviors in both research and everyday clinical settings. We do, nevertheless, address measures of repetitive behaviors and motor movements because they are responsive to certain medications. In all cases, drug therapies are palliatives; they do not alter underlying pathophysiology in such a way as to "cure" the behavioral disturbance. Therefore, drug discontinuation is often (but not always) associated with some degree of behavioral deterioration in the absence of alternative compensatory intervention.

In this chapter we first address several variables and general concepts relevant to either the development or selection of assessment instruments for use in research and everyday clinical settings. We next describe the types of behavior and emotional problems experienced by individuals with ASD and the prevalence of use of psychotropic medicines. We conclude with descriptions of a number of measures that could be used to assess drug response as well as side effects. We focus mainly on clinician- and caregiver-completed rating scales, owing to the fact that little has been done with self-report measures or direct observations. Instruments were selected based on their track record, unique features, or potential with this population. We encountered at least two challenges in trying to identify suitable instruments. First, ASD are quite heterogeneous. They occur over the life span, and there is great variability in functional level and symptomatology. Practical considerations preclude our covering all possible combinations of target symptoms and patient characteristics. Second, there is a small database in ASD from which to make recommendations. Progress in evidenced-based drug assessment procedures for individuals with ASD generally lags far behind research in comparable areas with non-ASD patient populations. Therefore, it was often necessary to draw examples from the treatment of other disorders (e.g., attention deficit hyperactivity disorder [ADHD]) to illustrate important concepts and indicate directions for future research.

GENERAL CONSIDERATIONS

Before discussing suitable measures for assessing drug response in individuals with ASD, there are several important issues that require some reflection as they have implications for selecting instruments for assessing response to psychotropic medication. The first issue is how measures become evidence-based. Other issues pertain to the conceptualization of "illness," intellectual and maturational characteristics, differences in informant perspective, and rationales for treatment. All of these issues impact the development and selection of assessment instruments. Although they are certainly recognized in the literature, their collective role in shaping health care for individuals with ASD is rarely discussed, let alone integrated into a well-defended strategy for assessing response to intervention.

HOW MEASURES BECOME "EVIDENCED-BASED"

Although space limitations preclude a detailed discussion of how measures become "evidence-based," this topic is arguably more interesting than the measures themselves which can be ascertained from a literature search. Briefly, for a measure to be shown to be sensitive to treatment effects it must of course be used in a clinical trial. The selection of measures for use in research is based on a number of considerations, including the findings of prior studies, personal experience with and awareness of available measures, administrative and practical considerations (e.g., amount of time it will take to complete them, costs to purchase them), proprietary considerations if the trial is funded by a drug company (i.e., measure used in prior studies of FDA-approved drugs), and peer pressure either through the review process (which now includes institutional review boards) or directly from funding agencies.

Although one could argue that these same considerations determine in part the types of treatments that are selected for study, there are nevertheless several important factors that impact the process of scale development and selection, three of which are noted here. First, there are measures not currently in use that may be superior to existing measures but remain undocumented simply because they are not studied. This raises the issue of whether psychopharmacologists should be more actively involved in scale development and psychometric research by examining the relative sensitivity of different measures in the same clinical trial. The best way to determine the superior clinical utility of one measure over another is to actually compare them in the same circumstances (at the same time with the same patients). Although this may sound simple, in reality it is not, because this requires patients, caregivers, and clinicians to complete multiple measures which may be impractical owing to time constraints. Our personal experience indicates that this concern is often greatly exaggerated. Second, relatively low prevalence disorders such as ASD often receive a comparable amount of research support. Therefore, the ability to systematically study relative clinical utility is greatly restricted by the actual amount of research being conducted. Lastly, there has been and continues to be a general reluctance in the scientific community to embrace or fund the development of new measures. Curiously, we do not have this same indifference to new therapies; evidently there is something very unsettling about scientific progress in the taxonomy of behavioral disturbance, a topic we return to later. Collectively, the confluence of these and other variables has resulted in a quandary in the development of instrumentation for assessing treatment effects.

CONCEPTUALIZATION OF BEHAVIORAL AND EMOTIONAL PROBLEMS

Perhaps the single most important issue in the generation of guidelines for evidence-based assessment is the conceptualization of behavioral and emotional problems in people with ASD. One simple example can illustrate just how important this is. If one adopts a diagnostic model (i.e., a medical model) and assumes that behaviors and symptoms in people with ASD are features of conventional psychiatric syndromes, then it stands to reason that measures demonstrated clinically useful for assessing response to medication in non-ASD individuals are likely to be effective for people with ASD. Nevertheless, certain modifications to the instrument may be necessary depending on the intellectual level and whether the core features of ASD alter the clinical presentation of the psychiatric syndrome. If this assertion is correct, it offers enormous economies of scale by capitalizing on a vast worldwide research literature not only about assessment, but also response to treatment. Alternatively, if one assumes that behaviors and emotional problems associated with ASD are phenocopies (i.e., appear similar to psychiatric syndromes but are really epiphenomena associated with the ASD diathesis or unique ASD behavioral syndromes), then it would make more sense to generate assessment instruments unique to this group of individuals. In other words, a taxonomy of behavior and emotional problems would be generated for ASD, and then assessment instruments and treatments would be developed around this model. In practicality, measures inherently based on both conceptual strategies are widely used in clinical trials and everyday clinical settings with little regard for this apparent contradiction. In this chapter we must struggle with this same issue. To better understand this controversy and its implications for assessing response to treatment, we briefly contrast each conceptual model.

CATEGORICAL VERSUS DIMENSIONAL MODELS OF BEHAVIOR AND EMOTIONAL PROBLEMS

For numerous reasons (some more obvious than others) many practical issues associated with the assessment of behavioral disturbance and response to intervention are inextricably linked to conceptualizations about the taxonomy of behavior and emotional problems. One of the most fundamental pertains to whether behavior and emotional problems are best conceptualized as categories (i.e., disorders) or dimensions (i.e., varying degrees of severity along a continuum).

The preeminent categorical model is the *Diagnostic and Statistical Manual of Mental Disorders* promulgated by the American Psychiatric Association (1994). This model defines psychiatric syndromes not only in terms of specific symptoms, but also other prerequisite (e.g., age of onset and duration of symptoms) and exclusion (e.g., presence of co-occurring symptoms or other disorders that best characterize the emotional or behavioral symptoms) criteria. In some cases a specific symptom must be present (e.g., bipolar disorder or generalized anxiety disorder). It is also necessary to establish that symptoms impair academic, social, or occupational functioning based on information from the patient and collateral informants. In other words, a distinction is made between impairment and symptom severity; they are not synonymous (e.g., Winters et al., 2005). Nevertheless, the cutoff score (i.e., prerequisite number of symptoms) for a specific disorder is generally determined with respect to impairment such that individuals who are likely to meet all prerequisite symptoms are also likely to be impaired. Nevertheless, the findings of numerous studies show that for many disorders the number of individuals who meet all symptom criteria far exceeds the number of diagnosed and treated cases (e.g., Nolan et al., 2001). Conversely, there are also people who are academically, socially, or occupationally impaired and who, because they do not exhibit all the prerequisite behavioral symptoms (i.e., borderline cases), are considered not to have a psychiatric disorder.

In the categorical model, the symptoms that define a specific psychiatric disorder are generally determined from observation of the behavioral characteristics (clinical features) of expert-diagnosed cases. In recent years much attention has been given to distinguishing one disorder from another (differential diagnosis) and better understanding the co-occurrence of different types of disorders (comorbidity). The scientific procedure for validating psychiatric syndromes generally follows the guidelines set forth by Robins and Guze (1970) and Feighner et al. (1972). These include demonstrating that individuals diagnosed as having a specific disorder are unique from individuals who do not, and are also different from individuals with similar disorders. The biologic and environmental variables of greatest interest are those believed to be implicated in some way to the etiology of the syndromes. Although this discussion may seem a bit tangential to the topic of evidence-based assessment, it is not. Psychotropic medications are generally (but not always) approved by the Food and Drug Administration (FDA) in the United States for use for specific disorders. For example, specific stimulant and non-stimulant medications are approved for ADHD, not "attention problems." Therefore, evidence-based measures for assessing response to medication are generally validated with regard to an internationally accepted diagnostic (categorical) model, but more on this later.

A dimensional model of behavior and emotional problems rests on different premises and methods. The first step consists of generating a list of behaviors and symptoms of interest for a particular group of individuals. This list is typically generated from patient charts, other instruments, personal experience, or existing definitions of the disorder. Syndromes or dimensions are derived with the assistance of multivariate statistical procedures (e.g., factor analytically driven techniques) and are based on the covariation of symptoms or behaviors. In this sense, each rating scale is its own taxonomy of behavior and emotional problems. Syndromes are validated against criteria external to the analysis. Drug response measures generally (but not always) focus on negativistic behaviors with higher scores indicating more severe symptoms and lower scores denoting minimal symptom severity. Unlike the categorical model, impairment is not considered when defining a syndrome. The model is based on symptom severity, and impairment is implicit once symptoms are beyond a certain threshold. An objective, but arbitrary cutoff indicates that a person is very different from everyone else (i.e., potentially has a disorder). Cutoffs are typically defined as scores above 1.5 or 2.0 standard deviations (SD) from the normative sample. When a cutoff score is used to identify people with a disorder, the dimensional model of course becomes a categorical model. Because aberrant behaviors are not normally distributed, approximately 4 to 6 percent of individuals in normative samples receive scores above two SDs above the mean (e.g., Gadow and Sprafkin, 2002). In the dimensional model, the prevalence of all behavior "disorders" is the same when the same statistical cutoff (e.g., >2 SDs) is applied to all dimensional syndromes. Generally speaking, assessment instruments based on the dimensional model do not assess duration of symptoms, premorbid functioning, or impairment, nor do they specify key features of the syndrome. All of these characteristics can of course be established as part of a clinical interview.

In real world settings, treatment evaluation is a poorly conceptualized mishmash of both models. The DSM-IV categorical model is generally applied to diagnosis (i.e., determining who should be treated), whereas treatment response is measured with scales based on a dimensional model of behavior and emotional problems. Increasingly, however, instrument developers have used the symptoms from the DSM categorical model to generate dimensional rating scales to evaluate response to medication. This is less the case for ASD because the DSM-IV categorical model is generally interpreted as not recognizing psychiatric comorbidity in individuals with ASD. In other words, many other psychiatric diagnoses are precluded in the presence of ASD. Therefore, dimensional models are often applied for both "diagnosis" of syndromes and assessment of treatment response, which has the distinct advantage of assessing treatment in terms of the behaviors that define the disorder. The significance of this issue with regard to generating guidelines for evidenced-based medication assessment of behavioral disturbance cannot be underestimated.

PATIENT CHARACTERISTICS

Maturational and intellectual levels are two characteristics that impact significantly instrument development and selection. Age figures importantly in the construction and selection of both dimensional and categorical assessment instruments because human behavior (and behavior and emotional problems) changes over time. For example, personality disorders are thought of as adult disorders. Conversely, other disorders such as elective mutism, encopresis, and separation anxiety are generally thought of as primarily disorders of childhood. However, this is not a static situation. For example, ADHD, which was once thought to be a disorder of childhood is now recognized as an adult disorder as well (e.g., Sprafkin et al., 2007). Moreover, oppositional defiant disorder (ODD) and conduct disorder (CD) may also have relevance for adulthood, both as dimensions and categories (e.g., Gadow et al., 2007). In the case of ASD, relatively very little research has focused on age-related differences in the assessment of behavior and emotional problems compared with non-ASD individuals. This is likely a reflection of the fact that traditionally studied samples were comprised primarily of youngsters with intellectual disability (ID). However, now with our arguably more informed notions about the breadth of the ASD phenotype, we are hopeful that research will emerge on the behavioral and emotional problems of higher-functioning people with ASD as well as those encountered in adulthood.

For over three decades, investigators have examined the relation between intellectual ability and behavior and emotional problems. Many researchers have reported only weak associations between these variables (e.g., Brown et al., 2004; Eyman et al., 1981; Rojahn and Tassé, 1996; Watson et al., 1988), particularly for ratings of DSM-defined symptoms (e.g., Gadow et al., 2004, 2005; Pearson and Aman, 1994; Sprafkin et al., 2002). Nevertheless, findings in the extant literature are mixed owing to diverse methodologies including the specific types of behaviors studied (e.g., anxiety vs. self injury), sample heterogeneity (e.g., percentage with ID, level of ID, ASD subtypes), and type of assessment measure (e.g., designed specifically for ID or typically developing populations, categorical vs. dimensional). The significant issue here is that the items in many (but not all) instruments generally reflect the behaviors that developers deem to be problematic for the population of interest. For example, children with ASD and severe ID engage in behaviors that occur with very low frequency in the general population (e.g., self-injury, stereotypies, pica, rumination). One would therefore predict associations between IQ and rating scale scores for measures that include items pertaining to these behaviors, especially for samples with diverse intellectual ability. Conversely, DSM-IV symptoms are generally conceptualized with regard to disorders in individuals with average IQ. Not unexpectedly, studies of preschoolers, children, adolescents, and adults that have examined the relation between these symptoms and IQ have found little relation for most syndromes. Two exceptions in ASD are anxiety and language disorders. We and others have found that level of functioning is positively correlated with symptoms of anxiety (Lecavalier, 2006; Sukhodolsky et al., 2007; Weisbrot et al., 2005) and language problems (Gadow et al., 2004).

In summary, from a practical perspective, where age and intellectual ability are relevant considerations, it is prudent to select evidence-based measures that appropriately consider these variables. However, we caution against simply assuming that a particular measure is necessarily inappropriate or ineffective in the absence of information supporting such a claim. Nevertheless, it is safe to assume that a scale specifically designed for behavior problems peculiar to individuals with ASD and ID will be more suited for assessing treatment effects in this subsample of the patient population. Moreover, as previously noted, ASD or ID may alter the typical clinical presentation of behavioral syndromes and therefore require a unique set of drug assessment instruments. Unfortunately, this topic has received very little attention in the pharmacotherapy literature, and the relative clinical superiority of standard measures specifically adapted for lower-functioning individuals is virtually unstudied.

INFORMANT AGREEMENT

For several decades, researchers have documented relatively poor agreement between child, parent, and teacher reports of the frequency and severity of child behavior and emotional problems in both non-ASD (e.g., Achenbach et al., 1987; Offord et al., 1996) and ASD (Gadow et al., 2004, 2005, 2006; Lecavalier et al., 2006) samples. This is also true for DSM-IV-based diagnostic constructs in both non-ASD (e.g., Gadow et al., 2004) and ASD (Gadow et al., 2004, 2005) samples. Although there is much discussion of how to combine information from multiple informants, there is no consensus on how this should be done (e.g., Bird et al., 1992; Piacentini et al., 1992) and some evidence indicating that this may be counterproductive, at least with regard to the validation of behavioral syndromes (e.g., Drabick et al., 2007a; Gadow et al., 2004, 2006; Offord et al., 1996). The importance of source specificity to the conceptualization of psychopathology is underscored by the fact that the associated risk/protective factors and co-occurring psychiatric symptoms of teacher- versus parent-defined behavioral syndromes are dissimilar (e.g., Gadow et al., 2007; Lecavalier, 2006), which suggests possible differences in the etiology of problem behaviors and therefore their response to intervention.

A much less appreciated implication of informant disagreement pertains to the notion of rate dependency in treatment response; namely, more impaired individuals generally evidence greater therapeutic improvement than less impaired individuals. Therefore, perceived differences in therapeutic improvement are also linked to the perceived severity of the problem behavior(s). In other words, teacher ratings of drug response in children with teacher-defined syndromes are likely to be larger than for teacher ratings of parent-defined syndromes. Setting variables also appear to impact the rater's ability to discern drug effects. In this regard, there are numerous published studies showing differences between parent and teacher ratings of drug response in children with ADHD (e.g., Gadow et al., 1995). In general, their findings indicate that teacher ratings appear to be more sensitive indicators of stimulant response and differences between doses of stimulant medication than parent ratings, even when using identical measures.

Several explanations have been offered for the commonly observed discrepancy in parent and teacher ratings of child behaviors, each of which likely contributes to informant disagreement. Perhaps the most popular is the fact that teachers, unlike parents, have an opportunity to observe the behavior of a large group of children in the same setting and make inferences as to what constitutes deviations from the norm. Equally important is the long-established observation that children behave differently in different settings, and this is well illustrated from research on children with ADHD (e.g., Ellis et al., 1974; Whalen et al., 1978, 1979). In addition, discrepancies in parent and teacher ratings seem to reflect differences in the types of behavior that are most important to each informant (e.g., Drabick et al., 2007a). Children may also be more likely to make comments about their internal state to parents than to teachers (Drabick et al., in press).

These issues have important implications for developing evidence-based strategies for assessing response to psychotropic medication in ASD. Findings of therapeutic improvement from different informants are likely to be discrepant, and as previously noted, explanations for which are diverse and complex. At the individual patient level, differences in informant report can result in a quagmire of vexing clinical management issues, especially for more complex cases of which challenging behaviors in ASD qualify. Although the notion that an individual may exhibit symptoms in one setting and not in another is "inconvenient," there are countless examples in medicine where this is the case. Owing to the fact that most psychotropic drugs are long-acting, treatment will inevitably extend to settings where behavior is not problematic in some individuals. For all the aforementioned reasons, assessment measures that have parallel formats (parent and teacher versions for children, and collateral self-report versions for adults) are desirable.

RATIONALE FOR TREATMENT

One of the least discussed and researched topics in child psychopathology is the rationale for treatment, which has direct bearing on the selection of appropriate measures for assessing treatment effects (Gadow, 1991). A rationale for treatment should be able to describe well-documented drug effects and delineate their short- and long-term implications for the individual. In other words, it should be testable. Central to the aforementioned categorical model of behavior and emotional problems is the notion that effective therapy should reduce the severity of the symptoms of the disorder and in so doing result in improved social, academic, or vocational functioning. In reality, however, most evidence-based drug-response measures for emotional and behavioral problems focus exclusively on symptom reduction and not on the enhancement of adaptive behavior. Implicit in both categorical and dimensional models of behavior and emotional problems is the notion that effective pharmacotherapy should make the patient behave in a manner that is more similar to individuals who are not behaviorally disabled (behavioral normalization). Optimally, treatment should reduce symptom severity to a level below the categorical or dimensional cutoff score. As previously discussed, although the categorical model requires impairment in social, academic, or vocational functioning for diagnosis, clinically significant improvement in these areas is not a prerequisite for drug approval or prescription.

Effective pharmacotherapy could also have favorable long-term consequences. The residual benefits of treatment include a significant alteration in the course of the disorder manifest as less symptomatic adolescent or adult outcome or more pronounced development of adaptive behavior. Unfortunately, the residual benefits of treatment with regard to the latter outcome have not been demonstrated (or investigated) for individuals with ASD. Studies on the residual benefits are beset with a legion of methodological aggravations and are not usually initiated until long after the treatment practice is well established. Not surprisingly therefore, these benefits are commonly inferred to exist simply on the basis of short-term efficacy studies.

Perhaps the thorniest issue for developing a rationale of treatment is the criterion for behavioral improvement. In other words, how big of an improvement is necessary to justify prescribing medications that are associated with certain risks? Are standards the same for individuals with a developmental disability (DD)? Is any degree of behavioral improvement justifiable? The most rigorous (and rarely achieved) criterion is behavioral normalization. The FDA does not require behavioral normalization as a criterion for drug approval. Nevertheless, if this is adopted as a useful concept for adjusting dose of medication, then evidence-based measures will require normative data. Although it is a fairly straightforward procedure to obtain such data, behavioral normalization is more conceptually problematic for individuals with a DD. For example, is the goal of treatment to effect behavioral change that is typical of other individuals with a DD or is the criterion behavior that of the general population? In other words, who is the comparison group?

There are a number of additional reasons that are commonly given for prescribing psychopharmacological palliatives (a few of which are noted here), but generally their empirical bases in individuals with ASD have either not been investigated or convincingly substantiated. Drug therapy is also perceived as having secondary benefits (therapeutic improvements that are not target symptoms or primary diagnostic features of the disorder), which are usually serendipitous but nevertheless can become important reasons for maintaining treatment. For example, symptom suppression or enhancement of adaptive behavior may lead to (secondary) improvement in self-esteem, especially when this is associated with marked reductions in negative statements by peers and care providers. Bradley (1957) was one of the first psychopharmacologists to state that this was an important justification for pharmacotherapy of disruptive behavior disorders.

Another potential secondary benefit of pharmacotherapy is the facilitation of a less restrictive educational or vocational placement or living arrangement (e.g., increased opportunity to interact with nondisabled peers), which is presumed to have important therapeutic and positive life-adjustment implications for the individual. For example, behavioral improvement may allow a child with ASD to remain in the regular classroom instead of being placed in a self-contained class. Whether less restrictive placement is in fact beneficial for a child, and in what ways, is a matter of considerable controversy.

Medication may alter the behavior of care providers or peers in socially significant ways (e.g., increased amount of teaching time, higher levels of peer productivity, less personal injury or property damage, greater marital satisfaction or family stability). For example, a major complaint of teachers about disruptive hyperactive children with ADHD is that they lower the overall level of classroom performance by increasing the rate of negativistic behaviors in classmates. Although there is some evidence that this may be true in specific cases, the effect that pharmacotherapy has on this phenomenon is relatively unstudied in public school settings (e.g., Gadow et al., 1992; Nolan and Gadow, 1997). In other words, researchers generally do an excellent job of describing symptom suppression, but they are less successful when it comes to demonstrating the link between symptom suppression and the reason for prescribing medication.

In real world settings, the selection and especially the interpretation of findings of drug response assessment measures either implicitly or explicitly speaks to the aforementioned issues. Moreover, rationales for treatment are not governmentally sanctioned; rather, they are personal constructs and likely vary from person to person. At the most basic level, instrumentation needs to address the objectives of treatment in a reliable and accurate way and with appropriate consideration to patient and informant characteristics. Because it is highly unlikely that all participants, active or passive, will be in uniform agreement on all concerns, therein lay the art of clinical management. Ideally, to as great a degree as possible, the measures selected for evaluating clinical response to medication should embrace the considerations of all participants. In reality, however, this is unattainable. Practically, therefore, one should strive to achieve the standards set forth in "best practices guidelines" established by relevant professional societies.

BEHAVIORAL AND EMOTIONAL PROBLEMS IN PEOPLE WITH ASD

In clinical practice the item content of evidence-based measures of drug response should match the emotional or behavioral problems for which medication is prescribed. Although this seems self evident, in actuality it is much more complicated. Very briefly, some important problems for the psychopharmacology of ASD are these: (a) there are no FDA-approved drugs for the core features of ASD; (b) medications for individuals with ASD are generally prescribed for behavioral disturbances; (c) there is no consensus taxonomy for either a categorical or dimensional model of psychopathology in ASD; (d) at the time of this writing, there is only one FDA-approved indication for a medication (risperidone) for behavioral disturbance (irritability and aggression) in autism; and (e) DSM-IV guidelines are generally interpreted as indicating that behavioral disturbances in ASD are not "true" psychiatric syndromes. In addition, the most researched conceptual model for behavior and emotional problems in ASD is dimensional, and this strategy generally does not address impairment over and above symptom severity or the perceived need for intervention. To complicate matters even more, when a physician in the United States diagnoses and writes a prescription for a behavior or emotional problem in a patient with ASD, health care providers generally do not require a diagnosis other than ASD. Conversely, the diagnosis can be a non-ASD DSM-IV-defined disorder without any mention of ASD. For these and other reasons, it is very difficult to obtain information about the exact reasons for which medication is prescribed to individuals with ASD. In this section, we briefly review what is currently known about the problem behaviors for which evidence-based measures need be applied.

Early group studies of children who would now be diagnosed with autistic or Asperger's disorder reported relatively high rates of psychiatric symptoms (e.g., Rutter et al., 1967; Simmons, 1974; Wing, 1981), and numerous case studies (reviewed by Gillberg and Billstedt, 2000; Sverd, 2003) describe a variety of conventional psychiatric syndromes in this patient population. More recently, investigators using psychiatric interviews with small samples of children with ASD have reported that many youngsters with Asperger's disorder (e.g., Green et al., 2000; Wozniak et al., 1997) or autistic disorder (e.g., Leyfer et al., 2006; Muris et al., 1998) meet diagnostic criteria for specific psychiatric disorders, most notably ADHD, and anxiety and mood disorders.

DIMENSIONAL RATING SCALES

For several decades, researchers have been assessing the prevalence and severity of psychopathology in children with ASD using rating scales based on a dimensional model of behavior and emotional problems. Comparing and interpreting these findings has been complicated by the fact that different instruments were used, and although the percentage of individuals receiving "severe" scores are often reported, it is difficult to know what these scores mean in terms of impairment of social, academic, or vocational functioning, or the perceived need for intervention. With these limitations in mind, we briefly describe the findings of two noteworthy studies. Both of these studies were conducted using community-based samples and had high participation rates.

In their longitudinal study of behavior and emotional problems in youngsters with ID (total $n = 590$), Tonge and Einfeld (2003) examined a subgroup of 118 children with autism. All children were rated on the *Developmental Behaviour Checklist* [described below]. At the beginning of the study, 74 percent of children with autism (mean age of 8.5 years) were above the cutoff considered clinically significant for caseness. They were the subgroup with the highest rates of behavior and emotional problems, and scores were quite stable over time.

Lecavalier (2006) collected parent and teacher ratings of behavior and emotional problems with the *Nisonger Child Behavior Rating Form* [described below] for a sample of 487 youngsters with ASD (mean age of 9.6 years). Children were recruited in public schools across Ohio. Parent ratings suggested that 52 percent of the sample was free of significant behavior and emotional problems, whereas 9 percent had several elevated subscale scores. Similarly, teacher ratings suggested that 55 percent of the sample was relatively free of behavior and emotional problems, and 13 percent of the sample had several elevated subscale scores.

It has been shown that autism is a risk marker for behavior and emotional problems (Holden and Gitlesen, 2006; McClintock et al., 2003). Indeed, compared to their counterparts with ID only, individuals with a diagnosis of autism are significantly more likely to engage in self-injury, aggression, and disruptive behavior, which occur more often as the level of functioning decreases.

DSM-BASED DISORDERS

There is a growing body of evidence indicating that behavioral syndromes in ASD are phenotypically similar to conventional DSM-IV-defined psychiatric syndromes. For these disorders, conventional treatment-response measures may be appropriate, or at the very least, suitable with minor modifications. Described here are disorders for which this may apply.

Attention Deficit Hyperactivity Disorder (ADHD)

Although there has long been reports of relatively high rates of hyperactivity and attention deficits in children with ASD (e.g., Ando and Yoshimura,

1979; Chung et al., 1990; Ghaziuddin and Greden, 1998; Kim et al., 2000; Rutter et al., 1967; Wozniak et al., 1997), until recently there has been little systematic study of ADHD symptoms defined according to DSM-IV criteria in this clinical population. In two recent studies, Gadow et al. (2004, 2005) used parent- and teacher-completed versions of DSM-IV-referenced rating scales, the Early Childhood Inventory-4 (ECI-4) (Gadow and Sprafkin, 1994, 2000) and the Child Symptom Inventory-4 (CSI-4) (Gadow and Sprafkin, 2002), to evaluate large samples of clinically-referred children with ASD. Findings indicated that over 40 percent of 3 to 5 year olds and over 50 percent of 6 to 12 year olds met symptom criteria for at least one DSM-IV subtype of ADHD. Interestingly, screening prevalence rates of ADHD subtypes in the ASD samples were comparable to non-ASD clinic-referred children, and the severity of ADHD symptoms were similar across ASD subtypes (i.e., autistic disorder, Asperger's disorder, PDD-NOS). Along the same lines, in his community-based study of children with ASD, Lecavalier (2006) found that the most frequently endorsed problems were those relating to ADHD. For instance, the following items were reported to be moderate or severe problems (parents/teachers): difficulty concentrating (49/50 percent), easily distracted (60/60 percent), and fidgeting, wriggling, squirming (42/44 percent).

Although a number of studies have investigated differences between ADHD subtypes in non-ASD samples, usually with a DSM-IV-referenced rating scale, this is not the case for children with ASD. To address this issue in greater detail, Gadow et al. (2006) used the ECI-4 and CSI-4 to classify children with ASD. In this study parents and teachers completed the CSI-4 for 6- to 12-year-old children ($N = 301/191$) with ASD and clinic controls, respectively. Children were sorted into one of four groups: ADHD inattentive (I) type, ADHD hyperactive-impulsive (H) type, ADHD combined (C) type, and a comparison group without ADHD symptoms (NONE). Study findings provided tentative support for an ADHD syndrome in children with ASD and preliminary evidence for the external validity of DSM-IV-defined ADHD subtypes in children with ASD. Findings for 3–5 year olds were similar.

Oppositional Defiant Disorder (ODD)

DSM-IV-defined ODD also appears to be common in children with ASD. For example, 2 recent studies found the percentages of 3–5 and 6–12 year olds with ASD and ODD to be 13 percent and 27 percent based on parent ratings, respectively, and 21 percent and 25 percent based on teacher ratings, respectively (Gadow et al., 2004, 2005). Interestingly, these symptom prevalence rates were comparable to the rates for ODD in non-ASD children referred for child psychiatric outpatient clinic evaluation. Moreover, there were other similarities (age, gender, and rater differences) in clinical characteristics associated with ODD in ASD, clinic-based, and community-based samples, which support the notion that ODD may be a unique behavioral syndrome in children with ASD, and equally important, may be the same (or a similar) disorder as observed in non-ASD children.

Given the high rate of ADHD and ODD co-occurrence in both ASD and non-ASD samples, Gadow et al. (2007) investigated whether ODD was a unique clinical entity separate from ADHD in 608 children with ASD (ages 3–12 years). Parents and teachers completed the ECI-4 or CSI-4. The sample was separated into four groups: ODD, ADHD, ODD + ADHD, and neither (NONE). Comparison samples were clinic ($n = 326$) and community controls ($n > 800$). In the ASD sample, all three ODD/ADHD groups were clearly differentiated from the NONE group, and the ODD + ADHD group had the most severe co-occurring symptoms, medication use, and environmental disadvantage. There were few differences between ASD + ODD and ASD + ADHD groups, but findings for ASD and control samples were similar which supports the notion of overlapping mechanisms in the pathogenesis of ODD.

Conduct Disorder (CD)

As with other psychiatric syndromes, there are reports in the literature describing CD in individuals with ASD. Nevertheless, studies comparing rates of CD in ASD and other samples actually indicate that this disorder is less common than expected compared with other disorders. In fact, CD screening prevalence rates in ASD are more similar to special and regular education students than clinic-referred non-ASD outpatients (Gadow et al., 2004, 2005). For example, the percentage of 6–12 year old boys with ASD who met criteria for DSM-IV-defined CD according to the CSI-4 (parent/teacher ratings) was as follows: ASD (8/9 percent), non-ASD outpatients (23/22 percent), special education (3/0 percent), and regular education (2/2 percent).

Anxiety Disorders

Anxiety is now recognized as being a relatively common occurrence in children with ASD (Green et al., 2000; Kim et al., 2000; Lecavalier, 2006) with frequency rates and symptom severity levels much higher than community samples (Gadow et al., 2004, 2005; Kim et al., 2000; Sofronoff et al., 2005) and more comparable to clinically-referred non-ASD children (Gadow et al., 2004, 2005; Sofronoff et al., 2005). For example, Gadow et al. (2004, 2005) reported that the percentage of 6–12 year old children with ASD who met criteria for DSM-IV anxiety syndromes (parent/teacher ratings) according to the ECI-4 and CSI-4 were as follows: GAD (31/28 percent), specific phobia (58/34 percent), Social Anxiety Disorder (9 percent, parent ratings only), social phobia (11 percent, teacher ratings only), any anxiety subtype (66/56 percent). Similarly, in his sample of community-based young people with ASD, Lecavalier (2006) found the following symptoms of anxiety to be moderate or severe problems (parents/teachers): nervous/tense (21/18 percent), fearful/anxious (17/11 percent), and worried (14/14 percent).

Depression

Because depression commonly co-occurs with anxiety, it is not surprising that depression is reported in individuals with ASD given their high rates of anxiety (e.g., Ghaziuddin and Greden, 1998; Kim et al. 2000). However, there is little research on depression in this patient population. Using the CSI-4, Gadow et al. (2004, 2005) reported that the percentage of 6–12 year old children with ASD who met criteria for DSM-IV depression syndromes (parent/teacher ratings) were as follows: Major Depressive Disorder (6/3 percent) and dysthymia (15/13 percent). These rating scales symptoms categories are not mutually exclusive. Lecavalier (2006) found the following symptoms of mood problems to be moderate or severe problems (parents/teachers) in his community-based sample of youngsters with ASD: easily frustrated (62/54 percent); crying (23/23 percent), irritable (19/23 percent), temper tantrums (29/30 percent), and unhappy/sad (6/9 percent).

Other DSM-based Disorders

Other disorders in individuals with ASD that have received research attention in recent years are mania (Wozniak et al., 1997), obsessive-compulsive disorder (Scahill et al., 2006), sleep disorder (DeVincent et al., 2007), feeding disorders (Ledford and Gast, 2006), and tic disorder (Gadow and DeVincent, 2005). Stereotypies are also prevalent in people with ASD, particularly in individuals functioning in the ID range, with estimates ranging from 5–20 percent. The prevalence of stereotypical behavior is inversely related to level of functioning and positively correlated with the presence of self-injurious behaviors (Bodfish et al., 2000; Matson et al., 1996; Matson et al., 1997).

Psychotropic Drug Studies

Psychotropic drug studies are also a source of information about the behavior and emotional problems in ASD. As an illustration, antipsychotics have been used to treat stereotypical behavior, motor tics, aggression, irritability, self-injury, sleep problems, inattention, and overactivity. Readers interested in more in-depth discussions of psychotropic drug therapy for ASD are referred to the chapter on this topic in this text, as well as other excellent reviews (e.g., Handen and Lubetsky, 2005; Malone et al., 2005).

PREVALENCE OF DRUG THERAPY

Just as knowledge about the relative prevalence of behavior and emotional problems is helpful in generating guidelines for evidence-based assessment, so too is pharmaco-epidemiology. These studies seek to describe specific drugs used in everyday clinical settings and the reasons for prescribing them. In the previous section we indicated the need to match the features of behavior and emotional problems with specific types of measures, and a similar concern applies to the assessment of adverse drug reactions (side effects). Unfortunately, different classes of drugs are associated with different types of adverse events, which generally require the use of measures tailored for specific groups of drugs, a topic to which we return later in the chapter. In this section, we describe the findings of recent treatment prevalence studies.

A number of studies have examined the prevalence of use of psychotropic medicines in people with DD (see Valdovinos et al., 2003), but few have focused exclusively on people with ASD. Aman and colleagues conducted three large-scale surveys of psychotropic medicine use in people with ASD. The first survey was conducted in North Carolina in 1995 (Aman et al., 1995) with 859 individuals, aged 1 to 82 years. The researchers found that 31 percent of the sample was taking some psychotropic medication. This figure increased to 39 percent when considering antiepileptic drugs, and 42 percent when including megavitamins.

In their second survey conducted in 1999, Aman et al. (2003) assessed medication use in 417 individuals in Ohio (ages 2–46 yrs), of whom 46 percent were taking some psychotropic agent. The figure rose to 55 percent if antiepileptic drugs and vitamins were included. The most commonly prescribed medicines were antidepressants (22 percent), antisychotics (15 percent), antihypertensives (13 percent), and stimulants (11 percent).

The third survey was conducted in North Carolina in 2001 (Langworthy-Lam et al., 2002) and included 1538 individuals (ages 3–56 yrs) of whom 46 percent were receiving some type of psychotropic drug; 6 percent were taking vitamin supplements; and 12 percent were taking antiepileptic drugs. The most commonly prescribed classes of medicines were antidepressants (22 percent), antipsychotics (17 percent), and stimulants (14 percent). Prevalence of the various types of psychotropic medicines were nearly identical to those reported by Aman et al. (2003).

Aman et al. (2005) analyzed the data from their three surveys. The prevalence of use of any psychotropic medicine increased from 31 percent in the first North Carolina survey to 45 percent in the second one. Significant increases in use over time were noted in antipsychotics, antidepressants, psychostimulants, and antihypertensives. The only significant regional difference was found in the rate of autism supplement use, with the second North Carolina study reporting 6 percent and the Ohio study reporting 10 percent. Across the three studies, greater age, more severe autism and ID, residence outside of home, and more restrictive educational placement were consistently associated with a greater likelihood of medication use. The vitamin and supplement usage was associated with younger age and higher parental education.

Two studies focused on specific subpopulations of people with ASD. Martin et al. (1999) studied 109 clinic-referred young people with Asperger's disorder and high-functioning autism (mean age 14 years). They found that 55 percent of the sample was receiving some type of psychotropic medication. The most commonly prescribed category of psychotropic medicines were antidepressants (32 percent), stimulants (20 percent), antipsychotics (17 percent), and antihypertensives (6 percent). Of those taking medicines, the most commonly treated target symptoms were anxiety-related (65 percent), inattention, distraction, hyperactivity (50 percent), and disruptive, violent, self-injurious behaviors (43 percent). This is the only study to have collected information on the reason for prescribing the medicines.

Witwer and Lecavalier (2005) examined the one-year treatment rates and patterns of 353 children with ASD (mean age 10 years) attending public schools across Ohio. In this survey, parents also completed measures of social competence, problem behavior, and adaptive behavior. Results indicated that 47 percent were administered at least one psychotropic medication in the past year. In addition, 17 percent received some type of specially formulated vitamin or supplement; 16 percent were on a modified diet; 12 percent were taking some combination of psychotropic medication and an alternative treatment; and 5 percent were prescribed an antiepileptic. As reported in the Aman studies, greater age and lower adaptive skills were associated with higher levels of medication use. As a group, youngsters who received drug therapy had lower social competence scores and higher problem behavior subscale scores on the *Nisonger Child Behavior Rating Form.*

Collectively, the results of these studies indicate that psychotropic drug therapy is relatively common in people with ASD. Moreover, the most frequently prescribed drugs are antipsychotics, antidepressants, and stimulants. Patient characteristics associated with higher rates of pharmacotherapy include older age and lower levels of functioning.

MEASURES OF THERAPEUTIC IMPROVEMENT

In this section, we focus on standardized behavior rating scales completed by parent, teacher, direct care staff, or clinicians, owing to the fact that much less has been done with self-report, collateral-report (e.g., spouse), direct observation, or laboratory measures. We define *rating scale* as a measure with a built-in system for quantifying behaviors or other states. Most measures contain multiple items rated on a metric related to frequency or severity. By *standardized*, we mean that the contents of the scale, instructions, or scoring system do not change with use. We make a distinction between the terms "normed" and "standardized," often used interchangeably in the literature. Developing norms refer to obtaining ratings on a large number of individuals (ideally, representative of a given population). These normative data can be based on different groups, such as community-based or outpatient populations, and serve as a basis for comparing individual scores. Therefore, a measure can be standardized without having norms.

Rating scales have a variety of strengths and weaknesses (Lecavalier and Aman, 2005). Among their strengths are their structured content (compared with anecdotal report), ease of completion, cost-effectiveness, and flexibility. Among the disadvantages of rating scales are their subjectivity, "halo errors" (i.e., the tendency to exaggerate severity in one domain of behavior as a consequence of the perceived severity of another domain), and regression towards the mean (i.e., a statistical phenomenon where, in repeated assessment, extreme scores change in the direction of the mean score). In psychotropic drug studies of disruptive behavior, however, when severe scores improve, mild scores generally do not worsen (i.e., change in the direction of the mean score).

Rating scales can be grouped according to the type and number of behavioral domains, dimensions, or syndromes they are designed to evaluate. Global measures such as the *Clinical Global Impressions Scale* and the *Developmental Disabilities Modification of the Children's Global Assessment Scale* [described below] provide a single index to evaluate treatment responses. Symptom-based measures can be broadband or specific. Broadband measures (containing items assessing a wide range of behaviors) have considerable practical advantages. First, comorbidity is the rule and not the exception (Gadow et al., 2004, 2005; Lecavalier, 2006). In other words, individuals with ASD typically exhibit a wide range of problem behaviors (symptoms) or multiple behavioral syndromes (disorders). Even when a problem behavior does not reach the clinical threshold for a diagnosis, symptom improvement may be perceived as beneficial. Second, the subscales of broadband instruments generally share the same metric, and their psychometric properties are based on the same individuals, settings, and informants. Third, it is generally more cost-effective and efficient to administer one broadband measure than several different narrowband instruments. This having been said, narrowband measures dominate the clinical literature, and the assessment of pharmacotherapy for behavior and emotional problems in persons with ASD is no exception.

Regardless of their content or the method underlying their development, rating scales need to be evaluated in terms of their reliability and validity. Reliability refers to the consistency of ratings and has three major components: internal consistency, temporal stability, and inter-rater agreement. Validation is an ongoing process and addresses what the instrument measures and the precision of the measurement. The three general types of validity are content, construct, and criterion validity. We refer the reader to articles by Cichetti (1994) and Meyers and Winters (2002a) for a discussion of psychometrics and guidelines for evaluating normed and standardized assessment instruments.

Our selection of evidence-based measures for assessing response to psychotropic drugs is based on the following criteria and assumptions. To be considered evidence-based, priority was given to measures with acceptable psychometric properties and sensitivity for assessing drug effects as demonstrated in published clinical trials involving individuals with ASD. In the absence of research indicating that validated drug-response measures for non-ASD individuals are inappropriate for people with ASD, it seems ill-advised to rule them out. Nevertheless, space constraints precluded review of the entire assessment literature, and therefore only representative and well-established non-ASD measures shown to be sensitive to psychotropic drug effects are noted. Failure to cite major instruments should be considered an oversight and not a judgment of their merits. Readers interested in additional discussion of this and related topics are referred to other reviews of treatment response measures for ASD (e.g., Aman et al., 2004) and rating scales for typically developing (Collett et al., 2003; Meyers and Winters, 2002b; Winters et al., 2005) or ID populations (Lecavalier and Aman, 2005).

In this chapter, rating scales are grouped according to their scope (global, broadband, narrowband), implicit taxonomy (dimensional, DSM-referenced), and content (problem behaviors, functioning, adaptive behavior). Moreover, in our sections about narrowband scales, we also make a distinction between behavioral domains (ADHD, aggression, anxiety, mood, etc.).

GLOBAL DIMENSIONAL SCALES

Clinical Global Impressions Scale (CGI)

The CGI (NIMH, 1976) is a clinician-completed measure with two main subscales of one item each, rated on a 7-point scale. For the Severity of Illness subscale, the clinician rates the individual's condition from "not at all ill" to "among the most severely ill." The Global Improvement subscale assesses change from "very much worse" through "no change" to "very much improved." The CGI is a rating scale in its simplest form, provides the bottom-line, and is ever present in pharmacological trials. It has been used in several drug studies of youngsters with ASD (e.g., Hellings et al., 2005; Hollander et al., 2006; RUPP, 2002, 2005).

BROADBAND DIMENSIONAL SCALES

Aberrant Behavior Checklist (ABC)

The ABC (Aman et al., 1985a, 1985b) was primarily developed as an outcome measure for treatment studies. It is completed by parents, teachers, or other caregivers. It was derived by factor analysis and contains 58 items, distributed on five factors: (a) Irritability, Agitation, Crying (15 items); (b) Lethargy, Social Withdrawal (16 items); (c) Stereotypic Behavior (7 items); (d) Hyperactivity/Noncompliance (16 items); and (e) Inappropriate Speech (4 items). The findings of psychometric studies have consistently been positive and supportive of the original factor structure and reliability/validity estimates (see Aman, 2003). Normative data have been presented for children and adolescents with ID recruited from public schools (Brown et al., 2002; Marshburn and Aman, 1992) and adults with ID recruited from group homes (Aman and Singh, 1994). This scale was one of the first credible instruments for assessing behavior and emotional problems in people with ID. More than 200 studies using the ABC have been published, several of which were drug trials of individuals with ASD (e.g., Arnold et al., 2006; Handen et al., 2000; Hellings et al., 2005;

RUPP, 2002, 2005). The Irritability subscale has been used as a primary outcome measure in several of these studies. Its items include the following: Injures self, Aggressive to others, Screams, Temper tantrums, Irritable, Yells, Depressed, Demands, Cries over minor annoyances, Mood changes, Cries and screams, Stamps feet or bangs, Deliberately hurts himself/herself, Does physical violence, Has temper outbursts.

Nisonger Child Behavior Rating Form (NCBRF)

The NCBRF (Aman et al., 1996; Tassé et al., 1996) has a parent and teacher version, with identical content and similar factor structures. Each version contains two sections, Social Competence and Problem Behaviors. The Social Competence Section contains 10 items rated on a 4-point scale and distributed on two subscales: Compliant/Calm and Adaptive/Social. The Problem Behavior Section contains 66 items, also rated on a 4-point scale and distributed on six subscales: Conduct Problem, Insecure/Anxious, Hyperactive, Self-Injury/Stereotypic, Self-Isolated/Ritualistic, and Overly Sensitive (parent)/Irritable (teacher). Lecavalier et al. (2004) showed that the original factor structure for the NCBRF held fundamentally true for youngsters with ASD. Lecavalier (2006) also provided some preliminary norms for the ASD population based on the ratings by 353 parents and 437 teachers. The NCBRF was used as the primary outcome measure in large clinical trials of risperidone in non-ASD children with disruptive behavior disorders, and the Conduct Problems subscale in particular was particularly sensitive to the effects of treatment (Aman et al., 2002; Snyder et al., 2002). To our knowledge, this rating scale has not been used in clinical trials for children with ASD. The social competence items might make this scale attractive for certain applications.

Developmental Behaviour Checklist (DBC)

The DBC measures behavior and emotional problems in youngsters with ID (Einfeld and Tonge, 1992, 2002). Items are rated on a 3-point scale that ranges from 0 (not true) to 2 (very true or often true). The parent and teacher versions contain a total of 96 and 93 items, respectively. Einfeld and Tonge (2002) revised the DBC's initial factor structure. Subscales were labeled the following way: Disruptive and Antisocial Behavior (27 items), Self-Absorbed (31 items), Communication Disturbance (13 items), Anxiety (9 items), and Social Relating Disturbance (10 items). The Self-Absorbed subscale contains a number of items such as pica and self injury that appear to be related to lower levels of functioning. A score of 46 or greater was determined to be the optimal clinical cutoff point. There is a significant amount of supportive psychometric data, and normative data based on large community-based samples for parent and teacher ratings have been presented (Einfeld and Tonge, 2002). At the time of this writing, an adult version of the DBC is being validated and normed in Australia. Worthy of mentioning is the fact that Brereton et al. (2002) developed a 29-item algorithm to screen for autism. In a brief report based on 37 children, Clark et al. (2003)

reported the DBC to be sensitive to change. Many studies using the DBC have included children with ASD, but we are not aware of its being used in drug trials.

Pervasive Developmental Disorder Behavior Inventory (PDDBI)

The PDDBI (Cohen and Sudhalter, 2005) is designed to measure response to treatment in children with ASD between the ages of 1.5 and 12.5 years of age. There are parent and teacher versions, containing 188 and 180 items, respectively. Items are rated on a 3-point scale, and divided in two sections: Problem Behavior and Adaptive. The Problem Behavior domains include: Sensory/Perceptual Approach Behaviors, Ritualism/Resistance to Change, Specific Fears, Arousal Regulation Problems, Aggressiveness, Social Pragmatic Problems, and Semantic Pragmatic Problems. Adaptive domains include Social Approach Behaviors, Learning, Memory, and Receptive Language; and Expressive Language Skills. The domains were defined on an a priori basis and were further divided into subcategories. Normative data are based on the ratings of 369 parents and 277 teachers recruited from a variety of geographical areas and research and clinical settings (Cohen and Sudhalter, 2005) The findings of preliminary reliability and validity studies are encouraging (Cohen, 2003; Cohen et al., 2003). The presence of adaptive and problem behavior sections could make it appealing for certain applications. At the time of this writing, no data on sensitivity to change are available.

NARROWBAND DIMENSIONAL SCALES

Children's Yale-Brown Obsessive Compulsive Scale Modified for Pervasive Developmental Disorders (CYBOCS-PDD)

The CYBOCS-PDD (Scahill et al., 2006) is a modified version of the CYBOCS (Scahill et al., 1997), itself an adaptation of the YBOCS (Goodman et al., 1989a,b). This modified version of the instrument was designed to rate the severity of compulsive symptoms in children and adolescents with ASD (items measuring obsessions were excluded). The CYBOCS-PDD is completed within a semi-structured interview by a trained clinician, and scoring is based on the interviewer's judgment. Using a list of compulsions and rituals, the four most severe behaviors are identified. Five items (Time spent, Distress, Interference, Resistance, and Degree of control) are then rated on a 5-point Likert scale ranging from 0 (Never) to 4 (Extreme) based on the four compulsions combined. The CYBOCS-PDD was administered to 172 medication-free children with ASD (88 percent with autism; average age of 8.2 years) participating in clinical trials of methylphenidate (RUPP, 2002) and risperidone (RUPP, 2005). The tool performed somewhat differently for children with IQs above and below the ID range, although most differences were not significant. The 5-item CYBOCS-PDD seems reliable, distinct from other measures of repetitive behavior, and sensitive to drug effects (McDougle et al., 2005).

ADHD Symptom Checklist-4 (ADHD-SC4)

The ADHD-SC4 (Gadow and Sprafkin, 1997) is one of many ADHD rating scales that includes the DSM-IV symptoms of ADHD inattentive, hyperactive-impulsive, and combined types. It also includes a DSM-referenced subscale for ODD, the Peer Conflict Scale (which captures many DSM-IV CD symptoms), and the Stimulant Side Effects Checklist. The ADHD-SC4 contains 50 items and is completed by parents or teachers. Normative data are available for children aged 3–18 years. Norms were based on parent ($n = 1844$) and teacher ratings ($n = 2715$) of community-based samples. The reliability and validity of the ADHD-SC4 and its sensitivity to stimulant drug effects have been demonstrated in a number of studies (Gadow and Sprafkin, 1997; Nolan et al., 1999, 2001; Sprafkin et al., 2001). A similar DSM-IV-referenced ADHD rating scale was sensitive to atomoxetine drug effects in children with ASD and ADHD symptoms (Arnold et al., 2006).

Behavior Problem Inventory (BPI-01)

The BPI-01 contains 49 items distributed onto three subscales (Rojahn et al., 2001). The three subscales are Self-Injurious Behavior (14 items), Stereotyped Behavior (24 items), and Aggressive/Destructive Behavior (11 items). Each of the three sections has a broad definition describing the range of behaviors to be rated in the past two months, and a residual item for behaviors that were not explicitly listed among the items, yet met one of the generic behavior problem definitions (e.g., "other stereotyped behavior"). Each item is rated on a frequency (0 = Never, through 4 = Hourly) and severity scale (0 = No problem, 3 = Severe problem). Factor analysis (Rojahn et al., 2001) of the ratings of 432 adolescents and adults recruited from a developmental center (93 percent with severe and profound ID) confirmed the arbitrary item assignments. This sample also served to generate normative data. Reliability and validity estimates are reasonably strong (Rojahn et al., 2001). These estimates were obtained by interviewing direct caregivers. In many settings, the tool is likely to be used as a paper–pencil instrument with less support and psychometric properties should be investigated in this fashion. The BPI-01 was used in two trials of risperidone in non-ASD children, and the Aggressive subscale was sensitive to treatment in both instances (Aman et al., 2002; Snyder et al., 2002). Self-injury, stereotypy, and aggression are all fairly common in individuals with ASD. When these behaviors are the target of treatment, the BPI-01 should be considered. Compared to other broadband instruments, the BPI-01 offers a much more detailed picture. For instance, the ABC contains only four items that directly assess aggression towards others and self-injurious behaviors.

Repetitive Behavior Scale-Revised (RBS-R)

The RBS-R is an empirically-derived scale containing 43 items measuring six dimensions of repetitive behavior: stereotyped behavior, self-injurious behavior, compulsive behavior, ritualistic behavior, sameness behavior, and restricted behavior (Bodfish et al., 2000). The scale was developed by compiling items from existing behavior rating scales measuring repetitive behaviors and from clinical experience (Bodfish et al., 1999). Items are evaluated on a 4-point Likert scale ranging from (0) "Behavior does not occur" to (3) "Behavior occurs and is a severe problem." The scale was used to measure repetitive behavior in people with ID and ASD, and preliminary data suggest good psychometric properties. Recently, Lam and Aman (in press) assessed the RBS-R's factor structure in a sample of 307 children and adults with ASD. The participants were recruited from the Autism Society of South Carolina and served to generate preliminary norms. Analyses essentially confirmed the original item assignments; the most apparent difference was that their 5-factor solution collapsed the original Ritualistic Behavior and Sameness Behavior subscales into one (labeled "Ritualistic/Sameness Behavior"). To our knowledge, the RBS-R not been used in clinical trials with people with ASD.

Overt Aggression Scale (OAS)

The OAS (Yudofsky et al., 1986) was designed to measure aggressive or violent behavior and is divided into two sections. The first section consists of four categories: Verbal Aggression, Physical Aggression, Physical Aggression Against Self, and Physical Aggression Against Other People. Within each category, there are four descriptors, and aggressive behavior is rated according to its severity. Items are weighted differentially in an effort to equate across different forms of aggression (e.g., 1–4 for verbal aggression, but 3–6 for physical aggression). The second section of the scale rates interventions at the time of the aggressive incident. Interventions are also rated according to their severity (e.g., from verbal redirection to physically holding the person) and scores are weighted accordingly. The OAS was developed for incident reporting in inpatient psychiatric settings, but has been used in a variety of other settings and populations. It was modified for retrospective rating (instead of incident reporting) and used as a caregiver- and clinician-completed rating scale (e.g., Coccaro et al., 1991; Sorgi et al., 1991). It was recently used as a parent- and teacher-completed rating scale in a small study of valproate in children with autistic disorder and performed well (Hellings et al., 2005). There is little psychometric information available on the OAS, and normative data are not available. The OAS was developed to track an individual's aggression and has the advantage of being tied to treatment.

Other Measures

A few additional measures are worth noting with regard to specific internalizing symptoms. There are few specific measures of anxiety and mood symptoms that have been used in individuals with ASD. Sukhodolsky et al. (2007) recently generated an anxiety scale for children and adolescents with ASD based on the anxiety items in the Child and Adolescents Symptom Inventories. Initial analyses indicated acceptable psychometric properties, and this measure may prove useful in drug trials. Another measure, the Pediatric Anxiety Rating Scale (PARS; RUPP, 2002), was used in a large multisite trial of flu- voxamine in non-ASD children and adolescents. The PARS is a clinician- completed scale with acceptable reliability and validity that may be suited for medication evaluations with or without modifications in children with ASD. The Anxiety, Depression and Mood Scale (ADAMS; Esbensen et al., 2003) is an empirically driven caregiver-completed measure containing 28-items rated on a 4-point scale. Items are distributed on five subscales: Manic/Hyperactive Behavior, Depressed Mood, Social Avoidance, General Anxiety, and Compul- sive Behavior. The ADAMS appears to be a psychometrically sound instrument for screening anxiety, depression, and mood disorders in adults with ID. It has not been used in ASD populations or clinical trials. Finally, the General Behavior Inventory (GBI; Depue et al., 1981) assesses symptoms of mania/hypomania as well as depression. The GBI contains 73 items rated on 4-point scale which are distributed on two subscales: Hypomanic/biphasic and Depressive. The GPI was designed as a self-report scale for adults and has been modified for use as a parent-report measure for children and adolescents between the ages of 5 and 17 years (Youngstrom et al., 2001). It is a well-validated instrument, but has yet to be used in clinical trials with ASD populations.

DSM-REFERENCED BROADBAND SCALES

Child Symptom Inventory-4 (CSI-4)

The CSI-4 (Gadow and Sprafkin, 2002) is a DSM-IV-referenced rating scale for 5–12 year olds to be completed by parents (97 items) and teachers (77 items). Subscales represent the most commonly encountered childhood disorders and include ADHD, ODD, CD, GAD, Separation Anxiety Disorder, Social Phobia, Major Depressive Disorder, Dysthymic Disorder, and the triad of ASD symp- toms.Items are evaluated on a 4-point Likert scale ranging from 0 (never) to 3 (very often). There are two scoring procedures: Screening Cutoff (categorical) and Symptom Severity (dimensional) scores. The Screening Cutoff score is based on the number of positive symptoms that meet the minimum necessary for a DSM-IV diagnosis. Symptom Severity is the sum of all items for each disorder. Numerous studies indicate that the CSI-4 has satisfactory internal consistency, reliability, and convergent and discriminant validity in community-based, clinic- referred non-ASD, and ASD samples (Gadow and Sprafkin, 2006). Symptom Count scores show acceptable levels of sensitivity and specificity for screen- ing many disorders including ASD when compared with structured psychiatric interviews and chart diagnoses. Symptom severity scores show moderate-to-high correspondence with psychiatric diagnoses but are minimally correlated with age, IQ, or SES. Normative data are available and based on several groups, including community-based, clinic-referred non-ASD, and ASD samples. There are parallel versions for 3–5 year olds, the Early Childhood Inventory-4 (ECI-4; Gadow and Sprafkin, 1994, 2000) and 12–18 year olds, the Adolescent Symptom

Inventory-4 (ASI-4, Gadow and Sprafkin, 1997). As previously noted, the CSI-4 and ECI-4 have been used in large-scale studies of behavior and emotional problems in children with ASD, but their sensitivity to drug effects in this population is unstudied.

Assessment of Dual Diagnosis (ADD)

The ADD (Matson, 1997) was developed to screen adults with mild and moderate ID for psychiatric problems. It contains 79 DSM-IV-referenced items distributed into 13 subscales: Mania, Depression, Anxiety, Post Traumatic Stress Disorder, Substance Abuse, Somatoform Disorder, Dementia, Conduct Disorder, PDD, Schizophrenia, Personality Disorders, Eating Disorders, and Sexual Disorders. Each item of the ADD is scored on a 3-point Likert scale for behavior exhibited during the prior month in terms of its frequency, duration, and severity. Matson and Bamburg (1998) reported good reliability on a sample of 101 adults living in residential facilities and group homes. Preliminary psychometric properties were obtained by having trained interviewers score the responses of direct care staff. The initial psychometric data are encouraging, although it is difficult to know the effects of having interviewers complete the scale. Future studies need to examine the ADD's reliability and validity when used as a paper-and-pencil rating scale as this is likely how it will be administered in most circumstances. The ADD has not been used in drugs trials for ASD, but some subscales/rating dimensions might be useful in this capacity.

Diagnostic Assessment of the Severely Handicapped-II (DASH-II)

The DASH-II (Matson, 1998) was developed to evaluate behavior and emotional problems in adults with severe and profound ID. It contains 84 items representing 13 diagnostic categories based on the DSM-III-R: Anxiety, Depression, Mania, Autism and other PDDs, Schizophrenia, Stereotypies, Self-Injurious Behavior, Elimination Disorders, Eating Disorders, Sleep Disorders, Sexual Disorders, Organic Syndromes, and Impulse Control and Other Miscellaneous Behaviors. The DASH-II is not exhaustive of all DSM disorders, but it covers conditions commonly seen in people with ID (e.g., stereotypic and self injurious behaviors) as well as disorders frequently encountered in the general population (e.g., mood and sleep disorders). Items are scored on a 3-point Likert scale according to three dimensions (frequency, duration, severity) for the previous two weeks. Factor analysis of the items in a sample of 451 people with ID (89 percent with profound ID; average age of 48 years) indicated five factors labeled Emotional Lability/Antisocial, Language Disorder, Dementia/Anxiety, Sleep Disorder, and Psychosis (Sturmey et al., 2004). Cutoff scores suggesting a high risk of pathology and normative data have been proposed (Matson, 1998). Reliability estimates vary significantly by subscale and dimension rated (Matson, 1998). A series of studies have reported on the validity of subscales relevant to ASD such as Mania, Anxiety, PDD/Autism, Depression, Stereotypies, and Self-Injury subscales (Matson et al., 1996, 1997a,b, 1999; Matson and

Smiroldo, 1997). Much like the ADD, the DASH-II was developed with the ratings of trained interviewers. There has been a significant amount of empirical work on the DASH-II and, despite the fact that certain subscale scores have low reliability, it is one of the most widely-used scales for adolescents and adults with severe and profound ID. To our knowledge, it has not been used in drugs trials for ASD, but some subscales and dimensions might be relevant to this population.

GLOBAL FUNCTIONING MEASURE

Developmental Disabilities Modification of the Children's Global Assessment Scale (DDCGAS)

The DDCGAS (Wagner et al., 2007) is a modification of the CGAS (Shaffer et al., 1983). It is a clinician-completed global measure of functioning designed to be used in treatment studies. The rating is intended to be based on all available sources of information and across four domains of functioning, including self-care, communication, social behavior, and school/academic functioning. It yields scores ranging from 1 to 100, where 1 represents the most impaired functioning and 100, superior functioning. Each decile (e.g., 1–10, 11–20) has a descriptive header (e.g., "Moderate impairment in functioning in most domains") and a scoring grid was developed that assigns a level of impairment (none, slight, moderate, severe, extreme) to the four key domains of functioning. The rating compares the child with a DD to his or her typically developing same-age peers. The DD-CGAS does not measure symptoms per se, but is built with the assumption that symptoms will have an impact on functioning. Initial reliability and validity data are quite encouraging, and the DDCGAS was shown to be sensitive to change in a small open-label trial (Wagner et al., 2007). It is distinct from adaptive behavior (correlation of 0.50 with adaptive behavior composite scores) and global symptom ratings (correlation of 0.48 with the CGI severity) and seems to be sensitive to the effect of core social and communication deficits, irritability, obsessive compulsive symptoms, and noncompliance on functioning. The DDCGAS can accommodate for significant variability in level of functioning and be an adjunct to other specific measures of functioning.

BROADBAND MEASURES OF ADAPTIVE BEHAVIOR

Deficits in adaptive functioning are not core symptoms of autism, but they are observed in the vast majority of individuals with ASD. Several investigators have raised the need for the identification of reliable and socially valid outcome measures that are sensitive to change in treatment studies with this population (Scahill and Lord, 2004). Although an exhaustive review of the literature about this topic goes far beyond the scope of this chapter, we present two measures with potential in the ASD population.

Vineland Adaptive Behavior Scales-II (VABS-II)

The VABS-II (Sparrow et al., 2005) measures four areas of adaptive functioning (Communication, Daily Living, Socialization, Motor Skills) and has a section on problem behavior. It is available in three different editions (survey, expanded, and classroom) when used as a semi-structured interview. It is also available as a parent/caregiver rating scale. It was normed on a large representative national sample and has very good psychometric properties (Sparrow et al., 2005). Items are rated on a 3-point rating scale, where 0 = Never, 1 = Sometimes or Partially, and 2 = Usually. Recently, Williams et al. (2006) showed that raw scores, age-equivalents, and special norm percentile scores of the previous edition of the instrument (Sparrow et al., 1984) were all sensitive to change in a risperidone study in children with autism. Vineland age-equivalent scores appear to be most useful in assessing change with treatment over time. The VABS-II has a rich history and, compared to other adaptive behavior scales, has more item density at lower ends.

Matson Evaluation of Social Skills for Individuals with Severe Mental Retardation (MESSIER)

The MESSIER (Matson, 1995) was designed for adults with severe and profound ID. It contains 85 items rated on a 4-point scale, where 0 = Never, 1 = Rarely, 2 = Some, and 3 = Often. Items were grouped into six clinically derived subscales: Positive Verbal (e.g., says please), Positive Nonverbal (e.g., waves hello appropriately), General Positive (e.g., has a friend), Negative Verbal (e.g., talks with food in mouth), Negative Nonverbal (e.g., pushes, hits, kicks, etc. peers or caregivers), and General Negative (e.g., is timid or shy in social situations). The MESSIER is the social skills rating scale with the most published psychometric data in the ID field. Its authors have reported good reliability (Matson et al., 1999) and validity (LeBlanc et al., 1999; Matson et al., 1998). The MESSIER has been administered to large samples of adults with severe and profound ID, and these data could be used as norms. For instance, Matson et al. (1998) obtained ratings on 892 adults living in a state residential facility. At the time of this writing, the tool is being used in one pharmacological trial of risperidone in ASD.

OTHER DOMAINS

There are other developments in assessment that have implications for the psychopharmacology of ASD, three of which are quality of life, consumer satisfaction, and cognition. However, this undertaking is much more ambitious than a simple focus on symptom reduction. For example, quality of life measures typically examine school functioning, relations with parents and peers, functioning in the neighborhood, personal happiness, and family life. Similarly, consumer satisfactions and cognitive functioning are equally complex. Unfortunately, important as these areas are to understanding the impact of psychotropic drug therapy on individuals with ASD, at present very little research has been directed toward this effort (Aman et al., 2004).

MEASURES OF ADVERSE EVENTS

As previously discussed, three of the most commonly prescribed groups of medications for behavior and emotional problems in people with ASD are antidepressants, antipsychotics, and stimulants, and their associated side effects are diverse owing to widely different mechanisms of action. Progress in the development of assessment instruments for evaluating adverse events (AEs) is hindered by almost all the same factors that stall advances in the assessment of therapeutic effects, and then some. For example, the role of caregivers, let alone the patient, in evaluating side effects other than responding to the verbal inquiries of the clinician is greatly underappreciated. This is most clearly evidenced by the all but complete absence of psychometrically sound, behaviorally oriented measures of AEs for individuals with ASD. In fact, investigators often fail to even describe how AEs were assessed in drug studies.

There are many reasons for this situation, several of which are noted here. First, by necessity, AEs must be infrequent enough for drug products to be commercially successful and therefore for manufacturers to recoup their research, development, and marketing costs. Therefore, a true test of the safety of a particular medication requires very large samples to adequately assess low frequency reactions. The difficulty in conducting such research is compounded when the disorder is also low in frequency. In other words, although one can study treatment sensitivity to therapeutic effects with smaller and arguably even with uncontrolled trials, this is certainly not true for AEs. Second is the problem of validity. Take for example "drowsiness." When viewed as an AE, how often do researchers actually validate ratings of drowsiness against some objective criterion such as on-task behavior or ability to concentrate? The fact of the matter is this is almost never done. What typically passes for validity of an AE measure is a comparison between drug and placebo response. If difference in scores are statistically significant, this is often the sole evidence for validity. Third, there is generally little or no commercial value in marketing AE measures; therefore, there is little money to develop them. Normative data, for example, are often simply too costly to obtain. Lastly, the amount of psychometric evidence is for the most part positively correlated with the severity of physical symptoms. Laboratory measures of biologic function, for example, which in some cases are subject to governmental oversight, are generally perceived as being reliable and valid when used appropriately. Nevertheless, in real world settings there can be considerable variability in these measures as well. At the other end of the continuum, behavioral assessment of more subtle aspects of cognitive impairment (e.g., Aman et al., 2004) or "personality changes" receive relatively little attention as AEs.

Given the focus of our chapter, we do not review the frequency of AEs or the relative safety of specific drug products; rather, we describe evidence-based assessment instruments. Readers interested in reviews of drug effects are referred to the chapter about this topic in this volume as well as other excellent reviews (e.g., Aman et al., 2005; Handen and Lubetsky, 2005; Kalachnik, 1999; Malone et al., 2005). Our discussion is further limited to behavioral assessment; review of the psychometric characteristics of laboratory tests is clearly beyond the scope of this text. Because there are so few large-scale drug studies of people with ASD that have used formal AE instruments, especially measures designed for use by non-clinicians, we also draw on the non-ASD literature.

ANTIPSYCHOTICS

One clinician-completed rating scale of AEs in children and adolescents with ASD is the Side Effects Review (SER; RUPP, 2005). The SER lists 29 commonly reported AEs associated with atypical antipsychotics as indicated from material in the package insert, published journal articles, and clinical experience of its authors. AEs are rated on a scale ranging from 0 (not present) to 3 (severe, requires immediate intervention). In one report, there were seven items for which differences between drug and placebo were significantly different (Aman et al., 2005). Additional information about the psychometric properties of the SER are not currently available. Nevertheless, given the large number of individuals with ASD who have been evaluated with the SER in controlled drug trials, we included it in Appendix A.

Extrapyramidal syndromes are movement disorders generally associated with antipsychotic medications, but they can be induced by other drugs as well. Clinician-completed ratings scales are generally used to measure these reactions, and they are among the most well studied, behaviorally-oriented AE measures. Several representative scales are briefly noted here, none of which were developed exclusively for individuals ASD. The Abnormal Involuntary Movement Scale (AIMS; Campbell and Palij, 1985) is a clinician-rated review of tremor, dyskinesia, and other neuromotor side effects. The AIMS takes 8–12 minutes to administer, using a combination of history and inspection. The Simpson-Angus Rating Scale (SARS; Simpson and Angus, 1970) complements the AIMs in assessing extrapyramidal side effects (rigidity, dystonia, and abnormal glabellar reflex) of antipsychotics. It takes 8–12 minutes and is administered by clinician examination. The Barnes Akathisia Scale (BAS; Barnes, 1989) is a 4-item, clinician-completed scale with the first three items scored from 0 to 3 and the last item rated 0 to 5. Higher scores reflect greater symptomatology. It includes two items pertaining to objective observation/clinical judgment by the rater and two items relating to the patient's subjective experience of restlessness.

STIMULANTS

Recent studies of stimulants in patients with ASD have generally used clinician-completed rating scales with items based on information reported in the package insert and controlled trials of non-ASD individuals. In general, other than significant mean differences between drug and placebo for specific symptoms, their psychometric properties are unreported. The RUPP Autism Network (2002), for example, used a parent-completed rating scale to monitor the AEs associated with methylphenidate therapy for hyperactivity and inattention symptoms in children and adolescents with ASD (see Appendix B). Four items indicated differences between doses of methylphenidate and placebo. Arnold et al. (2006) developed a 16-item scale with a 0–6 point severity rating to evaluate AEs associate with atomoxetine therapy for children and adolescents with ASD and prominent ADHD symptoms. Specific items were presented in a table, four of which indicated drug-placebo differences. Handen et al. (2000) also used a stimulant side effect checklist (Handen et al., 1991) based on AEs listed in the package insert. Their 13-item scale required teachers to rate severity using a 6-point Likert scale. In their study of methylphenidate in children with ASD and comorbid ADHD symptoms, the percentage experiencing side effects was reported.

Another measure, the Stimulant Side Effects Checklist (SSEC; Gadow, 1986), was developed to obtain ratings of AEs from parents and teachers of non-ASD children with ADHD. The SSEC contains 12 items rated on a 4-point scale (0 = never; 3 = very often). Items can also be grouped to form three indexes: a 4-item Mood index (irritability, unusually cheerful, sad, anxious), a 4-item Attention-Arousal index ("spaced out," overly quiet, lethargic, withdrawn), and 3-item Physical Complaints index (sleep, appetite, somatic). One item addresses abnormal movements. The SSEC has been used to evaluate side effects in several single- and double-blind studies of children with ADHD (Gadow and Sprafkin, 1997; Gadow et al., 1995, 1999; Nolan et al., 1999; Sprafkin and Gadow, 1996) and is included in the ADHD Symptom Checklist-4. Psychometric analyses include convergent and divergent validity with regard to other measures (Sprafkin et al., 2001), and normative data for teacher ratings of non-ASD 5–12 year olds (Gadow and Sprafkin, 1997).

OTHER DRUGS AND MEASURES

For the third group of most commonly prescribed drugs for people with ASD, the antidepressants, particularly the SSRIs, there is no widely accepted side effects rating scale for this patient population. As with other drug classes, idiosyncratic measures based on package insert information and findings from published studies is the rule. Antiepileptics are another group of drugs that are commonly prescribed for individuals with ASD owing to the relatively high rate of seizure disorders in this clinical population (Tuchman, 2004). We include comment of these drugs here because they are generally prescribed for long periods, have psychotropic properties, and are implicated in behavioral toxicity. One measure that may be useful for assessing AEs associated with antiepileptics is the Scale for the Evaluation and Identification of Seizures, Epilepsy, and Anticonvulsant Side Effects (Matson et al., 2005). Preliminary findings are encouraging. There are two additional broadband measures of AEs developed for individuals with ID that certainly warrant noting, the Matson Evaluation of Drug Side Effects (Matson et al., 1998) and the Monitoring of Side Effects System (Kalachnik, 1986).

SUMMARY

ASDs are complex neurodevelopmental syndromes that are associated with high rates of behavior and emotional problems and psychotropic drug therapy. One of the keys to valid psychopharmacology research and clinical management is the use of sound instrumentation. In fact, good assessment instruments are at the heart of any successful initiative to better understand the causes and treatment of behavior and emotional problems in this (and any) population.

The current state of affairs with respect to evidenced-based assessment research in ASD is quite limited and confined almost exclusively to a small number of more recently conducted, controlled clinical trials. There are numerous reasons for this situation and little indication this will change in the foreseeable future. Many of the instruments used in earlier studies are unpublished and difficult to obtain. Information substantiating their psychometric properties is generally limited, owing primarily to a lack of funding to support the required research.

The scientific community has yet to generate a consensus-driven taxonomy of behavioral and emotional problems for this clinical population, which has been a major stumbling block. Nevertheless, advances have been made, partly in response to the needs of the pharmaceutical industry. The list of available measures is opportunistic in that it is not based on relative comparisons of sensitivity in measuring drug response within the context of the same clinical trial. Researchers and clinicians alike must consider a number of issues when developing, selecting, and using instruments to measure treatment effects. They cannot assume that available scales are suitable for every situation and should carefully examine reliability, validity, and normative data.

The field is in need of a concerted effort to elucidate and validate a taxonomy of behavior and emotional problems for this patient population. More attention also needs to be paid to the broader ASD phenotype as well as adults. Few measures have normative data which allow making comparisons of symptom severity to the general population of individuals with ASD. Much more research is needed in the development of measures to assess anxiety and mood symptoms and the adverse effects of psychotropic drugs. Equally important is research into assessment modalities other than caregiver reports to include patient self-report, direct observations, and laboratory measures, as well as other aspects of functioning that go beyond simple symptom suppression.

REFERENCES

Achenbach, T.M., McConaughy, S.H., and Howell, C.T. (1987). Child/adolescent behavioral and emotional problems: Implications of cross-informant correlations for situational specificity. *Psychological Bulletin*, **101**, 213–232.

Aman, M.G. (2003). *Annotated Bibliography on the Aberrant Behavior Checklist (June 2003 update)*. Columbus, OH: Ohio State University.

Aman, M.G., Arnold, E., McDougle, C.J., et al. (2005). Acute and long-term safety and tolerability of risperidone in children with autism. *Journal of Child and Adolescent Psychopharmacology*, **15**, 869–884.

Aman, M.G., DeSmedt, G., Derivan, A., et al. (2002). Double–blind, placebo-controlled study of Risperidone for the treatment of Disruptive Behaviors in Children with Sub average Intelligence. *American Journal of Psychiatry*, **159**, 1337–1346.

Aman, M.G., Lam, K.L., and Collier-Crespin, A. (2003). Prevalence and patterns of use of psychoactive medicines among individuals with autism in the Autism Society of Ohio. *Journal of Autism and Developmental Disorders*, **33**, 527–534.

Aman, M.G., Lam, K.S.L., and Van Bourgondien, M.E. (2005). Medication patterns in patients with autism: Temporal, regional, and demographic influences. *Journal of Child and Adolescent Psychopharmacology*, **15**, 116–126.

Aman, M.G., Novotny, S., Samango-Sprouse, C., et al. (2004). Outcome measures for clinical trials in autism. *Central Nervous System Spectrum*, **9**, 36–47.

Aman, M.G., Sarphare, G., and Burrow, W. (1995). Psychoactive drugs in group homes: Prevalence and relation to demographic/psychiatric variables. *American Journal of Mental Retardation*, **99**, 500–509.

Aman, M.G. and Singh, N.N. (1994). *Aberrant Behavior Checklist – Community. Supplementary Manual*. East Aurora, NY: Slosson Educational Publications.

Aman, M.G., Singh, N.N., Stewart, A.W., and Field, C.J. (1985a). The Aberrant Behavior Checklist: A behavior rating scale for the assessment of treatment effects. *American Journal of Mental Deficiency*, **89**, 485–491.

Aman, M.G., Singh, N.N., Stewart, A.W., and Field, C.J. (1985b). Psychometric characteristics of the Aberrant Behavior Checklist. *American Journal of Mental Deficiency*, **89**, 492–502.

Aman, M.G., Tassé, M.J., Rojahn, J., and Hammer, D. (1996). The Nisonger CBRF: A child behavior rating form for children with developmental disabilities. *Research in Developmental Disabilities*, **17**, 41–57.

American Psychiatric Association (1994). *Diagnostic and statistical manual of mental disorders (4th ed.)*. Washington, DC: Author.

Ando, H., and Yoshimura, I. (1979). Effects of age on communication skill levels and prevalence of maladaptive behaviors in autistic and mentally retarded children. *Journal of Autism and Developmental Disorders*, **9**, 83–93.

Arnold, L.E., Aman, M.G., Cook, A.M., et al. (2006). Atomoxetine for hyperactivity in autism spectrum disorders: Placebo-controlled crossover pilot trial. *Journal of the American Academy of Child and Adolescent Psychiatry*, **45**, 1196–1205.

Barnes, T.R.E. (1989). A rating scale for drug-induced akathisia. *British Journal of Psychiatry*, **154**, 672–676.

Bird, H.R., Gould, M.S., and Staghezza, B. (1992). Aggregating data from multiple informants in child psychiatry epidemiological research. *Journal of the American Academy of Child and Adolescent Psychiatry*, **31**, 78–85.

Bodfish, J.W., Symons, F.W., and Lewis, M.H. (1999). *The Repetitive Behavior Scale.* Western Carolina Center Research Reports.

Bodfish, J.W., Symons, F.J., Parker, D.E., and Lewis, M.H. (2000). Varieties of repetitive behavior in autism: Comparisons to mental retardation. *Journal of Autism and Developmental Disorders,* **30**, 237–243.

Bradley, C. (1957). Characteristics and management of children with behavior problems associated with organic brain damage. *Pediatric Clinics of North America,* **4**, 1049–1060.

Brereton, A.V., Tonge, B.J., Mackinnon, A.J., and Einfeld, S.L. (2002). Screening young people for autism with the Development Behavior Checklist. *Journal of the American Academy of Child and Adolescent Psychiatry,* **41**, 1369–1375.

Brown, E.C., Aman, M.G., and Havercamp, S.M. (2002). Factor analysis and norms on parent ratings with the Aberrant Behavior ChecklistCCommunity for young people in special education. *Research in Developmental Disabilities,* **23**, 45–60.

Brown, E., Aman, M.G., and Lecavalier, L. (2004). Empirical classification of behavioral and psychiatric problems in children and adolescents with mental retardation. *American Journal on Mental Retardation,* **109**, 445–455.

Campbell, M. and Palij, M. (1985). Measurement of side effects including tardive dyskinesia. *Psychopharmacology Bulletin,* **9** *(Special Issue),* 1063–1082.

Chung, S.Y., Luk, S.L., and Lee, P.W. (1990). A follow-up study of infantile autism in Hong Kong. *Journal of Autism and Developmental Disorders,* **20**, 221–232.

Cichetti, D.V. (1994). Guidelines, criteria, and rule of thumb for evaluating normed and standardized assessment instruments in psychology. *Psychological Assessment,* **6**, 284–290.

Clark, A.R., Tonge, B.J., Einfeld, S.L., and Mackinnon, A. (2003). Assessment of change with the Developmental Behaviour Checklist. *Journal of Intellectual Disability Research,* **47**, 210–212.

Coccaro, E.F., Harvey, P.D., Kupsaw-Lawrence, E., et al. (1991). Development of neurophar-macologically based behavioural assessments of impulsive aggressive behaviour. *Journal of Neuropsychiatry and Clinical Neuroscience,* **3**, s44–s51.

Cohen, I.L. (2003). Criterion-related validity of the PDD Behavior Inventory. *Journal of Autism and Developmental Disorders,* **33**, 47–53.

Cohen, I.L., Schmidt-Lackner, S., Romanczyk, R., and Sudhalter, V. (2003). The PDD Behavior Inventory: A rating scale for assessing response to intervention in children with pervasive developmental disorder. *Journal of Autism and Developmental Disorders,* **33**, 31–45.

Cohen, I.L. and Sudhalter, V. (2005). *The PDD Behavior Inventory.* Lutz, FL: Psychological Assessment.

Collett, B.R., Ohan, J.L., and Meyers, K.M. (2003). Ten-year review of rating scales. VI: Scales assessing externalizing behaviors. *Journal of the American Academy of Child and Adolescent Psychiatry,* **42**, 1143–1170.

Depue, R.A., Slater, J.F., Wolfstetter-Kausch, H., et al. (1981). A behavioral paradigm for identifying persons at risk for bipolar depressive disorder: A conceptual framework and five validation studies. *Journal of Abnormal Psychology,* **90**, 381–437.

DeVincent, C.J., Gadow, K.D., Delosh, D., and Geller, L. (2007). Sleep disturbance and its relation to DSM-IV psychiatric symptoms in preschool-aged children with pervasive developmental disorder and community controls. *Journal of Child Neurology,* **22**, 161–169.

Drabick, D.A.G., Gadow, K.D., and Loney, J. (in press). Co-occurring ODD and GAD symptom groups: Source-specific syndromes and cross-informant comorbidity. *Journal of Clinical Child and Adolescent Psychology.*

Drabick, D.A.G., Gadow, K.D., and Loney, J. (2007a). Source-specific oppositional defiant disorder: Comorbidity and risk factors in referred elementary school boys. *Journal of the American Academy of Child and Adolescent Psychiatry,* **46**, 92–101.

Einfeld, S.L. and Tonge, B.J. (1992). *Manual for the Developmental Behaviour Checklist.* Clayton, Malbourne, and Aydney: Monash University Center for Developmental Psychiatry and School of Psychiatry, University of New South Wales.

Einfeld, S.L. and Tonge, B.J. (2002). *Manual for the Developmental Behaviour Checklist (Second Edition)*. Clayton, Malbourne, and Sydney: Monash University Center for Developmental Psychiatry and School of Psychiatry, University of New South Wales.

Ellis, M.J., Witt, P.A., Reynolds, R., and Sprague, R.L. (1974). Methylphenidate and the activity of hyperactives in informal settings. *Child Development*, **45**, 217–220.

Esbensen, A.J., Rojahn, J., Aman, M.G., and Ruedrich, S. (2003). The reliability and validity of an assessment instrument for anxiety, depression and mood among individuals with mental retardation. *Journal of Autism and Developmental Disorders*, **33**, 617–629.

Eyman, R.K., Borthwick S.A., and Miller C. (1981). Trends in maladaptive behavior of mentally retarded persons placed in community and institutional settings. *American Journal of Mental Deficiency*, **85**, 473–477.

Feighner, J.P., Robins, E., Guze, S.B., et al. (1972). Diagnostic criteria for use in psychiatric research. *Archives of General Psychiatry*, **26**, 57–63.

Gadow, K.D. (1986). *Stimulant Side Effects Checklist*. Department of Psychiatry, State University of New York, Stony Brook.

Gadow, K.D. (1991). Clinical issues in child and adolescent psychopharmacology. *Journal of Consulting and Clinical Psychology*, **59**, 842–852.

Gadow, K.D. and DeVincent, C.J. (2005). Clinical significance of tics and attention-deficit hyperactivity disorder (ADHD) in children with pervasive developmental disorder. *Journal of Child Neurology*, **20**, 481–488.

Gadow, K.D., DeVincent, C.J., and Drabick, D.A.G. (2007). *Oppositional Defiant Disorder as a Clinical Phenotype in Children with Pervasive Developmental Disorder*. Manuscript submitted for publication.

Gadow, K.D., DeVincent, C., and Pomeroy, J. (2006). ADHD symptom subtypes in children with pervasive developmental disorder. *Journal of Autism and Developmental Disorders*, **36**, 271–283.

Gadow, K.D., DeVincent, C.J., Pomeroy, J., and Azizian, A. (2004). Psychiatric symptoms in preschool children with PDD and clinic and comparison samples. *Journal of Autism and Developmental Disorders*, **34**, 379–393.

Gadow, K.D., DeVincent, C.J., Pomeroy, J., and Azizian, A. (2005). Comparison of DSM-IV symptoms in elementary school-aged children with PDD versus clinic and community samples. *Autism*, **9**, 392–415.

Gadow, K.D., DeVincent, C. Schneider, J., and Drabick, D.A.G. (2007). *Predictors of psychiatric syndromes in children with autism spectrum disorders*. Manuscript submitted for publication.

Gadow, K.D., Drabick, D.A.G., Loney, J., et al. (2004). Comparison of ADHD symptom subtypes as source-specific syndromes. *Journal of Child Psychology and Psychiatry*, **45**, 1135–1149.

Gadow, K.D., Paolicelli, L.M., Nolan, E.E., et al. (1992). Methylphenidate in aggressive hyperactive boys: II. Indirect effects of medication on peer behavior. *Journal of Child and Adolescent Psychopharmacology*, **2**, 49–61.

Gadow K.D., Sverd, J., Sprafkin, J., et al. (1995). Efficacy of methylphenidate for attention-deficit hyperactivity disorder in children with tic disorder. *Archives of General Psychiatry*, **52**, 444–455.

Gadow, K.D. and Pomeroy, J.C. (1990). A controlled case study of methylphenidate and fenfluramine in a young mentally retarded, hyperactive child. *Australian and New Zealand Journal of Developmental Disabilities*, **16**, 323–334.

Gadow, K.D. and Sprafkin, J. (1994). *Early Childhood Inventory-4 norms manual*. Stony Brook, NY: Checkmate Plus.

Gadow, K.D. and Sprafkin, J. (1997). *Adolescent Symptom Inventory-4 screening manual*. Stony Brook, NY: Checkmate Plus.

Gadow, K.D. and Sprafkin, J. (2000). *Early Childhood Inventory-4 screening manual*. Stony Brook, NY: Checkmate Plus.

Gadow, K.D. and Sprafkin, J. (2002). *Child Symptom Inventory-4 Screening and Norms Manual*. Stony Brook, NY: Checkmate Plus.

Gadow, K.D. and Sprafkin, J. (2006). *The Symptom Inventories: An Annotated Bibliography* [On-line]. Available: www.checkmateplus.com

Gadow, K.D., Sprafkin, J., Schneider, J., et al. (2007). ODD, ADHD, versus ODD + ADHD in clinic and community adults. *Journal of Attention Disorders*, **11**, 374–383.

Gadow, K.D., Sprafkin, J., and Weiss, M. (2004). *Adult Self Report Inventory-4 and Adult Inventory-4 manual*. Stony Brook, NY: Checkmate Plus.

Ghaziuddin, M. and Greden, J. (1998). Depression in children with autism/pervasive developmental disorders: A case-control family history study. *Journal of Autism and Developmental Disorders*, **28**, 111–115.

Gillberg, C., and Billstedt, E. (2000). Autism and Asperger syndrome: Coexistence with other clinical disorders. *Acta Psychiatrica Scandinavica*, **102**, 321–330.

Goodman, W.K., Price, L.H., Rasmussen, S.A., et al. (1989a). The Yale-Brown obsessive compulsive scale, II: Validity. *Archives of General Psychiatry*, **46**, 1012–1016.

Goodman, W.K., Price, L.H., Rasmussen, S.A., et al. (1989b). The Yale-Brown Obsessive Compulsive Scale, I: Development, use, and reliability. *Archives of General Psychiatry*, **46**, 1006–1011.

Green, J., Gilchrist, A., Burton, D., and Cox, A. (2000). Social and psychiatric functioning in adolescents with Asperger syndrome compared with conduct disorder. *Journal of Autism and Developmental Disorder*, **30**, 279–293.

Handen, B.L., Feldman, H., Gosling, A., et al. (1991). Adverse effects of methylphenidate among mentally retarded children with ADHD. *Journal of the American Academy of Child and Adolescent Psychiatry*, **30**, 241–245.

Handen, B.L., Johnson, C.R., and Lubetsky, M. (2000). Efficacy of methylphenidate among children with autism and symptoms of attention-deficit hyperactivity disorder. *Journal of Autism and Developmental Disorders*, **30**, 245–255.

Handen, B.L. and Lubetsky, M. (2005). Pharmacotherapy in Autism and Related Disorders. *School Psychology Quarterly*, **20**, 155–171.

Hellings, J.A., Nickel, E.J., Weckbaugh, M., et al. (2005). The overt aggression scale for rating aggression in outpatient youth with autistic disorder: Preliminary findings. *Journal of Neuropsychiatric & Clinical Neurosciences*, **17**, 29–35.

Hellings, J.A., Weckbaugh, M., Nickel, E.J., et al. (2005). A double-blind, placebo-controlled study of Valproate for aggression in youth with pervasive developmental disorders. *Journal of Child and Adolescent Psychopharmacology*, **15**, 682–692.

Holden, B. and Gitlesen, J.P. (2006). A total population study of challenging in the county of Hedmark, Norway: Prevalence, and risk markers. *Research in Developmental Disabilities*, **27**, 456–465.

Hollander, E., Wasserman, S., Swanson, E.N., et al. (2006). A double-blind placebo-controlled pilot study of alanzapine in childhood/adolescent pervasive developmental disorder. *Journal of Child and Adolescent Psychopharmacology*, **16**, 541–548.

Kalachnik, J. (1986). Assessment sheet for Monitoring of Side Effects System (MOSES). In *Drug Therapy for Behavior Disorders: An Introduction* (A. Poling, K. Gadow, and J. Cleary, eds.) pp. 153–155. New York: Pergamon Press.

Kalachnik, J.E. (1999). Measureing side effects of psychopharmacologic medication in individuals with mental retardation and developmental disabilities. *Mental Retardation and Developmental Disabilities Research Review*, **5**, 348–359.

Kim, J.A., Szatmari, P., Bryson, S., et al. (2000). The prevalence of anxiety and mood problems among children with autism and Asperger syndrome. *Autism*, **4**, 117–132.

Lam, K.L.S. and Aman, M.G. (in press). The repetitive behavior scale-revised: Independent validation in individuals with autism spectrum disorders. *Journal of Autism and Developmental Disorders*, **37**, 855–866.

Langworthy-Lam, K.L., Aman, M.G., and Van Bourgondiem, M.E. (2002). Prevalence and patterns of use of psychoactive medicines in individuals with autism in the Autism Society of North Carolina. *Journal of Child and Adolescent Psychopharmacology*, **12**, 311–321.

LeBlanc, L.A., Matson, J.L., Cherry, K.E., Bamburg, J.W. (1999). An examination of the convergent validity of the Matson Evaluation of Social Skills for Individuals with Severe Retardation (MESSIER) with sociometric ranking. *British Journal of Developmental Disabilities*, **45**, 85–91.

Lecavalier, L. (2006) Behavior and emotional problems in young people with pervasive developmental disorders: Relative prevalence, effects of subject characteristics, and empirical classification. *Journal of Autism and Developmental Disorders*, **36**, 1101–1114.

Lecavalier, L. and Aman, M.G. (2005). Rating instruments. In *Behavior Modification for Persons with Developmental Disabilities: Treatments and Supports: Volume One* (J.L. Matson, R.B. Laud, and M.L. Matson, eds.) pp. 160–189. Kingston, NY: National Association for the Dually Diagnosed Press.

Lecavalier, L., Aman, M.G., Hammer, D., et al. (2004). Factor analysis of the nisonger child behavior rating form in children with autism spectrum disorders. *Journal of Autism and Developmental Disorders*, **34**, 709–721.

Lecavalier, L., Leone, S., and Wiltz, J. (2006). The impact of behaviour problems on caregiver stress in young people with autism spectrum disorders. *Journal of Intellectual Disability Research*, **50**, 172–183.

Ledford, J.R. and Gast, D.L. (2006). Feeding problems in children with autism spectrum disorders: A review. *Focus on Autism and Other Developmental Disabilities*, **21**, 153–166.

Leyfer, O.T., Folstein, S.E., Bacalman, S., et al. (2006). Comorbid psychiatric disorders in children with autism: Interview developmental rates of disorders. *Journal of Autism and Developmental Disorders*, **36**, 849–861.

Malone, R.P., Gratz, S.S., Delaney, M.A., and Hyman, S.B. (2005). Advances in drug treatments for children and adolescents with autism and other pervasive developmental disorders. *CNS Drugs*, **19**, 923–934.

Marshburn, E.C. and Aman, M.G. (1992). Factor validity and norms for the Aberrant Behavior Checklist in a community sample of children with mental retardation. *Journal of Autism and Developmental Disorders*, **22**, 357–373.

Martin, A., Scahill, L., Klin, A., Volkmar, F.R. (1999). Higher-functioning pervasive developmental disorders: rates and patterns of psychotropic drug use. *Journal of the American Academy of Child and Adolescent Psychiatry*, **38**, 923–931.

Matson, J.L. (1995). *Manual for the Matson Evaluation of Social Skills for Individuals with Severe Retardation*. Baton Rouge, LA: Scientific Publishers, Inc.

Matson, J.L. (1998). *Manual for the Diagnostic Assessment for the Severely Handicapped-II*. Baton Rouge, LA: Louisiana State University.

Matson, J.L. (1997). *Manual for the Assessment of Dual Diagnosis*. Baton Rouge, LA: Louisiana State University.

Matson, J.L., Baglio, C.S., Smiroldo, B.B., et al. (1996). Characteristics of autism as assessed by the Diagnostic Assessment for the Severely Handicapped – II (DASH-II). *Research in Developmental Disabilities*, **17**, 1–9.

Matson, J.L. and Bamburg, J.A. (1998). Reliability of the Assessment of Dual Diagnosis (ADD). *Research in Developmental Disabilities*, **19**, 89–95.

Matson, J.L., Carlisle, C.B., and Bamburg, J.W. (1998). The convergent validity of the Matson Evaluation of Social Skills for individuals with Severe Retardation. *Research in Developmental Disabilities*, **19**, 493–500.

Matson, J.L., Hamilton, M., Duncan, D., et al. (1997a). Characteristic of stereotypic movement disorder and self-injurious behavior as assessed by the Diagnostic Assessment for the Severely Handicapped II (DASH-II). *Research in Developmental Disabilities*, **18**, 457–469.

Matson, J.L., Laud, R.B, Gonzalez, M.L., et al. (2005). The reliability of the scale for the evaluation and identification of seizure, epilepsy, and anticonvulsant side Effects-B (SEIZES B). *Research in Developmental Disabilities*, **26**, 593–599.

Matson, J.L., LeBlanc, L.A., and Weinheimer, B. (1999). Reliability of the Matson Evaluation of Social Skills in Individuals with Severe Retardation (MESSIER). *Behavior Modification*, **23**, 647–661.

Matson, J.L., Mayville, E.A., Bielecki, J., et al. (1998). Reliability of the Matson Evaluation of Drug Side Effects (MEDS). *Research in Developmental Disabilities*, **19**, 501–506.

Matson, J.L., Rush, K.S., Smiroldo, B.B., et al. (1999). Characteristics of depression as assessed by the Diagnostic Assessment for the Severely Handicapped II (DASH-II). *Research in Developmental Disabilities*, **20**, 305–313.

Matson, J.L. and Smiroldo, B.B. (1997). Validity of the mania subscale of the Diagnostic Assessment for the Severely Handicapped – II (DASH-II). *Research in Developmental Disabilities*, **18**, 1–5.

Matson, J.L., Smiroldo, B.B., Hamilton, M., and Baglio, C.S. (1997b). Do anxiety disorders exist in people with severe and profound mental retardation? *Research in Developmental Disabilities*, **18**, 39–44.

McClintock, J., Hall, S., and Oliver, C. (2003). Risk markers associated with challenging behaviours in people with intellectual disabilities: A meta-analytic study. *Journal of Intellectual Disability Research*, **47**, 405–416.

McDougle, C.J., Scahill, L., Aman, M.G., et al. (2005). Risperidone for the core symptom domains of autism: Results from the study by the autism network of the Research Units on Pediatric Psychopharmacology. *American Journal of Psychiatry*, **162**, 1142–1148.

Meyers, K. and Winters, N.C. (2002a). Ten-year review of rating scales, I: Overview of scale functioning, psychometric properties, and selection. *Journal of the American Academy of Child and Adolescent Psychiatry*, **41**, 114–122.

Meyers, K. and Winters, N.C. (2002b). Ten-year review of rating scales, II: Scales for internalizing disorders. *Journal of the American Academy of Child and Adolescent Psychiatry*, **41**, 634–659.

Muris, P., Steerneman, P., Merckelbach, H., et al. (1998). Comorbid anxiety symptoms in children with pervasive developmental disorders. *Journal of Anxiety Disorders*, **12**, 387–393.

National Institute of Mental Health. (1976). Clinical Global Impressions (CGI). In *ECDEU Assessment Manual for Psychopharmacology Revised* (W. Guy, ed). pp. 217–222. Rockville, MD: U.S. National Institutes of Health, Psychopharmacology Research Branch.

Nolan, E.E. and Gadow, K.D. (1997). Children with ADHD and tic disorder and their classmates: behavioral normalization with methylphenidate. *Journal of the American Academy of Child and Adolescent Psychiatry*, **36**, 597–604.

Nolan, E.E., Gadow, K.D., and Sprafkin, J. (1999). Stimulant medication withdrawal during long-term therapy in children with comorbid attention-deficit hyperactivity disorder and chronic multiple tic disorder. *Pediatrics*, **103**, 730–737.

Nolan, E.E., Gadow, K.D., and Sprafkin, J. (2001). Teacher reports of DSM-IV ADHD, ODD, and CD symptoms in schoolchildren. *Journal of the American Academy of Child and Adolescent Psychiatry*, **40**, 241–249.

Offord, D.R., Boyle, M.H., Racine, Y., et al. (1996). Integrating assessment data from multiple informants. *Journal of the American Academy of Child and Adolescent Psychiatry*, **35**, 1078–1085.

Pearson D.A. and Aman, M.G. (1994). Ratings of hyperactivity and developmental indices: Should clinicians correct for developmental level? *Journal of Autism and Developmental Disorders*, **24**, 395–411.

Piacentini, J.C., Cohen, P., and Cohen, J. (1992). Combining discrepant diagnostic information from multiple sources: A re complex algorithms better than simple ones? *Journal of Abnormal Child Psychology*, **20**, 51–63.

Research Units on Pediatric Psychopharmacology (RUPP) Autism Network (2002). Risperidone in children with autism and serious behavioral problems. *New England Journal of Medicine*, **347**, 314–321.

Research Units on Pediatric Psychopharmacology (RUPP) Anxiety Study Group (2002). The Pediatric Anxiety Rating Scale (PARS): Development and psychometric properties. *Journal of the American Academy of Child and Adolescent Psychiatry*, **41**, 1061–1069.

Research Units on Pediatric Psychopharmacology (RUPP) Autism Network. (2005). Randomized, controlled, crossover trial of methylphenidate in pervasive developmental disorders with hyperactivity. *Archives of General Psychiatry*, **62**, 1266–1274.

Robins, E. and Guze, S. (1970). Establishment of diagnostic validity in psychiatric illness: Its application to schizophrenia. *American Journal of Psychiatry*, **126**, 983–987.

Rojahn, J. and Tassé, M.J. (1996). Psychopathology in mental retardation. In *Manual of Diagnosis and Professional Practice in Mental Retardation* (J.W. Jacobson and J.A. Mulick, eds.) pp. 147–156. Washington DC: APA.

Rojahn, J., Matson, J.L., Lott, D., et al. (2001). The behavior problems inventory: An instrument for the assessment of self-injury, stereotyped behavior and aggression/destruction in individuals with developmental disabilities. *Journal of Autism and Developmental Disorders*, **31**, 577–588.

Rutter, M., Greenfield, D., and Lockyer, L. (1967). A five to fifteen year follow-up study of Infantile Psychosis: II. Social and behavioral outcome. *British Journal of Psychiatry*, **113**, 1183–1190.

Scahill L. and Lord, C. (2004). Subject selection and characterization in clinical trials in children with autism. *CNS Spectrums*, **9**, 22–32.

Scahill, L., McDougle, C.J., Williams, S.K., et al. (2006). Children's Yale-Brown obsessive compulsive scale modified for pervasive developmental disorders. *Journal of the American Academy of Child and Adolescent Psychiatry*, **45**, 1114–1123.

Scahill, L., Riddle, M.A., McSwiggin-Hardin, M., et al. (1997). Children's Yale-Brown Obsessive Compulsive Scale: reliability and validity. *Journal of the American Academy of Child and Adolescent Psychiatry*, **36**, 844–852.

Shaffer, D., Gould, M.S., Brasic, J., et al. (1983). A children's global assessment scale (CGAS). *Archives of General Psychiatry*, **40**, 1228–1231.

Simmons, J.M. (1974). Observations on compulsive behavior in autism. *Journal of Autism and Childhood Schizophrenia*, **4**, 1–10.

Simpson, G.M. and Angus, J.W. (1970). A rating scale for extrapyramidal side effects. *Acta Psychiatrica Scandinavica*, **212**, 11–19.

Snyder, R., Turgay, A., Aman, M.G., et al. (2002). Effects of risperidone on conduct and disruptive disorders in children with subaverage IQ's. *Journal of the American Academy of Child and Adolescent Psychiatry*, **41**, 1026–1036.

Sofronoff, K., Attwood, T., and Hinton, S. (2005). A randomized controlled trial of a CBT intervention for anxiety in children with Asperger syndrome. *Journal of Child Psychology and Psychiatry*, **46**, 1152–1160.

Sorgi, P., Ratey, J., Knoedler, D.W., et al. (1991). Rating aggression in the clinical setting. A retrospective adaptation of the overt aggression scale: Preliminary results. *Journal of Neuropsychiatry*, **3**, S52–S56.

Sparrow, S., Balla, D., and Cichetti, D. (1984). *The Vineland Adaptive Behavior Scales: Interview Edition, Survey Form*. Circle Pines, MN: American Guidance Service.

Sparrow, S., Cicchetti, D., and Balla, D. (2005). *The Vineland Adaptive Behavior Scales Second Edition, Survey Forms Manual*. Circle Pines, MN: American Guidance Service.

Sprafkin, J. and Gadow, K.D. (1996). Double-blind versus open evaluations of stimulant drug response in children with attention-deficit hyperactivity disorder. *Journal of Child and Adolescent Psychopharmacology*, **6**, 215–228.

Sprafkin, J., Gadow, K.D., and Nolan E.E. (2001). The utility of a DSM-IV-referenced screening instrument for attention-deficit/hyperactivity disorder. *Journal of Emotional and Behavioral Disorders*, **9**, 182–191.

Sprafkin, J., Gadow, K.D., Salisbury, H., et al. (2002). Further evidence of reliability and validity of the Child Symptom Inventory-4: Parent Checklist in clinically referred boys. *Journal of Clinical Child and Adolescent Psychology*, **31**, 513–524.

Sprafkin, J., Gadow, K.D., Weiss, M.D., et al. (2007). Psychiatric comorbidity in ADHD symptom subtypes in clinic and community adults. *Journal of Attention Disorders*, **11**, 114–124.

Sturmey, P., Matson, J.L., and Lott, J.D. (2004). The factor structure of the DASH-II. *Journal of Developmental and Physical Disabilities*, **16**, 247–255.

Sukhodolsky, D.G., Scahill, L., Gadow, K.D., et al. (2007). Parent-rated anxiety symptoms in children with pervasive developmental disorders: Frequency and association with core autism symptoms and cognitive functioning. *Journal of Abnormal Child Psychology*.

Sverd, J. (2003). Psychiatric disorders in individuals with pervasive developmental disorder. *Journal of Psychiatric Practice*, **9**, 111–127.

Tassé, M.J., Aman, M.G., Hammer, D., and Rojahn, J. (1996). The Nisonger child behavior rating form: Age and gender effects and norms. *Research in Developmental Disorders*, **17**, 59–75.

Tuchman, R. (2004). AEDs and psychotropic drugs in children with autism and epilepsy. *Mental Retardation and Developmental Disabilities*, **10**, 135–138.

Tonge, B.J. and Einfeld, S.L. (2003). Psychopathology and intellectual disability: The Australian child to adult longitudinal study. In *International Review of Research in Mental Retardation* (L.M. Glidden, ed). (Vol. 26, pp. 61–91). San Diego, CA: Academic Press.

Valdovinos M.G., Schroeder S.R., and Kim G. (2003). Prevalence and correlates of psychotropic medication use among adults with developmental disabilities: 1970–2000. In *International Review of Research in Mental Retardation* (L.M. Glidden, ed). pp. 175–220). San Diego, CA: Academic Press.

Wagner, A., Lecavalier, L., Arnold, L.E., et al. (2007). Developmental Disabilities Modification of Children's Global Assessment Scale (DD-CGAS). *Biological Psychiatry*, **61**, 504–511.

Watson J.E., Aman, M.G., and Singh, N.N. (1988). The psychopathology instrument for mentally retarded adults: Psychometric characteristics, factor structure, and relationship to subject characteristics. *Research in Developmental Disabilities*, **9**, 277–290.

Weisbrot, D.M., Gadow, K.D., DeVincent, C.J., and Pomeroy, J. (2005). The presentation of anxiety in children with pervasive developmental disorders. *Journal of Child and Adolescent Psychopharmacology*, **15**, 477–496.

Whalen, C.K., Collins, B.E., Henker, B., et al. (1978). Behavior observations of hyperactive children and methylphenidate (Ritalin) effects in systematically structured classroom environments: Now you see them, now you don't. *Journal of Pediatric Psychology*, **3**, 177–184.

Whalen, C.K., Henker, B., Collins, B.E., et al. (1979). A social ecology of hyperactive boys: Medication effects in structured classroom environments. *Journal of Applied Behavioral Analysis*, **12**, 65–81.

Williams, S.K. Scahill, L. Vitiello, B., et al. (2006). Risperidone and Adaptive Behavior in Children with Autism. *Journal of the American Academy of Child and Adolescent Psychiatry*, **45**, 431–439.

Wing, L. (1981). Asperger's syndrome: a clinical account. *Psychological Medicine*, **11**, 115–129.

Witwer, A. and Lecavalier, L. (2005). Treatment incidence and patterns in children and adolescents with autism spectrum disorders. *Journal of Child and Adolescent psychopharmacology*, **15**, 671–681.

Winters, N.C., Collett, B.R., and Myers, K.M. (2005). Ten-year review of rating scales, VII: scales assessing functional impairment. *Journal of the American Academy of Child and Adolescent Psychiatry*, **44**, 309–338.

Wozniak, J., Biederman, J., Faraone, S.V., et al. (1997). Mania in children with pervasive developmental disorder revisited. *Journal of the American Academy of Child and Adolescent Psychiatry*, **36**, 1552–1559.

Youngstrom, E.A., Findling, R.L., Danielson, C.K., and Calabrese, J.R. (2001). Discriminative validity of parent report of hypomanic and depressive symptoms on the General Behavior Inventory. *Psychological Assessment*, **13**, 267–276.

Yudofsky, S.C., Silver, J.M., Jackson W., et al. (1986). The Overt Aggression Scale or the objective rating of verbal and physical aggression. *American Journal of Psychiatry*, **143**, 35–39.

APPENDIX A: SIDE EFFECTS REVIEW FORM USED
IN RISPERIDONE STUDY (RUPP, 2005)

Participant: _____
Information Source: _____

a. Does your child have any current health
   complaints?   ☐ Yes   ☐ No

b. Has your child had any recent injuries
   or illnesses?   ☐ Yes   ☐ No

c. Has your child seen a doctor for
   any reason?   ☐ Yes   ☐ No

d. Is your child taking any new medications
   (over the counter or prescription)?   ☐ Yes   ☐ No

*You may need to update the Concomitant Medications and/or Adverse
Events form if there has been a change in severity since baseline.**

Side Effect	Absent	Mild* No intervention required	Moderate* Some intervention required	Severe* Immediate intervention required
1. Difficulty falling asleep or difficulty staying asleep	0	1	2	3
2. Tired during the day, wants to take naps, sleepy	0	1	2	3
3. Difficulty in waking up in the morning	0	1	2	3
4. Shakiness in arms, legs, or hands (tremors)	0	1	2	3
5. Twisting or repetitive tongue movements	0	1	2	3
6. Muscles appearing stiff or "stuck"	0	1	2	3
7. Eyes appearing "stuck" in one position	0	1	2	3
8. Headaches	0	1	2	3
9. Dizziness or loss of balance	0	1	2	3
10. Constipation	0	1	2	3
11. Diarrhea/loose stools	0	1	2	3

Side Effect	Absent	Mild* No intervention required	Moderate* Some intervention required	Severe* Immediate intervention required
12. Dyspepsia (acid stomach)	0	1	2	3
13. Nausea or vomiting	0	1	2	3
14. Anxiety	0	1	2	3
15. Excessive saliva, drooling	0	1	2	3
16. Excessive appetite	0	1	2	3
17. Dry mouth/high beverage intake	0	1	2	3
18. Blurred Vision	0	1	2	3
19. Urinary Problems	0	1	2	3
a) enuresis, bed-wetting	0	1	2	3
b) trouble emptying/voiding the bladder	0	1	2	3
c) other, urinary problems (specify: _____)	0	1	2	3
20. Rhinitis (runny nose)	0	1	2	3
21. Gynecomastia (abnormally enlarged breasts)	0	1	2	3
22. Galactorrhea	0	1	2	3
23. Menstrual problems □ N/A	0	1	2	3
24. Coughing	0	1	2	3
25. Tachycardia (perception of rapid heart beat)	0	1	2	3
26. Seizures	0	1	2	3
27. Skin rash	0	1	2	3
28. Tinnitus (ringing in the ears)	0	1	2	3
29. Weight Gain	0	1	2	3
30. Other _____	0	1	2	3

31. Sleep Patterns Usual Time Child __ __ : __ __ Usual Waking Time __ __ : __ __

Use 24 Hour Clock Falls Asleep h h m m h h m m

32. Does the subject have any peculiar habits?
(please only answer at screening/baseline) □ Yes □ No □ N/A

If yes, specify _____

33. Has there been any change in eating habits since the □ Yes □ No □ N/A
screening/baseline visit? **(please only answer after baseline)**

If yes, specify: _____

AEs were defined as follows:

(a) Mild AE: poses no interference and no intervention is required
(b) Moderate AE: poses some interference OR requires intervention
    (e.g., lowering dose)
(c) Severe AE: poses some interference AND requires intervention.
(d) Serious AE are defined as follows:
    – Life threatening
    – Potential for permanent disability
    – Requiring hospitalization (or prolonging hospitalization)

Attribution of AE was classified as follows:

– Definite: AE is clearly related to study drug
– Probable: AE is likely to be related to the study drug
– Possible: AE may be related to study drug
– Unlikely: AE is doubtfully related to the study drug
– Unrelated: AE is clearly not related to the study drug.

APPENDIX B: SIDE EFFECTS REVIEW FORM USED IN METHYLPHENIDATE STUDY (RUPP, 2002)

Participant: _____
Information Source: _____
Date: _____

Directions: For each behavior, please circle the number corresponding to the degree of the behavior as observed over the past week. If absent, or if you have not seen the problem, circle "0".

Mild = causes little or not interference in every day life (e.g., behavior occurs occasionally and is low in intensity)
Moderate = causes some interference in every day life (e.g., behavior occurs occasionally and is high in intensity or behavior occurs frequently and is low in intensity)
Severe = causes clear and substantial interference in every day life (e.g., behavior occurs frequently and is high in intensity)

BEHAVIOR	Absent	Mild	Moderate	Severe
1. Irritable, easily annoyed, (emotionally over-reactive)	0	1	2	3
2. Crabby, whiny	0	1	2	3
3. Tearful, prone to crying	0	1	2	3

BEHAVIOR	Absent	Mild	Moderate	Severe
4. Sad, unhappy, depressed	0	1	2	3
5. Social withdrawal, talks or interacts little	0	1	2	3
6. Staring, daydreaming	0	1	2	3
7. Dull, not alert	0	1	2	3
8. Drowsy, sleepy	0	1	2	3
9. Insomnia	0	1	2	3
10. Nightmares	0	1	2	3
11. Eating less or skipping meals	0	1	2	3
12. Diarrhea, loose bowel movements	0	1	2	3
13. Encopresis (soiling of self not due to diarrhea)	0	1	2	3
14. Bed or pants wetting	0	1	2	3
15. Dizzy, balance unstable	0	1	2	3
16. Headaches	0	1	2	3
17. Stomachaches, nausea, vomiting	0	1	2	3
18. Anxiety, fear, nervousness	0	1	2	3
19. Restless, high activity level	0	1	2	3
20. Easily excited	0	1	2	3
21. Excessive talking	0	1	2	3
22. Excessively happy, silly	0	1	2	3
23. Bizarre behavior	0	1	2	3
24. Repetitive tongue movements	0	1	2	3
25. Muscle twitches or sudden sounds	0	1	2	3
26. Gets stuck on repetitive activities	0	1	2	3
27. Stereotypic movements (deliberate, repetitive movements with no apparent function: e.g., rocks body back and forth; shake hand(s) in front of eyes)	0	1	2	3
28. Self Injury (deliberately hurts self – e.g., bites, hits, scratches, or otherwise injures self)*	0	1	2	3
29. Repetitive picking at hair, skin, fingernails or biting fingernails*	0	1	2	3
30. Other (specify) _____	0	1	2	3
31. Other (specify) _____	0	1	2	3

*If picking or nail biting causes self-injury, rate the degree of self-injury on item 28. Also rate the picking or nail biting on item 29.

Do you have any additional comments about possible side effects?

PART

III

INTERVENTIONS

Derby Hospitals NHS Foundation
Trust
Library and Knowledge Service

9

CHALLENGING BEHAVIORS

OLIVER C. MUDFORD, ANGELA M.
ARNOLD-SARITEPE, KATRINA J. PHILLIPS,
JANINE MAARI LOCKE, I-CHEN SHARON HO,
AND SARAH ANN TAYLOR

University of Auckland, Auckland, New Zealand

INTRODUCTION

Over the past 50 years an extensive body of research literature has investigated many aspects of challenging behavior in people with autism spectrum disorders (ASD). The quantity of research perhaps reflects the impact that challenging behavior has on individuals with ASD and those that care about them, and for them. Challenging behavior has a range of negative effects for the individual performing the behaviors and for those around them (e.g., Emerson et al., 2000). Physical injuries, increased risk of isolation, neglect, and abuse from others are some of the consequences for the individual. Challenging behavior not only interferes with adaptive behavior instruction for the person and others around them, it also decreases the range of options in living, educational, and working environments. Those who live with people with challenging behavior (e.g., parents or residential staff), or are involved in their education and training, can suffer injury and/or increased stress.

This chapter samples the recent research literature regarding challenging behaviors in which the participants were identified by the researchers as being diagnosed with an ASD, i.e., autism, pervasive developmental disorders (PDD), or PDD-NOS (Not Otherwise Specified). We have not attempted a comprehensive review of research on all aspects of challenging behaviors studied over the past 50 years.

WHAT IS CHALLENGING BEHAVIOR?

Challenging behaviors are those that "present a significant challenge to carers and support agencies" (Emerson et al., 2000, p. 197). Any behavior performed to excess in frequency or intensity, and beyond the immediate resources available for effective treatment, can be called challenging behavior. The most frequently cited examples of challenging behaviors are aggressive, self-injurious, antisocial, offensive, disruptive, and destructive behaviors. Any others that impair a person's learning or safety (e.g., non-compliance, running away from required care) or reduce the likelihood of regular community integration through stigmatizing behaviors (e.g., idiosyncratic stereotyped repetitive behaviors, like hand-flapping or rocking) can be labeled as challenging behaviors. Depending on the theoretical perspectives of researchers, challenging behaviors are considered sometimes as "externalizing behaviors" (e.g., Donenberg and Baker, 1993), problem behaviors (e.g., Campbell, 2003), maladaptive behaviors (e.g., Dawson et al., 1998), as symptoms of emotional and behavioral disorders (e.g., Hill and Furniss, 2006), or indicative of psychiatric disorders (e.g., Gadow et al., 2004).

The presence of challenging behaviors is a primary reason for referral for professional assistance for people with autism spectrum disorders (ASDs). A recent study of 6701 child and youth referrals to community mental health centers included 48 young people with autism and 76 with Asperger's Disorder (Mandell et al., 2005). The primary reasons identified for referral that were most often (>5 percent) cited for autism were hyperactivity, aggression, poor peer interaction, social avoidance, and "strange" behaviors. With Asperger's, common primary problems were similar but attention difficulties or noncompliance featured as well. Other challenging behaviors cited less frequently as primary concerns and that rarely feature in the treatment literature included verbal abuse (e.g., death threats), sexualized behaviors, and inappropriate bowel movements for children with Asperger's.

PREVALENCE OF CHALLENGING BEHAVIORS IN AUTISTIC SPECTRUM DISORDERS (ASDs)

A random telephone survey of >85 000 families was conducted in 2003–2004 by the US National Survey of Children's Health. One of the items was "Has a doctor or health professional ever told you that your child has autism?"; 483 respondents replied affirmatively (Gurney et al., 2006). The estimated national prevalence of ASDs was calculated to be about 53 per 10 000 in the 3–17 year age group, with some 324 000 children affected. Further item responses showed that 59 percent of children with ASDs had a health professional's diagnosis of behavioral or conduct problems. This was more than ten times the prevalence of such problems among the estimated 61 million US children without ASD.

Comparable findings were reported from interviewing parents of 205 children with diagnosed ASDs in a region of Australia (Icasiano et al., 2004). The regional prevalence of ASDs at ages 2–17 years was estimated at 39 per 10 000. Forty-seven percent of the sample had a diagnosed intellectual disability, also known as mental retardation. The majority of children were described as having moderate or severe obsessive-ritualistic behaviors (65 percent) or behaviors associated with aggression or anger (63 percent).

The prevalence of self-injurious behaviors in a sample of 222 children with ASD aged 2–7 years was found to be 53 percent in a French study across 51 agencies (Baghdadli et al., 2003). Close to 15 percent of the sample were reported to have severe self-injurious behavior. Most (96 percent) of the children had more than mild deficits in adaptive behaviors, suggesting intellectual disability. Risk of self-injurious behavior was increased in children with fewer speech and communication skills.

Obsessional and compulsive behaviors with people with higher function-ing ASDs (e.g., Asperger's Disorder) can be considered challenging behav-iors in that they can interfere with people's functional activities to a disabling extent. Structured interviews with 40 adults with ASD but without intellectual disability showed that obsessional thoughts took up one or more hours per day for 39 percent of the sample (Russell et al., 2005). Compulsive behaviors (i.e., rituals) reported by 25 to 60 percent of individuals interviewed were check-ing, cleaning, repeating, hoarding, and arranging. Performance of these behaviors required more than 1 hour per day for 26 percent of the sample. A majority (56 percent) of interviewees reported at least moderate anxiety from interruptions to obsessional or compulsive rituals (Russell et al., 2005).

To summarize: These studies are difficult to compare as they used different methods for participant or informant selection, e.g., total population sample stud-ies (Gurney et al., 2006), total ASD population study (Icasiano et al., 2004), and consecutive UK clinical referrals (Russell et al., 2005). Data were derived from survey items describing different behaviors, classifications of behaviors, and inter-pretations of behaviors. For example, we do not know how or whether "behavioral or conduct problems" (Gurney et al., 2006), "obsessional/ritualistic" and "aggres-sion/anger behaviors" (Icasiano et al., 2004), "obsessional/compulsive behaviors" (Russell et al., 2005) are comparable. However, in some respects this diver-sity of approach and method can strengthen a conclusion: Regarding prevalence of challenging behaviors, recent studies from a variety of countries agree that challenging behaviors are problematic for the majority of children and adults across the autistic spectrum.

ASSOCIATION OF CHALLENGING BEHAVIORS WITH ASDs AND INTELLECTUAL DISABILITY

The question to be approached in this section is: Is the high prevalence of challenging behaviors in ASD populations related to co-occurring intellectual disability? McClintock et al. (2003) reported the results of meta-analysis of prevalence studies on challenging behaviors of individuals with intellectual disability. It was found that a diagnosis of autism was more likely to be correlated with higher levels of property destruction, aggression, and self-injurious behavior than the absence of autism. Self-injurious behavior, but not aggression, was more likely to be reported for individuals with communication deficits (as in Baghdadli et al., 2003).

Holden and Gitlesen (2006) investigated the prevalence of challenging behaviors in a Norwegian sample of 826 adults and children with intellectual disability. The sample included 53 participants with a diagnosis of autism. Challenging behaviors were reported for 11.1 percent of the whole sample, but significantly more often (35.8 percent) among those with autism. Hill and Furniss (2006) used the DASH-II (Matson et al., 1996) to quantify dimensions of challenging behaviors for 69 individuals with ASD and 13 without ASD. All participants had a diagnosis of severe intellectual disability. The ASD group scored higher (i.e., more aberrant) on all eight DASH subscales of emotional and behavioral disturbance analyzed, significantly so on five of these. Elevated scores for participants with ASD and intellectual disability over those with intellectual disability but not ASD had been found also by Matson et al. (1996) and others (Bradley et al., 2004). Similar results using different measures were reported for repetitive behaviors, interfering compulsions, and self-injurious behaviors (Bodfish et al., 2000).

Murphy et al. (2005) conducted a total population study in a defined area in London, UK. They surveyed the carers of 141 people with severe intellectual disability and/or autism, with an average age of 21 years, who had responded to a similar survey 12 years before. Interviewers asked about challenging behaviors of several categories including stereotypies, and behaviors that were judged as being performed with either social awareness or limited social awareness. "Socially aware" behaviors included teasing, lying, and bullying. Those with less awareness included destruction, aggression, and difficult public behavior. The latter category of challenging behaviors was more often associated with people with an ASD diagnosis.

To summarize this section, recent research using a variety of methods shows that people with ASDs are more vulnerable than others with similar levels of intellectual disability to developing challenging behaviors. People with ASD and more severe deficits in communication skills are more likely than others to develop self-injurious behavior.

CHRONICITY OF CHALLENGING BEHAVIORS AND EFFECTS ON CARERS

A recent study investigated the course of challenging behaviors and their relation to maternal well-being through the preschool years (Eisenhower et al., 2005). Parent-reported levels of problem behavior for 3-year-old children with autism were found to be higher than for their age-peers with similar degree of intellectual disability without autism, with 46 percent of problem behavior scores in the borderline or clinical range. Continuing elevated levels of problem behaviors were reported for the same group of children at ages 4 and 5 years. The mothers of children with autism reported higher levels of negative impact (stress and depression), and this correlated with levels of problem behaviors. Similar findings have been reported by other researchers: Herring et al. (2006) who assessed child problem behaviors and mothers' and fathers' mental health when their children's ages averaged 3 years and 5 years; and Icasiano et al. (2004). Lecavalier et al. (2006) surveyed a wider age-range (3–18 years) of children and youth with ASDs and the stress levels for their parents and teachers. Teachers' and, again, parents' (86 percent of whom were mothers) stress levels increased with higher levels of challenging behaviors. The effects of challenging behaviors on mental health were replicated with mothers of young adults (16–26 years) with ASD (Blacher and McIntyre, 2006). Finally, in this section, the previously cited study by Murphy et al. (2005) showed that challenging behaviors most often associated with ASDs did not change significantly over 12 years from ages 9 to 21 years.

In summary: Challenging behaviors are often a long-term problem for children and young adults with ASDs. There was little information about what interventions had been used to attempt to reduce challenging behaviors in the samples described, so research to date cannot indicate whether challenging behaviors are chronic in the ASD population in the absence of (or despite) treatment. Negative effects for parents and teachers increase with more severe challenging behaviors.

APPROACHES TO INTERVENTION

The presence of challenging behaviors in people with autism attracts recommendations for a multitude of intervention approaches from many professional and paraprofessional groups, and from non-professionals. Pharmacological and behavioral approaches to remediating challenging behaviors have received much (and continuing) research effort, whereas there is a distinct lack of evidence for recommending other proposed interventions (see, Jacobson et al., 2005).

PREVALENCE OF BIOLOGICAL AND BEHAVIORAL INTERVENTIONS

Aman et al. (2005) reviewed three studies of the use of biological agents (medications and supplements) by >2800 people aged 1–82 years with ASDs. In the more recent studies conducted in 1999 and 2001, about 65 percent of individuals were receiving one or more biological treatments. Witwer and Lecavalier (2005) surveyed biological treatments used over 12 months in 2002–2003 with 353 children and youth (ages 3–21 years) across public schools in Ohio. Psychotropic medications, i.e., drugs that change behaviors, were given to 47 percent of the sample. The likelihood of receiving medication increased over age and with more problematic behaviors. A survey of medication use by 109 clinic-referred children and adults with ASDs and IQ > 70 (i.e., higher functioning ASDs) was conducted in 1997 by Martin et al. (1999). Fifty-five percent were receiving psychotropic medications at the time, although close to 70 percent had taken them when past use was counted. More than half of the respondents who were taking medication received more than one psychotropic agent.

Emerson et al. (2000) surveyed procedures for the management and intervention for challenging behaviors in residential services in the British Isles. "Management" can be viewed as a reactive response to a behavior when it occurs, whereas "interventions" can be considered as proactive interventions planned to reduce the frequency, duration, or severity of the behaviors. Participants, whose mean age was in their 40s, lived in group homes ($N = 281$, of whom 35 percent had an ASD diagnosis), residential campuses (133, 47 percent ASD), and "intentional communities" (86, 38 percent ASD). Over all settings, 53 percent of residents were reported to have moderate or severe challenging behavior in the past month. Management of these behaviors included sedation with medication (35 percent of cases), physical restraint in 44 percent (of whom half received sedation as well), seclusion (20 percent), and mechanical restraint (3 percent). Treatment with psychotropic medications was prescribed for 49 percent of individuals with moderate or severe challenging behaviors, and only 15 percent had a written behavioral intervention program.

The foregoing brief review of recent studies suggests that psychopharmacology for challenging behaviors is prevalent. Review of the evidence-base for prescribing psychotropic medications is beyond the scope of this chapter. However, Aman et al. (2005) describe the research literature on use of psychotropics for challenging behaviors such as self-injurious behavior, aggression, destruction, stereotypy and obsessions in ASDs as "fairly unsophisticated" (p. 123). Emerson et al. (2000) noted the high reliance on medication in the absence of clear empirical evidence for benefits. They contrasted this with the relative disuse of behavioral interventions, for which there was a strong researched evidence base for recommendation. The evidence base for the effects of dietary supplements or elimination diets for people with ASD is insufficient for recommendations (e.g., Christison and Ivany, 2006; Nye and Brice, 2005).

To summarize: Children and adults with ASDs, from those with severe intellectual disability to those in the normal range of general ability, are at high risk from receiving intrusive and restrictive behavior management strategies and/or treatments that have not been rigorously researched. This point had been made by Emerson et al. (2000) as well as others, and review of more recent research suggests that the situation has not changed markedly; however, see Aman et al. (2005), which includes updated brief reviews of the effects of medications for challenging behaviors with ASDs.

BEHAVIORAL INTERVENTIONS

The methods by which behavioral treatments for significant behavior problems have been evaluated, and the results from studies using behavioral methods, comprise the science called Applied Behavior Analysis (ABA; Cooper et al., 2007). Assessment and intervention for challenging behaviors has been the source of much ABA research. By 2002, there had been more than 700 research reports on the effects of behavioral interventions for people with autism (Mudford, 2004; for detailed reviews, see Campbell, 2003; Matson et al., 1996).

The effectiveness and acceptability of behavioral interventions have been improved over the last 15 years or so with the widespread use of functional assessment to enable effective interventions tailored for individuals' challenging behaviors (Campbell, 2003; Pelios et al., 1999). We review this approach to interventions in some detail.

BEHAVIORAL ASSESSMENT WITH CHALLENGING BEHAVIORS

Behavioral assessment for an individual's challenging behavior seeks to determine the nature of environmental variables that affect the occurrence of the behavior. Behavioral assessment concentrates especially on why the behavior is continuing to occur, not on why it might have started occurring originally. Advised by the results of initial assessment, intervention is designed to change the environment so that the behavior is reduced or eliminated. Note that "individual" and "behavior" are singular nouns in this introductory explanation: It cannot be assumed that a behavior (e.g., self-biting) is affected by the environment in the same way for all individuals; neither can it be assumed that all the challenging behaviors of an individual are affected by the environment in the same manner.

Assessment is guided by an initial assumption that the challenging behavior serves a *function* for the individual. That is, the behavior continues to occur because (in the past) it has been successful in bringing about an environmental change that acts as a reinforcer for the behavior. The process of investigating environmental variables to check if they may be reinforcers for a challenging behavior is known as *functional assessment.*

Reinforcers can be positive or negative. Positive reinforcers are those which involve the addition of something to the individual's environment (e.g., attention from a carer following self-biting). Negative reinforcers are changes that remove something from the environment (e.g., teacher withdraws a task demand following the same behavior). Negatively reinforced behaviors are known as *escape* behaviors if they result in escaping from a nonpreferred situation (the teacher's demand), or as *avoidance* behaviors if they function to avoid the nonpreferred situation in the first place, for example, refusing to go to into the classroom where demands are likely. Reinforcement can involve environmental changes outside (external) and inside (internal) the body of the individual. The examples just given so far are of external reinforcers, and they are also examples of socially-mediated reinforcers since they require changes to the environment involving other people, i.e., carer or teacher. Nonsocial external reinforcers do not require other people to do something, e.g., the behavior of wrecking a locked kitchen door may be positively reinforced by access to tangible items like food, knives, or drinks.

Positive and negative internal reinforcers are often called *automatic* reinforcers, since it is assumed that the behavior automatically produces reinforcement without any involvement of the external social or nonsocial environment. Automatically reinforced behaviors have been known also as self-stimulatory behaviors, and automatic reinforcers as sensory or perceptual reinforcers (Rapp and Vollmer, 2005). Automatic reinforcers can be positive consequences (i.e., "pleasure") following a behavior, e.g., dizziness that some report as euphoric following breath-holding, partial self-strangulation, and Valsalva maneuvers. Negative automatic reinforcers can be related to the concept of "relief" from internal discomfort, e.g., self-scratching reducing an itch, or face-punching to alleviate toothache.

FUNCTIONAL ASSESSMENT METHODS

Functional assessment usually starts with *interviews* with the client and/or others who know the client's behavior well (O'Neill et al., 1997). The interviewer asks about the challenging behaviors of the client and, particularly, what happens before (antecedent conditions) and after (consequences, i.e., potential reinforcers) each instance of the challenging behavior. *Rating scales* may be a helpful addition in interviews (e.g., Dawson et al., 1998).

Interviews about a challenging behavior are usually insufficient to determine behavioral function for the purposes of developing an effective intervention. *Direct observation* by a behavior analyst is the required next step in functional assessment. This entails recording of the behavior of concern and its antecedents and consequences as they occur in the natural settings in which the behavior is a problem. This can help develop hypotheses about the function of a challenging behavior by supporting or contradicting the information provided during interviews. The hypotheses derive from correlations between recorded occurrences of the behavior and the probability of the behavior being followed by particular consequences (e.g., McKerchar and Thompson, 2004). Although sometimes an effective intervention can be planned on the basis of assessment at this point (e.g., Anderson and Long, 2002), with other cases correlational information can mislead the behavior analyst as to the maintaining reinforcer for challenging behaviors (e.g., Hall, 2005).

The gold standard for functional assessment is called *functional analysis*. This involves experimental manipulation of the antecedents and consequences of a challenging behavior. There are variations in methods used, but analyses following (or derived from) those demonstrated by Iwata et al. (1982/1994) may produce most valid results (Hanley et al., 2003). Whether a functional analysis or assessment method is "valid" is best judged by outcomes for individuals whose challenging behaviors have been treated using interventions selected on the basis of the function identified by the method used.

The original Iwata et al. (1982/1994) procedure used four 15-min. conditions alternated randomly and repeated over several days. Standard conditions are called: attention, demand, alone, and control. In the attention condition, the client may engage in a preferred activity (e.g., toys for children) while a therapist is in the same room but not interacting with the client. Following an occurrence of the challenging behavior, the therapist provides attention. High rates of behavior occurring in this condition would suggest that attention functions as a reinforcer for the behavior.

In the demand condition, the client is required to complete a task with prompting from the therapist. Contingent on the occurrence of the target behavior, the therapist allows the participant to have a break from the task. High rates of behavior occurring in this condition would suggest that escape from task demands functions as reinforcement for the challenging behavior.

In the alone condition, the client is alone in a room and without materials for preferred activities. High rates of behavior in this condition suggest that the challenging behavior is maintained by automatic reinforcement.

Finally, in the control condition, the client and therapist engage together with the client's preferred toys or materials. No demands are made of the client, and attention is provided frequently. This condition attempts to create an enriched environment that is designed to minimize the probability of challenging behavior occurring if the behavior is externally reinforced, or if an automatically reinforced behavior can be replaced by activities in the enriched environment (e.g., Horner, 1980).

Many variations have been made to the typical functional analysis described (Hanley et al., 2003). As an example, in a brief functional analysis (Northup et al., 1991) conditions are run for 5 min. and the entire analysis can be completed in an hour in cases where there is a high rate of challenging behavior, and there is only one function of the behavior. Also, as will be seen in the following review of interventions derived from functional assessment, functional analysis technology has expanded to include other reinforcers (e.g., challenging behaviors reinforced by tangibles) and conditions (e.g., challenging behavior occurring around transitions from one activity to another). Another example of idiosyncratic function hypothesized for some individuals with ASD is reinforcement by access to perseverative stereotyped behaviors (Reese et al., 2003).

The use of functional assessment with people with ASDs and challenging behaviors has grown considerably (Matson and Nebel-Schwalm, 2006). Hanley et al. (2003) found 58 research articles published by 2000 reporting functional analyses that included participants with autism. Interventions for challenging behaviors in people with ASDs are more effective if they are designed following functional assessment, particularly functional analysis (Campbell, 2003).

FUNCTIONS OF CHALLENGING BEHAVIORS

There has been some research of an epidemiological nature concerning the relative prevalence of behavioral functions for challenging behaviors in ASDs, developmental disabilities, and other clinical populations. Hanley et al. (2003) reviewed the published research data and reported that social-negative consequences were the maintaining reinforcers in 34 percent of cases, social-positive (including tangible reinforcers) in 35 percent, automatic in 16 percent, unknown in 4 percent, with the rest showing multiple functions. They acknowledge that the low rate of "unknown" function reported in the research may have been an underestimate of the proportion of referred cases for which functional assessment did not find a function on which to base intervention. In behavior-analytic clinical practice, the proportion of failures of current functional assessment methods may be closer to the 16 percent reported by Page et al. (2007). It is worth noting that Page et al. (2007) found that 38 percent of their clinical sample showed multiple functions for challenging behaviors. Treatment is more complex when more than a single function is maintaining an individual's challenging behaviors.

Regarding ASDs specifically, Matson et al. (1996) found that the challenging behaviors of this population were more likely to be nonsocially reinforced than in persons with intellectual disability. Reese et al. (2005) found also that 23 children with ASDs, as a group, were different from children without ASD in terms of challenging behavior functions. They reported that nonsocial functions predominated in stating that: "Those with autism reliably exhibited disruptive behavior to gain or maintain access to items with which to engage in repetitive behavior, or to avoid idiosyncratically unpleasant sensory stimuli" (Reese et al., 2005, p. 425). Taylor and Carr (1992) reported that the challenging behaviors of three children with autism were reinforced by social avoidance. That is, the behaviors served the function of having others leave them alone. Further research on common and idiosyncratic functions of challenging behaviors across the whole spectrum of ASD, especially regarding those performed by individuals with Asperger's Disorder or higher functioning autism, is needed.

BEHAVIORAL INTERVENTIONS SELECTED BY MAINTAINING FUNCTION

In most recent research reports, selection of an intervention is based on the results of functional assessment and functional analysis. When function is identified, an intervention is designed to: alter the antecedent events that set the occasion for the behavior; remove the reinforcing contingencies that maintain behavior; or strengthen competing behavior.

The manipulation of the antecedent event has been used to reduce challenging behavior for a long time. Moving the desk of a disruptive student closer to the teacher is a common practice that teachers use to decrease disruption. Examples of interventions that manipulate antecedent events include functional communication training (FCT) and noncontingent reinforcement (NCR). Functional communication training (FCT) involves the teaching of communicative alternatives to challenging behavior. For example, the child who throws the desk whenever work is presented is taught to functionally communicate "I want a break" verbally or through the use of alternative acceptable communication. Noncontingent reinforcement (NCR) is an antecedent intervention that delivers reinforcers, often the maintaining reinforcer, on a response-independent time schedule. This means that the reinforcer is provided to the individual after a certain time interval has elapsed, irrespective of what behavior has occurred during the interval.

The removal of reinforcement contingencies generally involves withholding reinforcement from the targeted behavior (e.g., extinction) and/or reinforcing other behavior (e.g., differential reinforcement). Extinction reduces behavior by withholding the reinforcer that maintains it. The reinforcer can be positive, as in the case of the child who received the candy bar when having a tantrum in the checkout aisle of the supermarket, or negative as in the case of the child who does not go to school after saying it has a stomachache, although there is no indication of ill health. In the above examples, extinction would consist of no longer giving the child the candy bar and not letting the child who claims to have the stomachache stay home from school. An alternative to the removal of reinforcement is the provision of reinforcement contingent on the target behavior not occurring for a specified period of time (differential reinforcement of other behavior, or DRO) or the reinforcement of a behavior that is an alternative to the challenging behavior (differential reinforcement of alternative behavior or DRA). For example, if the goal was to reduce finger nail-biting, reinforcement for every 5-minute period in which no finger nail-biting occurred would be a DRO. If finger nail-painting was reinforced, this would be a DRA.

Interventions that strengthen competing behaviors include those that specifically teach a skill alternative to the challenging behavior (e.g., FCT), as well as skill-acquisition programs that have been shown to have a collateral reductive effect on challenging behaviors (e.g., Picture Exchange Communication System, Frost and Bondy, 1994; social stories, Gray, 2000).

When determining which of the empirically researched intervention strategies to use, the behavior analyst relies on the identified maintaining function of the challenging behavior. As noted previously, common maintaining functions include positive reinforcement, negative reinforcement, and automatic reinforcement. While it would simplify matters for the interventionist if all challenging behaviors had a single function, this is not the case and multifunctional behaviors often require a multicomponent intervention package in which each function is addressed.

CHALLENGING BEHAVIOR MAINTAINED BY POSITIVE
REINFORCEMENT

Challenging behaviors can function to gain access to preferred items or activities that other people can provide, or the attention of others. These behaviors are said to be maintained by social positive reinforcement. The research provides examples (FCT, NCR) of a number of interventions that, either alone or in conjunction with one another, have decreased the occurrence of challenging behaviors in individuals with autism.

Functional communication training has often been used to decrease challenging behavior maintained by positive reinforcement. This is possibly due to its efficacy in decreasing the behavior while teaching an alternative behavior that provides the individual the ability to obtain the reinforcement. FCT teaches an alternative communicative response to gain access to the reinforcing item, activity, or attention. The request topography depends on the individual's skill repertoire and may take the form of manual signs, picture or card exchange, or verbal request. While FCT is generally referred to as a form of intervention in its own right, FCT interventions are DRA, where the reinforced alternative behavior is communicative.

Sigafoos and Meikle (1996) found that the aggression, self-injury, and destructive behaviors of two boys with autism and moderate to severe intellectual disabilities were maintained by access to tangible items (e.g., food, drink, and toys) and to adult attention. Following assessment, the teacher taught the children to recruit these reinforcers in a more socially acceptable manner. One child had no expressive speech and was taught to tap the teacher's hand to gain attention in addition to using a picture point system to request choice of a tangible item. The second child had some speech and was taught to say the teacher's name, or the name of the preferred object, to gain attention or the tangible items respectively. Initially the communicative request was prompted 1 sec. after the removal of attention or the desired object, thus limiting the opportunity for the challenging behaviors to occur. The latency to the prompt was subsequently extended to 3 sec. Results showed that FCT, in conditions with tangible items, decreased the challenging behaviors to zero and the number of communicative responses increased to 100 percent of opportunities. This behavior change was maintained at a 2- and 4-week follow-up. FCT was able to decrease the challenging behaviors to zero for most attention sessions and maintenance probes generally still showed zero rates. However, in comparison to the tangible conditions, the number of independent communicative responses was lower. The authors suggest that this may be due to attention being available at times outside of the training sessions. The major limitation of this study, and many FCT studies, is that the communicative response was taught in very controlled settings and no data were provided on generalization to functional environments.

Moes and Frea (2002) provided parent training in FCT. All parents had children with a diagnosis of autism and varying levels of intellectual disability.

Following the training, when the parent implemented FCT, the occurrence of the challenging behaviors generally decreased, and communicative responses of the child increased. However, the results were somewhat variable, and did not generalize to untrained settings. A subsequent training session individualized the FCT for each family. For example, they involved more members of the family and identified situations where FCT could be used in the natural environment. Following this, the problem behaviors stabilized at zero or near zero. The decrease in challenging behaviors and the increase in communicative responses generalized to untrained settings. The change in behaviors across all settings was maintained 14 months later. In addition, the results of a social validity questionnaire found that the parents' perception of the sustainability of the FCT intervention was increased following the individualization of the intervention.

When selecting the type of communicative response, it is important to consider the efficiency of the communicative response in comparison to the challenging behavior. If the communicative response requires more effort, obtains less reinforcement, or the reinforcement is delayed, it is unlikely that the FCT will be effective (Buckley and Newchok, 2004; Horner and Day, 1991). Research has shown that individuals can be taught to tolerate obtaining less and/or more delayed reinforcement, once the communicative response has been learnt, using schedule-thinning procedures (see Hanley et al., 2001, for a general comparison of schedule-thinning procedures during FCT). Schedule thinning can be achieved by extending the delay to reinforcement following the communicative response (e.g., Hagopian et al., 2005), alternating a period where the communicative response is reinforced on an FR1 with increasing period of extinction (e.g., Hagopian et al., 2005), extending the interval in an FI schedule (Marcus and Vollmer, 1996), or only reinforcing responses which fall above a certain inter-response time (i.e., differential reinforcement of low rates of behavior; e.g., Durand and Carr, 1992). Some research has suggested that the provision of an alternative activity during schedule thinning may make the process more efficacious. For example, providing access to preferred activities that have, in the past, been associated with lower levels of the challenging behavior (Hagopian et al., 2005) or providing a work task (Fisher et al., 2000).

Although FCT is regularly combined with extinction, it has also been combined with other reductive procedures such as time-out from positive reinforcement. Wacker et al. (1990) worked with a boy with autism and severe to profound intellectual disability who exhibited hand biting that was maintained by access to a tangible item. Wacker et al. found that timeout and FCT combined were more efficacious than FCT alone or the combination of DRO and time-out. Durand and Carr (1992) compared the effectiveness of FCT (asking "Am I doing good work?") or time-out on two groups of children, whose challenging behavior had been identified as being maintained by attention. They found that both FCT and time-out reduced the levels of challenging behavior. However, FCT was able to maintain low levels of challenging behavior when a therapist, naïve to the children's history of intervention, conducted experimental sessions.

This maintenance in the FCT condition is probably due to the children being able to recruit attention in an appropriate manner. The lack of maintenance in the time-out procedure highlights the need to teach a replacement behavior or to implement the intervention across settings when using a reductive procedure such as time-out. The major limitation of Durand and Carr (1992) is the inadequate experimental control in the comparisons of treatments. While this limits our ability to draw conclusions, the results do highlight the need to include appropriate means of gaining reinforcement when using reductive interventions.

A different approach to using knowledge of maintaining reinforcers to reduce behaviors is NCR. Marcus and Vollmer (1996) compared the effects of FCT, NCR and DRO on a boy's tantrum behavior that was maintained by access to toys. They found that NCR on a continuous schedule and FCT with schedule thinning were able to decrease the level of tantrum behavior to zero or near zero. In comparison, the level of tantrums during the DRO was above that in baseline. While these results do support the effectiveness of NCR, it should be noted that the NCR was on a continuous schedule and, as such, may not be a practical intervention in some situations. In addition, the results may have been affected by order effects during intervention.

One limitation of NCR is that the behavior may occur at the end of the fixed-time interval and may be inadvertently reinforced, creating an intermittent schedule of reinforcement. A way to avoid this is to use a hold. This means if the behavior occurs at the end of the interval, reinforcement is withheld for a brief period until after the challenging behavior ceases. Hagopian et al. (2000) compared the effects of NCR with extinction (including a 5-sec. hold period) to NCR without extinction, on aggressive behavior maintained by access to tangible items in a boy diagnosed with autism and severe intellectual disability. The data showed that the NCR schedule without extinction reduced behaviors to zero. However, this only occurred when the schedule was continuous. When it was thinned to a fixed time (FT)15-sec. schedule the behaviors returned to baseline levels. When NCR was combined with extinction and a hold period, the schedule was able to be thinned out to an FT 85-sec. schedule. There was, however, an initial increase in challenging behavior at the beginning of the schedule thinning, possibly an extinction burst. These results suggest that in order for schedule thinning during NCR to be effective, it should be combined with extinction. It would be of interest to assess if, like FCT, the addition of alternative competing stimuli during schedule thinning enhances its effectiveness.

The research on challenging behaviors in children with autism, which have been identified as being maintained by social-positive reinforcement (e.g., attention or access tangible items), suggests FCT and NCR to be the most frequently used interventions. The advantage of FCT is that it provides the child with an alternative means of independently gaining the reinforcement, thus increasing the chances of the behavior maintaining and generalizing. Nonetheless, more research is required on specific training with parents in which they learn how to facilitate FCT in the natural environment. The major disadvantage of FCT appears to be the sometimes lengthy training process followed by the need to conduct schedule thinning. In comparison, NCR requires little training either of the individual or of the behavior change agent. However, NCR still requires schedule thinning and there is no evidence that NCR can be maintained through all waking hours for weeks, or even months. An FT 5-min. schedule has commonly been used as a terminal criterion (Kahng et al., 2000). While this seems to be practical from the perspective of those administering the intervention, there is no evidence that this is more effective than a shorter or longer time interval.

There is an abundance of literature on common reductive strategies for challenging behaviors maintained by social-positive reinforcement that is exhibited by individuals with intellectual disability. However, the literature appears to be limited for the ASD population, especially the part of the population that does not have intellectual disability.

CHALLENGING BEHAVIOR MAINTAINED BY NEGATIVE REINFORCEMENT

Many of the challenging behaviors observed in individuals with autism may be maintained by negative reinforcement. For example, when disruptive or aggressive behavior during instructional sessions results in the removal of aversive demands, the behaviors are negatively reinforced.

A number of effective intervention strategies can be used to treat behavior that has been shown to be maintained by negative reinforcement or escape. These strategies include training the individual to request a break (FCT or differential negative reinforcement), providing frequent breaks during aversive tasks independent of the behavior (non-contingent negative reinforcement), reinforcing task compliance or any other behavior (differential reinforcement), and preventing the termination or avoidance of the aversive activity following the behavior (escape extinction).

Functional communication training involves training an individual to request termination or removal of an aversive stimulus. However, in the case of requesting breaks (escape) from a task, the individual can limit his/her learning opportunities if breaks are requested too frequently. Therefore, after initial FCT training, breaks can be provided contingent on a predetermined number of task responses and appropriate requesting (Lalli et al., 1995) or by training a request for assistance rather than a break (Braithwaite and Richdale, 2000).

The majority of research on FCT interventions for negatively reinforced behavior focuses on teaching requests for escape from tasks or activities (Day et al., 1994; DeLeon et al., 2001; Fisher et al., 2005; Hagopian et al., 2001, et al., 2004; Lalli et al., 1995; Neidert et al., 2005). Yi et al. (2006) trained two boys and a girl diagnosed with autism to use alternative responses to refuse nonpreferred items. Functional assessment had shown that challenging behaviors (including slapping, pushing, and pinching) were negatively reinforced by the removal of nonpreferred items. Two of the children were trained to say "No thanks" and "No, don't do that", the third child was taught to sign refusal. The data from the final phase showed that trained alternative responses were used on every appropriate occasion (with one exception) and challenging behaviors were reduced to zero. For each participant the responses were generalized to 7 untrained items. It should be noted, however, that all the participants had a history of intensive discrete trial teaching. Their history of learning may have affected the relative ease with which the new responses were trained.

Noncontingent escape (NCE) is a variation of NCR where the reinforcer is the removal of aversive stimuli. The reinforcer is provided independent of the occurrence of the behavior. Similarly, differential negative reinforcement of other behavior (DNRO) provides escape from the aversive stimuli contingent on the absence of the problem behavior for a predetermined interval of time. Kodak et al. (2003) compared the effectiveness of NCE and DNRO interventions for disruptive behavior in two boys with autism. Initially NCE sessions consisted of a continuous break, i.e., no demands were made. Then, if problem behavior remained below a criterion, NCE intervals were gradually increased until they reached 2 min. in duration. DNRO sessions began with a continuous break, and then the intervals were gradually increased by the same increments as in the NCE sessions; however breaks were provided contingent on the absence of the behavior within the intervals. The results showed both interventions produced large decreases in problem behavior and increases in compliance. Although it was unclear why the latter occurred, the authors suggested that compliance may have been adventitiously reinforced, or that the establishing operation for escape was reduced by the provision of frequent breaks, or that praise may have become reinforcing following the reduction of escape behavior.

Ringdahl et al. (2002) found DRA to be effective in reducing the challenging behaviors (destruction, aggression, and self-injury) of an 8-year-old girl with autism. A 1-min. break from instruction was provided contingent on independent completion of the task and the absence of problem behavior. Results showed that the intervention was more effective in reducing challenging behavior when DRA was combined with instructional fading, that is, the sessions started with no instruction and the number of instructions were then gradually increased contingent on the absence of problem behavior. The authors hypothesized that instructional fading may decrease the value of escape as a reinforcer because, to begin with, much of the session is a break. It was also suggested that a gradual introduction to tasks may establish a history of reinforced compliance which makes future compliance more likely.

Using *escape extinction* by eliminating the escape contingency for the behavior is another approach to treating challenging behaviors maintained by negative reinforcement. It is usually used in combination with other intervention strategies such as NCR (Mace et al., 1998), DRO (Progar et al., 2001), DRI (Ricciardi and Luiselli, 2003), or DRA (Najdowski et al., 2003). Escape extinction can be difficult to implement as it requires the therapist to persist with the delivery of the task or stimulus in the presence of the challenging behavior. Hoch et al. (2002) demonstrated that aggression and self-injurious behavior could be decreased without the use of escape extinction (i.e., the challenging behavior continued to be reinforced with escape), while also increasing task completion. The intervention provided escape with access to preferred activities contingent on task completion, thereby increasing reinforcement for task completion (when compared to reinforcement for the problem behavior). The low levels of challenging behavior were maintained as the response requirements were increased.

Other research has assessed preference of positive or negative reinforcement during treatment for escape-maintained behavior (DeLeon et al., 2001; Fisher et al., 2005). DeLeon et al. found edible reinforcers (potato chips) were more effective at reducing challenging behavior (self-injurious behavior, aggression, disruption) and increasing compliance than the provision of breaks in a 10-year-old girl with autism. However, following an increase in task requirements, preference shifted from positive reinforcement to a variable pattern of positive and negative reinforcement. Problem behaviors became more variable with an increase in task requirements. Fisher et al. found that one participant with autism showed a clear preference for positive over negative reinforcement (even when both were available). It was suggested that the presence of positive reinforcement reduced the aversiveness of the task, and communication for a break was no longer required. Similar preferences were not observed for the second participant. Both of the above-mentioned studies used escape extinction as part of the intervention.

The topography of the challenging behavior and the aversive stimulus being escaped or avoided may determine which intervention strategies will be most appropriate for the particular situation. For example, when the challenging behavior endangers an individual or therapist, escape extinction (e.g. prompting continuation of tasks) may not be feasible and escape becomes unavoidable. For this reason, strategies that increase a functional target behavior (e.g. reinforcing task completion or FCT) may be of more benefit to the client than those that only aim to reduce the behavior (i.e., escape extinction, DNRO and NCE). When a high level of escape is provided in instructional fading or reinforcement rich schedules, this can reduce the individual's need to perform the challenging behavior because the reinforcer is readily available. A disadvantage of instructional fading or providing escape (whether it is noncontingent or following a trained request) is that learning opportunities for the client may be reduced. Therefore it is important to ensure schedules are thinned effectively or a task criterion is set if breaks are requested too frequently.

CHALLENGING BEHAVIOR MAINTAINED BY AUTOMATIC REINFORCEMENT

Many challenging behaviors exhibited by individuals with ASD are maintained by automatic reinforcement (Reese et al., 2005). Automatic reinforcement refers to situations where the reinforcer for the challenging behaviors is produced by the behavior itself. When the automatically reinforced behavior is positively reinforced (automatic positive reinforcement), it is assumed that the behavior is producing a sensory stimulative effect (i.e., visual, auditory, olfactory, tactile, or proprioceptive stimulation). In comparison, when the automatically reinforced behavior is negatively reinforced (i.e., automatic negative reinforcement), it is assumed that pain attenuation may be the cause of the behavior (e.g., toothache, headache, gastric disorders). Consequently, it is of foremost importance to ascertain the function of the target challenging behavior in order to seek the appropriate intervention (i.e., behavioral interventions for positive automatic reinforcers versus medical attention for presumed negative automatic functions). In addition, if the behavior is found to be positively reinforced, it is ideal to determine the sensory consequences.

The main interventions for the reduction of *positively* automatically reinforced challenging behaviors are: *extinction* (i.e., blocking and sensory masking) by masking, changing, or removing the sensory effects of the behavior; *response blocking; stimulus substitution* (i.e., substituting the maintaining functional reinforcer of problematic behavior with a more appropriate matched stimulus); *unmatched stimulus access* (i.e., stimulus that is not the functional reinforcer); *environmental enrichment* (providing free access to preferred stimuli); *differential reinforcement* (i.e., differential reinforcement of alternative or incompatible behavior using contingent access to competing or highly preferred reinforcers); *contingent aversive stimulation* (or other behavioral punishment, such as overcorrection); and *self-management* strategies.

The literature shows that response blocking is not always effective in the treatment of automatically reinforced behaviors. McCord et al. (2005) found response blocking to be effective in reducing pica when consistently implemented early in the behavior chain (i.e., a sequence of antecedent behaviors that has in the past lead to the occurrence of pica). However, it has also been demonstrated to be less effective when compared with environmental enrichment, and can amplify the challenging behavior upon its discontinuation (Rapp, 2006). Response blocking has also been found to be associated with undesirable side effects (e.g., increases in other stereotypic responses, elicited aggression) (Hagopian and Adelinis, 2001; Lerman et al., 2003).

Extinction can also take the form of sensory masking. For example, Moore et al. (2004) used protective equipment (e.g., helmet, gloves) as a method of sensory extinction to reduce self-injurious behavior maintained by automatic reinforcement. Extinction procedures are generally not used in isolation, but combined with the use of differential reinforcement strategies. Richman et al. (1998) found that extinction combined with differential reinforcement of alternative behavior was effective in reducing behavior maintained by automatic reinforcement.

Environmental enrichment has been a focus of research on nonsocially mediated behaviors. Environmental enrichment can be facilitated by being combined with differential reinforcement strategies, or with prompts to interact with competing stimuli. Britton et al. (2002) found that environmental enrichment can be enhanced by experimenter prompts for the participant to interact with the preferred stimuli.

Most research has found that environmental enrichment is most effective when highly preferred stimuli are used (Vollmer et al., 1994). However, there are conflicting findings as to which of the two stimuli types (matched vs unmatched stimuli) are most effective at reducing the occurrence of automatically reinforced behavior. Ahearn et al. (2005) found that both types of stimulations produced significant reductions in the rates of challenging automatically reinforced behaviors. In comparison, Piazza et al. (2000) found that matched stimulation was more effective in reducing challenging behaviors.

Nevertheless, environmental enrichment research has employed both the use of matched and unmatched stimuli in providing noncontingent access to individuals with ASDs exhibiting nonsocially mediated challenging behaviors (e.g., Healey et al., 2001; Rapp, 2006; Sidener et al., 2005; Vollmer et al., 1994). Patel et al. (2000) found that a behavior identified as positively automatically reinforced was effectively eliminated by using stimulus substitution (identified via an antecedent and preference assessment) in a differential reinforcement procedure (i.e., differential reinforcement of other behavior using functional stimuli as reinforces). Van Camp et al. (2001) found that the efficacy of environmental enrichment can be enhanced by placing highly preferred stimuli in the environment, increasing the effort of the aberrant response, and implementing the intervention in environments that have been found to correlate to low levels of aberrant behavior. Rincover et al. (1979) used the alternative sensory reinforcer found as reinforcement for a DRA procedure (i.e., appropriate toy play).

While maintaining variables for automatically reinforced behaviors may be identified and substituted by more appropriate stimuli, this is not always possible because reinforcement contingencies of the aberrant behavior may not be clear cannot be withheld (Lerman and Vorndran, 2002). However, ethical concerns are raised by nonreinforcement based interventions employed to decrease automatically reinforced behaviors (Behavior Analyst Certification Board, 2004). Due to this, research in this area often combines the use of punishment with a positive-reinforcement based intervention. Falcomata et al. (2004) combined the use of response cost with environmental enrichment intervention and found that it was effective in reducing vocalizations that were maintained by automatic reinforcement. It can also be beneficial to implement punishment as a means to decrease the challenging behavior in order to be able to reinforce an alternative behavior, which is more likely to occur when the rate of a frequent or continuous challenging behavior has been reduced (e.g., Tomporowski, 1983).

A common punishment procedure used in reducing automatically reinforced behaviors is overcorrection (Cole et al., 2000). Overcorrection is a procedure that requires the individual to "*overcorrect* the environmental effects of an inappropriate act (and) . . . intensively to practise overly correct forms of relevant behavior" (Foxx and Azrin, 1973, p. 2). Ricciardi et al. (2003) reduced pica by implementing an overcorrection procedure. However, overcorrection procedures can be difficult and time-consuming to apply (Forehand and Baumeister, 1976), and should be combined with other positive-reinforcement based interventions.

A weakness in the previous literature on nonsocially mediated behaviors is that most research has failed to investigate the maintenance of the effects of functionally based interventions. It is also a limitation inherent within interventions designed for reducing automatically reinforced behaviors that most individuals do not learn complete independence in using the apparatus (e.g., competing stimulus) involved in minimizing the behavior. Most learners are dependent on some manipulation on the part of an instructor or therapist in providing the apparatus, or via prompting strategies and highly controlled environmental conditions. Consequently, the learners' reliance on these conditions can impede the opportunities for learning (Taylor et al., 2005). This limitation can somewhat be minimized by the use of self-management strategies. However, self-management strategies require the learner to be able to exhibit self-management responses (i.e., self-monitoring and self-reinforcement) (Mancina et al., 2000; Newman et al., 1997), therefore the intervention is somewhat restricted to higher-functioning individuals with ASD (Shabani et al., 2001). Koegel and Koegel (1990) found that children with severe autism who had some language skills and necessary motor skills can learn to use a self-management strategy to reduce stereotypic behavior. Independence can also be facilitated by carefully planned fading procedures (e.g., fading of sensory extinction materials, reinforcement or punishment schedules, or elements of punishers) (Aiken and Salzberg, 1984; Jenson et al., 1985).

The existing literature on ameliorating challenging behaviors that are maintained by automatic reinforcement is encouraging and increasingly resourceful. However, research needs to incorporate more sophisticated functional assessments, which extend beyond the point at which the researcher can assume that the challenging behavior is automatically reinforced, to determine the specific sensory domain that is stimulated to provide the maintaining reinforcer. Continued research is also required to investigate particular interventions on various topographies of sensory specific nonsocially mediated responding, as well as the longevity of the treatment effects.

MULTI-COMPONENT INTERVENTIONS FOR CHALLENGING BEHAVIOR MAINTAINED BY MULTIPLE FUNCTIONS

The treatment of severe, long lasting challenging behaviors usually involves multicomponent treatment packages that include FCT, differential reinforcement, choice, environmental enrichment, highly structured activities, access to community activities and modification of living arrangements (e.g., Foxx and Garito, 2007; Foxx and Meindl, 2007). Foxx and Meindl (2007) developed a program for reducing the aggressive/destructive behaviour of a 13-year-old boy with autism who had been excluded from school and other community settings. The results of the functional assessment showed that the behaviors functioned to escape academic or social demands and to obtain desired items. An intervention package, including a high density of positive reinforcement, tokens, choice making, response cost, overcorrection, and physical restraint, resulted in a reduction of challenging behavior to near zero levels. The success of the intervention generalized across settings and was maintained a year later.

Foxx and Garito (2007) describe a similar intervention package for the severe behaviour of another child. Despite no functional assessment, the result of the intervention package was a marked reduction in challenging behavior. Both studies by Foxx and colleagues make use of negative consequences for the occurrence of problem behaviors, the use of which is viewed unfavorably by some. Elsewhere, Foxx (2005) argued that nonaversive interventions involving only reinforcement-based and antecedent change procedures have not been demonstrably effective with severe, dangerous multifunctional challenging behaviors.

While effective in reducing behaviors, the use of multicomponent intervention packages makes it difficult to ascertain which strategy, or combination of strategies, is effective. Another example is of a study that reported the use of an intervention package that included a change of dwelling, medications, restraint, and restraint-fading to reduce challenging behaviors with an adult with autism (Jenson et al., 2001). Further research on intervention strategies for severe multifunctional challenging behaviors is clearly warranted.

CHALLENGING BEHAVIOR REDUCTION AS A POSITIVE SIDE EFFECT OF OTHER BEHAVIORAL INTERVENTIONS

A number of intervention strategies have emerged that specifically target the behavioral deficits observed in people with ASD. Interventions such as PECS (Frost and Bondy, 1994), Social Stories (Gray, 2000) and visual supports (Quill, 1995) are all strategies that have sought to increase communication and social behaviors. These interventions have been well received in wider clinical practice particularly as anecdotal reports suggested that decreases in challenging behaviors occurred at the same time as their introduction. When these interventions are put in place, functional assessment of existing challenging behaviors does not always occur.

PECS is a pictorial system that was developed for children with social-communication deficits. It consists of a series of phases or steps that people move through to develop their communication skills. The initial phase requires the learner to initiate a request for a preferred item by handing over a picture card. Later phases involve ensuring the learner is able to seek out and persist with communicative partners, in addition to discriminating between pictures and building sentences. Until recently, support for the use of PECS as a tool to teach communication, was largely anecdotal. Charlop-Christy et al. (2002) demonstrated that teaching communication following the PECS procedure did lead to an increase in initiations, requesting and commenting behavior in three boys aged between 3 and 12 years. Further to the measurement of communicative behaviors, the authors also collected data on the rate of challenging behaviors in the participants. The findings indicate that increased communication skills occurred in conjunction with a decrease in challenging behavior (tantrums, grabbing, out of seat, disruptions). While interpretation of this finding is limited due to the lack of experimental control, it is consistent with research that shows an inverse relation between communication skills and challenging behaviors (Carr and Durand, 1985; Durand and Carr, 1991).

The use of visual supports to aid in transitions is another common clinical strategy for children with autism. Visual supports are tools that enable people to keep track of the day's events to help in the development of understanding of time and an appreciation of environmental sequences (Twatchman, 1995). Following a functional assessment Dooley et al. (2001) found the challenging behavior of a 3-year-old boy with PDD to be associated with difficulties during transitions. It was hypothesized that switching activities was unsettling and that the challenging behaviors served a communicative purpose. A PECS-based schedule board was introduced where the child was required to select an activity from the board, find the match for the activity, complete the activity, take the picture back to the activity schedule, and deposit the picture in a container. A decrease in challenging behavior was observed once the schedule was introduced and this maintained throughout the school year, while the schedule was in use. Similarly, Schmit et al. (2000) found a photographic cuing package to decrease tantrums associated with transitions for a 6-year-old boy with autism. Prior to a transition, the child was presented with a photographic cue (with a printed word) that represented the next activity to occur. A verbal prompt was also given. A multiple baseline across settings design showed a reduction in tantrums as the intervention was introduced. Furthermore, the authors report that the child became more independent without having to have an adult guide him from activity to activity.

The use of Social Stories (Gray, 2000) as an intervention to reduce challenging behavior is a further example of an intervention to receive widespread clinical support in the absence of supporting literature. A social story is a short story that is written in a child-specific format describing a social situation. Specific guidelines for the construction of the stories aim to teach the child to manage their own behavior during a given social situation. Scattone et al. (2002) utilized social stories as an intervention for three children between 7 and 15 years who displayed challenging behavior. A multiple baseline across participants design showed the introduction of social stories to decrease the incidence of challenging behavior. Similarly, Crozier and Tincani (2005) found modified social stories to decreases the disruptive behavior of an eight-year-old boy, but also found that the procedure resulted in greater decreases in challenging behavior when it was paired with verbal prompts to engage in the alternative behavior as outlined in the social story. Both these studies are limited through the lack of identification of the functions of the challenging behavior.

Choice making has been shown to have a reductive effect on challenging behavior. Following a functional analysis, which showed the maintaining variables for the challenging behavior of two children was both positive and negative, Harding et al. (2002) conducted a choice assessment to evaluate the relative influence of preferred toys and parent attention on the behavior. Intervention comprised of providing the children the opportunity to choose a higher quality and greater amount of reinforcement for compliance with parental instruction, rather than challenging behavior. An increase in compliance and a decrease in challenging behavior was observed in both children.

In a further example of choice, Newman et al. (2002) compared teacher choice of teaching program order and reinforcers with students choosing order of programs and reinforcers. When choice was provided, a decrease in challenging behavior of all three male participants was observed. The function of the challenging behaviors was not determined.

While early research shows some support for the notion that acquisitional interventions for people with ASD can result in a decrease in challenging behavior, the relationship remains a correlation. Consistent application of functional assessment that identifies the reinforcers maintaining the challenging behavior and tighter experimental control would be useful in determining the benefits. The advantage of PECS, social stories and visual supports (including choice) is that they are appealing to the consumer and are accepted widely in the clinical community. If they are to continue to be found to be effective, further research may also seek to address the issue of procedural integrity as the application of clinical strategies tends to drift over time.

CONCLUDING SUMMARY AND RECOMMENDATIONS

Behaviors that are problematic enough for health care professionals to record, parents to report, or individuals to describe affect a majority (or close to that) of people with ASDs (see section on "Prevalence of Challenging Behaviors in Autistic Spectrum Disorders"). Further research is needed regarding the prevalence of challenging behaviors for planning for future provision of services to help affected individuals. With ASDs being recognized increasingly frequently, especially for people without intellectual disability, such studies may be particularly important for those higher ability subgroups of ASD.

There is evidence that challenging behaviors occur with higher prevalence among individuals with ASDs compared to those with intellectual disability without an ASD diagnosis (see section on "Association of Challenging Behaviors with ASDs and Intellectual Disability"). Also, a small body of existing data suggests that the functions of challenging behaviors for individuals with ASD are more likely to be related to automatic reinforcement (see section on "Functional Assessment Methods"). With automatically reinforced behaviors being more difficult to assess for function and to treat, this adds to the challenges for services and professionals who seek to help reduce challenging behaviors (see section on "Challenging Behavior Maintained by Automatic Reinforcement"). Further research related to these issues is required to indicate the extent of differences in professional training and expertise required for those working with ASDs compared with those whose experience has been predominantly with intellectual disabilities in general. The added complexities with an ASD population may have led the Autism Special Interest Group (2004) of the Association for Behavior Analysis International to recommend extra criteria for a justifiable claim for professional expertise in assessment and intervention for behavior analysts (see www.BACB.com) who specialize in ASDs. Our interpretations of the recent research reviewed for this chapter strengthen the view that the Autism SIG's recommendations should be taken seriously by professionals, services who employ them, and consumers, e.g., people with ASDs and their parents, teachers, and other carers.

Two approaches to intervention for challenging behaviors have received considerable research effort and continue to do so: psychopharmacology and Applied Behavior Analysis. We did not review the psychopharmacology research, but we reviewed examples from the ABA research literature to illustrate the variety of interventions that may be selected depending on the functional characteristics of an individual's challenging behavior (see section on "Behavioral Interventions Selected by Maintaining Function"). Although the *efficacy* of these treatments based on the science of ABA has been demonstrated in the published research, there is at present a relative lack of research on the *effectiveness* of the approach. An efficacious treatment is one that has been demonstrated as beneficial in carefully controlled scientific studies. An effective treatment is one that is still beneficial when used "in the wild", i.e., in typical environments such as homes and schools when conducted by regular carers like parents and teachers (see, Chambless and Hollon, 1998).

In the section "Prevalence of Biological and Behavioral Interventions", we noted that researchers have found that a large proportion of people with challenging behaviors are prescribed medications or other biological treatments for which there is insufficient evidence to describe their use as "evidence-based". Restraint procedures and other reactive management methods appear to be quite common as well. With further evidence of the *effectiveness* of interventions based on functional assessment of behavior, we expect that the Applied Behavior Analysis approach to reducing challenging behaviors should become the norm for interventions.

The associations between language deficits, challenging behaviors, their treatment using functional communication methods, and what we labeled "acquisitional" interventions (see section on "Challenging Behavior Reduction . . . ") leads to recommendation for early interventions that may help avoid the development of severe chronic challenging behaviors. Review of behavioral early intervention is beyond the scope of this chapter, but the teaching of communication skills may reduce the likelihood of challenging behaviors developing that serve an aberrant communicative function.

REFERENCES

Ahearn, W.H., Clark, K.M., DeBar, R., and Florentino, C. (2005). On the role of preference in response competition. *Journal of Applied Behavior Analysis*, **38**, 247–250.

Aiken, J.M. and Salzberg, C.L. (1984). The effects of a sensory extinction procedure on stereotypic sounds of two autistic children. *Journal of Autism and Developmental Disorders*, **14**, 291–299.

Aman, M.G., Lam, K.S.L., Van Bourgondien, M.E. (2005). Medication patterns in patients with autism: Temporal, regional, and demographic influences. *Journal of Child and Adolescent Psychopharmacology*, **15**, 116–126.

Anderson, C.M. and Long, E.S. (2002). Use of a structured descriptive assessment methodology to identify variables affecting problem behavior. *Journal of Applied Behavior Analysis*, **35**, 137–154.

Autism Special Interest Group (2004). *Revised Guidelines for Consumers of Applied Behavior Analysis Services to Individuals with Autism and Related Disorders*. Association for Behavior Analysis International. Retrieved February 27th, 2007 from http://www.abainternational.org/Special_Interests/autism_guidelines.asp

Behavior Analyst Certification Board. (2004). *Behavior Analyst Certification Board Guidelines for Responsible Conduct for Behavior Analysts*. Retrieved February 9th 2007, from http://www.bachallenging behavior.com/pages/conduct.html

Baghdadli, A., Pascal, C., Grisi, S., and Aussilloux, C. (2003). Risk factors for self-injurious behaviours among 222 young children with autistic disorders. *Journal of Intellectual Disability Research*, **47**, 622–627.

Blacher, J. and McIntyre, L.L. (2006). Syndrome specificity and behavioural disorders in young adults with intellectual disability: Cultural differences in family impact. *Journal of Intellectual Disability Research*, **50**, 184–198.

Bodfish, J.W., Symons, F.J., Parker, D.E., and Lewis, M.H. (2000). Varieties of repetitive behavior in autism: Comparisons to mental retardation. *Journal of Autism and Developmental Disorders*, **30**, 237–243.

Bradley, E.A., Summers, J.A., Wood, H.L., and Bryson, S.E. (2004). Comparing rates of psychiatric and behavioral disorders in adolescents and young adults with severe intellectual disability with and without autism. *Journal of Autism and Developmental Disorders*, **34**, 151–161.

Braithwaite, K.L. and Richdale, A.L. (2000). Functional communication training to replace challenging behaviors across two behavioral outcomes. *Behavioral Interventions*, **15**, 21–36.

Britton, L.N., Carr, J.E., Landaburu, H.J., and Romick, K.S. (2002). The efficacy of noncontingent reinforcement as treatment for automatically reinforced stereotypy. *Behavioral Interventions*, **17**, 93–103.

Buckley, S.D. and Newchok, D.K. (2004). Differential impact of response effort within a response chain on use of mands in a student with autism. *Research in Developmental Disabilities*, **26**, 77–85.

Campbell, J.M. (2003). Efficacy of behavioral interventions for reducing problem behaviors in persons with autism: A quantitative synthesis of single-subject research. *Research in Developmental Disabilities*, **24**, 120–138.

Carr, E.G. and Durand, V.M. (1985). Reducing behavior problems through functional communication training. *Journal of Applied Behavior Analysis*, **18**, 111–126.

Chambless, D.L. and Hollon, S.D. (1998). Defining empirically supported treatments. *Journal of Consulting and Clinical Psychology*, **66**, 7–18.

Charlop-Christy, M.H., Carpenter, M., Le, L., et al. (2002). Using the picture exchange communication system (PECS) with children with autism: Assessment of PECS acquisition, speech, social-communicative behavior, and problem behavior. *Journal of Applied Behavior Analysis*, **35**, 213–231.

Christison, G.W. and Ivany, K. (2006). Elimination diets in autism spectrum disorders: Any wheat amidst the chaff? *Journal of Developmental & Behavioral Pediatrics*, **27**, S162–S171.

Cole, G.A., Montgomery, R.W., Wilson, K.M., and Milan, M.A. (2000). Parametric analysis of overcorrection duration effects. *Behavior Modification*, **24**, 359–378.

Cooper, J.O., Heron, T.E., and Heward (2007). *Applied Behavior Analysis* (2nd ed.). Upper Saddle River, NJ: Pearson.

Crozier, S. and Tincani, M.J. (2005). Using a modified social story to decrease disruptive behavior of a child with autism. *Focus on Autism and Other Developmental Disabilities*, **20**, 150–157.

Dawson, J.E., Matson, J.L., and Cherry, K.E. (1998). An analysis of maladaptive behaviors in persons with autism, PDD-NOS, and mental retardation. *Research in Developmental Disabilities*, **19**, 439–448.

Day, H.M., Horner, R.H., and O'Neill, R.E. (1994). Multiple functions of problem behaviors: Assessment and intervention. *Journal of Applied Behavior Analysis*, **27**, 279–289.

DeLeon, I.G., Neidert, P.L., Anders, B.M., and Rodriguez-Catter, V. (2001). Choices between positive and negative reinforcement during treatment for escape-maintained behavior. *Journal of Applied Behavior Analysis*, **34**, 521–525.

Donenberg, G., and Baker, B.L. (1993). The impact of young children with externalizing behaviors on their families. *Journal of Abnormal Child Psychology*, **21**, 179–198.

Dooley, P., Wilczenski, F.L., and Torem, C. (2001). Using an activity schedule to smooth school transitions. *Journal of Positive Behavior Interventions*, **3**, 57–61.

Durand, V.M. and Carr, E.G. (1991). Functional communication training to reduce challenging behavior: Maintenance and application in new settings. *Journal of Applied Behavior Analysis*. **24**, 251–264.

Durand, V.M. and Carr, E.G. (1992). An analysis of maintenance following functional communication training. *Journal of Applied Behavior Analysis*, **25**, 777–794.

Eisenhower, A.S., Baker, B.L., and Blacher, J. (2005). Preschool children with intellectual disability: Syndrome specificity, behaviour problems, and maternal well-being. *Journal of Intellectual Disability Research*, **49**, 657–671.

Emerson, E., Robertson, J., Gregory, N., et al. (2000). Treatment and management of challenging behaviours in residential settings. *Journal of Applied Research in Intellectual Disabilities*, **13**, 197–215.

Falcomata, T.S., Roane, H.S., Hovanetz, A.N., Kettering, T.L., and Keeney, K.M. (2004). An evaluation of response cost in the treatment of inappropriate vocalizations maintained by automatic reinforcement. *Journal of Applied Behavior Analysis*, **37**, 83–87.

Fisher, W.W., Adelinis, J.D., Volkert, V.M., et al. (2005). Assessing preferences for positive and negative reinforcement during treatment of destructive behavior with functional communication training. *Research in Developmental Disabilities*, **26**, 153–168.

Fisher, W.W., Thompson, R.H., Hagopian, L.P., et al. (2000). Facilitating tolerance of delayed reinforcement during functional communication training. *Behavior Modification*, **24**, 3–29.

Forehand, R., and Baumeister, A. (1976). A deceleration of aberrant behavior among retarded individuals. In *Progress in Behavior Modification* (M. Hersen, R.M. Eisler and P.M. Miller, eds.) pp. 77–145. New York: Academic Press.

Foxx, R.M. (2005). Severe aggressive and self-destructive behavior: The myth of the non-aversive treatment of severe behavior. In J.W. Jacobson, R.M. Foxx and J.A. Mulick (Eds.) *Controversial* therapies for developmental disabilities: Fad, fashion, and science in professional practice (pp. 295–310). Mahwah, NJ: Lawrence Erlbaum.

Foxx, R.M. and Azrin, N.H. (1973). The elimination of autistic self-stimulatory behavior by over-correction. *Journal of Applied Behavior Analysis*, **6**, 1–14.

Foxx, R.M. and Garito, J. (2007). The long term successful treatment of the very severe behaviors of a preadolescent with autism. *Behavioral Interventions*, **22**, 69–82.

Foxx, R.M. and Meindl, J. (2007). The long term successful treatment of the aggressive/destructive behaviors of a preadolescent with autism. *Behavioral Interventions*, **22**, 83–97.

Frost, L.A. and Bondy, A.S. (1994). *The Picture Exchange Communication System Training Manual*. Cherry Hill, NJ: Pyramid Educational Consultants.

Gadow, K.D., DeVincent, C.J., Pomeroy, J., and Azizian, A. (2004). Psychiatric symptoms in preschool children with PDD and clinic and comparison samples. *Journal of Autism and Developmental Disorders*, **34**, 379–393.

Gray, C. (2000). *Writing Social Stories with Carol Gray*. Arlington, TX: Future Horizons.

Gurney, J.G., McPheeters, M.L., and Davis, M.M. (2006). Parental report of health conditions and health care use among children with and without autism. *Archives of Pediatrics and Adolescent Medicine*, **160**, 825–830.

Hagopian, L.P. and Adelinis, J.D. (2001). Response blocking with and without redirection for the treatment of pica. *Journal of Applied Behavior Analysis*, **34**, 527–530.

Hagopian, L.P., Contrucci Kuhn, S.A., Long, E.S., and Rush, K.S. (2005). Schedule thinning following communication training using competing stimuli to enhance tolerance to decrements in reinforcer density. *Journal of Applied Behavior Analysis*, **38**, 177–193.

Hagopian, L.P., Crockett, J.L., van Stone, M., et al. (2000). Effects of noncontingent reinforcement on problem behavior and stimulus engagement: The role of satiation, extinction, and alternative reinforcement. *Journal of Applied Behavior Analysis*, **33**, 433–449.

Hagopian, L.P., Toole, L.M., Long, E.S., et al. (2004). A comparison of dense-to-lean and fixed lean schedules of alternative reinforcement and extinction. *Journal of Applied Behavior Analysis*, **37**, 323–337.

Hagopian, L.P., Wilson, D.M., and Wilder, D.A. (2001). Assessment and treatment of problem behavior maintained by escape from attention and access to tangible items. *Journal of Applied Behavior Analysis*, **34**, 229–232.

Hall, S.S. (2005). Comparing descriptive, experimental and informant-based assessments of problem behaviors. *Research in Developmental Disabilities*, **26**, 514–526.

Hanley, G.P., Iwata, B.A., and McCord, B.E. (2003). Functional analysis of problem behavior: A review. *Journal of Applied Behavior Analysis*, **36**, 147–185.

Hanley, G.P., Iwata, B.A., and Thompson, R.H. (2001). Reinforcement schedule thinning following treatment with functional communication training. *Journal of Applied Behavior Analysis*, **34**, 17–38.

Harding, J.W., Wacker, D.P., Berg, W.K., et al. (2002). Assessment and treatment of severe behavior problems using choice making procedures. *Education and Treatment of Children*, **25**, 26–46.

Healey, J.J., Ahearn, W.A., Graff, R.B., and Libby, M.E. (2001). Extended analysis and treatment of self-injurious behavior. *Behavioral Interventions*, **16**, 181–195.

Herring, S., Gray, K., Taffe, J., et al. (2006). Behaviour and emotional problems in toddlers with pervasive developmental disorders and developmental delay: Associations with parental mental health and family functioning. *Journal of Intellectual Disability Research*, **50**, 874–882.

Hill, J. and Furniss, F. (2006). Patterns of emotional and behavioural disturbance associated with autistic traits in young people with severe intellectual disabilities and challenging behaviours. *Research in Developmental Disabilities*, **27**, 517–528.

Hoch, H., McComas, J.J., Thompson, A.L., and Paone, D. (2002). Concurrent reinforcement schedules: behavior change and maintenance without extinction. *Journal of Applied Behavior Analysis*, **35**, 155–169.

Holden, B. and Gitlesen, J.P. (2006). A total population study of challenging behaviour in the county of Hedmark, Norway: Prevalence, and risk markers. *Research in Developmental Disabilities*, **27**, 456–465.

Horner, R.D. (1980). The effects of an environmental enrichment program on the behavior of institutionalized profoundly retarded children. *Journal of Applied Behavior Analysis*, **13**, 473–491.

Horner, R.H. and Day, H.M. (1991). The effects of response efficiency on functionally equivalent competing behaviors. *Journal of Applied Behavior Analysis*, **24**, 719–732.

Icasiano, F., Hewson, P., Machet, P., et al. (2004). Childhood autism spectrum disorder in the Barwan region: A community based study. *Journal of Paediatrics and Child Health*, **40**, 696–701.

Iwata, B.A., Dorsey, M.F., Slifer, K.J., et al. (1982). Toward a functional analysis of self-injury. *Analysis and Intervention in Developmental Disabilities*, **2**, 1–20. Reprinted in *Journal of Applied Behavior Analysis* 1994, **27**, 197–209.

Jacobson, J.W., Foxx, R.M., and Mulick, J.A. (2005). *Controversial Therapies for Developmental Disabilities: Fad, Fashion, and Science in Professional Practice.* Mahwah, NJ: Lawrence Erlbaum.

Jenson, W.R., Rovner, L., Cameron, S., et al. (1985). Reduction of self-injurious behavior in an autistic girl using a multifaceted treatment program. *Journal of Behavior Therapy and Experimental Psychiatry*, **16**, 77–80.

Kahng, S.W., Iwata, B.A., Thompson, R.H., and Hanley, G.P. (2000) A method for identifying satiation versus extinction effects under non contingent reinforcement schedules. *Journal of Applied Behavior Analysis*, **33**, 419–432.

Kodak, T., Miltenberger, R.G., and Romaniuk, C. (2003). The effects of differential negative reinforcement of other behavior and noncontingent escape on compliance. *Journal of Applied Behavior Analysis*, **36**, 379–382.

Koegel, R.L. and Koegel, L.K. (1990). Extended reductions in stereotypic behavior of students with autism through a self-management treatment package. *Journal of Applied Behavior Analysis*, **23**, 119–127.

Lalli, J.S., Casey, S., and Kates, K. (1995). Reducing escape behavior and increasing task completion with functional communication training, extinction, and response chaining. *Journal of Applied Behavior Analysis*, **28**, 261–268.

Lecavalier, L., Leone, S., and Wiltz, J. (2006). The impact of behaviour problems on caregiver stress in young people with autism spectrum disorders. *Journal of Intellectual Disability Research*, **50**, 172–183.

Lerman, D.C., Kelley, M.E., Vorndran, C.M., and Van Camp, C.M. (2003). Collateral effects of response blocking during the treatment of stereotypic behavior. *Journal of Applied Behavior Analysis*, **36**, 119–123.

Lerman, D.C. and Vorndran, C.M. (2002). On the status of knowledge for using punishment: Implications for treating behavior disorders. *Journal of Applied Behavior Analysis*, **35**, 431–464.

Mace, A.B., Shapiro, E.S., and Mace, F.C. (1998). Effects of warning stimuli for reinforcer withdrawal and task onset on self-injury. *Journal of Applied Behavior Analysis*, **31**, 679–682.

Mancina, C., Tankersley, M., Kamps, D., et al. (2000). Brief report: Reduction of inappropriate vocalization for a child with autism using a self-management treatment program. *Journal of Autism and Developmental Disorders*, **30**, 599–606.

Mandell, D.S., Walrath, C.M., Manteuffel, B., et al. (2005). Characteristics of children with autistic spectrum disorders served in comprehensive community-based mental health settings. *Journal of Autism and Developmental Disorders*, **35**, 313–321.

Marcus, B.A. and Vollmer, T.R. (1996). Combining noncontingent reinforcement and differential reinforcement schedules as treatment for aberrant behavior. *Journal of Applied Behavior Analysis*, **29**, 43–51.

Martin, A., Scahill, L., Klin, A., and Volkmar, F.R. (1999). Higher-functioning pervasive developmental disorders: Rates and patterns of psychotropic drug use. *Journal of the American Academy of Child and Adolescent Psychiatry*, **38**, 923–931.

Matson, J.L., Baglio, C.S., Smiroldo, B.B., et al. (1996). Characteristics of autism as assessed by the Diagnostic Assessment for the Severely Handicapped – II (DASH-II). *Research in Devlopmental Disabilities*, **17**, 135–143.

Matson, J.L., Benavidez, D.A., Compton, L.S., et al. (1996). Behavioral treatment of autistic persons: A review of research from 1980 to the present. *Research in Developmental Disabilities*, **17**, 433–465.

Matson, J.L. and Nebel-Schwalm, M. (2006). Assessing challenging behaviors in children with autism spectrum disorders: A review. *Research in Developmental Disabilities* doi10.1016/j.ridd.2006.08.001.

McClintock, K., Hall, S., and Oliver, C. (2003). Risk markers associated with challenging behaviours in people with intellectual disabilities: A meta-analytic study. *Journal of Intellectual Disability Research*, **47**, 405–416.

McCord, B.E., Grosser, J.W., Iwata, B.A., and Powers, L.A. (2005). An analysis of response-blocking parameters in the prevention of pica. *Journal of Applied Behavior Analysis*, **38**, 391–394.

McKerchar, P.M. and Thompson, R.H. (2004). A descriptive analysis of potential reinforcement contingencies in the preschool classroom. *Journal of Applied Behavior Analysis*, **37**, 431–444.

Moes, D.R. and Frea, W.D. (2002). Contextualized behavioral support in early intervention for children with autism and their families. *Journal of Autism and Developmental Disorders*, **32**, 519–533.

Moore, J.W., Fisher, W.W., and Pennington, A. (2004). Systematic application and removal of protective equipment in the assessment of multiple topographies of self-injury. *Journal of Applied Behavior Analysis*, **37**, 73–77.

Mudford, O.C. (2004). Autism and pervasive developmental disorders. In *Behavior Modification for Persons with Developmental Disabilities: Treatments and Supports* (J.L. Matson, R.B. Laud, and M.L. Matson, eds.) pp. 213–252. Kingston, NY: NADD Press.

Murphy, G.H., Beadle-Brown, J., Wing, L., et al. (2005). Chronicity of challenging behaviours in people with severe intellectual disabilities and/or autism: A total population sample. *Journal of Autism and Developmental Disorders*, **35**, 405–418.

Najdowski, A.C., Wallace, M.D., Doney, J.K., and Ghezzi, P.M. (2003). Parental assessment and treatment of food selectivity in natural settings. *Journal of Applied Behavior Analysis*, **36**, 383–386.

Neidert, P.L., Iwata, B.A., and Dozier, C.L. (2005). Treatment of multiply controlled problem behavior with procedural variations of differential reinforcement. *Exceptionality*, **13**, 45–53.

Newman, B., Needleman, M., Reinecke, D.R., and Robek, A. (2002). The effect of providing choices on skill acquisition and competing behavior of children with autism during discrete trial instruction. *Behavioral Interventions*, **17**, 31–41.

Newman, B., Tuntigian, L., Ryan, C.S., and Reinecke, D.R. (1997). Self-management of a DRO procedure by three students with autism. *Behavioral Interventions*, **12**, 149–156.

Northup, J., Wacker, D., Sasso, G., et al. (1991). A brief functional analysis of aggressive and alternative behavior in an outclinic setting. *Journal of Applied Behavior Analysis*, **24**, 509–522.

Nye, C. and Brice, A. (2005). Combined vitamin B6-magnesium treatment in autism spectrum disorder. *Cochrane Database of Systematic Reviews*, **1**, 2007.

O'Neill, R.E., Horner, R.H., Albin, R.W., et al. (1997). *Functional Assessment and Program Development for Problem Behavior: A Practical Handbook* (2nd ed.). Pacific Grove, CA: Brooks-Cole.

Page, T.J., Perrin, F.A., Tessing, J.L., et al. (2007). Beyond treatment for individual behavior problems: An effective residential continuum of care for individuals with severe behavior problems. *Behavioral Interventions*, **22**, 35–45.

Patel, M.R., Carr, J.E., Kim, C., et al. (2000). Functional analysis of aberrant behavior maintained by automatic reinforcement: Assessments of specific sensory reinforcers. *Research in Developmental Disabilities*, **21**, 393–407.

Pelios, L., Morren, J., Tesch, D., and Axelrod, S. (1999). The impact of functional analysis methodology on treatment choice for self-injurious and aggressive behavior. *Journal of Applied Behavior Analysis*, **32**, 185–195.

Piazza, C.C., Adelinis, J.D., Hanley, G.P., et al. (2000). An evaluation of the effects of matched stimuli on behaviors maintained by automatic reinforcement. *Journal of Applied Behavior Analysis*, **33**, 13–27.

Progar, P.R., North, S.T., Bruce, S.S., et al. (2001). Putative behavioral history effects and aggression maintained by escape from therapists. *Journal of Applied Behavior Analysis*, **34**, 69–72.

Quill, K.A. (ed.) (1995). *Teaching Children with Autism: Strategies to Enhance Communication and Socialization*. Albany, NY: Delmar.

Rapp, J.T. (2006). Toward an empirical method for identifying matched stimulation for automatically reinforced behavior: A preliminary investigation. *Journal of Applied Behavior Analysis*, **39**, 137–140.

Rapp, J.T. and Vollmer, T.R. (2005). Stereotypy I: A review of behavioral assessment and treatment. *Research in Developmental Disabilities*, **26**, 527–547.

Reese, R.M., Richman, D.M., Belmont, J.M., and Morse, P. (2005). Functional characteristics of disruptive behavior in developmentally disabled children with and without autism. *Journal of Autism and Developmental Disorders*, **35**, 419–428.

Reese, R.M., Richman, D.M., Zarcone, J., and Zarcone, T. (2003). Individualizing functional assessments for children with autism: The contribution of perseverative behavior and sensory disturbances to disruptive behavior. *Focus on Autism and Other Developmental Disabilities*, **18**, 89–94.

Ricciardi, J.N. and Luiselli, J.K. (2003). Behavioral intervention to eliminate socially mediated urinary incontinence in a child with autism. *Child & Family Behavior Therapy*, **25**, 53–63.

Ricciardi, J.N., Luiselli, J.K., Terrill, S., and Reardon, K. (2003). Alternative response training with contingent practice as intervention for pica in a school setting. *Behavioral Interventions*, **18**, 219–226.

Richman, D.M., Wacker, D.P., Asmus, J.M., and Casey, S.D. (1998). Functional analysis and extinction of different behavior problems exhibited by the same individual. *Journal of Applied Behavior Analysis*, **31**, 475–478.

Rincover, A., Cook, R., Peoples, A., and Packard, D. (1979). Sensory extinction and sensory reinforcement principles for programming multiple adaptive behavior change. *Journal of Applied Behavior Analysis*, **12**, 221–233.

Ringdahl, J.E., Kitsukawa, K., Andelman, M.S., et al. (2002). Differential reinforcement with and without instructional fading. *Journal of Applied Behavior Analysis*, **35**, 291–294.

Russell, A.J., Mataix-Cols, D., Anson, M., and Murphy, D.G.M. (2005). Obsessions and compulsions in Asperger syndrome and high-functioning autism. *British Journal of Psychiatry*, **186**, 525–528.

Scattone, D., Wilczynski, S.M., Edwards, R.P., and Rabian, B. (2002). Decreasing disruptive behaviors of children with autism using social stories. *Journal of Autism and Developmental Disorders*, **32**, 535–543.

Schmit, J., Alper, S., Raschke, D., and Ryndak, D. (2000). Effects of using a photographic cueing package during routine school transitions with a child who has autism. *Mental Retardation*, **38**, 131–137.

Shabani, D.B., Wilder, D.A., and Flood, W.A. (2001). Reducing stereotypic behavior through discrimination training, differential reinforcement of other behavior, and self-monitoring. *Behavioral Interventions*, **16**, 279–286.

Sidener, T.M., Carr, J.E., and Firth, A.M. (2005). Superimposition and withholding of edible consequences as treatment for automatically reinforced stereotypy. *Journal of Applied Behavior Analysis*, **38**, 121–124.

Sigafoos, J. and Meikle, B. (1996). Functional communication training for the treatment of multiply determined challenging behavior in two boys with autism. *Behavior Modification*, **20**, 60–84.

Taylor, B.A., Hoch, H., and Weissman, M. (2005). The analysis and treatment of vocal stereotypy in a child with autism. *Behavioral Interventions*, **20**, 239–253.

Taylor, J.C. and Carr, E.G. (1992). Severe problem behaviors related to social interaction: I. Attention seeking and social avoidance. *Behavior Modification*, **16**, 305–335.

Tomporowski, P.D. (1983). Training an autistic client: The effect of brief restraint on disruptive behavior. *Journal of Behavior Therapy & Experimental Psychiatry*, **14**, 169–173.

Twatchman, D. (1995). Methods to enhance communication in verbal children, In *Teaching Children with Autism: Strategies to Enhance Communication and Socialization* (K. Quill, ed.) pp. 133–162. Albany, NY: Delmar.

Van Camp, C.M., Vollmer, T.R., and Daniel, D. (2001). A systematic evaluation of stimulus preference, response effort, and stimulus control in the treatment of automatically reinforced self-injury. *Behavior Therapy*, **32**, 603–613.

Vollmer, T.R., Marcus, B.A., and LeBlanc, L. (1994). Treatment of self-injury and hand mouthing following inconclusive functional analyses. *Journal of Applied Behavior Analysis*, **27**, 331–344.

Wacker, D.P., Steege, M.W., Northup, J., et al. (1990). A component analysis of functional communication training across three topographies of severe behavior problems. *Journal of Applied Behavior Analysis*, **23**, 417–429.

Witwer, A., and Lecavalier, L. (2005). Treatment incidence and patterns in children and adolescents with autism spectrum disorders. *Journal of Child and Adolescent Psychopharmacology*, **15**, 671–681.

Yi, J.I., Christian, L., Vittimberga, G., and Lowenkron, B. (2006). Generalized negatively reinforced manding in children with autism. *The Analysis of Verbal Behavior*, **22**, 21–33.

10

COMMUNICATION INTERVENTION FOR CHILDREN WITH AUTISM SPECTRUM DISORDERS

RALF W. SCHLOSSER[1] AND JEFF SIGAFOOS[2]

[1]*Northeastern University, Boston, MA, USA*
[2]*Victoria University of Wellington, New Zealand*

INTRODUCTION

Aberrant speech and language patterns are defining characteristics of autism and related conditions within the autism spectrum. Diagnostic criteria for autism, Asperger's syndrome, and the pervasive developmental disorders all include reference to delayed, deviant, or atypical speech and language development (American Psychiatric Association, 1994). More generally, individuals within the autism spectrum often have deficits in functional communication. For example, some individuals may fail to develop any appreciable amount of spoken language and for all intents and purposes could be considered mute. In the absence of speech, some individuals may develop problem behaviors such as aggression or self-injury to fill the communicative void. Others may acquire speech, but use it only in a rote and nonfunctional way, such as by simply repeating words or phrases that they have heard in the past. This pattern of persistent nonfunctional repetition of speech is known as echolalia. Other children may acquire speech, but engage in bizarre or unusual talk, such as insisting on talking at length about vacuum cleaners.

Given this range of presenting communication problems, all individuals within the autism spectrum could potentially benefit from communication intervention. Communication intervention is thus likely to be a vital component in the overall habilitative plan for individuals with autism spectrum disorders (ASD). Thus, it is clear that communication intervention is likely to be a high priority for a large number of children with autism. Data suggest that the best outcomes for individuals with ASD accrue when intervention begins early and makes use of empirically supported procedures (Lovaas, 1987). In this chapter, we therefore focus on reviewing evidence-based procedures for enhancing communication skills of children with ASD. This focus on children is consistent with emphasis on providing early intervention. When focused on this target population, clinicians will no doubt encounter many children who present the very beginning stages of communication development. Many of these children are likely to have little or no functional speech and thus the initial intervention target is likely to involve teaching imitative speech and/or developing functional communication using augmentative and alternative communication (AAC) modes, such as manual signs or picture-based communication systems. Depending on the source consulted, up to 50 percent of the population is estimated to fail to develop functional speech skills (Peeters and Gillberg, 1999) and hence, may benefit from AAC intervention.

The purpose of this chapter is to synthesize the evidence on communication interventions for children with autism. The focus is intervention for children at the beginning stages of communication intervention. Procedures for teaching speech are included as are procedures for developing functional use of AAC systems. Our review is intended to provide a summary of current best practice in beginning and early communication intervention for children with ASD.

METHODS

CRITERIA FOR INCLUSION AND EXCLUSION

In order to be included, a study had to meet the following criteria: (1) the participants had to be children (under the age of 21 years) and have a diagnosis of autism or Pervasive Developmental Disorders – Not Otherwise Specified (PDD-NOS); (2) the intervention had to be communication-based; (3) the outcome had to relate to one of the following communication skills: comprehension, production, and social use of language form (phonology, syntax, morphology), content (semantics), and use (pragmatics); (4) the design had to be a quasi-experimental group design or single-subject experimental design (preexperimental designs such as AB-designs or case studies are excluded); (5) the intervention approach had to be examined across several studies in support of its effectiveness.

PROCEDURES

When available, we relied on aggregated or synthesized effectiveness data and quality appraisals generated elsewhere through reviews of the literature (Bopp et al., 2004; Campbell, 2003; Goldstein, 2002; Mancil, 2006; McConachie and Diddle, 2007; McConnell, 2002; Odom et al., 2003; Schlosser and Wendt, in press; Schwartz and Nye, 2006; Wendt, 2006). When possible, we relied first on systematic reviews rather than nonsystematic reviews or narrative reviews. Systematic reviews ". . . adhere closely to a set of scientific methods that explicitly aim to limit systematic error (bias), mainly attempting to identify, appraise, and synthesize all relevant studies (of whatever design) in order to answer a particular question (or set of questions)" (Petticrew and Roberts, 2006, p. 9). Because of their rigor and transparency, systematic reviews are better tools to inform clinical practice decisions than narrative reviews (Schlosser, 2007; Schlosser, Wendt, and Sigafoos, 2007).

Schlosser and Wendt (in press), for example, calculated effect sizes (for group studies) and the percentage of nonoverlapping data (PND, for single-subject experimental designs) of several AAC interventions. In addition, they appraised the quality of the evidence classifying it as conclusive, preponderant, suggestive, or inconclusive based on how the study fulfilled three internal validity aspects (design and implementation, inter-observer agreement, and treatment integrity). Intervention approaches that are considered invalid such as facilitated communication (Probst, 2005) will not be addressed. Moreover, interventions for which the evidence is largely inconclusive will not be elaborated upon (e.g., Buckley and Newchock, 2005; Son et al., 2006).

SPEECH-BASED INTERVENTIONS

SHAPING IMITATIVE SPEECH

The pioneering work of Lovaas et al. (1966) has produced what is today one of the more well-established approaches for teaching imitative speech to children with autism. The program is based on sound, empirically validated principles of learning. The program involves several steps. The first is based on the strengthening effects of reinforcement with the aim being to increase the frequency of vocalizations produced by the child. To achieve this, the child is reinforced with access to a highly preferred item for any vocalization. Lovaas et al. showed that this contingency produced an increase in the frequency of vocalizations. The second step makes use of differential reinforcement in that only vocalizations that occur in response to a verbal model from the interventionist are reinforced. For example, the instructor would say a word such as "ba" and any vocalization that occurred within 6 seconds would be reinforced. Again, data show that this differential reinforcement is effective in bringing the child's vocalizations under the control of the model. The third step applied shaping principles in that reinforcement is now only delivered when the form of the child's vocalization sounds similar to the interventionist's model. By gradually increasing the complexity of the model (ba, ball, I want the ball), the aim is to teach imitation of speech. This approach to teaching imitative speech has good evidence to support its effectiveness. However, the approach may not be effective for all children and often requires a considerable period of intensive intervention before acquisition of imitative speech is evident.

STIMULUS–STIMULUS PAIRING

A variation of the shaping approach is the recent work on stimulus–stimulus pairing for developing speech in children with ASD (Sundberg et al., 1996). There is emerging evidence supporting the effectiveness of this procedure. Specifically, the interventionist models a speech sound or word (e.g., *da, gee, oh*) and at the same time delivers a reinforcer to the child. The rationale being that this pairing of vocal model with a reinforcer will eventually make the child's own vocalizations automatically reinforcing and thus the child's propensity to emit speech will increase. Data indicate that after approximately 300–400 such pairings, some children with autism and language delays may begin to spontaneously imitate the target sounds (Miguel, Carr, and Michael, 2002; Yoon and Bennett, 2000). While additional research is needed to establish the reliability of these initial findings, it would appear that this stimulus–stimulus pairing procedure is a promising approach for inducing imitative speech.

REPLACING ECHOLALIA

Some children have speech, but simply repeat words or phrases that they hear other people say. Because this echolalia is not functional, the aim of intervention is to replace echolalia with functional use of speech. Along these lines, there has been some success in replacing echolalia with functional speech using prompting, shaping, and fading procedures (Lovaas, 1977). Generally, the interventionist sets the occasion for a response by presenting a discriminative stimulus (e.g., holding up a book and asking, "What is this?"). During the initial phases of intervention, the child is immediately prompted to say "Book." Because the prompt is immediate, the child is most likely to echo only the last word (book), rather than the entire initial question. This echoic prompt is then faded by speaking the word "book" with less and less volume and emphasis over successive learning opportunities.

A well-established variation of this approach is known as the cues-pause-point procedure (Foxx et al., 1987; McMorrow and Foxx, 1986; McMorrow et al., 1987). The procedure involves a series of steps that occur during intervention sessions. First, the interventionist prompts the child to remain silent by holding up a finger to the lips. If any child verbalizations occur at this point, the interventionist gives corrective feedback ("No" or "Shh"). This corrective feedback is referred to as the pause prompt. Once the child has paused, the interventionist points to a discriminative stimulus and asks, "What is this?" The pause prompt is then removed, which is intended to signal to the child that it can now make a response. Data show that this procedure is highly effective for replacing echolalia with correct naming of objects.

MILIEU-BASED INTERVENTIONS

Goldstein (2002) reviewed 12 studies investigating the use of time delay, milieu teaching, and natural language paradigm interventions. His review is systematic in terms of extracting some of the data from the original studies (e.g., appraisal of quality, design, participant characteristics, independent variables, dependent variables, generalization assessed), but falls short on effectiveness judgments, which appear to be subjective. In addition, the review does not specify where and how the search for studies was conducted. Hence, the conclusions reached in this review were discussed with these limitations in mind.

Time delay is a technique whereby a pause is inserted between the presentation of a stimulus and a prompt or a sequence of prompts. Depending on the exact delivery of the prompts, we distinguish between constant time delay and progressive time delay. Time delay lends itself readily for use in natural settings although its use is also frequent in discrete-trial interventions such as the speech-based interventions described earlier. According to Goldstein (2002), time delay is effective in producing rapid and often generalized language production, although it is many times unclear whether it is time delay that is responsible and/or the frequently combined correction and modeling procedures.

Milieu teaching is a family of procedures that aim to elaborate on the child's desires and wants in the natural environment. Milieu teaching approaches include incidental teaching involving the mand-model procedure and time delay, and following the child's lead and interests (natural language paradigm). Goldstein (2002) corrected the common misconception that milieu teaching is used only for teaching requesting, noting the following other intervention goals that have been targeted: preverbal communication (e.g., eye contact, joint attention), spontaneous productions, descriptions of drawings and card play, social amenities, positive interactions with peers, answers to questions, phoneme production, and increased talking. Although generally viewed as effective, Goldstein (2002) argued that there is no compelling evidence that milieu teaching is any more effective than discrete-trial instruction.

COMMUNICATION PARTNER INTERVENTIONS

In communication intervention the role of communication partners cannot be overemphasized. If communication is viewed as a transactional process between a sender and a receiver, the communication partner's contribution to the success of an interaction is critical (Schlosser et al., 2007). Parents constitute one group of partners that are part of children's natural environment, especially when these children are young. Other partner groups are teachers and related staff in classrooms, day care centers, and peers.

Goldstein (2002) reviewed three studies that focused on the effectiveness of parent training programs exclusively, two studies that targeted entire classroom staff, and one study that involved day care center staff as well as parents of children with autism. Although each of these studies reported moderate to significant effects for the children involved, Goldstein (2002) cautioned about the low confidence we can place in these results due to numerous shortcomings in design (except one study using a randomized control trial), lack of treatment integrity, and sketchy descriptions of interventions.

McConachie and Diggle (2007) conducted a more recent and rigorous systematic review of parent-implement intervention programs in early intervention involving children with ASD. Based on a randomised control trial (RCT) by Aldred et al. (2004), they conclude that the children in the parent training group had statistically significant lower ratings on the Autism Diagnostic Observation Schedule score for social-communication impairments and score for social interaction than the routine care group. Further, based on a meta-analysis of two studies (Alfred et al., 2004; Drew et al., 2002), McConachie and Diggle (2007) conclude that parent-implemented intervention resulted in greater number of words understood and on words said as measured by the MacArthur Communication Development Inventory. In sum, it appears that there is growing evidence that parent-implemented interventions can work and do work in improving language and communication skills of young children with ASD. At the same time, McConachie and Diggle (2007) point out that much more research remains to be done to examine whether these interventions work in daily practice.

SOCIAL INTERACTION INTERVENTIONS

Due to social interaction and communication being at the core of the deficit faced by children with ASD, interventions that promote social interactions are crucial. Goldstein (2002) included five such studies in his review. In two of the reviewed studies, peers of children with autism were successfully taught to share and give play directions or to attend to, comment, or respond to children with autism. Several studies were effective in teaching children with ASD to interact within scripted conversation and managed to engage in untrained variations of the scripts. Only one study effectively tackled the frequently observed difficulty of children with ASD in initiating conversations through a combination of modeling, rehearsal, and token reinforcement.

McConnell (2002) reviewed the literature on social skills interventions for young children with autism. Although this review presents with many fine characteristics of systematic reviews such as the systematic appraisal of each study's internal validity, external validity, and generalization, the search was limited to PsycINFO and no attempt was made to calculate effect sizes. Thus, the conclusions of this review, in particular those that speak to the effectiveness of interventions, may be overextending the methodology utilized. Interventions were grouped into the following categories: (a) ecological variations, (b) collateral skills interventions, (c) child-specific interventions, (d) peer behavior, and (e) comprehensive interventions. Ecological variations were defined as modifications in activity structure, schedule or nature and composition of peer groups. McConnell concludes that "ecological variations can, under some conditions, produce weak to moderate effects on the social interactions of young children with autism, but these effects appear variable across investigations, intervention strategies, and children... As a result, ecological variations in and of themselves may be viewed as necessary, but sometimes not sufficient, for producing changes in the social interaction" (p. 360). Collateral skill interventions were defined as those that target other skills (e.g., participation) in order to achieve improvements in social skills. McConnell concludes that these interventions may increase social interaction by facilitating the contact between children with autism and their peers. The third group, child-specific interventions are procedures aimed at increasing skills (or frequency and quality) of social behaviors by the children with ASD. According to McConnell, child-specific interventions can lead to increased social interactions, but the heavy emphasis on initiating rather than maintaining conversations and the weak reinforcing qualities of social interaction by itself, raises questions about the long-term effectiveness of this intervention. Peer-mediated interventions are directed to alter the behavior of other children in order to facilitate interactions with children who have autism. McConnell concludes that these interventions "have demonstrated powerful and robust treatment effects across a number of children, investigators, and intervention variations" (p. 364). At the same time, he cautions that peer-mediated interventions have logical limitations due to the required continuous access to "trained" peers, unless these interventions can show effects that generalize to untrained peers and situations. Finally, comprehensive interventions incorporate two or more of the previously discussed interventions into one package. Based on a relatively small base of seven empirical studies, McConnell concludes that interventions directed to both young children with autism and their nondisabled peers can produce pronounced effects on social interaction and generalization across settings.

AAC INTERVENTIONS

Children who do not have any functional speech often benefit from AAC intervention involving aided methods such as exchange-based approaches and pointing-based approaches (i.e., communication boards, wallets, speech generating devices) and/or unaided approaches such as the use of manual signing and gestures. We have chosen to review interventions for which there is a body of research evidence in their support, including the Picture Exchange Communication System, speech-generating devices, and manual signs and gestures.

PICTURE EXCHANGE COMMUNICATION SYSTEM

The Picture Exchange Communication System (PECS) (Frost and Bondy, 2002) has gained increased popularity over the past decade. PECS is considered a manualized treatment for beginning communicators. It is arranged across 6 phases. In *Phase I: Physical Exchange*, children are trained to exchange a graphic symbol for a desired object. In *Phase II: Expanding Spontaneity*, children are taught to exchange a symbol with a communication partner who is not in their immediate vicinity. In *Phase III: Picture Discrimination*, the child learns to discriminate among symbols to request preferred objects. Then, in *Phase IV: Sentence Structure*, the learner is taught to apply an "I want" symbol to a blank sentence strip, combine it with the symbol for a desired object, and to exchange the sentence strip with a communication partner. In *Phase V: Responding to "What do you want,"* a learner is taught to respond to a direct question. Finally, in *Phase VI: Responsive and Spontaneous Commenting*, children are taught to build upon acquired skills by encouraging them to respond to additional questions (i.e., "What do you see?") and engage in spontaneous commenting.

Schlosser and Wendt (in press) reviewed the PECS interventions. In order to be considered for their review, the study had to include children with autism or PDD-NOS and make explicit reference to the PECS manual in describing their intervention procedures. Studies with other populations (e.g., Bock et al., 2005) and studies using preexperimental designs or program evaluations were excluded (e.g., Carr and Felce, 2006a,b; Liddle, 2001; Magiati and Howlin, 2003; Schwartz et al., 1998). The following studies were rated inconclusive and, as such, bear no practical implications (Beck et al., 2006; Buckley and Newchock, 2005; Frea et al., 2001; Ganz and Simpson, 2004; Marckel et al., 2006; Son et al., 2006; Travis, 2006; Yokoyama et al., 2006). The suggestive or better studies varied in terms of the phases of PECS instruction investigated. Some studies focused only on the first phase of teaching the exchange while others examined several phases (I–III, I–IV, etc.).

Two group studies yielded conclusive evidence. Yoder and Stone (2006a,b) compared PECS with Responsive Education and Prelinguistic Milieu Teaching (RPMT) in 36 children with ASD. The first study focused solely on speech production as outcomes and found that the PECS was more successful than the RPMT in terms of nonimitative spoken communicative acts and the number of different nonimitative words. An additional exploratory analysis showed that growth rate of the number of different nonimitative words was faster with PECS than with RPMT for children who began treatment with relatively high object exploration. The RPMT group, however, did better than the PECS group in children who began treatment with relatively low object exploration skills. The second study involved the same participants (Yoder and Stone, 2006b) and yielded that RPMT facilitated generalized turn-taking and generalized initiating joint attention more than did the PECS. This applied only to children with some preexisting joint attention skills. Children with very little preexisting joint attention skills, on the other hand, did better with PECS than RPMT.

Among the suggestive or better studies, four studies examined whether PECS instruction is effective in and of itself (Charlop-Christy et al., 2002; Ganz et al., 2007; Kravits et al., 2002; Tincani et al., 2006). Kravits et al. (2002) yielded fairly effective results in terms of requesting, commenting, and expansions in one elementary-aged child. PECS was highly effective in terms of requesting (Tincani et al., 2006) and ranged from fairly effective to highly effective in enhancing eye contact, joint attention or play as well as requests and initiations in three children with autism (Charlop-Christy et al., 2002). In the same study, PECS was found fairly to highly effective in improving imitative speech production for one of the three participants, but was of unreliable effectiveness for the others. In addition, PECS was unreliable in improving the mean length of utterances (MLU) and elicited speech productions across all three participants. Charlop-Christy et al. (2002) also assessed the effects of PECS for reducing two types of problem behavior, tantrums/out-of-seat behavior and disruptions/grabbing. The frequency of these problem behaviors was monitored separately for play and work settings involving two participants, Jake and Kyle. The impact of PECS on reducing the frequency of disruption/grabbing can be considered to be highly effective (outcome metrics could not be applied to the tantrums/out-of-seat behavior), but does not seem to result in the complete suppression of the behavior. Because these effects were obtained without a prior functional assessment into the functions that maintained the problem behavior, it is unclear whether the appropriate communicative behaviors taught were functionally equivalent to the functions served by the problem behaviors. Ganz et al. (2007) evaluated the effects of PECS instructions, Phases I–IV, in three children. Results indicated that the intervention was highly effective in improving requesting, but minimal changes (in the ineffective range) were noted in speech production.

Two studies compared PECS with manual signing (Anderson, 2001; Tincani, 2004). Schlosser and Wendt (in press) combined the PND outcome scores from both studies for each intervention variable for a further statistical comparison of PECS versus manual signs. For acquisition, PECS was statistically found more effective than manual signs. Based on these results, the PECS intervention can be interpreted as "fairly effective" for teaching requesting skills, whereas the manual signs intervention would be rated as ineffective. Although both of the above studies also monitored speech production, only the study by Tincani lent itself to PND calculations. Both participants yielded gains in speech production with manual signing and with PECS that were highly effective, but manual signing still led to better speech production than PECS.

Three suggestive studies explored the effectiveness of various *innovations* to the PECS protocol (Angermeier et al., 2006; Sidener et al., 2005; Tincani et al., 2006). For instance, Tincani et al. (2006) studied the effects of reinforcement of vocalizations during Phase IV instruction (which is not part of the protocol), combining an AAC intervention with a speech-based intervention. This innovation resulted in improved word approximations, but was not as effective in improving word vocalizations. These data were obtained with only one child, and hence the generalizability of these results is rather limited. Sidener et al. (2005) examined two strategies for dealing with the problem of keeping the frequency of newly acquired requesting skills through exchanges at practical levels. Often, the high frequency requests preclude the teaching of anything else. The authors concluded that the use of multiple schedules is an effective strategy whereas delay-to-reinforcement was ineffective. The data did not lend itself to PND calculations making it difficult to verify the effectiveness of this strategy. Finally, Angermeier et al. (2006) studied whether graphic symbols that look more like their referents (i.e., highly iconic) are more readily acquired during the early phases of the PECS protocol than graphic symbols that look less like their referents (i.e., low iconicity). Typically, the PECS protocol suggests the use of Picture Communication Symbols (PCS), a highly iconic set of graphic symbols. The study found no differences between symbols high in iconicity versus low in iconicity (Blissymbols) in terms of requesting. This suggests that practitioners may be free to choose either type of symbols early on in the PECS protocol (Phase I & II).

In summary, the aggregated evidence suggests that PECS is more effective/efficient than manual signing in terms of requesting. Because the quality of this evidence was deemed high, practitioners can place confidence in these findings. When the treatment goal is speech production, however, the appraised evidence to date has not yet reached a sufficient threshold to inform practice in favor of manual signing or PECS. The companion studies by Yoder and Stone (2006a,b) offer conclusive evidence that informs decision-making. The PECS seems to be a more effective choice than RPMT in terms of speech production whereas RPMT seems to be the better choice in terms of generalized turn taking and initiating joint attention. Hence, it is important for the practitioner to try and prioritize these goals. The companion studies by Yoder and Stone further suggest that it may be critical to assess whether or not a child comes to the task with object exploration and/or joint attention skills.

INTRODUCING SPEECH GENERATING DEVICES

Speech generating devices (SGDs) provide digitized and/or synthetic speech when activated. In recent years we have seen a spurt of research activity in this area. Again we rely on the effectiveness analyses and appraisals by Schlosser and Wendt (in press). Intervention studies involving the use of SGDs evaluated their effects of SGDs as part of a treatment package or evaluated speech output as an independent variable. The following studies were deemed inconclusive (Dyches, 1998; Sigafoos et al., 2003; Son et al., 2006).

Three studies, all rated as "suggestive," evaluated the effects of a treatment package involving SGDs (Olive et al., 2006; Schepis et al., 1998; Sigafoos et al., 2004). Schepis et al. (1998) found that the use of naturalistic teaching strategies to introduce an SGD resulted in highly effective increases in communicative interactions by four children with autism. Similarly, Olive et al. (2006) found that enhanced milieu teaching for introducing an SGD resulted in fairly to highly effective SGD use and overall communication for all of their three child participants. Interestingly, the intervention, however, was unreliable in improving vocalizations in two children. Finally, a study by Sigafoos et al. (2004) yielded that SGD use can be taught successfully and very effectively to two youngsters with autism as a repair strategy when prelinguistic requests do not seem to be recognized by their communication partner. Treatment involved planned ignoring of prelinguistic behaviors and least-to-most prompting in SGD use. In sum, based on this evidence it is plausible that treatment packages involving SGDs improve a variety of communicative functions and behaviors in children with autism.

Several studies aimed to evaluate the specific effect of providing access to speech output in comparison to not having speech output during intervention in teaching spelling (Schlosser and Blischak, 2004; Schlosser et al., 1998), speech production (Parsons and La Sorte, 1993; Schlosser et al., 2007), and requesting (Schlosser et al., 2007; Sigafoos et al., 2003). Two studies examined the effects of three feedback conditions (with speech, with print from the Liquid Crystal Display, and speech and print) during copy-cover-compare instruction on spelling acquisition. Based on conclusive evidence, the intervention was found similarly effective across these feedback conditions in that all participants reached criterion (Schlosser et al., 1998; Schlosser and Blischak, 2004). Based on the differential number of trials to criterion, the authors hypothesized that there appear to be two distinct profiles of feedback efficiency. Children with a primarily *visual profile* spell words most efficiently when feedback involves print. Children with a primarily *auditory profile* spell words most efficiently when feedback involves speech.

One study, yielding preponderant evidence, examined the effects of teaching requesting of preferred objects with an SGD with the speech on and with the speech off to five children with autism (Schlosser et al., 2007). There were no consistent differences across conditions and children. Specifically, the outcomes for two children were considered fairly effective, for one child it was of questionable effectiveness, and for one child the outcome was deemed unreliable. It is possible that the intervention was not carried out long enough to yield higher acquisition levels. In the same study, the effects on elicited vocalizations were monitored as well in both conditions alongside effects on requesting. Interestingly, four of the children remained at 0 percent even after intervention and only one child made minimal gains.

In a study yielding suggestive evidence, Parsons and La Sorte (1993) found that six learners with autism produced many more spontaneous vocalizations when learning with a software that provided speech as compared to one without speech. A closer look at these seemingly contradictory findings suggests that a number of methodological differences could account for these discrepant results. For example, in this study any speech productions were counted whereas in the Schlosser et al. (2007) study the vocalizations had to be addressing the specific objects that were taught to request with the SGD. Based on two studies it seems premature to draw any implications for practice in any specific direction.

In summary, based on the appraised evidence concerning the use of treatment packages involving SGDs, it seems counterproductive that SGDs be automatically discounted as an AAC option for children with autism. The automatic exclusion is grounded in the generally held belief that children with autism tend to process visual stimuli more readily than auditory stimuli. The evidence suggests that it is plausible to explore the use of SGDs with these children. In fact, it may be much more productive to view processing strengths of children with autism relative to specific task-demands such as spelling with an SGD (see Schlosser and Blischak, 2004) rather than having generalized statements dictate treatment choices.

INTRODUCING NON-ELECTRONIC SELECTION-BASED SYSTEMS WITH GRAPHIC SYMBOLS

As early as the 1980s authors have drawn attention to the potential benefits of graphic symbols due to their nontransient nature (e.g., Mirenda and Schuler, 1988). Graphic symbols in the studies reviewed here included the following: Blissymbols, colored photographs, line drawings, Picture Communication Symbols (PCS), Premack, Orthography, and Rebus. Selection-based nonelectronic systems involve communication boards, communication wallets, and the like. The child points to a graphic symbol in order to communicate a message. We will rely on the effectiveness and quality judgments produced by Schlosser and Wendt (in press). The following studies were deemed inconclusive and are therefore not discussed further (Dexter, 1998; Hamilton and Snell, 1993; Spencer, 2002).

Three studies indicate that there is suggestive to conclusive evidence that teaching the use of graphic symbols is effective in promoting the acquisition of requesting in children with autism (Johnston et al., 2003; Kozleski, 1991; Sigafoos, 1998). Children in these studies were successfully taught to request to play and to gain access to preferred objects and activities. In one of these studies, Kozleski (1991) compared multiple graphic symbol sets/systems and noted that sets/systems that bear a greater visual resemblance between symbol and referent appear to be acquired more readily than graphic symbols that do not bear that resemblance to their referents. In their integrative review, Schlosser and Sigafoos (2002) argued, however, that Kozleski's assertion is difficult to sustain because iconicity was not manipulated a priori.

One study provided suggestive evidence that graphic symbols used as visual supports may be highly effective in reducing the latency between an instructional cue and beginning new activities in children with autism (Dettmer et al., 2000). Transitions are difficult to handle for children with autism. If this evidence were substantiated further in future research, it would be a welcome addition to an empirically-based repertoire for teaching children with autism the use of graphic symbols not only for expressive purposes but also for receptive goals. The study by Hetzroni and Shalem (2005) offers preponderant evidence that children with autism are able to learn to match orthographic symbols to corresponding logos in an effective manner. While matching is an important skill for enabling communication involving symbols, matching by itself does not constitute a communicative act.

In summary, the use of graphic symbols with selection-based nonelectronic communication systems enjoys most empirical support for teaching requesting. However, this research cannot yet productively inform choices of one graphic symbol set/system over others. Future research that manipulates iconicity and other symbol characteristics prospectively is needed. The evidence in support of using graphic symbols as part of visual schedules is limited to only one study and as such still emerging. Children with autism seem to be able to match graphic symbols to orthographic symbols, but it is yet to be examined whether this matching could lead to enhanced communication.

TEACHING MANUAL SIGNS AND GESTURES

Manual signs and gestures do not require any external aids or devices external to the body (Lloyd et al., 1997). Hence, they cannot be "left behind" or break down like the aided methods described earlier. Manual signing was introduced in the 1970s and has been used with this population for more than 30 years. Manual signs can refer to a natural sign language such as American Sign Language or to the production of manual signs as a code for a spoken language such as Signing Exact English (Blischak et al., 1997). Gestures are body movements or sequences of coordinated body movements to represent a referent without the linguistic features of manual signs (e.g., pointing, yes-no headshake). Individuals with autism, however, rarely use gestures as an alternative communication strategy, even if they have difficulty speaking (Loveland et al., 1988).

As before we rely heavily on the effectiveness judgments and quality appraisals developed by Schlosser and Wendt (in press). The following studies were rated as inconclusive: Brady and Smouse (1978), Hundert (1981), Rotholz et al. (1989), and Saraydarian (1994).

Most studies primarily monitored symbol acquisition as an outcome variable. Among the conclusive evidence, one study monitored the acquisition of sign items for six participants as part of a study comparing acquisition and use of manual signs versus PECS (Anderson, 2001). Although overall the PECS training was superior, the study demonstrated that all participants were very successful in acquiring manual signs as well. Buffington et al. (1998) successfully taught four children to use gestures in combination with speech (saying "look") for indicating tasks.

Among the preponderant evidence, Tincani (2004) compared manual signing with PECS in terms of requesting and speech production. As discussed earlier for PECS, manual signing was fairly effective for two participants in terms of requesting, but not as effective as PECS. Another two participants were highly successful in increasing their vocalizations after manual signing, yielding superior findings over PECS.

The majority of studies produced suggestive evidence, including a study by Carr et al. (1978), which evaluated the impact of prompting, fading, and stimulus rotation on sign production. The procedure yielded highly effective expressive sign labeling. Carr and Kemp (1989) found that an intervention was highly effective in terms of teaching the use of pointing (to replace leading) for requests in all four participants. Carr and Kologinsky (1983), Experiment 1, found that a combination of prompting, fading, differential reinforcement, and incidental teaching was highly effective in yielding spontaneous requesting. This intervention also resulted in the children being able to generalize those requests across communication partners. In Experiment 2, the same authors investigated whether targeted prompting and reinforcement increase signed requesting and its generalization across adults and settings. The intervention was highly effective for three participants in terms of requesting. It also proved to be highly effective for all children when generalization across settings was targeted. In terms of generalization across partners, the treatment turned out to be highly effective for one participant and fairly effective for another. Subsequently, Carr et al. (1987) examined the effects of prompting, fading, stimulus rotation, and differential reinforcement on descriptive signing of action–object phrases in three children. This teaching procedure was highly effective in that they learned signed action–object phrases and were able to generalize those to new situations. Keogh et al. (1987) evaluated the effects of a treatment package that included verbal prompts, modeling, physical guidance, positive reinforcement, fading and chaining procedures to teach one participant an interactive signing dialogue within a naturalistic snack time routine. The intervention was highly effective in increasing the child's sign repertoire but was ineffective in terms of generalizing signed communication to new partners. In a related study, the same participant was taught a behavioral script to sign interactively with other children in a play situation (Sommer et al., 1988). For sign acquisition as well as for generalizing signed communication to another play situation, the intervention was rated of questionable effectiveness. Schepis et al. (1982) investigated the effects of modified incidental teaching strategies on manual sign acquisition in four participants. Mixed rates of success for learning manual signing were yielded. The intervention was highly effective in terms of expressive signing for one participant, fairly effective for another, of questionable effectiveness for the third and ineffective for the fourth child. In the only study in this category looking at *receptive* speech and receptive signing, Carr and Dores (1981) found that simultaneous communication was highly effective for three learners.

A second line of research compared the effects of simultaneous communication versus sign-alone training and/or oral training. Barrera et al. (1980) taught expressive language to one child using three different instructional methods: simultaneous communication, sign-alone training, and oral training. Increases were noted as the number of words successfully produced either through expressive signing or oral speech. While sign-alone and oral training were of questionable effectiveness, simultaneous communication was fairly effective. Remington and Clarke (1983) compared simultaneous communication with sign-alone training in two learners and found that both were highly effective in increasing sign production and speech comprehension. However, there were no differences between conditions.

In conclusion, manual signing and gestures demonstrate strong intervention effectiveness for symbol acquisition and production, as well as speech comprehension and production. A systematic review by Schwartz and Nye (2006) also supported the effectiveness of manual signing for children with autism in terms of the sign production or speech production. The interventions were manual sign instruction or simultaneous communication. At the same time, Schwartz and Nye (2006) cautioned that there is a shortage of high quality research on manual signing (for a commentary on this review see Brady, 2007). While this seems accurate based on their body of included studies (the latest included study was from 1988), the more recent evidence reviewed here and by Schlosser and Wendt (in press) has yielded some higher quality studies.

Thus, manual signing and gestures represent a very effective communication option for children with autism. This success can be explained in a number of ways. For example, learning manual signs or gestures may be an easier option than speech because many children with autism have difficulty echoing sounds, but they can usually imitate a few fine or gross motor movements demonstrated by their communication partners (Sundberg and Partington, 1998). Also, individuals without a strong vocal imitative repertoire might more readily learn to imitate motor movements than to echo words (Sundberg, 1993). As pointed out by Sundberg and Partington (1998), motor imitation is an easier behavior to teach because the teacher can make use of physical prompting and fading procedures. Unlike with speech, manual sign instruction also benefits from the fact that for many of the signs they strongly resemble the object they represent (Loncke and Bos, 1997). A major drawback of manual signs and gestures, however, relates to the demands it places on the communication partners (Mirenda and Erickson, 2000). Partners who are not skilled in manual signing and/or gestures will have great difficulty understanding the individual with autism who had that training (see Rotholz et al., 1989). Clearly, the learning demands for family members, teachers, classmates, and community members who need to communicate with a child with autism via manual signing or gestures are heavy, if independence from an interpreter is desired. Nevertheless, manual signs and/or gestures can play a significant role as one component of a multimodal communication system that works across different communication environments including partners with and without experience in using manual signs and/or gestures.

FUNCTIONAL COMMUNICATION TRAINING

Functional Communication Training (FCT) is a positive behavioral support intervention that involves the teaching of an appropriate alternative communicative response that serves the same function as the problem behavior (Durand, 1990) (see also Chapter 6 of this book). For example, a child whose self-injurious behavior has been determined to serve an escape function (to get out of difficult tasks) could be taught to sign "break" in order to take a break before returning to the task. There is a strong correlation between the ability to communicate and the prevalence of problem behavior in children with developmental disabilities. That being said, problem behavior is also prevalent in children with autism and other developmental disabilities who are speaking. It is being used with speaking as well as nonspeaking children. As such FCT can be considered a hybrid of the previously discussed speech-based interventions and AAC interventions.

Two recent reviews have dealt with the effectiveness of FCT in individuals with autism (Bopp et al., 2004; Mancil, 2006). An earlier review by Campbell (2003) was highly systematic including six studies on FCT up to 1998, but did not separate analysis for FCT from other positive behavioral interventions. Therefore we will only present the findings from the other two reviews and appraise their quality.

Bopp et al. (2004) identified 16 FCT studies involving 19 children with ASD ranging in chronological age between 3 years and 14 years. Two studies were classified as case studies and one as an AB design (Class III studies) while all others were single-subject experimental designs (Class II studies). The most common single AAC technique used in both school and home settings was manual signing (used with 6 of the 19 participants), followed by picture symbols or line drawings (3 participants), printed words (2 participants), speech generating devices (2 participants), and gestures (1 participant). Instruction was provided outside of the classroom in four of the nine school-based studies

(44.4 percent), in the classroom in three (33.3 percent), and in an unspecified location in the remaining two (22.2 percent). In terms of intervention procedures, prompting/fading, specifically graduated guidance, was the most common technique used to elicit the new communicative behaviors. In the majority of studies, problem behavior was dealt with through extinction, ignoring, and/or immediate redirecting to the new communicative behavior. In all studies, an immediate or gradual substantial reduction in problem behavior was reported, but fewer than half included an evaluation of generalization of the new communicative behavior and only two studies offered maintenance data. The authors conclude that the studies reviewed reflect "moderate clinical certainty" (Miller et al., 1999) with regard to recommendations based on them. Thus, SLPs and others who implement FCT/AAC interventions can be reasonably confident that their efforts are derived from research evidence related to outcomes. Drawing from two sources (Schlosser, 2007; Schlosser et al., 2007), 12 key questions will be asked in order to appraise the review by Bopp et al. (2004).

1. *Was there a Protocol?* A protocol is necessary for the rigorous implementation of a review. No reference was made to a protocol.
2. *Is a Concise Research Question stated?* The presence of a concise question or purpose statement is an indicator that the review represents a systematic effort. This review's self-stated purpose says that it is a tutorial, the aim of which is "to summarize the research regarding the use of FCT/AAC interventions and visual schedule, and to provide suggestions for the roles that speech language pathologists can play . . . " (p. 5). This purpose does not explicitly state that the authors will be drawing conclusions about the effectiveness of FCT interventions even though this is what was done.
3. *Were the inclusion/exclusion criteria complete, sufficiently operationalized, and consistent with the purpose of the review?* The criteria for selecting studies were not reported. For example, although all studies seemed to involve children with ASD, it was unclear whether that was by design or by coincidence (i.e., Were studies with learners with other developmental disabilities without ASD excluded?; Were studies with adults with ASD excluded by design?). The lack of inclusion criteria may explain why three studies involving preexperimental designs were included; because the review draws conclusions about the effectiveness of FCT such designs should have been excluded.
4. *Were the sources searched carefully balanced to minimize source selection bias?* The data sources consulted used to arrive at the selected studies were not reported.
5. *Was the search conducted to minimize database bias?* Because the sources were not specified, most likely the answer to this question is "no."
6. *Was the search strategy appropriate?* The search strategy was not reported.

7. *Was the search designed to minimize publication bias?* Because the search strategy and sources were not reported, most likely the answer is "no."

8. *Was the search comprehensive?* Based on the answers to Questions 4 through 7, the search was not comprehensive.

9. *Was the selection of studies done in a reliable manner?* The reporting of inter-rater agreement data for including and excluding studies did not occur.

10. *Were the data from the studies extracted in a reliable manner?* Although data seem to have been extracted from the original studies rather systematically (as indicative by the tables), there were no inter-rater agreement data reported for data extraction.

11. *Were the criteria to arrive at judgments of effectiveness clearly stated?* Vote count was used for effectiveness judgments in reducing problem behavior; ISR-PB = immediate (within 3 sessions/days) and substantial reduction in identified problem behavior; GSR-PB = gradual and substantial reduction in identified problem behavior. The use of vote count is considered an unreliable method for determining effect size. For instance it is unclear how "substantial reduction" was defined. Given that FCT involves the replacement of problem behavior with appropriate communication it would have been prudent to analyze the effectiveness of the new communicative behavior rather than focusing solely on the reduction of problem behavior.

12. *Were the criteria used to arrive at judgments of quality stated?* The quality of the evidence was appraised in terms of the design hierarchy by the American Academy of Neurology (Miller et al., 1999). While this is positive, quality assessment should involve more than just design considerations such as inter-observer agreement and treatment integrity.

In sum, while the authors may have fallen victim to competing demands within one and the same article (review and tutorial), there are numerous limitations that render this review to be of rather poor transparency and unsystematic. Hence, its conclusions need to be viewed with a healthy dose of skepticism.

Mancil (2006) conducted another review in which he synthesized FCT studies using speech as well as FCT studies using AAC. Drawing from two sources (Schlosser, 2007; Schlosser et al., 2007), 12 key questions will be asked of the systematic review by Mancil (2006).

1. *Was there a Protocol?* A protocol is necessary for the rigorous implementation of a review. Mancil (2006) may have had such a protocol, but he does not make a reference to one being developed and used.

2. *Is a Concise Research Question stated?* The presence of a concise question or purpose statement is an indicator that the review represents a systematic effort. Mancil (2006) states: ". . . the purpose of this

review is to examine functional communication training, particularly, the environments and individuals involved in the training and the effectiveness of FCT with children who have a diagnosis of Autism Spectrum Disorders" (p. 214). Based on this statement it is clear to the reader what the author of this review is trying to accomplish.

3. *Were the inclusion/exclusion criteria complete, sufficiently operationalized, and consistent with the purpose of the review*? Mancil (2006) put forth the following criteria for inclusion in his review: "(a) at least one participant of the study was a child with an autism spectrum disorders diagnosis, (b) the function of the challenging behavior was determined by the functional behavior assessment (FBA) process, and (c) the primary intervention was functional communication training." These criteria specify many important criteria for inclusion. For instance, it is clear that studies in which FCT is combined with another treatment are eligible. Also, only studies involving children (not adults) with ASD qualified. Operational definitions were not provided although both FBA and FCT have been described in the preceding literature review. There were, however, many critical elements missing. For instance, it was not stated whether there were any temporal constraints imposed. Similarly, were there any language constraints imposed? Based on the description of the search (not the inclusion criteria), it appears that only English studies qualified, but this can only be inferred. Finally, the purpose of the study (i.e., "effectiveness of FCT") requires that only those designs be included that can establish cause–effect relations, yet, no such inclusion criterion was stated. In sum, while there were few positive aspects to the inclusion criteria, the overall response to this question was negative.

4. *Were the sources searched carefully balanced to minimize source selection bias*? Potential sources include general-purpose databases, search engines, meta-search engines, professional journals, bibliographies, trial registers, conference proceedings, chapters in books, books, and dissertations and theses. Source selection biases may be introduced through an inappropriate mix of sources such as the exclusive use of general-purpose databases. Mancil (2006) relied on general-purpose databases but also hand searched four journals and examined the bibliographies of retrieved articles for additional studies. Thus, while many sources were not searched, it is fair to say that three of the critical sources were utilized.

5. *Was the search conducted to minimize database bias*? Database bias occurs when the selection of databases consulted by the reviewer is inadequate either in terms of quantity or type. Mancil (2006) searched ERIC, Education, PsycINFO, and Academic Search Premier. It is commendable that four different databases had been searched. The only

others that may have led to further evidence are the Cumulative Index of Nursing and Allied Health Literatures (CINAHL) and Medline.

6. *Was the search strategy appropriate?* Mancil (2006) reported that he used various combinations of the following terms: functional communication training, functional equivalence training, autism, autism spectrum disorder, and communication. These terms certainly seem generally appropriate. However, it is unclear whether these were used as free-text terms or thesaurus-based terms. Because the keywords vary across databases, it would have been advantageous had these been listed for each database along with the specific combinations.

7. *Was the search designed to minimize publication bias?* Publication bias may be introduced when a systematic review relies exclusively on peer-reviewed articles. Mancil (2006) represents such a case because no attempt was made to locate any kind of unpublished studies (e.g., dissertations, theses, conference papers). By excluding unpublished evidence, the reviewer may run the risk of overestimating the yielded effectiveness of an intervention.

8. *Was the search comprehensive?* Based on the answers to Questions 4 through 7, our confidence that the search was comprehensive is not very strong. While there were some positive aspects in the search methodology, overall there were too many shortcomings to convince us fully that the search was indeed comprehensive.

9. *Was the selection of studies done in a reliable manner?* In order to determine reliability of selection, at least two raters should independently code a reasonable percentage of the total number of studies for inclusion into the systematic review? Mancil (2006) appeared to have made these decisions himself.

10. *Were the data from the studies extracted in a reliable manner?* The reader should get an indication that the coding of each study was done reliably. In Mancil's (2006) review all the coding appeared to be completed by the author himself.

11. *Were the criteria to arrive at judgments of effectiveness clearly stated?* These criteria should be stated and operationalized. Mancil (2006) provided tables for the major findings of each study. For the problem behavior results, the tables listed judgments such as the following: "DB [disruptive behavior] decreased to 0.5 percent,"and "Reduction in HF [hand flapping]." The first example seems to be based on the value of the last datapoint in the original study, but it is unknown what the baseline level was. The second example neither indicates the degree of reduction nor the method how this was determined (if any, or whether the results reported by the authors of the original study were taken at face value). For the results on appropriate communicative behavior, examples of judgments are "manding increased," "signing was maintained," and

"communication increased." These examples illustrate similar problems as discussed earlier. Thus, the answer to this question is a clear "no."

12. *Were the criteria used to arrive at judgments of quality stated?* The criteria used to arrive at these quality assessments should be made explicit and defined. Mancil (2006) made explicit that three quality considerations were extracted from each study: research design, reliability, and treatment fidelity. These are very important quality indicators and, therefore, it is commendable to include these as part of data extraction. In terms of research design, the name of the design used was provided in a table and a few examples of the most often used designs were described in the text. Unfortunately, a proper appraisal of the implementation of the designs were lacking. Designs have to be implemented in a certain way in order to establish experimental control and some designs establish better control than others. The designs of all studies appear to be better than preexperimental, alleviating the earlier stated concern about the absence of a design criterion for including studies (see No. 3). It remains unknown whether this was planned or occurred by coincidence. In terms of reliability and treatment fidelity, the results section revealed that all of the included studies reported acceptable levels of fidelity of implementation and "high inter-rater agreement" (p. 221). Subsequently, a few examples of such reliability percentages are listed. Although this speaks highly for the included studies, the reviewer never stated upfront what they considered to be "high reliability" or sound treatment fidelity and what was unacceptable.

In summary, among communication interventions, FCT is one of those few and far between interventions with a critical mass of studies. For instance, Bopp et al. identified 16 studies and Mancil (2006) included 8 studies. Thus, these studies really lend themselves to a systematic review and meta-analyses. Unfortunately, the two reviews discussed here are not adequately transparent and systematic to trust their conclusions. This should not lead the practitioner to conclude that FCT is not an effective method for replacing communication-based problem behaviors. Actually, both reviews arrived at the conclusion that FCT was effective. Based on our knowledge of the individual studies it is fairly safe for us to say that it is rather a shortcoming in the systematic review methodology employed than any question about the effectiveness of FCT in individual studies.

SUMMARY

Due to core deficits in communication, social interaction, and language, children on the autism spectrum are likely candidates for communication inter-vention. In this chapter, we aimed to synthesize the evidence on communication interventions, in particular at the beginning stages of communication. Interven-tions were grouped into speech-based interventions, milieu-based interventions, communication partner interventions, social interaction interventions, AAC interventions, and FCT. Whenever available, we have relied on systematic reviews of the evidence before less systematic reviews before individual studies. Hence, practitioners can feel confident that the interventions discussed represent the current best practice in beginning and early communication intervention for children with ASD.

REFERENCES

Aldred, C., Green, J., and Adams, C. (2004). A new social communication intervention for children with autism: a pilot randomized controlled treatment study suggesting effectiveness. *Journal of Child Psychology and Psychiatry*, **45**, 1420–1430.

American Psychiatric Association (1994): *Diagnostic and Statistical Manual of Mental Disorders* (4th edition). Washington DC, American Psychiatric Association.

Anderson, A.E. (2001). *Augmentative Communication and Autism: A Comparison of Sign Language and the Picture Exchange Communication System*. Unpublished doctoral dissertation, University of California, San Diego.

Angermeier, K., Schlosser, R.W., Luiselli, J.K., et al. (2006). *Effects of Iconicity on Symbol Learning with the Picture Exchange Communication System in Children with Autism Spectrum Disorders*. Manuscript under review.

Barrera, R.D., Lobato-Barrera, D., and Sulzer-Azaroff, B. (1980). A simultaneous treatment comparison of three expressive language training programs with a mute autistic child. *Journal of Autism and Developmental Disorders*, **10**, 21–37.

Beck, A.R., Stoner, J.B., Bock, S.J., and Parton, T. (in press). Comparison of PECS and the use of a VOCA: A Replication. Education and Training in Developmental Disabilities.

Blischak, D.M., Lloyd, L.L., and Fuller, D.R. (1997). In *Augmentative and Alternative Communication: A Handbook of Principles and Practices* (L.L. Lloyd, D.R. Fuller, and H.H. Arvidson, eds.) pp. 38–42. Needham Heights, MA: Allyn and Bacon.

Bock, S.J., Stoner, J.B., Beck, A.R., Hanley, L. and Prochnow, J. (2005). Increasing functional communication in non-speaking preschool children: comparison of PECS and VOCA. *Education and Training in Developmental Disabilities*, **40**, 264–278.

Bopp, K.D., Brown, K.E., and Mirenda, P. (2004). Speech-language pathologists' roles in the delivery of positive behavior support for individuals with developmental disabilities. *American Journal of Speech-Language Pathology*, **13**, 5–19.

Brady, D.O. and Smouse, A.D. (1978). A simultaneous comparison of three methods for language training with an autistic child: An experimental single case analysis. *Journal of Autism and Childhood Schizophrenia*, **8**, 271–279.

Brady, N.C. (2007). Data seem to support manual sign interventions for children with autism, but more high-quality research is needed [Abstract]. *Evidence-Based Communication Assessment and Intervention*, **1**, 16–17. Abstract of Schwartz, J.B. and Nye, C. (2006). A systematic review, synthesis, and evaluation of the evidence for teaching sign language to children with autism. *EBP Briefs*, **1**, 1–17.

Buckley, S.D. and Newchok, D.K. (2005). Differential impact of response effort within a response chain on use of mands in a student with autism. *Research in Developmental Disabilities*, **26**, 77–85.

Buffington, D.M., Krantz, P.J., McClannahan, L.E., and Poulson, C.L. (1998). Procedures for teaching appropriate gestural communication skills to children with autism. *Journal of Autism and Developmental Disorders*, **28**, 535–545.

Campbell, J.M. (2003). Efficacy of behavioral interventions for reducing problem behaviors in persons with autism: a quantitative synthesis of single-subject research. *Research in Developmental Disabilities*, **24**, 120–138.

Carr, E.G. and Dores, P. (1981). Patterns of language acquisition following simultaneous communication with autistic children. *Analysis and Intervention in Developmental Disabilities*, **1**, 347–361.

Carr, D. and Felce, J. (2006a). The effects of PECS teaching to phase III on the communicative interactions between children with autism and their teachers. *Journal of Autism and Developmental Disorders*, DOI 10.1007/s10803–006–0203–1. Published on-line www.springerlink.com, September 28, 2006.

Carr, D. and Felce, J. (2006b). Brief report: Increase in production of spoken words in some children with autism after PECS teaching to Phase III. *Journal of Autism and Developmental Disorders*, DOI 10.1007/s10803–006–0204–0. Published on-line, www.springerlink.com, September 21, 2006.

Carr, E.G., Binkoff, J.A., Kologinsky, E., and Eddy, M. (1978). Acquisition of sign language by autistic children. I: Expressive labeling. *Journal of Applied Behavior Analysis*, **11**, 489–501.

Carr, E.G. and Kemp, D.C. (1989). Functional equivalence of autistic leading and communicative pointing: Analysis and treatment. *Journal of Autism and Developmental Disorders*, **19**, 561–578.

Carr, E.G. and Kologinsky, E. (1983). Acquisition of sign language by autistic children II: Spontaneity and generalization effects. *Journal of Applied Behavior Analysis*, **16**, 297–314.

Carr, E.G., Kologinsky, E., and Leff-Simon, S. (1987). Acquisition of sign language by autistic children III: Generalized descriptive phrases. *Journal of Autism and Developmental Disorders*, **17**, 217–229.

Charlop-Christy, M., Carpenter, M., Le, L., et al. (2002). Using the Picture Exchange Communication System (PECS) with children with autism: Assessment of PECS acquisition, speech, social-communicative behavior, and problem behavior. *Journal of Applied Behavior Analysis*, **35**, 213–231.

Dettmer, S., Simpson, R.L., Smith Myles, B., and Ganz, J. (2000). The use of visual supports to facilitate transitions of students with autism. *Focus on Autism and Other Developmental Disabilities*, **15**, 163–169.

Dexter, M.E. (1998). *The Effects of Aided Language Stimulation upon Verbal Output and Augmentative Communication During Storybook Reading for Children with Pervasive Developmental Disabilities*. Unpublished doctoral dissertation, The Johns Hopkins University, Baltimore.

Drew, A., Baird, G., Baron-Cohen, S., Cox, A., et al. (2002). A pilot randomized controlled trial of a parent training intervention for preschool children with autism. *European Child and Adolescent Psychiatry*, **11**, 266–272.

Durand, V.M. (1990). *Severe Behavior Problems: A Functional Communication Training Approach*. New York: Guilford Press.

Dyches, T.T. (1998). Effects of switch training on the communication of children with autism and severe disabilities. *Focus on Autism and other Developmental Disabilities*, **13**, 151–162.

Frea, W.D., Arnold, C.L., and Wittinberga, G.L. (2001). A demonstration of the effects of augmentative communication on the extreme aggressive behavior of a child with autism within an integrated preschool setting. *Journal of Positive Behavior Interventions*, **3**, 194–198.

Foxx, R.M., McMorrow, M.J., Faw, G.D., et al. (1987). Cues-pause-point language training: Structuring trainer statements to students with correct answers to questions. *Behavioral Residential Treatment*, **2**, 103–115.

Frost, L.A. and Bondy, A.S. (2002). *The Picture Exchange Communication System Training Manual* (2nd ed.). Newark, DE: Pyramid Educational Consultants, Inc.

Ganz, J.B. and Simpson, R.L. (2004). Effects on communicative requesting and speech development of the Picture Exchange Communication System in children with characteristics of autism. *Journal of Autism and Developmental Disorders*, **34**, 395–409.

Ganz, J.B., Simpson, R.L., and Corbin-Newsome, J. (2007). The impact of the Picture Exchange Communication System on requesting and speech development in preschoolers with autism spectrum disorders and similar characteristics. *Research in Autism Spectrum Disorders*, doi:10.1016/j.rasd.2007.04.005, published on-line, www.sciencedirect.com, May 25, 2007.

Goldstein, H. (2002). Communication intervention for children with autism: A review of treatment efficacy. *Journal of Autism and Developmental Disorders*, **32**, 373–396.

Hamilton, B.L. and Snell, M.E. (1993). Using the milieu approach to increase communication book use across environments by an adolescent with autism. *Augmentative and Alternative Communication*, **9**, 259–272.

Hetzroni, O.E. and Shalem, U. (2005). From logos to orthographic symbols: A multilevel fading computer program for teaching nonverbal children with autism. *Focus on Autism and Other Developmental Disabilities*, **20**, 201–212.

Hundert, J. (1981). Stimulus generalization after training an autistic deaf boy in manual signs. *Education and Treatment of Children*, **4**, 329–337.

Johnston, S., Nelson, C., Evans, J., and Palazolo, K. (2003). The use of visual supports in teaching young children with autism spectrum disorder to initiate interactions. *Augmentative and Alternative Communication*, **19**, 86–103.

Keogh, D., Whitman, T., Beeman, D., et al. (1987). Teaching interactive signing in a dialogue situation to mentally retarded individuals. *Research in Developmental Disabilities*, **8**, 39–53.

Kozleski, E. (1991). Visual symbol acquisition by students with autism. *Exceptionality*, **2**, 173–194.

Kravits, T.R., Kamps, D.M., Kemmerer, K., and Potucek, J. (2002). Increasing communication skills for an elementary-aged student with autism using the Picture Exchange Communication System. *Journal of Autism and Developmental Disorders*, **32**, 225–230.

Liddle, K. (2001). Implementing the Picture Exchange Communication System (PECS). *International Journal of Language and Communication Disorders*, **36** *(Suppl.)*, 391–395.

Lloyd, L.L., Fuller, D.R., and Arvidson, H.H. (Eds.) (1997). *Augmentative and Alternative Communication: A Handbook of Principles and Practices*. Needham Heights, MA: Allyn & Bacon.

Loncke, F. and Bos, H. (1997). Unaided AAC symbols. In *Augmentative and Alternative Communication: A Handbook of Principles and Practices* (L.L. Lloyd, D.R. Fuller, and H.H. Arvidson, eds.) pp. 80–106. Needham Heights, MA: Allyn and Bacon.

Lovaas, O.I. (1977). *The Autistic Child: Language Development Through Behavior Modification.* New York: Irvington Publishers.

Lovaas, O.I. (1987). Behavioral treatment and normal educational and intellectual functioning in young autistic children. *Journal of Consulting and Clinical Psychology*, **55**, 3–9.

Lovaas, O.I., Berberich, J.P., Perloff, B.F., and Schaeffer, B. (1966). Acquisition of imitative speech by schizophrenic children. *Science*, **151**, 705–707.

Loveland, K.A., Landry, S.H., Hughes, S.O., et al. (1988). Speech acts and the pragmatic deficits of autism. *Journal of Speech and Hearing Research*, **31**, 593–604.

Magiati, I. and Howlin, P. (2003). A pilot evaluation study of the Picture Exchange Communication System (PECS) for children with autistic spectrum disorders. *Autism*, **7**, 297–320.

Mancil, G.R. (2006). Functional communication training: A review of the literature related to children with autism. *Education and Training and Developmental Disabilities*, **41**, 213–224.

Marckel, J.M., Neef, N.A., and Ferreri, S.J. (2006). A preliminary analysis of teaching improvisation with the Picture Exchange Communication System to children with autism. *Journal of Applied Behavior Analysis*, **39**, 109–115.

McConachie, H. and Diggle, T. (2007). Parent implemented early intervention for young children with autism spectrum disorder: A systematic review. *Journal of Evaluation of Clinical Practice*, **13**, 120–129.

McConnell, S.R. (2002). Interventions to facilitate social interaction for young children with autism: Review of available research and recommendations for educational intervention and future research. *Journal of Autism and Developmental Disorders*, **32**, 351–372.

McMorrow, M.J. and Foxx, R.M. (1986). Some direct and generalized effects of replacing an autistic man's echolalia with correct responses to questions. *Journal of Applied Behavior Analysis*, **19**, 289–297.

McMorrow, M.J., Foxx, R.M., Faw, G.D., and Bittle, R.G. (1987). Cues-pause-point language training: Teaching echolalics functional use of their verbal labeling repertoires. *Journal of Applied Behavior Analysis*, **20**, 11–22.

Miguel, C.F., Carr, J.E., Michael, J. (2002). The effects of a stimulus-stimulus pairing procedure on the vocal behavior of children diagnosed with autism. *The Analysis of Verbal Behavior*, **18**, 3–13.

Miller, R.G., Rosenberg, J.A., Gelinas, D.F., et al. (1999). Practice parameter: The care of the patient with amyotrophic lateral sclerosis (an evidence-based review): Report of the Quality Standards Subcommittee of the American Academy of Neurology. *Neurology*, **52**, 1311–1323.

Mirenda, P. and Erickson, K.A. (2000). Augmentative communication and literacy. In *Autism Spectrum Disorders: A Transactional Developmental Perspective* (A.M. Wetherby and B.M. Prizant, eds.) pp. 333–367. Baltimore: Paul H. Brookes Publishing Co.

Mirenda, P. and Schuler, A. (1988). Augmenting communication for persons with autism: Issues and strategies. *Topics in Language Disorders*, **9**, 24–43.

Odom, S.L., Brown, W.H., Frey, T., et al. (2003). Evidence-based practices for young children with autism: Contribution for single-subject design research. *Focus on Autism and Other Developmental Disabilities*, **18**, 166–175.

Olive, M., de la Cruz, B., Davis, T.N., et al. (2006). The effects of enhanced milieu teaching and a voice output communication aid on the requesting of three children with autism. *Journal of Autism and Developmental Disorders*. DOI 10.1007/s10803–006–0243–6.

Parsons, C.L. and La Sorte, D. (1993). The effect of computers with synthesized speech and no speech on the spontaneous communication of children with autism. *Australian Journal of Human Communication Disorders*, **21**, 12–31.

Peeters, T. and Gillberg, C. (1999). *Autism: Medical and Educational Aspects*. London: Whurr.

Petticrew, M. and Roberts, H. (2006). *Systematic Reviews in the Social Sciences: A Practical Guide*. Malden, MA: Blackwell Publishing Co.

Probst, P. (2005). "Communication unbound – or unfound"? – An integrative review on the effectiveness of Facilitated Communication (FC) in nonverbal persons with autism and mental retardation. *Zeitschrift für Klinische Psychologie, Psychiatrie und Psychotherapie*, **53**, 93–128.

Remington, B. and Clarke, S. (1983). Acquisition of expressive signing by autistic children: An evaluation of the relative effects of simultaneous communication and sign-alone training. *Journal of Applied Behavior Analysis*, **16**, 315–328.

Rotholz, D.A., Berkowitz, S.F., and Burberry, J. (1989). Functionality of two modes of communication in the community by students with developmental disabilities. A comparison of signing and communication books. *Journal of the Association for Persons with Severe Handicaps*, **14**, 227–233.

Saraydarian, K.A. (1994). *Simultaneous Referent Recognition-Production Training for Nonverbal Children with Autism*. Unpublished doctoral dissertation, Columbia University Teachers College, New York, New York.

Schepis, M.M., Reid, D.H., Behrmann, M.M., and Sutton, K.A. (1998). Increasing communicative interactions of young children with autism using a voice output communication aid and naturalistic teaching. *Journal of Applied Behavior Analysis*, **31**, 561–578.

Schepis, M.M., Reid, D.H., Fitzgerald, J.R., et al. (1982). A program for increasing manual signing by autistic and profoundly retarded youth within the daily environment. *Journal of Applied Behavior Analysis*, **15**, 363–379.

Schlosser, R.W. (2007). Appraising the quality of systematic reviews. *Focus: Technical Brief No. 17*, 1–8.

Schlosser, R.W. and Blischak, D.M. (2004). Effects of speech and print feedback on spelling in children with autism. *Journal of Speech, Language and Hearing Research*, **47**, 848–862.

Schlosser, R.W., Blischak, D.M., Belfiore, P.J., et al (1998). The effects of synthetic speech output and orthographic feedback on spelling in a student with autism: A preliminary study. *Journal of Autism and Developmental Disorders*, **28**, 319–329.

Schlosser, R.W. and Sigafoos, J. (2002). Selecting graphic symbols for an initial request lexicon: Integrative review. *Augmentative and Alternative Communication*, **18**, 102–123.

Schlosser, R.W., Sigafoos, J., Rothschild, N., et al. (2007). Speech and language disorders. In *A Comprehensive Guide to Intellectual and Developmental Disabilities* (I. Brown, and M. Percy, eds.) pp. 383–400. Baltimore: Paul H. Brookes Publishing Co.

Schlosser, R.W. and Wendt, O. (in press). Augmentative and alternative communication interventions for children with autism. In *Effective Practices for Children with Autism: Educational and Behavior Support Interventions that Work* (J.K. Luiselli, Dennis C. Russo, and Walter P. Christian, eds.) pp. TBD. Oxford University Press.

Schlosser, R.W., Wendt, O., and Sigafoos, J. (2007). Not all systematic reviews are created equal: Considerations for appraisal. *Evidence-Based Communication Assessment and Intervention*, **1**, 138–150.

Schwartz, I.S., Garfinkle, A.N., and Bauer, J. (1998). The Picture Exchange Communication System: communicative outcomes for young children with disabilities. *Topics in Early Childhood Special Education*, **18**, 144–159.

Schwartz, J.B. and Nye, C. (2006). A systematic review, synthesis, and evaluation of the evidence for teaching sign language to children with autism. *EBP Briefs*, **1**, 1–17.

Sidener, T.M., Shabani, D.B., Carr, J.E., and Roland, J.P. (2005). An evaluation of strategies to maintain mands at practical levels. *Research in Developmental Disabilities*, **27**, 632–644.

Sigafoos, J. (1998). Assessing conditional use of graphic mode requesting in a young boy with autism. *Journal of Developmental and Physical Disabilities*, **10**, 133–151.

Sigafoos, J., Didden, R., and O'Reilly, M. (2003). Effects of speech output on maintenance of requesting and frequency of vocalizations in three children with developmental disabilities. *Augmentative and Alternative Communication*, **19**, 37–47.

Sigafoos, J., Drasgow, E., Halle, J.W., et al. (2004). Teaching VOCA use as a communicative repair strategy. *Journal of Autism and Developmental Disorders*, **34**, 411–422.

Sommer, K.S., Whitman, T.L., and Keogh, D.A. (1988). Teaching severely retarded persons to sign interactively through the use of a behavioral script. *Journal in Developmental Disabilities*, **9**, 291–304.

Son, S.H., Sigafoos, J., O'Reilly, M., and Lancioni, G.E. (2006). Comparing two types of augmentative and alternative communication for children with autism. *Pediatric Rehabilitation*, **9**, 389–395.

Spencer, L.G. (2002). *Comparing the Effectiveness of Static Pictures vs. Video Modeling on Teaching Requesting Skills to Elementary Children with Autism*. Unpublished doctoral dissertation, Georgia State University, Atlanta.

Spillane, M.M. (1999). *The Effect of Instructional Method on Symbol Acquisition by Students with Severe Disabilities*. Unpublished doctoral dissertation, University of Nebraska, Lincoln, USA.

Sundberg, M.L. (1993). Selecting a response form for nonverbal persons: Facilitated communication, pointing systems, or sign language? *The Analysis of Verbal Behavior*, **11**, 99–116.

Sundberg, M.L., Michael, J., Partington, J.W., and Sundberg, C.A. (1996). The role of automatic reinforcement in early language acquisition. *The Analysis of Verbal Behavior*, **13**, 21–37.

Sundberg, M. and Partington, J. (1998). *Teaching Language to Children with Autism or Other Developmental Disabilities* (Version 7.1) [Computer manual]. Pleasant Hill, CA: Behavior Analysts.

Tincani, M. (2004). Comparing the picture exchange communication system (PECS) and sign-language training for children with autism. *Focus on Autism and other Developmental Disabilities*, **19**, 152–163.

Tincani, M., Crozier, S., and Alazetta, L. (2006). The Picture Exchange Communication System: Effects on manding and speech development for school-aged children with autism. *Education and Training in Developmental Disabilities*, **41**, 177–184.

Travis, J. (2006). *The Effectiveness of the Picture Exchange Communication System (PECS) as an Augmentative Communication System for Children with Autism Spectrum Disorders (ASD): A South African Pilot Study*. Unpublished Master's thesis, University of Cape Town, Cape Town, South Africa.

Wendt, O. (2006). *The Effectiveness of Augmentative and Alternative Communication for Individuals with Autism Spectrum Disorders: A Systematic Review and Meta-analysis*. Unpublished doctoral dissertation, Purdue University, West Lafayette, IN.

Yoder, P.J. and Stone, W.L. (2006a). A randomized comparison of the effect of two prelinguistic communication interventions on the acquisition of spoken communication in preschoolers with ASD. *Journal of Speech, Language, and Hearing Research*, **49**, 698–711.

Yoder, P. and Stone, W. (2006b). Randomized comparison of two communication interventions for preschoolers with Autism Spectrum Disorders. *Journal of Consulting and Clinical Psychology*, **74**, 426–435.

Yokoyama, K., Naoi, N., and Yakamoto, J.-I. (2006). Teaching verbal behavior using the Picture Exchange Communication System (PECS) with children with autism spectrum disorders. *Japanese Journal or Special Education*, **43**, 485–503.

Yoon, S. and Bennett, G.M. (2000). Effects of a stimulus-stimulus pairing procedure on conditioning vocal sounds as reinforcers. *The Analysis of Verbal Behavior*, **17**, 75–88.

11

TEACHING ADAPTIVE
SKILLS TO PEOPLE WITH
AUTISM

KAREN SHERIDAN AND TROY RAFFIELD

Pinecrest Developmental Center, Pineville, LA, USA

INTRODUCTION

Considering the emphasis on integration of persons with autism and other developmental disabilities into community settings, it is important for treatment providers to focus their interventions on skills that can promote independence and facilitate community placement. Skill acquisition in the domain of adaptive functioning is particularly important when considering transition to community-based living. One unpublished study reported that staff ratings on factors related to people's group home placement success were significantly predicted by IQ score and the adaptive behavior composite (ABC) score of the Vineland Adaptive Behavior Scales (VABS). Staff ratings for people's success living in supervised apartment placement were predicted by number of psychotropic medications, age, gender, and ABC score on the VABS (Sheridan and Campbell, 2004). In addition, adaptive skills can be associated with quality of life factors. For example, one study found that level of daily living skills positively predicted life circumstances as assessed on eight life areas such as material well-being, physical well-being, community access, daily routines, choice opportunities, contact with family and friends, residential well-being, and general information (Vine and Hamilton, 2005). Therefore, adaptive skills training is an important contribution to success in community placement, promotion of integration into the community, and quality of life for people.

Deficits in adaptive behavior are often associated with the diagnosis of autism. For example, one study compared the adaptive functioning of people with autism/PDD to a group of participants diagnosed with a psychotic disorder or behavior problems with similar levels of intellectual disabilities as the group with autism. The participants diagnosed with autism/PDD were found to have lower levels of social and adaptive skills as compared to the two other groups (Matson et al., 2003); therefore, interventions targeting this domain of skills are especially crucial to this population.

When selecting adaptive interventions for people with pervasive developmental disorders or autism, several factors should be taken into consideration. People with autism may show relative strengths in the areas of concrete thinking, rote memory, and understanding of visuo-spatial relationships, but relative weaknesses in the areas of abstract thinking, social cognition, and communication (Quill, 1995). Data from cognitive assessments show that children with autism perform better on tasks involving form discrimination, matching, copying exact duplications, and puzzle assembly (DeMyer, 1975). People with autism display memory skills, such as immediate rote memory, cued recall, and paired-associative learning (Boucher, 1981; Prior, 1979; Sigman et al., 1987). However, Boucher (1981) found that children with autism showed significantly poorer performance on a recent events memory (REM) task as compared to a matched group (on age, sex, and nonverbal mental age) of participants with intellectual disabilities and a group of matched peers (on age and sex) who functioned at a normal level.

Another consideration when structuring an adaptive training intervention with people with autism is stimulus overselectivity. Stimulus overselectivity is a term that was introduced in 1971 to describe the problems this group has with responding to multiple cues in the environment; therefore, they were more likely to selectively respond to only a limited number of cues (Lovaas and Schreibman, 1971; Lovaas et al., 1979). However, in later studies, this phenomenon was also found with other groups such as people with intellectual disability and has been associated with mental age in some research (Lovaas et al., 1979). Stimulus overselectivity has been identified as a possible reason why some children treated with behavior modification methods show treatment effects that are reversible, context-specific, and slow in progression; therefore, making generalization of interventions more difficult (Lovaas et al., 1973).

It is important that adaptive skills training programs selected by clinicians address the challenges and use the strengths associated with this population. Some common methods of instruction in adaptive skills and the possible advantages and/or disadvantages to their use with persons with autism will be discussed.

APPLIED BEHAVIOR ANALYSIS

Applied behavior analysis is an approach to influencing socially important behavior by utilizing principles of behavior modification discovered through decades of laboratory and applied research. Applied behavior analysts very much consider themselves 'applied behavioral scientists' in that they emphasize the importance of a scientific approach to understanding and influencing human behavior. Centrally important practices include: hypothesis generation and testing, examination of objective data, use of operational definitions, experimental control, and replication of results (Baer et al., 1968; Cooper et al., 2007). Common procedural tools of the applied behavior analyst include the delivery of reinforcing or punishing consequences contingent upon a certain response, task analysis, modeling, role-playing, fading of prompts, and chaining. Not surprisingly, much of the research on training adaptive behavior skills makes use of such interventions.

Applied behavior analysis has demonstrated a substantial amount of empirical support when used in training communication skills with children with autism (Lovaas, 1987; Cohen et al., 2006; Sallows and Graupner, 2005). In a classic study by Lovaas (1987), trained therapists used a discrete trial teaching style, involving reinforcement and fading of prompts, in instructing a group of children with autism. Following an intensive treatment phase (40 hours per week for two or more years), forty-seven percent of the participants scored within the normal range on an IQ test.

Although applied behavior analysis has shown success when used in treatment of people with autism, problems with generalization have been noted (Horner et al., 1988). There are also concerns in some applied settings with respect to the degree of expertise and amount of staff time that are required for proper implementation of intensive procedures that have been shown to be effective in published research. Moreover, punitive procedures may not be consistent with the implementation of the positive behavior support philosophy of service delivery to persons with developmental disabilities that many facilities have adopted.

The positive behavior support approach represents a confluence of three major factors: applied behavior analysis, the normalization movement, and person-centered values. The positive behavior support approach emphasizes behavioral methods that prevent problem behavior rather than consequential methods that are implemented following the behavior. This approach also promotes the ideal that people with intellectual disabilities should be living in the same settings and given the same opportunities as other people. In addition, this approach supports the idea that treatment strategies should not only be judged on their efficacy, but on how they enhance choice opportunities and personal dignity of the people for which they are used. Because this method emphasizes ecological validity, interventions often teach adaptive skills in a classroom setting and generalize this training to the home and community settings (Carr et al., 2002).

TASK ANALYSIS

A common method for teaching various adaptive skills is the utilization of task analysis (Horner and Keilitz, 1975). To develop a task analysis, a target skill must be broken down into smaller components and listed as steps in the number of their occurrence in performing the skill (Sulzer-Azaroff and Mayer, 1977).

This method can be especially advantageous for use in people with autism and intellectual disabilities because it can be individualized according to the skill level of the trainee. Task analysis involves breaking tasks into smaller, more digestible parts making trainees less overwhelmed by the task; therefore, this method may help with stimulus overselectivity often associated with autism. Finally, once a task analysis of a skill is developed, the skill can be taught via forward or backward chaining methodology (Matson et al., 1996).

VISUALLY CUED INSTRUCTION

Visually cued instruction seems to be a favorable method of teaching people with autism and can be used in combination with task analysis. For example, children exposed to visual displays of task analyses are able to learn and maintain the skills with less reliance on trainer prompting than skills taught without visual cues (Quill, 1995). Some research has shown that when visual cues are used with a prompt hierarchy to teach daily living skills, participants have shown to improve acquisition, generalization, and maintenance of these skills (Pierce and Screibman, 1994).

Visual cues have been used successfully to develop interventions for people with autism within the communication domain. For example, the picture exchange communication system (PECS), which utilizes picture cues to facilitate communication, has been shown in some studies to increase verbal speech in children with autism (Charlop-Christy et al., 2002; Kravits et al., 2002; Ganz and Simpson, 2004). In addition, photographic activity schedules have been used to help children with autism demonstrate the ability to independently change activities and perform daily living skills without immediate supervision (MacDuff et al., 1993; Pierce and Schreibman, 1994). Use of visual cues in treatment of people with autism seems to capitalize on their strengths, such as concrete thinking, and has been shown to promote generalization.

Computers are beginning to be used as a mode of delivering visual instructions of task analyses to trainees. For example, one study used a palm-top computer to store information regarding one or two selected tasks. Pictorial representations of each step of the task were presented on the screen. The computer had a latency function that required a certain interval of time before a new step instruction could be presented. In addition, prompt and reinforcement functions were provided. In this study, the computer-based system was compared to a card-based system. Most participants reported a preference for using the computer-based system and, overall, exhibited a higher level of correct performance of the tasks when using the computer-based system than when using the card-based system (Lancioni et al., 1998). Although the computer-based instruction system makes use of concrete cues which may be helpful in training a person with autism, this type of assistive device may be costly and somewhat difficult to use, especially for those whose functioning falls toward the lower end of the spectrum.

MODELING

PEER/ADULT

The utilization of "peer models" to instruct persons with autism to perform adaptive skills is based on the notion of observational learning (Bandura, 1969). According to this notion, various skills can be learned vicariously, through observation and performance of that skill by a typical peer, or normal functioning counterpart. Subsequently, the trainee is allowed an opportunity to imitate or reproduce the skill they had observed (Robertson and Biederman, 1989). Egel et al. (1981) found that the use of normal peer models improved responding of four children with autism on five different discrimination tasks. In addition, another study found that typical peer models were able to influence voice loudness and increase labeling vocabulary of children with autism (Coleman and Stedman, 1974). One study with a group of students with intellectual disabilities successfully used another peer with an intellectual disability to serve as a skill trainer (Wacker and Berg, 1989). However, results of the use of this intervention may be dependent upon level of functioning. Results of a study by Varni et al. (1979) indicated that children with autism who functioned at the lower end of the spectrum were only able to learn a subset of responses modeled by adults. Considering these results, stimulus overselectivity may be more problematic in children with autism who have more severe intellectual disabilities and they may not be able to learn as readily by observation. However, matching the "model" used in training to the trainee's age and gender has been shown to directly impact the chances of the "model" being imitated by the trainee (Bandura et al., 1963; Rosekrans, 1967).

VIDEOTAPE

The use of videotape modeling in training of daily living skills is also based on the principle of observation learning. However, the "model" used in this modality is videotaped performing the skill, instead of a live performance, and the tape is subsequently shown to the trainee. Once the trainee has viewed the videotape, he or she is given the opportunity to imitate the skill performed in the video clip (Shipley-Benamou et al., 2002). A variant of video tape modeling training is known as video prompting. With video prompting, trainees view one individual step in the task analysis, the video is stopped, and trainees are immediately given an opportunity to perform that step before they view the next step on the video (Sigafoos et al., 2005).

Several advantages exist to video modeling as a teaching method for children with autism. For example, this procedure may counteract the effects of stimulus overselectivity (Koegel et al., 1989). Because a video requires a person to only attend to a small spatial area (television monitor) and a minimum amount of language, children may be more obliged to attend to the message (Sherer et al., 2001). Another advantage to this method is the decreased need for an adult to facilitate the learning process. Finally, motivation may also be increased due to the viewing of a video being a low-demand task and watching television seems to be enjoyable to most people. A potential drawback to this methodology occurs in the area of generalization such as that gains may not be present once the trainer (or video viewing of the trainer) is removed (Horner et al., 1988).

SELF-MODELING

Self-modeling is a method that uses the video representation of the trainee engaging in the task that is being trained. A self-modeling video is usually produced by having a trainee perform the skill being trained as proficiently as possible (usually with incentives, rehearsal, etc.) and then editing out any errors or distractions. Similar forms of self-observation can be done with other modalities, such as audiotapes, imagination, role-play, or photographs presented in serial order (Dowrick, 1999). This type of intervention would share the advantages and disadvantages of video modeling, but it would also present a unique advantage to people with autism. Because generalization is particularly challenging with this population, watching themselves perform the target skill may make generalization easier as it eliminates the need to "transfer" the skill from model to trainee.

NATURAL, SIMULATED, OR VIRTUAL ENVIRONMENTS

When training adaptive skills, clinicians may want to consider making the training setting as comparable to the environment in which the skill will most likely be applied in real life. Therefore, the most obvious choice may be to train skills in the natural environment. Interventions in the natural environment provide in vivo opportunities for people with developmental disabilities to learn a skill. The main benefit to this type of training is that skills are taught under the actual circumstances that would be encountered in the real world; therefore, there are no problems with the transfer of stimulus control often associated with simulated methods (Bates et al., 2001). Some evidence has shown that in vivo training may be more effective than simulated instruction (Bates et al., 2001; Coon et al., 1981). Because this procedure does not have the "transfer" problems of so many other treatments, it may be especially advantageous for the autism population. However, other problems must be considered regarding this method such as cost, transportation issues, scheduling, and consequences of errors during training.

To address the challenges presented by training in the natural environment, simulated environments were developed for use in the instruction of community skills with people with developmental disabilities. For example, instruction is often held in a classroom-type setting that has been designed to approximate the natural stimulus conditions and behavioral topographies frequently encountered in real world settings. Support for this method of instruction has been varied in the research literature. Some studies have shown positive results, while others have found this intervention to be ineffective or not as successful as training in the naturalistic setting (Neef et al., 1978; Shafer et al., 1986; McDonnell et al., 1984; Morrow and Bates, 1987). The advantages of simulation are the reduced cost, more opportunities for practice of the selected skill, reduced social consequences for trainee's mistakes, and less conflict with school scheduling (Nietupski et al., 1986). However, this type of intervention may be problematic for implementation with the autism population. Because of stimulus overselectivity, they may not be as likely to generalize skills learned in a simulated setting to a real world setting. However, some research has shown that persons with mild intellectual disability may be more successful in generalizing skills learned in simulation instruction to a community setting than persons with moderate intellectual disability (Bates et al., 2001). Considering these results, people with autism, who function at a high level, may be better candidates for this type of instruction.

Virtual environments (VEs) are three-dimensional, computer-generated environments that allow the user to experience the environment in "real time", as if he/she were actually walking through the scene in real life (Parsons et al., 2004). Some studies have noted that persons with autism spectrum disorders were able to understand and use virtual environments. For example, Parson et al. (2004) found that participants with autism spectrum disorders demonstrated a basic understanding of the virtual environment as a depiction of the real world. However, these individuals were more likely to bump into, or walk between, other people in the virtual environment as compared with other participants that had been matched to them on VIQ and PIQ scores. In addition, another study found that two children with autism complied with wearing a virtual reality helmet, were able to identify recognizable objects and characteristics of the objects in their environment while using the helmet, and were able to find and approach objects in their environment while using the helmet (Strickland et al., 1996).

Training that utilizes virtual reality may be helpful in addressing some of the challenges of providing training in the natural environment. Virtual environments can be manipulated in ways real world environments cannot and be structured according to the individual's needs. For example, virtual environments can be designed to be a simple construction of the real world environment and, as the individual masters the skill being trained, can become more complex such as it would be in the natural environment. Virtual environments can be structured to highlight important characteristics of the task for the trainee, or a virtual tutor can assist throughout the task. Virtual environments have been recommended for use in training individuals with autism. The above features may be beneficial in promoting flexibility and generalization of skills and reducing stimulus overselectivity in this population. Because individuals with autism may have limited language skills, virtual environments may be helpful in communicating rules and abstract concepts without using language (Parsons and Mitchell, 2002). However, this method of training is not without its drawbacks. For example, the "fully-immersive system" version of virtual reality, which includes head-mounted displays, are very expensive and heavy which may cause users to experience "cybersickness," characterized by symptoms of nausea, headaches, and dizziness (Cobb et al., 1999). To avoid these problems, desktop versions of virtual environments may be used which only require a joystick and a mouse, and are less likely to elicit symptoms of "cybersickness" (Nichols, 1999).

CONSTANT TIME DELAY (CTD)

Constant time delay (CTD) is described as a response prompting method. When applied, a controlling prompt is faded according to an interval of time until the stimulus control (e.g. task request) is transferred to the discriminative stimulus. In the beginning of this application, zero-second time delay trials are presented in which the controlling prompt is given immediately following the discriminative stimulus. After these trials, the prompt is delivered after a selected time interval has passed (e.g. 3, 4, or 5 sec.). This interval stays the same throughout the remaining trials until mastery is achieved (Touchette, 1971). This method has been shown to be effective with the autism population in training skills (Ault et al., 1988; Yilmaz et al., 2005). Because the prompts are eventually faded, this may promote generalization of skills with this group.

SELF-MANAGEMENT

Another method of instruction utilized alone and in conjunction with other modalities of training adaptive skills is self-management. Self-management programs are usually characterized by self-evaluation of performance, self-monitoring, self-selection of reinforcers, and self-delivery of reinforcers. The goal of these programs is to teach trainees to observe their own behavior and maintain appropriate responding in the absence of the trainer (Stahmer and Schreibman, 1992). The advantage of these programs is their efficiency and potential to promote generalization of skills, which is especially difficult to achieve when training people with autism. This method was shown to provide a reduction in stereotypic behavior in children with autism when used in conjunction with reinforcement for appropriate behavior (Koegel and Koegel, 1990). However, trainees, who function at a lower level, may not be able to perform some of the requirements of these programs.

There are a variety of methods that have been used in teaching adaptive skills to people with intellectual disabilities. Each strategy has its own set of strengths and weaknesses. Many of these interventions have been used both in isolation and as components of treatment packages. When choosing and implementing an intervention, individualization should be considered in order to facilitate positive treatment effects. Applications, methodologies and future directions of research will be discussed.

Derby Hospitals NHS Foundation
Trust
Library and Knowledge Service

VOCATIONAL SKILLS

Because people with developmental disabilities are becoming increasingly able to secure employment in the community, vocational skills training is becoming a more essential component of preparation for community transition. One study of four supported workers with autism suggested that job-site plus simulation training resulted in an increased level of skill or faster skill acquisition than job-site training alone on three of four tasks. However, one shortcoming of this study is the amount of instruction time was not controlled across both training methods; therefore, when the supported workers received simulation training plus job-site training they also received more instruction time than with the job-training alone (Lattimore et al., 2006).

A study was conducted comparing groups who received video self-modeling, small cash incentives, and attention/control in order to increase work productivity. The self-modeling group was video taped at work, mistakes were edited out of the video, and the participants were allowed to watch the video in the middle of the work day. The cash incentive group earned one point for every 10 percent of work productivity they achieved and they were given a ten cent pay increase for every point earned. The control group met briefly with the experimenter to check their hours, output, and to discuss their general work performance. Participants in the self-modeling group were found to demonstrate the most gains (15 percent increase), followed by the cash incentives group (3 percent), and attention/control group (−3 percent regression). A similar pattern was observed during a 4-month follow-up (Dowrick and Hood, 1981).

Training individuals with developmental disabilities to decrease their need for supervision is very important in a vocational setting. Successful unsupervised job performance could lead to more earning potential and job opportunities for individuals and more cost efficiency for providers. Self-recording and picture cues were used to train three individuals with mental retardation on how to independently change job tasks in a vocational setting. Praise was given to participants when they responded appropriately to the intervention and corrective feedback was also given when they responded inappropriately. All of the participants showed increased levels of independent task change after the implementation of the intervention, and gains were maintained for more than 10 weeks posttreatment (Connis, 1979). A later study found that students with intellectual disabilities in a vocational training program were also successful in independently changing work tasks throughout the day, without trainer prompts, when an intervention using self-management and picture cues was implemented. These results were maintained after supervision was reduced. Two of the participants were able to maintain their skills even when novel tasks were introduced on their picture schedule suggesting generalization of their training (Sowers et al., 1985).

Wacker and Berg (1983) found that five adolescents with intellectual disabilities were able to use picture prompts to acquire and generalize their performance of complex vocational tasks. Another study used peer tutors to train adolescents with intellectual disabilities on a target vocational task. Trainees showed improvement on this task at posttreatment when compared to baseline. Peer trainers were also successful in instructing trainees on a second generalization task.

A second study by these researchers was conducted with peer trainers teaching trainees to use picture prompts to complete one or two more complex tasks. During the posttreatment phase, trainees exhibited improved performance on these tasks. In addition, trainees were able to independently perform a novel generalization task using novel picture prompts. One concern the authors cited with using peer trainers was the incidence of the trainers' using unnecessary prompts. These trainers' unnecessary prompts did not seem to influence the results of this particular study but they may need to be tracked in subsequent studies using this technique (Wacker and Berg, 1989).

Some research found that a treatment package using preinstruction, instructional feedback, and picture prompts, was successful in teaching three adults with intellectual disabilities how to manage time in the job setting. When the first two components of the intervention were withdrawn, two out of the three participants were able to maintain high levels of responding; however, one participant's correct responding was reduced. Preinstruction was reinstated with this participant and correct responding increased. At follow-up, the first two components of the treatment were again withdrawn and this individual maintained the skills (Sowers et al., 1980).

DOMESTIC SKILLS

As individuals with intellectual disabilities move into the community, they will need to complete a greater number of domestic tasks. Training on such tasks can ensure that they will be able to successfully contribute to the maintenance of their household. A study of three children with autism used a video modeling system to teach daily living skills. The primary researcher videotaped the performance of various tasks (making orange juice, cleaning a fish bowl, and feeding a cat) from the point of view of the person completing each task. Following the baseline and intervention conditions, a no-video phase and a month follow-up were also conducted to determine if skills acquired were maintained. All three participants improved skill performance from baseline to video and no-video phases. All participants also maintained skill performance from 80 percent to 100 percent appropriate responding during the 1-month follow-up. Modifications to the method during the intervention phase were made for one participant who became distracted. This was remedied by lowering the position of the television monitor to eye level and adding a gestural prompt to cue the participant to attend to the video. Replication probes were also conducted in the participants' homes during each phase of the study, except the follow-up phase when probes were only conducted in two of the three participants' homes. Similar results were found in this setting with all three participants reaching 100 percent appropriate responding during the video and no-video phase. Follow-up data in the home for two of the three participants ranged from 75 percent to 100 percent appropriate responding (Shipley-Benamou et al., 2002).

A study of three children with autism was conducted to investigate the use of pictorial self-management in the training of daily living skills, such as setting a table, making lunch, or getting dressed. The participants were given a book of pictures that represented selected steps taken from a task analysis of their selected target skills. The final page of the book had a smiley face sticker that represented the completion of the task and was used as a prompt for self-reinforcement. The training consisted of three phases. During Phase 1, the children were trained to discriminate among the pictures representing the steps of their selected skills. In Phase 2, they were taught to select their own reinforcer, turn the pages of the book without assistance, perform motor actions, and self-reinforce. In the final phase, the trainer's presence was faded. All three children showed increases in on-task behavior and decreases in inappropriate behavior following the treatment. Two of the three children were able to perform all of their targeted skills in a generalized setting. All of the children were able to complete their targeted skills at a 2-month follow-up, although there was some variability in their performance (Pierce and Schreibman, 1994).

Laarhoven and Laarhoven-Myers (2006) conducted an adapted alternating treatment design study of video rehearsal, video rehearsal plus photos, and video rehearsal plus in vivo prompting to teach daily living skills such as cooking a microwave pizza, folding clothes, and cleaning a table. Their sample consisted of participants with developmental disabilities, one of which had a diagnosis of autism. All procedures were associated with increases in correct responding. However, video rehearsal plus prompting and video rehearsal plus photo conditions showed more efficiency in that fewer sessions were needed to meet mastery criterion. Two of the three participants showed more independent responding during the video in vivo phase, while the other individual showed more independent correct responding during the video photo phase.

Another study utilized video prompting to teach three male adults with developmental disabilities how to make microwave popcorn. A task analysis was modeled from the perspective of the person performing the task (only hands were shown) during the video clips and voice-over instructions were also included. One modification to the environment was made to help participants with two steps in the task analysis. A cardboard template was used to cover all of the buttons on the microwave except the "popcorn" button (which activated a preset time interval on the microwave needed to cook popcorn) and the start button. Two out of the three participants achieved 100 percent mastery of the task analysis in five to nine sessions and were able to maintain 80–100 percent mastery during the follow-up phase. One participant was not able to achieve mastery criterion in the training phase. The researchers suggested that this participant seemed disinterested in eating popcorn and his performance seemed to decline following a family death (Sigafoos et al., 2005).

A study by Lancioni et al. (1998) compared the use of a computer-based system versus a card-based system to promote task performance in three participants with severe disabilities. Results showed that the computer-based system produced a significantly higher level of correct task performance of food preparation and cleaning/table setting skills when compared with the card-based system. In addition, two out of the three participants reported a preference for the computer-based system as opposed to the card-based system.

Meal planning is also an important domain in which people with developmental disabilities need to acquire skills in order to facilitate good nutritional habits to maintain their health. One mealtime planning training program was found to be effective in increasing health food choices with three males with dual diagnosis of intellectual disability and psychiatric illness. Results were maintained at a 2-month follow-up (Arnold-Reid et al., 1997).

SELF-CARE

The ability to independently complete self-care skills enables individuals with developmental disabilities to more easily transition to community settings. A pivotal task that increases independence is toileting. Cicero and Pfadt (2002) implemented a toileting procedure with three children with autism that used a combination of positive reinforcement, graduated guidance, scheduled practice trials, and forward prompting. Participants were able to spontaneously request the toilet and cease urinary accidents within seven to eleven days. The results were also found to generalize to the home setting over the same time frame without implementation of a formal gennernalization phase. Gains were maintained at 6-month and one-year intervals per teacher and parent interviews.

In another study with a 7-year-old girl diagnosed with pervasive developmental disorder, a transfer-of-stimulus control prompting procedure was used in toilet training. The procedure consisted of the girl wearing a disposable undergarment, a stimulus associated with urination, while sitting on the toilet. The participant was reinforced for urination while sitting on the toilet (regardless of the presence of the disposable undergarment). The disposable undergarment was eventually faded out by changing its physical characteristics which entailed cutting progressively larger holes in the disposable undergarment as training proceeded. Urinary incontinence was eliminated and self-initiated toileting began during the tenth week of training (Luiselli, 1996).

Azrin and Foxx (1971) implemented an intensive training program with nine people with profound intellectual disabilities living in an institution. The program utilized an automatic apparatus for signaling elimination, shaping procedure for independent toileting, cleanliness training (as a consequence for accidents), and staff reinforcement for correct toileting behavior and dry pants. This program resulted in rapid reduction of incontinence and eventually led to near-zero levels. This program became widely used when training people with developmental disabilities when several studies using these same procedures showed success (Azrin et al., 1971; Sadler and Merkert, 1977; Smith, 1979). This method has also shown effectiveness when used with children with autism (Ando, 1977).

One research study implemented an intervention for personal hygiene following bowel movements with three adults with developmental disabilities, including one participant who had a diagnosis of autistic disorder. This program used task analysis, correspondence training (using verbal behavior to mediate a behavior chain), and general case instruction (training examples that represent real world counterparts). All of the participants demonstrated significant improvement in hygiene skills as compared to baseline. Generalization to other settings was achieved and maintained over a 9-month time period (Stokes et al., 2004). In another study, females with intellectual disabilities were taught menstrual care skills, involving a treatment package including task analysis. Participants showed increases in skills at posttreatment and the gains were maintained up to 5 months after the study (Richman et al., 1984).

A study of three children with autism was conducted to train self-help skills which included shoe tying, tooth brushing, hair combing, putting on pants, shirt, and socks, and eating and drinking. The intervention involved modeling, verbal instructions, prompting, and edible and social reinforcement. Participants showed an increase in the number of steps they could perform correctly in the task analysis of each skill following the treatment. Two of the three participants were able to maintain or increase their skill level at follow-up while the other participant showed some regression but still maintained a skill level above baseline (Matson et al., 1990).

A cognitive-behavioral intervention was used to train a man with an intellectual disability in grooming skills. This intervention involved a task analysis of a set of grooming skills which included four picture drawings that described each step in the sequence. These pictures were placed in a manual for the participant's use. This study used a multiple baseline design across three grooming skills which included tooth brushing, shaving, showering, and washing of arms and face. After the baseline phase of the study, the participant received four sessions of personal teaching on health education and one session of instructed practice with the pictorial instruction manual. The methodology produced rapid learning of all three skills; however, shaving was actually mastered by the participant in the baseline phase. The authors could not give a clear explanation of the acquisition of the shaving skill at baseline but suggested that shaving may have been mastered quickly because it involved the least amount of steps for mastery. Mastery of each skill was maintained at 1 month follow-up (Saloviita and Tuulkari, 2000). In another study, three males with intellectual disabilities were taught to self-initiate morning grooming behaviors using pictorial cues and reinforcement. Improvement in skills was found at posttreatment. However, a slight skill regression was noted in the follow-up phase (Thinesen and Bryan, 1981).

A program using task analysis was implemented to teach tooth brushing to eight participants with intellectual disabilities, which consisted of four people in an experimental group and four people in a systematic replication group. Four procedures were applied successively to the training of each step in the task analysis. For example, the trainer would provide no help to the trainee in the first 5 seconds and would increase level of prompting (verbal instruction, demonstration + verbal instruction, physical guidance + instruction) until the trainee was able to complete that step. The experimental group was reinforced for correct responding with social praise and tokens while the replication group was reinforced with social praise only. All participants were able to improve their toothbrush skills posttreatment as compared to baseline levels (Horner and Keilitz, 1975).

One unique intervention taught women with intellectual disabilities to select clothing according to community norms. This program used a puzzle simulation of a woman with various pieces of colored clothing, sized in proportion to the puzzle. The color coordination training utilized modeling, instructions, practice, praise, and feedback in order to facilitate learning. All of the participants demonstrated higher levels of correct responding as compared to baseline and were able to generalize their new skills to actual clothing. These results were maintained over a 7 to 14 week follow-up period (Nutter and Reid, 1978).

COMMUNITY SKILLS

Community skills are needed in order to facilitate independence and favorable impressions of people with intellectual disabilities by the larger community. Blew et al. (1985) compared modeling and peer tutoring in teaching community skills to children with autism. Two male participants were taught community skills (checking out a library book, buying a snack, buying an item at a convenience store, and crossing the street) using both of these methods. Modeling showed no effects on the baseline performance of one participant and only minimal increases (23 percent, 27 percent, and 0 percent) from baseline percentages of the other participant. Prior to the peer tutoring condition, tutors attended a pretraining session with the participants to establish rapport and become familiar with the discrete trial teaching style utilized during the intervention phase. For one participant, the peer tutoring phase produced improved performance on all three skills. When baseline was reintroduced, this participant maintained gains, achieving 80 percent mastery, on the community skill of buying an item at the convenience store. Performance of the other two skills initially decreased, but reached mastery level when the peer tutoring condition was reintroduced. For the second participant, peer tutoring also improved skill performances. Mastery criteria for buying a snack at a restaurant was met after a second peer tutoring phase was introduced following a return to baseline. The two other community skills reached mastery after only one peer tutoring phase.

Three males with intellectual disabilities were taught the following skills needed when going to a restaurant: locating, ordering, paying, eating, and exiting.

Methods used in this intervention included modeling, role playing, photo slide sequences, and using a simulated ordering counter. Participants had substantial improvement in their restaurant skills following training as compared to baseline. Skills were found to generalize to community settings and were maintained at a 1-year follow-up. However, two of the participants showed a slight regression in skills from posttreatment (86 percent–70 percent; 80 percent–5 percent) (van den Pol et al., 1981).

Bates et al. (2001) compared two conditions, simulation instruction plus community instruction versus community instruction only, in teaching four community skills (grocery shopping, use of commercial laundromat, purchasing soda in restaurant, and cleaning a restroom). This sample consisted of participants with mild and moderate intellectual disabilities. Ten participants from each skill level were assigned to each condition. The assignment to condition was alternated for each task. Both participants with mild and moderate intellectual disabilities showed significant improvement in pre- and posttest scores regardless of whether they had received previous simulation instruction with a few minor exceptions. Also, in community instruction only condition, performance levels of both persons with mild and moderate intellectual disabilities were recorded at 90 percent or higher. Overall, persons with mild intellectual disability showed better task performance than their counterparts with moderate intellectual disabilities on simulated tasks and in the community setting. People with mild intellectual disabilities were more likely than people with moderate intellectual disabilities to achieve generalization of skills to the community subsequent to simulation instruction. Groups from both levels of functioning had some regression in skills at follow-up but were still able to maintain performance levels that were significantly improved from pre-community instruction assessment levels.

Because of a substantial number of individuals with developmental disabilities that are obtaining jobs, training on money management and other money skills is needed. Colyer and Collins (1996) trained students with mild and moderate intellectual disabilities on the "next dollar" strategy of making a purchase. This strategy teaches individuals to present the next dollar amount higher than the price given when making a purchase (McDonnell et al., 1984). Three out of the four participants were able to reach mastery level during the treatment phase and showed generalization of this skill in the community. However, the training procedure was modified somewhat for one participant. This participant was trained to ask for the price to be restated prior to counting out money to make a purchase in order to avoid confusion. A tangible reinforcement system (presentation of a penny) was used when this participant demonstrated appropriate responding (Colyer and Collins, 1996).

Lowe and Cuvo (1976) taught coin summation to four persons with intellectual disabilities. The program used modeling, modeling with subject involvement, and independent counting by the participant. A significant increase was found on pretest to posttest scores. Trace et al. (1977) implemented an intervention teaching coin equivalence with an experimental group. The training included a chain of naming, selecting and counting, and depositing monetary values into a coin machine. The experimental group showed a significant increase in skills pretest to posttest and showed significantly higher posttest scores when compared to the control group. Another study used a decreasing prompt hierarchy or a time-delay method to teach four students with moderate intellectual disabilities to cash checks and use an automatic teller. Although both strategies led to skill acquisition, participants were able to reach mastery more quickly with the decreasing prompt hierarchy method. Maintenance of skills was achieved at 4 and 8 week follow-up (McDonnell and Ferguson, 1989).

Because the earning potential of persons with intellectual disabilities is growing, purchasing skills are needed in order for these individuals to spend their money independently. Three individuals with autism were trained on a task analysis about purchasing items in one setting (high school cafeteria or nearby convenience store). The introduction of this training resulted in the increased level of appropriate social and operational responses as compared to baseline performance. However, data were gathered in three probe settings where generalization of purchasing skills failed to occur. The experimenters then introduced generalization training which consisted of video modeling of a same-aged, normal functioning peer performing the task analysis they had been taught in the original purchasing training. Trainers also asked participants a series of questions about the video. This video modeling procedure resulted in generalization in the probe settings for all participants (Haring et al., 1987). Similarly, a study by Alcantara (1994) used video modeling to teach children with autism to make purchases in the community and participants were able to generalize their skills to an untrained setting.

Virtual environments have been developed to help people with intellectual disabilities purchase items at the grocery store. One study with young people with severe intellectual disabilities found that the group of participants who received an intervention using a virtual supermarket were more efficient during grocery shopping (Standen et al., 1998). In another study, a 2-D virtual reality (VR) program and a conventional program were compared to teach grocery shopping skills to people with intellectual deficits. Both programs seemed to improve participants' skills in this domain. No significant difference in effectiveness was found between the two programs (Tam et al., 2005).

Pedestrian skills are needed for individuals with developmental disabilities so that they can safely navigate where they live. Batu et al. (2004) taught pedestrian skills (how to cross the street with overcrossing, pedestrian lights, and crossing the street without traffic patrol or facilitators) to a group of participants using most-to-least prompting. The intervention was found to be successful and participants were able to generalize their skills to a naturalistic setting. Similarly, Page et al. (1976) conducted a study using a simulated environment to train pedestrian skills. Skills taught included street crossing in sequence, intersection recognition, pedestrian-light skills, and skills for different stop sign conditions. Participants were able to transfer the skills they learned in the simulated environment to a real world setting and maintained skills two to six weeks after the intervention was stopped. Another study trained four males with profound intellectual disabilities living in an institution to walk independently from their living area to school. The program used a backward chaining format and included instructions, practice, social praise, feedback, verbal reprimands, prompts, and edible reinforcers. Participants were able to walk independently to school from their living area during 86–100 percent of the sessions. During the maintenance phase, participants were able to walk to school and back to their living area, even though walking back had not been trained. Follow-up showed that gains were maintained at 1 and 8 week reassessment (Gruber et al., 1979).

The use of public transportation is also a valuable skill in which to train individuals with intellectual disabilities. Individuals who obtain this skill are allowed more independence to move freely in the community. One study compared public transportation training in the classroom to in vivo training. The intervention included components such as role playing, manipulating the actions of a doll on a simulated model, and responding to questions about slide sequences. Skills taught with this treatment package included locating, signaling, boarding, riding and exiting a bus. Participants who received classroom instruction and in vivo training showed skill acquisition following treatment; however, the classroom-based program was found to take less training sessions and was more cost efficient (Neef et al., 1978).

LEISURE SKILLS

In addition to gaining skills in core adaptive areas, individuals with developmental disabilities also benefit from learning skills that enhance the quality of their leisure time. Yilmaz et al. (2005) conducted a study using constant time delay (CTD) in training children with autism in aquatic play skills. The participants showed an increase in performance of target skills and were able to maintain skills through maintenance phases. Another study also used a constant time delay intervention in the teaching of leisure skills, such as playing a variety of games, to three participants with developmental disabilities (including one participant with an autism diagnosis). This procedure was found to be effective for all of the participants. The trainees were able to maintain a mean of 87.5 percent accuracy of responding over a 5-month period in which they no longer received any instruction. Self-determined behavior during unstructured free time at school also increased over the study period (Wall et al., 1999).

Silliman and French (1993) conducted a study comparing the use of verbal praise, music reinforcement, and no treatment on the soccer ball kicking behavior of children 10–17 year olds with profound intellectual disabilities. Although all three groups showed improvement on their ball kicking accuracy, descriptive data showed that groups receiving verbal praise and music reinforcement had higher scores than the control group. In another study, adolescents with mild intellectual disabilities were trained to keep their heart rates above a certain level with the use of a heart monitor while pedaling an exercise bicycle. Most subjects were able to acquire this skill posttraining (Ellis et al., 1993). In addition, individuals with severe and profound intellectual disabilities, living in an institution, were found to improve in their physical endurance and ability to exercise following participation in two exercise programs (Tomporowski and Jameson, 1985).

METHODOLOGICAL ISSUES

There are a number of issues to consider when inspecting the research that has been conducted on adaptive skills interventions. Most of the research that has been done in this domain has used samples of participants with intellectual disabilities or developmental disabilities, not particularly autism. Although, some studies have looked at the use of these interventions within the autism spectrum (Blew et al., 1985; Cicero and Pfadt, 2002; Lattimore et al., 2006; Pierce and Schreibman, 1994; Shipley-Benamou et al., 2002;), it is important to consider how these interventions may or may not be adapted for use with people with autism spectrum disorders. For example, persons with autism with severe communication deficits may not respond well to interventions based on verbal instructions. Also, people with autism with severe nonsocial behaviors (such as hand flapping or scratching the face) may respond better to interventions with elements of role-play which involve activities that require their hands to be engaged. This method may reduce the incidence of nonsocial behavior (because of the competing response provided by the training activity) to enable the person to focus better on the task. However, because autism and mental retardation have a high comorbidity rate and have been found to share characteristics such as stimulus overselectivity (Lovaas and Schreibman, 1971), concrete thinking (Blake, 1976), and communication problems (Abbeduto et al., 2001), interventions used previously for persons with intellectual disabilities could be reasonably modified or applied to treat people with autism spectrum disorders.

The most obvious limitation of research in this domain is the lack of true experimental design in the majority of the studies. For example, most of the research reported does not use control groups which limits the ability to make conclusions about causality. Single-case designs, such as AB and multiple baseline, are often used when studying these interventions. This body of research is also constrained by its small sample sizes. Because of this, applicability to the larger population of people with intellectual disabilities and developmental disabilities is unknown.

FUTURE DIRECTIONS

There is substantial room for growth in the research of interventions that train adaptive skills with the autism population. For example, researchers should investigate interventions for a variety of adaptive skills with persons with autism spectrum disorders. Since the majority of studies in this domain have been conducted with people with intellectual disabilities without a diagnosis of autism, researchers need to examine the differential effects of various interventions with participants with different levels of functioning within the autism spectrum. Because this spectrum of disorders is so heterogeneous, it is not reasonable to assume that interventions found to be effective with the higher end of this continuum can be successfully applied to individuals functioning on the lower end or vice versa. In addition, future studies should be conducted that examine the effectiveness of interventions designed to build upon the needs of people with autism, such as treatment programs utilizing visual modalities and promoting generalization.

Future research also needs to remedy the methodological shortcomings that are prevalent in the current body of studies. Although studies with control groups would be ideal, this is not always an option because of practical or ethical concerns. For example, treatment facilities may not have the staff resources to conduct sophisticated experimental studies that include all the proper experimental controls and methodological refinements characteristic of 'true' experimental designs. In addition, these facilities could not deny treatment to participants in a control group because of the ethical ramifications. Therefore, more comparison and/or wait-list groups may be utilized in lieu of control groups. Comparison groups could be formed to investigate different modalities of treatment or wait-list participants could receive the treatment at a later time. These provisions would give every participant the chance to receive some type of treatment and allow the researcher access to some form of comparison data.

In addition, increasing sample sizes and matching subjects on relevant variables, such as IQ, communication level, sensory issues, and diagnoses, would represent progress. Many of the current studies in this domain of research use multicomponent treatment packages. Researchers should assess the treatment effects of each component individually to isolate elements most responsible for promoting skill acquisition in persons with autism.

Considering the normalization movement, studies using in vivo interventions may be needed to investigate generalization of skills and external validity. Because people with autism often have trouble with generalization, studying the differential effects of simulated versus real-world settings may provide more information on how well people with autism can transfer their skills to community settings.

CONCLUSION

The research on adaptive skills interventions for use with people with autism spectrum disorders has been limited. However, many studies have been conducted using samples of participants with intellectual and developmental disabilities. Research on interventions utilizing different modalities of instruction, such as applied behavior analysis, task analysis, visually cued instruction, modeling (peer/adult, videotape, self-modeling), natural/simulated/virtual environments, constant time delay, and self-management have been reviewed. This body of studies remains susceptible to methodological weaknesses, such as lack of control groups and small sample sizes. Future investigations should address these concerns and provide more attention to the differential effects of these interventions with different functioning levels of autism. Clinicians treating people with autism should be careful to choose interventions that have shown favorable results in past studies, and also individualize the interventions to the person's strengths or weaknesses.

REFERENCES

Abbeduto, L., Evans, J., and Dolan, T. (2001). Theoretical perspectives on language and communication problems in mental retardation and developmental disabilities. *Mental Retardation and Developmental Disabilities*, **7**, 45–55.

Ando, H. (1977). Training autistic children to urinate in the toilet through operant conditioning techniques. *Journal of Autism and Childhood Schizophrenia*, **7**, 151–163.

Alcantara, P. (1994). Effects of videotape instructional package on purchasing skills of children with autism. *Exceptional Children*, **61**, 40–55.

Arnold-Reid, G., Schloss, P., and Alper, S. (1997). Teaching meal planning to youth with mental retardation in natural settings. *Remedial and Special Education*, **18**, 166–173.

Ault, M., Wolery, M., Gast, D., et al. (1988). Comparison of response prompting in teaching numeral identification to autistic subjects. *Journal of Autism and Developmental Disorders*, **18**, 627–636.

Azrin, N., Bugle, C., and O'Brien, F. (1971). Behavioral engineering: Two apparatuses for toilet training retarded children. *Journal of Applied Behavior Analysis*, **4**, 249–253.

Azrin, N. and Foxx, R. (1971). A rapid method of toilet training the institutionalized retarded. *Journal of Applied Behavior Analysis*, **4**, 89–99.

Baer, D.M., Wolf, M.M., and Risley, T.R. (1968). Some current dimensions of applied behavior analysis. *Journal of Applied Behavior Analysis*, **1**, 91–97.

Bandura, A. (1969). *Principles of Behavior Modification*. New York: Holt, Rinehart, & Winston.

Bandura, A., Ross, D., and Ross, S. (1963). Imitation of film-mediated aggressive models. *Journal of Abnormal and Social Psychology*, **66**, 3–11.

Bates, P., Cuvo, T., Miner, C., and Korabek, C. (2001). Simulated and community-based instruction involving persons with mild and moderate mental retardation. *Research in Developmental Disabilities*, **22**, 95–115.

Batu, S., Ergenekon, Y., Erbas, D., and Akmanoglu, N. (2004). Teaching pedestrian skills to individuals with developmental disabilities. *Journal of Behavioral Education*, **13**, 147–164.

Blake, K. (1976). Abstractness and concreteness and retarded and normal pupils' sentence comprehension. *Journal of Research and Development in Education*, **9**, 90–91.

Blew, P., Schwartz, I., and Luce, S. (1985). Teaching functional community skills to autistic children using nonhandicapped peer tutors. *Journal of Applied Behavior Analysis*, **18**, 337–342.

Boucher, J. (1981). Memory for recent events in autistic children. *Journal of Autism and Developmental Disorders*, **11**, 293–301.

Carr, E., Dunlap, G., Horner, R., et al. (2002). Positive behavior support: Evolution of an applied science. *Journal of Positive Behavior Interventions*, **4**, 4–16, 20.

Charlop-Christy, M.H, Carpenter, M., Le, L., et al. (2002). Using the picture exchange communication system (PECS) with children with autism: Assessment of PECS acquisition, speech, social-communicative behavior, and problem behavior. *Journal of Applied Behavior Analysis*, **35**, 213–231.

Cicero, F. and Pfadt, A. (2002). Investigation of a reinforcement-based toileting training procedure for children with autism. *Research in Developmental Disabilities*, **23**, 319–331.

Cobb, S., Nichols, S., Ramsey, A., and Wilson, J. (1999). Virtual reality-induced symptoms and effects. *Presence*, **8**, 169–186.

Cohen, H., Amerine-Dickens, M., Smith, T. (2006). Early intensive behavioral treatment: Replication of the UCLA model in a community setting. *Journal of Developmental & Behavioral Pediatrics*, **27**, S145–S155.

Coleman, S. and Stedman, J. (1974). Use of a peer model in language training in an echolalic child. *Journal of Behavior Therapy and Experimental Psychiatry*, **5**, 275–279.

Colyer, S. and Collins, B. (1996). Using natural cues within prompt levels to teach the next dollar strategy to students with disabilities. *The Journal of Special Education*, **30**, 305–318.

Connis, R. (1979). The effects of sequential pictorial cues, self-recording, and praise on the job task sequencing of retarded adults. *Journal of Applied Behavior Analysis*, **12**, 355–361.

Coon, M., Vogelsberg, R., and Williams, W. (1981). Effects of classroom public transportation instruction of generalization of the natural environment. *Journal of the Association for Persons with Severe Handicaps*, **6**, 46–53.

Cooper, J.O., Heron, T.E., Heward, W.L. (2007) *Applied Behavior Analysis (2nd Ed.)*. Columbus, OH: Prentice Hall.

DeMyer, M. (1975). The nature of neuropsychological disability in autistic children. *Journal of Autism and Childhood Schizophrenia*, **5**, 109–128.

Dowrick, P. (1999). A review of self modeling and related interventions. *Applied & Preventive Psychology*, **8**, 23–39.

Dowrick, P. and Hood, M. (1981). Comparison of self-modeling and small cash incentives in a sheltered workshop. *Journal of Applied Psychology*, **66**, 394–397.

Egel, A., Richman, G., Koegel, R. (1981). Normal peer models and autistic children's learning. *Journal of Applied Behavior Analysis*, **14**, 3–12.

Ellis, D., Cress, P., and Spellman, C. (1993). Training students with mental retardation to self-pace while exercising. *Adapted Physical Activity Quarterly*, **10**, 104–124.

Ganz, J. and Simpson, R. (2004). Effects on communicative requesting and speech development of the picture exchange communication system in children with characteristics of autism. *Journal of Autism and Developmental Disorders*, **34**, 395–409.

Gruber, B., Reeser, R., Reid, D. (1979). Providing a less restrictive environment for profoundly retarded persons by teaching independent walking skills. *Journal of Applied Behavior Analysis*, **12**, 285–297.

Haring, T., Kennedy, C., Adams, M., and Pitts-Conway, V. (1987). Teaching generalization of purchasing skills across community settings to autistic youth using videotape modeling. *Journal of Applied Behavior Analysis*, **20**, 89–96.

Horner, R., Dunlap, G., and Koegel, R. (1988). *Generalization and Maintenance: Life-style Changes in Applied Settings*. Baltimore, MD: Paul H. Brooks Publishing.

Horner, R. and Keilitz, I. (1975). Training mentally retarded adolescents to brush their teeth. *Journal of Applied Behavior Analysis*, **8**, 301–309.

Koegel, R. and Koegel, L. (1990). Extended reductions in stereotypic behavior through self-management in multiple community settings. *Journal of Applied Behavior Analysis*, **23**, 119–128.

Koegel, R., Schreibman, L., Good, A., et al. (1989). *How to Teach Pivotal Behaviors in Children with Autism: A Training Manual*. San Diego: University of California.

Kravits, T., Kamps, D., Kemmerer, K., and Potucek, J. (2002). Brief report: Increasing communication skills for an elementary-aged student with autism using the picture exchange communication system. *Journal of Autism and Developmental Disorders*, **32**, 225–230.

Laarhoven, T. and Laarhoven-Myers, T. (2006). Comparison of three video-based instructional procedures for teaching daily living skills to persons with developmental disabilities. *Education and Training in Developmental Disabilities*, **41**, 365–381.

Lancioni, G., van den Hof, E., Boelens, H., et al. (1998). A computer-based system providing pictorial instructions and prompts to promote task performance in persons with severe developmental disabilities. *Behavioral Interventions*, **13**, 111–122.

Lattimore, L., Parson, M., Reid, D. (2006). Enhancing job-site training of supported workers with autism: A reemphasis on simulation. *Journal of Applied Behavior Analysis*, **39**, 91–102.

Lovaas, O. (1987). Behavioral treatment and normal educational and intellectual functioning in young autistic children. *Journal of Consulting and Clinical Psychology*, **55**, 3–9.

Lovaas, O., Koegel, R., and Schreibman, L. (1979). Stimulus overselectivity in autism: A review of research. *Psychological Bulletin*, **6**, 1236–1254.

Lovaas, O., Koegel, R., and Simmons, J., Long, J. (1973). Some generalization and follow-up measures on autistic children in behavior therapy. *Journal of Applied Behavior Analysis*, **6**, 131–165.

Lovaas, O. and Schreibman, L. (1971). Stimulus overselectivity of autistic children in a two stimulus situation. *Behavior Research and Therapy*, **9**, 305–310.

Lowe, M. and Cuvo, A. (1976). Teaching coin summation to the mentally retarded. *Journal of Applied Behavior Analysis*, **9**, 483–489.

Luiselli, J. (1996). A case study evaluation of a transfer-of-stimulus control toilet training procedure for a child with pervasive developmental disorder. *Focus on Autism and Other Developmental Disabilities*, **11**, 158–162.

MacDuff, G., Krantz, P., and McClannahan, L. (1993). Teaching children with autism to use photographic activity schedules maintenance and generalization of complex response chains. *Journal of Applied Behavior Analysis*, **26**, 89–97.

Matson, J., Benavidez, D., Compton, L., et al. (1996). Behavioral treatment of autistic persons: A review of research from 1980 to the present. *Research in Developmental Disabilities*, **17**, 433–465.

Matson, J., Mayville, E., Lott, J., et al. (2003). A comparison of social and adaptive functioning in persons with psychosis, autism, and severe or profound mental retardation. *Journal of Developmental and Physical Disabilities*, **15**, 57–65.

Matson, J., Taras, M., Sevin, J., et al. (1990). Teaching self-help skills to autistic and mentally retarded children. *Research in Developmental Disabilities*, **11**, 361–378.

McDonnell, J. and Ferguson, B. (1989). A comparison of time delay and decreasing prompt hierarchy strategies in teaching banking skills to students with moderate handicaps. *Journal of Applied Behavior Analysis*, **22**, 85–91.

McDonnell, J., Horner, R., and Williams, J. (1984). Comparison of three strategies for teaching generalization grocery purchasing to high school students with severe handicaps. *Journal of the Association for Persons with Severe Handicaps*, **9**, 123–133.

Morrow, S. and Bates, P. (1987). The effectiveness of three sets of school-based instructional materials and community training on acquisition and generalization of community laundry skills by students with severe handicaps. *Research in Developmental Disabilities*, **8**, 113–136.

Neef, N., Iwata, B, and Page, T. (1978). Public transportation training: In vivo versus classroom instruction. *Journal of Applied Behavior Analysis*, **11**, 331–344.

Nichols, S. (1999). Physical ergonomics of virtual environment use. *Applied Ergonomics*, **30**, 79–90.

Nietupski, J., Hamre-Nietupski, S., Clancy, P., and Veerhusen, K. (1986). Guidelines for making simulation an effective adjunct to in vivo community instruction. *Journal of the Association for persons with severe handicaps*, **11**, 12–18.

Nutter, D. and Reid, D. (1978). Teaching retarded women a clothing selection skill using community norms. *Journal of Applied Behavior Analysis*, **11**, 475–487.

Page, T., Iwata, B., and Neef, N. (1976). Teaching pedestrian skills to retarded persons: Generalization from the classroom to the natural environment. *Journal of Applied Behavior Analysis*, **9**, 433–444.

Parsons, S. and Mitchell, P. (2002). The potential of virtual reality in social skills training for people with autistic spectrum disorders. *Journal of Intellectual Disability Research*, **46**, 430–443.

Parsons, S., Mitchell, P., Leonard, A. (2004). The use and understanding of virtual environments by adolescents with autistic spectrum disorders. *Journal of Autism and Developmental Disabilities*, **34**, 449–466.

Pierce, K. and Schreibman, L. (1994). Teaching daily living skills to children with autism in unsupervised settings through pictorial self-management. *Journal of Applied Behavior Analysis*, **27**, 471–481.

Prior, M. (1979). Cognitive abilities and disabilities in autism: A review. *Journal of Abnormal Child Psychology*, **2**, 357–380.

Quill, K. (1995). Visually cued instruction for children with autism and pervasive developmental disorders. *Focus on Autistic Behavior*, **10**, 10–20.

Richman, G., Reiss, M., Bauman, K., and Bailey, J. (1984). Teaching menstrual care to mentally retarded women: Acquistion, generalization, and maintenance. *Journal of Applied Behavior Analysis*, **17**, 441–451.

Robertson, H. and Biederman, G. (1989). Modeling, imitation, and observational learning in remediation experimentation 1979–1988: An analysis of the validity of research designs and outcomes. *Canadian Journal of Behavioural Science*, **21**, 174–197.

Rosekrans, M.A (1967). Imitation in children as a function of perceived similarity to social model and vicarious reinforcement. *Journal of Personality and Social Psychology*, **7**, 307–315.

Sadler, O. and Merkert, F. (1977). Evaluating the Foxx and Azrin toilet training procedure for retarded children in a day training center. *Behavior Therapy*, **8**, 499–500.

Sallows, G. and Graupner, T. (2005). Intensive behavioral treatment for children with autism: Four-year outcome and predictors. *American Journal on Mental Retardation*, **110**, 417–438.

Saloviita, T. and Tuulkari, M. (2000). Cognitive-behavioral treatment package for teaching grooming skills to a man with an intellectual disability. *Scandinavian Journal of Behaviour Therapy*, **29**, 140–147.

Shafer, M., Inge, K., and Hill, J. (1986). Acquisition, generalization, and maintenance of automated banking skills. *Education and Training of the Mentally Retarded*, **21**, 265–272.

Sherer, M., Pierce, K., Paredes, S., et al. (2001). Enhancing conversation skills with children with autism via video technology: Which is better "self" or "other" as a model? *Behavior Modification*, **25**, 140–158.

Sheridan, K. and Campbell, M. (2004). *Predicting Client Success in Traditional Group Homes and Supervised Apartments*. Poster presented at the annual meeting of the American Association of Mental Retardation (AAMR). October 27–30, 2004, Philadelphia, Mississippi.

Shipley-Benamou, R., Lutzker, J., and Taubman, M. (2002). Teaching daily living skills to children with autism through instructional video modeling. *Journal of Positive Behavior Interventions*, **4**, 165–175.

Sigafoos, J., O'Reilly, M., Cannella, H., et al. (2005). Computer-presented video prompting for teaching microwave oven use to three adults with developmental disabilities. *Journal of Behavioral Education*, **14**, 189–201.

Sigman, M., Ungerer, J., Mundy, P., and Sherman, T. (1987). Cognition in autistic children. In *Handbook of Autism and Pervasive Developmental Disorders* (D. Cohen and A. Donnellan, eds.) pp. 103–120. New York: Wiley.

Silliman, L. and French, R. (1993). Use of selected reinforcers to improve the ball kicking of youths with profound mental retardation. *Adapted Physical Activity Quarterly*, **10**, 52–69.

Smith, P. (1979). A comparison of different methods of toilet training the mentally handicapped. *Behaviour Research & Therapy*, **17**, 33–43.

Sowers, J., Rusch, F., Connis, R. and Cummings, L. (1980). Teaching mentally retarded adults to time-manage in a vocational setting. *Journal of Applied Behavior Analysis*, **13**, 119–128.

Sowers, J., Verdi, M., Bourbeau, P., and Sheehan, M. (1985). Teaching job independence and flexibility to mentally retarded students through the use of a self-control package. *Journal of Applied Behavior Analysis*, **18**, 81–85.

Stahmer, A. and Schreibman, L. (1992). Teaching children with autism appropriate play in unsupervised environments using a self-management package. *Journal of Applied Behavior Analysis*, **25**, 447–459.

Standen, P., Cromby, J., and Brown, D. (1998). Playing for real. *Mental Health Care*, **1**, 412–415.

Stokes, J., Cameron, M., Dorsey, M. and Fleming, E. (2004). Task analysis, correspondence training, and general case instruction for teaching personal hygiene skills. *Behavioral Interventions*, **19**, 121–135.

Strickland, D., Marcus, L., Mesibov, G., and Hogan, K. (1996). Brief report: Two case studies using virtual reality as a learning tool for autistic children. *Journal of Autism and Developmental Disabilities*, **26**, 651–659.

Sulzer-Azaroff, B. and Mayer, G. (1977). *Applying Behavior Analysis Procedures with Children and Youth*. New York: Holt, Rinehart, and Winston.

Tam, S., Wai-Kwong Man, D., Chan, Y., et al. (2005). Evaluation of a computer-assisted, 2-D virtual reality system for training people with intellectual disabilities on how to shop. *Rehabilitation Psychology*, **50**, 285–291.

Thinesen, P. and Bryan, A. (1981). The use of sequential pictorial cues in the initiation and maintenance of grooming behaviors and mentally retarded adults. *Mental Retardation*, **19**, 246–250.

Tomporowski, P., Jameson, L. (1985). Effects of a physical fitness training program on the exercise behavior of institutionalized mentally retarded adults. *Adapted Physical Activity Quarterly*, **2**, 197–205.

Touchette, P. (1971). Transfer of stimulus control: Measuring the moment of transfer. *Journal of the Experimental Analysis of Behavior*, **15**, 347–354.

Trace, M. Cuvo, A., and Criswell, J. (1977). Teaching coin equivalence to the mentally retarded. *Journal of Applied Behavior Analysis*, **10**, 85–92.

van den Pol, R., Iwata, B., Ivancic, M., et al. (1981). Teaching the handicapped to eat in public places: acquisition, generalization and maintenance of restaurant skills. *Journal of Applied Behavior Analysis*, **14**, 61–69.

Varni, J., Lovaas, O., Koegel, R., and Everett, N. (1979). An analysis of observational learning in autistic and normal children. *Journal of Abnormal Child Psychology*, **7**, 31–43.

Vine, X. and Hamilton, D. (2005). Individual characteristics associated with community integration of adults with intellectual disability. *Journal of Intellectual and Developmental Disability*, **30**, 171–175.

Wacker, D. and Berg, W. (1983). Effects of picture prompts on the acquisition of complex vocational tasks by mentally retarded adolescents. *Journal of Applied Behavior Analysis*, **16**, 417–433.

Wacker, D. and Berg, W. (1989). Evaluation of the generalized effects of a peer-training procedure with moderately retarded adolescents. *Journal of Applied Behavior Analysis*, **22**, 2261–273.

Wall, M., Gast, D., and Royston, P. (1999). Leisure skills instruction for adolescents with severe or profound developmental disabilities. *Journal of Developmental and Physical Disabilities*, **11**, 193–219.

Yilmaz, I., Birkan, B., Konukman, F., and Erkan, M. (2005). Using a constant time delay procedure to teach aquatic play skills to children with autism. *Education and Training in Developmental Disabilities*, **40**, 171–182.

12

COMPREHENSIVE TREATMENT PACKAGES FOR ASD: PERCEIVED VS PROVEN EFFECTIVENESS

RAYMOND G. ROMANCZYK[1], JENNIFER M. GILLIS[2], SARA WHITE[1], AND FLORENCE DIGENNARO[1]

[1]State University of New York at Binghamton, Binghamton, NY, USA
[2]Auburn University

INTRODUCTION

Autism spectrum disorders (ASD) by definition have broad impact upon the individual. Thus, it would seem reasonable that comprehensive treatment would be recommended. In turn, when specific etiological pathways and pathogenesis are identified, then focused treatment may be merited if the pathogenic mechanisms are discrete and modifiable. However, until such identification takes place, the common wisdom in the field is that children should receive comprehensive treatment.

The extant and growing treatment research literature is imbalanced in that there are far more research reports on highly specific treatment procedures, and relatively much less on comprehensive treatment packages. This is no doubt in part due to the high cost of evaluating treatment packages because of issues of recruitment, control groups, procedural integrity, nonoverlapping ancillary treatment services, and measurement methodology, to name a few. Such discussion, however, begs the question as to what is a comprehensive treatment package and what constitutes evidence-based evaluation for treatment packages?

MODEL PROGRAMS APPROACH

The Committee on Educational Interventions for Children with Autism (National Research Council, 2001) utilized specific selection criteria in their search for model programs, based on published reports and frequency of citation. They identified 10 programs based on their criteria, to illustrate "state-of-the-art" model approaches. These 10 programs were:

1. Children's Unit at the State University of New York at Binghamton.
2. Denver Model at the University of Colorado Health Sciences Center.
3. Developmental Intervention Model at The George Washington University School of Medicine.
4. Douglass Developmental Center at Rutgers University.
5. Individualized Support Program at the University of South Florida at Tampa.
6. Learning Experiences, an Alternative Program for Preschoolers and their Parents (LEAP) Preschool at the University of Colorado School of Education.
7. Pivotal Response Model at the University of California at Santa Barbara.
8. Treatment and Education of Autistic and Related Communication Handicapped Children (TEACCH) at the University of North Carolina School of Medicine at Chapel Hill.
9. The University of California at Los Angeles (UCLA) Young Autism Project.
10. Walden Early Childhood Programs at the Emory University School of Medicine.

The Committee reviewed these programs in order to examine if common elements existed. They stated: "An overview of well-known model approaches to early autism intervention reveals a consensus across programs on the factors that result in program effectiveness. Similarities far outweigh differences in ten state-of-the-art programs that were selected for comparison" (p. 140).

Odom et al. (in press) recently contacted the programs originally identified by the Committee to ascertain current status, and update current research support. They point out that the majority are center based, have emphasis on family participation, are skill focused, and "utilize behavioral approaches grounded in the theory of applied behavior analysis" (p. 12).

Analysis of model programs can be useful in identifying what appear to be common elements, and therefore infer that the common components are perhaps necessary elements. But such comparative examination does not lend itself to component analysis and cost-benefit analysis. It is also unlikely that direct comparison of various model programs will occur. Because treatment programs are typically evaluated by incremental improvements in child skills, rather than remission of symptoms, it is essential that direct comparisons be attempted.

An excellent example of the need for direct comparisons is the recent comparative study by Howard et al. (2005). The authors compared an applied behavior analysis program with both an intensive eclectic program (a combination of various popular treatment methods including sensory integration, TEACCH, Picture Exchange Communication System (PECS), discrete trial training, as well as normative classroom activities, 1:1 or 1:2 staff–child ratio, 30 h per week of services, designed for children with autism, and having experienced, credentialed staff) and a nonintensive public early intervention program not specifically designed for children with autism (credentialed staff, using developmentally appropriate activities, small groups, emphasis on language, play, and sensory activities, and 15 h per week of services).

Thus, they compared what might be termed colloquially, a "narrow" ABA (applied behavior analysis) program, a comprehensive program integrating a number of approaches, and a "generic" special education program. Contrary to what many practitioners might predict, the ABA program was significantly superior to the other two programs, with the two remaining programs not differing from each other in outcome. Thus great care must be used in assuming that one can examine various treatment approaches that purport to produce change and extract the "best" components to assemble into a "comprehensive" program. While such a course may make common sense, this study demonstrates the need for further empirical evaluation.

EVIDENCED-BASED TREATMENT

Evidence-based and "manualized" treatment packages are topics of interest for the broad array of human service providers as well as the funding sources for those services. In 1995 the American Psychological Association's (APA) Division 12 (Clinical Psychology) Task Force developed criteria for empirically supported therapies (EST) in order to provide guidelines for researchers, practitioners, and consumers to evaluate psychological treatments or interventions. They established three categories to describe degrees of evidence available: well established, probably efficacious, and experimental (c.f. Chambless and Ollendick, 2001). However, the specific methodology presented, as well as other similar processes of evaluation, are sadly underutilized. Not surprisingly, since the number of individuals with ASD needing services is large and rapidly increasing, there is growing "entrepreneurship" in the worst sense of the word (Romanczyk and Gillis, 2007). Using knowledge of the developing standard of care that requires use of evidence-based treatment, many practitioners are simply marketing their services by using the term "evidence based." The problem lies in agreement as to what constitutes "evidence." We hold that it is the result of methodologically sound experimental research, while many others use the term very casually to include anecdote and simple case record review.

BEST PRACTICE GUIDELINES

Best practice guidelines incorporate evidence-based treatment, but go beyond that base and are intended to inform consumers and service providers about the current status of optimal care guidelines as compared to generally accepted practice parameters for specific conditions or disorders. Such guidelines are not mandatory, but instead, guidelines are intended to set a higher standard for care. While there are numerous position papers and advocacy group "mandates," such presentations are not best practice guidelines, as best practice is based primarily in fact, not opinion. There is an accepted methodology for evaluating treatments in order to produce best practice guidelines (Holland et al., 2005).

The Agency for Health Care Policy and Research (AHCPR) was established in 1997. Evidence-based Practice Centers (EPCs) were established. These Centers ". . . develop evidence reports and technology assessments on topics relevant to clinical, social science/behavioral, economic, and other health care organization and delivery issues – specifically those that are common, expensive, and/or significant" (http://www.ahrq.gov/clinic/epc/).

The AHCPR clinical practice guideline methodology uses principles for developing practice guidelines recommended by the US Institute of Medicine (IOM, 1992). This AHCPR methodology is considered to be the standard for developing evidence-based clinical practice guidelines (Eddy and Hasselblad, 1994; Holland, 1995; Schriger, 1995; Woolf, 1991, 1994).

The National Autism Center (http://www.nationalautismcenter.org/index.php) has begun a multiyear review of the research literature on autism intervention. Its methodology goes beyond previous comprehensive reviews in that detail will be provided on the specific published research articles using a "Scientific Merit Rating Scale." This scale will assist in quantifying the "strength of findings" by directly assessing the numerous and complex issues of methodological rigor and data analysis. This process will allow the reader to identify the strengths and weaknesses of research articles and thus evaluate their overall importance and impact. Once this process has been completed, the next step will be the development of standards for treatment, based on the results of the review.

COMPREHENSIVE TREATMENT PACKAGES

There is not a generally accepted definition of "comprehensive treatment package." It is a term that makes intuitive sense but becomes difficult to apply consistently when evaluating specific therapeutic procedures or intervention programs. Odom et al. (in press), offers a definition that incorporates many of the aspects also highlighted by the Committee on Educational Interventions for Children with Autism. Odom et al. (in press), state: "Comprehensive treatment models typically consist of multiple components (e.g., child-focused instruction, family-focused support), a broad scope (i.e., they may address several developmental domains or skill areas), intensity (i.e., they often occur over an entire instructional day or in multiple settings such as a school/clinic and home), and longevity (i.e., they may occur over a month or even years)" (p. 11).

This type of definition incorporates procedural characteristics, and similar to the Committee on Educational Interventions for Children with Autism, attempts to address the issue of treatment "dosage" (i.e., parameters of intensity and duration of treatment). We offer a somewhat different, though not incompatible, approach to comprehensive treatment, choosing to focus on symptomatology rather than procedure.

Three core characteristics are presented in DSM-IV TR (*Diagnostic and Statistical Manual of Mental Disorders*: DSM-IV-TR, American Psychiatric Association, 2000) that are central to the pervasive developmental disorders (PDD): impairment of social interaction, impairment of communication, and characteristic behavior patterns. The spectrum of the PDDs (aka ASD), all contain these characteristics, but they all differ in the degree and nature of these characteristics. Thus, a comprehensive treatment program needs to address these core areas and the individual differences in the expression of related problems, as well as comorbid conditions. While it can be argued that biological treatments intended to impact causative mechanisms for the disorder would indirectly address these core deficits, to date no medical intervention has demonstrated such an effect. Further, there is no agreement across (or within) the many fields involved in service delivery and research, as to what measures should be used to evaluate treatment outcome. In the absence of such agreement, a review of the broad field of treatment for ASD becomes difficult and typically results in choice of arbitrary criteria (arbitrary in the sense that there is not consensus). We have chosen to focus on a survey of both sources of recommendations for the lay and professional public, and also published reviews of the literature, in an effort to address both the range of interventions recommended as well as the evaluation of data presented in support of interventions.

SURVEY OF STATUS OF INTERVENTION TYPES AND RESEARCH SUPPORT

The use of internet search engines is ubiquitous for both professionals and consumers. With this as a starting point, we identified 16 web-based sources of information concerning ASD that represented both private, professional groups, and government efforts. Our goal was to have a representative cross section of frequently visited sites. The sites we selected were:

ASAT
Autism Network Resources for Physicians
Autism Society of America

Autism Speaks
autism_resources.com
AutismToday.com
CAN
Centers for Disease Control
National Research Council – Educating Children With Autism
Healing Arts
Kyle's Treehouse
National Autism Association
NIMH
remedyfind.com
Spectrum Magazine
Wikipedia

Each site was reviewed and interventions presented for ASD were tabulated by site. A total of 414 interventions were identified. These interventions represented a diversity of biological, educational, psychological, and experiential (i.e., participation in interactive activities), and combinational approaches. The range of conceptual models represented were of such extent and ambiguity that categorization was not practical.

The tabulation produced a very surprising outcome with respect to consistency of interventions listed across web sites. It was anticipated that a least a small group of interventions would be consistently listed across web sites, indicating a general consensus of opinion for a subset of the large number of extant interventions. The data revealed a very different pattern as presented in Figure 12.1.

Figure 12.1 illustrates the diversity and disarray of evaluation of interventions for ASD. The clear majority of interventions, almost 80 percent, are mentioned in

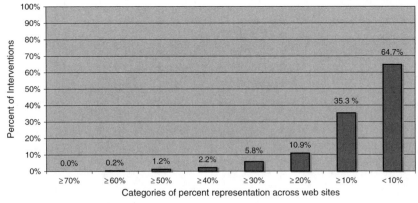

FIGURE 12.1 The percentage of interventions presented on the sample of web sites that occurred at specific frequencies across web sites.

only one or two sources of a total of 16. Fully one-third occur in only 1 of 16 web sites. Note that only 1.2 percent of interventions are mentioned in at least one half of the sites. It is thus not surprising that a common complaint of consumers is that sources for information on intervention for ASD are overwhelmingly confusing and contradictory.

Using a criterion that an intervention must appear in at least one-third of the web sites, only 14 interventions met this criterion, and are presented in Table 12.1. There was an almost equal distribution of biomedical, six, and experiential (broadly defined), eight. Examining the group of 14, one finds little in the way of consistency, whether for conceptual model, procedure, strength of underlying research base for components, difficulty of implementation, professional discipline, or cost.

In order to examine the research support for the 414 treatments identified in our survey, we turned to published, peer-reviewed outlets. The term "autism treatment review" was entered into the PsycINFO, ERIC, and www.scholar.google.com databases in late February and early March 2007. In addition, during this same time period the term "comprehensive autism treatment" was entered into the PsycINFO and ERIC databases. Finally, a search was conducted on www.scholar.google.com for each of the treatments listed in Table 12.1 with the term "review autism" (e.g., "facilitated communication review autism"). Sources published between 2000 and 2007 that contained

TABLE 12.1   Interventions appearing in at least one-third of sources.

Intervention	Biomedical?	Comprehensive?	Hits (%)
Diet: gluten-free; casein-free	Y	Y	63
Creative arts therapy: music therapy	N	Y	56
Occupational therapy: sensory integration therapy	N	Y	56
Treatment and Education of Autism and Related Communication Handicapped Children (TEACCH)	N	Y	56
Secretin	Y	Y	50
ABA	N	Y	44
Speech therapy	N	N	44
Relationship development intervention (RDI)	N	Y	44
Vitamin B_6 (pyridoxine)	Y	Y	44
ABA: Lovaas	N	Y	38
Chelation therapy: DMSA	Y	Y	38
Hyperbaric oxygen treatment (HBOT)	N	Y	38
Facilitated communication	N	Y	38
Vitamin B_{12}	Y	Y	38

reviews of both research and the extant literature were retained for further analysis. The reviews identified are marked with an asterisk in the references list. Coding procedures consisted of identifying interventions reviewed and/or summarized and the corresponding research support cited within the review. Interestingly, a total of exactly 100 treatment approaches/procedures were identified using this procedure. The reviews were then aggregated by treatment to allow assignment of strength of evidence rankings for each of the treatments associated with one or more reviews. Inter-rater agreement for assignment of reviews to treatments was 100 percent. The following definitions were then used to determine the strength of evidence for the individual treatments:

1. Review opinion "strong" – At least two studies with control groups that show significant changes across all three areas of symptoms OR at least three studies with control groups that show significant changes in two of the three areas of symptoms.
2. Review opinion "moderate" – One study with a control group that shows significant changes across all three areas of symptoms OR two studies with control groups that show significant changes in two of the three areas of symptoms OR three or more group studies with or without control groups that show significant changes in any area OR five or more group or single subject studies that show significant changes in any area.
3. Review opinion "limited" – Some research supporting effectiveness, but does not meet criteria of strong or moderate support.
4. Review opinion "limited – single subject research only" – Some research supporting effectiveness, but research is from single subject studies only.
5. Review opinion "mixed" – Meets criteria for strong, moderate, or limited support but also has studies indicating no effect of treatment or studies with ambiguous results.
6. Review opinion "outcome research unavailable" – No research supporting positive effect, but no research indicating no effect.
7. Review opinion "not supported" – No research supporting positive effect AND one to two studies indicating no effect.
8. Review opinion "not recommended" – No research supporting positive effect AND three or more studies indicating no effect AND/OR evidence of harm to participants.

Of the 100 treatment procedures and approaches identified, and evaluated, having appeared in at least one published review, a large percentage (45 percent) did not have outcome research available. Although there were a handful of descriptive programmatic summarizations in this category of programs that did not present themselves as research studies, (e.g., descriptions of the program strategies used at schools for children with autism spectrum disorders that rely on the utilization of empirically supported treatments, such as the Alpine Learning Group and the Children's Unit for Treatment and Evaluation), many of the approaches lacking research were common, individual treatments promoted for general use (e.g., aquatic therapy, occupational therapy, and pet/animal therapy). Twenty-three percent of the treatments had some support in favor of the approach (2 percent strong, 7 percent moderate, and 14 percent limited), having met the definitional requirements to be rated as having support for the procedure. The interventions in these three categories were:

STRONG RESEARCH SUPPORT

- Discrete trial instruction (ABA)
- UCLA Young Autism Project (ABA – Lovaas)

MODERATE RESEARCH SUPPORT

- Applied behavior analysis
- Stimulants
- Denver Model
- Pivotal Response Model of University of California at Santa Barbara
- Walden Early Childhood Programs at Emory University
- Douglass Developmental Disabilities Center
- Lifeskills and Education for Students with Autism and other Pervasive Developmental Disorders (LEAP)
  (Note that five of these treatment approaches are center-based programs.)

LIMITED RESEARCH SUPPORT

- Autism Preschool Program
- Child's talk
- Floortime/Developmental Individual Difference
- Incidental teaching
- Scottish Centre for Autism
- Touch therapy
- Treatment and Education of Autism and Related Communication Handicapped Children (TEACCH)
- Princeton Child Development Institute (PCDI)
- Oxytocin infusion
- Antihypertensive medication
- Atypical antipsychotics
- Vitamin B_{12}

LIMITED RESEARCH SUPPORT – SINGLE SUBJECT ONLY

- Hyperbaric oxygen treatment (HBOT)
- Exercise

Unfortunately, none of the aforementioned treatment approaches may be considered "comprehensive" by our definition. That is, no treatment, with at least some empirical support, demonstrated improvements in *all* of the core areas of autism. This was due either to a failure to measure changes in these areas, or that there was not a significant change due to treatment. This speaks to the heart of the intervention evaluation process. There are no generally agreed upon measurement instruments, methodology, nor focus in such research. We feel the standard of improvements in *all* of the core areas of autism is a reasonable criteria for "comprehensive" treatment evaluation.

Also, not all of the above interventions should be considered to have equal research "weight." We used a rating system designed to minimize bias and to objectively apply clear criteria. However, not all reviews provided equal detail as to research study methods and outcome. As an example, while both are categorized under "Limited Research Support," HBOT and exercise have significantly different research support. The HBOT research consists of simple case study using an AB design, the weakest of the single subject design methodologies. In contrast, research on exercise were based on more sophisticated reversal and counterbalanced alternating treatment designs. Thus it is important to emphasize the degree of heterogeneity in research design and methodology quality within and across our rating categories.

Twelve percent of the treatment approaches received a ranking of "mixed" due to research showing effectiveness of procedures, as well as findings that were not in support of treatment effectiveness. Treatments falling within this category included:

- Gluten-free/casein-free diet (GFCF diet)
- Ketogenic diet
- Sensory integration training
- Vision therapy
- Immunotherapy
- Anticonvulsants
- Cyproheptadine
- Developmental – pragmatic interventions/developmentally based interventions
- Speech therapy
- Haloperidol
- Naltrexone
- Risperdal

This category encompassed interventions with variability in rigor showing support for procedures, ambiguity in the findings and evidence failing to show support for treatment procedures. For example, there were more studies showing ambiguous results for GFCF ($N = 8$) than studies showing a positive effect ($N = 5$). Additionally, only one of the studies in support of the diet had a control group. Therefore, it is important to evaluate the interventions rated as having "mixed" support against a backdrop of the scientific rigor and methodology used to investigate effectiveness. As this chapter was based solely on reviews of research that others completed, it was often difficult to fully determine the complete details of all of the studies. Many review articles did not fully describe the methodology used in the studies investigating the intervention approaches. Because full review of all of the research literature on all possible treatments for autism is beyond the scope of this chapter, we urge professionals to make these comparisons before adopting or recommending treatment approaches.

Five percent of the interventions had studies failing to show efficacy (patterning, digestive enzymes, carnosine supplementation, famatodine, and essential fatty acids/omega 3 fatty acids). The findings were ambiguous for these five treatment approaches. In addition, there was one study with a control group that clearly failed to show a positive effect for patterning.

Finally, 15 percent of the treatment approaches were not recommended due to: (1) substantial research demonstrating ineffectiveness of procedures; or (2) some research showing support, but evidence of harm to recipients of the treatment. These included:

■ Auditory integration training
■ Facilitated communication
■ Holding therapy
■ Music therapy
■ Chelation
■ Antibiotics
■ Antifungal medication
■ Antiviral medication
■ Fefluramine
■ Secretin
■ Selective serotonin reuptake inhibitors (SSRIs)
■ Tricyclic antibiotics
■ Dimethylglycine
■ Megavitamin therapy
■ Vitamin B_6

Parents and professionals are strongly cautioned to select alternatives to the foregoing treatments when choosing an intervention approach.

Finally, we compared the strength of evidence rankings with the 14 interventions from Table 12.1. A majority of these interventions (64 percent) either had no outcome research ($N = 1$; relationship development intervention), were not recommended ($N = 5$; music therapy, secretin, vitamin B_6, chelation therapy, and facilitated communication), or had mixed results ($N = 3$; GFCF diet, sensory integration, and speech therapy). Only one was listed as having strong research support (ABA: Lovaas), and only one approach was rated as having met the requirements as having moderate research support backing its procedures (i.e., ABA: General), whereas 21 percent had limited empirical evidence ($N = 2$;

TEACCH, and vitamin B_{12}) or limited evidence with only single subject research support ($N = 1$; HBOT).

What do these data tell us? First, there are a myriad of interventions presented as options for autism when one accesses the internet for information. If a parent were to select from the most frequently cited interventions, he or she would be more likely to select an intervention that lacks sufficient empirical evidence (i.e., does not have strong or moderate support for its procedures) than one with evidence from carefully controlled studies. Based on examination of current reviews of published treatment approaches for autism, a bleak picture is painted with respect to outcome research. Only two interventions met the criterion for a ranking of "strong" evidence (e.g., discrete trial instruction, a specific component of ABA methodology, and the UCLA Young Autism Project (Lovaas), also based on ABA methodology). Although there were a handful of interventions ranked as "moderate" and "limited" support, only 23 percent of interventions had some type of support with concurrent absence of evidence indicating no effect, or ill effect, of treatment. These results are presented in Table 12.2.

CONSUMER PERSPECTIVE

Decision-making strategies. Families want the best for their children. However, with over 400 "treatments" for individuals with ASD advertised and available, and in the absence of widely disseminated specific guidelines to assist in making treatment decisions, families often find themselves in a difficult situation: What treatment do we select? How do we know that is the best one? Who do we go to? These questions are common amongst families of children with ASD. We have broadly characterized previously some of the strategies that families use to select treatment options (Romanczyk and Gillis, 2005). These strategies/beliefs are briefly presented in a colloquial language format as follows:

- "They know what's best" – Trust is placed in a service provider to choose. Trust may be based on both positive as well as negative characteristics, such as reputation, personal likable qualities, willingness to spend time with parents, promises of effectiveness, minimizing child's deficits, and offering a good prognosis.
- "Hedge your bets" – Do a little bit of everything in the belief that it can't hurt. This approach assumes that all components are compatible with one another and that the balance and sequence between approaches is not important and that the amount (or dosage) of an intervention approach is not critical.
- "Fanatical focus" – Pursue a single course with overwhelming intensity and focus that goes beyond the typical recommendations. Based on the false belief that if a specific "dosage" is good, then increasing it is better. Such extreme focus is often based on a lack of understanding of the

TABLE 12.2 Support for 100 interventions based on analysis of published reviews.

Intervention	Number of studies in support	Number of single subject studies in support	Number of studies in support with a control group	Number of studies with ambiguous results	Number of studies with negative results	Number of review articles indicating potential harm due to treatment	Number of descriptive or opinion-based reviews that mention treatment	Review opinion
Discrete trial (ABA)	8	0	6	0	0	0	4	Strong support
University of California Los Angeles Young Autism Project	5	0	5	0	0	0	5	Strong support
Applied behavior analysis (ABA)	3	0	2	0	0	0	8	Moderate support
Denver Model	5	0	0	0	0	0	4	Moderate support
Douglass Developmental Disabilities Center	3	0	2	0	0	0	5	Moderate support
Lifeskills and Education for Students with Autism and other Pervasive Developmental Disorders (LEAP)	3	0	0	0	0	0	4	Moderate support
Pivotal Response Model at University of California at Santa Barbara	3	0	0	0	0	0	1	Moderate support
Stimulants (e.g., methylphenidate, pemoline)	3	0	3	0	0	0	3	Moderate support

(*Continues*)

TABLE 12.2 (Continued)

Intervention	Number of studies in support	Number of single subject studies in support	Number of studies in support with a control group	Number of studies with ambiguous results	Number of studies with negative results	Number of review articles indicating potential harm due to treatment	Number of descriptive or opinion-based reviews that mention treatment	Review opinion
Walden Early Childhood Programs at Emory	3	0	0	0	0	0	3	Moderate support
Antihypertensives (e.g., (clonidine, propanolol)	2	0	0	0	0	0	3	Limited support
Atypical antipsychotics (e.g., olanzapine, quetiapine)	1	0	0	0	0	0	4	Limited support
Autism Preschool Program	1	0	1	0	0	0	0	Limited support
Child's talk	1	0	1	0	0	0	0	Limited support
Exercise	4	4	0	0	0	0	0	Limited support
Floortime/developmental individual difference (DIR)	1	0	1	0	0	0	7	Limited support
Hyperbaric oxygen treatment	1	1	0	0	0	0	0	Limited support
Incidental teaching	1	0	0	0	0	0	2	Limited support
Oxytocin infusion	1	0	0	0	0	0	1	Limited support
Princeton Child Development Institute (PCDI)	1	0	0	0	0	0	2	Limited support

Scottish Centre for Autism	1	0	0	0	0	0	Limited support
Touch therapy	1	1	0	0	0	0	Limited support
Treatment and Education of Autism and Related Communication Handicapped Children (TEACCH)	1	1	0	0	0	11	Limited support
Vitamin B_{12}	1	0	0	0	0	1	Limited support
Anticonvulsants (e.g., lamotrigine)	1	0	0	1	0	1	Mixed support
Cyproheptadine	1	0	1	0	0	1	Mixed support
Developmental – pragmatic interventions/ Developmentally based interventions	3	1	0	1	0	0	Mixed support
Gluten-free casein-free (GFCF) diet	5	1	8	0	0	3	Mixed support
Haloperidol	1	1	0	1	0	2	Mixed support
Immunotherapy (e.g., transfer factor, pentoxifylline, or intravenous immune globulin)	3	0	1	4	0	2	Mixed support
Ketogenic diet	1	0	1	0	0	2	Mixed support
Naltrexone	6	2	1	3	0	3	Mixed support

(Continues)

TABLE 12.2 (*Continued*)

Intervention	Number of studies in support	Number of single subject studies in support	Number of studies in support with a control group	Number of studies with ambiguous results	Number of studies with negative results	Number of review articles indicating potential harm due to treatment	Number of descriptive or opinion-based reviews that mention treatment	Review opinion
Risperdal/risperdone	11	0	3	0	1	0	3	Mixed support
Sensory integration training	8	6	1	2	0	0	5	Mixed support
Speech therapy	2	2	0	0	1	0	2	Mixed support
Vision therapy (e.g., prisms)	2	0	0	1	0	0	3	Mixed support
Alpine Learning Group	0	0	0	0	0	0	1	Outcome research unavailable
Amphetamines	0	0	0	0	0	0	1	Outcome research unavailable
Antidepressants (e.g., buproprion)	0	0	0	0	0	0	2	Outcome research unavailable
Anxiolytics (e.g., buspirone, lorazepam, clonazepam)	0	0	0	0	0	0	4	Outcome research unavailable
Aquatic therapy	0	0	0	0	0	0	1	Outcome research unavailable
Art therapy	0	0	0	0	0	0	1	Outcome research unavailable
Assistive technology	0	0	0	0	0	0	1	Outcome research unavailable

Augmentative communication	0	0	0	0	2	Outcome research unavailable
Behavioral therapy	0	0	0	0	1	Outcome research unavailable
Brain surgery	0	0	0	0	1	Outcome research unavailable
Children's Unit for Treatment and Evaluation	0	0	0	0	2	Outcome research unavailable
Corticosteroids (e.g., prednisone)	0	0	0	0	2	Outcome research unavailable
Craniosacral manipulations	0	0	0	0	4	Outcome research unavailable
Fast ForWord	0	0	0	0	2	Outcome research unavailable
Feingold diet	0	0	0	0	1	Outcome research unavailable
Gentle teaching	0	0	0	0	2	Outcome research unavailable
Giant steps	0	0	0	0	1	Outcome research unavailable
Higashi school	0	0	0	0	2	Outcome research unavailable
Horseback riding	0	0	0	0	1	Outcome research unavailable

(*Continues*)

TABLE 12.2 (*Continued*)

Intervention	Number of studies in support	Number of single subject studies in support	Number of studies in support with a control group	Number of studies with ambiguous results	Number of studies with negative results	Number of review articles indicating potential harm due to treatment	Number of descriptive or opinion-based reviews that mention treatment	Review opinion
Individualized Support Program at University of South Florida Tampa	0	0	0	0	0	0	1	Outcome research unavailable
Interactive metronome	0	0	0	0	0	0	1	Outcome research unavailable
Joint action routines	0	0	0	0	0	0	1	Outcome research unavailable
Lithium	0	0	0	0	0	0	1	Outcome research unavailable
Low phenylalanine diet	0	0	0	0	0	0	2	Outcome research unavailable
Low tryptophan diet	0	0	0	0	0	0	1	Outcome research unavailable
Melatonin	0	0	0	0	0	0	1	Outcome research unavailable
Miller method	0	0	0	0	0	0	1	Outcome research unavailable
Mineral supplements (e.g., calcium or folic acid)	0	0	0	0	0	0	4	Outcome research unavailable
Neuroleptics	0	0	0	0	0	0	2	Outcome research unavailable

Occupational therapy	0	0	0	1	Outcome research unavailable
Options/Son-Rise	0	0	0	3	Outcome research unavailable
Pet/animal therapy	0	0	0	1	Outcome research unavailable
Pharmacotherapy	0	0	0	1	Outcome research unavailable
Picture Exchange Communication System (PECS)	0	0	0	3	Outcome research unavailable
Pivotal response training	0	0	0	3	Outcome research unavailable
Play therapy	0	0	0	3	Outcome research unavailable
Positive behavioral support (PBS)	0	0	0	1	Outcome research unavailable
Relationship development intervention	0	0	0	1	Outcome research unavailable
Serotonin and norepinephrine reuptake inhibitors (SNRIs) (e.g., venlafaxine)	0	0	0	2	Outcome research unavailable
Social pragmatic communication approach	0	0	0	2	Outcome research unavailable
Specific carbohydrate diet	0	0	0	2	Outcome research unavailable

(Continues)

TABLE 12.2 (Continued)

Intervention	Number of studies in support	Number of single subject studies in support	Number of studies in support with a control group	Number of studies with ambiguous results	Number of studies with negative results	Number of review articles indicating potential harm due to treatment	Number of descriptive or opinion-based reviews that mention treatment	Review opinion
Tryptophan and tyrosine supplementation	0	0	0	0	0	0	2	Outcome research unavailable
Van Dijk circular approach	0	0	0	0	0	0	1	Outcome research unavailable
Verbal behavior analysis (VBA)	0	0	0	0	0	0	1	Outcome research unavailable
Vitamin supplementation (e.g. vitamin A, vitamin C)	0	0	0	0	0	0	2	Outcome research unavailable
Carnosine supplementation	0	0	0	1	0	0	0	Not supported
Digestive enzymes	0	0	0	1	0	0	0	Not supported
Essential fatty acids/omega 3 fatty acids or polyunsaturated fatty acid	0	0	0	1	0	0	1	Not supported
Famatodine (pepcid)	0	0	0	1	0	0	1	Not supported
Patterning	0	0	0	1	1	0	0	Not supported
Antibiotics (e.g., D-cycloserine, vancomycin)	2	0	0	0	0	1	2	Not recommended
Antifungal medication	0	0	0	1	0	2	2	Not recommended

								Not recommended
Antiviral medications (e.g., amantadine)	0	0	0	0	1	1	2	Not recommended
Auditory integration training	1	0	1	6	4	3	6	Not recommended
Chelation	0	0	0	0	3	4	2	Not recommended
Dimethylglycine (DMG)	0	0	0	0	2	1	3	Not recommended
Facilitated communication	3	3	0	6	21	1	10	Not recommended
Fenfluramine	0	0	0	2	0	1	1	Not recommended
Holding therapy						1	2	Not recommended
Mega vitamin therapy	1	0	0	0	2	1	5	Not recommended
Music therapy	0	0	0	0	3	0	5	Not recommended
Secretin	4	0	2	0	19	0	8	Not recommended
Selective serotonin reuptake inhibitors (SSRIs) (e.g., fluvoxamine, fluoxetine, paroxetine)	2	0	1	0	1	1	7	
Tricyclic antidepressants (e.g., clomipramine, desipramine)	4	0	2	1	0	5	3	Not recommended
Vitamin B$_6$ (pyidoxine)	6	0	0	5	2	1	2	Not recommended

empirical literature and lack of appropriate child-centered assessment and evaluation information.

- "Hope for the best" – Forgo formal treatment and participate in typical activities that are available. Often influenced by family members who don't "trust" professionals, have examples of family members or knowledge of other families where someone was slow to develop and ultimately "turned out fine."
- "Cure du Jour" – Pursue each new treatment as they appear and drop the current program. This approach stems from the "new is better" philosophy and often reflects being overly influenced by marketing, "breakthrough" announcements in the media, and the simple repetition of history.
- "A friend told me" – Do what seemed to work for the child of someone you know or have read about. Since autism spectrum disorders encompass a broad heterogeneity of specific child characteristics and expression of severity, this approach ignores important child characteristics.
- "Guru selection" – Following and believing in a single, specific "expert." The approach is packaged in the context of the "expert" having made "breakthroughs," is outside the "establishment," and use of seemingly impressive case studies to prove the approach works.

These decision-making strategies are common and do not come as a surprise to most clinicians and professionals in the field of ASD. However, without providing families with decision-making tools, these strategies will continue to be used and this may lead to the continuation of the selection and delivery of unproven or even dangerous treatments when more effective interventions are available.

Identifying and categorizing existing treatments for children with ASD is helpful in assisting with the decision-making process. Unfortunately, as determined from our review, most research on comprehensive treatment packages for ASD yields heterogeneous results, meaning that some children experience significant gains and others do not. The field of ASD lacks the ability to determine, a priori, which treatment package is going to result in the most positive treatment gains for one child over another.

Most consumers, parents, and professionals look to the internet when interested in a subject area, including ASD and treatments. Given the results from Table 12.1, where the percentage of hits are displayed for 14 interventions, it would appear that consumers would look to such "popular" treatments, and thus misinterpret these as "the best or most effective" treatments because they are mentioned frequently. Without a critical examination of these treatments, parents and many professionals are reduced to using the internet and trying to find chapters or books for parents/professionals that provide treatment recommendations. Rarely do consumers have the ability to examine or read primary sources (i.e., journal articles) of treatments for ASD. Service coordinators or case workers bear the burden of recommending comprehensive treatments to families or attempting to put together a number of separate treatments for a comprehensive treatment package for the child and family. This is understandably difficult, as service coordinators are typically seeing parents soon after they have received a diagnosis of ASD for their child, which is undoubtedly during an emotionally taxing period coupled with the urgency to begin treatment as soon as possible.

This is an interesting dilemma: The marketing of ineffective treatments on the internet may be able to guide decisions of parents/consumers much like commercials advocate consumers to buy one type of laundry detergent over another. It is not clear how to easily and effectively mend this situation.

REVIEW OF IMPORTANT FAMILY FACTORS IN COMPREHENSIVE TREATMENT

An important consideration when implementing a comprehensive treatment package for children with ASD is the family context. By family context, we mean the family's priorities for change in their child, the family's level of involvement in the intervention for the child, family stress level, socioeconomic status, services available to the family, etc. In order for external validity of a comprehensive treatment package to be fully assessed, these factors related to family needs are important. Treatment packages should take into account the child's strengths and weaknesses as well as the family's needs. This next section of the chapter provides information on parental perceptions of interventions, parental stress, social support, and siblings. These four important family factors need to be taken into consideration when choosing a comprehensive treatment for a child with ASD.

Parental Perceptions of Interventions. Hume et al. (2005) conducted a large-scale study of parent perceptions of early intervention and early childhood education for young children with ASD. The authors surveyed 195 parents whose children received a range of services. The results of the survey indicated that most (73.8 percent) children receive intervention in public preschool settings or in the home (16.4 percent). The three most frequently reported intervention services received included speech therapy (89.2 percent), occupational therapy (83.1 percent) and classroom aides (46.7 percent). Children received the highest number of hours of intervention for discrete trial training (16.2 h), classroom aide (15.4 h), and augmentative communication (11.6 h). The authors found that the majority of families were satisfied with the interventions received and agreed that each intervention the child was receiving contributed strongly to the child's development. The top four interventions rated by families as having a strong impact to the child's development were speech therapy, sensory integration, discrete trial training, and social supports. It is interesting and also alarming that sensory integration was perceived as having a significant impact on a child's growth given the lack of empirical support for its efficacy in treatment of ASD (Baranek, 2002). Another treatment lacking in empirical support, but favored highly was Floortime. Floortime (Developmental, Individual Differences, Relationship-based model) was reported as having perceived positive outcomes to social, cognitive and speech development. Other interventions that were reported to have perceived positive outcomes to these areas of development by parents were integration with typical peers and parent training.

Parents also reported that parent participation was encouraged, but less than a quarter of parents reported receiving parent training as an intervention. In addition, less than a quarter of parents reported having a case manager or coordinator of intervention services. Even though the number of hours of each intervention received varied, 66 percent of families reported receiving less than 25 h of services per week. This study included parents' reports about practices of EI and school age interventions for ASD, and parents' perceptions as to the influence of interventions on several areas of development. The authors note the inherent response bias in the study and that parents may not necessarily be accurate judges of developmental change or progress. However, this study does provide useful information about the types of interventions received and parental perception of such interventions.

One must ask why such a response bias might occur. That is, why did a very high percentage of parents report that all interventions were effective or helpful in treating their child with ASD? Several factors are possible contributing factors.

Parental Stress. It is common for parents to experience varying levels of stress who are raising typically developing toddlers. Parenting a toddler with ASD has shown to even more stressful (Baker-Ericzén et al., 2005). In fact, two-thirds of mothers of children with ASD experience significantly higher levels of stress than parenting children without ASD (Tomanik et al., 2004). Other studies confirm significantly elevated stress levels in both parents of children with ASD compared to parents of typically developing children (Baker-Ericzén et al., 2005; Hastings, 2003). The sources of parental stress include specific child characteristics as well as care taking issues (Baker-Ericzén et al., 2005; Bebko et al., 1987; Kelly and Booth, 1999; Moes, 1995). Some of the child-specific characteristics related to stress include the difficulty children have with expressive language, disruptive behaviors, and cognitive impairments. In addition, treatment decision-making can also be a stress-inducing task for parents of children with ASD (Guralnick, 2000). This is due to the difficulty parents might have with deciding which treatment option to obtain for their child with ASD. After receiving an initial diagnostic evaluation, parents are then bombarded with large amounts of information related to the diagnosis, prognosis, range of treatment options, etc., which can be stress-inducing (Guralnick, 2000).

Interventions aimed at reducing parental stress have been documented in the literature. Some interventions that have reduced parental stress include parent education and training programs, parent support groups, teaching parents relaxation techniques and other cognitive and behavioral strategies for coping and stress reduction (Feldman and Werner, 2002; Hawkins and Singer, 1989; Nixon and Singer, 1993; Santelli et al., 2002). A study by Siklos and Kerns (2006) identified specific needs of parents of children with ASD in British Columbia, Canada. Parents indicated that having more consistent services and professionals knowledgeable in ASD is a frequently reported need.

Social support. It has been well documented that parents of children with ASD who receive social support tend to have higher and healthy levels of adaptation (Bristol, 1984, 1987; Sanders and Morgan, 1997; Siklos and Kerns, 2006). These social supports include support from spouse, immediate family, extended family, friends, and support groups. A study by Konstantareas and Homatidis (1989) compared amount of support received by parents of children with ASD to parents of typically developing children. According to this study, both parents receive an equal amount of social support. However, parents of children with ASD reported a higher frequency of aggravations compared to typically developing children (Konstantareas, 1991). This increase in reported aggravations may lead to increased stress reported by parents of children with ASD. Thus, the actual amount of social support may not be the critical factor in predicting healthy adaptation, but rather the perception of social support.

The importance of beliefs about social support is evidenced by several studies showing that perceived support leads to healthy adaptation (Bristol, 1984; Wolf et al., 1989). With regard to what the social supports for families should look like, Agosta (1989) offers three essential components: (1) parents should be able to make informed decisions about the services their child receives; (2) the entire family should be able to receive support services; and (3) each family is different and will have different needs, and the services available to family should be flexible in meeting individual family needs. This emphasis of evaluating family needs and quality of life is also an important element of the suggestions made by investigators of the Early Child Outcome (ECO) project (ECO, 2005).

Siblings. Evaluating family needs also includes evaluating siblings' needs, adaptation, and development. Hastings (2003) suggest that siblings of children with ASD exhibited poorer psychological adjustment compared to siblings of normally developing children. This finding is consistent with previous studies examining psychological adjustment in siblings (Fisman et al., 2000; Lardieri et al., 2000). However, there are also a number of studies reporting contradictory results; siblings of children with ASD are at no more increased risk for the development of adjustment difficulties or behavioral problems than siblings of typically developing children (Burton and Parks, 1994; McHale and Gamble, 1987). Recent research has begun to evaluate why the discrepancy in previous findings exist. One such reason could be due to the heterogeneity of ASD; perhaps the more severe a child's disability the worse the sibling adjustment. Verte et al. (2003) examined sibling adjustment to having a sibling with high functioning autism (HFA). These authors found that siblings of children with HFA between the ages of 6 and 11 years exhibited a higher number of externalizing behaviors than siblings of typically developing children. This is most likely accounted for by attention seeking behavior (Boyce and Barnett, 1993), given the elevated stress families experience and the increased amount of attention typically given to the child with HFA. However, in terms of self-concept, children with more positive self-concept exhibited higher levels of social competence, regardless of having a sibling with HFA.

RECOMMENDATIONS

Researchers must continue to increase the number of empirical studies evaluating the effectiveness of different comprehensive treatments. Parents, service coordinators, and case workers must be taught how to be critical in selecting treatments and to examine the support or lack of support for such treatments. Given the data regarding parent perceptions of treatment, it is crucial to use additional measures of treatment outcome. The involvement of and consideration for family needs is an area that we recommend be included in comprehensive treatment packages based on the available research regarding parental stress, social support and sibling adjustment. Social support, and even the perception of social support, is critical for parents, in terms of reducing stress and selecting treatments. It has been shown that siblings may experience adjustment difficulties, including behavior problems, especially at young ages. Assessing these variables is important for recommending and selecting specific treatments for families, especially since early on in the treatment process is typically the most stressful.

Treatment outcome research remains poor with regard to the assessment of comprehensive treatments for ASD. It is clear that there are comprehensive treatments being recommended and implemented for ASD, which have no research support for their efficacy. As outlined in Table 12.2, treatments that have been shown to cause harm are nevertheless supported by agencies, providers, and parents as viable treatments. This is disappointing, but not surprising. Even in the era of "empirically supported treatments," the use of ineffective, sham, or harmful treatments for ASD continues despite evidence against specific treatments or the lack of evidence for specific treatments.

It is important to emphasize that ASD are not disorders of arrested development. Children with ASD change over time in the absence of formal treatment. Therefore, the standard that should be used to evaluate treatments is not simply "Has the child's behavior changed from point A to point B?", but rather, "Does the treatment produce a rate of change that exceeds no treatment, comparison treatments, as well as appropriate control conditions?" In addition, measurement of change of all core deficit areas of ASD is imperative to determine whether a treatment is "comprehensive" or core-specific. It is also critical that assessment of change be performed trans-situationally, not simply within the treatment milieu. Such simple standards would greatly clarify the efficacy of the plethora of treatments offered for ASD. It is unfortunately the case that at this time most children are receiving what must be termed "experimental" treatments (i.e., treatments that have not been empirically tested and supported) in the absence of informed consent by parents and guardians. Because there are multiple consumers of a given treatment for ASD, personal evaluation of effectiveness by caregivers can be influenced by many factors that are independent of child success (Romanczyk and Gillis, 2007). It is because of these issues of multiple consumers and nonsuccess-related factors that the popularity and frequency of use of treatments do not correlate with extensiveness and strength of research support.

REFERENCES

Review articles used in the analysis of treatments are marked with an asterisk.

Agosta, J. (1989). Using cash assistance to support family efforts. In *Support for Caregiving Families: Enabling Positive Adaptation to Disability* (G.H. Singer and L.K. Irvin, eds.). Baltimore: Paul H. Brookes.

American Psychiatric Association (2000). *Diagnostic and Statistical Manual of Mental Disorders: DSM-IV-TR (Fourth Edition, Text Revision)*. Washington, DC: American Psychiatric Association.

Baker-Ericzén, M.J., Brookman-Frazee, L., and Stahmer, A. (2005). Stress levels and adaptability in parents of toddlers with and without autism spectrum disorders. *Research & Practice for Persons with Severe Disabilities*, **30**, 194–204.

*Ball, C.M. (2004). Music therapy for children with autistic spectrum disorder. In Bazian Ltd (eds.) *STEER: Succinct and Timely Evaluated Evidence Reviews*, **4**(1), Bazian Ltd and WessexInstitute for Health Research & Development, University of Southampton. [WWW document] URL http://www.signpoststeer.org/

Baranek, G.T. (2002). Efficacy of sensory and motor interventions for children with autism. *Journal of Autism and Developmental Disorders*, **32**, 397–422.

*Bebko, J.M., Konstantareas, M.M., and Springer, J. (1987). Parent and professional evaluations of family stress associated with characteristics of autism. *Journal of Autism & Developmental Disorders*, **17**, 565–576.

*Benham, A.L. and Slotnick, C.F. (2006). Play therapy: integrating clinical and developmental perspectives. In *Handbook of Preschool Mental Health* (J.L. Luby, ed.) pp. 331–371. New York: The Guilford Press.

*Bodfish, J.W. (2004). Treating the core features of autism: Are we there yet? *Mental Retardation and Developmental Disabilities Research Review*, **10**, 318–326.

*Bosa, C.A. (2006). Autism: psychoeducational intervention. *Revista Brasileira de Psiquiatria*, **28** (Suppl. I), S47–S53.

Boyce, G.C. and Barnett, W.S. (1993). Siblings of persons with mental retardation: a historical perspective and recent findings. In *The Effects of Mental Retardation, Disability and Illness on Sibling Relationships: Research Issues and Challenges* (Z. Stoneman and P. Waldman, eds.) pp. 145–184. Paul H. Brookes Publishing Company: Baltimore, New York.

Bristol, M. (1984). Family resources and successful adaptation to autistic children. In *The Effects of Autism on the Family* (E. Schopler and G. B. Mesibov, eds.) pp. 289–310. New York: Plenum Press.

Bristol, M.M. (1987). Mothers of children with autism or communication disorders: Successful adaptation and the double ABCX model. *Journal of Autism and Developmental Disorders*, **17**, 469–486.

*Brown, K.A. and Patel, D.R. (2005). Complementary and alternative medicine in developmental disabilities. *Symposium on Developmental and Behavioral Disorders – II*, **72**, 949–952.

*Bryson, S.E., Rogers, S.J., and Fombonne, E. (2003). Autism spectrum disorders: Early detection, intervention, education, and psychopharmacological management. *Canadian Journal of Psychiatry*, **48**, 506–516.

Burton, S.L. and Parks, A.L. (1994). Self-esteem, locus of control and career aspirations of college-age siblings of individuals with disabilities. *Social Work Research*, **18**, 178–185.

Chambless, D.L. and Ollendick, T.H. (2001). Empirically supported psychological interventions: controversies and evidence. *Annual Review of Psychology*, **52**, 685–716.

*Christison, G.W. and Ivany, K. (2006). Elimination diets in autism spectrum disorders: Any wheat amidst the chaff? *Developmental and Behavioral Pediatrics*, **27**, S162–S171.

*Coakley, T., Richards, D., Bellevue, M., et al. (2002). *Autistic Spectrum Disorder: Intervention Guidance for Service Providers and Families of Young Children with Autistic Spectrum Disorder*. Hartford, CT: Connecticut State Department of Mental Retardation.

*Connecticut Birth to Three System (2002). *Autism Spectrum Disorder: Intervention Guidance for Service Providers and Families of Young children with Autistic Spectrum Disorder*. Hartford, CT: Connecticut State Department of Mental Retardation.

*Corsello, C.M. (2005). Early intervention in autism. *Infants and Young Children*, **18**, 74–85.

*Dawson, G. and Watling, R. (2000). Interventions to facilitate auditory, visual, and motor integration in autism: a review of the evidence. *Journal of Autism and Developmental Disorders*, **30**, 415–421.

*Dempsey, I. and Foreman, P. (2001). A review of educational approaches for individuals with autism. *International Journal of Disability, Development, and Education*, **48**, 103–116.

*des Portes, V., Hagerman, R.J., and Hendren, R.L. (2003). Pharmacotherapy. In *Autism Spectrum Disorders: A Research Review for Practitioners* (S. Ozonoff, S.J. Rogers, and R.L. Hendren, eds.) pp. 161–186. Arlington, VA: American Psychiatric Publishing, Inc.

Eddy, D.M. and Hasselblad, V. (1994). Analyzing evidence by the confidence and profile method. In *Clinical Practice Guideline Development: Methodology Perspectives* (AHCPR Publication No. 95-0009). (K.A. McCormick, S.R. Moore, and R.A. Siegel, eds.). Rockville, MD: US Department of Health and Human Services, Agency for Health Care Policy and Research, Public Health Service.

*Erickson, C.A., Stigler, K.A., Corkins, M.R., et al. (2005). Gastrointestinal factors in autistic disorder: a critical review. *Journal of Autism and Developmental Disorders*, **35**, 713–727.

*Esch, B.E. and Carr, J.E. (2004). Secretin as a treatment for autism: a review of the evidence. *Journal of Autism and Developmental Disorders*, **34**, 543–556.

*Faja, S. and Dawson, G. (2006). Early intervention for autism. In *Handbook of Preschool Mental Health* (J.L. Luby, ed.) pp. 388–416. New York: The Guilford Press.

Feldman, F.A. and Werner, S.E. (2002). Collateral effects of behavioral parent training on families of children with developmental disabilities and behavior disorders. *Behavioral Interventions*, **17**, 75–83.

Finn, P., Both, A.K., and Bramlett, R.E. (2005). Science and pseudoscience in communication disorders: criteria and applications. *American Journal of Speech-Language Pathology*, **14**, 172–185.

Fisman, S.M.B., Wolf, L.M.S., Ellison, D., and Freeman, T.M.D. (2000). A longitudinal study of siblings of children with chronic disabilities. *Canadian Journal of Psychiatry*, **45**, 369–375.

*Fisman, S. and Wolf, L. (1991). The handicapped child: psychological effects of parental, marital, and sibling relationships. *Psychiatric Clinics of North America*, **14**, 199–217.

*Francis, K. (2005). Autism interventions: a critical update. *Developmental Medicine and Child Neurology*, **47**, 493–499.

*Gabriels, R.L. (2002). Therapy: laying the foundation for individual and family growth. In *Autism – From Research to Individualized Practice* (R.L. Gabriels and D.E. Hill, eds.) pp. 91–126. London: Jessica Kingsley Publishers Ltd.

*Goldstein, H. (2000). Commentary: Interventions to facilitate auditory, visual, and motor integration: "show me the data". *Journal of Autism and Developmental Disorders*, **30**, 423–425.

*Goldstein, H. (2002). Communication intervention for children with autism: a review of treatment efficacy. *Journal of Autism and Developmental Disorders*, **32**(5), 373–396.

*Gupta, S. (2000). Immunological treatments for autism. *Journal of Autism and Developmental Disorders*, **30**, 475–479.

Guralnick, M.J. (2000). An agenda for change in early childhood inclusion. *Journal of Early Intervention*, **23**, 213–222.

*Hansen, R.L. and Ozonoff, S. (2003). Alternative theories: assessment and therapy options. In *Autism Spectrum Disorders: A Research Review for Practitioners* (S. Ozonoff, S.J. Rogers, and R.L. Hendren, eds.) pp. 187–208. Arlington, VA: American Psychiatric Publishing, Inc.

*Harris, S.L., Handleman, J.S., and Jennett, H.K. (2005). Models of educational intervention for students with autism: home, center, and school-based programming. In *Handbook of Autism and Pervasive Developmental Disorders*. 3rd ed. (F.R. Volkmar, R. Paul, A. Klin, and D. Cohen, eds.). Hoboken, NJ: John Wiley & Sons, Inc.

Hastings, R.P. (2003). Child behavior problems and partner mental health as correlates of stress in mothers and fathers of children with autism. *Journal of Intellectual Disability Research. Special Issue on Family Research*, **47**, 231–237.

Hawkins, N. and Singer, H.S. (1989). A skills training approach for assisting parents to cope with stress. In *Support for Caregiving Families: Enabling Positive Adaptation to Disability* (G.H.S. Singer and L.K. Irvin, eds.) pp. 71–83. Baltimore, MD: Paul H. Brookes Publishing Co.

Howard, J.S., Sparkman, C.R., Cohen, H.G., et al. (2005). A comparison of intensive behavior analytic and eclectic treatments for young children with autism. *Research in Developmental Disabilities*, **26**, 359–383.

Holland, J.P. (1995). Development of a clinical practice guideline for acute low back pain. *Current Opinion in Orthopedics*, **6**, 63–69.

Holland, J.P., Noyes-Grossier, D., Holland, C.L., et al. (2005). Rationale and methodology for developing guidelines for early intervention services for young children with developmental disabilities. *Infants and Young Children*, **18**(2), 119–135.

Hume, K., Bellini, S., and Pratt, C. (2005). The usage and perceived outcomes of early intervention and early childhood programs for young children with autism spectrum disorder. *Topics in Early Childhood Special Education*, **25**, 195–207.

Kelly, J.F. and Booth, C.L. (1999). Child care for infants with special needs: issues and applications. *Infants and Young Children*, **12**, 26–33.

*Kerbeshian, J., Burd, L., and Avery, K. (2001). Pharmacotherapy of autism: a review and clinical approach. *Journal of Developmental and Physical Disabilities*, **13**, 199–228.

*Knivsberg, A.M., Reichelt, K.L., and Noland, M. (2001). Reports on dietary interventions in autistic disorder. *Nutritional Neuroscience*, **4**, 25–37.

Konstantareas, M.K. (1991). Autistic, learning disabled and delayed children's impact on their parents. *Canadian Journal of Behavioural Science*, **23**, 358–375.

Konstantareas, M.K. and Homatidis, S. (1989). Assessing child symptom severity and stress in parents of autistic children. *Journal of Child Psychology and Psychiatry*, **30**, 459–470.

Lardieri, L.A., Blacher, J., and Swanson, H.L. (2000). Sibling relationships and parent stress in families of children with and without learning disabilities. *Learning Disability Quarterly*, **23**, 105–116.

*Levy, K., Kim, A.H., and Olive, M.L. (2006). Interventions for young children with autism: a synthesis of the literature. *Focus on Autism and Other Developmental Disabilities*, **21**, 55–62.

*Levy, S.E. and Hyman, S.L. (2002). Alternative/complementary approaches to treatment of children with autism spectrum disorders. *Infants and Young Children*, **14**(3), 33–42.

*Levy, S.E. and Hyman, S.L. (2005). Novel treatments for autistic spectrum disorders. *Mental Retardation and Developmental Disabilities Research Review*, **11**, 131–142.

*Luby, J.L.(ed.) (2006). Psychopharmacology. In *Handbook of Preschool Mental Health*, pp. 311–330. New York: The Guilford Press.

*Manning-Courtney, P., Brown, J., Molloy, C.A., et al. (2003). Diagnosis and treatment of autism spectrum disorders. *Current Problems in Pediatric and Adolescent Health Care*, **33**, 283–304.

*Mastergeorge, A.M., Rogers, S.J., Corbett, B.A., and Solomon, M. (2003). Nonmedical interventions for autism spectrum disorders. In *Autism Spectrum Disorders: A Research Review* *for Practitioners* (S. Ozonoff, S.J. Rogers, and R.L. Hendren, eds.) pp. 133–160. Arlington, VA: American Psychiatric Publishing, Inc.

McHale, S.M. and Gamble, W.C. (1987). Sibilng relationships and adjustment of children with disabled and nondisabled brothers and sisters. *Developmental Psychology*, **25**, 421–429.

*Millward, C., Ferriter, M., Calver, S., and Connell-Jones, G. (2004). Gluten- and casein-free diets for autistic spectrum disorder. *Cochrane Database of Systematic Reviews*, **2**. Art. No.: CD003498. DOI: 10.1002/14651858.CD003498.pub2.

Moes, D. (1995). Parent education and parenting stress. In *Teaching Children with Autism: Strategies for Initiating Positive Interactions and Improving Learning Opportunities* (R.L. Koegel and L.K. Koegel, eds.) pp. 79–93. Baltimore, MD: Paul H. Brookes Publishing Co.

*Mostert, M.P. (2001). Facilitated communication since 1995: A review of published studies. *Journal of Autism and Developmental Disorders*, **31**, 287–313.

National Research Council (2001). *Educating Children with Autism*. Washington, DC: National Academy Press.

Nixon, C.D. and Singer, G.H. (1993). Group cognitive behavioral treatment for excessive parental self-blame and guilt. *American Journal on Mental Retardation*, **97**, 665–672.

*Nye, C. and Brice, A. (2003). Combined vitamin B_6-magnesium treatment in autism spectrum disorder (Cochrane Review). In *The Cochrane Library*, **1**. Oxford: Update Software.

Odom, S.L., Rogers, S., McDougle, C.J., et al. (2007). Early intervention for children with autism spectrum disorder. In *Handbook of Developmental Disabilities* (S.L. Odom, R.H. Horner, M.E. Snell, and J. Blacher, eds.). New York: Guilford Press.

*Page, T. (2000). Metabolic approaches to the treatment of autism spectrum disorders. *Journal of Autism and Developmental Disorders*, **30**, 463–469.

*Rogers, S.J. and Ozonoff, S. (2006). Behavioral, educational, and developmental treatments for autism. In *Understanding Autism: From Basic Neuroscience to Treatment* (S.O. Moldin and J.L.R. Rubenstein, eds.). Boca Raton, FL: Taylor & Francis Group, LLC.

Romanczyk, R.G. and Gillis, J.M. (2005). Treatment approaches for autism: evaluating options and making informed choices. In *Autism: Identification, Education and Treatment*. 3rd ed. (D. Zager, ed.). Hillsdale, NJ: Lawrence Erlbaum Associates.

Romanczyk, R.G. and Gillis, J.M. (2007). Practice guidelines for autism education and intervention: Historical perspective and recent developments. In *Effective Practices for Children with Autism: Educational and Behavior Support Interventions that Work* (J.K. Luiselli, D.C. Russo and W.P. Christian, eds.). NY, NY: Oxford University Press.

Sanders, J.L. and Morgan, S.B. (1997). Family stress and adjustment as perceived by parents of children with autism or Down syndrome: implications for intervention. *Child and Family Behavior Therapy*, **19**, 15–32.

Santelli, B., Ginsberg, C., Sullivan, S., and Niederhauser, C. (2002). A collaborative study of parent to parent programs: implications for positive behavior support. In *Families and Positive Behavior Support: Addressing Problem Behavior in Family Contexts; Families and Positive Behavior Support; Addressing Problem Behavior in Family Contexts; Family, Community & Disability* (J.M. Lucyshyn and G. Dunlap, eds.) pp. 439–456. Baltimore, MD: Paul H. Brookes Publishing Co.

*Scott, J. and Baldwin, W.L. (2005). The challenge of early intensive intervention. In *Autism Spectrum Disorders* (D. Zager, ed.). Mahwah, NJ: Lawrence Erlbaum Associates, Inc.

Schriger, D.L. (1995). Training panels in methodology. In *Clinical Practice Guideline Development: Methodology Perspectives* (K.A. McCormick, S.R. Moore, and R.A. Siegel, eds.) (AHCPR Publication No. 95-0009). Rockville, MD: U.S. Department of Health and Human Services, Agency for Health Care Policy and Research, Public Health Service.

Siklos, S. and Kerns, K.A. (2006). Assessing need for social support in parents of children with autism and down syndrome. *Journal of Autism and Developmental Disorders*, **36**, 921–933.

*Simpson, R.L. (2005). Evidence-based practices and students with autism spectrum disorders. *Focus on Autism and Other Developmental Disabilities*, **20**, 140–149.

*Sinha Y., Silove N., Wheeler D., and Williams K. (2007). Auditory integration training and other sound therapies for autism spectrum disorders. *Cochrane Database of Systematic Reviews*, **1**. Art. No.: CD003681. DOI: 10.1002/14651858.CD003681.pub2.

*Sinha, Y., Silove, N., and Williams, K. (2006). Chelation therapy and autism. *British Medical Journal*, **333**, 7571.

*Sinha, Y., Silove, N., Wheeler, D., and Williams, K. (2006). Auditory integration training and other sound therapies for autism spectrum disorders: a systematic review. *Archives of Disease in Childhood*, **9**, 1018–1022.

*Stackhouse, T.M., Graham, N.S., Laschober, J.S., (2002). Occupational therapy intervention and autism. In *Autism – From Research to Individualized Practice* (R.L. Gabriels and D.E. Hill, eds.) pp. 155–178. London: Jessica Kingsley Publishers Ltd.

*Sturmey, P. (2005). Secretin is an ineffective treatment for pervasive developmental disabilities: a review of 15 double-blind randomized controlled trials. *Research in Developmental Disabilities*, **26**, 87–97.

*Tanguay, P.E. (2000). Pervasive developmental disorders: a 10-year review. *Journal of the American Academy of Child and Adolescent Psychiatry*, **39**, 1079–1095.

Tomanik, S., Harris, G.E., and Hawkins, J. (2004). The relationship between behaviours exhibited by children with autism and maternal stress. *Journal of Intellectual & Developmental Disability*, **29**, 16–26.

U.S. Institute of Medicine (1992). Committee on clinical practice guidelines. In *Guidelines for Clinical Practice: From Development to Use*. (M.J. Field and K.N. Lohr, eds.). Washington, DC: National Academy Press.

Verte, S., Roeyers, H., and Buysse, A. (2003). Behavioral problems, social competence and self-concept in siblings of children with autism. *Child: Care, Health, and Development*, **29**, 193–205.

Wolf, L.C., Noh, S., Fisman, S.N., and Speechley, M. (1989). Brief report: psychological effects of parenting stress on parents of autistic children. *Journal of Autism and Developmental Disorders*, **19**, 157–166.

Woolf, S.H. (1991). *AHCPR Interim Manual for Clinical Practice Guideline Development* (AHCPR Publication No. 91-0018). Rockville, MD: U.S. Department of Health and Human Services, Agency for Health Care Policy and Research, Public Health Service.

Woolf, S.H. (1994). An organized analytic framework for practice guideline development: using the analytic logic as a guide for reviewing evidence, developing recommendations, and explaining the rationale. In *Clinical Practice Guideline Development: Methodology Perspectives* (K.A. McCormick, S.R. Moore, and R.A. Siegel, eds.) (AHCPR Publication No. 95-0009). Rockville, MD: U.S. Department of Health and Human Services, Agency for Health Care Policy and Research, Public Health Service.

13

PHARMACOTHERAPY

LUKE Y. TSAI

University of Michigan Medical School, MI, USA

INTRODUCTION

It is clear that pervasive developmental disorders (PDDs) (autism spectrum disorder, ASD) have neurobiological etiologies. At present, however, no specific biological markers have been identified as the causes of PDDs that include autistic disorders, Asperger's disorder, Rett's disorder, childhood disintegrative disorder, and pervasive developmental disorder not otherwise specified (PDDNOS) according to DSM-IV of American Psychiatric Association (1994). Hence, etiologically based treatments or interventions have not been developed to "cure" individuals with PDDs. Currently, comprehensive intervention including parental counseling, behavior modification, special education in a highly structured environment, social skill training, sensory integration training, music therapy, vocational training, and medication treatment (pharmacotherapy) has been emphasized. The nonmedical treatments or interventions of PDDs have been described in other chapters of this book. The present chapter is written for parents and other caregivers of persons with PDDs with intent to help them gain more knowledge of when and how pharmacotherapy can and should be used as an important part of the comprehensive treatment PDDs. For the purpose of presentation, the term ASD will be used as a synonym of PDDs throughout the remaining sections of this chapter. However, due to very low prevalence rates of Rett's disorder and childhood disintegrative disorder, the literature review and the suggested pharmacotherapy are mainly relevant to the populations with autistic disorder, Asperger's disorder, and PDDNOS.

For this chapter, multiple literature searches were carried out using Entrez PubMed Database (www.pubmed.gov) which is a service of the US National Library of Medicine and the National Institute of Health. PubMed includes over 16 million citations from MEDLINE and other life science journals for biomedical articles back to the 1950s. However, for the present chapter, only those English-language studies published between 1994 and 2006 are reviewed. The main reason for this decision is that the current psychiatric diagnostic system of the American Psychiatric Association (*Diagnostic and Statistic Manual of Mental Disorder, 4th Edition*) (DSM-IV)) was established in 1994 (APA, 1994). Hence, most research reports published since 1994 tend to be based on the current diagnostic concept and system.

Multiple searches were done on psychotropic medications including anticonvulsants that had been studied in persons with ASD. A search that did not use any specific drug names was also performed. The present review of relevant literature does not include studies of vitamins and other supplements.

Although the main theme of this book is about "future direction in evidence intervention with older learners with ASD," there is very limited, if any, study of clinical conditions in the adults with ASD that may benefit the use of psychotropic medications as well as study of adverse and/or side effects of the psychotropic medications in adults with ASD.

RATIONALES FOR PHARMACOTHERAPY IN ASD

ASD HAS NEUROBIOLOGICAL DYSFUNCTIONS THAT MAY INVOLVED NEUROTRANSMITTERS

Neuroscientists have identified several types of neurotransmitters including catecholamine transmitters (epinephrine, norepinephrine, and dopamine), serotonin, acetylcholine, gamma-aminobutyric acid (GABA), and certain other amino acids and neuropeptides are connected to many human behaviors. For example, epinephrine and norepinephrine appear to be involved in emotional states such as arousal, rage, fear, anxiety, pleasure, stress response, motivation, and exhilaration. In addition, they also impact cardiovascular and respiratory function, eating and drinking, neuroendocrine regulation, activity level, selective attention, movement, memory, cognition, and learning.

Dopamine is crucial to every voluntary movement, and also is involved in cognition, eating and drinking, neuroendocrine regulation, sexual behavior, selective attention, etc.

Serotonin seems to play a crucial role in sleep and wakefulness, in certain types of sexual activity, and perhaps in modulating and balancing a wide range of synaptic activities such as body temperature, pain, sensory perception, immune response, motor function, neuroendocrine regulation, appetite, learning, memory, and learning.

Neuroscientists have also found that neuropsychiatric disorders are related to altered or dysregulated neurotransmitter systems. For example, Shortage of serotonin in the frontal lobes and in the brain's limbic system (where emotions come from) seems to relate to impulsivity. Individuals with inadequate serotonin are unable to connect disagreeable consequences with what provoked them. A serotonergic defect involving the basal ganglia may cause obsessive–compulsive symptoms in some people. The well-known psychotherapeutic medication, fluoxetine (Prozac) is a serotonin reuptake inhibitor (SRI) that can increase the availability of serotonin in the particular neural network relating to obsessive–compulsive disorder (OCD) and to improve the symptoms of OCD.

ASD is characterized by deficits in language usage, impairments in social reciprocity, and the presence of behavioral rigidity. ASD also has many coexisting neuropsychiatric disorders. (This aspect will be reviewed in the next section.) It is quite reasonable to speculate that ASD is related to dysfunctions of certain neurotransmitter systems and that certain medications may be appropriate and effective in improving ASD and coexisting neuropsychiatric disorders.

ASD HAS MANY COEXISTING NEUROPSYCHIATRIC DISORDERS THAT TEND TO RESPOND TO PHARMACOTHERAPY

Co-existing Neuropsychiatric Disorders in Autistic Disorder

Many children and adolescents with autistic disorder also develop other behavioral and/or psychiatric symptoms in addition to the core autistic symptomatologies. These additional symptoms may be considered as clinical manifestations of comorbid psychiatric disorders. In fact, there is an accumulation of case reports describing specific types of psychiatric disorders occurring in individuals with autistic disorders. Literature shows that children and adolescents with autistic disorder, about 60 percent had poor attention and concentration; 40 percent were hyperactive; 43–88 percent exhibited morbid or unusual preoccupation; 37 percent had obsessive phenomena; 16–86 percent showed compulsions or rituals; 50–89 percent demonstrated stereotyped utterance; 70 percent exhibited stereotyped mannerism; 17–74 percent had anxiety or fears; 9–44 percent showed depressive mood, irritability, agitation, and inappropriate affect; 24–43 percent had a history of self-injury; and 8 percent experienced tics. In the past, the medical community considered these additional symptoms as "associate features" of autistic disorder. Today, however, there are increasing numbers of investigators who argue for considering these additional behaviors/symptoms as features of coexisting neuropsychiatric disorders such as attention deficit hyperactivity disorder (ADHD), affective/mood disorders, anxiety disorder including OCD, and Tourette's disorder (reviewed by Tsai, 2005).

Follow-up studies of adults reported stereotyped/repetitive behaviors were noted in about 30–50 percent of the participants (Ballaban-Gil et al., 1996; Howlin et al., 2000, 2004). Ballaban-Gil et al. (1996) also reported that about 49 percent of adults engaged in self-injurious behavior.

At some stage during childhood, particularly under 8 years of age, the majority of autistic children were reported as having sleep problems including one or more of extreme sleep latencies (difficulty falling sleep); lengthy periods of night waking, shortened night sleep; early waking; and excessive daytime sleepiness (Elia et al., 2000; Patzold et al., 1998; Takase et al., 1998; Taira et al., 1998; Tsai et al., 1997). Tsai et al. (1997) surveyed parents of 226 (181 boys and 45 girls) children and adolescents with autistic disorder and found that about

10 percent of the children were considered as having severe sleep problem and about 22 percent as having moderate sleep problem.

Gail Williams et al. (2004) surveyed sleep problems in 210 children with autism and found that sleep problems are frequently reported by parents of children with autism with prevalence estimates of 44–83 percent for sleep disorders in this population. These individuals tend to keep the whole family awake every night because of their unusual sleep patterns. Other investigators, however, questioned parental oversensitivity to sleep disturbance of their autistic children (Hering et al., 1999; Schreck and Mulick, 2000).

Individuals with autism are particularly vulnerable to the development of seizure disorders (also called epilepsy). During the first decade of life, the incidence of epilepsy in children with autism is higher than that in the general population. Epilepsy has been noted in 4–42 percent of autistic persons (Giovanardi Rossi et al., 2000). Several reports have suggested that many autistic individuals first develop seizures in adolescence (Rutter, 1984). Volkmar and Nelson (1990) reported that risk for developing seizures in children with autism is highest during early childhood. A prospective study of epilepsy in children with autistic spectrum disorder found that about 5 percent of those with an autistic condition had epilepsy. Most had onset of seizures before the age of 1 year (Wong, 1993). A retrospective study of 60 individuals (mean age 17 years and 2 months), the prevalence of EEG paroxysmal abnormalities without epilepsy was 6.7 percent; seizure onset was after age 12 years in 66.7 percent of cases; the most common type of epilepsy was partial in 45 percent (Rossi et al., 1995) to 65.2 percent (Giovanardi Rossi et al., 2000). Rossi et al. (1995) noted that electroencephalogram (EEG) paroxysmal abnormalities were mostly focal and multifocal. Females with autism seemed to be more frequently affected by seizures than were males (Elia et al., 1995). Individuals with autism and with both a severe mental deficit and a motor handicap are at the greatest risk for seizure disorder. Follow-up studies of adults with autism have reported seizure disorders in 15–38 percent of the participants (Danielsson et al., 2005; Howlin et al., 2004; Wolf and Goldberg, 1986).

COEXISTING NEUROPSYCHIATRIC DISORDERS IN ASPERGER'S DISORDER

Information about comorbid neuropsychiatric disorders of Asperger's disorder has been quite limited due to its relatively short history of being recognized as a distinct clinical entity by professionals in the United States. Furthermore, there is no established method for clinicians to validly assess comorbid neuropsychiatric disorders in this population. Nonetheless, there are reported cases of psychiatric disorders that have been associated with Asperger's disorder such as Tourette's disorder; ADHD; affective illness or mood disorders; anxiety disorder; OCD; and schizophrenia (reviewed by Tsai, 2005). Green et al. (2000) examined psychiatric and social functioning in 20 individuals with Asperger's disorder aged 11–19 years with full-scale intelligence quotient (IQ) scores above 70. The researchers found that 35 percent of the adolescents met the ICD-10 (WHO, 1992) criteria for generalized anxiety disorder, 10 percent met the criteria for a specific phobia, and 30 percent had two or more additional psychiatric diagnoses.

Polimeni et al. (2005) asked 52 parents of children with Asperger's disorder to complete a survey on their child's sleep patterns, the nature and severity of any sleep problems and success of any treatment attempted. The results showed a high prevalence of sleep problems (73 percent).

Little is known about the risk for psychiatric disorders in adulthood for individuals with Asperger's disorder. In a follow-up study of 85 adults with Asperger syndrome, Tantam (1991) reported that 30 (35 percent) met the criteria for a psychiatric disorder other than a developmental disorder (criteria taken from the ninth revision of the *International Classification of Diseases*, World Health Organization, 1977). Tantam noted that the proportion was likely higher than that to be found in an unselected community sample, as psychiatric disorder was one factor leading to psychiatric referral. Nevertheless, there was a higher than expected risk of psychosis, with mania (occurring in 9 percent) being more common than schizophrenia (3.5 percent). The single most common disorder was depression, occurring in 15 percent of the adults with Asperger's disorder. Anxiety disorder was also common, reaching clinically significant severity in 7 percent; it is often associated with depression.

Tani et al. (2003) studied sleep problems in 20 adults with Asperger's disorder without medication. The results showed that the adults with Asperger's disorder had frequent insomnia based on the sleep questionnaire 90 percent (18/20), the sleep diary 75 percent (15/20), and in free description, 85 percent (17/20). The study also found that there was a substantial psychiatric comorbidity with only four participants with Asperger's disorder devoid of other axis-I or axis-II disorders.

Howlin (2000) reviewed the issue of co-morbid disorders and noted what little is known about outcome for individuals with Asperger's disorder. She concluded: "more research into psychiatric conditions in adulthood is badly needed, not only to identify the true level of risk, but also to improve knowledge amongst clinicians about how psychiatric disorders in this group are manifest" (p. 76).

COMORBID NEUROPSYCHIATRIC DISORDER OF PDDNOS

Information of comorbid neuropsychiatric disorders of PDDNOS has been quite limited, if any, due to very few investigators have studied this subtype of PDD.

Gillberg and Coleman (1996) reported that the overall prevalence of medical disorders in atypical autism (i.e., PDDNOS) was similar to that found in typical autism (about 24 percent).

Volkmar et al. (1988) concluded that 25 percent of the atypical autism group had some evidence of organicity.

COMORBID NEUROPSYCHIATRIC DISORDER OF AUTISM SPECTRUM DISORDER

When autistic disorder and Asperger's disorder are viewed together as ASD, some clinicians have cited anxiety as a common feature of ASD (Attwood, 1998; Tantam, 2000). Kim et al. (2000) examined the prevalence of anxiety and mood problems in a sample of 59 children with autism and Asperger's disorder with IQ scores above the cutoff for intellectual disabilities. The researchers found that 13.6 percent of the children in the study scored at least two standard deviations above the mean on a parent report measure of generalized anxiety and on the internalizing factor, which includes generalized anxiety, separation anxiety, and depression.

Allik et al. (2006) studied several aspects of sleep–wake behavior, including insomnia, using a structured pediatric sleep questionnaire in thirty-two 8- to 12-year-old children with Asperger's disorder/high function autism (HFA). These children's parents reported difficulties with initiating sleep and daytime sleepiness and 10 of the 32 children with Asperger's disorder/HFA (31.2 percent) fulfilled the study definition of pediatric insomnia.

IMPORTANCE OF LEARNING ABOUT PHARMACOTHERAPY IN ASD

HIGH PREVALENCE OF THE USE OF PSYCHOTROPIC MEDICATIONS ASD POPULATIONS

In 1995, Autism Society of North Carolina did a survey of medication patterns. Caregivers of 1595 index cases were sent survey questionnaires by mail, and repeat questionnaires were sent twice if no reply was received. A total of 838 care providers (53 percent) responded to the survey. More than 50 percent of the sample was taking some psychotropic, antiepileptic, vitamin, or "medical" agent (Aman et al., 1995).

Martin et al. (1999b) reviewed the rates and pattern of psychotropic drug use in 109 high functioning PDD children, adolescent, and adults enrolled into the Yale Child Study Center's Project on Social Learning Disabilities. In all, 55 percent of these individuals were taking psychotropics.

Langworthy-Lam et al. (2002) carried out a mail survey of 3228 families that were members of the Autism Society of North Carolina. Some 1538 member families within the society (48 percent) responded to the survey. The survey noted that 703 (45.7 percent) individuals with autism were taking psychotropic drugs, and 191 (12.4 percent) were taking antiepileptic drugs (AEDs).

The Autism Society of Ohio carried out a survey of prevalence and patterns of use of psychoactive medicines among individuals with ASD (Aman et al., 2003). In all, 747 families were surveyed and 417 families (55.8 percent) replied. A total of 45.6 percent were taking some form of psychotropic agent and 11.5 percent were taking AEDs.

Derby Hospitals NHS Foundation
Trust
Library and Knowledge Service

Witwer and Lecavalier (2005) examined the treatment rates and patterns in children and adolescents with ASD. Data were collected on 353 nonreferred children and adolescents with ASD from public schools across Ohio. Parents provided information on the use of psychotropic medicines, vitamins, supplements, and modified diets. The results showed that 46.7 percent of the children and adolescents with ASD had taken at least one psychotropic medication in the past year. In addition, 11.9 percent had some combination of psychotropic medication and an alternative treatment, and 4.8 percent had taken an anticonvulsant.

Green et al. (2006) developed an Internet survey to identify treatments used by parents of children with autism. The survey listed 111 treatments and was distributed via colleagues and through chapters of the Autism Society of America and Autism Organizations Worldwide. A total of 552 parents submitted usable returns during the 3-month survey period. About 52 percent of parents were currently using at least one medication to treat their child.

The above survey studies found that not all the medications taken by the surveyed populations were effective. In other words, some individuals might have received the wrong or ineffective medications or were taking the wrong dosages. The findings also seemed to support the growing concern of some professionals that the increased reliance on pharmacotherapy may represent a trend in which quality programming for persons with ASD is being replaced by attempts to find a quick cure to emotional and behavioral problems through the use of medications.

To effectively advocate for persons with ASD, therefore, caregivers not only need to learn why, when, and how the psychotherapeutic medications should be prescribed, they must also learn when to resist pressures from others for getting pharmacotherapy for their children with ASD. One should keep in mind that unnecessary pharmacotherapy not only does not help, it also can unwittingly promote chronic illness. The individuals being put on unnecessary medications may come to believe that their problems only respond to medication, and the more medications are taken, the stronger the misconception becomes. Furthermore, pharmacotherapy can also cause individuals suffer from side and/or adverse effects.

On the other hand, to render appropriate and effective pharmacotherapy to persons with ASD, physicians should begin to practice evidence-based medicine.

EVIDENCE-BASED PHARMACOTHERAPY

The specific term evidence-based medicine was introduced in 1990 to refer to a systematic approach to helping practitioners apply scientific evidence to decision making at the point of contact with a specific person. Doctors practice evidence-based medicine will search medical journals and databases for specific research studies that applied randomized controlled trials. These studies evaluate a drug by giving it to a randomly selected group of individuals, while others receive an alternative treatment; sometimes a placebo is used. If the participants on the drug fare better than the other on an alternative treatment, a series of complicated statistical analyses can determine if the drug is the reason. When a doctor finds a certain drug that has helped large groups of people, he/she then applies the information to his/her own clients, under the statistical assurance that what holds true for groups is likely to be valid for individuals.

Currently, there are no established guidelines or policies of evidence-based medicine for ASD. Nevertheless, it is important to do a up-to-date literature review of published pharmacotherapy studies to help caregivers to gain some knowledge of more appropriate and effective pharmacotherapy in ASD.

REVIEW OF RELEVANT PHARMACOTHERAPY IN ASD

Many psychotropic medications have been tried in ASD populations. The following review is based on multiple literature searches using Entrez PubMed Database. Multiple searches were carried out on psychotropic medications including anticonvulsants that had been studied in persons with ASD. The present review of relevant literature, however, does not include studies of vitamins and other supplements. This review also does not include general review articles.

STUDIES OF USE OF PSYCHOTROPIC MEDICATIONS IN AUTISTIC DISORDER POPULATIONS

A literature review search using PubMed Database with the key words "autistic syndrome/disorder and medication treatment" yields the following publications. Some of them are case reports; others are small sample size studies that combined individuals with atypical autism.

ATYPICAL NEUROLEPTICS (ANTIPSYCHOTICS)

Risperidone (Risperdal)

Risperidone has been reported to be effective in treating symptoms relating to OCD, and PDD including repetitive behavior, aggression, anxiety or nervousness, depression, irritability, self-injury, and overall behavioral symptoms (Arnold et al., 2003; Croonenberghs et al., 2005; Crosland et al., 2003; Findling et al., 1997; Fisman and Steele 1996; Horrigan and Barnhill 1997; Malone et al., 2002; McCracken et al., 2002; McDougle et al., 1995a,b, 1998, 2005; Perry et al., 1997; Posey et al., 1999; Purdon et al., 1994; Scahill et al., 2002; Shea et al., 2004; Zuddas et al., 2000).

Although it is believed that risperidone has a low tendency to produce extrapyramidal side effects (EPS), withdrawal dyskinesias was noted (Malone et al., 2002). Weight gain seems to be common (Findling et al., 1997; Horrigan and Barnhill 1997; Malone et al., 2002; McCracken et al., 2002; Zuddas et al., 2000). The rate of increase lessened over a period of time, and after drug withdrawal, considerable weight loss was observed in the individuals who had previously shown the most significant increase of weight (Zuddas et al., 2000). It can also cause side effects of somnolence, increased dream activity, anxiety, dry mouth, dizziness, constipation, micturition disturbances, nausea, dyspepsia, rhinitis, rash, and tachycardia.

Olanzapine (Zyprexa)

Five of six children treated with olanzapine showed Clinical Global Impression (CGI) Scale improvement (Malone et al., 2001). Weight gain is common with olanzapine treatment.

Quetiapine Fumarate (Seroquel)

In an open-label quentiapine treatment in six autistic children, Martin et al. (1999a) reported no significant improvement based on CGI Scale, and that quetiapine was poorly tolerated and associated with serious side effect.

Zaiprasidone (Geodon)

Twelve individuals with autism or PDDNOS specified were treated with zaiprasidone for at least 6 weeks. Six (50 percent) of the 12 participants were considered responders based on a CGI Scale. It appeared that zaiprasidone had the potential for improving symptoms of aggression, agitation, and irritability. Most common side effect was transient sedation. Significant weight gain was not observed in the short-term open-label trial (McDougle et al., 2002).

STIMULANTS

Methylphenidate

Quintana et al. (1995) reported modest but statistically significant improvement on methylphenidate in 10 autistic children. Handen et al. (2000) reported that eight of thirteen autistic children showed positive response on methylphenidate, based upon a minimum 50 percent decrease on the Conners Hyperactivity Index. Stimulants are frequently reported to exacerbate irritability, insomnia, and aggression in clinical population (Posey and McDougle, 2000).

Recently, Posey et al. (2007) report a study in which 72 children were enrolled in the trial, but 6 (8 percent) were excluded because of the inability to tolerate methylphenidate in the test-dose phase. Sixty-six children (aged 5–11 years) with autism ($n=47$), Asperger's disorder ($n=5$), or PDDNOS ($n=14$) completed the test-dose phase and entered the double-blind crossover phase. Of the 66 participants, 58 children were able to complete all 4 weeks of the crossover, with the remainder leaving either as a result of adverse events or for other reasons. The results showed that methylphenidate was associated with significant improvement that was most evident at the 0.25- and 0.5-mg/kg/day doses. Hyperactivity and impulsivity improved more than inattention.

ANTIDEPRESSANTS AND ANTIOBSESSIVE–COMPULSIVE MEDICATIONS (SPECIFIC SEROTONIN REUPTAKE INHIBITORS – SSRIS)

Fluoxetine (Prozac)

Improvements in social functioning and increased interest in the environment were reported in an open prospective study of fluoxetine treatment of six children between 4 and 8 years with autism (Peral et al., 1999). Fluoxetine has also been reported to reduce overall autistic symptoms (Buchsbaum et al., 2001; DeLong et al., 1998; Fatemi et al., 1998), but it also induce significant side effects, including restlessness, hyperactivity, agitation, vivid dreams, decreased appetite, and insomnia (Fatemi et al., 1998).

Fluvoxamine (Luvox)

Fluvoxamine was reported as more effective than placebo in a short-term treatment of symptoms of autism (i.e., social relatedness, repetitive thoughts and behavior, maladaptive behavior, and aggression) in 15 adults (McDougle et al., 1996).

Sertralin (Zoloft)

Sertralin was reported as effective in reducing self-injury and aggression in individuals with autism and intellectual disabilities (Hellings et al., 1996), and in transition-associated anxiety and agitation in autistic children (Steingard et al., 1997).

Venlafaxine (Effexor)

Low dosage of venlafaxine was reported as effective in six individuals with autism. Improvement was noted in repetitive behaviors and restricted interests, social deficits, communication and language function, inattention, and hyperactivity (Hollander et al., 2000).

TRICYCLIC ANTIOBSESSIONAL ANTIDEPRESSANTS

Clomipramine (CMI or Anafranil)

Published open trial studies with the less selective medication clomipramine have shown inconsistent findings and some have indicated that younger children respond less well (Brasic et al., 1994; McDougle et al., 2000). A study of seven young children with autism reported that CMI was not therapeutic and was associated with serious untoward effects (Sanchez et al., 1996).

Brodkin et al. (1997) investigated short-term efficacy and tolerability of clomipramine in a consecutive series of adults with PDDs. Thirty-five adults with PDDs (18 with autistic disorder, 6 with Asperger's disorder, and 11 with PDDNOS) entered a 12-week prospective open-label trial of clomipramine. The initial sample included behavioral ratings were obtained at baseline and after 4, 8, and 12 weeks of clomipramine. Eighteen (55 percent) of the 33 participants who completed the trial were categorized as treatment responders based on scores of "much improved" or "very much improved" on the CGI global improvement item. Ten (63 percent) of 16 participants with autistic disorder, 2 (33 percent) of 6 participants with Asperger's disorder, and 6 (55 percent) of 11 participants with PDDNOS were considered responders to clomipramine treatment. In those 18 participants, clomipramine significantly reduced total repetitive thoughts and behavior and also aggression, and improved some aspects of social relatedness, such as eye contact and verbal responsiveness. The level of autistic behavior, as measured by the Autism Behavior Checklist (ABC) score, and full-scale intelligence quotient (IQ) were not significantly associated with global treatment response. Whereas clomipramine was well tolerated by most participants, 13 had clinically significant adverse effects. Three participants had seizures during clomipramine treatment, including two who had prior seizure disorders and were taking anticonvulsants. Of the 32 participants who had no history of prior seizures, only one had a seizure during clomipramine treatment. There were no adverse cardiovascular or extrapyramidal effects.

ANTIANXIETY MEDICATIONS

Buspirone (BuSpar)

McCormick (1997) carried out a study in which an autistic child received placebo for 3 weeks and buspirone for 3 weeks; there was a 1-week interval between the two treatments. The outcome was measured by using Conners abbreviated parent and teacher questionnaires and by determining the number of daily performance tasks completed by the child at school. Buspirone was found to be safe and efficacious, without side effects, for decreasing hyperactivity and increasing completed performance tasks.

OPIATE ANTAGONISTS

Naltrexone

Naltrexone has been reported to have positive effects on hyperactivity, social relatedness, and self-injury (Kolmen et al., 1995, 1997). A double-blind placebo-controlled crossover study in 23 autistic children, aged 3–7 years, with a mean daily dosage of 1 mg/kg of naltrexone for 4 weeks, the teachers reported a decrease in hyperactivity and irritability, but effects on social and stereotypic behavior could not be demonstrated (Willemsen-Swinkels et al., 1995b, 1996). Other investigators did not find the above reported effects (Feldman et al., 1999; Gillberg, 1995). Willemsen-Swinkels et al. (1995a) reported increased incidence of stereotyped behavior by naltrexone treatment.

ANTICONVULSANTS

The following review focus on anticonvulsants being tried to treat nonepileptic symptom(s).

Divalproex Sodium (Depakote)

Hollander et al. (2001) reported that 10 of 14 participants with autism on divalproex sodium were rated as having sustained response to treatment. It appeared that the responders were those who had associated features of affective instability, impulsivity, and aggression as well as those with a history of EEG abnormalities or seizures.

In a more recent study, Hollander et al. (2006) evaluated the use of divalproex in the treatment of repetitive, compulsive-like symptoms ASD. Thirteen individuals with ASD participated in an 8-week, double-blind, placebo-controlled trial of divalproex sodium versus placebo. There was a significant group difference on improvement in repetitive behaviors as measured by the Children's Yale-Brown Obsessive Compulsive Scale (C-YBOCS).

Anagnostou et al. (2006) investigated whether pretreatment with divalproex sodium decreases the irritability experienced by autistic individuals in association with fluoxetine treatment. Thirteen children (mean age 9.5 years) were recruited. Ten children were diagnosed with autistic disorder, two with Asperger syndrome (no language delay at 36 month), and one with PDDNOS. This double-blind, placebo-controlled treatment trial of divalproex sodium consisted of two phases. In the first phase, 13 children were randomized to divalproex sodium versus placebo. In the second phase, starting at week 8, six boys were started on fluoxetine (four were pretreated with divalproex and two were pretreated with placebo). All children on phase 2 were maintained at the same divalproex versus placebo dose as in week 8 of the first phase. During the second 8-week phase, participants were evaluated weekly for the first 4 weeks and biweekly for the next 4 weeks in a double-blind fashion by the treating physician. The results from this study suggest that pretreatment with divalproex may be effective in preventing symptoms of activation in children with ASD treated with fluoxetine at standard titration.

Valproate (Depakene)

Hellings et al. (2005) carried out a prospective double-blind, placebo-controlled study in 30 individuals (20 boys, 10 girls), 6–20 years of age, with PDD and significant aggression. These participants were randomized and received treatment with valproate (VPA) or placebo (PBO) for 8 weeks. The results showed no treatment difference between the VPA and the PBO groups. Increased appetite and skin rash were significant side effects. Only one participant was dropped from the study owing to side effects, notably a spreading skin rash, which then resolved spontaneously. Two participants receiving VPA developed increased serum ammonia levels, one with slurred speech and mild cognitive slowing.

Topiramate (Topamax) (TPM)

Canitano (2005) carried out an open study over an observation period of 18 months of 10 children and adolescents, eight males and two females, age ranged from 8 to 19 years with a diagnosis of autistic disorder or PDD not otherwise specified according to DSM-IV. Starting dosage of TPM was 0.5 mg/kg followed by titration of 0.5 mg/kg on a weekly basis, up to 1–3 mg/kg/day as the maintenance dosage. Eight participants were undergoing long-term treatment with risperidone, one with pimozide and one was temporarily not on antipsychotics. Six participants took TPM on a regular basis and four dropped out. Variable degrees of weight reduction were observed in four participants. However, two participants showed weight increase. Behavioral adverse effects were observed in three participants causing rapid withdrawal of the medication.

Hardan et al. (2004) conducted an open-label retrospective study to assess the effectiveness and tolerability of topiramate in children and adolescents with PDD. Individuals were included if concomitant medications remained unchanged. Treatment response was assessed using the Global Improvement item of the CGI Scale (CGI-GI), based on a review of medical records and the Conners Parent Scale (CPS), as completed by parents. Fifteen children and adolescents were identified (12 males, 3 females; mean age of 14.7 years), including 11 with autistic disorder, two with Asperger's disorder, and two with PDDNOS. Treatment duration was 25 ± 16 weeks, and the mean dose was 235 ± 88 mg. The results of the study showed that eight participants (four with autistic disorder, two with Asperger's disorder, and two with PDDNOS) were judged to be responders, as defined by a score of 1 or 2 on the CGI-GI. Differences between the baseline and the end-of-trial period were observed in the following CPS subscales: conduct, hyperactivity, and inattention. No differences were noted in the psychosomatic, learning, and anxiety subscales. Three participants discontinued topiramate because of side effects, with two participants experiencing cognitive difficulties and one participant developing a skin rash.

Mazzone and Ruta (2006) reported a study of five boys, aged 9–13 years, with a diagnosis of DSM-IV autistic disorder, two boys with mild intellectual disability and three with moderate intellectual disability. Two boys received add-on SSRI drug from 6 months (sertraline) for obsessive behavior and one was undergoing long-term therapy with risperidone. Duration of treatment ranged from 10 to 33 weeks, with a mean of 22 weeks. TPM was started at the dose of 0.5 mg/kg/day for 2 weeks, followed by increments of 0.5 mg/kg/day at 2-week intervals, up to a maximum of 2.5 mg/kg/day (mean TPM dose was 2.1 mg/kg/day). Treatment response was assessed using the CGI Scale and Child Behavior Checklist (CBCL). Two boys were judged to be responders, as defined by a score of 1 or 2 on the CGI and they improved hyperactivity, interpersonal behavior, irritability or anger, anxiety, and depression reaction. These two boys also showed good improvement on two subscales of the CBCL (anxious/depressed and attention problems). The three other boys did not show any clinically significant improvement (one discontinued treatment after 10 weeks). Adverse effects were mild and TPM was well tolerated. One boy developed mild sedation. Weight and body mass index (BMI) (kg/m^2) were significantly reduced in one boy (about 6 kg over a period of 12 weeks/BMI change – 2.1), slightly reduced in another boy (about 1.9 kg over 12 weeks/BMI change – 0.9), and unchanged in the others.

Carbamazepine (Tegretal)

Renier (2004) used carbamazepine to treat an autistic child with spitting seizures. By increasing the dose of carbamazepine, spitting behavior disappeared.

OTHER MEDICAL TREATMENT AGENTS

Melatonin

Giannotti et al. (2006) investigated the long-term effectiveness of controlled-release melatonin in 25 children, aged 2.6–9.6 years with autism without other coexistent pathologies and was evaluated openly. Sleep patterns were studied using Children's Sleep Habits Questionnaire (CSHQ) and sleep diaries at base-line, after 1, 3, and 6 months melatonin treatment, and 1 month after discontinuation. The study found that during treatment sleep patterns of all children improved. After discontinuation of the treatment, 16 children returned to pre-treatment score. Readministration of melatonin was again effective. Treatment gains were maintained at 12- and 24-month follow-ups. No adverse side effects were reported.

Hayashi (2000) gave melatonin at a dose of 6 mg at 9:00 pm (C1) or 11:00 pm (C2) to a 14-year-old autistic male with severe intellectual disability and sleep disturbance. His parents kept a sleep diary. In C1, he often experienced early morning waking and fragmented night sleep but in C2, night sleep was prolonged and sleep–wake rhythm was improved. Suitable medication time, therefore, improved the sleep–wake rhythm.

Secretin

After the initial report of positive effect of secretin treatment in three children with autism (Horvath et al., 1998), many children with autism have received secretin treatment. However, several large sample controlled studies have failed to demonstrate any significant treatment effect for autism (Chez et al., 2000; Coniglio et al., 2001; Dunn-Geier et al., 2000; Roberts et al., 2001; Sandler et al., 1999). A worsening in the autistic symptoms during secretin treatment was noted by Robinson (2001).

Neuropeptide ORG 2766 – ORG 2766, a synthetic analogue of adrenocorti-cotropic hormone, was given to 50 children with autism, aged 7 to 15 years and with a Performance IQ of more than 60, ORG 2766 failed to improve social and communicative behavior at the group level (Buitelaar et al., 1996).

Niaprazine

Niaprazine, a histamine H1-receptor antagonist with marked sedative proper-ties, was administered at 1 mg/kg/day for 60 days in 25 individuals with autism.

A positive effect was noted in 52 percent of participants, particularly on hyper-kinesias, unstable attention, resistance to change and frustration, mild anxiety sign, aggression, and sleep problems (Rossi et al., 1999).

R-THBP (6R-L-erythro-5,6,7,8-tetrahydrobiopterin)

R-THBP, a cofactor for tyrosine hydroxylase in the biosynthetic pathway of catecholamines and serotonin, was reported as effective in autistic children's social functioning – mainly eye contact and desire to interact, and in the number of words or sounds which the child used (Fernell et al., 1997; Komori et al., 1995).

STUDIES OF USE OF PSYCHOTROPIC MEDICATIONS IN ASPERGER'S DISORDER POPULATIONS

Empirical studies of medication treatment of Asperger's disorder are scarce. A literature review search using PubMed Database with the key words Asperger syndrome/disorder and medication treatment yields only a few publications. Some of them are case reports; others are small sample size studies that combined individuals with autistic disorder and Asperger's disorder as one group.

Fluvoxamine (Luvox)

Furusho et al. (2001) reported that an 8-year-old boy with Asperger's disorder could not sleep at night, recalling his awful experience, and kept crying every night and refused to go to school. He was treated with fluvoxamine, a selective SRI, at the dose of 25 mg daily. Four weeks after the treatment, his repetitive behavior and hyperactivity decreased and night crying diminished. Although he still has difficulties in communicating with others, he is now able to attend extracurricular classes in a private school.

Frazier et al. (2002) reported a 13.5-year-old boy with diagnoses of Asperger's disorder and bipolar disorder (mixed, with psychotic features). He had a long history of aggression and unsafe behaviors. After treatment for many years with various psychotropic medications, the authors believed that finally a combination of 1 mg of oral clonazepam twice a day, 2100 mg/day of lithium, and 3 mg/day of risperidone led to a marked reduction in his behavioral symptoms. Later his mood normalized and his aggressive, extreme compulsive and disruptive behaviors stopped.

Aripiprazole (Abilify)

Staller (2003) reported that a 34-year-old white man with lifelong, disabling Asperger's disorder and a 20-year history of failed psychotherapeutic and pharmacologic interventions was prescribed aripiprazole. This led to dramatic symptomatic improvement, including improved sociability; increased self-awareness; reduced rigidity, anxiety, and irritability; and reduced preoccupation with circumscribed esoteric interests.

Oxytocin

Hollander et al. (2003) examined the impact of oxytocin on the repetitive behaviors in 15 adults with autism or Asperger's disorder via randomized double-blind oxytocin and placebo challenges. The primary outcome measure was an instrument that rated six repetitive behaviors: need to know, repeating, ordering, need to tell/ask, self-injury, and touching. Adults with ASD showed a significant reduction in repetitive behaviors following oxytocin infusion in comparison to placebo infusion.

Citalopram (Celexa)

Namerow et al. (2003) assessed the effectiveness and tolerability of the selective serotonin reuptake inhibitor citalopram in the treatment of individuals with PDDs. The medical charts of 15 children and adolescents (aged 6–16 years) with Asperger's syndrome, autism, or PDDNOS treated with citalopram were retrospectively reviewed. The final dose of citalopram was 16.9 ± 12.1 mg/day with a treatment duration of 218.8 ± 167.2 days. Independent ratings of the CGI Severity and Improvement Scales allowed comparison between baseline and PDD symptoms at the last visit. Eleven adolescents (73 percent) exhibited significant improvement in PDD, anxiety, or mood CGI score. Anxiety symptoms associated with PDDs improved significantly in 66 percent of participants, and mood symptoms improved significantly in 47 percent of participants. Mild side effects were reported by five participants (33 percent).

Guanfacine (Tenex)

Posey et al. (2004) used open-label guanfacine to treat 80 children and adolescents with PDDs (10 females, 70 males) (aged 3–18 years). It was found that guanfacine treatment was effective in 19 of 80 (23.8 percent) participants. Individuals with PDDNOS (11 of 28 responders; 39.3 percent) and Asperger's disorder (2 of 6 responders; 33.3 percent) showed a greater rate of global response than those with autistic disorder (6 of 46 responders; 13.0 percent). Further, there was a trend for individuals without comorbid intellectual disabilities (9 of 24 participants; 37.5 percent) to respond at a greater rate than those with intellectual disabilities (10 of 56 participants; 17.9 percent). Symptom improvement was seen in hyperactivity, inattention, insomnia, and tics. Guanfacine was well tolerated, and did not lead to significant changes in blood pressure or heart rate.

Risperidone (Risperdal)

Rausch et al. (2005) studied 13 male children and adolescents aged 6–18 years who were diagnosed with Asperger's disorder by DSM-IV criteria and were enrolled in a 12-week, prospective, open-label pilot study. All participants were started on risperidone 0.25 mg twice a day. Doses were increased based on clinical indication and tolerability. The primary efficacy variable was the Scale for the Assessment of Negative Symptoms (SANS). Each participant's baseline score served as his control. Secondary efficacy measures included the

Positive and Negative Syndrome Scale (PANSS), Brief Psychiatric Rating Scale, Montgomery–Asberg Depression Rating Scale, Global Assessment Scale (GAS), and a modified Asperger Syndrome Diagnostic Scale (ASDS). It was found that a statistically significant improvement from baseline for last-observation-carried-forward (LOCF) analyses as well as for analyses of 12-week completers ($N=9$) in the primary outcome measure, SANS scores. There was also statistically significant improvement in all secondary efficacy measurements.

Sertralin (Zoloft)

In 2005, Australian investigators (Mathai et al., 2005) reported lessons learnt in conducting a clinical drug trial of sertralin in 12 children with Asperger's disorder. However, the result from the study has not been published.

The above review of published studies shows that the use of newer antipsychotic agents and the SSRIs appear to be growing in ASD. This is because the older, "typical" antipsychotics (e.g., haloperidol) and the nonselective serotonin reuptake medications (e.g., desipramin) are poorly tolerated by many individuals with ASD.

The present review finds that there is some evidence supporting the use of some atypical antipsychotics in the treatment of some behavioral problems associated with ASD. The evidence includes several open trials and two placebo-controlled trials of atypical antipsychotics in ASD, all reporting significant improvements in at least half of the individuals studied. However, in these studies most of the improvements were seen in such nonspecific behavioral problems as aggression, self-injurious behavior, irritability, and anxiety. With respect to the core features of ASD, improvements were reported for some of the repetitive behavioral features of ASD but not for the social or communication deficits. Furthermore, the atypical antipsychotics are also clearly associated with side effects, particularly weight gain and sedation, in a significant minority of cases treated. Such side effects have limited the use of atypical antipsychotics in some individuals with ASD.

There is also some evidence supporting the use of SSRIs in the treatment of older individuals with ASD. The evidence includes several positive case series and open studies reporting improvements in both repetitive behavior and social-communication symptoms in adults with ASD. There are also positive double-blind, placebo-controlled trials with SSRIs in adults reporting significant improvements in the overall functioning, in repetitive thoughts and behaviors, and maladaptive behaviors. However, the evidence of the effects of SSRIs in children is more equivocal.

The findings from the above published studies must be interpreted with caution, given that all the studies reviewed have demonstrated consistent methodological weaknesses (e.g., small sample size, open label or retrospective studies, heterogeneous population due to use of loose diagnosis, lack of control trials, nonblind measuring of treatment effects, reliance on global ratings of improvement and generalized behavior rating scales which do not focus on specific topographies of behavior, short-term studies). Most of the reported treatment effects also have not been replicated by other investigators. Therefore, it is not clear how these data can be generalized to other populations with ASD.

It is clear that there is no single best medication to treat a person with ASD. Many psychotropic medications have been tried in ASD population as reviewed above. As described above, individuals with ASD tend to be placed on psychotropic medications that usually do not show clear benefit. On the other hand, new psychotropic medications appear on market very few months. There is an urgent need to establish a mechanism (e.g., evidence-based medicine committee at a national organization of ASD) that will be responsible for setting up-to-date evidence-based guidelines or policies for pharmacotherapy in ASD population. Such mechanism will enable doctors to sift through all the information to assemble the best, most updated, and appropriate options of pharmacotherapy for individuals with ASD.

Nonetheless, the psychopharmacological field has compiled sufficient knowledge of pharmacotherapy from the fields of other psychiatric disorders. The following sections will describe and discuss some important aspects or issues that the caregivers of persons with ASD may benefit from becoming familiar with them.

PERFORM A COMPLETE FUNCTIONAL BEHAVIOR ANALYSIS PRIOR TO PHARMACOTHERAPY

There is a wide range of inappropriate and undesirable behaviors exhibited by individuals with ASD. Most of the behaviors are learned as individuals react to their environment and people in it. However, some of the behaviors are symptoms of coexisting neuropsychiatric disorders. It is critical to be able to distinguish the types of behaviors (i.e., learned challenging behaviors versus neuropsychiatric symptoms) so that effective intervention plan can be implemented to improve these individuals' behaviors.

Didden et al. (1997) carried out a meta-analysis of 482 empirical studies on treatment of problematic behaviors of individuals with intellectual disabilities. Many of the problematic behaviors also tend to exist in ASD population. The meta-analysis identified a total of 64 treatment procedures that included pharmacotherapy. The results from the meta-analysis show that those treatment studies began with a "functional analysis" tended to yield significant improvement whereas pharmacotherapy studies showed the least effectiveness because they usually did not perform a functional analysis before the initiation of therapy.

It is clear from the above report of meta-analysis that a complete functional behavioral analysis should be carried out by an experienced and qualified professional (usually a psychologist or a behavioral therapist) before the decision is made to refer an individual with ASD for pharmacotherapy. The results from the functional behavioral analysis should be presented at a follow-up team meeting. A decision of referring the person for a medical assessment and to obtain pharmacotherapy would be considered as appropriate when the team members agree that the behaviors of concern are not "learned or maladapted behaviors" and that particular individual has not responded to non-medical an intervention prior to the performance of functional behavioral analysis.

Due to the space limitation of this chapter, those readers who are not familiar with "functional behavioral analysis" are strongly encouraged to learn it from appropriate resources.

BASELINE MEDICAL ASSESSMENT

An effective pharmacotherapy begins with a functional analysis and then follows with a thorough medical assessment. The pretreatment assessment is essential for detecting many medical conditions such as seizure disorder, meningitis, lead poisoning, brain tumors, endocrinological disorders, and chromosomal abnormalities that can cause or exacerbate behavioral, emotional, communicative, or cognitive problems in persons with ASD. The pretreatment assessment is also essential for establishing the baseline physical, psychological, behavioral, and cognitive status prior to medication treatment.

The following sections will describe the methods of gathering information for medical assessment and diagnosis in individuals with autism.

Interviewing and observing behaviors – Formal and informal interviews and observation of behaviors comprise one method for gathering in-depth information about the child, parents, caregivers, and interaction between them. Child-rearing methods, discipline, and parental or caregiver's attitudes and perceptions of their child's behavior, can be explored. The commonly used interview formats include the following: unstructured interview, structured interview, semi-structured interview, symptom checklists, and computer-based interview. The interviews can be carried out as the following formats: interviewing the parents, caregivers, and child together; interviewing the parents and/or other caregivers without the presence of the child; interviewing the child alone; observing the child playing without the presence of the parents and/or other caregivers; observing the child playing or interacting with the parents and/or other caregivers.

For more detailed information regarding the rationales and usefulness of "interviewing and observing behaviors," the readers of this chapter are encouraged to read such information from other resources (e.g., Tsai, 2001).

Physical and neurological assessment – Because different behavior problems, symptoms, or side effects of medications may mimic other medical or psychiatric disorders, the physical and neurological assessment may reveal medical problems or disorders previously missed; new, unrelated medical problems or disorders; incorrect earlier diagnoses; or adverse effects associated with various treatments. It is very important to make an accurate differential diagnosis that will directly impact on the nature and course of medication to be prescribed. The other major reason for a careful and complete physical and neurological assessment is to establish the baseline physical and neurological status prior to medication therapy for monitoring and prevention of the development of side effects.

Simple measures such as recording of both standing and supine blood pressure, pulse, height, and weight (e.g., weight loss caused by stimulant and weight gain caused by neuroleptics) should also be included. A complete documentation of present illness, past medical history including immunizations and hospitalizations, medical review of systems, history of allergies, other prescribed or illicit drug or alcohol use, and a family neuropsychiatric history should be done. It should be emphasized here that the above assessment procedures should be continuous throughout the course of the treatment to ensure the efficacy of psychopharmacotherapy.

Problems encountered during physical and neurological assessment – Performing a complete physical and neurological assessment in some individuals with autism can be a real challenge, and the physician needs special training and experience in working with these individuals. This is particularly true in individuals with low cognitive and communicative functions. It may be impossible to explain the examination procedure to them to get their cooperation during the assessment. Some individuals may resist any physical contact and may even react violently to the usual examination procedure. The assistance of parents and/or caregivers who are familiar with the individual's behavior patterns and means of communication can be most helpful. In some really difficult cases, the physician may have to compromise with the situation and focus on just obtaining the essential information, or he may have to rely on a recent documentation of another physician's physical examination obtained when the individual was cooperative.

Laboratory tests – Although the laboratory tests can never replace clinical acumen in any medical specialty, they can play a significant role in explaining and quantifying biological factors associated with various medical and psychiatric disorders. The role of the laboratory tests in the evaluation of behavioral problems has become increasingly prominent as a supplement to the crucial clinical history and physical examination. In some individuals, supplementary laboratory and diagnostic tests may be needed when specific clues from the history, physical examination, or initial laboratory screens or tests suggest a medical or psychiatric condition that might have caused or exacerbated the behaviors or symptoms of concern. Judicious use of laboratory parameters may thus be valuable to the physician in answering specific questions of evaluation.

Not all the laboratory measures and tests promoted by nonmedical professionals or the media needed to be done as routine screens or tests. Particularly, many tests recommended by advocacy groups and/or media tend to be new tests that may not be supported by scientific evidence demonstrating that they meet minimum criteria of effectiveness. Inaccurate, false-positive results can cause profound anxiety and require additional testing that can be increasingly invasive and costly. They can also deplete society's limited medical resources. Physicians can and should refuse to order tests that would violate their medical and ethical judgment.

On the other hand, some physicians who do not have much knowledge, training, and experience in working with individuals with ASD may order unnecessary medical tests. The parents or nonmedical caregivers should inquire the reason(s) for the tests and how the results aid in the assessment and/or intervention of the child. Physicians have a responsibility to inform the caregivers of the limitations and risks of the tests they would like to pursue. If the caregivers are not satisfied with the explanation(s) given by the assessing physician and if there is no life-threatening urgency, they should seek a second opinion before agreeing to take the tests.

It is the physical condition of the child and the physician's medical knowledge and experience that determine which laboratory tests should be done to aid the assessment. Wasteful laboratory tests that have limited clinical utility should be avoided.

It can be said that very few diagnoses of mental or psychiatric disorders can be confirmed by current laboratory tests. Hence, laboratory studies should be ordered only for (1) specific diagnostic considerations (e.g., thyroid studies to evaluate depression), and (2) baseline assessment where the proposed medication(s) could alter organ systems (e.g., assessments of thyroid function before lithium is instituted).

The following are some laboratory tests that tend to be considered to support or to confirm the clinical diagnoses of certain medical and/or neurological disorders that also have behavioral symptoms as part of the clinical manifestations. The other function of these tests is to confirm that the behaviors of concern are side effects of psychotherapeutic medication(s) taken by the individual with autism. Due to space limitation, the readers of this chapter are encourage to obtain more details from other resources of the following laboratory tests: electrocardiogram (ECG), EEG, catecholamine and enzyme assays, brain imaging, lumbar punctures, electromyogram (EMG), polysomnography (PSG), metabolic screening, thyroid function tests, liver and kidney function tests, serum measures, chromosomal analysis, illicit drug screening, and toxicology screening.

Speech/Language and Cognitive Function Assessments – Psychotherapeutic medications and anticonvulsants may alter speech and language development and/or performance (e.g., neuroleptics, stimulants, tricyclic antidepressants can alter speech production, rate, volume, and coherence) in persons with autism. Psychotherapeutic medications may also affect these individuals' cognitive function or performance (e.g., fenfluramine may have a retarding effect on discrimination learning). It is important to have a documentation of baseline speech/language and cognitive function. These assessments should be carried out by a qualified and experienced speech pathologist and a psychologist, respectively.

PHARMACOTHERAPY SHOULD BE CARRIED OUT
BY A TEAM

As mentioned above, pharmacotherapy in ASD is just part of a comprehensive treatment plan. There should be a multidisciplinary treatment approach. The prescribing physician must take into account the input of parents, other caregivers (psychologists, special education teachers, speech and language pathologists, occupational therapists, physical therapists, etc.), and the individual with ASD. The inclusion of nonmedical professionals in the treatment team recognizes the large psychosocial component of intervention in ASD. The prescription and management of medications, however, should be done by a physician specialized in developmental, behavioral, and psychiatric disorders (i.e., a developmental neurologist, developmental/behavioral pediatrician, and psychiatrist). The physician works closely with the individuals with ASD, and their parents and other caregivers. This is the only way to ensure that the most effective use of psychotherapeutic drugs is achieved with a minimum risk of side effects or complications.

CHOOSING AN EFFECTIVE MEDICATION AND INDIVIDUALIZING DOSAGE

Until a well-established guidelines or policies of pharmacotherapy for ASD is available, the decision about the choice of medication is influenced substantially by the confidence the prescribing physician has in the accuracy of the diagnosis, estimates of the extent and severity of the disease, and previous experience with certain disorders and medications used to treat those disorders. Based on the best available information, the physician must decide on an initial medication from a group of reasonable alternatives. Many factors, including a cost-benefit analysis of diagnostic tests of the efficacy (e.g., test for blood level) and monitoring of side effects (e.g., ECG monitoring for cardiac side effects), availability and specificity of alternative therapies (e.g., melatonin for certain type of sleep problem), and the likelihood of a reduction in future utilization of expensive health care (e.g., use lithium to prevent relapse of mania and readmission to an inpatient unit), will influence the assessment of selecting the medication.

Variation in pharmacokinetic properties of a medication (e.g., rates of the absorption and distribution of the drug in the body, and length of the drug being metabolized and excreted from the body) as well as the individual's physiological and pathological variations in organ function (e.g., kidney or liver diseases) will also influence the selection of the medication. These variations also will influence the design of a rational individualized dosage regimen

MONITORING OF PHARMACOTHERAPY EFFECTS

Dosage regulation of any medication depends on reliable measurement of changes or improvements of targeted behaviors. However, most individuals with

ASD are unable to report accurately their responses to the treatments. On the other hand, a positive treatment effect may be a decrease in the frequency or severity of a long-standing problem behavior. However, this change may not be readily apparent in the clinician's office. Therefore, the measuring of treatment response must rely on objective techniques that are reliable (i.e., repeatable over time or across observers) and valid (i.e., reflect what is actually being measured) for data collection from caregivers.

There are various measuring techniques that can be employed. These techniques include direct behavioral observations, behavioral rating scales, self-reports, standardized tests, learning and performance measures, mechanical movement monitors, and global impression. On the other hand, it is also crucial that the assessment strategies are sensitive to changes produced by the medication and are practical, economic, safe, and ethical (Tsai, 2001). Due to space limitations here, the readers should and can obtain more detailed information from other resources.

RECOGNITING ADVERSE OR SIDE EFFECTS CAUSED BY PHARMACOTHERAPY

In pharmacotherapy of ASD, the focus tends to be on obtaining positive results. However, all psychotherapeutic medications have a potential to produce adverse reactions or side effects. Hence, recognizing and managing adverse and/or side effects of the psychotherapeutive medications are also crucial in the optimal use of the psychotherapeutic medications. Side effects may range from a minor nuisance to a potentially fatal reaction. If unrecognized, the medication-induced side effects can affect an individual's outcome adversely, both in terms of medical and psychiatric well-being. This is particularly true in individuals with ASD. Because of their cognitive and communication disabilities, they may not be able to comprehend or to recognize the medication-induced adverse and/or side effects. Hence they are incapable of alerting or informing their caregivers about the development of the adverse and/or side effects. They may become frightened or suspicious if a sudden change or dysfunction occurs following the administration of medication(s). Such feelings may trigger tantrums or interfere with compliance. It has been reported that psychotherapeutic medication-induced side effects are the reason for discontinuation in 25–33 percent of those who stop pharmacotherapy (Tsai, 2001). Therefore, the importance of actually monitoring drug response cannot be overemphasized.

SIDE EFFECTS OF PSYCHOTHERAPEUTIC MEDICATIONS

Since multiple adverse/side effects can be caused by one medication and that same type of side effects can be produced by many different psychotherapeutic medications, there is not enough space here to describe which side effect tends to be induced by what medications. The following are the commonly seen psychotherapeutic medication-induced adverse/side effects: (1) *behavioral effects* include: jitteriness syndrome, sedative effect, impaired memory, disinhibition, hostility, and aggression, switch mania, paranoid psychosis, work and school phobia, sleep disturbances, withdrawal reactions, and dependence; (2) *neuromuscular effects* include problems with muscles (tension, tremor, twitching, cramps, and/or pains), daytime myoclonus, nocturnal myoclonus, tremor of upper extremities, impaired motor function (decline in speed, accuracy, attention and coordination, falls and impaired automobile driving), extrapyramidal symptoms (EPS) (acute dystonia, neuroleptic-induced parkinsonism, acute akathisia, akinesia, tardive dyskinesia, neuroleptic malignant syndrome (NMS); (3) *convulsive effects* of seizures are rare but serious side effects had been reported; (4) *cardiovascular effects* include hypertensive reaction, orthostatic hypotension, conduction delays (increased PR, QRS, or QT interval in ECG); (5) *gastrointestinal effects* include dry mouth, dysphagia, gastroesophageal reflux, withdrawal reactions (nausea, vomiting, anorexia, abdominal pain, diarrhea, and increased salivation), constipation, or abnormal distension; (6) *endocrine and metabolic effects* include weight gain, hyperprolactinemia, hypothyroidism, nephrogenic diabetes insipidus (NDI) (polyuria and polydipsia), and hypercalcemia; (7) *hematologic reactions* include aplastic anemia, agranulocytosis, eosinophilia, thrombocytopenia (diminished number of platelets); (8) *hepatic effects* include liver diseases (hepatocellular hepatotoxicity, hepatocellular degeneration, necrosis, or steatosis); (9) *genitourinary system effects* include: polyuria, incontinence and enuresis, urinary retention, and renal failure; (10) *reproductive and adverse sexual effects* include decreased or increased libido, decreased or increased erection and congestion–lubrication, decreased emission, delayed or inhibited orgasm and may cause impotence, menstrual irregularities, amenorrhe, gynecomastia in males, breast enlargement or galactorrhea, and testicular swelling.

More detailed descriptions of the above adverse/side effects can be found in other resources (e.g., Tsai, 2001).

One general strategy for dealing with psychotherapeutic medication-induced adverse/side effects is to change the medication if possible. Of course, the best way to deal with the problem is to know how to prevent their development.

PREVENTION OF DEVELOPMENT OF SIDE EFFECTS

It is essential that the clinician is knowledgeable of the full range of adverse/side effects of the medication(s) being prescribed and knows how to manage side effects should they arise. In general, "mechanism-based" adverse drug reactions or side effects (e.g., a decrease in blood pressure when using clonidine (Catapres) to treat ADHD due to Catapres' antihypertension pharmacological property) are relatively easier to predict based on preclinical and clinical pharmacology studies. However, the relatively rare and severe "idiosyncratic" adverse reactions or side effects (e.g., severe dermatologic, hematologic or hepatologic toxicities), which result from an interaction of the medication with unique host factors that are unrelated to the principal action of the medication, are more difficult to predict. In addition, it is clear that a population risk of the rare "idiosyncratic" adverse reactions is not distributed evenly across the population. Some individuals, because of unique genetic or environmental factors, are at an extremely high risk, while the remainder of the population may be at low or no risk. Understanding the genetic and environmental bases of idiosyncratic adverse events will certainly improve the overall safety of pharmacotherapy. The following are general guidelines to avoid the development of side effects:

1. Obtain a complete family history including medication treatments and responses and a complete medical history (including responses to previous medication treatment) of the individual.
2. Treatment should begin with one medication.
3. Avoid giving the same medication that had demonstrated previous side effects in the individual.
4. Avoid giving *preventive* anti-side-effect medication, such as antiparkinsonian agent.
5. If the individual does not respond to the medication of first choice, it is discontinued gradually while a second medication is instituted and its dosage is increased.
6. Use the lowest possible maintenance doses in the therapeutic range once it has been established.
7. If indicated, regularly monitor the blood level of the medication, blood counts, blood pressure, pulse rate, ECG, liver function, height, and weight.
8. Regularly perform a complete physical and neurological examination and monitor side effects using published side effects rating scales.
9. After the optimal effect of a medication has been established, give periodic drug holidays, at least once every 4–6 months.
10. When a decision of discontinuation of a medication has been made, in most cases, the medication should be tapered and withdrawn gradually.

It is also critical to alert and educate parents and caretakers regarding the potential side effects of the chosen medication as well as the therapeutic benefits. When a psychotherapeutic medication or anticonvulsant is prescribed, the person with ASD, his/her family members and other caretakers should have complete information about the recommended pharmacotherapy. Some physicians may not disclose all the information due to various reasons. By asking the following questions, one will gain a better understanding of the recommended psychotherapeutic medications:

■ What is the name of the medication, and what is it supposed to do?
■ What is known about the medication's effectiveness in persons with similar symptoms and in individuals with ASD?

- How will the medication help me/my child?
- Do members of the school staff (supervisors at job place) need to be informed about this medication?
- What is the recommended dosage? How often will the medication be taken? What times of day should the medicine be taken?
- Is there any laboratory test, such as heart function or blood tests that need to be done before taking the medication? Will any test needs to be done while using the medication?
- What foods, drinks, other medications, or activities should one avoid while taking the prescribed medication?
- How long does it take before I/we see improvement?
- How the response to the medication will be monitored and if necessary who will help make dosage changes?
- What are the side effects, and what should one do if they occur?
- How long will the medication be needed? What factors will lead to a decision to stop the medication?
- Is there any written information available about the medication? Is it available?

CLINICAL INDICATIONS FOR PHARMACOTHERAPY IN ASD

From the above literature review, the available evidence suggests that the current pharmacotherapy in ASD is not effective in the treatment of core symptoms of ASD. However, there are symptoms of the frequently coexisting neuropsychiatric disorders appear to be responsive to some psychotropic medications. In some of the following conditions or symptoms, the recommendation of use of certain medications is based on well-documented research in other psychiatric disorders as well as based on some evidence from the available pharmacotherapy studies of ASD. In other conditions or symptoms, the suggestions of use of certain medications are made based on the limited clinical and empirical experiences of the present author.

1. Typical features of OCD, particularly ego-dystonic obsessions and compulsions; resistance to change – clomipramine, or one of the SSRIs may be considered first in individuals who do not have seizure disorders. One of the SSRIs should be considered in individuals also with seizure disorders.
2. Perseveration of talking or making statements, asking same or various questions, playing toys, games, or activities; abnormal attachments; stereotyped movements – most psychotropic medications provide very minimal effect. Behavioral modification treatment may be more helpful in decreasing the frequency and intensity of these symptoms or behaviors.

3. Disturbance of motility, short attention, impulsive behaviors, or symptoms of ADHD – atomoxetine (Strattera), clonidine (Catapres), guanfacine, or imipramine (Tofranil) may be considered in the low or middle functioning autistic individuals with or without other neurological disorders such as seizure disorders, and Tourette's disorder, etc. Haloperidol (Haldol), risperidone, or naltrexone may be considered in individuals who do not respond to atomoxetine, clonidine, guanfacine, or imipramine. In high functioning individuals without other neurological disorders, stimulants such as methylphenidate, dextroamphetamine (Dexedrin), or dextroamphetamine saccharate and sulfate combined amphetamine sulfate and aspartate (Adderall) may be tried first. Atomoxetine, guanfacine, clonidine, imipramine, haloperidol, risperidone, or naltrexone may be considered in individuals who do not respond to stimulants or in those who have other neurological disorders.

4. Motor and/or vocal tics, Tourette's disorder, and stereotyped movements or behaviors of tic disorders – haloperidol or pimozide (Orap) should be considered first. Risperidone, clonidine, or fluoxetine may be tried in individuals who do not respond to haloperidol or pimozide. In some cases, the combination of haloperidol or pimozide with fluoxetine may be needed.

5. In depressed individuals with strong family history of unipolar affective illness, tricyclic antidepressant such as desipramine (Norpramin), venlafaxine, bupropion, SSRIs serotonin reuptake blockers such as fluoxetine, sertraline, fluvoxamine, paroxetine, citalopram (Celexa), or escitalopram (Lexapro) may be considered. Close monitoring of the drug response is critical in these individuals because the present author and other clinicians had experienced depression episode being switched to hypomanic episode in some cases. Lithium, or divalproex may be the drug of choice in individuals with family history of bipolar affective illness and who develop manic-like episode.

6. Some people with ASD may become aggressive and physically attack other people. Some of the aggressive behaviors may relate to frustrations of these individuals. Much of the aggressive behaviors, however, do not seem to have any clear cause. In individuals who exhibit frequent aggressive behaviors and who do not respond to behavioral interventions, haloperidol, risperidone, apripiprazole, olanzapine, quentiapine, or trazodone (Desyrel), may be the drug of first choice. Carbamazepine, Lithium or Inderal may be considered in individuals who fail to respond to haloperidol, risperidone, apripiprazole, olanzapine, quentiapine, or trazodone treatment.

7. Unusual sleeping patterns may develop in some children and adolescents with ASD. Some children develop complete reversed sleep pattern, that is, they sleep during the day and awake during the night. The key to solve such a problem is to reverse the sleep cycle through a well-planned regimen. Some individuals with ASD seem to need much longer time to

settle down for sleep (i.e., having initial insomnia), and/or need less sleep. Melatonin should be considered first. Some individual may respond to antihistamines such as Benadryl, or other medications such as Vistaril (Atarax), or clonidine. However, in daily practice, it is not unusual for parents of autistic children to report paradoxical excitatory responses with antihistamines. In other more severe cases, antidepressant such as imipramine or trazodone, or hypnotic such as zolpidem (Ambient) may be considered for short-term use.

8. Self-injury – Effective pharmacotherapy for SIB has not been established. At present, if self-injurious behaviors develop as a part of Tourette's disorder, the above medications for Tourette's disorder should be considered first. Naltrexone, trazodone or fluoxetine may be considered in individuals who do not respond to the above medications and if effective intensive behavioral treatment is not available to these individuals.

9. Excessive fear, worry, anxiety or generalized anxiety – Buspirone should be tried first. One of the SSRIs may be tried in individuals who do not respond to buspirone.

10. In the individuals with ASD who develop clear delusions, hallucinations, and bizarre behaviors including catatonia, atypical antipsychotic medications such as risperidone, clozapine (Clozaril), olanzapine, quentiapine, or apripiprazole should be considered first. Haloperidol or thioridazine (Navane) is the second line of drugs of choice.

11. Enuresis – Some children with autism tend not to respond to toilet training before age seven. In the treatment of enuresis in children over 7 years who fail to respond to nonmedical means, imipramine and desmopressin (DDAVP) may be considered.

12. Social withdrawal – In individuals who are not interested in social activities, naltrexone and fluoxetine may be considered. In individuals whose social withdrawal is related to depressive disorder, one of the SSRIs may be considered.

13. Seizure disorders – Effective treatment can be achieved if an accurate early diagnosis of seizure type can be established. Effective treatment of an individual with ASD and seizure requires active interactions between multiple factors including medical, psychological, and environmental. Nonetheless, these individuals are likely to require long-term anticonvulsant treatment. The selection of the medication for the treatment depends on the type of seizure and a neurologist specializing in seizure disorders best manages the use of medications. In general, management of seizures in individuals with ASD is the same as that in individuals with epilepsy but without ASD. However, when psychotherapeutic medications are considered in persons with ASD and seizure disorder, the potential alterations in seizure threshold and the interactions between psychotherapeutic medications and anticonvulsants should be assessed.

GETTING MEDICAL INFORMATION ONLINE

Nowadays, if one knows how to sort out outdated reports, misinformation, and out-and-out charlatanism, Internet can be a great resource for obtaining rich and lifesaving information. Here are a few credible web sites for readers of this chapter to begin looking for medical information:

http://medlineplus.gov – The National Library of Medicine's comprehensive health-information portal.

www.healthfinder.gov – A health library sponsored by the US Department of Health and Human Services.

www.clinicaltrials.gov – Lists experimental treatments one may be eligible to receive.

www.psych.org – Straightforward general information from the American Psychiatric Association.

www.aacap.org – General information provided by the American Academy of Child and Adolescent Psychiatry.

www.autism-society.org – A nonprofit organization (Autism Society of America) sponsored site.

www.medem.com – A partnership among medical societies to foster doctor–patient communication; includes an online medical library.

www.webmd.com – A for-profit news and information service with interactive activities.

SUMMARY

Although the main theme of this book is about "evidence-based assessment and intervention across lifespan of ASD," there is very limited, if any, study of clinical conditions in the adults with ASD that may benefit from the use of psychotropic medications as well as study of adverse and/or side effects of the psychotropic medications in adults with ASD. On the other hand, there is evidence that children and adolescents with ASD are frequently being placed on a wide range of psychotropic medications for their "problem behaviors" that may be considered as features of many coexisting neuropsychiatric disorders of ASD.

The current definitions and diagnostic criteria of certain DSM-IV psychiatric disorders (e.g., generalized anxiety disorder and OCD) call for the individuals to verbally report their feelings, emotions, problems, etc. before diagnoses can be made by the clinicians. Many individuals with ASD, particularly those who are nonverbal and lower functioning are not capable of providing such information. Hence, many clinicians are reluctant to make additional psychiatric diagnosis in these individuals. On the other hand, even verbal children or adolescents with ASD may not know whether their symptoms are due to comorbid neuropsychiatric disorders. Thus, they usually do not report or complain of their symptoms.

Therefore, to study the drug response of coexisting symptoms or neuropsychiatric disorders as well as to render more effective treatment to people with ASD, the current assessment technology must be refined and advanced.

The present review finds that there is some evidence supporting the use of some atypical antipsychotics and SSRIs in the treatment of some of the behavioral problems associated with ASD. However, most of the reviewed studies have significant methodological weaknesses. The results from those studies are not quite ready to be used to establish the urgently needed evidence-based guidelines or policies for pharmacotherapy of ASD.

Future research of pharmacotherapy in ASD should emphasize the following:

1. A committee at the national level should be formed to refine the current DSM-IV definitions and diagnostic criteria of certain coexisting psychiatric disorders so that they are more valid and can be reliably applied to ASD populations. A "gold standard" for determining the validity of diagnostic instruments to assess the comorbid neuropsychiatric disorders in ASD population should also be established.

2. Based on multicenter corroborative investigations that will enlarge the sample size, enhance the inter-rater reliability in diagnosis to obtain more homogeneous groups of participants for study, and ensure the consistency of assessment of treatment results.

3. At the initial stage of a drug study, the selection of the participants should base on DSM-IV concept of subtypes of PDD. Such approach will enable the study of drug treatment response in individuals with different clinical disorders. Only when there is sufficient data indicating no significant difference of drug response between the three disorders (i.e., autistic disorder, Asperger's disorder, and PDDNOS) in a certain study, then all the participants can be lumped together as an ASD group.

4. Employ standardized controlled study design which would enable the comparison of efficacy between different medications, between medication treatment and nonmedication intervention such as behavioral treatment, and the efficacy of the combination of both treatments.

5. A committee for establishing evidence-based medicine for ASD should be formed at the national level. Multiple literature searches should be done on each of the psychotropic medications that have been used by most clinicians in ASD populations. The literature searches will include published research studies, abstracts, review articles, and textbooks. All the relevant materials will be reviewed and evaluated by each of the committee members. Appropriate publications will then be selected for grading the "strength of evidence" which will considers both the treatment efficacy and adverse/side effects of the drug. A standardized formula that considers the inclusion of diagnosis, sample size, age, gender, treatment protocol, validity of conclusions, and potential sources of bias should be used as the base for grading. The committee should establish guidelines that would incorporate criteria for identifying

"well-established" and "probably efficacious" interventions as proposed by the Task Force of Section on Clinical Child Psychology, the Division of Clinical Psychology, and the American Psychological Association (Lonigan et al., 1998). All selected publications should be graded by all the committee members. A draft of the guideline should include "strength of evidence" of each psychotropic medication for treatment of certain symptom, symptom cluster, or comorbid neuropsychiatric disorder(s). Such initial draft should then be sent to nationally recognized experts in ASD for their reviews and inputs. Final guidelines will be established after incorporating the inputs of external experts.

REFERENCES

Allik, H., Larsson, J.O., and Smedje, H. (2006). Insomnia in school-age children with Asperger syndrome or high-functioning autism. *BMC Psychiatry*, **6**, April 28, 18.

Aman, M.G., Van Bourgondien, M.E., Wolford, P.L., and Sarphare, G. (1995). Psychotropic and anticonvulsant drugs in subjects with autism: Prevalence and patterns of use. *Journal of American Academy of Child and Adolescent Psychiatry*, **34**, 1672–1681.

Aman, M.G., Lam, K.S.L., and Collier-Crespin, A. (2003). Prevalence and patterns of use of psychoactive medicines among individuals with autism in the Autism Society of Ohio. *Journal of Autism & Developmental Disorders*, **33**, 527–534.

American Psychiatric Association (1994). *Diagnostic and Statistic Manual of Mental Disorders (4th ed.)*. Washington DC: American Psychiatric Association.

Anagnostou, E., Esposito, K., Sooryya, L., et al. (2006). Divalproex versus placebo for prevention of irritability associated with fluoxetine treatment in autism spectrum disorder. *Journal of Clinical Psychopharmacology*, **26**(40), 444–446.

Arnold, L.E., Vitiello, B., McDougle, C., et al. (2003). Parent-defined target symptoms respond to risperidone in RUPP autism study: Customer approach to clinical trials. *Journal of the American Academy of Child and Adolescent Psychiatry*, **42**(12), 1443–1450.

Attwood, T. (1998). *Asperger's Syndrome: A Guide for Parents and Professionals*. Philadelphia: Jessica Kingsley.

Ballaban-Gil, K., Rapin, I., Tuchman, R., and Shinnar, S. (1996). Longitudinal examination of the behavioral, language, and social changes in a population of adolescents and young adults with autistic disorder. *Pediatric Neurology*, **15**(3), 217–223.

Brasic, J.R., Barnett, J.Y., Kaplan, D., et al. (1994). Clomipramine ameliorates adventitious movements and compulsions in prepubertal boys with autistic disorder and severe mental retardation. *Neurology*, **44**, 1309–1312.

Brodkin, E.S., McDougle, C.J., Naylor, S.T., et al. (1997). Clomipramine in adults with pervasive developmental disorders: A prospective open-label investigation. *Journal of Child and Adolescent Psychopharmacology*, **7**, 109–121.

Buchsbaum, M.S., Hollander, E., Hazenedar, M.M., et al. (2001). Effect of fluoxetine on regional cerebral metabolism in autistic spectrum disorder: A pilot study. *International Journal of Neuropsychopharmacology*, **4**, 119–125.

Buitelaar, J.K., Dekker, M.E., van Ree, J.M., et al. (1996). A control trial with ORG 2766, an ACTH-(4–9) analog, in 50 relatively able children with autism. *European Neuropsyhopharmacology*, **6**, 13–19.

Canitano, R. (2005). Clinical experience with Topiramate to counteract neuroleptic induced weight gain in 10 individuals with autistic spectrum disorders. *Brain and Development*, **27**, 228–232.

Chez, M.G., Buchanan, C.P., Bagan, B.T., et al. (2000). Secretin and autism: a two-part clinical investigation. *Journal of Autism and Developmental Disorders*, **30**, 87–94.

Coniglio, S.J., Lewis, J.D., Lang, C., et al. (2001). A randomized, double-blind, placebo-controlled trial of single-dose intravenous secretin as treatment for children with autism. *Journal of Pediatrics*, **138**, 649–655.

Croonenberghs, J., Fegert, J.M., Findling, R.L., et al. (2005). Risperidone in children with disruptive behavior disorders and subaverage intelligence: A 1-year, open-label study of 504 patients. *Journal of the American Academy of Child and Adolescent Psychiatry*, **44**(1), 64–72.

Crosland, K.A., Zarcone, J.R., Lindauer, S.E., et al. (2003). Use of functional analysis methodology in the evaluation of medication effects. *Journal of Autism and Developmental Disorders*, **33**(3), 271–279.

Danielsson, S., Gillberg, I.C., Billstedt, E., et al. (2005). Epilepsy in young adults with autism: a prospective population-based follow-up study of 120 individuals diagnosed in childhood. *Epilepsia*, **46**(6), 918–923.

DeLong, R., Teague, L.A., and McSwain-Kamran, M. (1998). Effects of fluoxetine treatment in young children with idiopathic autism. *Developmental Medicine & Child Neurology*, **40**, 551–562.

Didden, R., Duker, P.C. and Korzilius, H. (1997). Meta-analytic study on treatment effectiveness for problem behaviors with individuals who have mental retardation. *American Journal on Mental Retardation*, **101**, 387–399.

Dunn-Geier, J., Ho, H.H., Auersperg, E., et al. (2000). Effect of secretin on children with autism: a randomized controlled trial. *Developmental Medicine & Child Neurology*, **42**, 796–802.

Elia, M., Ferri, R., Musumeci, S.A., Del Gracco, S., et al. (2000). Sleep in subjects with autistic disorder: a neurophysiological and psychological study. *Brain and Development*, **22**:88–92.

Elia, M., Musumeci, S.A., Ferri, R., and Bergonzi, P. (1995). Clinical and neurophysiological aspects of epilepsy in subjects with autism and mental retardation. *American Journal of Mental Retardation*, **100**, 6–16.

Fatemi, S.H., Realmuto, G.M., Khan, L., and Thuras, P. (1998). Fluoxetine in treatment of adolescent patients with autism: a longitudinal open trial. *Journal of Autism and Developmental Disorders*, **28**, 303–307.

Feldman, H.M., Kolmen, B.K., and Gonzaga, A.M. (1999). Naltrexone and communication skills in young children with autism. *Journal of American Academy of Child & Adolescent Psychiatry*, **38**, 587–593.

Fernell, E., Watanabe, Y., Adolfsson, Y.,et al. (1997). Possible effects of tetrahydrobiopterin treatment in six children with autism-clinical and position emission tomography data: a pilot study. *Developmental Medicine & Child Neurology*, **39**, 313–318.

Findling, R.L., Maxwell, K., and Wiznitzer, M. (1997). An open clinical trial of risperidone monotherapy in young children with autistic disorder. *Psychopharmacology Bulletin*, **33**, 155–159.

Fisman, S. and Steel, M. (1996). Use of risperidone in pervasive developmental disorders: a case series. *Journal of Child & Adolescent Psychopharmacology*, **6**, 177–190.

Frazier, J.A., Doyle, R., Chiu, S. and Coyle, J.T. (2002). Treating a child with Asperger's disorder and comorbid bipolar disorder. *American Journal of Psychiatry*, **159**(1), 13–21.

Furusho, J., Matsuzaki, K., Ichihashi, I., et al. (2001). Alleviation of sleep disturbance and repetitive behavior by a selective serotonin re-uptake inhibitor in a boy with Asperger's syndrome. *Brain and Development*, **23**(2), 135–137.

Gail Williams, P., Sears, L.L. and Allard, A. (2004). Sleep problems in children with autism. *Journal of Sleep Research*, **13**(3), 265–268.

Gillberg, C. (1995). Endogenous opioid and opiate antagonists in autism: brief review of empirical findings and implications for clinicians. *Developmental Medicine and Child Neurology*, **37**, 239–245.

Gillberg, C. and Coleman, M. (1996). Autism and medical disorders: a review of the literature. *Developmental Medicine and Child Neurology*, **38**, 191–202.

Giannotti, F., Cortesi, F., Cerquiglini, A., and Bernabei, P. (2006). An open-label study of controlled-release melatonin in treatment of sleep disorders in children with autism. *Journal of Autism and Developmental Disorders*, **36**, 741–752.

Giovanardi Rossi, P., Posar, A., and Parmeggiani, A. (2000). Epilepsy in adolescents and young adults with autistic disorder. *Brain and Development*, **22**, 102–106.

Green, J., Gilchrist, A., Burton D., and Cox, A. (2000). Social and psychiatric functioning in adolescents with Asperger syndrome compared with conduct disorder. *Journal of Autism and Developmental Disorders*, **30**(4), 279–93.

Green, V.A., Pituch, K.A., Itchon, Choi, A., et al. (2006). Internet survey of treatments used by parents of children with autism. *Research in Developmental Disabilities*, **27**, 70–84.

Handen, B.L., Johnson, C.R., and Lubetsky, M. (2000). Efficacy of methylphenidate among children with autism and symptoms of attention-deficit hyperactivity disorder. *Journal of Autism & Developmental Disorders*, **30**, 245–255.

Hardan, A.Y., Jou, R.J., and Handen, B.L. (2004). A retrospective assessment of Topiramate in children and adolescents with pervasive developmental disorders, *Journal of Child and Adolescent Psychopharmacology*, **14**, 426–432.

Hayashi, E. (2000). Effect of melatonin on sleep-wake rhythm: the sleep diary of an autistic male. *Psychiatry and Clinical Neuroscience*, **54**, 383–384.

Hellings, J.A., Kelley, L.A., Gabrielli, W.F., et al. (1996). Sertraline resonse in adults with mental retardation and autistic disorder. *Journal of Clinical Psychiatry*, **57**, 333–336.

Hellings, J.A., Weckbaugh, M., Nickel, E.J., et al. (2005). A double-blind, placebo-controlled study of valproate for aggression in youth with pervasive developmental disorders. *Journal of Child and Adolescnt Psychopharmacology*, **15**, 682–692.

Hering, E., Epstein, R., Elroy, S., et al. (1999). Sleep patterns in autistic children. *Journal of Autism & Developmental Disorders*, **29**, 143–147.

Hollander, E., Dolgoff-Kaspar, R., Cartwright, C., et al. (2001). An open trial of divalproex sodium in autism spectrum disorders. *Journal of Clinical Psychiatry*, **62**, 530–534.

Hollander, E., Kaplan, A., Cartwright, C., and Reichman, D. (2000). Venlafaxine in children, adolescents, and young adults with autism spectrum disorders: an open retrospective clinical report. *Journal of Child Neurology*, **15**, 132–135.

Hollander, E., Novotny, S., Hanratty, M., et al. (2003). Oxytocin infusion reduces repetitive behaviors in adults with autistic and Asperger's disorders. *Neuropsychopharmacology*, **28**(1), 193–198.

Hollander, E., Soorya, L., Wasserman, S., et al. (2006). Divalproex sodium vs. placebo in the treatment of repetitive behaviors in autism. *International Journal of Neuropsychopharmacology*, **9**, 209–213.

Horrigan, J.P. and Barnhill, L.J. (1997). Ridperidone and explosive aggressive autism. *Journal of Autism Developmental Disorders*, **27**, 313–323.

Horvath, K., Stefanatos, G., Sokolski, K.N., et al. (1998). Improved social and language skills after secretin administration in patients with autistic spectrum disorders. *Journal of Associated Academic Minority Physicians*, **9**, 9–15.

Howlin, P. (2000). Autism and intellectual disability: Diagnostic and treatment issues. *Journal of the Royal Society of Medicine*, **93**(7), 351–355.

Howlin, P., Goode, S., Hutton, J. and Rutter, M. (2004). Adult outcome for children with autism. *Journal of Child Psychology and Psychiatry*, **45**(2), 212–229.

Howlin, P., Mawhood, L. and Rutter, M. (2000). Autism and developmental receptive language disorder – a follow-up comparison in early adult life. II: Social, behavioural, and psychiatric outcomes. *Journal of Child Psychology and Psychiatry*, **41**(5), 561–578.

Kim, J.A., Szatmari, P., Bryson, S.E., et al. (2000). The prevalence of anxiety and mood problems among children with autism and Asperger syndrome, *Autism*, **4**, 117–132.

Kolmen, B.K., Feldman, H.M., Handen, B.L., and Janosky, J.E. (1995). Naltrexon in young autistic children: a double-blind, placebo-controlled crossover study. *Journal of American Academy of Child and Adolescent Psychiatry*, **34**, 223–231.

Kolmen, B.K., Feldman, H.M., Handen, B.L., and Janosky, J.E. (1997). Naltrexone in young autistic children: replication study and learning measures. *Journal of American Academy of Child & Adclescent Psychiatry*, **36**, 800–802.

Komori, H., Matsuishi, T., Yamada, S., et al. (1995). Cerebralspinal fluid biopterin and biogenic amine metabolites during oral R-THBP therapy for infantile autism. *Journal of Autism & Developmental Disorders*, **25**, 183–193.

Langworthy-Lam, K.S., Aman, M.G., and Van Bourgondien, M.E. (2002). Prevalence and patterns of use of psychoactive medicines in individuals with autism in the Autism Society of North Carolina. *Journal of Child & Adolescent Psychopharmacology*, **12**, 311–321.

Lonigan, C.J., Elbert, J.C. and Johnson, S.B. (1998). Empirically supported psychosocial interventions for children: An overview. *Journal of Clinical Child Psychology*, **27**(2), 138–145.

Malone, R.P., Cater, J., Sheikh, R.M., et al. (2001). Olanzapine versus haloperidol in children with autistic disorder: an open pilot study. *Journal of American Academy of Child & Adolescent Psychiatry*, **40**, 887–894.

Malone, R.P., Maislin, G., Choudhury, M.S., et al. (2002). Risperidone treatment in children and adolescents with autism: short- and long-term safety and effectiveness. *Journal of American Academy of Child & Adolescent Psychiatry*, **41**, 140–147.

Martin, A., Koenig, K., Scahill, L., and Bregman, J. (1999a). Open-label quetiapine in the treatment of children and adolescents with autistic disorder. *Journal of Child & Adolescent Psychopharmacology*, **9**, 99–107.

Martin, A., Scahill, L., Klin, A. and Volkmar, F.R. (1999b). Higher-functioning pervasive developmental disorders: Rates and patterns of psychotropic drug use. *Journal of American Academy of Child and Adolescent Psychiatry*, **38**, 923–931.

Mathai, J., Bourne, A., and Cranswick, N. (2005). Lessons learnt in conducting a clinical drug trial in children with Asperger Syndrome. *Australasian Psychiatry*, **13**(2), 173–175.

Mazzone, L. and Ruta, L. (2006). Topiramate in children with autistic disorders. *Brain and Development*, **28**, 668.

McCormick, L.H. (1997). Treatment with buspirone in a patient with autism. *Archive of Family Medicine*, **6**, 368–370.

McCracken, J.T., McGough, J., Shah, B., et al. (2002). Risperidone in children with autism and serious behavioral problems. *New England Journal of Medicine*, **347**, 314–321.

McDougle, C.J., Fleischmann, R.L., Epperson, C.N., et al. (1995a). Risperidone addition in fluvoxamine-refractory obsessive-compulsive disorder: three cases. *Journal of Clinical Psychiatry*, **56**, 526–528.

McDougle, C.J., Holmes, J.P., Carlson, D.C., et al. (1998). A double-blind, placebo-controlled study of risperidone in adults with autistic disorder and other pervasive developmental disorders. *Archive of General Psychiatry*, **55**, 633–641.

McDougle, C.J., Kem, D.L., and Posey, D.J. (2002). Case series: Use of ziprasidone for maladaptive symptoms in youths with autism. *Journal of American Academy of Child & Adolescent Psychiatry*, **41**, 921–927.

McDougle, C.J., Kresch, L.E., Goodman, W.K., et al. (1995b). A case-controlled study of repetitive thoughts and behavior in adults with autistic disorder and obsessive-compulsive disorder. *American Journal of Psychiatry*, **152**, 772–777.

McDougle, C.J., Kresch, L.E., and Posey, D.J. (2000). Repetitive thoughts and behavior in pervasive developmental disorders: Treatment with serotonin reuptake inhibitors. *Journal of Autism and Developmental Disorders*, **30**(5), 427–435.

McDougle, C.J., Naylor, S.T., Cohen, D.J., et al. (1996). A double-blind, placebo-controlled study of fluvoxamine in adults with autistic disorder. *Archives of General Psychiatry*, **53**, 1001–1008.

McDougle, C.J., Scahill, L., Aman, M.G., et al. (2005). Risperidone for the core symptom domains of autism: Results from the study by the autism network of the research units on pediatric psychopharmacology. *American Journal of Psychiatry*, **162**(6), 1142–1148.

Namerow, L.B., Thomas, P., Bostic, J.Q., et al. (2003). Use of citalopram in pervasive developmental disorders. *Journal of Developmental Behavior Pediatrics*, **24**(2), 104–108.

Patzold, L.M., Richdale, A.L., and Tonge B.J. (1998). An investigation into sleep characteristics of children with autism and Asperger's Disorder. *Journal of Paediatric Child Health*, **34**, 528–533.

Peral, M., Alcami, M., and Gilaberte, I. (1999). Fluoxetine in children with autism. *Journal of American Academy of Child and Adolescent Psychiatry*, **38**, 1472–1473.

Perry, R., Pataki, C., Munoz-Silva, D.M., et al. (1997). Risperidone in children and adolescents with pervasive developmental disorder: pilot trial and follow-up. *Journal of child & Adolescent Psychopharmacology*, **7**, 167–179.

Polimeni, M.A., Richdale, A.L., and Francis, A.J. (2005). A survey of sleep problems in autism, Asperger's disorder and typically developing children. *Journal of Intellectural Disability Research*, **49**, 260–268.

Posey, D.J., Aman, M.G., McCracken, J.T., et al. (2007). Positive effects of methylphenidate on inattention and hyperactivity in pervasive developmental disorders: An analysis of secondary measures. *Biological Psychiatry*, **61**, 538–544.

Posey, D.J. and McDougle, C.J. (2000). The pharmacotherapy of target symptoms associated with autistic disorder and other pervasive developmental disorders. *Harvard Review of Psychiatry*, **8**, 45–63.

Posey, D.J., Puntney, J.I., Sasher, T.M., et al. (2004). Guanfacine treatment of hyperactivity and inattention in pervasive developmental disorders: A retrospective analysis of 80 cases. *Journal of Child and Adolescent Psychopharmacology*, **4**(2), 233–241.

Posey, D.J., Walsh, K.H., Wilson, G.A., and McDougle, C.J. (1999). Risperidone in the treatment of two very young children with autism. *Journal of Child & Adolescent Psychopharmacology*, **9**, 273–276.

Purdon, S.E., Lit, W., Labelle, A., and Jones, B.D. (1994). Risperidone in the treatment of pervasive developmental disorder. *Canadian Journal of Psychiatry*, **39**, 400–405.

Quintana, H., Brimaher, B., Stedge, D., et al. (1995). Use of Methylphenidate in the treatment of children with autistic disorder. *Journal of Autism and Developmental Disorders*, **25**, 283–294.

Rausch, J.L., Sirota, E.L., Londino, D.L., et al. (2005). Open-label risperidone for Asperger's disorder: negative symptom spectrum response. *Journal of Clinical Psychiatry*, **66**(12), 1592–1597.

Renier, W.O. (2004). Compulsive spitting as manifestation of temporal epilepsy. *European Journal of Pediatric Neurology*, **8**, 61–62.

Roberts, W., Weaver, L., Brian, J., et al. (2001). Repeated doses of porcine secretin in the treatment of autism: a randomized, placebo-controlled trial. *Pediatrics*, **107**, E71.

Robinson, T.W. (2001). Homeopathic Secretin in autism: a clinical pilot study. *British Homeopath Journal*, **90**, 86–91.

Rossi, P.G., Parmeggiani, A., Bach, V., et al. (1995). EEG features and epilepsy in patients with autism. *Brain & Development*, **17**, 169–174.

Rossi, P.G., Posar, A., Parmeggiani, A., et al. (1999). Niaprazine in the treatment of autistic disorder. *Journal of Child Neurology*, **14**, 547–550.

Rutter, M. (1984). Autistic children growing up. *Developmental Medicine and Child Neurology*, **26**, 122–129.

Sanchez, L.E., Campbell, M., Small, A.M., et al. (1996). A pilot study of clomipramine in young autistic children. *Journal of American Academy of Child and Adolescent Psychiatry*, **35**, 537–544.

Sandler, A.D., Sutton, K.A., DeWeese, J., et al. (1999). Lack of benefit of a single dose of synthetic human secretin in the treatment of autism and pervasive developmental disorder. *New England Journal of Medicine*, **341**, 1801–1806.

Scahill, L., McCracken, J.T., McGough, J., et al. (2002). Risperidone in children with autism and serious behavioral problems. *New England Journal of Medicine*, **347**(5), 314–321.

Schreck, K.A. and Mulick, J.A. (2000). Parental report of sleep problems in children with autism. *Journal of Autism and Developmental Disorders*, **30**, 127–135.

Shea, S., Turgay, A., Carroll, A., et al. (2004). Risperidone in the treatment of disruptive behavioral symptoms in children with autistic and other pervasive developmental disorders. *Pediatrics*, **114**(5), e634–e641.

Staller, J.A. (2003). Aripiprazole in an adult with Asperger disorder. *Annal of Pharmacother*apy, **37**(11), 1628–1631.

Steingard, R., Zimnitzky, B., DeMaso, D.R., et al. (1997). Sertraline treatment of transition-associated anxiety and agitation in chidren with autistic disorder. *Journal of Child & Adolescent Psychopharmacology*, **7**, 9–15.

Taira, M., Takase, M., and Sasaki, H. (1998). Sleep disorder in children with autism. *Psychiatry & Clinical Neuroscience*, **52**, 182–183.

Takase, M., Taira, M., and Sasaki, H. (1998). Sleep-wake rhythm of autistic children. *Psychiatry and Clinical Neuroscience*, **52**, 181–182.

Tani, P., Lindberg, N., Nieminen-von Wendt, T., et al. (2003). Insomnia is a frequent finding in adults with Asperger syndrome. *BMC Psychiatry*, **16**(3), 12.

Tantam, D. (1991). Asperger syndrome in adulthood. In *Autism and Asperger Syndrome* (U. Frith, ed.) pp. 147–183. Cambridge: Cambridge University Press.

Tantam, D. (2000). Psychological disorder in adolescents and adults with Asperger Syndrome. *Autism*, **4**, 47–62.

Tsai, L.Y. (2001). *Taking the Mystery Out of Medication in Autism/Asperger Syndromes*. Arlington, Texas, Future Horizons Inc.

Tsai, L.Y. (2005). Autistic Disorder. In *Essentials of Child and Adolescent Psychiatry* (D. Mina and J.W. Wiener, eds.) pp. 137–183. Washington DC: American Psychiatric Press.

Tsai, L.Y., Chu, E., and Biederman, I. (1997). Sleep problems and effective treatment in children with autism. *Proceeding of Autism Society of America National Conference*, Orlando, July 8–12.

Volkmar, F.R. and Nelson, D.S. (1990). Seizure disorders in autism. *Journal of American Academy of Child and Adolescent Psychiatry*, **29**(1), 127–129.

Volkmar, F.R., Cohen, D.J., Hoshino, Y., et al. (1988). Phenomenology and classification of the childhood psychoses. *Psychological Medicine*, **18**, 191–201.

World Health Organization. (1977). *International Classification of Diseases*, (9th rev. ed.). Geneva, Switzerland: Author.

Willemsen-Swinkels, S.H., Buitelaar, J.K., Nijhof, G.J., and van England, H. (1995a). Failure of naltrexone hydrochloride to reduce self-injurious and autistic behavior in mentally retarded adults. Double-blind placebo-controlled studies. *Archives of General Psychiatry*, **52**, 766–773.

Willemsen-Swinkels, S.H., Buitelaar, J.K., and van Engeland, H. (1996). The effect of chronic naltrexone treatment in young autistic children: a double-blind placebo-controlled crossover study. *Biological Psychiatry*, **39**, 1023–1031.

Willemsen-Swinkels, S.H., Buitelaar, J.K.,Weijnen, F.G., and van Engeland, H. (1995b). Placebo-controlled acute dosage naltrexone study in young autistic children. *Psychiatry Research*, **58**, 203–215.

Witwer, A. and Lecavalier, L. (2005). Treatment incidence and patterns in children and adolescents with autism spectrum disorders. *Journal of Child & Adolescent Psychopharmacology*, **15**(4), 671–681.

World Health Organization (1992). The ICD-10 classification of mental and behavioral disorders: Clinical descriptions and diagnostic guidelines. Geneva: World Health Organization.

Wolf, L. and Goldberg, B. (1986). Autistic children grow up: An eight to twenty-four year follow-up study. *Canadian Journal of Psychiatry*, **31**(6), 550–556.

Wong, V. (1993). Epilepsy in children with autistic spectrum disorder. *Journal of Child Neurology*, **8**, 316–322.

Zuddas, A., Di Martino, A., Muglia. P. and Cianchetti, C. (2000). Long-term risperidone for pervasive developmental disorder: Efficacy, tolerability, and discontinuation. *Journal of Child & Adolescent Psychopharmacology*, **10**, 79–90.

INDEX

Derby Hospitals NHS Foundation
Trust
Library and Knowledge Service